UMI ANNUAL SUNDAY SCHOOL LESSON
C O M M E N T A R Y

PRECEPTS
FOR
LIVING

M I S S I O N   S T A T E M E N T

*We are called
of God to create, produce, and distribute
quality Christian education products;
to deliver exemplary customer service;
and to provide quality Christian
educational services which will empower
God's people, especially within the Black
community, to evangelize, disciple,
and equip people for serving Christ,
His kingdom, and Church.*

Urban Ministries, Inc.
The African American Christian Publishing
& Communications Co.

UMI ANNUAL SUNDAY SCHOOL LESSON
COMMENTARY
PRECEPTS FOR LIVING
2004–2005
INTERNATIONAL SUNDAY SCHOOL LESSONS
VOLUME 7
URBAN MINISTRIES, INC.

Melvin E. Banks, Sr., Litt.D., Founder and Chairman
C. Jeffrey Wright, J. D., President and CEO

All art: Copyright© 2004 Urban Ministries, Inc.
Bible art: Fred Carter

Unless otherwise indicated, all Scripture references are taken from the
authorized King James Version of the Bible.

CONTRIBUTORS

Editorial Staff
Carl Ellis,
Editor

Katara A. Washington,
Director of Editorial

Kathryn Hall,
Managing Editor

Herb Jackson,
Contributing Writer

Cheryl Wilson,
Editorial Assistant

Evangeline Carey,
Editorial Assistant

Megan Bell,
Copy Editor

Denise Gates,
Copy Editor

Production
Shawan Brand,
Assoc. Dir. Production
Tiphany Pugh,
Product Manager

Layout & Design
Larry Taylor Design, Ltd.

Bible Illustrations
Fred Carter

Contributing Writers
Essays
Evangeline Carey
Aja Carr
Lisa Crayton
Rukeia Draw
Charlesetta Watson-Holmes
Judith St. Clair Hull, Ph.D.
LaTonya Mason
Cedric McCay
Barbara Carr-Phillips
Philip Rodman
Kathy Steward
Connie Taylor
Katara A. Washington

Bible Study Guides
Evangeline Carey
Olivia Cloud
Lisa Crayton
Robert Dulin
Annette Goodwin-Dammer
Richard Gray, Ph.D.
Charlesetta Watson-Holmes
Victoria Johnson
Jennifer King
Lynn Lillard
Vanessa Lovelace
Keyonda McQuarters
Mary S. Minor
Patricia Owens

Jerii Rodman
Philip Rodman
Fred Thomas
Diane Turner
Gwendolyn Weathers
Charles Woolery
Rosalyn Yilpat

More Light On The Text
Moussa Coulibaly, Ph.D.
Richard Gray, Ph.D.
Emily Jenkins
Marcel Kerr
Esther Kibor
Jennifer King
Vanessa Lovelace
C. Fyne Nsofor
Dr. A. Okechukwu
Ogbonnaya
Samuel Olarewaju
Joseph Parker
Michelle Taylor
Reuben Unaegbu

TABLE OF CONTENTS

Fall Quarter, 2004

Winter Quarter, 2004–2005

CYCLE OF 2004-2007

Arrangement of Quarters According to the
Church School Year, September through August

	FALL	WINTER	SPRING	SUMMER
2004-2005	The God of Continuing Creation (Bible Survey) Theme: Creation (13)	Called To Be God's People (Bible Survey) Theme: Call (13)	God's Project: Effective Christians (Romans & Galatians) Theme: Covenant (13)	Jesus' Life, Teachings, and Ministry (Matthew, Mark, Luke) Theme: Christ (13)
2005-2006	You Will Be My Witness (Acts) Theme: Community (13)	God's Commitment—Our Response (Isaiah, 1 & 2 Timothy) Theme: Commitment (13)	Living in and as God's Creation (Psalms, Job, Ecclesiastes, Proverbs) Theme: Creation (13)	Called To Be a Christian Community (1 & 2 Corinthians) Theme: Call (13)
2006-2007	God's Living Covenant (Old Testament Survey) Theme: Covenant (13)	Jesus Christ: A Portrait of God (John, Philippians, Colossians, Hebrews, 1 John) Theme: Christ (13)	Our Community Now and in God's Future (1 John, Revelation) Theme: Community (13)	Committed To Doing Right (Various prophets, 2 Kings, 2 Chronicles) Theme: Commitment (13)

THE WHITE HORSE

by Evangeline Carey

The white horse on the cover of this edition of *Precepts For Living* should draw our attention to the end times and God's ultimate victory over Satan, false powers, and all the forces of evil. In keeping with the 2004-2005 theme, the white horse heralds the culmination of the Christian struggles here on earth. For those who have had their transgressions pardoned, who have been redeemed by the blood of the Lamb, and who have their identity in Jesus, the symbolic horse declares the authenticity of the eternal life God offers. The symbolic white horse should remind and give all believers everywhere confidence and hope that in the end, when all is said and done, God will win the final battle between good and evil.

Revelation 19:11-13 states: "And I saw heaven opened, and behold a white horse; and he that sat upon him was called Faithful and True, and in righteousness he doth judge and make war. His eyes were as a flame of fire, and on his head were many crowns; and he had a name written, that no man knew, but he himself. And he was clothed with a vesture dipped in blood: and his name is called The Word of God."

While banished to the island of Patmos (off the Coast of Asia) by the Roman Emperor Domitian from A.D. 81-96, the apostle John wrote the book of Revelation. During his deferment, God gave John a vision of the future, when time is no more. Unbelievers will be busy worshiping the Antichrist and Jesus will step out from heaven on the sands of time, *riding a white horse*, leading an army of angels, and ushering in the great Judgment Day. In this passage of Scripture, God through John reveals that the spotless Lamb that was slain is no longer the humble suffering servant, the victim He was in His first coming. As you recall, Jesus had been rejected by many of the people He came to save, falsely accused, tried, convicted, beaten, spat upon, cursed, mocked, and hung on a cruel Cross to pay the penalty for the sins of all believers. On His Second Coming, He makes a triumphant entry as the righteous Judge, the Conqueror, the Victor. Jesus comes to make war, not peace, and defeat His enemies that have allied with Satan. He comes with great wrath to purge and make right that which has been made wrong.

God wants all soldiers of the Cross to know that Jesus will return still as the sovereign God, with all power and authority in His hands. On that day, everyone will know without a doubt that He is the Son of God and Lord of the universe. Everyone will know that He is faithful and true, King of kings, and Lord of lords! When Jesus steps out of heaven this time, He is not coming as our Redeemer. The invitation to accept Jesus Christ as Lord and Saviour will be withdrawn. In fact, it will be "payday" for humankind. The day of toiling, praying, and pressing the battle on for all Christians will be over. It will be time to receive our heavenly crown. Those who are yet unbelievers (not born again) will be judged, found wanting, and receive their just reward as well.

The white horse, therefore, symbolizes a time of God's absolute, glorious, and eternal victory. No longer will the enemies of God overcome the saints of God. Those who have been saved by His divine power, who have been standing on the promises of God, standing on the Solid Rock, and walking in the light of God will then experience the land of Beulah, "that blessed, blessed land of light, where the flowers bloom forever, and the sun is always bright."

Study the 2004-2005 *Precepts For Living Annual Sunday School Commentary,* and be blessed with faith and hope because Jesus is coming back again!

Evangeline Carey is an Adult Sunday School Teacher with more than 25 years of experience. She is a freelance writer and holds a bachelor's degree in sociology and psychology.

SEPTEMBER 2004
QUARTER AT-A-GLANCE

The God of Continuing Creation

Throughout the Bible, God reveals Himself as the God of creation. Not only has He created heaven and earth, but He has also created humanity with a special plan and purpose. God created people to be in fellowship with Him and with one another.

UNIT 1. CREATED FOR A PURPOSE

In the first lesson, we see that God created Adam and Eve. In the second lesson, He re-created the human race after the flood. In the third and fourth lessons, we see how God delivered the Israelites and established them as His people.

LESSON 1: September 5
From the Dust of the Ground
Genesis 2:4b-7, 15-24

This first lesson focuses on the creation of Adam and Eve. God created them with a purpose. He gave them responsibilities, including tending the Garden of Eden and naming the birds and animals. God also gave them a boundary: They were not to eat of the Tree of the Knowledge of Good and Evil. This first couple, Adam and Eve, were created to fellowship with God and with each other.

LESSON 2: September 12
Beginning Again
Genesis 6:5-8; 7:1-5, 17, 23; 8:14-16; 9:1

God was grieved over the sinfulness of humanity, so He decided to re-create humanity through the family of Noah, who pleased God. After constructing the ark, Noah gathered the animals according to God's plan. When the flood came, only those in the ark were saved. After the rain, God called Noah, his family, and all of the animals out of the ark. Then God told Noah to be fruitful and multiply.

LESSON 3: September 19
God Raises Up a Deliverer
Exodus 3:1-12

This Scripture passage begins with Moses tending his father-in-law's flocks out in the wilderness. Suddenly he sees a bush that is burning but is not being consumed, so he draws near to get a closer look. Then God speaks to Moses from the bush and tells him that He has seen the misery of the Israelites and is going to use Moses to bring the people out of Egypt.

LESSON 4: September 26
Becoming God's People
Deuteronomy 29:2-15

After the Israelites had wandered in the wilderness for 40 years, the Lord was ready to confirm His covenant with the people. God made a covenant with the Israelites and established them as His special people, but they were to keep their part of the covenant by obeying God's Word.

UNIT 2. GOD'S CREATIVITY CONTINUES

God continues His creativity in a series of re-creations in the latter days of Israel's history. God made a wonderful covenant with David in which He promised him an eternal dynasty. Later in Judah's history the people were taken into exile in Babylon, but God did not forget His people. He loved them and promised to bring them back.

LESSON 5: October 3
Creating a New Dynasty
2 Samuel 7:18-29

In this Scripture passage, David humbly accepts God's wonderful covenant promise to him and praises God for His promise. God promised that through David's descendants, He would establish a royal dynasty that would last forever. This promise was fulfilled in Jesus.

1

LESSON 6: October 10
Creating a Redeemed People
Isaiah 43:1-2, 10-13, 18-19

The people were in exile in Babylon, but God had not forgotten His people. He promised to be with His people as they passed through the waters. The Lord God is the only Saviour. God was doing a new thing: He was going to re-create His people.

LESSON 7: October 17
Creating a New Covenant
Jeremiah 29:10-14; 31:31-34

When 70 years of exile were over, God promised to bring His people back to the land. God's plans were to prosper them when they sought Him with all their heart. He was going to make a new covenant with His people, a covenant of the heart. Under the new covenant, His people would obey and recognize Him and forgiveness would be available to all.

LESSON 8: October 24
Creating a New Hope
Ezekiel 37:1-14

Ezekiel's prophecy of a valley full of dry bones, which the Lord was going to bring back to life, was a message of hope that signified the renewal of the people of Israel. Israel was in what seemed like a hopeless situation in exile. The bones and flesh coming together to create bodies and life being breathed into the bodies echo God's creation of Adam. This restoration of Israel is another re-creative act of God.

LESSON 9: October 31
Creating a Renewed Trust
Psalm 73:1-3, 12-13, 16-18, 21-26

Sometimes the godly are tempted to envy those who are materially successful but do not follow the Lord. However, this kind of success is very precarious; it can be lost very quickly and without warning. But God is good to those who follow Him. We may not be rich or famous, but we have God. Therefore, we can encourage ourselves to trust in the Lord, who will one day reward those who follow Him.

UNIT 3. A NEW CREATION

This last unit focuses on the work of God in offering to make us new in Christ. In the first lesson, the law is turned upside down and, rather than being a set of external rules, becomes plant-ed within. The second lesson teaches us that our bodies will some day be made anew. In the third lesson, we learn that when we believe in Jesus as Saviour, we become new creatures in Him. And in the last lesson of this quarter, we see that we as a body (the Church) are made one.

LESSON 10: November 7
A New Approach
Matthew 5:17-18, 21-22, 27-28, 31-35, 38-39, 43-44

Jesus addresses the superficial view of the law and explains that He did not come to abolish the law, but to plant it within the heart. Jesus does not excuse hateful name-calling but makes it equivalent to murder. Lust is the same as adultery. Divorce is excused only when there is unfaithfulness. The follower of the Lord does not need to swear by an oath, but must always speak the truth. Jesus also tells His followers to love their enemies.

LESSON 11: November 14
A New Body
1 Corinthians 15:42-57

God will re-create the human body of the believer as a heavenly body after the resurrection, and our new eternal bodies will be imperishable, glorious, and powerful. The creation of Adam is contrasted with the resurrection of Christ, who is the first to appear in a spiritual body. Christ, the last Adam, is from heaven and His body is heavenly. When we receive Christ as Saviour, we can look forward to being raised in our resurrection bodies.

LESSON 12: November 21
A New Creature in Christ
2 Corinthians 5:11-21

Paul tells us that those who are in Christ are new creations. God creates us anew when we receive Christ as Saviour. Everything about us is new. God reconciles us to Himself through His Son.

LESSON 13: November 28
A New Relationship
Ephesians 2:11-21

Not only does God create us anew as individuals, but He also creates us as one body in Christ. In New Testament days, Gentile believers and Jewish believers were made one. Today, people of different cultures, races, and origins are made one in Christ. Jesus is our peace; He has broken down the walls that would divide us.

THE GOD OF CONTINUING CREATION

by Katherine Steward

One needs only to watch a brilliant sunset, sit in the grass under a star-filled sky, or touch the tiny fingers of a newborn child to marvel at the awesome work of our Creator, God the Father. The familiar passage in Genesis 1, where God speaks light, sky, water, land, etc. into being, culminates in the creation of man, His prize work. As we read this account, it is necessary to stop and try—as much as our human understanding will allow—to appreciate the majesty and wonder of creation and to acknowledge our value amidst God's "good" work (Genesis 1:31). It is also necessary to realize that God's creative work did not end after the six days of Creation. It did not end when He declared all that He made "good." As illustrated throughout the Bible, God is a God of *continuing* creation. His creative work continues even to this day as believers are made new creations through Christ Jesus.

Creation of Man

Adam was created from the "dust of the ground" (Genesis 2:7) as a void, lifeless shell. It was not until God Himself breathed life into his nostrils that he became a viable, functional being, created in God's image (Genesis 1:27). Humankind was created with the ability to reflect God's character. We were created with the ability to think for ourselves; to be morally responsible and creative in our own right; and to express love, patience, kindness, forgiveness, and other characteristics that reflect God. We were created with the ability to establish and enjoy relationships. Humankind was created for a purpose. We were created to have fellowship with God, to honor God, and to cultivate the land He created (1:28). Through sin, however, the perfect fellowship

between God and man was broken (see Genesis 3).

One might wonder why Adam and Eve, the first man and woman God created, would disobey a Father who so lovingly and so abundantly provided for them. The answer is the same as it is with God's children today: They were human, created with free will and the ability to choose. God created us with free will so that our obedience to and love for God would be given by choice, not by force.

As we all can attest, people sometimes make bad or ill-advised choices. They don't always consider the consequences of their choices and as a result must live with those consequences. People often choose to go their own way rather than yield to the Creator. If Adam and Eve had considered the consequences of their actions, then arguably they may not have sinned against their Creator.

By the time of Noah, sin was rampant and wickedness abounded on earth (6:5). The earth was now far from the paradise that the Creator had intended and where He had enjoyed fellowship with Adam. Instead, God looked upon His creation with sadness. He was grieved (6:6). His creation had chosen sin and rebellion over Him.

It had become necessary for God to impose judgment on His creation, as He cannot tolerate sin and allow it to go on indefinitely. He decided to destroy what He had created: "I will destroy man whom I have created from the face of the earth" (6:7). God would destroy, through a great flood, a world that had become flooded with evil.

In the midst of judgment, God's loving, merciful, and redemptive nature shone through as He found just one person—Noah—who was faithful and who walked with the Lord (6:9). God decided to save Noah and his family, and after the rest of

3

creation had been wiped from the earth, Noah and his family would be charged to repopulate the earth (9:1). God's creation would be given a second chance. God, the Creator, is faithful to those who love and obey Him.

Creation of a Covenant

"With thee will I establish my covenant" (Genesis 6:18). These words were uttered by God as He created a covenant with Noah that He would never again destroy the earth with a flood (9:8-11). A covenant is a promise or a mutual agreement to do or to refrain from certain acts. Throughout history, God made covenants with His people. In Genesis 15:12-21, God made a covenant with Abram (Abraham) that his descendants would be as numerous as the stars in the sky, that he would be the "father of many nations" (17:4). At Mount Sinai, God established a covenant with the people of Israel (Exodus 19:5). This covenant was renewed in Deuteronomy 29. God also created a covenant with David, promising to extend his dynasty forever (2 Samuel 7:11-16). This promise was, of course, fulfilled through Jesus, a direct descendant of David (Luke 1:32-33).

In order for Old Testament covenants to remain valid, each side (God and man) had to honor the terms of the covenant. God would keep His promises if the people fulfilled their obligations. For Israel, this meant being faithful and obedient to God's laws. The covenants also required a blood sacrifice for the atonement for sin. If a blood sacrifice was not offered, the people's sin would be held against them. Unfortunately, Israel could not honor the terms of the covenant. Their disobedience and inability to honor the covenants led to exile, captivity, and destruction.

Once again, though, God's loving, merciful, and redemptive nature shone through as He promised to create yet another covenant with humankind. This covenant would differ from the covenants of old in that God's laws would be written on people's hearts and forgiveness would be available to all people (Jeremiah 31:31-33). Jesus would come to earth to establish this covenant, and His death and the shedding of His innocent blood would bind it for all eternity.

Re-creation through Jesus

Since the fall of man in the Garden of Eden, humanity has been separated from God and headed for eternal death. Our sinful nature—and the desire to please it—is the problem. Jesus is the solution. God came to earth in the flesh—Jesus—to reconcile us to and restore our relationship with God and to once and for all break the power of sin. In order to do that, Jesus had to give His life; His shed blood cleanses us of all our sins and provides the only way back to God (John 14:6). When we accept by faith what Jesus did, when we die to sin (Romans 6:1-14) and are born again in Jesus, we are re-created—created anew—with a new spirit and a new nature that is no longer under sin's control. "Therefore if any man be in Christ, he is a new creature: old things are passed away; behold, all things are become new" (2 Corinthians 5:17). Our hearts and our consciences are transformed. We are changed on the inside.

As a new creation, we no longer live for ourselves, but for God. We no longer try to live in resistance to the law, but in compliance with the law, for we understand that true freedom comes from obedience. As a new creation, we see and respond to people differently, showing love to those we may not have loved before and striving to be peacemakers. As a new creation, we are able to do "good works" (Ephesians 2:8-10) and pray that God will give us strength to perform the works He has prepared for us to do. As a new creation, we become "ambassadors" for God; we are called to be involved in the ministry of reconciling others to God (2 Corinthians 5:20) by helping them to know how they, too, can become new creations through Christ Jesus.

So while it may be nice on occasion to watch a brilliant sunset, sit in the grass under a star-filled sky, or touch the tiny fingers of a newborn child to appreciate the wonder of creation, one who has been made anew through Christ Jesus has to go no further than the closest mirror to marvel at the awesome work of our Creator, God the Father.

Katherine Steward is the Editor of *Preschool Playhouse®* and *Juniorway®* at Urban Ministries, Inc. She holds a bachelor's and a master's degree in psychology.

EXPANDING THE BOUNDARIES OF CHRISTIAN EDUCATION:

Reaching the Unchurched Community

by Charlesetta Watson Holmes

Lakeshia, pregnant with her fourth child, sits on her front porch smoking a cigarette. Her three barely clothed children have not eaten in three days. Gas and electric services have been shut off and her welfare check is late. Sherry, a graduate student from MIT, works as a software engineer in a prestigious firm. She makes a six-figure salary and ponders over where to go for her two-week vacation, Bermuda or Alaska. What do these two women have in common? From the above description it is hard to tell; however, both of these women are part of a growing group called the "unchurched" community, individuals who are part of a generation who never grew up in church.

The unchurched community includes emotionally, intellectually, and economically impoverished individuals. The intellectually unsaved individual feels that he or she does not need God. Intellectually, this person understands the concept of God, but emotionally he or she feels that success is a result of self-sufficiency. Emotionally and economically unsaved individuals have a particular need they would like God to meet. "Prosperity" messages have lured the unchurched into vacant pews. When the bona fide Word of God is taught, the unchurched discover that the prerequisite to God's blessings is a genuine relationship with Jesus Christ. Desiring to avoid relationship, commitment, and accountability, the unchurched take flight, leaving the pews empty again.

The Sunday School program is the staple of church growth and has long survived every theological fad that has been used to attempt to teach God's Word. Moreover, Sunday School has provided basic fundamental principles for teaching and reinforcing the Word of God. The challenge for Christian education today is to offer programs that reach the "impoverished minds" of both the "Lakeshias" and "Sherrys" of this age. In order to achieve this kind of evangelistic endeavor, the church must reevaluate its educational programs. This process may involve modifying programs and staffing and redirecting resources; however, only God can redefine a church's mission. In order to achieve evangelistic success in the unchurched community, we must first look at our greatest example, Jesus Christ.

Jesus Christ was a master teacher. Through Him, God the Creator demonstrated how to teach the masses. In Jesus' day, diversity existed among the people. Jesus' disciples came from a variety of socioeconomic backgrounds. Yet Jesus had no problem attracting the masses from both sides of the track; He taught all, whether rich, poor, old, or young. Jesus' purpose was to redeem mankind. In the Gospel of John, the writer tells how Jesus, the only One who has ever seen God, came to earth to introduce God and to reconcile man, the "creation," back to his Creator (John 1:8).

During His earthly ministry, Jesus completed the task of reconciling those who believed in Him back to the Creator. He taught the Word of God to the masses and instructed His disciples to do the same. God's redemptive plan for mankind was orchestrated through His Son, Jesus Christ. It is through Christ that the "creation" is transformed into a "new creation" molded into the image of God. It is through our newly created existence that we gain access to the unconditional love of God. It is God's agape love that beckons the church to reach out to the unsaved. It is the church's responsibility to take the Word of God to a diversified group of unbelievers, the "melting pot" of the unchurched community, and introduce them to their original owner, God the Creator.

This massive undertaking requires the church to increase its boundaries in Christian education. Adjusting the educational curriculum may be necessary; however, the key is to modify the curriculum without compromising the integrity of God's Word. Expanding the "nets" (the evangelistic thrust) that capture the "fish" (unsaved individuals) warrants close observation of the techniques Jesus used to haul in the "catch." Jesus was not only the master teacher but also the master fisherman. The following steps can be utilized in reaching the unchurched community.

1. Put Out a Little from the Land

In Luke 5:1-11, we read how Jesus entered Simon's (Peter's) boat in order to speak to the masses of people. He asked Simon to "thrust out a little from the land" (Luke 5:3). Jesus asked Simon to move the boat a little bit into the water so He could sit down and teach the people. First, make sure Jesus is "aboard" every evangelistic effort. Be sure that His teaching is in effect. Only God can draw the unsaved. Before launching major projects into the "deep waters" of the larger community, start with the local areas around the church. Fellowship with local churches and business persons, and perform demographic studies to determine the individuals living in the local community. Saturate the community with the Word of God.

2. Put Out into the Deep Water

Jesus instructed Simon to launch into the deep. When God instructs the church to further its evangelistic efforts beyond the local community, move! The Lord instructed Simon to "let down your nets" for a catch (Luke 5:4). The nets are the church's available resources. There is a big difference between using "bait" and "letting down a net" to catch the unsaved. Bait, if improperly used, can be construed as manipulation. Remember that what-ever is used to attract the "catch" will be required to keep them. A "net" inhibits the direction of the intended party, snatching them out of the drowning seas of sin and bringing them onto the dry ground of repentance and sanctification. Remember: It is God who calls the "fish" into the nets.

3. Put Away Assumptions

According to scholars, the fish referred to in this passage of Scripture represent 153 different species. When the "nets" come in, the diversity among the people will be impressive. There will be people from every walk of life. Both "Lakeshia" and "Sherry" will be among the catch. Don't make assumptions or judge individuals. Remember that the unsaved are "fish out of water" and are unfamiliar with the "dry land" (church).

4. Pull in Partners

When the nets began to break, Simon signaled for his partners, James and John, to help him bring in the nets. Simon called for skilled fishermen to help haul in the catch. When the increase comes in and the need to teach and serve is great, rely on "partners." Partners are individuals who are reliable "fishermen," trained individuals who can help disciple the unsaved. Partners might be clergy or laypersons who have been thoroughly trained in discipleship and teaching God's Word.

5. Put Aside Tradition

After the "catch" came in, Jesus redefined Simon and his partners' mission. He told them they would be "fishers of men." When God redirects the focus of the church, don't hold on to tradition—change the direction of the ministry.

Jesus trained His disciples in evangelism. Depend on the Creator. Only God knows the makeup of His creation. Allow His hand to direct the church's "fishing expedition." What "nets" are at your disposal?

Charlesetta Watson Holmes is a freelance writer for UMI and currently is a student at Monmouth University.

RENEWAL FOR BURNED-OUT BELIEVERS:

The God of Continuing Education

by LaTonya Mason

When the movie *The Sixth Sense* came out, there were many people parroting its famous line, "I see dead people." The child star of the movie coined the phrase when he went to a psychologist to seek help and refuge from dead, disturbed spirits whom he could see and communicate with. While I don't accept the movie's paranormal premises, I would like to use the phrase myself and relate it to what I have witnessed in the church. In the movie, people who were supposed to be dead were alive. In the church, I see dead people—believers who are supposed to be alive but are dead.

Simply defined, the word *dead* means to be without vitality and spirit, unresponsive, extinguished, and no longer functioning. So many people in the body of Christ are depressed, always tired, easily overwhelmed, and usually at the point of throwing in the towel. This is called "spiritual burnout" and is not new. In fact, many of the Bible's elect experienced it. In chapter 1 of his book, Job was commended as one who feared God and shunned evil; but by chapter 3, he was cursing the day he was born. Right after Elijah did a mighty exploit for the kingdom of God on Mount Carmel, he prayed for death because he was afraid of Jezebel. In most of his psalms, David fluctuated between "blessing the Lord at all times" and crying out for God's mercy and protection. Not everyone experiences burnout, but we can see that being a Christian does not exempt us from it. In fact, those who are willing to be on the "front line" of the battle are more susceptible. In his article, "The Cost of Caring," Dr. Summer H. Garte reports that the person who is dedicated, committed, and willing to spend great amounts of energy and time in service to other people is most vulnerable to burnout. He further says that "burnout victims" are those who have a strong need for approval and a "Messiah complex." There is a fine line between wanting to please God and seeking approval from man. Other factors that lead to burnout are overcommitment, chronic stress, misinterpretation of experiences, inadequate support, demanding perfection of oneself, and confusing roles.

Burnout is not the will of God for His children. In fact, He offers an alternative. In Matthew 11:28-29, Jesus asserts that there is a lighter burden for those of us who are heavy and oppressed. He even admonishes the overburdened and weary to come to Him so that He can give them rest. In verse 30 He says, "My yoke is easy, and my burden is light." In order to avoid burnout, we must be renewed through God's Word. If we are burned out, it is because we have believed the world's report on how to live and have taken on its burdens. Although the enemy is not to blame for burnout, he certainly uses it to his advantage. He knows that the body of Christ cannot function effectively or advance if its members are exhausted and inactive.

The following are suggestions that believers can apply to renew themselves and become resistant to burnout.

Pray. This sounds so simple that you may be tempted to read over it. But the truth is, if we spent more time in prayer asking for knowledge of God's will and wisdom, we would not take on half of the things that we do. Adequate time in prayer is a safeguard against making bad decisions.

Sometimes we refuse to pray because we are afraid of what God's answer may be. We need to be mindful that God cares for and loves us. He wants us to know His will and to experience the abundant life that He promised. But we must wait on Him in prayer to be renewed.

Learn how to say no without feeling guilty. It is false to think that being a good Christian means always saying yes. A good Christian follows the Golden Rule: "Love your neighbor as you love yourself." Super Christians reverse the command. They love others, and then if there is any love left over, they may direct it toward themselves, but only after looking for one more person to extend themselves to. How can you love or take care of another person when you are empty and lonely yourself? Super Christians keep giving and giving and giving and then they get angry when no one gives to them. Why would someone give to such a person? They give the illusion that they have it all. This sheds new light on the Golden Rule. If Christians do not take care of and love themselves, it is unfair to expect that someone else will. People will treat us the way we treat ourselves. So, if we disrespect ourselves, others will do the same. Good Christians are renewed by knowing that God already accepts them and that He gives the favor of men. That truth alone strengthens and rejuvenates us. We do not have to earn others' approval.

Be mindful of Christ's death. There are many believers who are strangers to their God-given covenant. They do not know the benefits of Christ's death. They stop at "He died for my sins." While that is true, it's just one-third of what He did. In Christ's death, the power of sin was abolished. He was beaten for our freedom and wholeness. We are not supposed to be sick, broke, or disgusted. Moreover, He was raised from the dead. In Him, we were raised too, and were put in a right relationship with God. We were justified. That means we can go to the throne of grace, humbly but boldly asking for God's provision. If He gave up His Son for us, why would He withhold the desires He placed in our hearts? In addition to His burial and resurrection, Christ also ascended into heaven to sit at the right hand of God to intercede for us. Remember when Jesus told Peter that Satan was trying to sift him as wheat, but that he need not worry because Jesus was praying for him? Well, He is doing the same for us. We spend so much time praying and pleading for God to intervene. We need to learn to rest, knowing that Jesus is praying for us. Being mindful of the threefold blessing of Christ's death immunizes our spirit against burnout and gives us strength to endure the trials of life.

Know who you are in Christ. As born-again believers, we know that we are the adopted sons and daughters of God and the siblings of Jesus Christ. We even bear His name and are known as Christians. God selected us and gave us the Bible as our adoption papers, which outline who we are, what we have, what we can do, and to whom we belong. Too many of us are living out our biological inheritances. We're broke because we come from a family background of poverty; we're sick because we have a family history of diseases; we're addicted to things and people because that's all we know. But the truth is that we have been adopted into a new family. We've been given a new inheritance and future. Our minds need to be renewed with the Word of God. There's no way we can be depressed, broke, frustrated, and sick while believing God's testimony.

I'm sure that there are more things that could be added to this list of ways to prevent burnout, but I think some basic essentials have been outlined. Let us not be like the church of Sardis in Revelation 3:1–2 (NIV), where John records the following message from God: "I know your deeds; you have a reputation of being alive, but you are dead. Wake up!"

LaTonya Mason is a freelance writer for UMIs *Inteen®* and *Young Adult Today®* publications. She holds a bachelor's degree in child psychology and a master's degree in counseling.

JAN ERNST MATZELIGER

(1852-1889) • *Inventor*

Persistence and optimism paid off for Jan Ernst Matzeliger, an African American inventor during the middle 1800s. While facing racial prejudice and massive discrimination in the U.S., he invented the "lasting machine," which revolutionized the shoe industry. His automated machine performed the final and important step of attaching the shoe's upper portion to the sole. In the past, people called "hand lasters" had performed this work. Thanks to Matzeliger, factories were able to turn out 150 to 700 pairs of shoes a day as opposed to the 50 pairs produced previously.

Matzeliger was born in the Republic of Suriname (Dutch Guiana) in South America to a Surinamese Black slave mother and a wealthy White Dutch father from Holland who was an engineer in charge of government machine shops. At age 10, Matzeliger also went to work in a machine shop. Then, at the age of 19, he acquired a job on an East Indian merchant ship and spent two years at sea. When the ship docked in Philadelphia, Matzeliger decided to stay in the U.S.

While in America, he worked various jobs. In 1876, he settled in Lynn, Massachusetts, where he secured a job with the shoe manufacturing company that helped him launch his career. Even though he was successful doing manual labor at the factory, Matzeliger was not satisfied with his education and station. Therefore, he enrolled in night school where he studied physics and improved his English. He also painted and gave art lessons.

During the day, Matzeliger studied the hand lasters in the factory as they did their jobs, and at night he worked on his design using salvaged scraps. He tried to duplicate the movements of the lasters and finally did so by making drawings. He worked for six months on a simple machine made of wire, wood, and cigar boxes. In four years, he had perfected a machine made of scrap iron.

His boss tried to buy his design for $50, but Matzeliger refused. He later refused an offer of $1,500 and kept perfecting his invention. He also secured a patent. After 10 years of sweat and hard work (with little encouragement and monumental discouragement) spending five to six cents a day for food, sacrificing sleep, and enduring public laughter at his efforts, he finally developed and perfected the advanced model of the lasting machine that recast the shoemaking industry.

Sixty-five years later, the United Shoe Machinery Corporation, which used Matzeliger's invention and dominated the U.S. shoemaking industry, was worth over one billion dollars. Matzeliger's hometown, Lynn, became the "Shoe Capital of the World." In addition, a school founded in Lynn to train young men to run the lasting machine still produces more than 200 graduates each year, who in turn educate others in the U.S. and abroad in the use of Matzeliger's lasting machine.

Matzeliger died August 24, 1889 from tuberculosis. Because the North Congregational Church was the only church in Lynn that did not turn him away due to his skin color, he left a large portion of his estate to them. A life-size portrait of Matzeliger still hangs on the wall of the church that opened its doors to this inventor.

For further information on Jan Ernst Matzeliger visit *www.bridgew.edu/HOBA/Inductees/Matzeliger.htm* or *www.africanpubs.com/Apps/bios/0957MatzeligerJan.asp.*

Evangeline Carey is a freelance author with more than 350 published works. She holds a bachelor's degree in sociology/psychology and studied extensively at Moody Bible Institute in Chicago.

TEACHING TIPS

1. Words You Should Know

A. Soul (Genesis 2:7) *nephesh* (Heb.)—The whole human person, physical and spiritual. The term "being" best expresses this biblical concept.

B. Adam (v. 19) *àdam* (Heb.)—The original Hebrew word for mankind or human beings.

2. Teacher Preparation

A. Pray for the students in your class, asking God to open their hearts to today's lesson.

B. Read and study the FOCAL VERSES, paying attention to the Lord's relationship with Adam.

C. Carefully review the Bible Study Guide, making notes for clarification.

D. Share a personal thought with the class about how you feel knowing you were uniquely created in the image of God.

3. Starting the Lesson

A. Before the class arrives, write the words *Adam* and *sovereignty* on the board.

B. After the students arrive and are settled, lead the class in prayer. Pray specifically for godly insights on the lesson and blessings on the lives of the students.

4. Getting into the Lesson

A. Ask volunteers to read IN FOCUS and then discuss the meaning of the story.

B. Ask volunteers to read THE PEOPLE, PLACES, AND TIMES and BACKGROUND.

C. Ask students to read the FOCAL VERSES together, then have a student read the corresponding IN DEPTH section. Allow time for discussion between each section.

5. Relating the Lesson to Life

A. Spend time answering the questions in the DISCUSS THE MEANING section.

B. Ask if any student has an insight that he or she would like to share regarding today's lesson.

6. Arousing Action

A. Read LESSON IN OUR SOCIETY to the class. Tell your class that during the month they will create a small garden and invite someone to share it with them. Direct the students to read the MAKE IT HAPPEN section and discuss it in class.

B. Tell the students to complete SEARCH THE SCRIPTURES as a review during the week.

C. End the class with prayer.

"And the LORD God formed man of the dust of the ground, and breathed into his nostrils the breath of life; and man became a living soul"

(Genesis 2:7).

WORSHIP GUIDE

For the Superintendent or Teacher
Theme: From the Dust of the Ground
Theme Song: "Have Thine Own Way, Lord!"
Scripture: Genesis 2:7
Song: "I Believe in Miracles"
Meditation: Holy Father, You are the Master Potter, and we are but clay to be molded to Your will. Thank You for life and the privilege of growing into Your kingdom.

FROM THE DUST OF THE GROUND

Bible Background • GENESIS 2
Printed Text • GENESIS 2:4-7, 15-24
Devotional Reading • PSALM 150

LESSON AIM

By the end of the lesson, the students will be able to explain how man is unique to God's creation. They will also be able to articulate the significance of human companionship, even in the Garden of Eden.

KEEP IN MIND

"And the LORD God formed man of the dust of the ground, and breathed into his nostrils the breath of life; and man became a living soul" (Genesis 2:7).

FOCAL VERSES

Genesis 2:4 These are the generations of the heavens and the earth when they were created, in the day that the LORD God made the earth and the heavens,

5 And every plant of the field before it was in the earth, and every herb of the field before it grew: for the LORD God had not caused it to rain upon the earth, and there was not a man to till the ground.

6 But there went up a mist from the earth, and watered the whole face of the ground.

7 And the LORD God formed man of the dust of the ground, and breathed into his nostrils the breath of life; and man became a living soul.

2:15 And the LORD God took the man, and put him into the garden of Eden to dress it and to keep it.

16 And the LORD God commanded the man, saying, Of every tree of the garden thou mayest freely eat:

LESSON OVERVIEW

LESSON AIM
KEEP IN MIND
FOCAL VERSES
IN FOCUS
THE PEOPLE, PLACES, AND TIMES
BACKGROUND
AT-A-GLANCE
IN DEPTH
SEARCH THE SCRIPTURES
DISCUSS THE MEANING
LESSON IN OUR SOCIETY
MAKE IT HAPPEN
FOLLOW THE SPIRIT
REMEMBER YOUR THOUGHTS
MORE LIGHT ON THE TEXT
DAILY BIBLE READINGS

17 But of the tree of the knowledge of good and evil, thou shalt not eat of it: for in the day that thou eatest thereof thou shalt surely die.

18 And the LORD God said, It is not good that the man should be alone; I will make him an help meet for him.

19 And out of the ground the LORD God formed every beast of the field, and every fowl of the air; and brought them unto Adam to see what he would call them: and whatsoever Adam called every living creature, that was the name thereof.

20 And Adam gave names to all cattle, and to the fowl of the air, and to every beast of the field; but for Adam there was not found an help meet for him.

21 And the LORD God caused a deep sleep to fall upon Adam, and he slept: and he took one of his ribs, and closed up the flesh instead thereof;

22 And the rib, which the LORD God had taken from man, made he a woman, and brought her unto the man.

23 And Adam said, This is now bone of my bones, and flesh of my flesh: she shall be called Woman, because she was taken out of Man.

24 Therefore shall a man leave his father and his mother, and shall cleave unto his wife: and they shall be one flesh.

IN FOCUS

Malik and his wife Aisha drove to Saratoga,

Florida from Gary, Indiana with the desperate hope of finding work. A year later, they were living in their car. They were penniless, homeless, and helpless without money for car repairs, gasoline, or even food. For the last several months, the couple found themselves begging in front of grocery stores or street corners.

On an extremely hot day, Malik and Aisha found themselves walking the streets of Saratoga with a faint scent of urine reeking from Malik's ill-fitting clothes. Malik stared at his wife walking a few steps ahead of him and saw a well-dressed man approach her. The man put his hand on her shoulder and put some loose change in her hand. Before he walked away, he said what people often say, "God bless you my sister. Christ is the answer to your problems." Then the man marched across the street. Aisha smiled and turned to her husband. They moved to a bench next to a high iron fence. While counting their money they discovered they had enough for a couple of hamburgers. Malik took in his wife's woolen socks and thin shoulders and watched a smile grow under her matted hair. Smiling she said, "At least we're not poor today."

Just as Malik was about to curl up on the bench to sleep, he noticed the sign on the fence directly in front of him that read Antioch Theological Seminary. As if he were a man possessed, Malik sprang to his feet and ran through a crowd of shocked students who were walking the clean sidewalks and manicured lawns inside the fence screaming at them, "I want to see the face of God." Aisha ran close behind him as he charged up the concrete stairs leading to the library and through the heavy glass doors. He yelled, "Where is he?" When Malik approached the aging librarian, he was out of breath. The librarian remained calm. Malik leaned over the counter, panting and demanding, "I want to see the face of God. Where is he? Where is the God who everyone is telling me to believe in?"

The librarian thought to show him a picture of Christ in the Bible when Aisha grabbed her husband's hand and squeezed it. Then she kissed him and Malik burst into tears. Aisha said, "It's all right, you know I love you. Don't you love me?" The hurt in his wife's face touched his heart so deeply he pulled her into his arms. The librarian waved off the security guards who surrounded Malik and touched his hand, saying, "When you look into your wife's face you really are looking into the face of God."

When God created us, He created us in His image. No matter what our condition or circumstance, we each reflect His image as we go through life. God's perfect image is love.

THE PEOPLE, PLACES, AND TIMES

The Lord God. The principal meaning of God's name as used here (Heb. *Yahweh*, **Ya-way**) is the self-existent One or the eternal I AM. *Yahweh* has always existed and will never cease to exist.

Man. In the original Hebrew, the word for man is "Adam." In this sense, therefore, all mankind could rightly be called Adam.

The Garden of Eden. There remains today a great debate among scholars as to the exact location of the Garden of Eden. Suggested sites for the Garden include Asia, the Middle East, and Africa. Two of the Edenic rivers, the Pishon and the Gihon, flow through Africa. We may never know where on earth this garden of God was located, but we do know from Scripture that it was a paradise. Within this paradise, God placed the first man and woman, along with birds, animals, and trees with pleasant fruit to eat. This garden was also home to the Tree of Life, from which humans were encouraged to partake before the fall of mankind.

BACKGROUND

God created the heavens and the earth, and then He rested. The crowning achievement of His creative work was bringing into existence the first man and woman. The author of this portion of the Genesis narrative takes great care to detail how God created Adam and Eve. The writer also describes the creation of their place of habitation and the creation of the bird and animal life that shared their home.

God is cast in the light of a deliberate and intentional craftsman who brings into existence that which has never been. Not content just to fashion the objects of this creation from the essence of the earth, God imparts His image into His highest creation. God then begins to teach His newly created (Luke 3:37) son about his own uniqueness. This educational act culminates in God drawing a companion from the essence of man and delivering her as a helper.

AT-A-GLANCE

**1. God Creates a New Being
(Genesis 2:4b-7)
2. God Prepares Man for Righteousness
(vv. 15-17)
3. God's View of Man's Loneliness
(vv. 18-20)
4. God's Response to Man's Loneliness
(vv. 21-24)**

IN DEPTH

1. God Creates a New Being (Genesis 2:4b-7)

The heavens and earth were complete, and God had rested. Now it was time to bring into existence something brand new. It was time to create man. Before fashioning man, however, God prepared plants and herbs that eventually would make up the garden in which man would live and work. Finally, when the earth and plant life were prepared, God scooped a handful of dust from the earth and formed Adam. When God breathed into Adam's nostrils the breath of life, he became a living being.

2. God Prepares Man for Righteousness (vv. 15-17)

God made man to be a companion and friend. His great love for man was demonstrated by the care He took in planting the Garden of Eden for him. God and man would share fellowship in this garden paradise.

God also created Adam in a state of innocence, but not righteousness. Adam was to accomplish righteousness by fulfilling the terms of the Creation Covenant. In other words, he was to deliberately choose to remain loyal to God and to

not sin. Since the whole human race was in Adam, we were all involved in his choices. Yet God continues to show His love for us even though He knows that we will eventually disobey Him.

God desires that man seek righteousness. It is for that reason that once Adam was placed in the garden, God gave him several tasks: (1) to submit to God in all things; (2) to rule the creation according to God's will; (3) to experience oneness through marriage; (4) to fill the earth with God's people; (5) to care for, guard, and expand the garden; and (6) to partake of the Tree of Life.

Adam was to pass the test of loyalty by not eating from the Tree of the Knowledge of Good and Evil. Obedience to these tasks would guide man into righteousness and guarantee eternal life and fellowship with God.

3. God's View of Man's Loneliness (vv. 18-20)

One can feel lonely even though he shares an intimate fellowship with God and lives within a specially prepared paradise. God knew that His son (Adam) would be lonely. He wanted Adam to understand that he was created differently from the rest of creation. Adam occupied a special relationship with the Creator, and he would need someone like himself with whom to share his life and home.

After Adam was settled in the Garden of Eden, God caused the birds and animals of the earth to pass before man. Whatever Adam called them became their name. At the end of this experience, Adam realized that none of the living creatures he had just named was like him. He was unique to God's creation, and in a very real sense, he was alone.

4. God's Response to Man's Loneliness (vv. 21-24)

God allowed Adam to experience loneliness so that he would understand his own special place in the created order. Sharing God's image and His breath, Adam was created above the rest of the life on the earth. Once Adam had learned this, God, in an act of deep love and compassion, caused Adam to sleep and then took a portion of man and shaped it into a living companion.

When Adam woke up, God presented the

woman to him. Adam recognized that she was of the same essence as he. Though they were different physically, they were one and the same. In their union, neither would again be lonely in God's paradise.

SEARCH THE SCRIPTURES

1. Why did God plant the Garden of Eden for man (Genesis 2:7-8)?

2. Why was man forbidden to eat of the fruit of the Tree of the Knowledge of Good and Evil (v. 17)?

3. What is the significance of Adam's naming the animals (vv. 19-20)?

4. Why was Adam's helper formed from his rib (v. 23)?

DISCUSS THE MEANING

1. Do you think that there is special significance in the fact that God fashioned woman from the rib of man? What are some of the ways that this order of created activity affects the relationship between men and women?

2. God gave to man some of His authority over the earth and its animal and plant life. In what ways has man used this authority to order his life on the earth?

3. When God delegates some of His sovereignty to man, what does this say about the value God places on man?

LESSON IN OUR SOCIETY

In today's lesson, we see the deliberateness and care with which God created the first man, the first woman, and the world they were to inhabit. God acted very intentionally so that we would learn that our presence on the earth was not a mistake. No matter what fate befalls us during our time on the earth, the way in which we were created always reminds us of how special we are to God.

We have also come to understand that man was created in the image of God and entrusted by Him with power and authority over the earth. By creating man in His image and giving him delegated sovereignty over the earth, God is seeking to teach us how a proper relationship and the proper exercise of power can enrich each of our lives.

MAKE IT HAPPEN

We associate gardens with a sense of peace and tranquility. They invite us to relax in the midst of nature's beauty. Why not create a garden of your own? As a class, identify a small plot of land, obtain the necessary permission, and plant some flowers or a tree. Have the garden dedicated, and then invite your church family and community to share it with you. If you do not have access to an outdoor garden, you can create an indoor garden of sorts by asking students to bring plants to place around the Sunday School room.

FOLLOW THE SPIRIT

What God wants me to do:

_____

_____

REMEMBER YOUR THOUGHTS

Special insights I have learned:

_____

_____

MORE LIGHT ON THE TEXT

Genesis 2:4b-7, 15-24

4 These are the generations of the heavens and of the earth when they were created, in the day that the LORD God made the earth and the heavens,

The verse says the same things twice in reverse order: "the heavens and…the earth were created" and "made the earth and the heavens." This style is an ancient form of internal heading (see Genesis 5:1; 6:9; 10:1; 11:10, 27; 25:12, 19; 36:1; 37:2).

The term "generation" (Heb. *toledah*, **to-led-aw'**), which can be translated literally as "what comes after" or "what emerges from," describes something that is generated from something else. Thus, it does not describe the origin of the universe, but what immediately follows or arises from the heavens and earth. Therefore, in Genesis 2:4—4:26, we have a more detailed description of what God did on the sixth day of creation (1:24-31).

The combined name "the LORD God" (Heb. *yehovah elohiym*, **yeh-ho-vaw el-o-heem**) expresses the fact that Yahweh is one with Elohim. It establishes the unity of these two terms for Him, the

Adam and Eve: the highlight of God's creation.

man. Thus, the creation of the plants is not alluded to here, but simply the planting of the garden. The word "field" (Heb. *sadeh*, **saw-deh**), or garden, designates the open field of arable land or a definite portion of ground.

In the phrase "there was not a man to till the ground," there is a play on words. The words "man" (Heb. *adam*, **aw-dawm**) and "ground" (Heb. *adamah*, **ad-aw-maw**) are from the same Hebrew word *Édam*, which reminds us that we are created from the "dust of the ground."

6 But there went up a mist from the earth, and watered the whole face of the ground.

The term "mist" (Heb. *ed*, **ade**), or vapor, communicates a sense of enveloping. Moisture came up to water or envelop the earth. This detail is not mentioned in Genesis 1.

7 And the LORD God formed man of the dust of the ground, and breathed into his nostrils the breath of life; and man became a living soul.

Man consists of two elements: a physical, material side ("formed man of the dust"), showing that he has something in common with the physical environment, and an inner personality ("breathed into his nostrils the breath of life"), showing that he has something in common with God. The body of man consists entirely of basic substances similar to those found in the earth— "dust"(Heb. *aphar*, **aw-fawr**), or lumps of earth. God gave to man the "breath" (Heb. *neshamah*, **nesh-aw-maw**) of life in a special way that indicates that man exists on a much higher level than all other forms of life (cf. Genesis 1:26-27). Man is related to the physical world by virtue of his formation from the substance of the earth.

personal name and the title. Names were regarded not merely as labels but as symbols or keys to the nature or essence of the being or the thing (cf. Genesis 2:19).

5 And every plant of the field before it was in the earth, and every herb of the field before it grew: for the LORD God had not caused it to rain upon the earth, and there was not a man to till the ground.

The verse distinguishes between perennial wood plants that continue from year to year ("plant," Heb. *siyach*, **see'-akh**) and the green plants that spring up anew each year ("herb," Heb. *'eseb*, **eh'-seb**). The herbs spring up anew as the result of rains or of seeds sown by the hand of

At the same time, he is related to the nonphysical world because he was created in the image and likeness of God.

2:15 And the LORD God took the man, and put him into the garden of Eden to dress it and to keep it.

After the preparation of the garden, the Lord God placed man there "to dress it and to keep it." The statement contradicts the notion that work came as the result of the Fall. Genesis 1:28 indicates that God has given man jobs to do. These tasks are referred to here in 2:15 and more clearly defined as they relate to the garden in which man was placed. Paradise, the "garden" (Heb. *gan*, **gan**), does not equal a vacation or inactivity. The Garden of Eden, with all its precious trees, required dressing and keeping. It was intended to be dressed and kept by man, so that without human culture, plants degenerate and grow wild. Thus, the perfection of creation (1:31) did not exclude responsible work on man's part. The need to work and take care of the Garden of Eden implies that there were hostile forces against which man was to be on guard (cf. Genesis 3).

16 And the LORD God commanded the man, saying, Of every tree of the garden thou mayest freely eat: 17 But of the tree of the knowledge of good and evil, thou shalt not eat of it: for in the day that thou eatest thereof thou shalt surely die.

It was permissible for man to eat the fruit of all the trees in the garden with one exception: He should not eat "of the tree of the knowledge of good and evil." He was told to be obedient. Accompanying God's prohibition was the pronouncement of a serious penalty. If man disobeyed by eating from the Tree of the Knowledge of Good and Evil, he would come under judgment. He would experience the blessing of the Creation Covenant if he obeyed God's command and the curse of the Creation Covenant if he disobeyed (cf. Romans 6:23).

The term "in the day" (Heb. *yowm*, **yome**) is literally "on the day." The meaning of the phrase is, "you shall be doomed to death." The use of the infinitive absolute in Hebrew carries a wide range of meaning. In principle, man would immediately experience eternal death. However, in reality, man would not die instantly "in the day" he disobeyed (cf. Genesis 3). In fact, Adam lived 930 years (5:5). The punishment consisted of (1) subjection to physical decay and death (3:19; cf. the expression "and he died," which is repeated over and over in Genesis 5:5, 8, 11, and 14 regarding Adam and his descendants), (2) a ruined or damaged relationship with God, including man's removal from the presence of God (3:8-10, 22-24; Ephesians 2:2-3), (3) a ruined relationship toward God's creation (Genesis 3:12, 17-18; 4:23-24), and (4) a vulnerability to harassment by the enemy (3:15).

18 And the LORD God said, It is not good that the man should be alone; I will make him an help meet for him.

After the repeated statements in Genesis 1 that "it was good," it comes as a surprise to read "it is not good." Man was not created to be a solitary being. He is a social creature. He is made to enjoy other people. He needs a helper corresponding to him or alongside him. The Hebrew term for "help" (*ezer*, **ay-zer**) means to surround in the sense of protecting, helping, or supporting.

19 And out of the ground the LORD God formed every beast of the field, and every fowl of the air; and brought them unto Adam to see what he would call them: and whatsoever Adam called every living creature, that was the name thereof.

The Lord God invites Adam to name the animals He has created (cf. Genesis 1). In the ancient world, the act of naming is to give the description of the true nature. The names Adam gave to the animals expressed their true nature.

20 And Adam gave names to all cattle, and to the fowl of the air, and to every beast of the field; but for Adam there was not found an help meet for him.

Adam named the various animals. It is as if he was looking to see whether any animal could be an adequate companion for him. But there was no helper that corresponded to him. It was not good for man to be alone, and animal companionship was not enough to meet the need. The verb translated as "meet" usually means to suffice, reach, or be adequate.

21 And the LORD God caused a deep sleep to fall upon Adam, and he slept: and he took one of his ribs, and closed up the flesh instead thereof;

God caused man to fall into "a deep sleep" (Heb. *tardemah*, **tar-day-maw**, meaning lethargy or trance [cf. Genesis 15:12; Isaiah 29:10; Job 4:13; Proverbs 19:15]). This sleep is clearly different from ordinary sleep.

God took away one of the ribs of Adam and filled the empty place with flesh. The term "rib" (Heb. *tsela*, **tsay-law**) literally means "side" (see Genesis 2:12-22). To express close resemblance or kinship, the Hebrew language uses expressions like "the image" (Genesis 1:26) or "my bone and my flesh" (Genesis 29:14; Judges 9:2; 2 Samuel 5:1).

22 And the rib, which the LORD God had taken from man, made he a woman, and brought her unto the man.

God took the rib from man and made a woman. This creation of woman from man shows the complete and inherent unity of man and woman. She was formed for an inseparable unity and fellowship of life with man. She was brought to man wholly and exclusively by God.

23 And Adam said, This is now bone of my bones, and flesh of my flesh: she shall be called Woman, because she was taken out of Man.

In the woman, Adam discovered kinship. It was a cause of great, joyous astonishment to Adam. He describes his relation to the woman as "bone of my bones, and flesh of my flesh." He called her "woman" (Heb. *ishshah*, **ish-shaw**).

24 Therefore shall a man leave his father and his mother, and shall cleave unto his wife: and they shall be one flesh.

The word "therefore" (or "for this reason") indicates a close, binding unity of man and woman in the marriage bond. Marriage is designed to create distinct families—"a man [shall] leave his father and his mother."

The phrase "they shall be one flesh" expresses the unity of the two and the sanctity of their relationship (cf. Matthew 19:1-9; 5:32).

DAILY BIBLE READINGS

M: Praise the Lord
Psalm 148:1-6

T: Let All the Earth Praise God
Psalm 148:7-13

W: God's Creation is Good
Genesis 1:26-31

T: God Created Man
Genesis 2:4b-9

F: The Garden Is Watered by Rivers
Genesis 2:10-14

S: Man Is Placed in the Garden
Genesis 2:15-20

S: God Creates for Man
Genesis 2:21-25

God created us to have fellowship with Him and each other. Discover a deeper meaning of the word *fellowship* by doing a word study using one of the tools in your *Precepts For Living* CD-ROM library.

TEACHING TIPS

September 12
Bible Study Guide 2

1. Words You Should Know

A. Grace (Genesis 6:8) *chen* (Heb.)—God's unmerited favor.

B. Righteous (7:1) *tsaddiyq* (Heb.)—Being made right with God on the basis of faith.

2. Teacher Preparation

A. Pray for the students in your class, asking God to open their hearts to today's lesson.

B. Read and study the FOCAL VERSES, paying attention to God's feelings.

C. Carefully review the BIBLE STUDY GUIDE, making notes for clarification.

D. Share a personal thought with the class about a time when you were angry and how you reacted to that anger.

3. Starting the Lesson

A. Before the class arrives, write the words *Grace* and *Righteousness* on the board.

B. After the students arrive and are settled, lead the class in prayer. Pray specifically for godly insights into the lesson and blessings on the lives of the students.

4. Getting into the Lesson

A. Ask volunteers to read the IN FOCUS story and then spend time in discussion about what the story means.

B. Ask volunteers to read THE PEOPLE, PLACES, AND TIMES and BACKGROUND.

C. Ask students to read the FOCAL VERSES together, and then have a student read the corresponding IN DEPTH section. Allow time for discussion between each section.

5. Relating the Lesson to Life

A. Spend time answering the questions in DISCUSS THE MEANING.

B. Ask if any student has an insight regarding today's lesson that he/she would like to share.

6. Arousing Action

A. Read the LESSON IN OUR SOCIETY section to the class. Ask the students to select a partner and share an incident when they forgave someone or were forgiven by someone. After a brief discussion, direct the students to the MAKE IT HAPPEN section and discuss it as a class.

B. Tell the students to complete the SEARCH THE SCRIPTURES questions during the week to review the lesson.

C. End the class with prayer.

"And the bow shall be in the cloud; and I will look upon it, that I may remember the everlasting covenant between God and every living creature of all flesh that is upon the earth"

(Genesis 9:16).

BEGINNING AGAIN

Bible Background • GENESIS 6:5—9:17
Printed Text • GENESIS 6:5-8; 7:1-5, 17, 23; 8:14-16; 9:1
Devotional Reading • GENESIS 9:8-17

**SEPT
12TH**

LESSON AIM

By the end of the lesson, the students should understand that God always remembers His promises and that even when there are consequences for wrongdoing, God will leave room for second chances.

KEEP IN MIND

"And the bow shall be in the cloud; and I will look upon it, that I may remember the everlasting covenant between God and every living creature of all flesh that is upon the earth" (Genesis 9:16).

FOCAL VERSES

Genesis 6:5 And GOD saw that the wickedness of man was great in the earth, and that every imagination of the thoughts of his heart was only evil continually.

6 And it repented the LORD that he had made man on the earth, and it grieved him at his heart.

7 And the LORD said, I will destroy man whom I have created from the face of the earth, both man, and beast, and the creeping thing, and the fowls of the air; for it repenteth me that I have made them.

8 But Noah found grace in the eyes of the LORD.

7:1 And the LORD said unto Noah, Come thou and all thy house into the ark; for thee have I seen righteous before me in this generation.

2 Of every clean beast thou shalt take to thee by sevens, the male and his female: and of beasts that are not clean by two, the male and his female.

3 Of fowls also of the air by sevens, the male

LESSON OVERVIEW

LESSON AIM
KEEP IN MIND
FOCAL VERSES
IN FOCUS
THE PEOPLE, PLACES,
AND TIMES
BACKGROUND
AT-A-GLANCE
IN DEPTH
SEARCH THE SCRIPTURES
DISCUSS THE MEANING
LESSON IN OUR SOCIETY
MAKE IT HAPPEN
FOLLOW THE SPIRIT
REMEMBER YOUR THOUGHTS
MORE LIGHT ON THE TEXT
DAILY BIBLE READINGS

and the female; to keep seed alive upon the face of all the earth.

4 For yet seven days, and I will cause it to rain upon the earth forty days and forty nights; and every living substance that I have made will I destroy from off the face of the earth.

5 And Noah did according unto all that the LORD commanded him.

7:17 And the flood was forty days upon the earth; and the waters increased, and bare up the ark, and it was lift up above the earth.

7:23 And every living substance was destroyed which was upon the face of the ground, both man, and cattle, and the creeping things, and the fowl of the heaven; and they were destroyed from the earth: and Noah only remained alive, and they that were with him in the ark.

8:14 And in the second month, on the seven and twentieth day of the month, was the earth dried.

15 And God spake unto Noah, saying,

16 Go forth of the ark, thou, and thy wife, and thy sons, and thy sons' wives with thee.

9:1 And God blessed Noah and his sons, and said unto them, Be fruitful, and multiply, and replenish the earth.

IN FOCUS

Not long ago, a city dweller hoping to secure a less stressful life purchased a farm in the rural South. He looked forward to the rewards a farm life had to offer. It wasn't long before he realized that in order for him to have any hope of success as a farmer he would need the best mule in the county to help him work the land. After a short search, the man found the mule he wanted and purchased it from a wise old farmer, who promised to have one of his hands deliver the animal.

The new farmer could barely contain his excitement when the mule arrived, and he hurriedly hooked the animal to a plow. The mule promptly sat down and refused to move. The new farmer did everything he could think of to get the animal to pull the plow, but no matter what he tried, the animal remained fixed to that spot on the ground. Finally growing frustrated, the new farmer stormed back to the place where he had purchased the mule and complained to the old farmer. The old farmer could hardly believe the report he was hearing and asked to accompany the man back to his home so that he could see for himself what was happening.

After the two men arrived back at the farm, the new farmer repeated his efforts with the animal. No matter what he tried, the mule still refused to budge. Finally, the old farmer smiled and nodded his head knowingly. He picked up a two-by-four lying on the ground not far from the them, walked over to the mule, and whacked it between the eyes. The mule jumped to its feet with a start and dashed along the field pulling the plow behind. Then the old farmer turned to the new farmer and said simply, "Sometimes, you just have to know how to get their attention."

In this account of the flood and God's new covenant with creation, God was seeking to get our attention.

THE PEOPLE, PLACES, AND TIMES

Noah. Son of Lamech, Noah was born into a world that had become completely corrupted. However, because Noah found favor with God, he was declared righteous. Through Noah and his family, God preserved humanity and gave to the world a new beginning. Noah can be viewed, therefore, as the second father of humankind.

Many generations separated Noah and the earth's first couple. A canopy of water still hung in the heavens and provided shelter from the harmful effects of the sun. In that protected environment, life on earth flourished and mankind lived 900 years.

BACKGROUND

By the time of Noah's birth, God described humanity as very evil: "Every imagination of the thoughts of his heart was only evil continually." The descendants of Cain followed in his footsteps of sin. As they multiplied, they became a corrupting influence upon the world. The descendants of Seth, on the other hand, were to follow in his footsteps of faith. As they multiplied, they were to become a righteous witness to the world. However, all but a few of Seth's descendants followed the way of Cain. Among other things, they twisted God's Word to justify violence as the means of dealing with disagreements. Thus, violence and evil multiplied on the earth. Because of God's grace, they were living very long lives and were capable of very great wisdom; but they foolishly tried to use their God-given abilities against God.

The evil of man grieved God, and He determined that He would destroy all life on earth except for Noah, his family, and a set number of animals and birds.

> ## AT-A-GLANCE
>
> 1. God's Intense Grief
> (Genesis 6:5-8)
> 2. God's Saving Hand
> (Genesis 7:1-5, 17, 23)
> 3. God's Continuing Grace
> (Genesis 8:14-16; 9:1)

IN DEPTH

1. God's Intense Grief (Genesis 6:5-8)

How sad a time this must have been for the Creator. After God had carefully brought forth a beautiful and good creation, humans foolishly turned against Him and violated the terms of the Creation Covenant. Instead of pouring out His

The Ark shows that God gives second chances.

full judgment on mankind, God graciously established a Salvation Covenant. However, in spite of God's salvation promises, humans rejected God's call to faith. God gave them many encouragements to be fruitful and to multiply, but they refused to be obedient. Instead, mankind had become utterly depraved. Mankind had become so wicked that even at a subconscious level their imaginations and thoughts were evil. God was so grieved by this that He regretted ever creating man. Finally, God decided to pour out His judgment by destroying all life on earth.

However, God is faithful to His word and remembers His promise to Adam and Eve to provide a saviour and deliverer through whom man's broken relationship with Him will be restored (Genesis 3:15). This presents a dilemma for God. How can He wipe out life on earth and at the same time keep His promise to provide a saviour? God's solution was to raise up one righteous man and preserve him and his family from the coming destruction.

2. God's Saving Hand (Genesis 7:1-5, 17, 23)

Noah was not a perfect man. Like all of us, he had his share of sin and shortcomings. However, when God looked on Noah, He saw a man who put his trust in Him and His saving grace. God counted this faith as righteousness. He placed all of Noah's sin on the coming Redeemer, namely, His Son, Jesus Christ. Through God's grace, Noah was obedient. Thus, the human race was preserved in spite of God's judgment on sin through the flood.

3. God's Continuing Grace
(Genesis 8:14-16; 9:1)

Once God's judgment was complete, He gave instructions to Noah to take his family and the animals and disembark from the safety of the ark. Again, Noah obeyed God. Once all were safely out of the ark, God expressed His continuing grace to mankind by blessing Noah and his family and admonishing them to "be fruitful, and multiply."

SEARCH THE SCRIPTURES

1. Why did God regret making man (Genesis 6:5)?

2. What was destroyed in the flood (7:4)?

3. What did God do for Noah that communicated that He was giving mankind continuing grace (9:1)?

DISCUSS THE MEANING

1. How do you think Noah felt knowing the evil of the world in which he lived and hearing God say that He had found him to be righteous?

2. How do you think it was possible for it to rain for 40 days and 40 nights?

3. How did God ensure that the earth would be repopulated through Noah?

4. How was it possible for Noah to find grace in the eyes of the Lord?

LESSON IN OUR SOCIETY

Recently, a minister made national headlines when, after learning that his son had been shot and the person apprehended, he petitioned the criminal justice system for the felon to be sentenced to serve in his church. The courts complied with his request. Once the young shooter was in the church's custody, the pastor forgave him and helped him make a clean start.

Similarly, God's justice requires judgment for sin, but His grace makes forgiveness and redemption available to us through Jesus Christ.

MAKE IT HAPPEN

Have you ever done anything wrong? All of us have. How would you feel if you knew that God's judgment was coming and you would not be given a second chance? Write a poem from the perspective of a person on the outside of the ark. Use this to begin a discussion about our desire for second chances and our responsibility to give second chances to others.

FOLLOW THE SPIRIT

What God wants me to do:

_____

_____

REMEMBER YOUR THOUGHTS

Special insights I have learned:

_____

_____

MORE LIGHT ON THE TEXT

Genesis 6:5-8; 7:1-5, 17, 23; 8:14-16; 9:1

5 And GOD saw that the wickedness of man was great in the earth, and that every imagination of the thoughts of his heart was only evil continually.

God saw that the wickedness of man was great. He is not so far away that He takes no notice of what is happening. The deterioration of man into sin now comes to its greatest climax. His evil is described extensively. The intensity of the wickedness of man is shown with devastating force in the phrase "every imagination of the thoughts of his heart was only evil continually." The word "imagination" (Heb. *yetser*, **yay-tser**) is derived from the verb "to form" (Heb. *yatsar*, **yaw-tsar**; cf. Genesis 2:7) and implies purpose. Man was purposefully setting his mind on evil.

6 And it repented the LORD that he had made man on the earth, and it grieved him at his heart.

The verb "repented" (Heb. *nacham*, **naw-kham**)

has a root meaning of breathing deeply. It describes a change of mind or heart in an intransitive sense and is most frequently employed to indicate God's repentance. The verse raises the question: Can God repent? (cp. Exodus 32:14; Judges 2:18; 1 Samuel 15:11 with 1 Samuel 15:29; Psalm 110:4). The repentance of God is a human description (an anthropomorphic expression) conveying the poignancy of the situation and the serious breach that had taken place in the relationship of God to man. From a human's limited, earthly, finite perspective, it only appears that God's purposes have changed (see 1 Chronicles 21:15; Jeremiah 18:8; 26:3, 9; Amos 7:3, 6; Jonah 3:10). God's dealings with man are conditional upon the response of man (cf. Jeremiah 18:7-10; Deuteronomy 30:19).

7 And the LORD said, I will destroy man whom I have created from the face of the earth, both man, and beast, and the creeping thing, and the fowls of the air; for it repenteth me that I have made them.

The Lord decided to rub out of existence both man and his world. The verb "destroy" (Heb. *machah*, **maw-khaw**) has the meaning of wiping out or totally erasing something (see Genesis 7:4, 23; Exodus 32:32-33; 2 Kings 21:13; Psalm 51:1, 9; Isaiah 43:25; 44:22). It shows God's characteristic way of dealing with evil. He deals with it not with half-measures but with the simultaneous extremes of judgment and salvation.

Man's evil affects his environment, which was created for him. Thus, both man and his world would be wiped out (cp. Romans 8:19-23).

8 But Noah found grace in the eyes of the LORD.

The destruction, however, would not bring the human race to an end. God's mercy is shown in the midst of His wrath. He chose Noah, a man who would provide a way of salvation. The expression "to find grace" (Heb. *chen*, **khane**) is literally "to win favor in the eyes of" (see Genesis 39:21; Exodus 3:21; 33:12; Esther 2:15, 17; 5:2). God was pleased with, or attracted to, Noah. Noah did not deserve to be used by God; it was God's grace that saved him.

7:1 And the LORD said unto Noah, Come thou and all thy house into the ark; for thee have I seen righteous before me in this generation.

The Lord told Noah what he should do. He was to take his entire family into the ark (see Genesis 6:18; Romans 5:19; 1 Corinthians 7:14). He was reminded that the reason he was being spared was his righteous walk before God (see Genesis 6:9). The term "righteous" (Heb. *tsaddiyq*, **tsad-deek**) denotes conformity to an ethical or moral standard. Noah was not deviating from the norm set by God (cf. Ezekiel 14:14, 20).

The word "before" (Heb. *paniym*, **paw-neem** from *panah* meaning "to turn" or "to face") is a prepositional term meaning literally "to the face of" or "in my approving view." Noah was approved in the view of the Lord among all the people of the earth.

2 Of every clean beast thou shalt take to thee by sevens, the male and his female: and of beasts that are not clean by two, the male and his female.

Noah was instructed to bring into the ark seven pairs of clean animals and one pair of unclean— added details not mentioned in Genesis 6:18-20. The distinction between clean and unclean animals was probably for eating and for sacrificial purposes (cf. 8:20-21).

3 Of fowls also of the air by sevens, the male and the female; to keep seed alive upon the face of all the earth.

Noah was then to select seven pairs of every kind of bird. The ultimate purpose of the instructions given to Noah is "to keep seed alive upon the face of all the earth." Thus, every kind of living creature will survive the flood. The aquatic creatures were not mentioned, probably because they were immune from the danger presented by flood.

4 For yet seven days, and I will cause it to rain upon the earth forty days and forty nights; and every living substance that I have made will I destroy from off the face of the earth. 5 And Noah did according unto all that the LORD commanded him.

Noah carried out God's instructions with great

care (see Genesis 6:22). His obedience expressed his faith in the Lord, and many were saved through him (see Hebrews 11:7).

7:17 And the flood was forty days upon the earth; and the waters increased, and bare up the ark, and it was lift up above the earth. 7:23 And every living substance was destroyed which was upon the face of the ground, both man, and cattle, and the creeping things, and the fowl of the heaven; and they were destroyed from the earth: and Noah only remained alive, and they that were with him in the ark.

The flood wiped out every existing thing as the Lord had said (Genesis 7:4; see also 6:7). The list of animals given here is wider than the one in 6:7 and 7:14. It mentions birds and cattle as well as "the creeping things" (Heb. *remes*, **reh-mes**; see 1:25). "The creeping things" may be understood as all the countless kinds of animals that are not included in other categories.

8:14 And in the second month, on the seven and twentieth day of the month, was the earth dried.

The ground was sufficiently dry to allow men and animals to move around freely on the twenty-seventh of the second month. The word "dried" (Heb. *yabesh*, **yaw-bashe**) is a verb used here to mean "to become dry without moisture" or "to be dry and firm" (see 8:7, 14; Exodus 14:16, 21, 22; Joshua 2:10; Psalm 74:15). It is often used to portray dryness of vegetation. In Genesis 8:13 the word "dried" is a verb meaning "to be free of water" (Heb. *charab*, **khaw-rab**).

15 And God spake unto Noah, saying,

The initiative was from the Lord throughout (see 7:5, 9, 16; 8:1). The verse points out the fact that the saving of Noah and his family is exclusively an act of God. The whole scheme of salvation is centered on Noah; his family members are beneficiaries. Noah had shown self-discipline as he waited patiently for God's time and word (cp. 1 Samuel 13:9-14).

16 Go forth of the ark, thou, and thy wife, and thy sons, and thy sons' wives with thee. 9:1 And God blessed Noah and his sons, and said unto them, Be fruitful, and multiply, and replenish the earth.

Just as God had commanded Noah to enter the ark before the flood started, so now He ordered him to leave it with his family and all the animals. As in Genesis 6:18, the various members of Noah's family are listed. God commissioned Noah to refill the earth (cf. 1:28). By so doing, He renewed the blessing of creation (see 1:22, 28; 8:17; 9:7).

DAILY BIBLE READINGS

M: The Wickedness of Humans Is Great
Genesis 6:5-7
T: God Has Noah Build an Ark
Genesis 6:13-22
W: Noah Enters the Ark
Genesis 7:1-16
T: The Flood Comes
Genesis 7:17—8:5
F: Noah Leaves the Ark
Genesis 8:16-19
S: God Blesses Noah and His Family
Genesis 8:20—9:7
S: God Makes a Covenant
Genesis 9:8-17

Noah was pleasing to God. Find out more about the words *please* and *pleasing* by doing a search in the concordance resource that is available in the library of your *Precepts For Living* CD-ROM.

TEACHING TIPS

September 19
Bible Study Guide 3

1. Words You Should Know

A. Flock (Exodus 3:1) *tso'n* (Heb.)—A group of small cattle or sheep.

B. Taskmasters (v. 7) *nagas* (Heb.)—Rulers or oppressors.

C. Oppression (v. 9) *lachats* (Heb.)—Distress or pressure.

2. Teacher Preparation

A. Read the DEVOTIONAL READING.

B. Imagine how Moses felt not only to be called by God, but also to be selected to deliver His people out of bondage. How would you feel if God called you to deliver a correctional message to your family, coworkers, or friends?

C. Read the IN FOCUS and BACKGROUND sections.

3. Starting the Lesson

A. Open the lesson with prayer.

B. Ask a volunteer to read the FOCAL VERSES aloud.

C. Divide the class into two groups: the Moses group and the Pharaoh group. Have the Moses group tell how they would feel and what they would do if God called them to deliver His people.

D. Then ask the Pharaoh group to tell how they would react if the people under them demanded to be released from their authority. How would they feel if they were afflicted with the plagues that came upon Pharaoh?

4. Getting into the Lesson

A. Review the questions in the DISCUSS THE MEANING section.

B. Then have the groups come together to discuss their answers.

5. Relating the Lesson to Life

A. Ask class members to share a time when in obedience to God, they were led to do something difficult. For example, the Spirit of God may have impressed them to bring godly correction to someone based on His Word. How did they feel?

B. Have each person relate an experience when, like Pharaoh, they were the recipient of godly correction. How did they feel? How did they respond?

SEPT 19TH

6. Arousing Action

A. Encourage students to be more sensitive to the Spirit of God when God sends someone to speak words of correction or encouragement.

B. Remind students that whether they are the "deliverer" (Moses) or the "receiver" (Pharaoh), they should respond in the spirit of love.

WORSHIP GUIDE

For the Teacher or Superintendent
Theme: God Raises Up a Deliverer
Theme Song: "Trust and Obey"
Scripture: Exodus 3–4
Song: "Where He Leads Me I Will Follow"
Meditation: Dear Lord, help me to be sensitive to Your voice, that I might hear You when You call me. Heavenly Father, use me to help deliver Your children and point them to You, so they may worship You as well. Amen.

GOD RAISES UP A DELIVERER

Bible Background • EXODUS 3–4
Printed Text • EXODUS 3:1-12
Devotional Reading • EXODUS 3:13-17

LESSON AIM

By the end of the lesson, the students will learn how God can use anyone, not only to deliver His Word, but to act as His deliverer.

KEEP IN MIND

"Come now therefore, and I will send thee unto Pharaoh, that thou mayest bring forth my people the children of Israel out of Egypt" (Exodus 3:10).

FOCAL VERSES

Exodus 3:1 Now Moses kept the flock of Jethro his father in law, the priest of Midian: and he led the flock to the backside of the desert, and came to the mountain of God, even to Horeb.

2 And the angel of the LORD appeared unto him in a flame of fire out of the midst of a bush: and he looked, and, behold, the bush burned with fire, and the bush was not consumed.

3 And Moses said, I will now turn aside, and see this great sight, why the bush is not burnt.

4 And when the LORD saw that he turned aside to see, God called unto him out of the midst of the bush, and said, Moses, Moses. And he said, Here am I.

5 And he said, Draw not nigh hither: put off thy shoes from off thy feet, for the place whereon thou standest is holy ground.

6 Moreover he said, I am the God of thy father, the God of Abraham, the God of Isaac, and the God of Jacob. And Moses hid his face; for he was afraid to look upon God.

7 And the LORD said, I have surely seen the

LESSON OVERVIEW

LESSON AIM
KEEP IN MIND
FOCAL VERSES
IN FOCUS
THE PEOPLE, PLACES, AND TIMES
BACKGROUND
AT-A-GLANCE
IN DEPTH
SEARCH THE SCRIPTURES
DISCUSS THE MEANING
LESSON IN OUR SOCIETY
MAKE IT HAPPEN
FOLLOW THE SPIRIT
REMEMBER YOUR THOUGHTS
MORE LIGHT ON THE TEXT
DAILY BIBLE READINGS

affliction of my people which are in Egypt, and have heard their cry by reason of their taskmasters; for I know their sorrows;

8 And I am come down to deliver them out of the land of the Egyptians, and to bring them up out of that land unto a good land and a large, unto a land flowing with milk and honey; unto the place of the Canaanites, and the Hittites, and the Amorites, and the Perizzites, and the Hivites, and the Jebusites.

9 Now therefore, behold, the cry of the children of Israel is come unto me: and I have also seen the oppression wherewith the Egyptians oppress them.

10 Come now therefore, and I will send thee unto Pharaoh, that thou mayest bring forth my people the children of Israel out of Egypt.

11 And Moses said unto God, Who am I, that I should go unto Pharaoh, and that I should bring forth the children of Israel out of Egypt?

12 And he said, Certainly I will be with thee; and this shall be a token unto thee, that I have sent thee: When thou hast brought forth the people out of Egypt, ye shall serve God upon this mountain.

IN FOCUS

It was the first time God had called Lynn to minister His Word in front of a large crowd of people. Lynn was very nervous about this journey. Not only was this her first time ministering in front of a large crowd of people, it was also her first time in an airplane. During the entire flight, Lynn was so focused on her fear of flying that she could not even study her notes for her upcoming presentation. When the airplane arrived in Houston, the passenger sitting next to her inquired if Houston was her home. She responded that she was visiting the city to minister God's Word and that this was her first time flying in an airplane. Shocked, the passenger stated, "You seemed so calm, I would have never known that this was your first flight."

Upon arriving at the hotel, once again Lynn allowed doubt and fear to enter her thoughts. She began to wonder how she could take the written words that God had given her and express them verbally to His people. Again, she focused on her inabilities and not on God's ability to work through her. She began to question God's call on her life because she had not studied in seminary nor obtained a doctrinal degree.

Like Moses, Lynn chose to focus on doubting her abilities. Sometimes we think God cannot use us for one reason or another because we focus on our abilities instead of on His ability to work through us. Regardless of the circumstance, deliverance can only come when we step out of the way in submission to Christ. Lynn reminded herself of God's Word and promises, and by doing so, she received God's peace which says, "All is well." By yielding to God in spite of what she lacked in natural ability, God showed up supernaturally. Lynn's attitude changed because her perspective changed. She chose to stop focusing on doubting her abilities and focused on God's abundance. God is looking for a yielded vessel—a vessel that is willing to trust Him.

Thank God that He offers us His resources when He calls us to do a job for Him. Therefore, we do not have to hide behind our inadequacies, but we can look to God, our Source. He is our Lord, Savior, Redeemer, and Protector. He is our strength and shield.

THE PEOPLE, PLACES, AND TIMES

Moses as deliverer. God used Moses to deliver His people out of the hands of the Egyptians. Hebrews 11:23 reads, "By faith Moses' parents hid him for three months after he was born, because

they saw he was no ordinary child, and they were not afraid of the king's edicts" (NIV). From this verse, we see Moses was chosen as a child for a great destiny.

BACKGROUND

Moses fled Egypt fearing for his life after killing an Egyptian who was brutalizing an Israelite. Moses was trying to deliver his fellow Israelites from the bondage of the Egyptians. While in the wilderness, Moses met Jethro; in time, Jethro gave his daughter Zipporah to Moses in marriage. Zipporah bore children for Moses, and Moses began to tend to his father-in-law's sheep in the wilderness. God used the sheep to teach Moses patience and the wilderness to teach him humility. God used 40 years in the wilderness as a time of refining for Moses, to remove anything that would be a hindrance, not only to where God was taking Moses, but also what God would do through him.

While tending the sheep, Moses saw a bush on fire, yet it was not consumed by the fire. As Moses focused on this strange sight, God called to Moses from the burning bush. God told Moses to remove his sandals, because the place where he was standing was holy ground. God began to tell Moses about His passionate concern for His people. God revealed to Moses His plan to deliver them from Egyptian oppression and bring them before this very mountain to worship Him. He called and equipped Moses to play an important role in His plan. God not only told Moses that He would be with Him, He also shared with Moses who He was.

After 40 years of not speaking Egyptian, Moses' ability to speak the language had become quite rusty. The result was his slowness in speech (Exodus 4:10). Therefore, God allowed Moses' brother, Aaron, to be a spokesperson for him (vv. 14-16). God would give Moses the words to say, and Moses would in turn tell Aaron what the Lord had said so that Aaron could tell the people. When the Children of Israel heard what God had said to Moses, they believed and knelt down to worship God.

God hardened the heart of Pharaoh. Thus, Pharaoh spurned Moses' request to let God's people go. We do not know whether God hardened Pharaoh's heart to show forth His glory or for other reasons. But God wanted the Children of Israel to know without a shadow of a doubt that it was not Pharaoh's kindness, Moses' rod, or even Aaron's eloquent words that set them free. It was God Almighty: I AM THAT I AM. It was His power which released them. God provided Moses with a token for the Children of Israel to know that He had sent him. Moses met Aaron, his brother, in the wilderness and shared with him all that God had spoken and done. Aaron and Moses then went before the Children of Israel and shared with them what I AM THAT I AM had said. The Children of Israel were moved that God would look upon their afflictions and choose to deliver them. They then bowed their heads and began to worship God.

AT-A-GLANCE

1. God Appears to Moses in a Burning Bush (Exodus 3:1-4)
2. God Reveals His Plan (vv. 5-12)

IN DEPTH

1. God Appears to Moses in a Burning Bush (Exodus 3:1-4)

Before God appeared to him, Moses was hidden on the backside of the desert (v. 1). God used this time to build Moses' character, develop his personality, and mold and make him into what God wanted him to be—a true leader. He removed the ways of Egypt from Moses, refined the parts He needed to use—even Moses' temper—and produced patience in him by having him tend his father-in-law's sheep. Like people, sheep do not always move the way you want them to or as quickly as you would like. Therefore, God used these stubborn animals to teach Moses patience, the patience he would need in dealing with the Children of Israel—a stubborn, stiffnecked, hardheaded people. In fact, Moses went from the life of an Egyptian prince, where everything was done for him, to being a lowly shepherd, where he had to do everything for himself.

While Moses was tending the sheep, the angel of the Lord appeared to him in a flame out of the midst of a burning bush (v. 2). Deuteronomy 4:24 (NIV) says, "For the LORD your God is a consuming fire." God consumes us in order to refine us—but He will devour our enemies (9:3). God used a bush that was on fire, yet not consumed, to fascinate Moses. There are times in our lives when God will use something or someone to get our attention so He can speak to us. When God saw that He had Moses' attention, He called to him. Upon hearing God's call, Moses replied, "Here am I" (Exodus 3:4). God is trying to get our attention and then call us unto Himself. When we hear His call, we should respond like Moses: "Here am I." We should also allow Him to mold and make us into what He wants us to be.

2. God Reveals His Plan (vv. 5-12)

The afflictions of God's people had come before Him (vv. 7-9). He heard their cries and pleas for deliverance from the hands of hard taskmasters for 400 years. Yet God left them there in Egypt because they had to learn many valuable lessons as well as how to obey, love, and walk with Him. God told Moses that His passion was His children. In short, God had a passion, a purpose, and a plan! God's passion has always been the same—His children. His purpose has always remained the same—the deliverance of His passion, His children.

Before God could tell Moses His plan, Moses began to interrupt and express his doubt (which we all have) and to tell God all the reasons why he could not go (v. 11). All Moses could see was his own inadequacies and how big the job would be. He saw that working alone he could not accomplish the task, and indeed, he could not. In fact, God never told Moses that he would have to work alone.

God quieted Moses' fears with the assurance that He would be with him. He does the same for us by revealing that He will never leave us nor forsake us (Hebrews 13:5). God told Moses that His presence would be with him. After Moses had delivered God's people out of bondage, God wanted His people to come close and worship Him—as close as they could in their unregenerate flesh. Moses expressed doubt again. He told God that when he went before the Children of Israel they were going to ask him who sent him; who should he say (v. 13)? God knew Moses' frailty and that he was only dust (Genesis 2:7), as we are. God also knew the Children of Israel. He had made them as well. God told Moses to tell the Children of Israel that I AM THAT I AM had sent him (Exodus 3:14). God began to remind Moses of who He is to mankind, and with whom He made the covenant relationship (vv. 15-16). God always has a plan. He has not changed. Just as He had a purpose for Moses, He has a purpose for you and me, and He has provisions to bring it to pass.

SEARCH THE SCRIPTURES

1. Why was Moses out in the wilderness (Exodus 3:1)?

2. How did God use this time to prepare Moses to accomplish this purpose (vv. 1-12)?

3. What lessons can we learn from the burning bush and Moses' response?

4. What was God's plan (v. 10)?

DISCUSS THE MEANING

1. Discuss how God can call and use us to deliver people from bondage today.

2. Why does God call one person for a specific work and not another?

3. Why did God want to deliver His people? Why does He deliver people today?

4. When God calls, why should we respond in faith?

LESSON IN OUR SOCIETY

Nothing about us is a surprise to God; He is in charge of our past, present, and future. God led Moses to Jethro, the Midianite shepherd. God used Moses' job as a shepherd to prepare him to lead His sheep. God prepared Moses for greatness in the midst of bareness. Even when Moses doubted his ability to be used by God, he still allowed God to use him as His vessel. We also are called to guide the lost to God's Word and to minister to them under the anointing of our Heavenly Father. God is still looking for a people who will come to the mountain and worship Him. His purpose has never changed, nor has His plan or provisions.

MAKE IT HAPPEN

Are you passionate about what God is passionate about? If so, this week reflect on the ways God has sent people into your life to deliver you from sinful situations or actions that would have caused spiritual or physical harm, or even death. How can you allow God to use you to become more effective in ministering to others? When God is first in our lives, we will allow Him to use us for His purpose and we will want to complete His plan.

FOLLOW THE SPIRIT

What God wants me to do:

_____

_____

REMEMBER YOUR THOUGHTS

Special insights I have learned:

_____

_____

MORE LIGHT ON THE TEXT

Exodus 3:1-12

1 Now Moses kept the flock of Jethro his father in law, the priest of Midian: and he led the flock to the backside of the desert, and came to the mountain of God, even to Horeb.

Moses was carrying out his usual work as a shepherd. The verb "to keep" (Heb. *hayah*, **haw-yaw**) used in the sentence is a participle expressing the continuance of the occupation. It was his habitual occupation. Moses had become the shepherd of Jethro, his father-in-law. Jethro (Heb. *Yithrow*, **yith-ro'**), called Reuel in Exodus 2:18, is probably a title meaning "eminence" or "highness." The story took place many years after Moses fled from Egypt to Midian. According to Acts 7:30, it was 40 years later.

One day Moses led the sheep as far as Horeb, the mountain of God. Horeb is called the mountain of God either because God would first reveal Himself there to Moses and the Israelites (Exodus 3:1; 18:5; 24:13), or it was already known as a sacred place. Horeb and Sinai are two names for the same mountain or group of mountains (1 Kings 8:9; 19:8; Nehemiah 9:13; Psalms 68:8). Moses passed through the desert before reaching the pastureland of Horeb. The word "backside" (Heb. *achar,* **akh-ar'**) can be understood as the west side of the desert—for in Semitic thought, one faces east when giving compass directions.

Moses did not go to Horeb, the mountain of God, with a religious intention. He went just to take care of his father-in-law's flock.

2 And the angel of the LORD appeared unto him in a flame of fire out of the midst of a bush: and he looked, and, behold, the bush burned with fire, and the bush was not consumed.

Moses was going about his usual business when God appeared to him as an "angel." The term "angel" (Heb. *mal'ak,* **mal-awk'**) literally means "messenger." Here, the angel is not to be thought of as a supernatural messenger of Yahweh, but as a self-manifestation of Yahweh. The term is interchangeable with Yahweh (v. 4 speaks of Yahweh Himself calling out of the bush). It is a reverential way of referring to Yahweh, as His appearance in patriarchal stories shows (Genesis 16:7; 18:1; 19:1; 22:11; cf. Judges 6:12). At the same time, the angel is described as Yahweh and is distinguished from Him. This revelation prepares the reader of the Bible for the fuller revelation of God as three-in-one in the New Testament.

The Lord appeared to Moses in a flame of fire coming out of a bush. The term "bush" in Hebrew (Heb. *seneh,* **sen-eh'**) is similar in sound to Sinai (Heb. *Siynay,* **See-nah'ee**). This bush is referred to again in Deuteronomy 33:16. The Lord is called He "who dwelt in the bush." The word "fire" (Heb. *'esh,* **aysh**) in the Bible is often a symbol of the presence of God (Exodus 13:21; 19:18). It speaks of His holiness and of His anger in relation to sin (32:10). Moses' attention was drawn to the fact that though the fire was burning, the bush was not being consumed.

3 And Moses said, I will now turn aside, and see this great sight, why the bush is not burnt.

Moses decided to investigate more closely this strange event: the bush was burning, yet it was not consumed. He turned aside from the road or spot where he was standing to "see this great sight." The word "sight" (Heb. *mar'eh,* **mar-eh'**) is derived from the verb "to see" or "to look" (Heb. *ra'ah,* **raw-aw**) in a literal or figurative sense. The great sight caught so much of Moses' attention that he came near to it. The Lord used Moses' initial curiosity to attract him to the place.

4 And when the LORD saw that he turned aside to see, God called unto him out of the midst of the bush, and said, Moses, Moses. And he said, Here am I.

"The Lord saw": The transition from the angel (v. 2) to the Lord (v. 4) proves the identity of the two. Two names of God, Yahweh (a Jewish national name of God) and Elohim (Heb. *'Elohiym,* **El-o-heem'**, "the supreme God"), are interchanged, excluding the idea of Yahweh being only the God of Israel or merely a national God.

The Lord called Moses. He communicated with him personally and had called him by name. Moses responded, "Here am I" (cf. 1 Samuel 3).

5 And he said, Draw not nigh hither: put off thy shoes from off thy feet, for the place whereon thou standest is holy ground.

Moses was told not to come near. The term "draw nigh" (Heb. *qarab,* **kaw-rab'**) can be translated in modern language as "stop coming near, as you are doing." Moses did not recognize the presence or the nature of God. Later, after his experience with the Lord, he would be ready to draw near the Lord and intercede for others (see Exodus 32:30).

The Lord commanded Moses to take off his shoes. This practice, still observed in many religions, indicates the presence of God in the sanctuary (but see John 4:21-24; 1 Corinthians 6:19-20; Ephesians 3:14-21). Here, Moses must take off his shoes because he was standing on holy ground. The ground was made holy by the presence of God. The removal of shoes was intended to express not merely respect for the place itself; it was a sign of worship, a mark of reverence, and a sign of acceptance of a servant's position. It represented the removal of uncleanness caused by contact with the world. It was a recognition of

Moses shows respect for the Holy Sovereign God.

Yahweh's holiness. The place is holy as a result of Moses' experience there.

6 Moreover he said, I am the God of thy father, the God of Abraham, the God of Isaac, and the God of Jacob. And Moses hid his face; for he was afraid to look upon God.

The Lord explained to Moses why He had appeared to him. He was the God of Moses'

father. The term "father" (Heb. *'ab*, **awb**) has a literal and immediate meaning as well as a remote connotation (see Exodus 18:4; Genesis 46:3). The Lord was the same God who made the covenant promises to Abraham, Isaac, and Jacob, fathers of Moses and the Israelites. Each father stood out singly in distinction from the nation as having received the promise of seed directly from God (cf Matthew 22:32; Mark 12:26; Luke 20:37).

Those promises are now to be fulfilled (Exodus 8, 9). The phrase with a singular form of "father" occurs in Genesis 26:24; 31:5, 42, 53; 43:23; 46:1, 3; 49:25; 50:17; Exodus 15:2; 18:4.

Moses was afraid of the sight of the holy God. No sinful man can bear the sight of God (Exodus 33:20; Judges 6:22-23; 13:22; Isaiah 6:2, 5). When fragile and sinful humans encounter the holy God, the initial response is terror and an attempt to hide. However, the encounter is also an event of grace bringing hope and new life (cf. Genesis 28:17; 32:31; Exodus 19:21; 33:20; Leviticus 16:2; Numbers 4:20; Deuteronomy 5:24-25; Isaiah 6:5). The same fear struck the witnesses of the glory of Jesus manifested in His miracles, transfiguration, and resurrection (cf. Matthew 17:6; 28:4; Mark 1:27; 2:12; 4:41; 5:15, 42; 6:49-51; 16:5-8; Luke 4:36; 5:8-9, 26; 8:25,37, 56; 24:5, 37).

7 And the LORD said, I have surely seen the affliction of my people which are in Egypt, and have heard their cry by reason of their taskmasters; for I know their sorrows;

The Lord presented Himself as someone who cared. He saw the misery of His people in Egypt. He called them "My people." The verbs "have seen" (Heb. *ra'ah,* **raw-aw'**), "have heard" (Heb. *shama,* **shaw-mah'**), and "know" (Heb. *yada,* **yaw-dah'**) stress the Lord's sensitivity toward His people. He could see, hear, and know. He saw the misery of His people; He heard their cries for deliverance from their harsh slave masters. He knew their sorrows. He was going to do something about it.

8 And I am come down to deliver them out of the land of the Egyptians, and to bring them up out of that land unto a good land and a large, unto a land flowing with milk and honey; unto the place of the Canaanites, and the Hittites, and the Amorites, and the Perizzites, and the Hivites, and the Jebusites.

Yahweh had come down to deliver His people out the hands of the Egyptians (cf. Genesis 3:8; 11:5; Exodus 19:11, 18, 20; 34:5 speaks of Yahweh as coming virtually in bodily form to deliver Israel). He would lead them to the land promised to their fathers, a land good and large flowing

with milk and honey. The expression "milk and honey" (Heb. *chalab,* **khaw-lawb'** and *debash,* **deb-ash'**) describes a land with abundant food, a prosperous and fertile land. It is a proverbial description of Canaan symbolizing continuity, stability, and identity—things that only God can give to people.

The epithet "large" (Heb. *rachab,* **raw-khawb'**) is explained by the listing of the nations occupying the territory at that time (Genesis 10:6, 15-17, 19; 12:6; 15:20, 21; Numbers 13:29; 2 Samuel 11:3). They were not mutually related to each other as the 12 tribes of Israel were.

9 Now therefore, behold, the cry of the children of Israel is come unto me: and I have also seen the oppression wherewith the Egyptians oppress them.

Here, Yahweh repeated the fact that the cry of the people had reached Him (see v. 7). He knew of the sinful oppression by the Egyptians and the hardships to which they subjected His people.

10 Come now therefore, and I will send thee unto Pharaoh, that thou mayest bring forth my people the children of Israel out of Egypt.

"Now therefore" signifies the conclusion of the Lord's speech: Moses was selected for the work of redemption. God announced that He was going to save His people through Moses. Moses was the person chosen by Yahweh to achieve it. He was called and sent to Pharaoh to bring the Lord's people out of Egypt. God uses men and women to achieve His purposes. He does not need to do so. However, he invites us to share with Him in the fulfilling of His plans (John 20:21). He normally works through the willing obedience of His servants.

11 And Moses said unto God, Who am I, that I should go unto Pharaoh, and that I should bring forth the children of Israel out of Egypt?

Moses would have quickly welcomed the invitation from the Lord to free His people years earlier. Indeed, he had once tried to become the liberator of one Israelite from the power of the Pharaoh (Exodus 2:11-14). The years of hardship and bitterness in the Midian wilderness had changed him.

He was no longer the bold, impetuous, and impatient Moses he used to be. He was now timid and hesitant. He had learned his own weaknesses and limitations. This is the first of Moses' four protests against accepting the commission to lead Israel out of Egypt. He expressed his feeling of being inadequate and unworthy for the task. The three other protests are in Exodus 4:1, 10, and 13. Moses argued that he was not adequate to undertake the task of freeing his people. He expressed his reservations in the form of a question.

12 And he said, Certainly I will be with thee; and this shall be a token unto thee, that I have sent thee: When thou hast brought forth the people out of Egypt, ye shall serve God upon this mountain.

The Lord, in answer to Moses' fear, told him that He Himself would be with him. Where Moses' abilities might fail, there was to be a God of unlimited abilities. What Moses desired was some present assurance that God had truly sent him.

The Lord offered Moses a "sign" or "a token" (Heb. *'owth*, **oth**). The word "sign" covers a great variety of events and phenomena in the Bible and should not be restricted to too narrow a meaning. A sign is often a natural occurrence or a supernatural phenomenon that confirms the truth of what is said by God or by a prophet (see 1 Samuel 10:7, 9; 2 Kings 19:29; 20:8-9; Isaiah 7:11,14; Jeremiah 44:29). Here, the sign was that Moses' success in bringing the Israelites out of Egypt would prove the Lord was with him. They would serve God on this same mountain. In other words, the purpose of his mission would be accomplished. Moses received the guarantee that Yahweh was truly the One who sent him. The "I" in "I have sent thee" is emphatic.

The Israelites would serve God on the mountain of God. "To serve" (Heb. *abad*, **aw-bad**) has the meaning of service. Here, it is used in reference to God with the meaning of worship or obedience. The service offered to God is not a bondage, but rather a joyous and liberating experience. The service of the Lord was the basis of the whole drama of the plagues in Egypt (see 4:23; 7:16). The Israelites, by being free of Pharaoh's yoke, would not enter into a state of anarchical freedom. They would use their new freedom to serve God under a covenantal law. They would pass from the slave service of Pharaoh to the liberty of the service of God. This is a theme of the Exodus (cf. Matthew 6:24; Romans 6; Galatians 5:13; 1 Peter 2:16).

DAILY BIBLE READINGS

M: God Speaks to Moses
Exodus 3:1-6

T: God Calls Moses to Lead
Exodus 3:7-12

W: God Gives Moses Instructions
Exodus 3:13-22

T: God Gives Moses Special Powers
Exodus 4:1-9

F: Moses Still Feels Inadequate
Exodus 4:10-17

S: Moses Returns to Egypt
Exodus 4:18-23

S: The Israelites Believe Moses
Exodus 4:24-31

God raised up a deliverer for His people because they cried out to Him. Use your *Precepts For Living* CD-ROM to find out how often we are told to "pray" in the Bible.

TEACHING TIPS

September 26
Bible Study Guide 4

1. Words You Should Know

A. Maketh (Deuteronomy 29:12) *karath* (Heb.)—To cut or make. Usually used to denote the cutting of an animal in half and the makers of the covenant walking between the pieces to ratify it. By this they were saying, "If I fail to keep the terms of this covenant, may what we did to this animal happen to me."

B. Oath (v. 14) *'alah* (Heb.)—A solemn promise. Used in this case to express the solemn covenant between God and His people, especially the curse for breaking the covenant.

2. Teacher Preparation

A. Begin preparing for the lesson by reading Deuteronomy 27—30.

B. Next, focus on the FOCAL VERSES. Ask yourself how they apply to you personally. Be prepared to share your thoughts with the class.

3. Starting the Lesson

A. Begin the lesson with prayer, focusing on the LESSON AIM.

B. Review the highlights from last week's lesson. Then ask for a show of hands of those who implemented last week's MAKE IT HAPPEN section.

C. Ask for volunteers to share their experiences of implementing the section.

D. Ask for a volunteer to read the IN FOCUS story. After the reading, ask the class why it is important to remember historical events. Allow for discussion.

4. Getting into the Lesson

A. Ask the students why they think it is important to remember and rehearse the difficult times and situations God has brought them through. Allow for discussion.

B. Assign a student to read THE PEOPLE, PLACES, AND TIMES, and then ask the students to discuss the provision of the new covenant. See Jeremiah 1 for details.

C. Ask another student to read the BACK-GROUND information. Then ask the students if the formula mentioned in the section is applicable to today's Christians and how it applies to their lives.

5. Relating the Lesson to Life

A. Review the SEARCH THE SCRIPTURES questions to help the students think through the Scripture passage.

B. Direct the students' attention to the LESSON AIM. Ask them why it is important to remember and think about how God moved on their behalf in the past.

C. To help the students make a personal application of today's lesson, review the DISCUSS THE MEANING questions.

6. Arousing Action

A. Encourage the students to read and study next week's lesson and come prepared to share their insights with the class.

B. Review the MAKE IT HAPPEN section and challenge the students to implement the suggestion over the next week.

WORSHIP GUIDE

For the Superintendent or Teacher
Theme: Becoming God's People
Theme Song: "My Redeemer Lives"
Scripture: Deuteronomy 30:15-20
Song: "Think About His Love"
Meditation: Gracious Father, You sent Your only begotten Son into the world to redeem Your people from sin. You brought us into a new covenant relationship with You, sealed by the blood of Jesus. We thank You, Lord, for Your mercy and grace that guarantees us Your promises, Your presence, and Your paradise.

BECOMING GOD'S PEOPLE

Bible Background • DEUTERONOMY 29:1-29
Printed Text • DEUTERONOMY 29:2-15
Devotional Reading • DEUTERONOMY 30:15-20

LESSON AIM

By the end of the lesson, the students will understand how God delivered His people from bondage and provided for them during their 40 years of wandering. They will also be able to explain the importance of remembering and rehearsing how God provided and delivered them from past difficulties and determine to trust and obey God in their daily lives.

KEEP IN MIND

"That thou shouldest enter into covenant with the LORD thy God, and into his oath, which the LORD thy God maketh with thee this day: That he may establish thee today for a people unto himself, and that he may be unto thee a God, as he hath said unto thee, and as he hath sworn unto thy fathers, to Abraham, to Isaac, and to Jacob" (Deuteronomy 29:12-13).

FOCAL VERSES

Deuteronomy 29:2 And Moses called unto all Israel, and said unto them, Ye have seen all that the LORD did before your eyes in the land of Egypt unto Pharaoh, and unto all his servants, and unto all his land;

3 The great temptations which thine eyes have seen, the signs, and those great miracles:

4 Yet the LORD hath not given you an heart to perceive, and eyes to see, and ears to hear, unto this day.

5 And I have led you forty years in the wilderness: your clothes are not waxen old upon you, and thy

---

LESSON OVERVIEW

LESSON AIM
KEEP IN MIND
FOCAL VERSES
IN FOCUS
THE PEOPLE, PLACES, AND TIMES
BACKGROUND
AT-A-GLANCE
IN DEPTH
SEARCH THE SCRIPTURES
DISCUSS THE MEANING
LESSON IN OUR SOCIETY
MAKE IT HAPPEN
FOLLOW THE SPIRIT
REMEMBER YOUR THOUGHTS
MORE LIGHT ON THE TEXT
DAILY BIBLE READINGS

---

shoe is not waxen old upon thy foot.

6 Ye have not eaten bread, neither have ye drunk wine or strong drink: that ye might know that I am the LORD your God.

SEPT
26TH

7 And when ye came unto this place, Sihon the king of Heshbon, and Og the king of Bashan, came out against us unto battle, and we smote them:

8 And we took their land, and gave it for an inheritance unto the Reubenites, and to the Gadites, and to the half tribe of Manasseh.

9 Keep therefore the words of this covenant, and do them, that ye may prosper in all that ye do.

10 Ye stand this day all of you before the LORD your God; your captains of your tribes, your elders, and your officers, with all the men of Israel.

11 Your little ones, your wives, and thy stranger that is in thy camp, from the hewer of thy wood unto the drawer of thy water:

12 That thou shouldest enter into covenant with the LORD thy God, and into his oath, which the LORD thy God maketh with thee this day:

13 That he may establish thee to day for a people unto himself, and that he may be unto thee a God, as he hath said unto thee, and as he hath sworn unto thy fathers, to Abraham, to Isaac, and to Jacob.

14 Neither with you only do I make this covenant and this oath;

15 But with him that standeth here with us this day before the LORD our God, and also with him that is not here with us this day:

IN FOCUS

The year 1912 was a momentous one for the nation of South Africa. In that year, the African National Congress (ANC) was founded and one of the nation's greatest leaders was born. Walter Max Ulyate Sisulu was born in Ngcobo Transkei to Victor Dickenson, a White civil servant, and Alice Sisulu, a Black domestic worker.

The future leader obtained his education at the Anglican Missionary Institute, where it is reported that he took an enthusiastic interest in world history. The major inspiration of his youth is said to have been Marcus Garvey, the Jamaican immigrant, who championed the Black liberation struggle in the United States.

At the tender age of 14, Sisulu left school to work. Even though he had to quit school to help provide for himself and his family, Sisulu always understood that education was vital to his success. Instead of giving up on education, Sisulu continued his education through self-study.

As a young worker, Walter often found himself leading labor disputes. In 1940, he ventured into politics by joining the African National Congress. Sisulu recruited Nelson Mandela into the organization. Together, along with Oliver Tambo, they founded the Youth League, a radical wing of the ANC that advocated a more militant approach to dealing with the White government of South Africa.

The Youth League developed a strategy called the "Programme of Action," designed to pressure the government into abolishing its oppressive racist laws and granting equality to the masses of Black and colored people of the nation. After South Africa's all-White national election of 1948, the ANC adopted the "Programme of Action" as their official party policy. That same year, Sisulu became the party's secretary general.

In 1952, the ANC initiated the "Defiance Campaign." This campaign called for the ANC and all its followers to peacefully disregard all unjust laws. The White government cracked down on the ANC and others who participated in the campaign. They arrested more than 8500 people, including Walter Sisulu and Nelson Mandela.

In 1960, the White government passed legislation designed to keep the races separate. In response to these racist laws, the ANC organized a massive protest demonstration. The government reacted to the protest by arresting 18,000 protesters and banning the ANC. As a result, the party went underground and concluded that the only way to achieve their dream of racial equality was through military action. In November 1961, they established the military wing of the party called "Umkhonto We Siewe" (Spear of the Nation) and Sisulu was chosen to lead it.

The government's apartheid policy of discrimination and segregation enraged the citizens of color in South Africa and other African nations. It also drew criticism from most other countries and economic embargos from some. Under mounting civil unrest and global pressure, the South African government finally released Sisulu from prison on October 15, 1989. A year later, the government released Nelson Mandela and lifted the ban on the ANC. In April 1994, South Africa held its first election in which Blacks were allowed to vote. In the elections, Blacks finally gained control of the government.

On Monday, May 5, 2003, Walter Sisulu died in the arms of Albertina, his beloved wife of 59 years. South African President Thabo Mbeki praised the contributions of the man known in South Africa as the "quiet giant" with these words: "Our country and our people have lost one of our greatest sons, one of the architects of a nonracial and nonsexist society." Remembering the contributions of men like Walter Sisulu, Nelson Mandela, and Martin Luther King provides impetus to continue our struggle for national and global equality.

In today's lesson, Moses reviews the history of the Israelite's deliverance from Egyptian bondage and God's provision for them during their wilderness wanderings. He challenges them to always remember how God worked and provided for them in their time of need.

THE PEOPLE, PLACES, AND TIMES

God's Covenants with Abraham and His Descendants. These covenants are clear statements of God's purposes and intentions. God bound Himself by oath to honor all His promises. Through each covenant God was saying, "I will be your God and you will be my people." At the heart of these covenants were (1) the terms for God, (2) the terms for man, and (3) a statement of *cursings* for breaking the covenant and *blessings* for keeping it. God's terms include unbreakable promises. Our terms involve believing God's promises and acting on them through obedience to God's Word. It is our faith in God that brings the blessings of a covenant relationship with Him and the experience of His applied promises in our lives.

Three of the covenants God established with His people are:

1. The Abrahamic covenant, found in Genesis 17: "As for me, this is my covenant with you: You will be the father of many nations. No longer will you be called Abram; your name will be Abraham, for I have made you a father of many nations. I will make you very fruitful; I will make nations of you, and kings will come from you" (Genesis 17:4-6, NIV).

2. The Mosaic covenant (Exodus 19:1—Deuteronomy 30) defined the conditions by which God's people (the Israelites) would continue as God's chosen possession and reap His blessings. The promises of the Mosaic covenant were basically an extension of the Abrahamic. The people were to respond to God by keeping His commandants and offering the prescribed sacrifices. This covenant obligates God to give the land to the Israelites and their descendants forever as long as they remain faithful to Him and His law (see Deuteronomy 30:15-20; cf. 23:5).

3. The Davidic covenant, in which God promised that David's house or dynasty would endure forever. The high point of this covenant was the promise that a descendant from David's family line would be the eternal king who would rule over God's people and all the nations of the world (cf. Isaiah 9:6-37; Micah 5:2, 4). The fulfillment of the Davidic promise begins with the announcement of Jesus' birth by the angel Gabriel to Mary, the mother of Christ. It is completed in the future when Jesus assumes dominion over the everlasting kingdom in the new heaven and earth (Revelation 21—22).

Believers today, under the New Covenant, also express our faith by obedience to God. This obedient faith allows us to appropriate God's covenant promises while He accomplishes His will on earth through those who are in covenant relationship with Him.

BACKGROUND

Deuteronomy means "second law." The book consists of three farewell sermons delivered by the 123-year-old Moses at the entrance to the Promised Land. In this message, the old patriarch renewed the covenant for the sake of the new generation of Israelites.

Moses knew he would not be allowed to go into the Promised Land, so he wanted to make sure the new generation of Israelites kept God's Word close to their hearts and obeyed the instructions of the Lord. A characteristic of Deuteronomy is the admonition to "remember," which appears 13 times in the book. The people are admonished to remember all of God's gracious works on their behalf and to obey all previously revealed truth.

In his first sermon, Moses recaps the history of God's deliverance of the Israelites from Egyptian bondage and His daily provision for them throughout their 40 years of wandering in the wilderness (Deuteronomy 1:1—4:43).

In his second message, Moses restates the people's moral duties, describing how they should conduct themselves as God's people. It also emphasizes their ceremonial duties, such as sacrifices, and their civil and social duties related to the law and social justice (4:44—26:19).

In the final sermon (27:1—30:20), Moses outlines the terms under which the Israelites would enter into the Promised Land.

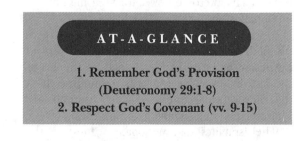

AT-A-GLANCE

1. Remember God's Provision
(Deuteronomy 29:1-8)
2. Respect God's Covenant (vv. 9-15)

IN DEPTH

1. Remember God's Provision (Deuteronomy 29:1-8)

Moses was God's appointed leader of the Israelites. Here, he demonstrates the two primary requisites of spiritual leadership. The phrase "the Lord commanded Moses" indicates that Moses spent time in communion with God and that he was obedient to all he heard from God. All great spiritual leaders spend a great amount of time communicating with God and then following His direction.

The Israelites were camped in Moab eagerly anticipating the command to finally enter the Promised Land. God had promised this land to their ancestors almost 700 years earlier, and now they were on the verge of claiming their birthright as children of Abraham. However, before they could enter the land, there were additional terms that had to be presented and agreed to. Moses called all the Israelites together to explain these terms (Deuteronomy 1:1; cf. 30:20).

A covenant is a formal agreement between God and His people. Like most ancient agreements, this one includes a recital of God's past dealings with the Israelites. The purpose of the recital is twofold. The first is to encourage the people to trust God in all circumstances. Just as God delivered them in the past, He would protect and care for them in the future. The second purpose was to incite the people to obedience. The list of curses would serve as a reminder of the consequences of disobeying God's commands.

The generation that died off in the wilderness was made up of all those who were over 20 years old at the time the Israelites left Egypt (see Numbers 14:28-30); so most of the Israelites had actually witnessed God's deliverance of His people in Egypt. They had seen miraculous demonstrations of His awesome power through mighty acts on behalf of the suffering Israelites.

Moses begins his recital by reminding the people of how God delivered them from slavery in Egypt and had cared and provided for them over the last 40 years. He begins by reminding them that they were eyewitnesses to God's triumph over Pharaoh, his subjects, and his entire country.

The Israelites had personally witnessed "the great temptations which thine eyes have seen, the signs, and those great miracles" (Deuteronomy 29:3). The word "temptations" would be better translated as "trials." Trials are not actually bad situations; they are internal responses to external adversity. They manifest as fear, anxiety, anger, and depression. Signs are extraordinary occurrences that point to supernatural causes. Miracles are incidents whereby God temporarily overrides the laws

of nature to accomplish His will. The 10 curses of Egypt (Exodus 7:14—11:6) were all miracles designed as trials for the Egyptians and signs for the Israelites.

God's grace toward the Israelites did not end after their deliverance from slavery. During the 40 years of wilderness wandering, neither their clothes nor their shoes wore out. Instead of eating bread, they were fed with manna from heaven. Instead of drinking wine, they were provided with fresh water through a small tree (15:22-25) and from stones (17:1-6; 20:1-11).

God protected them from the might of kings bent on their destruction. The Israelites defeated Sihon, the king of Heshbon (Numbers 21:21-35). The land of the two kings on the east side of the Jordan River was divided between the tribes of Reuben, Gad, and Manasseh after Israel defeated them.

In spite of all that the Israelites had seen, they did not understand the significance of what God had done on their behalf. "Yet the LORD hath not given you an heart to perceive, and eyes to see, and ears to hear, unto this day" (Deuteronomy 29:4). They knew the facts but they did not understand the truth. They had witnessed the miracles but they did not understand the signs.

Spiritual discernment comes only from the Holy Spirit. That is why Scripture tells us, "The man without the Spirit does not accept the things that come from the Spirit of God, for they are foolishness to him, and he cannot understand them, because they are spiritually discerned" (1 Corinthians 2:14, NIV). People without the Holy Spirit's illumination are unable to receive or properly understand God's message (cf. John 6:44; Romans 8:5-8). This explains why the Gospel appears foolish to unbelievers...they are spiritually blind, unable to comprehend the truths that belong to the spiritual realm.

2. Respect God's Covenant (vv. 9-15)

After rehearsing God's wondrous works on their behalf, Moses issues a two-part command: "Keep therefore the words of this covenant" (Deuteronomy 29:9). The word "therefore" looks back to the past history that Moses had gone over with them. On the positive side, if God were able to deliver His people from bondage and meet their every need during the 40 years in the desert, wouldn't He also meet the need of His covenant people who obeyed His will? Negatively, if God brought curses on Egypt because of their disobedience, He would not allow the disobedience of the Israelites to go unpunished.

Obedience is the key. "To keep" means to observe or to be constantly aware of the laws of God. The second part, "do them," is the reason for the awareness. We acquire knowledge of God's Word so that we may obey Him. Knowledge without obedience is the height of foolishness.

Moses emphasizes the solemnity of the occasion by reminding the people that they were standing in the very presence of God (Deuteronomy 29:10). All the people—regardless of rank, gender, or social standing—were bound by the precepts of the covenant. This new generation was entering into the covenant even as Abraham (Genesis 17) and the generation that perished in the wilderness had done before them.

The elements of the covenant were the same as those of the covenant God had made with their parents and forefathers. The purpose of this gathering was to renew their agreement to the covenant's terms and conditions. Because God originally cut this covenant with Abraham (15:9-21) and confirmed it with the first generation (Exodus 24:3-8), there was no need for any new animal sacrifice. Instead, God sealed the covenant with an oath. This oath bound God to carry out all His promises to the people. According to the writer of Hebrews, the oath also served as a reminder to future generations of the unchanging nature of God's promises (Hebrews 6:16-17).

All God's promises can be summarized into two fundamental promises. In this oath, God promises two things: "To confirm you this day as his people, that he may be your God as he promised you and as he swore to your fathers, Abraham, Isaac and Jacob" (Deuteronomy 29:13, NIV). Being God's people meant that the Israelites could depend on God for their protection, peace, and prosperity. Having the one true God as their God was an everlasting guarantee of God's close and personal presence among them and His unconditional love for them. These two promises are also foundational to the new

covenant (see Jeremiah 31:33; Hebrews 8:10). This covenantal relationship was not just for those who had assembled to ratify it; it included the future generations of believers (see Acts 3:25; Galatians 3:28).

The highest privilege in life is to enter into a covenant relationship with God. The New Covenant, which was sealed with the blood of Jesus, is the ultimate fulfillment of the Abrahamic and Mosaic covenants. Our Lord, who is the same yesterday, today, and forever (Hebrews 13:8), makes the same foundational promises to us that He made to the patriarchs and the Israelites. We will be His people and He will be our God. What more could anyone ask?

SEARCH THE SCRIPTURES

1. How did Moses describe the manifestation of God's power in defeating the Egyptians and procuring the freedom of the Israelites (Deuteronomy 29:3)?

2. In spite of all they had witnessed, why is it that the Israelites did not truly understand the significance of what God had done for them (v. 4)?

3. Which three tribes inherited the land the Israelites had won in battle on the east side of the Jordan River (v. 8)?

DISCUSS THE MEANING

1. How would you explain the difference between so-called common sense and spiritual discernment?

2. Many people limit prosperity to material blessings. What other ways can you think of that God might prosper those people who are in a new covenant relationship with Him?

LESSON IN OUR SOCIETY

Like the Israelites, we need to remember our legacy and how God is still emancipating and bringing us into the Promised Land. In times of trouble, we can rehearse how God provided when there was no other way. We can determine to daily love, trust, and obey Him because He is a God worthy to be praised. He is also faithful to His children.

MAKE IT HAPPEN

The foundational blessings of being God's

people are the guarantees of peace, prosperity, and protection. Over the next week, prayerfully study Psalm 91. Then make a list of how God has fulfilled these promises in your life.

FOLLOW THE SPIRIT
What God wants me to do:

_____

_____

REMEMBER YOUR THOUGHTS
Special insights I have learned:

_____

_____

MORE LIGHT ON THE TEXT
Deuteronomy 29:2-15
2 And Moses called unto all Israel, and said unto them, Ye have seen all that the LORD did before your eyes in the land of Egypt unto Pharaoh, and unto all his servants, and unto all his land;

The term "all Israel" (Heb. *kol-yisra'el*, **kole-yis-raw-ale**) is the nation of Israel with all its members (cf. vv. 10-11). Moses addresses Israel as a united community. As they face the future, they are urged to recall the past and "all that the LORD did before [their] eyes in the land of Egypt" (cf. Exodus 19:4). There are great lessons to be learned from the past.

By saying "Ye have seen all that the LORD did before your eyes," Moses knew unquestionably that some of the people who stood before him had not seen those things personally. Most of those who saw them had died in the desert. They had lacked the perception to understand what the Lord had shown them through signs and great miracles "in the land of Egypt."

3 The great temptations which thine eyes have seen, the signs, and those great miracles:

The words "temptations," "signs," and "miracles" are also used in the Exodus narrative (Exodus 4:8, 9, 17, 21, 28, 30; 7:3; 8:23; 10:1, 2; 11:9, 10). The word "temptations" (Heb. *massa*, **mas-saw**) refers to the testing of Pharaoh through the plagues. The word "signs" (Heb. *'oth*, **oth**) is any distinguishing mark, not necessarily of a

strange or miraculous nature, which points beyond itself to the thing signified. The word "miracles" (Heb. *mopet*, **mo-faith**) is an unusual phenomenon requiring explanation. Theses terms refer to the plagues brought upon Egypt (cf. Deuteronomy 4:34; 6:22; 7:19).

4 Yet the LORD hath not given you an heart to perceive, and eyes to see, and ears to hear, unto this day.

Those who witnessed the mighty acts of Jehovah did not understand them. They had lived in the midst of many manifestations of divine care and power, but they lacked the deeper insight needed to discern the deeper significance behind the external events. They needed the understanding that only the Lord could give.

The Lord had not given the people "heart[s] (Heb. *leb*, **labe**; the seat of man's intellect and will; see Deuteronomy 15:9; Isaiah 6:10; Jeremiah 5:21) to perceive" (Heb. *yada*, **yaw-dah**) or to know. He had not yet given the people "eyes to see, and ears to hear" because they were incredulous and disobedient. They failed to recognize the deeds of the Lord (cf. Isaiah 6:9-10; Jeremiah 1:17-19; Ezekiel 3:4-11; see 2 Corinthians 3:12-18). We must learn from their example not to delay any longer, but to wake up and pay attention to the deeds of God.

5 And I have led you forty years in the wilderness: your clothes are not waxen old upon you, and thy shoe is not waxen old upon thy foot.

The address of Moses, here, switches to give a direct quote from the Lord (cf. Amos 2:10). It is a rhetorical description of the care and provision of God for His people. The people were to remember the 40 years when God guided them through the desert to humble them and to prove the state of their hearts (Deuteronomy 8:2). During this time, God provided in a marvelous way for His people. Their clothes and shoes were not "waxen old" (Heb. *balah*, **baw-law**); literally, they did not "fall off from age" or "waste away through age" (see 8:4; Nehemiah 9:21).

6 Ye have not eaten bread, neither have ye drunk wine or strong drink: that ye might know that I am the LORD your God.

The Lord provided for the nourishment of His people. He fed them with manna. He intended to show them that man does not live by bread alone. The power to sustain life does not rest upon the nourishment of the body alone; life-giving power is found in every word that proceeds from the mouth of the Lord. His revealed will preserves life (see Deuteronomy 8:3; Isaiah 38:16; Genesis 27:40; Matthew 4:4).

The verb "know" (Heb. *yada*, **yaw-dah**) is used in the sense "to legally recognize or acknowledge" (see Deuteronomy 9:24; Genesis 18:19; Exodus 33:12; 2 Samuel 7:20; Isaiah 45:3). Israel is called to acknowledge the providential care of the Lord and obey Him as their God.

7 And when ye came unto this place, Sihon the king of Heshbon, and Og the king of Bashan, came out against us unto battle, and we smote them:

Further evidence of the Lord's care in the past years is pointed out. He gave strategic military victories to His people against all odds (see Deuteronomy 2:26—3:12). The reference is to the conquest of areas to the east of the Jordan River (cf. Numbers 21:21-35).

8 And we took their land, and gave it for an inheritance unto the Reubenites, and to the Gadites, and to the half tribe of Manasseh.

The Lord took the land of people who were utterly corrupt and gave it to Israel (see 9:4-5; Leviticus 18:24-25). Three tribes inherited the land east of the Jordan River: Reuben, Gad, and the half tribe of Manasseh (see Deuteronomy 3:12-22).

9 Keep therefore the words of this covenant, and do them, that ye may prosper in all that ye do.

An appeal is made to the people to faithfully observe all the terms of the covenant (see 8:18) and to act wisely. Bear in mind, however, that the Lord Himself is the wisdom of His people and that the search for this wisdom brings prosperity and salvation (see 6:6; 32:29; Joshua 1:7—8). Thus, the covenant has an immediate appeal, a present relevance. It inspires renewed confidence in the God who meets their immediate needs.

10 Ye stand this day all of you before the LORD your God; your captains of your tribes, your elders, and your officers, with all the men of Israel.

The verb "stand" (Heb. *natsab*, **naw-tsab**) has the reflexive meaning "you have taken your stand." The same usage is found in Joshua 24:1 and 1 Samuel 10:19.

The covenant assembly is described with great detail. The whole nation without a single exception stood before the Lord. The list starts with the tribal heads, the officials, and all the men of Israel. "Elders" (Heb. *zaqen*, **zaw-kane**) designates those traditionally responsible for the administration of justice in the community (see 16:18—17:7). The word "officers" (Heb. *shoter*, **sho-tare**) refers to those who were administrative assistants to the judges (see 16:18; 1:15).

11 Your little ones, your wives, and thy stranger that is in thy camp, from the hewer of thy wood unto the drawer of thy water:

The description of the covenant assembly continues with the children, the women, and the resident aliens (cf. Exodus 12:38; Numbers 10:29; 11:4). The word "stranger" (Heb. *ger*, **gare**) or "sojourner" refers to a landless and therefore economically weak individual who for some reason is living either temporarily or permanently away from the land of his own tribe or people (see Deuteronomy 1:16; 5:14; 14:29; 18:6). Usually a non-Israelite, he is regularly commended to the kindness of the people of God (see 14:29; 16:11, 14; 26:11).

Finally, the covenant assembly included the lowest servant, "the hewer of thy wood unto the drawer of thy water" (cf. Joshua 9:21, 23, 27). Although this person is socially inferior and responsible for the most menial task, he is important in the eyes of the Lord and to be included as part of the covenant people (cf. Deuteronomy 10:17; Acts 10:34; Romans 2:11; Galatians 2:6).

12 That thou shouldest enter into covenant with the LORD thy God, and into his oath, which the LORD thy God maketh with thee this day:

The purpose of the assembly was to "enter into covenant with the LORD," or literally, "that you may pass over into the covenant of the Lord" (see Genesis 15:17—18; 2 Chronicles 15:12). "To enter into" expresses entire entrance or to go completely through.

The word "oath" (Heb. *alah*, **aw-law**) also means "curse." Covenants were always confirmed or accompanied with an oath (cf. Genesis 26:28; Ezekiel 17:18). The oath by which allegiance to the covenant was sworn involved a self-cursing formula to guard against disobedience. A person who enters a covenant places himself in the position where curses will fall upon him if he violates the covenant obligations. Here, the people are summoned to enter into the covenant of the Lord, namely, to enter inwardly and make it an affair of the heart and life.

13 That he may establish thee to day for a people unto himself, and that he may be unto thee a God, as he hath said unto thee, and as he hath sworn unto thy fathers, to Abraham, to Isaac, and to Jacob.

The Lord, through the covenant, wanted to establish Israel as His people. "Establish" (Heb. *quwm*, **koom**) means to exalt or set up (Deuteronomy 27:9; 28:9; Exodus 19:5, 6).

He wanted to be their God in accordance with the promise made to the patriarchs. The correlation in the covenant between "a people unto himself" and "be unto thee a God" is a continuing theme in the Bible (cf. Deuteronomy 26:17-18; 28:9; Exodus 19:5).

14 Neither with you only do I make this covenant and this oath;

The covenant was made not only with those who were present. Its obligation extends beyond the generation which had direct and immediate experience of the Lord and His covenant.

15 But with him that standeth here with us this day before the LORD our God, and also with him that is not here with us this day:

Both those who were present and their descendants were included in this covenant to become a blessing for all nations (cf. 5:3; Joshua 24:25; John 17:20; Acts 2:39). Thus, present and future generations were to enter into a covenant relationship with God. The genealogical continuity of the covenant proceeds from the Lord's faithfulness in extending His blessing to all who obey Him. Each new generation must renew the covenant for itself and respond to the Lord. They must accept His Word for themselves in "this day" or "today." This Hebrew word *hayyome* (**hi-yome**) occurs six times in verses 2-15, 2 Corinthians 6:2, and Hebrews 2:3, indicating that the covenant is kept alive and forever contemporary.

DAILY BIBLE READINGS

M: Moses Reminds the Israelites
Deuteronomy 29:2-9
T: The Israelites Join the Covenant
Deuteronomy 29:10-15
W: Moses Warns the Israelites
Deuteronomy 29:16-21
T: The Reason for Devastation
Deuteronomy 29:22-29
F: God Will Forgive Those Who Return
Deuteronomy 30:1-5
S: God Will Prosper Those Who Believe
Deuteronomy 30:6-10
S: Obey God and Choose Life
Deuteronomy 30:11-20

Our obedience is more important to God than our sacrifice. By using the word search capability of your *Precepts For Living* CD-ROM, you can see how many times the words *obedience* and *obey* is used in the Bible.

TEACHING TIPS

October 3
Bible Study Guide 5

1. Words You Should Know

A. Redeem (2 Samuel 7:23) *padah* (Heb.)—To recover by paying a ransom; to rescue, set free, or deliver.

B. Confirmed (v. 24) *kuwn* (Heb.)—To be supported, established, and strengthened; to be securely determined.

2. Teacher Preparation

A. Prepare your heart by praying for yourself and your students by name.

B. Read the entire lesson several times, giving special attention to the LESSON AIM and asking the Lord for ways to make the lesson real to the students.

3. Starting the Lesson

A. Greet the students as they enter the classroom, and ask them to silently read the IN FOCUS section.

B. Allow the students to answer the questions and discuss their opinions and feelings about the situation.

4. Getting into the Lesson

A. Display the AT-A-GLANCE outline on the chalkboard or on poster board and have the students read it together to gain a preview of the focus and content of today's lesson.

B. Now have the students read the passage of Scripture from FOCAL VERSES, which is a transcript of David's prayer.

C. Ask: What do we discover about David by reading his prayer? Some answers are: (1) he considers himself a servant of God (7:19-21); (2) he respects God very highly (7:22); (3) he considers Israel to be a unique nation (7:23).

D. Use the AT-A-GLANCE outline and the FOCAL VERSES to lead the students through the lesson.

5. Relating the Lesson to Life

A. Allow the students to answer the SEARCH THE SCRIPTURES and DISCUSS THE MEANING questions.

B. Ask: If someone overheard you pray, what could they learn about you?

C. Give each student a 3 x 5" card and ask them to write a short prayer expressing thanks for God's goodness and their hope for future generations on the card. Collect the cards and redistribute them. Ask each person to read the prayer out loud and tell something positive that is revealed in the person's prayer.

OCT 3RD

6. Arousing Action

A. Review the MAKE IT HAPPEN activity and allow the class to brainstorm to develop a list of suggestions. Call for a vote to select one activity, and develop plans for class participation.

B. Remind the students to read the DAILY BIBLE READINGS this week.

WORSHIP GUIDE

For the Superintendent or Teacher
Theme: Creating a New Dynasty
Theme Song: "Standing on the Promises of God" (verses 1 and 2)
Scripture: John 1:11-12;
Philippians 4:19; 1 John 1:9
Song: "Standing on the Promises of God" (verses 3 and 4)
Meditation: Thank You, our Father, for the promises You have given us in Your Word. Help us to read them, memorize them, claim them as our own, and experience the reality of them in our daily lives.

CREATING A NEW DYNASTY

Bible Background • 2 SAMUEL 7
Printed Text • 2 SAMUEL 7:18-29
Devotional Reading • 2 SAMUEL 7:10-17

LESSON AIM

By the end of the lesson, the students will recall the importance of prayer and thanksgiving to God and recognize that their prayers and relationship with God can affect future generations.

KEEP IN MIND

"And thine house and thy kingdom shall be established for ever before thee: thy throne shall be established for ever" (2 Samuel 7:16).

FOCAL VERSES

2 Samuel 7:18 Then went king David in, and sat before the LORD, and he said, Who am I, O Lord GOD? and what is my house, that thou hast brought me hitherto?

19 And this was yet a small thing in thy sight, O Lord GOD; but thou hast spoken also of thy servant's house for a great while to come. And is this the manner of man, O Lord GOD?

20 And what can David say more unto thee? for thou, Lord GOD, knowest thy servant.

21 For thy word's sake, and according to thine own heart, hast thou done all these great things, to make thy servant know them.

22 Wherefore thou art great, O LORD God: for there is none like thee, neither is there any God beside thee, according to all that we have heard with our ears.

23 And what one nation in the earth is like thy people, even like Israel, whom God went to redeem for a people to himself, and to make him a name, and to do for you great things and terrible, for thy land, before thy people, which thou

LESSON OVERVIEW

LESSON AIM
KEEP IN MIND
FOCAL VERSES
IN FOCUS
THE PEOPLE, PLACES, AND TIMES
BACKGROUND
AT-A-GLANCE
IN DEPTH
SEARCH THE SCRIPTURES
DISCUSS THE MEANING
LESSON IN OUR SOCIETY
MAKE IT HAPPEN
FOLLOW THE SPIRIT
REMEMBER YOUR THOUGHTS
MORE LIGHT ON THE TEXT
DAILY BIBLE READINGS

redeemedst to thee from Egypt, from the nations and their gods?

24 For thou hast confirmed to thyself thy people Israel to be a people unto thee for ever: and thou, LORD, art become their God.

25 And now, O LORD God, the word that thou hast spoken concerning thy servant and concerning his house, establish it for ever, and do as thou hast said.

26 And let thy name be magnified for ever, saying, The LORD of hosts is the God over Israel: and let the house of thy servant David be established before thee.

27 For thou, O LORD of hosts, God of Israel, hast revealed to thy servant, saying, I will build thee an house: therefore hath thy servant found in his heart to pray this prayer unto thee.

28 And now, O Lord GOD, thou art that God, and thy words be true, and thou hast promised this goodness unto thy servant:

29 Therefore now let it please thee to bless the house of thy servant, that it may continue for ever before thee: for thou, O Lord GOD, hast spoken it: and with thy blessing let the house of thy servant be blessed for ever.

IN FOCUS

Earl labored over the barbecue grill. Smoky visions of his seven sons floated in his mind. Not one of his children had showed for his Fourth of July party. He turned over a steak and thought about the accident that had killed his first wife. It was a shame. His new wife Angela had brought him out of depression. Interrupting his thoughts, smiling Angela joined him.

"I think it's time to eat. Everybody is growling for food," she said, reading his thoughts. "It's your boys, isn't it? It's OK. I'll stall everyone. Go call them."

Earl called his oldest son Earl Jr. and tried an upbeat tone. "Hi, are my sons and grandchildren on the way?

After a pause, his son said, "None of us are coming."

Infuriated, Earl asked, "Why is that?"

In a heavy voice, Earl Jr. said, "It's the money from the house. You've given everything to Angela. She is a gold digger."

Earl closed his eyes and thought, "Lord, let me find the right words." Then he told his son, "You boys should never let money come between us. This is my business. Your bitterness will never change my relationship with Angela. And my house will always be open to my children."

Earl hung up the phone with pain but no guilt in his heart.

Did Earl's children place too much emphasis on tangible factors for their family unity? Should they have concentrated more on building spiritual relationships?

THE PEOPLE, PLACES, AND TIMES

Temple. When the Bible uses the word *temple* it usually refers to the temple of the Lord in Jerusalem in one of its three phases: Solomon's temple, Zerubabbel's temple, or Israel's third temple.

Solomon's temple was started in 957 B.C. (1 Kings 6:1-7) and finished seven years later (1 Kings 6:38). This temple was also called the "house of the LORD" (1 Kings 6:1). Zerubabbel's temple was Israel's second temple. It did not have the splendor of Solomon's temple. Zerubabbel had been appointed governor when the Jews were allowed to return to Canaan from Babylon. The temple he built was completed in 505 B.C.

Israel's third temple was started in 20 B.C. by King Herod. But it was not completely finished for 46 years (John 2:20), and work may have continued on it until it was destroyed by Titus in A.D. 70.

Blaiklock, Edward M. and R. K. Harrison, eds. *The New International Dictionary of Biblical Archaeology.* Grand Rapids: Zondervan, 1983.

BACKGROUND

Although Saul possessed military genius, his administration was marred by his spiritual short-sightedness. David understood the significance of Israel's worship of and obedience to God. He established a centralized capitol in Jerusalem to replace the old sanctuary at Shiloh. He implemented a judicial system (2 Samuel 14:4-17; 15:1-6) and allowed his administrators to carry out the daily duties of the king. By bringing the Ark of the Covenant, a symbol of the abiding presence of Yahweh (2 Samuel 7:2), to Jerusalem, he made Jerusalem the religious center of his kingdom. Even though he did not build Israel's temple, he purchased the site for it (2 Samuel 24:18-25).

In contrast to Saul's administration, which was marked by tension with Samuel, David had the apparent support of Nathan, the prophet (2 Samuel 7:1-3). While David "sat in his house, the LORD [having] given him rest round about from all his enemies" (2 Samuel 7:1), he confided in Nathan regarding his ambitions. Initially, Nathan responded to this by saying, "Go, do all that is in thine heart; for the LORD is with thee" (2 Samuel 7:3b). Later, under divine instructions, Nathan told David of the covenant relationship that the king and his seed were to enjoy with God. These instructions are called the Davidic Covenant. This covenant gave the Jews hope after the fall of Jerusalem (ca. 587 B.C.). This hope centered on the coming of David's great "son" to reign in future glory over Israel (Isaiah 9:6ff; 11:1ff). Today, our Christian faith traces Jesus Christ's kingship back to David (Matthew 2:1; Luke 1:32).

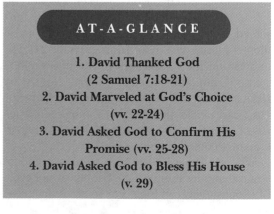

AT-A-GLANCE

1. **David Thanked God**
   (2 Samuel 7:18-21)
2. **David Marveled at God's Choice**
   (vv. 22-24)
3. **David Asked God to Confirm His Promise (vv. 25-28)**
4. **David Asked God to Bless His House (v. 29)**

IN DEPTH

1. David Thanked God (2 Samuel 7:18-21)

David had received divine instructions that he would not build a permanent dwelling place for the Lord. Upon hearing the Lord's words through Nathan, David went into the tent where the Ark of the Covenant was housed and prepared to pray. Verse 18 says, "Then went king David in, and sat before the LORD." Since there are no detailed descriptions of this position for prayer, it probably meant a kneeling position in which the worshiper sat back on his heels with his head erect.

One of the many contributions to Israel that David made were his frequent prayers. The Psalms contain some of David's most memorable prayers. David's prayer in 2 Samuel 7 began with thanksgiving. He humbly thanked God for the great things God had done and had promised to do.

Our prayers should always begin with thanksgiving and praise. It is good to express our gratitude for God's gracious promises and their fulfillment. In the New Testament, Paul tells us to give thanks in everything (1 Thessalonians 5:18). Gratitude shows our confident knowledge that God is the source of our blessings.

2. David Marveled at God's Choice (vv. 22-24)

David continues his prayer by marveling that God has chosen Israel and made a place for it by driving out other nations and their gods. He was also amazed that God had redeemed a nation of former slaves and had given them His name. The word "redeem" is translated from the Hebrew root, *padah*, which means to sever, ransom, or release. David remembered that God had ransomed Israel from Egyptian bondage to make them a special people for Himself (vv. 23-24). He understood the significance of the divine intervention into and through human history to redeem Israel. He was amazed that God had chosen Israel as His people. God's choice of Israel was a result of His grace and love, not their human accomplishments.

Whereas Israel looked back to all the important redemptive events of the Exodus from Egypt, Christians today can look back to the redemptive event on Calvary. Like David, we discover that our salvation is amazing in its nature. We are saved from the penalty and power of sin purely by God's grace (Romans 6:23; 7:6). In addition, our salvation is amazing in its scope and length. Anyone and everyone can be saved for eternity (John 3:16). Finally, we understand that our salvation is amazing in its results. Because of the salvation provided by Christ's sacrifice for us, by faith in Him even the most unproductive sinner can choose to live a productive life (John 15:16).

3. David Asked God to Confirm His Promise (vv. 25-28)

In this third part of David's prayer, he asked God to confirm His promise of perpetuating the house of David forever. When the Lord told David, "And thine house and thy kingdom shall be established for ever before thee: thy throne shall be established for ever" (2 Samuel 7:16), David was faced with the process of actualizing that promise. First, David's wife was childless (2 Samuel 6:23), showing that the process of perpetuating a family was halted initially. Second, the process continued to be a problem even after David fathered children through other wives. David's eldest son Amnon fell victim to his own immorality, and his son Absalom fell victim to his own ambition. Even Solomon was on the verge of losing the throne to his stepbrother, Adonijah.

What are we to do when our real-life situations seem to contradict God's promises? Like David, we pray and ask God to confirm His promises, and we rest our case with Him.

4. David Asked God to Bless His House (v. 29)

At the conclusion of this prayer, David asked God to bless his house forever. This is a noteworthy request. But what did he actually want? Was he referring to a house made of bricks, stucco, and lumber? No, here the Hebrew word translated as "house" is the word *bavith*, meaning a palace, temple, family, or dynasty.

It appears that David was exercising a fatherly concern for his children. Maybe he was aware of the vulnerability of Tamar, the ambitious nature of Absalom, and the licentious tendencies of Amnon; he obviously prayed for their welfare.

This example is reminiscent of Job. Job would rise early in the morning to offer burnt offerings for all his sons and daughters (Job 1:4-5). It is commendable to invite the pastor to a new house for the purpose of blessing it. But it is more commendable to pray consistently for our own children and other family members.

When we pray for wealth, success, money, cars, prestige, and power, we often are praying selfish prayers. Good parents pray for security, health, and safety for their children. They seek the stability of their family, rather than the acquisition of property, prestige, power, and prosperity. Parents that pray consistently and lead their families in prayer help their children to grow in Christian character, spiritual security, and genuine joyful living.

SEARCH THE SCRIPTURES

1. What was David's first response to the divine instructions by Nathan (2 Samuel 7:18)?

2. How did David begin his prayer (v. 18)?

3. What was the "small thing" to which David referred (v. 19)?

4. In what ways was Israel unlike other nations (vv. 23-24)?

5. How did God redeem Israel, and from whom (v. 23)?

6. What was the final request of David's prayer (v. 29)?

DISCUSS THE MEANING

1. David was the King of Israel, yet he listened to Nathan. How can listening to the right people improve the decisions we make?

2. David prayed while he was sitting. What is the correct posture for prayer?

3. The prayer of David began with thanksgiving. Why is thanksgiving an appropriate way to start praying?

4. David's prayer indicated that he had already claimed God's promises. Can we claim God's promises when we ask for what we want?

LESSON IN OUR SOCIETY

1. There is an old adage: "A family that prays together, stays together." Is there any validity to that adage in an era of disintegrating families?

2. Can savings bonds, real estate investments, stocks and bonds, and a guarantee of a college education for our children ensure a united family? Do you think these things are the answer to the problem of violence? In your opinion, what is the solution for many of the problems we face today? Discuss why you hold this opinion.

MAKE IT HAPPEN

Identify three or four ways that your Sunday School class can foster family unity. Decide on one way and make plans to put it into practice this week.

FOLLOW THE SPIRIT

What God wants me to do:

_____

_____

REMEMBER YOUR THOUGHTS

Special insights I have learned:

_____

_____

MORE LIGHT ON THE TEXT

2 Samuel 7:18-29

18 Then went king David in, and sat before the LORD, and he said, Who am I, O Lord GOD? and what is my house, that thou hast brought me hitherto?

David responded with prayer after the revelation given to him by the prophet Nathan (v. 17). He went into the sanctuary erected upon Zion and "sat before the Lord." "Sit" (Heb. *yashab*, **yaw-shab**) means to remain or to dwell (see Genesis 24:55; 29:19). David sat before the Lord in prayer.

David confessed his unworthiness of all the great things that the Lord had done for him, which He had increased still further by a glorious promise. David had come such a long way since the days when he was a shepherd boy. The word "house" (Heb. *bayith*, **bah-yith**) used here means family or dynasty (see Genesis 32:10).

19 And this was yet a small thing in thy sight, O Lord GOD; but thou hast spoken also of thy servant's house for a great while to come. And is this the manner of man, O Lord GOD?

God had shown sovereign graciousness to David. He made His plan known to David. The expression "a great while to come" (Heb. *rachowq*, **raw-khoke**) literally means "that which points to a remote period." God had spoken of the eternal establishment of David's house and throne. The word "manner" (Heb. *towrah*, **to-raw**) refers to the custom or law which determines or regulates the conduct of man. God had shown love and deference in the way He treated His servant David. David expressed praise for the grace of the Lord. He elevated David and treated him as a man of higher rank.

20 And what can David say more unto thee? for thou, Lord GOD, knowest thy servant.

David appealed to the omniscience of God, before whom his thankful heart lies open (see Psalm 27:3). He says to God that he can add nothing more that He does not already have. God knows His servant David better than anyone else.

21 For thy word's sake, and according to thine own heart, hast thou done all these great things, to make thy servant know them.

David ascribed to God all the blessings he received. God acted according to His own word (cf. 1 Samuel 16:12; 1 Chronicles 17:19). The promises that had just come to David were a sign of God's prearrangement and His faithfulness to keep His promises.

The Lord acted according to His own heart. "According to thine own heart" refers to the love and grace of Yahweh. He is gracious, merciful, and full of great kindness and truth (Exodus 34:6; Psalm 103:8).

The expression "great things" (Heb. *geduwlah*, **ghed-oo-law**) designates the greatness of the Lord.

22 Wherefore thou art great, O LORD God: for there is none like thee, neither is there any God beside thee, according to all that we have heard with our ears.

David admires the Lord's greatness and uniqueness. God is great, and immense in wisdom, kindness, and magnificent planning. In the great things He does, Yahweh proves the incomparable nature of His Deity. He alone is the true God (cf. Exodus 15:11; Deuteronomy 3:24; 4:35).

23 And what one nation in the earth is like thy people, even like Israel, whom God went to redeem for a people to himself, and to make him a name, and to do for you great things and terrible, for thy land, before thy people, which thou redeemedst to thee from Egypt, from the nations and their gods?

David marvels at what the Lord has done for Israel. His question is, "Is there any nation to which the deity worshiped by it went, as the true God went to Israel, to redeem it for His own people?" Yahweh is unique and has done a unique thing in His people, making them unique also. He made him a name. The Hebrew phrase *sum shem* (**soom shame**) is literally translated as "to put a name" and means to bestow on Israel a name or to put a mark on Israel showing that it belonged to God (see 2 Samuel 6:2). Giving a name to someone or something is a judicial act indicating ownership, possession, and protection (cf. 5:9; 12:28; Psalm 49:12; Isaiah 4:1; 63:19; Amos 9:12). David stressed the incomparable character of the things which God had done for His people (cf. 4:7, 34). He has acted as King, bringing redemption, release from bondage, glory for Himself, justice for the sins of the nations, banishment of sinful nations, and exaltation of His own people (cf. 10:21; Exodus 15:11).

24 For thou hast confirmed to thyself thy people Israel to be a people unto thee for ever: and thou, LORD, art become their God.

The Lord had acted sovereignly to bring about the creation of a people for Himself (cf. Exodus 19:3-6). He had become God to Israel (cf. 1 Samuel 12:22; Deuteronomy 26:17-18; 27:9; 29:12). He had attested and proved Himself to be Israel's God.

25 And now, O LORD God, the word that thou hast spoken concerning thy servant and concerning his house, establish it for ever, and do as thou hast said.

David turns the promise from the Lord into prayer and prays for its fulfillment. He prays that the Lord would carry out the word which He has spoken to His servant.

26 And let thy name be magnified for ever, saying, The LORD of hosts is the God over Israel: and let the house of thy servant David be established before thee.

"The LORD of hosts" (Heb. *yehovah sebaot,* **Yaway saw-baw-ot**) is a special name for God. It literally means "the Lord of armies" and is associated with Yahweh's kingship. Generally, it means that the Lord is the mightiest warrior or the all-powerful King (see 1 Samuel 17:45; Isaiah 31:4). He is Lord over Israel. The house of His servant David will be firmly established before Him. David expressed his prayer in the form of confident assurance.

27 For thou, O LORD of hosts, God of Israel, hast revealed to thy servant, saying, I will build thee an house: therefore hath thy servant found in his heart to pray this prayer unto thee.

"Reveal" (Heb. *gala ozen,* **gaw-law o-zen**) literally means "to open the ear" or "to uncover the ear" in order to disclose important information (cf. 1 Samuel 9:15; 20:2, 12,13; 22:8, 17; Ruth 4:4; Job 33:16; 36:10, 15).

David was bold in his prayer because God had opened his ear and given him His word. He asked for personal blessing upon his own household. The Lord promised to build David a "house" (Heb. *bayit,* **bah-yit**). The meaning of "house" here is not a physical structure but a dynasty.

28 And now, O Lord GOD, thou art that God, and thy words be true, and thou hast promised this goodness unto thy servant:

Here, David briefly sums up the two parts of his prayer of thanksgiving by saying "and now." He celebrates the greatness of the Lord and His promise (see vv. 18-24). He pleads God's promises.

"This goodness," or good thing (Heb. *hattoba,* **hazzot**), refers to the promise made by Yahweh to establish David's house forever (cf. v. 29). By promising "this goodness unto thy servant," the Lord brought David and his descendants into a covenantal relationship with Himself.

29 Therefore now let it please thee to bless the house of thy servant, that it may continue for ever before thee: for thou, O Lord GOD, hast spoken it: and with thy blessing let the house of thy servant be blessed for ever.

This verse is the substance of the prayer in verses 25-27. David pushes his request as high as it can go. He asks for eternal blessings. God has promised them forever, so David asks for the blessings to last forever. His faith is as big as the promise. The phrase "let be blessed" can be translated as "be pleased and bless" or "may it please you to bless" (see 1:5).

DAILY BIBLE READINGS

M: God's Steadfast Love Is Great
Psalm 86:8-13
T: David Moves the Ark of God
2 Samuel 6:1-5
W: David Brings the Ark to Jerusalem
2 Samuel 6:11-15
T: God Sends a Message to David
2 Samuel 7:1-9
F: God Makes a Covenant with David
2 Samuel 7:10-17
S: David Prays to God
2 Samuel 7:18-22
S: David Seeks God's Blessing
2 Samuel 7:23-29

TEACHING TIPS

October 10
Bible Study Guide 6

1. Words You Should Know

A. Redeemed (Isaiah 43:1) *ga'al* (Heb.)—To ransom, release, or deliver; to fulfill the duties of relationship. God is the Redeemer who purchased Israel from slavery in Egypt and from sin.

B. Former (v. 18) *ri'shown* (Heb.)—Former things in the prophetic context signify the past sins of Israel and God's judgment on them.

2. Teacher Preparation

A. Begin preparing for this lesson by reading Isaiah 43. Then prayerfully study the FOCAL VERSES for this week's lesson.

B. Pray that God will bless you with understanding as you study this week.

C. Finally, read BIBLE STUDY GUIDE 6.

3. Starting the Lesson

A. Open in prayer. Have a student read IN FOCUS.

B. Before beginning this lesson, briefly review the highlights of last week's lesson. Then ask for volunteers to share their experiences from last week's MAKE IT HAPPEN section.

C. Write on the chalkboard in large letters the word *PROMISE*. Then ask the students to share some incident where someone they trusted broke a promise and disappointed them. After the discussion, explain that the faith we place in God will never disappoint because He never fails to honor His promises.

4. Getting into the Lesson

A. Have a student read the BACKGROUND section and another read THE PEOPLE, PLACES, AND TIMES.

B. Write the AT-A-GLANCE outline on the chalkboard for the students to review as they discuss the lesson. Then, assign three students to read the FOCAL VERSES.

C. Give the students five minutes to read the first IN DEPTH section. After the reading, ask students the corresponding SEARCH THE SCRIPTURES questions.

5. Relating the Lesson to Life

A. Use the DISCUSS THE MEANING questions to help students understand how these truths relate to their lives.

B. The LESSON IN OUR SOCIETY section should also be used to help students see how the lesson relates to our society.

6. Arousing Action

A. Have the students read the KEEP IN MIND verse in unison, and ask one student to summarize what this verse is saying.

B. Read the MAKE IT HAPPEN assignment. Challenge the students to apply it to their lives this week.

C. Close by giving the students a time for silent prayer to thank God for the living hope that they have within them.

WORSHIP GUIDE

For the Superintendent or Teacher
Theme: Creating a Redeemed People
Theme Song: "My Redeemer Lives"
Scripture: Isaiah 43
Song: "Amazing Grace"
Meditation: Dear Lord, You are my God and I am Yours. You have called me into the Christian community with other believers. Help me to be a blessing to others even as You continue to be a blessing to me.

CREATING A REDEEMED PEOPLE

Bible Background • ISAIAH 43
Printed Text • ISAIAH 43:1-2, 10-13, 18-19
Devotional Reading • ISAIAH 42:5-13

LESSON AIM

By the end of the lesson, the students will understand God's message of hope to the captive Israelites in Assyria and Babylon, be able to explain why God's covenant relationship with His people binds Him to them forever and makes us His witnesses, and determine to trust God as they go through the trials and challenges of life.

KEEP IN MIND

"But now thus saith the LORD that created thee, O Jacob, and he that formed thee, O Israel, Fear not: for I have redeemed thee, I have called thee by thy name; thou art mine" (Isaiah 43:1).

FOCAL VERSES

Isaiah 43:1 But now thus saith the LORD that created thee, O Jacob, and he that formed thee, O Israel, Fear not: for I have redeemed thee, I have called thee by thy name; thou art mine.

2 When thou passest through the waters, I will be with thee; and through the rivers, they shall not overflow thee: when thou walkest through the fire, thou shalt not be burned; neither shall the flame kindle upon thee.

43:10 Ye are my witnesses, saith the LORD, and my servant whom I have chosen: that ye may know and believe me, and understand that I am he: before me there was no God formed, neither shall there be after me.

11 I, even I, am the LORD; and beside me there is no saviour.

LESSON OVERVIEW

LESSON AIM
KEEP IN MIND
FOCAL VERSES
IN FOCUS
THE PEOPLE, PLACES, AND TIMES
BACKGROUND
AT-A-GLANCE
IN DEPTH
SEARCH THE SCRIPTURES
DISCUSS THE MEANING
LESSON IN OUR SOCIETY
MAKE IT HAPPEN
FOLLOW THE SPIRIT
REMEMBER YOUR THOUGHTS
MORE LIGHT ON THE TEXT
DAILY BIBLE READINGS

12 I have declared, and have saved, and I have shewed, when there was no strange god among you: therefore ye are my witnesses, saith the LORD, that I am God.

13 Yea, before the day was I am he; and there is none that can deliver out of my hand: I will work, and who shall let it?

OCT 10TH

43:18 Remember ye not the former things, neither consider the things of old.

19 Behold, I will do a new thing; now it shall spring forth; shall ye not know it? I will even make a way in the wilderness, and rivers in the desert.

IN FOCUS

In 1994, the central African nation of Rwanda exploded into bloodshed. During one period called "the one-hundred-day massacre," the Rwandan Armed Forces, who were Hutu extremists, slaughtered nearly one million Tutsi and the Hutu moderates who supported them.

Barely a year after the genocide, Hutu and Tutsi widows who lost husbands during the slaughter gathered under a Eucalyptus tree. They formed a group to help survivors who had lost family members or had been maimed during the violence. Sitting side by side, the Hutu and Tutsi women wove elegantly patterned baskets that they planned to sell in Rwanda to help raise money.

The women sat very close together on a bench, cradling the coiling reed in their laps and using needles to sew the coils until each masterpiece was complete. Each basket takes about two to three weeks to complete. These lovely baskets came to symbolize new beginnings for the Hutu and Tutsi widows, whose tribes were once killing each other but are now working side by side to rebuild their lives.

In November 2003, Amber Chand, an Indian from Uganda, learned of the baskets at a Counsel for Peace conference in Geneva, Switzerland. Chand, who was expelled from Uganda during the reign of Idi Amim, was so moved by the story surrounding the baskets that she felt she had to do something. She visited Rwanda and met with several of the widows and witnessed how art and business could bring about peace and reconciliation. She called the baskets "vessels of peace," and the name stuck.

Eziba, a Boston-based company cofounded by Chand, began offering the peace baskets for sale on a worldwide basis through their website and catalog. The women now sell many more baskets that they ever hoped they'd sell in their native country. What started out as a way to overcome the grief and resentment, to move forward, and to restore some sanity to their lives has now become a way to help others whose lives have been scarred by violence.

In today's lesson, the prophet Isaiah delivers a message of comfort and new beginnings to those in the northern nation of Israel who had been taken captive by the Assyrians and to those in Judah who would soon go into exile in Babylon.

THE PEOPLE, PLACES, AND TIMES

God's Promises. A divine promise is an absolute assurance that flows into unfilled time. It is a future guarantee of companionship, comfort, and conquest.

BACKGROUND

Scripture declares that all things work together for the benefit of God's people (Romans 8:28). This means that sometimes even bad things happen for our benefit. So it was with the captivity of Judah. Before God sent His people into exile, He equipped them with certain precious promises to sustain them in captivity. One of these promises concerned the Israelites' release by a future Gentile king named Cyrus, who would allow the people to return and rebuild their land.

Isaiah first prophesied of Judah's Babylonian captivity after King Hezekiah's foolish act of presumption. The king had boastfully shown Babylonian emissaries all the treasures of his kingdom. God sent Isaiah to tell Hezekiah the day would come when all of Judah's treasures would be taken to Babylon. Isaiah also told him that some of his descendants would be carried into captivity to serve in the king's palace (Isaiah 39:1-6). However, the cause of Judah's downfall was not Hezekiah's foolishness, but the nation's sin.

After Hezekiah's death, his son, Manasseh, became king. Manasseh led the people into the darkest time of sin and idolatry in Judah's history, bringing God's judgment on the nation (2 Chronicles 33:1-9).

Later, Isaiah prophesied that God would appoint a ruler from the East. This ruler would conquer nations and carry out God's righteous plan of redemption. God would use this as yet unborn king to execute His wrath on Babylon and free His people. The Lord was going to do "a new thing" for His delivered people. They would receive a new time of forgiveness, restoration, and blessing (Isaiah 43:14-21).

God wanted His exiled people to do two things while in captivity: remember that they were special to Him and that He would never forget them (44:21), and repent—turn away from their wickedness and return to Him. If they repented, God would wipe away the cloud of sin that separated Him from His people (v. 22).

AT-A-GLANCE

1. Preserved in God (Isaiah 43:1-2)
2. Witnesses of God (vv. 10-13)
3. Power of God (vv. 18-19)

IN DEPTH

1. Preserved in God (Isaiah 43:1-2)

Isaiah begins this message of hope with the conjunction "but." Many times in Scripture, the word "but" signals a turning point. It highlights a situation that has reached a critical point and indicates that God is about to step in and turn things around. In this case, "but" signifies a turn-around from the last two verses of the preceding chapter: "But this is a people plundered and looted, all of them trapped in pits or hidden away in prisons. They have become plunder, with no one to rescue them; they have been made loot, with no one to say, 'Send them back'" (Isaiah 42:22, NIV). Who allowed Israel to be robbed and hurt? "Was it not the LORD, against whom we have sinned? For they would not follow his ways; they did not obey his law. So he poured out on them his burning anger, the violence of war. It enveloped them in flames, yet they did not understand; it consumed them, but they did not take it to heart" (vv. 24-25, NIV).

Assyria had already taken the 10 tribes making up the northern nation of Israel into captivity. A similar fate would soon befall the remaining nation of Judah at the hands of the Babylonians. The temple would be burned, Jerusalem destroyed, and the people taken in chains into Babylonian exile. The situation appeared hopeless; it seemed like the people of God would fade from the pages of history, never to be heard from again.

But then comes one of the most blessed words in Scripture: "but." God had outlined the penalty for disobedience before the Israelites entered the Promised Land (Deuteronomy 28:64-69). Later He announced the consequence of Israel's continued disobedience (Isaiah 42:24-26), but now God declares a message of hope in the midst of the people's despair.

It is one thing to counsel people not to lose hope; it is something different to command people to have hope. This kind of command must be based on the power of the commander to justify their hope. To illustrate His power, God begins by declaring who He is. He is the Lord, He is their Creator, and He is the One who formed them (Isaiah 43:1a).

"Lord" is most often a substitute for the name Yahweh. The ancient scribes held the holy name in such high reverence that they would not speak or write it, but instead substituted the title "Lord" in its place. Yahweh is God's covenant name. This name signifies the God of relationship and promise. It speaks of God's love for His people and His ability to fulfill every promise He makes.

The Israelites would associate this name with the God who delivered their forefathers from Egyptian bondage. If Yahweh, the God of the covenant, could deliver their forefathers from the bondage of Egypt, surely He could deliver them.

The reference to God as their creator has a double meaning. It harkens back to the dawn of time when God created the physical universe (Genesis 1:1-31). It also refers to the creation of God's people when He chose Abraham from among the millions of people in the world to father a nation of witnesses and servants.

God is the loving, powerful Deliverer who commands the people to "Fear not" (Isaiah 43:1a, 5). This command is based not only on who God is but also on who the Israelites are. They are God's redeemed. He delivered them from Egyptian bondage and personally named them (Genesis 32:27-28).

2. Witnesses of God (vv. 10-13)

In verses 5-9, God pulls back the curtain of time and gives the people a brief glimpse into their future. He begins His prophecy by once again commanding the people to "Fear not" (v. 5; see also v. 1). When the people of Judah were finally deported to Babylon, Jerusalem was destroyed and the temple was burned to the ground. With the holy city and their precious temple destroyed, the deported Israelites gave up all hope of ever returning to their homeland. Their God had turned them out because of their wickedness.

God summed up their feeling of hopelessness when He proclaimed through the prophet Ezekiel: "Then he said unto me, 'Son of man, these bones are the whole house of Israel': behold, they say, 'Our bones are dried, and our hope is lost: we are cut off for our parts'" (Ezekiel 37:11). Even though it appeared that their situation was hopeless, God instructed His people not to be afraid and not to worry because He would bring them back and restore them to the Promised Land. God would call His people back from around the world and reestablish the nation of Israel.

After prophesying their history in advance, God issues a challenge to the world and its false gods. He describes these confused pagans as having eyes that are blind and ears that are deaf. Even though the evidence of the one true God is all around them, they do not see it, hear it, or understand it. God challenges the pagan nations to bring forth witnesses who could testify of the ability of their gods to declare the future and then cause it to happen. Only the true God, who is the beginning and end of all things, can pull off such a feat.

In proving His own case, God declares that Israel is His witness. The Israelites can testify that God has never failed to bring about anything He declared. Not only are the Israelites His witnesses, they are His servants. They are to serve God by giving Him their complete obedience and unfettered worship. All the nations of the world would be drawn to God through the testimony of His servants. Their testimony would be based upon three premises: their knowledge of God's deliverance, protection, and care for them in the past; their faith in God to protect and care for them in the future; and their implicit understanding that He is the one true God, the singular Creator of all that is. Before Him, no god was created because there was no one to create it. He alone is the self-existent one, and aside from Him, they can depend on no one else to rescue them in times of trouble.

What proof does God offer to support His claim of sovereignty? He presents a threefold argument: "I have declared, and have saved, and I have shewed, when there was no strange god among you" (Isaiah 43:12). Only God can declare the future and bring it to pass. He alone delivered the Israelites from Egyptian bondage, and only He could reveal the future deliverance from Babylonian captivity. The miraculous testimony of the Israelites is proof that He is the one true God. He can deliver His people from any circumstance, but no one can deliver from His hand. His works are irreversible because there is no created thing or person powerful enough to alter what He has decreed.

It is comforting for God's people to know that He is able to deliver us from any situation and make us victorious. There is no god, person, or situation that can defeat Him or change the work of His hand. Our testimony of what God has done in our lives makes us living witnesses of His power, love, and goodness. It is our responsibility to be His witnesses to the unsaved world.

3. Power of God (vv. 18-19)

Isaiah frequently links the Babylonian exile and the Egyptian captivity. Just as God released Israel from Egypt with a mighty display of His power, that same awesome power would be displayed in their release from Babylon. Just as God had secured the release of Israel from Egypt and led her to the Promised Land, He would free His people from Babylonian captivity and regather them in their land to reclaim their heritage.

In verse 1, God describes Himself as Israel's creator and the one who formed them. Now, in this final passage of the chapter, God describes Himself as "your redeemer, the Holy One of Israel" (v. 14). As Israel's redeemer, God testifies to the closeness of their relationship. He is their kinsman-helper. This speaks of a close relative who has the responsibility to buy back a disadvantaged relative from indentured slavery.

God's holiness speaks of His pure and perfect nature and His singular right to judge what is right and pure. Because God is holy, He cannot tolerate sin and He must punish it. Israel's exile into Babylon is the result of the nation's slide into willful rebellion against God; this is the punishment the nation brought on herself. The people experienced the covenant curse for disobedience (Deuteronomy 28:15-36).

However, God also promised to redeem His fallen people: "Suppose all these things happen to you—the blessings and the curses I have listed—and you meditate on them as you are living among the nations to which the LORD your God has exiled you. If at that time you return to the LORD your God, and you and your children begin wholeheartedly to obey all the commands I have given you today, then the LORD your God will restore your fortunes. He will have mercy on you and gather you back from all the nations where he has scattered you" (Deuteronomy 30:1-3, NLT).

For the sake of His elect, God will bring down Babylon and all her nobles. The Lord emphasizes that the One making this declaration is the same One who made a way for His people to cross the Red Sea (v. 16; see Exodus 14:21-22). The same sea was turned into an avenue of escape for the fleeing Israelites and a graveyard for the pursuing armies and chariots of Egypt.

Although looking back at God's mighty works is a means of providing encouragement for the future, God tells the Israelites not to dwell on the past (Isaiah 43:18). This is because He is about to do a new thing. Freedom from Babylonian exile would be different from their release from Egypt. This time, God would not send a chosen Israelite as He did with Moses. He would send a foreign army. The glory of Babylon would be completely destroyed on a level comparable to the destruction of Sodom and Gomorrah (see Isaiah 13:13-20).

As for the Israelites, not only would God deliver them from exile, He would empower them to restore Jerusalem and the temple.

God's chosen people never need to fear. The Bible provides a long history of God's acts of deliverance for His people from various trials and tribulations. Modern day believers can offer millions of personal testimonies of how God delivered them from situations that appeared impossible at the time. God is still in the delivering business, and He stills commands His people to "fear not." He is the same God yesterday, today, and forever. What He has done for others, He will do for you.

SEARCH THE SCRIPTURES

1. Who allowed Israel to be conquered and taken into captivity, and why (Isaiah 42:24-25)?

2. What three reasons did God give to the Israelites for following His command not to be afraid (43:1)?

3. How does God describe the roles of the people He chooses (v. 10)?

4. Who is able to escape from God's hand and change the work that He does (v. 13)?

5. What did God tell the Israelites to forget and not to think about (v. 18)?

DISCUSS THE MEANING

1. In Scripture, God makes many promises to His people. How is He able to accomplish everything He promises? What are some of His most precious promises to you?

2. God promises to keep His people in perfect peace. How do the biblical accounts of God's deliverance of His people and the testimonies of other believers contribute to your sense of peace?

LESSON IN OUR SOCIETY

Even when we go through our trials and tribulations, we should keep in mind that we are God's special creation, we are redeemed, and He still loves us. Our problems can either make us bitter or better. We should pray that they make us better as we rely on God to carry us through.

MAKE IT HAPPEN

Did you know that worry indicates a lack of trust in God's ability to deliver you or bring you through your trial? Make a list of the things that worry you the most. Set aside 30 minutes each day for the rest of this week to spend time in prayer.

FOLLOW THE SPIRIT

What God wants me to do:

_____

_____

REMEMBER YOUR THOUGHTS

Special insights I have learned:

_____

_____

MORE LIGHT ON THE TEXT
Isaiah 43:1-2, 10-13, 18-19

Through the prophet Isaiah, God speaks forcefully yet lovingly to His people. Isaiah had the daunting task of prophesying to the Jewish people during a dark period in their history. The northern kingdom had already been taken into captivity, and foreign invaders were menacing Judah. The first part of the book of Isaiah, chapters 1 through 39, deals primarily with judgment. The Jews had repeatedly and stubbornly refused to be faithful to God. They carelessly dabbled in idol worship and foolishly mingled their culture

God can help all of us to feel safe.

and religion with those of the surrounding pagan nations.

Our lesson is from a portion of the second part of Isaiah's writings. In these final chapters, 40 through 66, Isaiah prophesies about God's truth being revealed in the Anointed One, Jesus. This section is often referred to as the "Book of Consolation." In chapter 43, God offers proof of both His deity and His unfailing love for His people. Most importantly, God speaks about His future purpose for His people.

1 But now thus saith the LORD that created thee, O Jacob, and he that formed thee, O Israel,
Fear not: for I have redeemed thee, I have called thee by thy name; thou art mine.

The chapter opens with God's declaration that He has "formed" Israel. Israel is unique in that it has been created by God Himself for His divine purpose. The sentiment in the latter part of the verse is echoed in Psalm 100:3: "Know ye that the LORD he is God: it is he that hath made us, and not we ourselves." The emphasis here is not on whom or what the nation is, but rather to whom they owe their existence.

Israel was God's special creation and a manifestation of His covenant with Abraham (Genesis 12:1-3). The nation is figuratively called "Jacob," referring to Israel's descendancy from Jacob, the grandson of Abraham and a patriarch of the nation. In the book of Genesis, Jacob's name is later changed to "Israel." Jacob literally means "supplanter" or "one who seizes." Figuratively, it means "one who deceives." Throughout most of his life, Jacob was a devious crook. He tricks his older brother Esau out of his birthright and steals his father's blessing from him. Much later in his life, Jacob attempts to heal the rift between himself and his brother. The night before Jacob would meet Esau, he would wrestle with an angel of the Lord. Because of his persistence, God would change his name to Israel, meaning "one who perseveres or contends." Figuratively, it means "one who prevails with God and man." The use of the name "Jacob" is important in our understanding that the nation of Israel was literally brought into existence or created by God. Just as God created a father of nations from a conniving trickster, He created a nation from a loose confederation of desert nomads.

This verse is clearly a message of consolation. In the consolation, we recognize that God is addressing the basic psychological needs of His special people and indeed of all mankind: to be recognized, accepted, and approved. God addresses the need for recognition by reminding them that He gave them their name and is now summoning them by that very name. The need for acceptance is implied in the fact that although God allowed pagan nations to discipline Israel, He is now redeeming them to Himself. Finally, the need for approval is apparent in the fact that God clearly has not turned His back on or abandoned them to their own fate. God's message to them is that they should "fear not" because He still cares.

Indeed, Israel is in dire need of such consolation. The northern kingdom of Israel goes into exile in 740 B.C. By the time of this writing, the southern kingdom of Judah is nationally crushed and spiritually disabled. God, however, is never disabled! He acts on Judah's behalf and works in the hearts and minds of pagan kings to liberate them and return the repentant remnant to their homeland in 537 B.C. In Isaiah 43:1, God speaks to His beloved people, exhorting them to remember who He is, what He has done, and what He will do on their behalf.

God has redeemed His people. The Hebrew word used here for "redeem" is ga'al (**gaw-al'**), which refers to ancient laws of kinship that allowed for the ransoming or repurchasing of near relatives. In this context, God is announcing that He intends to redeem or repurchase that which belongs to Him. This theme of the kinsman redeemer is prominent and prevalent in Israel's history and is seen throughout the Bible. Joseph redeems his family when they are enslaved in Egypt. By His power, God redeemed the Children of Israel from Egyptian bondage. The redemption of Ruth, the Moabitess by Boaz, actually prefigures the redemption of sinful mankind by Jesus Christ. So, too, would God's loving provision of redemption be extended to the freed exiles that He redeemed from Babylon.

In chapter 13, Isaiah prophesies that God would, through the armies of Media and Persia, ransom His chosen people (Isaiah 13:17-19). The final act of redemption however, would be completed when God sent forth His only Son, Jesus, the Christ. Paul writes that "God sent forth his Son, made of a woman, made under the law, to redeem them that were under the law, that we might receive the adoption of sons" (Galatians 4:4-5).

2 When thou passest through the waters, I will be with thee; and through the rivers, they shall not overflow thee: when thou walkest through the fire, thou shalt not be burned; neither shall the flame kindle upon thee.

The divine protection of God is continued in this verse. The allusion to passing through waters probably refers to the miraculous crossing of the Red Sea by the Israelites who were fleeing Pharaoh's mighty Egyptian army. Similarly, the safe passage of the Children of Israel across the Jordan River is evidence of the continuation of God's divine protection and providence for His beloved people. In each case, we see that the promises of God cannot be thwarted by natural phenomena. God is the ruler of the waters!

The second reference, that of walking through fire, probably alludes to the experience of the three Hebrew boys: Shadrach, Meshach, and Abednego (Heb. Hananiah, Mishael, and Azariah). These young men were thrown into a fiery furnace after demonstrating their integrity to the true God by refusing to bow down before a golden image of Nebuchadnezzar. Although the three were placed into a furnace that was seven times hotter than normal (Daniel 3:19-20), they escaped the furnace unharmed.

The promise of God's presence in any situation (flood or fire) should reassure modern–day saints. No matter where we are, God is there. No matter how dire our circumstances, the God who rules the wind and the waters walks before us. No matter how far away from His Word we stray, God stands ready to redeem us to Himself.

43:10 Ye are my witnesses, saith the LORD, and my servant whom I have chosen: that ye may know and believe me, and understand that I am he: before me there was no God formed, neither shall there be after me.

In this verse, the emphasis is on Israel's unique purpose. Israel has been personally selected to become a testimony of the majesty, graciousness, and goodness of God. The phrase that begins "I am he" serves, perhaps, to remind Israel of the folly of her past idolatrous ways. The various pagan gods that Israel had chosen to worship had been "formed" or created. However, God existed from the foundations of the earth. Before there were men to fashion or "form" the false gods of gold, silver, bronze, or clay, there was the one true God. The idol gods were powerless. God alone was able to create His witnesses who could testify of His mighty power and bear witness to His faithful loving-kindness.

Here, the Hebrew word for "witness" is *ed* (**ayd**), meaning a recorder or one who testifies. God's witnesses alone would be able to confirm "that not one thing hath failed of all the good things which the LORD your God spake concerning you; all are come to pass unto you, and not one thing hath failed thereof" (Joshua 23:14). God's witnesses would be able to proclaim that all of His promises will come true! God's miraculous deliverance was a result of His love and His desire that the nation of Israel be a faithful witness to Him.

11 I, even I, am the LORD; and beside me there is no saviour.

God has no competition. He stands alone in His ability to nurture, provide for, deliver, and redeem those whom He loves. Of all the world's religions, Christianity alone unequivocally guarantees the salvation of man. This is because only the Creator (God) provided a rescue or ransom (Jesus) for His most cherished creation.

12 I have declared, and have saved, and I have shewed, when there was no strange god among you: therefore ye are my witnesses, saith the LORD, that I am God.

God has provided His witnesses with a wealth of evidence; all they had to do was testify to His marvelous deeds. Having borne witness to His mighty works, the people of God would be able to declare, "We will not hide them from their children, shewing to the generation to come the praises of the LORD, and his strength, and his wonderful works that he hath done" (Psalm 78:4). Having witnessed what God had done, His people were fully expected to testify to the world of His goodness.

13 Yea, before the day was I am he; and there is none that can deliver out of my hand: I will work, and who shall let it?

God always was, is, and always will be. Unlike the idol gods, the one true God has no beginning and no end. In this verse, the prophet addresses Israel's future delivery from Babylonian captivity by reminding them of how God delivered them from Egyptian captivity. Neither Pharaoh, nor his mighty army, nor the scores of idol gods of Egypt could prevent Israel's deliverance. God had safely led the Children of Israel out of the hands of the Egyptians and through the scorching wilderness of the desert and had delivered them into the land of His promise. The same would be true of the mighty Babylonians. They would prove to be no obstacle to the powerful delivering hand of God.

The Hebrew verb used for "let" is *shuwb* (**shoob**), and in this verse it means "to halt or hinder." God is reminding His people that when He decides to move on their behalf, nothing and no one can stop Him. Jesus underscores this fact when He teaches, "I give unto them eternal life; and they shall never perish, neither shall any man pluck them out of my hand" (John 10:28). This is the consolation message for the present-day saint. We, the redeemed of the Lord, are being kept in Jesus' hand. Therefore, our hope is certain and our salvation is assured.

18 Remember ye not the former things, neither consider the things of old.

It is important to note that in this verse, the phrase "remember ye not" is not a command that Israel is to forget her past history. Indeed, Israel had been exhorted to remember God's past acts of salvation. Most notable, is the commandment that Israel "keep the Passover unto the LORD thy God" by celebrating their deliverance from Egyptian slavery (Deuteronomy 16:1). Instead, this verse suggests that they now prepare to bear witness to something "new" that God was about to do on their behalf.

19 Behold, I will do a new thing; now it shall spring forth; shall ye not know it? I will even make a way in the wilderness, and rivers in the desert.

The sense of barrenness that Israel must have felt during their Babylonian captivity was going to end. Because of His righteous nature, God had severely disciplined Israel, but He was now ready to restore His people. Like the first eruption of a plant after a frost-covered winter, the salvation of the nation would "spring forth." Isaiah is prophesying that deliverance is at hand. The prophet Jeremiah expressed the same sentiment when he prophesied, "He that scattered Israel will gather him, and keep him, as a shepherd doth his flock" (Jeremiah 31:10). The same God who had held back the walls of the Red Sea and led them across the treacherous desert would return them to the land of His promise. Again, Israel would be led

safely through a "wilderness" and their thirst satisfied with "rivers in the desert."

This divine promise did not expire. Through the shedding of Jesus' precious blood, we have been redeemed. Christians are God's special people: blood-purchased and covenant-bound. Today's saints can rest assured that God is continuing to do a "new thing" in our lives. The words of the hymn remind us: "Morning by morning new mercies I see; All I have needed, Thy hand has provided; Great is Thy faithfulness, Lord, unto me." Indeed, God's mercies are renewed day by day in the lives of those He has chosen, redeemed, and called to be His own.

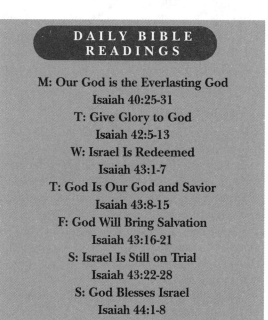

DAILY BIBLE READINGS

M: Our God is the Everlasting God
Isaiah 40:25-31

T: Give Glory to God
Isaiah 42:5-13

W: Israel Is Redeemed
Isaiah 43:1-7

T: God Is Our God and Savior
Isaiah 43:8-15

F: God Will Bring Salvation
Isaiah 43:16-21

S: Israel Is Still on Trial
Isaiah 43:22-28

S: God Blesses Israel
Isaiah 44:1-8

Why not meditate on the meaning of the word *new* as you prepare your lesson this week? You can use the concordance and dictionary in your *Precepts For Living* CD-ROM to gain more insight into this meaningful word.

TEACHING TIPS

October 17
Bible Study Guide 7

1. Words You Should Know

A. Thoughts (Jeremiah 29:11) *machashabah* (Heb.)—To plan, devise, or plot. Used to denote imagination, intention, or purpose.

B. House (31:31) *bayith* (Heb.)—In this case, the word refers to one's household, race, or descendants.

2. Teacher Preparation

A. Begin preparing for the lesson by reading the BIBLE BACKGROUND verses. Then prayerfully meditate on the DEVOTIONAL READING (Jeremiah 30:18-22).

B. Next, carefully study the MORE LIGHT ON THE TEXT section so that you will be prepared for the students' questions.

C. Review the TEACHING TIPS and plan how you will present the lesson.

3. Starting the Lesson

A. Concentrate on the LESSON AIM as you begin the lesson with prayer.

B. Have the students read the KEEP IN MIND verse aloud a few times in unison. Ask the students to write the verse on an index card, memorize it, and review it periodically during the week.

C. As the students enter class, select two students and assign each one to read a section of IN DEPTH. As a class, discuss what each of the students just read.

D. Ask the students why they believe it was necessary for God to implement a new covenant. Allow for discussion.

4. Getting into the Lesson

A. Begin the lesson by asking volunteers to read BACKGROUND and THE PEOPLE, PLACES, AND TIMES. This will help them to get a better understanding of the lesson.

B. Have the students read the FOCAL VERSES in unison according to the AT-A-GLANCE outline. Stop after each section to review the SEARCH THE SCRIPTURES questions.

5. Relating the Lesson to Life

A. Use the DISCUSS THE MEANING questions to stimulate discussion.

B. Examine the LESSON IN OUR SOCIETY section. Explore why so many people claim to be Christians, yet live immoral lifestyles.

6. Arousing Action

A. Review the MAKE IT HAPPEN section and encourage the students to seek out someone and strike up a conversation about the fear of death.

B. Assign the reading assignment for the week and encourage the students to use the DAILY BIBLE READINGS for their personal devotions.

C. Before closing the class, ask for prayer requests and praise reports. Then ask a volunteer to close the class with prayer.

WORSHIP GUIDE

For the Superintendent or Teacher
Theme: **Creating a New Covenant**
Theme Song: "This Is Love"
Scripture: Jeremiah 30:18-22
Song: "Deeper and Deeper"
Meditation: Lord, Your mercy is
infinite and Your grace overflows.
Keep me forever mindful of our
covenant relationship.

CREATING A NEW COVENANT

Bible Background • JEREMIAH 29:1-14; 31:31-34
Printed Text • JEREMIAH 29:10-14; 31:31-34
Devotional Reading • JEREMIAH 30:18-22

LESSON AIM

By the end of the lesson, the students will be able to explain how God chooses to move through the prayers of His people, understand that faith is the basis for our assurance of God fulfilling His promise, and determine to live each day mindful of their covenant relationship with God.

KEEP IN MIND

"But this shall be the covenant that I will make with the house of Israel; After those days, saith the LORD, I will put my law in their inward parts, and write it in their hearts; and will be their God, and they shall be my people" (Jeremiah 31:33).

LESSON OVERVIEW

LESSON AIM
KEEP IN MIND
FOCAL VERSES
IN FOCUS
THE PEOPLE, PLACES, AND TIMES
BACKGROUND
AT-A-GLANCE
IN DEPTH
SEARCH THE SCRIPTURES
DISCUSS THE MEANING
LESSON IN OUR SOCIETY
MAKE IT HAPPEN
FOLLOW THE SPIRIT
REMEMBER YOUR THOUGHTS
MORE LIGHT ON THE TEXT
DAILY BIBLE READINGS

FOCAL VERSES

Jeremiah 29:10 For thus saith the LORD, That after seventy years be accomplished at Babylon I will visit you, and perform my good word toward you, in causing you to return to this place.

11 For I know the thoughts that I think toward you, saith the LORD, thoughts of peace, and not of evil, to give you an expected end.

12 Then shall ye call upon me, and ye shall go and pray unto me, and I will hearken unto you.

13 And ye shall seek me, and find me, when ye shall search for me with all your heart.

14 And I will be found of you, saith the LORD: and I will turn away your captivity, and I will gather you from all the nations, and from all the places whither I have driven you, saith the LORD; and I will bring you again into the place whence I caused you to be carried away captive.

31:31 Behold, the days come, saith the LORD, that I will make a new covenant with the house of Israel, and with the house of Judah:

OCT 17TH

32 Not according to the covenant that I made with their fathers in the day that I took them by the hand to bring them out of the land of Egypt; which my covenant they brake, although I was an husband unto them, saith the LORD:

33 But this shall be the covenant that I will make with the house of Israel; After those days, saith the LORD, I will put my law in their inward parts, and write it in their hearts; and will be their God, and they shall be my people.

34 And they shall teach no more every man his neighbour, and every man his brother, saying, Know the LORD: for they shall all know me, from the least of them unto the greatest of them, saith the LORD: for I will forgive their iniquity, and I will remember their sin no more.

IN FOCUS

Frank was a young minister with a heavy heart for Sonny, one of the church's young men. He was in a jail cell for a series of sex and drug charges. Sonny was arrested on the eve of signing with the NBA. Now Frank sat in the church office with Senior Pastor Wright trying to find the right words to comfort the young man.

"I don't know what to tell Sonny when I visit him."

Pastor Wright peered over his glasses and said, "Tell him to pray."

Frank didn't think Pastor Wright understood. "But he's overcome so much. . . ."

Pastor Wright cut him off. "I know. I thought Sonny was too smart to get hung up in craziness."

Frank countered with some foolish thought. "The NBA should be abolished. It's a breeding ground for the seven deadly sins."

Pastor Wright came from behind his desk and sat next to Frank with a sideways look. "The NBA is not the root of all evil; it's the temptations abounding in our nation that seduce to immorality. Sonny has to pay for what he has done."

Frank's hands were wet; this was not the message he wanted. He probed for something else. "I understand the consequences for sin but it's the way he got trapped."

Rev. Wright nodded his head. "Our nation is so powerful, so affluent, it lures people into greedy, selfish, and decadent behavior. It grieves me that thousands of babies are aborted in the name of privacy and millions are demanding homosexual marriages." Rev. Wright stopped and smiled into Frank's eyes. "But this country is not cursed. Our currency still says, 'In God we trust.' We must trust God's grace to save our nation and our children."

Frank sank into his chair as a reprimanded child would do and recited a verse from his spirit. "If my people humble themselves, pray and seek God's face and repent. . . ."

Rev. Wright completed the verses for him. "Only then will they hear from heaven and God will forgive them and heal their land. That is the message to deliver to Sonny. Tell him to humble himself and repent."

In today's lesson, God reveals to a nation taken captive because of sin how He will answer their prayers of deliverance and establish an everlasting covenant with them.

THE PEOPLE, PLACES, AND TIMES

Israel's Captivity. In Deuteronomy 28, God tells the Israelites that if they fail to serve Him during their times of prosperity, He will cause them to suffer the consequences of their actions. "Because you did not serve the LORD your God joyfully and gladly in the time of prosperity, therefore in hunger and thirst, in nakedness and dire poverty, you will serve the enemies the LORD sends against you . . .Then the LORD will scatter you among all nations, from one end of the earth to the other" (Deuteronomy 28:47-48, 64, NIV).

The Children of Israel did exactly what God had warned them against: They turned away from the true God to follow false gods and pursue their own pleasures. Because of rebellion, God did indeed scatter them among the nations. The scattering of Israel occurred several times during their history. The northern kingdom of Israel was first taken captive by the Assyrians around 722-721 B.C. (see 2 Kings 17:6). The southern kingdom of Judah was later taken captive into Babylon in a series of three different deportations. The first deportation occurred around 605 B.C. when Judah's young nobility, including Daniel and his three friends—Shadrach, Meshach, and Abednego—were taken away (see Daniel 1:1-4).

In the second deportation around 597 B.C., 11,000 exiles were taken, including the prophet Ezekiel. In the third and final deportation, the rest of Judah, except for Jeremiah and the poorest and feeblest, were carried off. The final siege of Jerusalem lasted 18 months. One-third of the people died of starvation and disease, and another third was killed in battle or executed after the siege (2 Kings 25:1-21; Jeremiah 39:1-10; 52:4-11; Ezekiel 5:10-12).

God's promises of the consequences of sin never fail. Likewise, His promises of grace and restoration are always sure.

BACKGROUND

The controversy between Jeremiah and the false prophets of Judah began after the first deportation of 3,023 Israelites to Babylon (Jeremiah 23:9-15). The conflict continued, with each side delivering messages to support their view of the deliverance of the Israelite captives. According to the false prophet Hananiah (not Daniel's friend Shadrach), the captivity of the Israelites would be short-lived: "'Within two years I will bring back to this place all the articles of the

LORD's house that Nebuchadnezzar king of Babylon removed from here and took to Babylon. I will also bring back to this place Jehoiachin son of Jehoiakim king of Judah and all the other exiles from Judah who went to Babylon,' declares the LORD, 'for I will break the yoke of the king of Babylon'" (28:3-4, NIV).

However, the word of the Lord came to Jeremiah, the true prophet of God, with a message the people did not want to hear: "'This whole country will become a desolate wasteland, and these nations will serve the king of Babylon seventy years. But when the seventy years are fulfilled, I will punish the king of Babylon and his nation, the land of the Babylonians, for their guilt,' declares the LORD, 'and will make it desolate forever'" (25:11-12, NIV).

The conflict that began in Jerusalem as a war of words continued in Babylon with a war of letters. Shemaiah, a false prophet who had been carried into Babylon, continued the false teaching of Hananiah. He went so far as to send a letter to the priests in Jerusalem to incite them to persecute Jeremiah (29:24-29). Jeremiah answered Shemaiah's letter with a letter of his own to the captives in Babylon.

Our lesson this week begins with the letter Jeremiah wrote to the Jews who had been taken into Babylonian captivity during the first deportation of Judah around 595-597 B.C. The document—delivered by Elasah, the son of Shaphan, and Gemariah, the son of Hilkiah (29:3)—is considered to be one of the most important documents in the Old Testament.

The letter that the men delivered to the exiles contained four important truths about their new situation: (1) Settle down and start new lives (Jeremiah 29:6). God was telling the people to settle in and make the land of their exile their new home. (2) Be good productive citizens (v. 7). Since the people were going to be there for the long haul, they should attempt to make their new home a better place. (3) Don't be deceived by idols or false prophets (vv. 8-9). In a pagan society, there are many pitfalls from within and without. God's people must be alert for the false gods of the nations and the false prophets who dwell among them.

AT-A-GLANCE

1. A New Work (Jeremiah 29:10-14)
2. A New Covenant (Jeremiah 31:31-34)

IN DEPTH

1. A New Work (Jeremiah 29:10-14)

The final truth God wanted to convey to the exiles was that He had not forgotten about them. Although the generation that had originally been taken into captivity would probably die in the new land, God would indeed deliver His people 70 years from the date of the first deportation. In the letter written by the hand of Jeremiah but spoken by God, the Lord proclaims that at the appointed time He will visit His people and make good on His promise.

God acts according to a holy time schedule that no one can alter and fulfills His promises according to His redemptive purpose. In Paul's letter to the Galatians, we see the phrase, "But when the fulness of the time was come, God sent forth his Son made of a woman, made under the law" (Galatians 4:4). "The right time" refers to the completion of a predetermined length of time and of a predetermined set of circumstances. The 70 years marked "the right time" for the Israelites' redemption from exile.

Sometimes it may seem that the Lord has forgotten His people, but He is always working on our behalf. When it appears that nothing is going on and God is not answering our prayers, He is lining up events so that at the precise predetermined time He will move. God always works according to His divine schedule; but we can rest assured that He will never fail to make good His Word or His perfect timing.

God told Jeremiah that He had formed him in the womb of his mother. Before the prophet was born, the Lord sanctified him and ordained him to ministry (Jeremiah 1:5). Just as God had a plan and a ministry for Jeremiah, He has a plan for all His people. In the case of Israel, God's plans were to raise up an eternal King from among them who would reign and rule over the whole world, to save and provide for them in the land He promised them and to deliver them from captivity (see 23:5-8).

God's thoughts for His people are never evil; they are good and are designed to bring them peace and an "expected end" (Jeremiah 29:11b). The peace that God promised the Israelites refers to their physical and spiritual health (30:17), security in their cities (v. 18), happiness and joy (v. 19), and many children (v. 20). The expected end is simply the expectation that God will honor His promises. In this case, it means a return to the land of promise.

Before the Israelites' captivity, Jeremiah had prophesied that on the day the evil came upon them they would cry out to God and He would not hear them: "Therefore, thus saith the LORD, Behold, I will bring evil upon them, which they shall not be able to escape and though they shall cry unto me, I will not hearken unto them. Therefore pray not thou for this people, neither lift up a cry or prayer for them: for I will not hear them in the time that they cry unto me for their trouble" (Jeremiah 11:11, 14). The prayer that God ignored was the cry to escape the consequences of their actions. The prayer that God would answer would be the prayer of hope based on faith. At the end of their time in captivity, God Himself would stir the people up to pray. At that point, God says the people will "call upon me…pray unto me…seek me…search for me with all [their hearts]" (29:12-13). Although God had already determined the time and the method of their deliverance, He would only move in answer to their prayers.

In response to the prayers of His people, God says, "I will hearken unto you. I will be found of you. . .I will turn away your captivity. . .I will gather you from all the nations. . .I will bring you again into the place whence I caused you to be carried away captive" (Jeremiah 29:12, 13-14). God will align the will of the people with His will so they pray according to His will. Then He will answer them and give them the desires of their hearts.

It's comforting to know that none of the situations we encounter in life surprise God. He is not only aware of our circumstance, but He has predetermined our deliverance from the circumstance. His will is always to bring His people peace and to give the end that justifies their faith. That is why Christ said, "If ye abide in me, and my words abide in you, ye shall ask what ye will, and it shall be done unto you" (John 15:7).

2. A New Covenant (Jeremiah 31:31-34)

People are often shortsighted when it comes to the blessings and promises of God. As long as God fulfills our immediate needs and desires, we are satisfied. The ancient Israelites would have been more than satisfied with God restoring them to the land of their forefathers. However, when God told the people that He was thinking of them and had plans for their future (Jeremiah 29:11), He meant much more than simply restoring them to the land. God's purpose was never to simply restore Israel to the land; He intended to restore all humanity to Himself.

Israel had failed to keep the terms of the covenant—their contractual obligation agreed to at Mount Sinai (see Exodus 24:3-8; Deuteronomy 29:12-13); God now promised that one day in the future He would institute a new and better covenant with the entire reunited nation of Israel. The church is "grafted in" to Israel's promised covenant (see Romans 11:17-27).

The new covenant would enable all believers to have a personal relationship with God: "For they shall all know me, from the least of them unto the greatest of them" (Jeremiah 31:34). The new covenant would deal with the sin issue once and for all. Priests would no longer have to take animal sacrifices into the Holy of Holies to make atonements for the people. The blood of animals could only remind a person of his sin (Hebrews 10:1-4). The blood of Christ completely washes away all sin so that God no longer remembers it. As the writer of Hebrews states, "Then verily the first covenant had also ordinances of divine service, and a worldly sanctuary. But Christ being come an high priest of good things to come, by a greater and more perfect tabernacle, not made with hands, that is to say, not of this building; Neither by the blood of goats and calves, but by his own blood he entered in once into the holy place, having obtained eternal redemption for us" (Hebrews 9:1, 11-12).

The old covenant was inadequate and incomplete. It was a temporary provision that looked ahead to its ultimate fulfillment in Christ. Jesus is the mediator of the new covenant. His heavenly ministry is far superior to that of the old covenant priest who ministered in the earthly sanctuary. The new covenant is an agreement and a promise of God to bestow divine grace on all who respond to the Gospel of Jesus Christ with sincere faith and repentance.

SEARCH THE SCRIPTURES

1. What did God say He would do for the Israelites after their 70 years of captivity in Babylon (Jeremiah 29:10)?

2. What are the major effects of God's plans for His people (v. 11)?

3. How will God respond when the people call on Him in prayer (v. 12)?

DISCUSS THE MEANING

1. Isn't it awesome that the Creator of the universe thinks of each one of us and makes plans for us? What do you think God's plan is for your life? How does one go about finding out and fulfilling God's plan for his/her life?

2. How would you describe the new covenant promise of God to write His commandments on our hearts? Why is "heart writing" better than writing His law on stone?

LESSON IN OUR SOCIETY

As God's children, we too are in a covenant relationship with Him. Daily we can pray and ask Him to help us be mindful of this connection. We should always honor our agreement to be His people because indeed He is faithful as our God.

MAKE IT HAPPEN

Think about your own life. Have you responded to the Gospel of Jesus Christ with sincere faith and repentance? If you have, thank God for opening your heart and your eyes so that you could see the need for a Saviour. If you have not accepted Jesus as your Redeemer, do so today! Ask God to forgive you of your sins and receive the gift of His one and only Son.

FOLLOW THE SPIRIT

What God wants me to do:

_____

_____

REMEMBER YOUR THOUGHTS

Special insights I have learned:

_____

_____

MORE LIGHT ON THE TEXT
Jeremiah 29:10-14; 31:31-34

10 For thus saith the LORD, That after seventy years be accomplished at Babylon I will visit you, and perform my good word toward you, in causing you to return to this place.

Instrumentally, Jeremiah conveyed to the exiles in Babylon that they would be there seventy years. Instead, the exiles believed the false prophets. However, Jeremiah affirmed the lengthy exile. This is evident in the words "be accomplished" (Heb. *male,* **maw-lay**) meaning to accomplish, confirm, or fulfill.

Further, despite the dismal report, Jeremiah's message from God brings hope, expressed as "will visit" (Heb. *paqad,* **paw-kad**), which means to deliver or keep; "word" (Heb. *dabar,* **daw-bawr**), meaning decree; and "to return" (Heb. *shuwb,* **shoob**), which means bring (again, back, home again).

God has always and will always bring hope to us in times of need, even when we have broken His covenant and He must correct us. We can also be reassured that "God is not a man, that he should lie" (Numbers 23:19). The Word lets us know that if God said it, then He will perform it.

11 For I know the thoughts that I think toward you, saith the LORD, thoughts of peace, and not of evil, to give you an expected end.

In Proverbs 13:12 it says, "Hope deferred maketh the heart sick: but when the desire cometh, it is a tree of life." Clearly, God gives hope in this verse. He reveals His thoughts toward His people, thoughts of peace and not evil. In Hebrew, the word "evil" is *ra* (**rah**), which means grief, harm, or hurt.

Moreover, God has an expected good end for

us. The Hebrew word for "expected" is *tiqvah* (**tik-vaw**), which implies hope or something longed for. The word *end* (Heb. *achariyth*, **akh-ar-eeth**) suggests reward. God is our tree of life, bringing hope in trying times and an expected, rewarding end.

12 Then shall ye call upon me, and ye shall go and pray unto me, and I will hearken unto you.

Certainly, in this passage, God is revealing to His people that He is with them no matter what. Today, God is still giving us the same eternal message—He is with us through every trial and storm in our lives.

All we have to do is call upon Him. The Hebrew word for "call" is *qara* (**kaw-raw**), meaning cry (unto). Therefore, if we cry unto Him and pray, then He will "hearken" (Heb. *shama*, **shaw-mah**) meaning to give ear or listen intently.

13 And ye shall seek me, and find me, when ye shall search for me with all your heart.

This verse mirrors a verse in the New Testament, Matthew 7:7, which says, "Ask, and it shall be given you; seek, and ye shall find: knock, and it shall be opened unto you." Another verse is, Matthew 6:33: "Seek ye first the kingdom of God, and his righteousness; and all these things shall be added unto you." All these passages lead to the same highway, and that is of hope. God does not play hide and seek with us; rather, He wants us to find Him by seeking Him with our whole heart, especially in difficult times. The word *heart* in Hebrew is *lebab* (**lay-bawb**), which means "courage."

14 And I will be found of you, saith the LORD: and I will turn away your captivity, and I will gather you from all the nations, and from all the places whither I have driven you, saith the LORD; and I will bring you again into the place whence I caused you to be carried away captive.

Here, God gives the greatest hope to His people. He promises to take the exiles out of their dark situation into His marvelous deliverance from captivity. And greater still, He promises to return them to their own land. The old adage, "there's no place like home," certainly applies

Jeremiah: God's obedient and faithful messenger.

here, and God gives His people the hope of going home. A hopeful Hebrew word is "found," which is *matsa* (**maw-tsaw**), meaning "deliver." God is a deliverer.

31:31 Behold, the days come, saith the LORD, that I will make a new covenant with the house of Israel, and with the house of Judah:

Fortunately, God promises to establish a new covenant with His people. God's people broke the terms of the Sinai covenant that were written on stone, but the new covenant would be written on their hearts.

In Hebrews 8:7 it states, "For if that first covenant had been faultless, then should no place have been sought for the second."

32 Not according to the covenant that I made with their fathers in the day that I took them by the hand to bring them out of the land of Egypt; which my covenant they brake, although I was an husband unto them, saith the LORD:

This new covenant promises not to be like the covenant with the forefathers, which they broke. Instead, it will be a fresh new relationship between God and His people.

To better understand this new covenant, we must first define "covenant." A covenant, or, better still, a divine covenant, is a bond between a superior (God) and an inferior (man) that involves terms for each party. God's terms consist of promises, and man's terms involve repentance from sin, faith in God's promises, and obedience to God's Word.

God promises this new covenant out of love for His people in spite of themselves. He describes Himself as a "husband unto them" even though they broke the old covenant. We know that the Bible commands a husband to love his wife. Here, God demonstrates that type of love for His people through the new covenant. He never leaves them without hope.

33 But this shall be the covenant that I will make with the house of Israel; After those days, saith the LORD, I will put my law in their inward parts, and write it in their hearts; and will be their God, and they shall be my people.

Covenant relationship is established in this passage. Not only is there a new covenant but a stronger galvanization between God and His people. This covenant transcends stone (Ten Commandments) and permeates not only the inward parts but also the very hearts of man.

"Inward part" in Hebrew is *qereb* (**keh-reb**), which means "thought." The Hebrew word for "heart" is *leb* (**labe**) and means the will, center, or mind. Clearly, God's new covenant will permeate the very soul of His people.

34 And they shall teach no more every man his neighbour, and every man his brother, saying, Know the LORD: for they shall all know me, from the least of them unto the greatest of them, saith the LORD: for I will forgive their iniquity, and I will remember their sin no more.

Traditionally, all biblical covenants were sealed by the shedding of animal blood. This new covenant was no different except that it was a precursor to the greatest shedding of blood: that of our Lord and Saviour Jesus Christ. Jeremiah 31:31-34 are repeated again in Hebrews 8:6-12. Moreover, in Hebrews 8:6 it says, "But now hath he obtained a more excellent ministry, by how much also he is the mediator of a better covenant, which was established upon better promises."

The new covenant, a "better covenant established upon better promises," does what the old covenant failed to do—it removes sin through forgiveness and brings about cleansing.

"Forgive" in Hebrew is *calach* (**saw-lakh**), meaning "pardon" or "spare." On the other hand, "sin" in Hebrew is *chattaah* (**khat-taw-aw**), which means an offense. Jesus taught us about God's forgiveness, and it is the work of Jesus Christ on the Cross that fulfills the promise of the prophet Jeremiah.

DAILY BIBLE READINGS

M: God Will Restore the Exiles
Jeremiah 29:10-14

T: After Judgment Will Come Freedom
Jeremiah 30:2-9

W: Restoration Will Bring Abundance and Happiness
Jeremiah 30:18-22

T: God Is Always Faithful
Jeremiah 31:1-6

F: The Exiles Will Return with Joy
Jeremiah 31:7-14

S: God Restores All Who Are Responsible
Jeremiah 31:23-30

S: God Makes a New Covenant
Jeremiah 31:31-34

Use your *Precepts For Living* CD-ROM to do a cross-reference check on the word *covenant* as it is used in the Bible. Contrast the differences between the old and new covenants.

TEACHING TIPS

October 24
Bible Study Guide 8

1. Words You Should Know

A. Prophesy (Ezekiel 37:4) *naba'* (Heb.)—To speak by divine power.

B. Hear (v. 4) *shama'* (Heb.)—To hear with intelligence and with a mind and heart to obey.

C. Breath (v. 5) *ruwach* (Heb.)—Air for breathing; anything that passes quickly, like the wind.

2. Teacher Preparation

A. Get a Study Bible and read the introduction to Ezekiel and the notes about his life and times.

B. Also check to see if the Bible contains a biblical time line, which can be very helpful in understanding the events that took place before and after Ezekiel's time.

C. Materials needed: Bibles, chalkboard or newsprint (optional: copies of a biblical time line).

3. Starting the Lesson

A. Read the IN FOCUS section. Emphasize the fact that most people are facing impossible challenges personally and in the world today.

B. Have the class brainstorm about seemingly impossible situations they are personally facing or negative situations which our communities at large are experiencing. Record their responses on the chalkboard.

C. Read the FOCAL VERSES. Give each student a sheet of paper and ask them to write out a prayer that reflects their thoughts as they listen to this passage.

4. Getting into the Lesson

A. Read and discuss the BACKGROUND section.

B. You may want to show a biblical time line to give your students a better idea of when Ezekiel lived.

C. Read over the AT-A-GLANCE outline a number of times until the class knows the three sections well.

D. Lead the class through the IN DEPTH section and answer the SEARCH THE SCRIPTURES questions.

5. Relating the Lesson to Life

A. Lead the students in answering the DISCUSS THE MEANING questions.

B. Reserve time to discuss the LESSON IN OUR SOCIETY section. Ask who agrees and who disagrees with these statements, and why.

6. Arousing Action

A. Discuss MAKE IT HAPPEN. Have the students write down the answers to the questions in this section.

B. Give plenty of time at the end for the students to pray about their personal challenges, and have them share in prayer how the lesson has helped to give them renewed hope and direction.

C. Don't forget to mention impossible situations we are facing in our churches or communities. Have some students lead in prayer about these areas as well.

D. Assign the DAILY BIBLE READINGS for this week.

WORSHIP GUIDE

For the Superintendent or Teacher
Theme: Creating a New Hope
Theme Song: "Only Believe, All Things Are Possible"
Scripture: Ezekiel 37:1-11, 25-28
Song: "What a Mighty God We Serve"
Meditation: Lord, thank You for being a mighty God and allowing us to see You work in impossible situations. You are indeed able to give life to that which is dead. Amen.

CREATING A NEW HOPE

Bible Background • EZEKIEL 37
Printed Text • EZEKIEL 37:1-14
Devotional Reading • EZEKIEL 37:24-28

LESSON AIM

By the end of the lesson, the students should be able to explain the symbolism of the dry bones in the valley in relation to God's people, have restored hope concerning personal negative habits and/or loved ones who are lost, and trust God to help them overcome any impossible situation.

KEEP IN MIND

"And shall put my spirit in you, and ye shall live, and I shall place you in your own land: then shall ye know that I the LORD have spoken it, and performed it, saith the LORD" (Ezekiel 37:14).

FOCAL VERSES

Ezekiel 37:1 The hand of the LORD was upon me, and carried me out in the spirit of the LORD, and set me down in the midst of the valley which was full of bones,

2 And caused me to pass by them round about: and, behold, there were very many in the open valley; and, lo, they were very dry.

3 And he said unto me, Son of man, can these bones live? And I answered, O Lord GOD, thou knowest.

4 Again he said unto me, Prophesy upon these bones, and say unto them, O ye dry bones, hear the word of the LORD.

5 Thus saith the Lord GOD unto these bones; Behold, I will cause breath to enter into you, and ye shall live:

6 And I will lay sinews upon you, and will bring up flesh upon you, and cover you with skin, and put breath in you, and ye shall live; and ye shall

LESSON OVERVIEW

LESSON AIM
KEEP IN MIND
FOCAL VERSES
IN FOCUS
THE PEOPLE, PLACES, AND TIMES
BACKGROUND
AT-A-GLANCE
IN DEPTH
SEARCH THE SCRIPTURES
DISCUSS THE MEANING
LESSON IN OUR SOCIETY
MAKE IT HAPPEN
FOLLOW THE SPIRIT
REMEMBER YOUR THOUGHTS
MORE LIGHT ON THE TEXT
DAILY BIBLE READINGS

know that I am the LORD.

7 So I prophesied as I was commanded: and as I prophesied, there was a noise, and behold a shaking, and the bones came together, bone to his bone.

8 And when I beheld, lo, the sinews and the flesh came up upon them, and the skin covered them above: but there was no breath in them.

9 Then said he unto me, Prophesy unto the wind, prophesy, son of man, and say to the wind, Thus saith the Lord GOD; Come from the four winds, O breath, and breathe upon these slain, that they may live.

OCT
24TH

10 So I prophesied as he commanded me, and the breath came into them, and they lived, and stood up upon their feet, an exceeding great army.

11 Then he said unto me, Son of man, these bones are the whole house of Israel: behold, they say, Our bones are dried, and our hope is lost: we are cut off for our parts.

12 Therefore prophesy and say unto them, Thus saith the Lord GOD; Behold, O my people, I will open your graves, and cause you to come up out of your graves, and bring you into the land of Israel.

13 And ye shall know that I am the LORD, when I have opened your graves, O my people, and brought you up out of your graves,

14 And shall put my spirit in you, and ye shall live, and I shall place you in your own land: then shall ye know that I the LORD have spoken it, and performed it, saith the LORD.

IN FOCUS

Our God Is Able

All things are possible through Him,
yet we doubt sometimes
when it rains on our hopes
too long,
Or we don't feel as strongly convicted . . .
conflicted by sinful opportunities
multiplying on restless fingertips.

It was God's lips that created our world . . .
Six days spun as gold in artist's hands,
A chance to breathe life as He
molded Adam from dust,
Eve from trust.

God is worthy of all praise!
He raised men from deathbeds,
Emptied tombs,
Ordered dried bones to rise
from desert rooms;
Through prophesied eyes,
they stood
no longer disguised
and bore flesh
where bones
breathed wind.

God sliced the Red Sea
into halves
to form a path,
Shook the walls of Jericho to its knees,
Brought forth His son
through seeds harvested by an untouched
woman.

Only God could command the sun to "Stand
still";
Bid all seasons to do His will.
We speak His name
in remembrance

of all that has come before
and all
that remains to be seen.

God—is worthy of everything.
Today's lesson should inspire you to believe
God for something that seems humanly
impossible.

–Herb Jackson

THE PEOPLE, PLACES, AND TIMES

Ezekiel. The name means "God strengthens." Ezekiel was among the priests exiled to Babylon with King Jehoiachin (see 2 Kings 24:14-17). He is the son of Buzi, whose name appears in the opening lines of this, one of the major prophetic books. Ezekiel prophesied both in Jerusalem and while in exile.

Son of Man. A term which God used for the prophet Ezekiel and which became the symbolic name of the Messiah.

BACKGROUND

Ezekiel was a younger contemporary of Jeremiah. While Jeremiah ministered to the people still in Judah, Ezekiel prophesied to those already exiled to Babylon. Ezekiel and several other captives were taken in 597 B.C. The book of Ezekiel was probably written around 597 B.C. in Babylon during the time of the exile.

The book of Ezekiel records the prophet's life and ministry, beginning with his call as a prophet and commissioning as a watchman for Israel (chapters 1-3). The approaching siege and destruction of Jerusalem were recorded in the next section of the book (chapters 4-24). He, like Jeremiah and many of the other Old Testament prophets, makes it clear why God has to judge Judah. He focuses on Judah's idolatrous behavior and also on God's plans to judge the rebellion of the surrounding nations (chapters 25-32).

The book of Ezekiel ends with a message of hope. Ezekiel proclaims the faithfulness of God and foretells the future blessing for God's people (chapters 33-48). The dry bone prophecy in chapter 37 communicates hope and offers promises of future blessings.

AT-A-GLANCE

**1. God Poses a Revealing Question
(Ezekiel 37:1-3)
2. God Promises to Restore the People
(vv. 4-10)
3. God's Power Brings Restoration
(vv. 11-14)**

IN DEPTH

1. God Poses a Revealing Question (Ezekiel 37:1-3)

This section of Ezekiel does not have a heading or a date, yet its content was very important. For the sixth time in the book, the phrase "the hand of the LORD was upon me" was used (Ezekiel 37:1). This indicated a specific message, usually communicated in the form of a vision, that God wanted Ezekiel to deliver to His people.

In this particular vision, God supernaturally transported Ezekiel from his own home to a valley full of dead men's bones. The dry bones were a picture of the Jews in captivity—the 12 tribes all shattered and dead. God wanted to give them a visible picture of His promise to bring new life and restoration to the nation, both physically and spiritually.

God took Ezekiel "round about" (v. 2) and caused him to pass by the bones so he could have a clear vision of them. The bones were not under the ground nor piled up in a heap, but scattered over the ground, and they were very dry.

After giving Ezekiel an aerial view of the bones, God asked him a question: "Can these bones live?" Ezekiel answered, "Lord, you are the only one who knows." Ezekiel's response implied, according to human judgment, that it was inconceivable that dry bones could live. Ezekiel knew the power of God was essential to raise these very dry bones to life. God had declared it, and God would have to do it. God alone has the power to accomplish whatever He promises.

2. God Promises to Restore the People (vv. 4-10)

The bones, which symbolized God's chosen people, were slain or killed, not just dead (v. 9). Those who remained in captivity in Babylon were hopeless and helpless. Their nation had been completely devastated, and many of the people were violently murdered.

God told Ezekiel to speak to the bones and say, "O ye dry bones, hear the word of the LORD. Thus saith the Lord GOD unto these bones; Behold, I will cause breath to enter into you, and ye shall live" (vv. 4-5). When Ezekiel prophesied, a sound arose—rattling and shaking all across the valley. The bones of each body came together and attached to each other. While Ezekiel watched, muscles and flesh formed over the bones, and skin covered them. The form was not complete, however; the bodies had no breath. God instructed Ezekiel to call to the wind and say, "Come from the four winds, O breath" (v. 9). There takes place a reenactment of the act of creation, when God formed humanity from the dust of the ground and breathed into its nostrils the breath of life (see Genesis 2:7). Ezekiel spoke to the winds and the bodies began breathing. They lived! Once the bodies got onto their feet, they formed a great army.

The bones coming up out of the graves symbolized God raising up the 12 tribes of Israel once again. God's promise here goes beyond merely the physical and geographical restoration of Israel. He promises to breathe new spiritual life into His people so that their hearts and attitudes will be right with Him and united with one another.

3. God's Power Brings Restoration (vv. 11-14)

When Ezekiel spoke to the people, he felt he was speaking to the dead as he preached because they rarely responded to his message. In their hopelessness, the nation seemed dead; but these bones responded. Just as God brought life to the dead bones, he would bring life again to His spiritually dead people.

God would rescue His people from captivity and exile in Babylon and restore them to the their land. The same process is described throughout God's Word as the cleansing of our hearts by God's Spirit. That which may be dead in us, such as our ability to resist a bad habit or a habitual sin, can come alive as God ministers through us by the power of His Spirit and under the direction of His Word.

SEARCH THE SCRIPTURES

1. Who was the prophet sent to prophesy to the dry bones?

2. What was in the valley that the Lord showed to Ezekiel in a vision (Ezekiel 37:1)?

3. What did the dry bones need to hear in order to come alive (v. 4)?

4. The bones came together but something was missing. What (v. 5)?

DISCUSS THE MEANING

1. Are prophets sent out today to preach to people who are spiritually dry and starving? What has been the result?

2. The bones came together, but they were not empowered by the Holy Spirit. How is it possible for Christians to come together and not be empowered by God's Spirit?

3. Ezekiel was ordered to speak God's Word to the bones. Does the Word of God today have that much power? Why or why not?

4. Compare the reasons for Israel's hopelessness with the hopelessness of people today.

LESSON IN OUR SOCIETY

Your church may seem like a heap of dried-up bones to you—spiritually dead with no hope of vitality. But just as God promised to restore His nation, He can restore any church, no matter how dry or dead it may be. Rather than give up, pray for renewal because God can restore it to life. The hope and prayer of every church should be that God will put His Spirit into it (see Ezekiel 37:14). In fact, God is at work calling His people back to Himself and bringing new life into dead churches.

MAKE IT HAPPEN

Is there a situation in your life that seems impossible? Is it like the valley of dry bones— dead, unresponsive, lifeless? Only God knows if this situation can be restored. The first step is to ask Him about it. Consistently spend time in His Word and trust Him to speak to your particular situation. God can also use mature Christians to help you determine what you should do. Stay prayerful in seeking God's direction and wisdom.

FOLLOW THE SPIRIT

What God wants me to do:

_____

_____

REMEMBER YOUR THOUGHTS

Special insights I have learned:

_____

_____

MORE LIGHT ON THE TEXT
Ezekiel 37:1-14

1 The hand of the LORD was upon me, and carried me out in the spirit of the LORD, and set me down in the midst of the valley which was full of bones.

The vision of the dry bones concludes an oracle on future restoration of Israel that began at Ezekiel 36:16. Ezekiel 37:1-2 expresses the setting of the prophecy. The prophet saw the manner in which the prophecy unfolded as the Spirit of the Lord picked him up and transported him into the valley. The phrase "the hand of the LORD was upon me" describes the urgency and compulsion by which the prophet is overwhelmed. God's hand is a manifestation of God's power. The Hebrew word for "valley," *habbiq'ah*, is prefixed with the definite article *ha*. There is no particular valley mentioned. The valley was "full of bones," disjoined from one another and in an extreme state of deterioration. The vision illustrates the situation and condition of the people.

2 And caused me to pass by them round about: and, behold, there were very many in the open valley; and, lo, they were very dry.

The description is intended to show how many bones there were and how long they had been lying there in the valley. Ezekiel was made to pass around the bones to impress upon him their vast quantity and extreme dryness, indicating that life had left them a long time ago. As the recipient of the vision and an agent and witness of God, Ezekiel saw the skeletons of slaughtered men. They were so throughly bleached and dried by long exposure to the atmosphere that all apparent capability of life had left them. The prophet was astonished by what he saw, as his audience will be astonished by what they hear.

3 And he said unto me, Son of man, can these bones live? And I answered, O Lord GOD, thou knowest.

The question and answer are calculated to heighten the wonder of what is about to be related. Ezekiel recounts these details in the first person, according to what he saw and did. It is obvious that the possibility of a revival did not occur to the prophet. When the Lord asked him whether the bones could live, he acknowledged his lack of omniscience, replying that only the Lord knew. For the matter exclusively belonged to the grace and power of God as the One who alone can do what to human eyes looks impossible. The despair was logical; to hope that those who had been dead so long that their bones were bleached from years of exposure to the weather could live again was absurd. But faith understands that "the things which are impossible with men are possible with God" (Luke 18:27). Even when the situation seems hopeless, God can do the impossible.

4 Again he said unto me, Prophesy upon these bones, and say unto them, O ye dry bones, hear the word of the LORD. 5 Thus saith the Lord GOD unto these bones; Behold, I will cause breath to enter into you, and ye shall live: 6 And I will lay sinews upon you, and will bring up flesh upon you, and cover you with skin, and put breath in you, and ye shall live; and ye shall know that I am the LORD.

Ezekiel was commanded to prophesy to the dry bones and to proclaim God's purpose to endow them anew with powers and properties of life. The word was no sooner uttered when its effect took place. The prophecy was God's Word. Ezekiel was God's servant through whom hope and transformation would come to the people as God spoke. "I will cause breath to enter into you, and ye shall live" (v. 5) is a summary that anticipates the outcome. The Lord Himself would cause the bones to live. Tendons, flesh, skin, and breath, in that order, would come on the bones so that living people would be formed. Then this "resurrected" people would know that God was their Lord.

7 So I prophesied as I was commanded: and as I prophesied, there was a noise, and behold a shaking, and the bones came together, bone to his bone.

The prophet did exactly as the Lord commanded and proclaimed the words of the Lord to the dead, dry bones. While he was speaking, Ezekiel heard the rushing sound of God's mighty work and watched as the bones joined.

8 And when I beheld, lo, the sinews and the flesh came up upon them, and the skin covered them above: but there was no breath in them.

All the bones came together and took on themselves tendons, flesh, and skin. The bodies were complete, but there was no breath in them. There is no connection between this act of bones coming together and the resurrection, as some interpret it. It simply shows God in the act of reviving His people who had been "cut off" from the source of God's power and influence (v. 11) and had been abandoned. Yet the separation was a result of their own sin.

9 Then said he unto me, Prophesy unto the wind, prophesy, son of man, and say to the wind, Thus saith the Lord GOD; Come from the four winds, O breath, and breathe upon these slain, that they may live.

In obedience to another Word of God, the breath of life from God's Spirit penetrated the whole mass of bodies and transformed them into a host of valiant humans with healthy freshness and energy of life. The final act of power was needed to make them live. The Hebrew word translated as "spirit," "breath," and "wind" is *ru'ah*. The definite article used with *ru'ah* in this verse points specifically to God as the ultimate source of life, as found in Genesis 2:7. The breath of life is summoned from the four quarters or winds of the earth to breathe into the bodies and thus animate the whole people. The four winds may refer to God's omniscience. The Spirit of God is the agent of life and a sign of God's presence. God's Spirit renews humans and allows them to internalize His Word, which results in freedom.

10 So I prophesied as he commanded me, and the breath came into them, and they lived, and stood up upon their feet, an exceeding great army.

Ezekiel, as God's messenger, prophesies as God told him and the Spirit of God enters the completed bodies (v. 9), reviving them to life. The stiff corpses spring to their feet and become a mighty army. Instead of "a vast army," some translations use "an exceeding great force," which corresponds with the Hebrew word *hayil*, used in a double sense to imply superlative power. This is especially true when connected with personal resources and energy. The flesh-clothed skeletons that were revived to life become a vast multitude in full strength and vigor.

11 Then he said unto me, Son of man, these bones are the whole house of Israel: behold, they say, Our bones are dried, and our hope is lost: we are cut off for our parts. 12 Therefore prophesy and say unto them, Thus saith the Lord GOD; Behold, O my people, I will open your graves, and cause you to come up out of your graves, and bring you into the land of Israel. 13 And ye shall know that I am the LORD, when I have opened up your graves, O my people, and brought you up out of your graves, 14 And shall put my spirit in you, and ye shall live, and I shall place you in your own land: then shall ye know that I the LORD have spoken it, and performed it, saith the LORD.

Verses 11-14 give the explanation of the vision. What at first appears to be an expression of hopelessness, destruction, and despair is in fact a vision of the regathering and spiritual restoration of the nation of Israel. The phrase "these bones are the whole house of Israel" reveals that the vision does not describe the resurrection of individuals but the restoration of a nation. The Hebrew word for "graves" is *qeber* (keh'-ber), which means burying place, sepulchre, or tomb. The graves represent the foreign nations from which Israel would arise and return.

The experience of exile had left the nation devoid of hope, and the people regarded their exiled existence as an irretrievable end. Though addressed to Judah, the explanation of the vision refers to the whole house of Israel. The two warring nations (Israel and Judah) would become one under a new king. God would restore both life and unity.

Just as the dry bones could be restored into living beings only by the mighty act of God, the restoration of Israel would be accomplished only by God's power. God promises to breathe life into His people and bring them back to their land. This spiritual and physical restoration is God's promise of rich blessing.

DAILY BIBLE READINGS

M: God's Name Was Profaned
Ezekiel 36:16-22

T: God Will Give a New Heart
Ezekiel 36:23-32

W: The People Shall Know God
Ezekiel 36:33-38

T: Ezekiel Sees the Dry Bones
Ezekiel 37:1-6

F: The Dry Bones Live and Breathe
Ezekiel 37:7-14

S: Two Nations Shall Become One
Ezekiel 37:15-23

S: God Will Bless the New Nation
Ezekiel 37:24-28

Find out the full meaning of the word *dry* by using the reference tools in your *Precepts For Living* CD-ROM. Set yourself up on a systematic reading plan by using the CD-ROM so you can guard against spiritual dryness in your own life.

TEACHING TIPS

October 31
Bible Study Guide 9

1. Words You Should Know

A. Sanctuary (Psalm 73:17) *miqdash* (Heb.)—A consecrated, holy thing or place. In the Bible, the word usually referred to the tabernacle or the temple. This physical area was sacred because it was the place where God dwelt among His people. In some places in the Old Testament, the word is used metaphorically to refer to as a place of refuge.

B. Reins (v. 21) *kilyah* (Heb.)—The seat of the deepest emotions.

2. Teacher Preparation

A. Begin preparing for this lesson by reading Psalm 73 each day for at least five days. You are probably already in the habit of reading the DAILY BIBLE READINGS and the DEVOTIONAL READING as a part of your Sunday School lesson preparation.

B. Read over the FOCAL VERSES and the commentary in this BIBLE STUDY GUIDE. Review the questions in the SEARCH THE SCRIPTURES and DISCUSS THE MEANING sections. Go over the instructions in the MAKE IT HAPPEN section. You may want to have this chart ready ahead of time for the students to fill out.

3. Starting the Lesson

A. Read the LESSON AIM aloud together and have one or two students pray for the class based on it.

B. Divide the class into small groups. Ask each group to read the FOCAL VERSES, then rewrite the assigned verses in Psalm 73 in their own words. Allow each group to read their psalm.

C. Have the students read the IN FOCUS section.

4. Getting into the Lesson

A. Go over the AT-A-GLANCE outline several times.

B. Lead the class through the IN DEPTH section of the lesson, using the AT-A-GLANCE outline and SEARCH THE SCRIPTURES questions.

5. Relating the Lesson to Life

A. Lead the students in answering the DISCUSS THE MEANING questions. These questions should challenge the students to move toward the aim of the lesson.

B. Reserve time for discussion of the LESSON IN OUR SOCIETY. How have the students in your class allowed materialism to creep into their lives?

6. Arousing Action

A. Encourage each student to work through the chart found in the MAKE IT HAPPEN section. They may have a tendency to want to fold it up and say they will fill it out later, but be sure to leave time for this exercise and have them fill in the blanks before they leave. Have several Scriptures on hand to help them out.

B. Assign the DAILY BIBLE READINGS.

CREATING A RENEWED TRUST

Bible Background • PSALM 73
Printed Text • PSALM 73:1-3, 12-13, 16-18, 21-26
Devotional Reading • PSALM 91:1-10

LESSON AIM

By the end of the lesson, the students will recognize that the prosperity of the wicked is temporary, understand that trust in God can be renewed through worship, and acknowledge that pain and injustice are part of life.

KEEP IN MIND

"My flesh and my heart faileth: but God is the strength of my heart, and my portion for ever" (Psalm 73:26).

FOCAL VERSES

Psalm 73:1 Truly God is good to Israel, even to such as are of a clean heart.

2 But as for me, my feet were almost gone; my steps had well nigh slipped.

3 For I was envious at the foolish, when I saw the prosperity of the wicked.

73:12 Behold, these are the ungodly, who prosper in the world; they increase in riches.

13 Verily I have cleansed my heart in vain, and washed my hands in innocency.

73:16 When I thought to know this, it was too painful for me;

17 Until I went into the sanctuary of God; then understood I their end.

18 Surely thou didst set them in slippery places: thou castedst them down into destruction.

73:21 Thus my heart was grieved and I was pricked in my reins.

22 So foolish was I, and ignorant: I was as a beast before thee.

23 Nevertheless I am continually with thee: thou hast holden me by my right hand.

LESSON OVERVIEW

LESSON AIM
KEEP IN MIND
FOCAL VERSES
IN FOCUS
THE PEOPLE, PLACES,
AND TIMES
BACKGROUND
AT-A-GLANCE
IN DEPTH
SEARCH THE SCRIPTURES
DISCUSS THE MEANING
LESSON IN OUR SOCIETY
MAKE IT HAPPEN
FOLLOW THE SPIRIT
REMEMBER YOUR THOUGHTS
MORE LIGHT ON THE TEXT
DAILY BIBLE READINGS

24 Thou shalt guide me with thy counsel, and afterward receive me to glory.

25 Whom have I in heaven but thee? and there is none upon earth that I desire beside thee.

26 My flesh and my heart faileth: but God is the strength of my heart, and my portion for ever.

IN FOCUS

Catherine watched her ex-husband pull away from the house in his brand-new Lexus. He dropped off her three children, who were loaded down with bags from the mall. Even though the children were eager to show Catherine their brand-new outfits, she excused herself and sought the refuge of her bedroom. There she let the tears spill over. Five years ago, Catherine's husband had abandoned her for another woman. It had taken her three years of working day and night and also taking night classes to get a job that barely covered her monthly bills. She clung to the Lord, read her Bible daily, and trusted Him to get her through.

Yet there were times when her ex-spouse drove up in that new car that she felt envious. Why had God handed this selfish man so much wealth when she remained faithful to God but had to constantly endure hardship and pain?

Many of us ask this kind of question. This week's lesson offers answers and comfort.

THE PEOPLE, PLACES, AND TIMES

The Wicked. This term generally refers to people

who are morally wrong, perverted, or unrighteous. Those who are wicked are liable to punishment. The term *wicked* appears over 500 times in the Bible, mostly in Psalms, Proverbs, Job, and Ezekiel. The word points to the attitude and intentions of a person, not just their actions. They are usually guilty of violating the social rights of others through oppression, greed, exploitation, murder, dishonesty in business, and twisting justice. They hate the Lord and are hostile toward God and His people.

BACKGROUND

King David is believed to be the author of 73 psalms, the sons of Korah wrote 9 and Asaph (who wrote Psalm 73) is the author of 12.

Asaph was a Levite who was descended from Kohath. He was appointed by David as a director of choral music in the house of the Lord, and he was retained in the same capacity by Solomon in the temple (2 Chronicles 5:12).

Asaph and his clan, the Asaphites, composed the temple choir and were set apart specifically for the purpose of praising and worshiping the Lord. Psalm 73 could have been composed by Asaph personally or by his guild of temple singers. Asaph's numerous descendants are mentioned frequently in history. Ezra identifies him as the ancestor of the temple singers (Ezra 2:41).

AT-A-GLANCE

1. The Prosperity of Evildoers
(Psalm 73:1-3)
2. The Heart of the Righteous
(vv. 12-13)
3. The Future of the Wicked
(vv. 16-18)
4. The Benefits of the Righteous
(vv. 21-26)

IN DEPTH

1. The Prosperity of Evildoers (Psalm 73:1-3)

Psalm 73 starts out with a positive affirmation toward God. It is similar to the modern–day phrase recited at Christian gatherings: "God is good!" the leader says. The crowd responds, "All the time!"

The word *good* in this verse symbolizes all of God's graciousness and covenant blessings to His people. God's hand of blessings was upon those who had not worshiped idols or dealt dishonestly or deceitfully with God or other people. This person's heart was pure. Perfection is not the idea communicated here. Rather, it is a picture of one who in his deepest innermost being comes before God empty, sincerely desiring to be clean and pleasing toward Him—wanting His plans and purposes for his life.

After this outpouring of praise, Asaph confessed his problem. He poured his heart out before the Lord. Although this psalm is considered a testimony of trust and thanksgiving to God, it does not start out that way. Initially, Asaph expressed before God his attitude of confusion and complaint.

He admitted his thinking was about to cause him to fall into a lifestyle of whining, crying, and murmuring against Almighty God. What caused this dilemma in Asaph's mind? The psalmist was "envious at the foolish." In other words, he could not understand why the wicked seemed to proper and the godly and upright seemed to suffer.

Asaph failed to reconcile in his mind the suffering of the saints and the success of the sinners. How can God be "good all the time" while violent, oppressive people seem to obtain material wealth and stay healthy? People who have nothing to do with God appear to live in peace and prosperity, and all too often God's people suffer in pain and poverty.

Each one of us, if we are honest with ourselves, have at some point in our lives asked this kind of question.

2. The Heart of the Righteous (vv. 12-13)

In verses 3-12, Asaph described in detail evil individuals—people who have set their faces against God. Like the leaders in the Mafia, they seem to live in violence and harshness toward others. They employ conceit and violence as instruments of power. They are arrogant, and their filthy wealth surrounds them like a comforting blanket. Not only do we see their evil deeds and lifestyles, but the wicked are usually not quiet. Their mouths are full of propaganda and lies.

Asaph honestly and forthrightly posed his questions to God: "God, if You are all-powerful, all-seeing, and a just God, how can they get away with this? How can You allow them to go unpunished for their wrongdoing? The more evil they do, the more they increase in their wealth!"

Asaph lamented and continued to set his questions before the Lord. If people who are against God increase in health and riches, it doesn't really matter whether the righteous live a life pleasing to God or not. Asaph concludes that God is not good to the pure in heart; He is good to the wicked. "What kind of God are You?" the psalmist asks. "How can You allow drug dealers to live like kings, watch underground criminals continue to infiltrate society with pornography and gambling, and then sit back and do nothing?"

Asaph's questions begin to take on a more personal nature: "Why should I be righteous? Why should I make right choices? Why should I attempt to live a life pleasing to You? What difference does it make?" The psalmist says, "I have cleansed my heart in vain, and washed my hands in innocency" (v. 13).

Not only does the psalmist feel that his life has been lived in vain, but he also seems to have been plagued with some kind of chronic illness and seems to imply that God rebuked him on a daily basis. He repeatedly cleansed himself and repented, but his crisis continued. Asaph's theology (his belief system about God) and his day-to-day reality did not seem to match.

3. The Future of the Wicked (vv. 16-18)

Asaph handled his problem correctly. He did not look toward God with resentment. After pouring out his complaint and admitting his confusion, he goes to the sanctuary—the temple in Jerusalem. There the presence of the Lord abides. Asaph takes his dilemma before the Lord. He realized his thoughts were too troublesome or painful to put on the back burner of his mind.

When Asaph turns to the Lord for the answer, God is faithful. He replies to the cry and call of His talented musician. God does not spend time explaining the present good fortune of the wicked. He goes instead and shows Asaph their horrible end. While Asaph thought, "I am the one slipping," God shows him that the wicked are the ones who are in "slippery places." They will be "cast down" to "destruction." Their foundation is built on sand, and when the storms of life blow, they will not be able to stand (Matthew 7:24-27).

Not only will they fall in times of trouble, but their downfall will happen "in a moment." How many times do we hear stories of people who are rich and famous one day, but impoverished and destitute the next? God assures Asaph that the actions of the wicked will be judged. They will look in the mirror and wish someone else looked back. They will wish they had lived their lives differently. Many wicked people are featured in the media and are very visible. They have not covered up their wrongdoing or been ashamed of their lifestyles, but God will have the last word and the final decision concerning their lives.

4. The Benefits of the Righteous (vv. 21-26)

As Asaph reflects on the truth about the destructive end that the wicked will suffer, he is humiliated and broken. He is grieved and ashamed of his previous thoughts. He realized he had been trying to understand heavenly truth with earthly eyes. God's ways are not our ways, and His thoughts are not our thoughts (see Isaiah 55:9). Asaph now sees God from a different perspective. He no longer thought that God was unfair by rewarding the unrighteous and causing the righteous to suffer. Asaph now understands that believers benefit from making godly choices. Asaph concluded with a renewed mind and a refreshed spirit.

It pays to do all we can to keep our hearts and minds in tune with God. We benefit in our daily existence by being led and guided by the Lord. Daily we can choose to turn to Him and delight ourselves in His ways. Even though God's people go through difficulties and many times will be discouraged—our hearts and our flesh will fail (v. 26)—we have assurance that our strength will not be consumed or spent. We can look to the

Lord and rely on Him for strength. He is our rock and provision in this life.

God also gives His people assurance concerning life after death. Believers know where they will end up after death—in the loving, comforting arms of Jesus. Those who make wicked, evil choices that disregard the presence and power of God in this life will be lost and destroyed.

Asaph realized that God was the passion of his life. His present life and future existence were wrapped up in God. Asaph came to the conclusion that "God is indeed good—all the time!" He realized God was near him and was continually there for him. The writer of Hebrews encourages us to talk to God like a friend and close companion because we are His children. We are clean, washed, and have pure consciences before God because of Jesus Christ. We are encouraged to draw near to God—to come boldly into His presence (see Hebrews 4:15-16) based on our relationship with Him.

SEARCH THE SCRIPTURES

1. _____ is the author of Psalm 73.

2. God is good to those who are of a _____ (Psalm 73:1).

3. The psalmist was _____ of the _____ (v. 3).

4. The ungodly prosper in the _____ and increase in _____ (v. 12).

5. The psalmist thought he kept his _____ pure in _____ (v. 13).

6. His _____ and _____ failed, but God is his strength (v. 26).

DISCUSS THE MEANING

1. Why was it good for Asaph to ask questions like this?

2. Where did Asaph direct his questions, and why was this the best thing for him to do?

3. What conclusions did Asaph come to after his confrontation with God?

4. In what ways can you identify with Asaph?

LESSON IN OUR SOCIETY

Americans are surrounded by wealth. Money and fame are viewed as the ultimate goal in life. We grow up wishing Santa Claus would bring us everything on Christmas day. When the truck or doll is not under the tree, many times we make silent agreements telling ourselves, "Once I grow up I'm going to have everything I want. I'll never be disappointed again." Often this goal is achieved through illegal means, working ourselves to death, or attempting to use God like a genie.

One sign of maturity as an adult and as a Christian is being able to understand the difference between our wants and our needs—and being content with what God provides for us.

MAKE IT HAPPEN

Make a chart with these four headings:

• Wealthy ungodly people (These are people you know who are wealthy but do not honor God with their lives.)

• My thoughts (What are your thoughts about these people?)

• God's Word (List some Scriptures about wealth, money, the rich, etc.)

• Attitudes that need changing (What do I need to change about my thinking to have my thoughts more biblically centered?)

FOLLOW THE SPIRIT

What God wants me to do:

_____
_____

REMEMBER YOUR THOUGHTS

Special insights I have learned:

_____
_____

MORE LIGHT ON THE TEXT

Psalm 73:1-3, 12-13, 16-18, 21-26

1 Truly God is good to Israel, even to such as are of a clean heart.

The author of this psalm begins with a statement of assurance. He begins with the Hebrew word *'ak* (translated as "truly"). This indicates a sense of certainty and conviction that comes from a deep personal experience. It can also be translated as "surely." The psalmist is saying, "In any wise, God is good" or "Certainly, God is good." In spite of what may have happened, Asaph has

Our worship of Almighty God should never cease!

come to the conclusion that God is good. This is a "nevertheless" statement, which suggests that many things may have happened to shake the author's faith in the goodness of God.

The Hebrew word for God used here is not the sacred name of God. It is *elohiym* (**el-o-heem**), which is plural for *elowahh* meaning "god." In the ordinary sense, it would be translated as "gods." However, when used in this way, it indicates the absolute supremacy of the God of Israel. In a sense, it can also refer to the identity of *YAHWEH*,

the One who exceeds all other gods. This term also carries with it the idea of God as the Almighty Judge. As judges, the gods of the other nations could not be counted upon to be just. The psalmist was dealing with the question that often arises in human life. For example, "If God is so good, why does Israel suffer so much?" The suffering of the Children of Israel is well documented in Scripture. Similarly, the dispersion of our people around the world and the pain of forgotten connections is acute and may often seem unbearable. The prosperity of the wicked and of those who oppress the righteous raises serious questions about the goodness of God. But after examination, this psalmist arrived at the one conclusion which strengthens the heart: "Truly God is good to Israel."

The Hebrew word *towb*, or *tobe*, which means "good" when used of God's relation to His people, implies that God does beautifully. It means that God provided what is best and His bountiful provision is what cheers and puts the heart of Israel at ease in the midst of anxiety.

It can also mean that God bestows favor upon Israel. The author is not speaking of the future. He declares that God is good to Israel in the present . This fundamental truth is not limited to the Israelites; God's goodness is revealed to all those whose heart is in the right place. The word *baar*, which is combined to form the phrase *labaareey*, translates as "even to those that are of a clean heart." This can also mean those who are beloved by God. Those who are of a clean heart are clear in their interaction with God and the world. In fact, it is this purity of heart that keeps them from slipping into despair about the state of the world.

2 But as for me, my feet were almost gone; my steps had well nigh slipped. 3 For I was envious at the foolish, when I saw the prosperity of the wicked.

In this verse, the feet indicate firmness of purpose and the steps indicate the practical walk in the path laid down within the law of the Lord. The idea of feet slipping is a sign of moral uncertainty. The slippage of the foot is a symbolic expression of spiritual instability. The psalmist is on the verge of being carried away by a decline in moral and spiritual fervency. His thoughts took him on a downward spiral and his foundations were on the verge of being overthrown because of a prolonged concentration on the apparent injustice of God's way in the world. The author was about to turn aside from God's goodness. He was about to yield to despair.

"Why did I founder?" the author asks. He was envious of the foolish—not of the rich but of the foolish. He caused himself to become envious and stir up feelings of pain by constant conversa-

tion and meditation upon what the foolish have that he lacked. The word *qana'* (**kaw-naw**) means to exert zealous jealousy, which has the capacity to cloud one's judgment. The sight of the foolish and how well they were doing provoked his soul to jealous action. The word translated as "foolish" is the Hebrew word *halal* (**haw-lal**), which means to show off or to boast. It is the idea that those who boast are foolish.

The author of this song was despairing over those who commended themselves instead of God because of their possessions or their power. In the Bible, such boasting is always accompanied by wickedness. For the Lord hates the proud and rewards the humble (see 1 Peter 5:5).

The foolish were boastful because they were able to deal with their condition comfortably while glorying in themselves and feigning righteousness. The passage can also read, "I envied the outrageous and those who were renowned for doing evil." It was not just the fact they were foolish and wicked that made this writer concerned. The fact that in their wicked ways they seemed to prosper in everything they did is what ate at the core of his heart. In his view, the wicked seemed very happy. People sought them out as friends. Although they continued in their arrogant and wicked ways, they lived in health and prosperity.

73:12 Behold, these are the ungodly, who prosper in the world; they increase in riches.

After stating the reality concerning the condition of the wicked, he now concludes by saying, "Don't you see that I am right?" It is as though he is showing someone the ungodly. "Look," he seems to be saying, "is this person ungodly?" The implied answer is yes.

The word used for "world" in this passage is the Hebrew word *owlam* (**o-lawm** or **olam**), which means "through the ages." Asaph was convinced that the prosperity of the wicked is not a new thing. The word translated as "increase" here is the Hebrew word *sagah* meaning to enlarge, probably by evil machination and deceit. The word "riches" is translated from the Hebrew word *chayil* (**khah'-yil**). Some linguists think it means the use of force, either physical or spiritual, to gain what one desires. The measure of prosperity for this psalmist was material riches. In those days, an army or a band of soldiers could use force to obtain wealth. Many powerful nations prospered through wars undergirded by ruthlessness. When the psalmist looked at the world powers in his day—Assyria, Chaldea, Babylon, and Egypt—he noted they all prospered by destroying their neighbors. In his human perception, those who did wrong had it good.

13 Verily I have cleansed my heart in vain, and washed my hands in innocency.

"What's the use of being righteous?" he says. The phrase "washed my hands" is a metaphor for living life with integrity. Among the Igbos of West Africa, the washing of hands symbolizes righteousness. In the Old Testament, there are many places where the Law commands the people to wash. This washing is a sign that one is able to make a distinction between clean and unclean and between the holy and the unholy.

The word for "innocency" is the Hebrew phrase *ziykiytiy*, which comes from the word *zakah* (**zaw-kaw**) meaning to live a transparent lifestyle. He has worked hard to be innocent of crime. In a sense, his conscience was clear. As far as he was concerned, in the sight of God and humanity, he is counted as one who is pure. But when looking at the material result of his quest for righteousness, he was disappointed and begins to think that striving for moral integrity is a waste of time.

73:16 When I thought to know this, it was too painful for me;

Again he reminds the reader that this was not a casual observation. The word *chatab,* translated as "thought," means to plot deliberately or to overthrow the beliefs of others. It would seem that this author set out to show these "naive believers" in the goodness of God that they were wrong. He computed historical evidence. He marshaled eyewitness accounts of the prosperity of the wicked to show that God is not good to Israel. He held these arguments in his heart, they took hold of his imagination, and the result was pain and bitterness toward God.

17 Until I went into the sanctuary of God; then understood I their end.

This desire to show that God was not good after all continued "until." The Hebrew word for "until" indicates that he continued in this thought even as he proceeded to the place of worship. It could also mean that he thought about it during the meeting in the sanctuary. This makes sense as it was in the sanctuary that the people confirmed the goodness of the Lord to Israel. But it is much more than that. It points to what happened while he was in the sanctuary. It points to degrees of enlightenment that occur when one enters the presence of God among the people of faith. Before he went to the inner sanctuary, his heart was in the wrong place and his faith in the goodness of God was shaken. When he turned toward the divine sanctuary, his heart and his mind began to understand.

The Hebrew word for "sanctuary" is *miqdash* (**mik-dawsh** or **miqqedash**), as used in Exodus 15:17, which means the place of consecration. When he went to the sanctuary, his understanding was cleansed and wisdom was born within his soul.

18 Surely thou didst set them in slippery places: thou castedst them down into destruction.

What did he understand in the sanctuary? First, he came to know that although the wicked may prosper in this world, they were not as secure as they appeared. God has placed the wicked, even those in prosperity, in slippery places. In the sanctuary, where he met with God, the psalmist came to understand where God has placed the wicked in the scheme of things. God has appointed them for destruction. In fact, God has arrayed His army against them. Remember how the wicked got their wealth? They got it by raising up soldiers and using force. The same measure has been decreed in the heavens for them. The idea of slipperiness brings to mind the fact that they smoothly flatter themselves. As they have been forceful and smooth, God has marked them by allowing them to fall through their own smoothness. Neither their smooth talk nor their force can save them when they fall.

Second, God will cast them down to destruction.

The word *naphal* (**naw-fal**), which is translated as "castedst," implies that their fall will be accepted by many as the judgment of God. In fact, it means that when they slip, God will cast them down. It is not a fall from which one can get up; it is a fall that causes one to cease from being whatever it was that created the boastful attitude in the first place. They shall die, and their wealth shall be divided among those whom they have forced and oppressed. They will fall downward to a depth from which they cannot rise up again. They will move from fanfare to fugitive—from superiority to inferiority. God will judge them.

The wicked will be found wanting. The Lord will overthrow them and overwhelm them until they perish. As they have slain, so shall the Lord slay and smite them. The psalmist saw that the final end of the wicked is destruction. In contrast, in the end, Israel and those who are upright in the eyes of the Lord will inherit His goodness.

73:21 Thus my heart was grieved and I was pricked in my reins.

The first pain that the psalmist felt in verse 16 was a result of his misunderstanding the prosperity of the wicked. His weariness was a direct result of envy. In verse 21, his heart is grieved. He had been looking at the outward appearance of things. Now having entered into the Holy of Holies and seeing through the eyes of God, he was grieved. His inmost being was moved by what he saw. He finally saw that God is not indifferent to the plight of the righteous. More than that, he saw that God was not indifferent to the actions of the wicked. This realization caused him to rethink his previous position. He spoke harshly to himself and berated himself for lacking understanding. Such grief seems to be a sign of repentance. Understanding how far off he had been from the truth about God's goodness caused his heart to be pierced by the Spirit of the Lord. He became teachable and more eager to learn the ways of the Lord.

22 So foolish was I, and ignorant: I was as a beast before thee.

These are the words with which he berated himself. Though the wicked were foolish and boastful, he also was foolish. The word *ba'ar* (**bah'-ar**) simply means one who thinks mainly in terms of the concrete and who does not see the deeper meaning of a thing. It is equivalent to saying that one is stupid. The word translated as "ignorant" is the Hebrew word *la'*, which simply means "not," meaning that one is a negation of existence. It means that because he was acting foolishly he was less than nothing. He lacked the basic principle for living because his heart was not in the right place. By implication, it can mean that one is ignorant.

The final part of the verse supports the fact that he felt like nothing. He says, "I was as a beast before thee." The word he uses to describe himself is *behemah* (**be-hay-maw**). He was like a dumb beast as far as wisdom was concerned. He was similar to animals in that he based his argument against the goodness of God mainly upon what he saw and not on the perspective of God's divine plan.

23 Nevertheless I am continually with thee: thou hast holden me by my right hand.

His entrance into the sanctuary of the Lord allowed him to understand the perpetual presence of the Lord. Though he may have strayed in his thought, he is still with the Lord. Just because he wandered off does not mean that God wandered off also. What is amazing to him is God's continual goodness, even in the face of the psalmist's bad attitude. God continued to extend regular care to him. The fact that he doubted God's goodness to Israel does not mean that God ceased to be good.

God was continually with him even in the midst of his faithlessness. The wonderful message in this passage is that God continues to provide intimate care even when His children are shaky in their faith. The psalmist was blaming God, but God was with him. This verse explains why he almost slipped but did not fall like the wicked. He would have slipped and fell, but God held his right hand. God's hand seized and held him up. God was there to catch him on his way down. God provided a handle for his hand. It also means that even in his foolishness, God's power was available to him.

24 Thou shalt guide me with thy counsel, and afterward receive me to glory.

God is with him always to guide him. This guidance comes through the counsel of the Lord.

God will advise his heart, leading it away from foolishness. This could also mean that God will guide him by showing His plan for the wicked.

God's guidance and care prepares those who walk in the ways of righteousness for entrance into God's glory. After all is said and done, there is a future for the righteous. After the wealth and the kingdom of the wicked have disappeared by the same force with which they came, God will protect those who seek righteousness with all their heart. There is gain in following the Lord. The pursuit of holiness will bring forth blessings in the presence of God. For the psalmist, the one major assurance is that he will be received. *Laqach* (**law-kakh**), the Hebrew word for "receive," is a way of saying that God will take care of him. Though the world does not accept him and would rather praise the wicked, God will accept him and bring him into the presence of God. God will carry him away from the storm that will sweep the wicked away. The concept here is of the forceful redemption of those who are weaker from the hand of those who are stronger. God has reserved a place of victory. With God on his side, the psalmist knows that he will win.

25 Whom have I in heaven but thee? and there is none upon earth that I desire beside thee.

He now knows that help will come. "Whom have I in heaven but thee?" is a rhetorical question affirming the fact that God alone is his God. He is not looking for another God. The wicked have other gods. They count on the moon, the stars, and even other spirits to help them. They buy justice and sell favor. Many times the righteous do not have material wealth or power, so they cannot buy defense. But God is the defender of the poor. The psalmist is counting on God alone to be his advocate on this earth, not on the idols of the nations. He will not place another god in conjunction with God. He will not make other gods equal with the Holy One of Israel. For to do so is to go against his own soul and to stand in judgment of the Lord. This is an affirmation that his God is also the God of earth, not just a God who is in heaven and does not see the doings of human beings.

26 My flesh and my heart faileth: but God is the strength of my heart, and my portion for ever.

The word "flesh" here could mean his frail humanity. The human body will fail and human courage will give way to faintheartedness, but the strength of God will never fail; it never runs out. Our God can be counted on. He is the Rock on which we can stand firm without fear.

DAILY BIBLE READINGS

M: Sing for Joy to God
Psalm 84:1-7

T: Trust in God
Psalm 84:8-12

W: God Is Our Refuge
Psalm 91:1-10

T: The Wicked People Prosper
Psalm 73:1-9

F: Is Our Faith in Vain?
Psalm 73:10-14

S: The Prosperous Ones Are Destroyed
Psalm 73:15-20

S: Faith in God Renewed
Psalm 73:21-28

Use your *Precepts For Living* CD-ROM to find where the word *prosperity* is used in the Bible. Then, contrast the descriptions of the prosperity of the righteous with the prosperity of the wicked.

TEACHING TIPS

November 7
Bible Study Guide 10

1. Words You Should Know

A. Fulfil (Matthew 5:17) *pleroo* (Gk.)—To accomplish or perform what was foretold or prefigured in the Old Testament. It also meant that Christ performed perfect obedience in His person.

B. To Lust (v. 28) *epithymeo* (Gk.)—The phrase refers to the inclining of one's affections toward or setting one's heart on something or someone. To crave or covet a certain thing or person.

2. Teacher Preparation

A. As you study, ask God to give you an understanding of His Word and to direct and empower you in presenting the lesson to the class.

B. To gain additional insight into this week's lesson, study MORE LIGHT ON THE TEXT.

C. Prayerfully read the BIBLE BACKGROUND Scripture so that you will understand the context of the printed text.

D. During your personal devotions, meditate on the DEVOTIONAL READING for this week's lesson.

3. Starting the Lesson

A. Begin the class by asking the students the following two questions: How would you define the word *faithfulness*? What does it mean to obey God?

B. After a brief discussion of these questions, explain that today's lesson exhorts us to be faithful and explains that the true test of faithfulness is obedience to God in every situation.

C. Have one student read the IN FOCUS section for the lesson and another read the BACKGROUND information.

4. Getting into the Lesson

A. Write the AT-A-GLANCE outline on the board. Then have a student read the FOCAL VERSES for the first part of the outline. Have another student read the IN DEPTH section for those same verses. Ask the students what the main topic of the section is.

B. Refer to the SEARCH THE SCRIPTURES questions as you briefly discuss each section. Repeat the process until all three sections have been covered.

5. Relating the Lesson to Life

A. Use the DISCUSS THE MEANING questions to help the students understand how this passage relates to their daily lives.

B. Read the LESSON IN OUR SOCIETY section to contrast what is happening in society today with what God is commanding us to do.

6. Arousing Action

A. Sum up the lesson with the KEEP IN MIND verse. Have the students read it three times in unison; then have the class recite it from memory.

B. Challenge the students to implement the MAKE IT HAPPEN section beginning next week.

C. Assign homework for next week.

A NEW APPROACH

Bible Background • MATTHEW 5
Printed Text • MATTHEW 5:17-18, 21-22, 27-28, 31-35, 38-39, 43-44
Devotional Reading • MATTHEW 5:1-12

LESSON AIM

By the end of the lesson, the students will understand how the life and teachings of Jesus fulfilled the law, be able to explain the difference between external religious practice and true relational change, and determine to allow spiritual morality to guide their lives.

KEEP IN MIND

"Think not that I am come to destroy the law, or the prophets: I am not come to destroy, but to fulfil" (Matthew 5:17).

FOCAL VERSES

Matthew 5:17 Think not that I am come to destroy the law, or the prophets: I am not come to destroy, but to fulfil.

18 For verily I say unto you, Till heaven and earth pass, one jot or one tittle shall in no wise pass from the law, till all be fulfilled.

5:21 Ye have heard that it was said by them of old time, Thou shalt not kill; and whosoever shall kill shall be in danger of the judgment:

22 But I say unto you, That whosoever is angry with his brother without a cause shall be in danger of the judgment: and whosoever shall say to his brother, Raca, shall be in danger of the council: but whosoever shall say, Thou fool, shall be in danger of hell fire.

5:27 Ye have heard that it was said by them of old time, Thou shalt not commit adultery:

28 But I say unto you, That whosoever looketh on a woman to lust after her hath committed adultery with her already in her heart.

LESSON OVERVIEW

LESSON AIM
KEEP IN MIND
FOCAL VERSES
IN FOCUS
THE PEOPLE, PLACES, AND TIMES
BACKGROUND
AT-A-GLANCE
IN DEPTH
SEARCH THE SCRIPTURES
DISCUSS THE MEANING
LESSON IN OUR SOCIETY
MAKE IT HAPPEN
FOLLOW THE SPIRIT
REMEMBER YOUR THOUGHTS
MORE LIGHT ON THE TEXT
DAILY BIBLE READINGS

5:31 It hath been said, Whosoever shall put away his wife, let him give her a writing of divorcement:

32 But I say unto you, That whosoever shall put away his wife, saving for the cause of fornication, causeth her to commit adultery: and whosoever shall marry her that is divorced committeth adultery.

33 Again, ye have heard that it hath been said by them of old time, Thou shalt not forswear thyself, but shalt perform unto the Lord thine oaths:

34 But I say unto you, Swear not at all; neither by heaven; for it is God's throne:

35 Nor by the earth; for it is his footstool: neither by Jerusalem; for it is the city of the great King.

5:38 Ye have heard that it hath been said, An eye for an eye, and a tooth for a tooth:

39 But I say unto you, That ye resist not evil: but whosoever shall smite thee on thy right cheek, turn to him the other also.

5:43 Ye have heard that it hath been said, Thou shalt love thy neighbour, and hate thine enemy.

44 But I say unto you, Love your enemies, bless them that curse you, do good to them that hate you, and pray for them which despitefully use you, and persecute you.

IN FOCUS

A father takes his young daughter out for a

ride in the car. He places her in her car seat and carefully buckles her in. As he drives away, he looks back to see that his daughter has loosened the seatbelt and is standing up. "Honey, sit down and buckle yourself in," he says.

The little girl does as she is told, but a little later daddy looks in the rearview mirror and discovers that the little angel is standing up again. Losing his patience, he speaks gently but firmly to his little treasure, "Sit down, buckle yourself in, and do not stand up again!"

The little girl pouts, but does as her father says. For a while everything is fine, but then daddy looks back and his baby girl is standing up again. Now, he's angry! He pulls the car over, gets out, and quickly opens the back door. He places the child back into the seat and buckles her in. Then he glares at her and warns, "If you stand up again, it will be spanking time! Do you understand?"

"Yes, daddy, I understand," she replies.

They drive on and daddy's little heartthrob does not stand up again. As they near their house, the little darling speaks out.

"Daddy!"

"Yes, honey."

"I'm sitting down on the outside, but on the inside I'm still standing up."

In today's lesson, Jesus compares the external practice of religion to the internal building of Christlike character.

THE PEOPLE, PLACES, AND TIMES

Salt and Light. Before refrigeration, salt was used to preserve food. Meat would not keep for long unless it was salted. It meant the difference between life and death. Similarly, the followers of Christ preserve the best traditions and morality of their societies. They are the difference between life and death in their societies.

The addition of salt to food turns a bland meal into a delicious feast. Christians demonstrate to the world how a relationship with Christ adds zest to our mundane lives. It encourages unbelievers to "taste and see that the LORD is good" (Psalm 34:8).

Christ was the original Light of the world. When healing the blind man, Jesus explained to His disciples, "As long as I am in the world, I am the light of the world" (John 9:5). When He went back to heaven, He passed the obligation to illuminate to His disciples: "Ye are the light of the world. A city that is set on an hill cannot be hid" (Matthew 5:14). As light, we show the way. Jesus showed the way to the kingdom of heaven; we show the way to Jesus.

BACKGROUND

The Sermon on the Mount is an extension of the preaching Jesus used to launch His ministry, "Repent: for the kingdom of heaven is at hand" (Matthew 4:17). However, the teaching does not present the way to salvation; instead, it outlines the way of righteous living and contrasts it with the teachings of the scribes and Pharisees.

The sermon begins with an explanation of eight moral characteristics that lead to true happiness and blessings and should be true of all believers. These characteristics both demand and describe. They demand proper attitudes of believers, and they describe the blessings from the right attitudes. The demands and descriptions are given in an if/then relationship. If we are poor in spirit, then ours is the kingdom of heaven; if we mourn, then we shall be comforted; if we are meek, then we shall inherit the earth; if we hunger and thirst for righteousness, then we shall be filled; if we are merciful, then we shall obtain mercy; if we are peacemakers, then we shall be called the children of God; and if we rejoice during times of persecution, then great is our reward in heaven.

After His opening, Jesus launches right into the heart of His teaching. His audience knew that righteous living was required to enter into God's kingdom (Psalm 24:3-6). However, they had been taught that the religious practices of the Pharisees were sufficient. Jesus challenged that belief with the statement, "For I tell you that unless your righteousness surpasses that of the Pharisees and the teachers of the law, you will certainly not enter the kingdom of heaven!" (Matthew 5:20, NIV). Those who would be followers of Christ would not be called to a different standard of living, but to a higher standard of living.

1. Jesus Fulfills the Law
(Matthew 5:17-18)
2. Jesus Rejects Pharisaic
Interpretation of the Law
(vv. 21-22, 27-28, 31-35, 38-39, 43-44)

IN DEPTH

1. Jesus Fulfills the Law (Matthew 5:17-18)

Jesus' parents set godly examples for Him to follow by honoring the traditions of their religion (see Luke 2:21-24, 41). Jesus Himself came to fulfill the law. In the epic wilderness battle between the Saviour and the seducer, three times Jesus quotes from the book of Deuteronomy (Matthew 4:1-11). When He announced His ministry in a Galilean synagogue, Jesus quoted from the book of Isaiah (Luke 4:14-19). Throughout His ministry, Jesus refers back to writings of the prophets. Even in the last hours of His earthly life, our Saviour cries out in His agony by quoting a passage from David, "My God, my God, why have you forsaken me?" (Matthew 27:46, NIV; cf. Psalm 22:1).

What we know from Scripture is that not only did Jesus have an exceptional knowledge of the law, He also practiced absolute obedience to the law. However, over the centuries, the scribes had added their own interpretations to the law. These interpretations, known as the "oral law," were handed down from generation to generation. Later, Jewish scholars added commentaries to the oral law, now collectively known as the Talmud.

The Israelites had been taught that righteousness was achieved through the correct practice of their religion. Jesus understood that His call to internal righteousness rather than external religion would be misunderstood. It was absolutely necessary that the people understood that Jesus was not introducing a new religion. Our Lord illustrates this point by telling the people, "Do not think that I have come to abolish the Law or the Prophets; I have not come to abolish them but to fulfill them" (Matthew 5:17, NIV).

"The law and the prophets" is an expression used to describe the entire Old Testament. Christ affirms that His teachings are not meant to destroy or replace the Old Testament teachings, but to fulfill them. The teachings of Christ complete the law when they are fully realized in the lives of His followers. They are clarified when we understand the true meaning of the law as a means of demonstrating and not achieving our right standing with God.

The law is a revelation of the moral nature of God and His will for the lives of His people. As such, the law is timeless. As long as heaven and earth exist, "not the smallest letter, not the least stroke of a pen, will by any means disappear from the Law until everything is accomplished" (v. 18, NIV). However, believers should not view the law as a system of religion by which we can earn forgiveness for sin and right standing with God. Instead, the law should be seen as a moral code for those who have been saved by faith through grace. We are not saved by obedience to the law; rather, obedience to the law is an expression of our salvation (see Romans 6:15-22).

2. Jesus Rejects Pharisaic Interpretation of the Law (vv. 21-22, 27-28, 31-35, 38-39, 43-44)

Jesus calls on true believers to demonstrate a righteousness that surpasses the righteousness of the Pharisees. The phrases "You have heard" and "it has been said" do not refer to the teachings of Moses and the prophets, but rather to the imbalanced interpretations of the scribes and the Pharisees. The Old Testament prophets spoke for the Lord and began their pronouncements with the phrase, "This is what the Lord says" (see 2 Samuel 7:5; Isaiah 56:1). Jesus, on the other hand, did not simply quote God as instructed, He spoke with the authority of God. In His discussion of the futile religious system of the Pharisees, Jesus gives six examples of how the Pharisees failed to fulfill the law and how believers are to succeed in fulfilling it.

In the first example, Jesus quotes the sixth commandment: "Thou shalt not kill" (Matthew 5:21; cf. Deuteronomy 5:17). The law said that any person who took the life of another would forfeit their life in return (Leviticus 24:17) and then be subject to eternal judgment (Matthew 5:21b). To the scribes and Pharisees, the act of killing meant the actual taking of a life. But Jesus says that anything leading to murder is wrong. Not only must the act of murder be avoided, but the attitudes and emotions that lead to it are condemned. The physical act of murder is simply the last step in the process that began with envy, greed, anger, hatred, or fear.

The second issue Jesus confronts is again taken from the Ten Commandments: "Thou shalt not commit adultery" (Matthew 5:27; cf. Deuteronomy 5:18). He clarifies the meaning by saying, "But I say unto you, That whosoever looketh on a woman to lust after her hath committed adultery with her already in his heart" (Matthew 5:28). The word *adultery* means marriage breaker; it refers to the breaking of one's covenant vows. Before Jesus explained the true meaning of the law, people believed they could remain true to their spouses by refraining from the physical act while entertaining tantalizing fantasies of illicit relationships.

The "look" that Christ condemns here is not the sudden notice of a person's attractiveness or the sudden thought that Satan may bring to a person's mind. This lustful look is the approval of an immoral thought or desire. It is the unresisted and contemplated desire for sexual pleasure that leads to the physical act of adultery. Therefore, the sin actually begins with the thought and ends with the act.

After explaining how a person breaks the marriage vow through adultery, Jesus turns His attention to the subject of divorce. The Israelites were highly respected by the pagan nations of their day, who divorced in high numbers because of their low view of marriage. But even the Jews made ridding oneself of an unwanted wife a fairly simple process. . .all any husband (not wife) had to do was write a bill of divorcement charging the wife with uncleanness (see Deuteronomy 24:1).

Jesus argues that any man who divorces his wife for any cause except immorality "causeth her to commit adultery: and whosoever shall marry her that is divorced committeth adultery" (Matthew 5:32). Jesus squarely places the onus for the adul-

tery on the divorcing husband. He "causes" her to commit adultery. By divorcing her, the husband is forcing her to break the marriage vow. Later, Jesus would expand on this teaching to include the divorcing husband in the adultery: "Moses permitted divorce as a concession to your hard-hearted wickedness, but it was not what God had originally intended. And I tell you this, a man who divorces his wife and marries another commits adultery unless his wife has been unfaithful" (19:8-9, NLT). The institution of marriage is the spiritual fusion of two people (male and female) into one. Jesus argues that this fusion is permanent.

The next issue Jesus confronts is the need for basic honesty. The Old Testament strongly condemned false oaths (Exodus 20:7; Leviticus 19:12), but the Pharisees made distinctions between oaths that had to be kept and those that did not. Jesus condemned all oaths. God expects honesty from His people, so swearing and oath taking become unnecessary. Jesus said, "Just say a simple, 'Yes, I will,' or 'No, I won't.' Your word is enough" (Matthew 5:37, NLT). If we are known as truthful people, then our word alone should suffice (see James 5:12).

The "law of retaliation" (Matthew 5:38; cf. Exodus 21:24) was never meant to encourage revenge. In fact, the purpose of the law was to place limits on those seeking justice. The "law of retaliation" was a vast improvement over the old way of thinking, which held that if you hurt my family or me, I could take any extreme action against you. The law limits retaliation to the injury sustained. However, Jesus takes the law to a higher level: "But I say unto you, that ye resist not evil: but whosoever shall smite thee on thy right cheek, turn to him the other also" (Matthew 5:39). He encourages believers to imitate God, who returns good for evil. The words of Jesus are not necessarily to be taken literally. What He wants us to do is to meet reproach with restraint and to go out of our way to do good to those who have hurt us.

The final issue Jesus deals with in this teaching on the fulfillment of the law is the issue of love. Believers are most like God when we exercise unmerited love. It is easy to love those who are our friends. Jesus said, "even corrupt tax collectors do that much" (v. 46, NLT). The true test of Christian maturity is the ability to love a stranger or an enemy who has done you wrong. Believers are to be like Christ, who demonstrated the idea of love as He hung on the Cross and prayed for those who had put Him there (Luke 23:34). He commands His followers to do the same, "But I tell you, love your enemies! Pray for those who persecute you!" (Matthew 5:44, NIV).

SEARCH THE SCRIPTURES

1. What did Jesus say would pass away before even the smallest detail of the law would be made void (Matthew 5:18)?

2. What emotion did Jesus compare to murder (v. 22)?

3. How is it possible to commit adultery without actually engaging in illicit sex (v. 28)?

4. How should believers respond to people who have wronged them (v. 44)?

DISCUSS THE MEANING

1. It has often been stated by believers that the Old Testament Law no longer binds us, and this is true. Does this mean that the law is irrelevant to New Testament believers? If not, what part does it play in our lives?

2. Do you think that thinking about immoral sexual activity is just as bad as actually committing the act? If so, why? If not, why not?

LESSON IN OUR SOCIETY

Jesus challenges us to look at the motives behind our actions and thoughts. List several sins committed in today's society. What are some motives behind those sins? How are they anti-Christlike? How can we work to serve as examples of living according to Jesus' teachings?

MAKE IT HAPPEN

Take some time this week and review the six issues we studied. Pray and ask the Holy Spirit to reveal to you which of the areas you need to improve in. Then repent and ask God to help you grow in this area and make up your mind to do better. Be prepared to share your experience with the class next week.

FOLLOW THE SPIRIT

What God wants me to do:

_____

_____

REMEMBER YOUR THOUGHTS

Special insights I have learned:

_____

_____

MORE LIGHT ON THE TEXT

Matthew 5:17-18, 21-22, 27-28, 31-35, 38-39, 43-44

17 Think not that I am come to destroy the law or the prophets: I am not come to destroy, but to fulfil.

Jesus began His sermon with a description of the eight qualities that make up good Christian character. But before launching into the meat of His message, He prefaces what is about to follow. The preface is intended to prevent any misunderstanding of what He is about to say. Jewish teachers taught that flagrant disobedience to the law had the effect of abolishing it because disobedience was seen as rejection of the law's authority. Rebellion against the law was punishable by spiritual expulsion from the Jewish community. The charge of openly encouraging others to reject it would carry an even greater penalty.

Jesus did not oppose the law, but He opposed the deceptive interpretation of the law that emphasized following regulations over godly character. The Lord begins by explaining, "I am not come to destroy, but to fulfil." "Destroy" is used here in opposition to the word *fulfil*. "To destroy," from the Greek *katalyo*, means to bring to an end or abolish. "To fulfill," from the Greek *pleroo*, means to fully perform or to complete. It was not Jesus' intent to put an end to the law, because it was given as a system of legal statutes designed to facilitate government; a system of ceremonies designed to demonstrate the holiness necessary to approach God; and a system of types foreshadowing the kingdom of Christ.

Jesus fulfilled the legal requirements of the Law in His person by living a completely sinless life. He fulfilled the ceremonial requirements by offering His blood as a one-time sacrifice for all,

Jesus feeds His lambs and His sheep.

thus eliminating the need for periodic animal sacrifices and ceremonial practices that served as types. The writer of Hebrews explains it this way: "The law is only a shadow of the good things that are coming—not the realities themselves. For this reason it can never, by the same sacrifices repeated endlessly year after year, make perfect those who draw near to worship" (Hebrews 10:1, NIV). "When Christ came as high priest of the good things that are already here, he went through the greater and more perfect tabernacle that is not man-made, He did not enter by means of the blood of goats and calves; but he entered the Most Holy Place once for all by his own blood, having obtained eternal redemption" (9:11-12, NIV).

91

Regarding the prophets, the only way to destroy them would be to prevent the fulfillment of their predictions. Instead of coming to destroy either the law or the prophets, Jesus came to fulfill all the types of the law and all the unfulfilled predictions of the prophets.

18 For verily I say unto you, Till heaven and earth pass, one jot or one tittle shall in no wise pass from the law, till all be fulfilled.

The "jot" or *yod* (Heb.) was the smallest of the Hebrew alphabet—about the size of our apostrophe. The "tittle" was a little stroke of the pen used to distinguish the Hebrew letter *dalet* (d) from the letter *resh* (r). A good example of this is how we use a "tittle" in the center of the letter *e* to distinguish it from the letter *c*. This verse combined with verse 19 teaches both complete obedience to the law and the fact that it would remain in full force until Jesus completely fulfills it and demonstrates the precise accuracy of the prophets.

5:21 Ye have heard that it was said by them of old time, Thou shalt not kill; and whosoever shall kill shall be in danger of the judgment: 22 But I say unto you, That whosoever is angry with his brother without a cause shall be in danger of the judgment: and whosoever shall say to his brother, Raca, shall be in danger of the council: but whosoever shall say, Thou fool, shall be in danger of hell fire.

Although the law was to remain in force, Jesus called His disciples to move from external obedience to internal submission to the law written in their hearts. He begins by explaining some of the basic tenets of the law. The first principle He explains is the law against murder described in Exodus 20:13 and Deuteronomy 5:17. The Lord uses the phrase "Ye have heard" because most of the common people of His time knew the law only by its public reading and the exposition of the scribes that accompanied the readings. To them, the interpretation of the scribes carried the same authority as Scripture itself. The phrase "but I say" speaks with greater authority than other Jewish teachers and scribes claimed because they would generally cite another authority.

Jesus teaches that the external act of murder

results from an inner emotional state and describes three degrees of offense and three corresponding degrees of punishment. Silent rage, described as unjustified anger, was punishable by judgment. The Law of Moses provided for the appointment of judges (Deuteronomy 16:18). This tribunal was known as the judgment, and they were elders who determined the case of the manslayer (see Joshua 20:2-5). In determining the manslayer's case, the elders might confine the man in one of the cities of refuge or order him to be stoned to death.

The second degree was contemptuous speech, such as calling someone "Raca." This word is an expression of contempt of uncertain derivation thought to mean "empty-headed " or "spit out" (i.e., heretic). This internal act of murder was punishable by a trial before the Sanhedrin or council. The Sanhedrin was the chief court of the Jews, and common people held it in great awe.

The third degree was bitter reproach as evidenced by calling someone a "fool." To the Jews a fool is not a person who is mentally deficient but one who is morally perverse. David described the fool as being a corrupt person who does abominable deeds and no good works. Worst of all, he denies God in his heart (Psalm 14:1). The third punishment goes beyond human jurisdiction. It is the final punishment—being cast into hell. *Gehenna*, the Greek word for hell, is derived from the name Hinnom—a deep, narrow valley lying southeast of Jerusalem.

The Greek word *Gehenna*, which we translate as "hell," is first found in Joshua 18:16. It is the place where idolatrous people worshiped the god Molech by offering human sacrifice in the fires of Molech. Two Jewish kings (Ahaz, 2 Chronicles 28:3; and Manassah, 33:6) burned their children in the valley as sacrifices. This horrible practice of human sacrifice caused the valley to be associated in the mind of the Jews with sin and suffering and led to the application of its name which, in the Greek form, is the place of final and eternal punishment. Human sacrifice to Molech was entirely destroyed by King Josiah, who polluted the entire valley, making it unfit for even heathen worship.

The key to this passage is that while sin has stages, God takes note of it from the time it first begins to evolve in the heart, and a person's soul is put in danger long before his feelings bear their fruit of violence and murder.

5:27 Ye have heard that it was said by them of old time, Thou shalt not commit adultery: 28 But I say unto you, That whosoever looketh on a woman to lust after her hath committed adultery with her already in his heart.

Jesus returns to the Ten Commandments for his next teaching. As was the case with murder, Jesus again teaches against the thought which motivates the act. Lust, from the Greek *epithumo*, means to desire or long after. Therefore, the look of lust is a leering stare with immoral intent. The seedbed of sin is the heart, and the seed bag of the heart is the eye. Those who allow lustful leers to lead them to immoral imaginings and lustful desires are just as guilty before God as if they had committed the act.

5:31 It hath been said, Whosoever shall put away his wife, let him give her a writing of divorcement: 32 But I say unto you, That whosoever shall put away his wife, saving for the cause of fornication, causeth her to commit adultery: and whosoever shall marry her that is divorced committeth adultery.

In His next teaching, Jesus refers back to Deuteronomy 24:1, 3. Under Jewish law, adultery referred only to the woman's illicit behavior, not to the man's. Jesus' teaching on adultery (Matthew 5:28), where He specifically refers to the man's adultery, proves that He did not share or endorse their view. Because the specific law He is dealing with here refers to the woman, Jesus deals only with the issue of the wife.

The law of divorce permitted the husband to put away the wife when he found "some unseemly thing" in her. Jesus explained that the divorced woman is forced into a state of adultery. The mere fact of divorce did not make her an adulteress, but it brought her into a state of disgrace from which she invariably sought to free herself by contracting another marriage. This other marriage, which was due to her humiliating situation, drove her into a state of adultery.

Jesus explains that this law was given by Moses

on account of the hardness of the people's heart, i.e., to prevent greater evils (see Matthew 19:8). But here, Jesus limits the right of divorce to cases of fornication. "Fornication"—from the Greek *porneia*, from which we derive our English word "pornography"—refers to any type of sexual sin. In a marriage union, this fornication would be considered adultery.

It is implied that divorce for marital infidelity breaks the marriage bond, and it is therefore held almost universally that the innocent party to such a divorce can marry again. Of course, the guilty partner could not. No one is allowed by law to reap the benefits of his or her own wrongdoing.

33 Again, ye have heard that it hath been said by them of old time, Thou shalt not forswear thyself, but shalt perform unto the Lord thine oaths: 34 But I say unto you, Swear not at all; neither by heaven; for it is God's throne: 35 Nor by the earth; for it is his footstool: neither by Jerusalem; for it is the city of the great King.

It appears from Scripture (Leviticus 19:12; Numbers 30:2; Deuteronomy 23:21) that the law permitted oaths made unto the Lord. However, the Jews interpreted the law as giving them exemption from the binding effect of all other oaths. According to their interpretation, no oath was binding unless the sacred name of God was appealed to. So they invented many other oaths to suit their purposes, which would add weight to their statements or promises but would not leave them guilty of breaking the oath if they spoke untruthfully.

But Jesus showed that all oaths were ultimately referable to God, and that those who made them would be renounced if they did not keep them. To prevent this evil practice of loose swearing, Jesus lays down the prohibition, "Swear not at all." The Lord's injunction against swearing refers to making promises or giving one's word. With people of solid Christian character, a simple yes or no should suffice. There are some who refuse to take judicial oaths based on Jesus' teaching. However, judicial oaths were not included in the prohibition. This conclusion is reached when we interpret the prohibition in the light of Scripture as a whole. We find that God swore by himself

(Genesis 22:16-17; Hebrews 6:13; 7:21). The Lord Himself answered under oath before the Sanhedrin (Matthew 26:63).

5:38 Ye have heard that it hath been said, An eye for an eye, and a tooth for a tooth: 39 But I say unto you, That ye resist not evil: but whosoever shall smite thee on thy right cheek, turn to him the other also.

The "law of retaliation," as set forth in Leviticus 24:20 and quoted here by Jesus, referred to a legalized retribution that was enforced by a court. Old Testament law never permitted personal vengeance except in the case of a relative's murder (24:18-21). The law was designed to limit retaliation with a view to justice. However, the Pharisees misinterpreted the law as an encouragement for revenge.

Rather than revenge, Jesus taught nonresistance and gave an example of someone being struck on the cheek. The backhand blow to the right cheek was the most grievous insult possible. In fact, both Roman and Jewish law permitted persecution for this offense. Jesus' call to turn the other cheek is a call to a higher standard. The Lord is not speaking against proper justice for those who do evil, but rather is calling on His followers to love their enemies.

5:43 Ye have heard that it hath been said, Thou shalt love thy neighbour, and hate thine enemy. 44 But I say unto you, Love your enemies, bless them that curse you, do good to them that hate you, and pray for them which despitefully use you, and persecute you;

The law commanding love is found at Leviticus 19:18, while the sentiment "hate thy enemy" is not a precept of the law. However, the law forbade the Jews to make peace with the unrepentant Canaanites (Exodus 34:11-16; Deuteronomy 7:2; 23:6). Because they fought bloody wars with the

Canaanites at God's own command, they inevitably came to hate their enemies.

The command to love one's enemy appears to many persons to be impossible. The problem is they understand the word "love" as expressing the same feeling that is engendered by a friend or a near relative. However, love is much more than an emotion. It is best expressed by the action one takes on another's behalf. In this case, love may be best understood in the light of examples. The parable of the good Samaritan is given by Jesus for the express purpose of exemplifying it (Luke 10:35-37), as does Christ's own example in praying on the Cross for those who crucified Him.

DAILY BIBLE READINGS

M: Jesus Teaches About Blessings
Matthew 5:1-12

T: We Are to Obey God's Will
Matthew 5:13-20

W: A Teaching About Anger
Matthew 5:21-26

T: Teachings About Adultery and Divorce
Matthew 5:27-32

F: A Teaching About Taking Oaths
Matthew 5:33-37

S: A Teaching About Nonviolent Resistance
Matthew 5:38-42

S: A Teaching About Loving Enemies
Matthew 5:43-48

Jesus quotes from the Old Testament in Matthew 5. Find out where these quotes came from by clicking on the footnote numbers within these Bible verses on your *Precepts For Living* CD-ROM.

TEACHING TIPS

November 14
Bible Study Guide 11

1. Words You Should Know

A. Resurrection (1 Corinthians 15:42) *anastasis* (Gk.)—Rising or standing up again; to live again.

B. Corruption (v. 50) *phtora* (Gk.)—Indicates something that is decayed or perishing.

C. Sleep (v. 51) *koimao* (Gk.)—Indicates the dead or deceased.

D. The twinkling of an eye (v. 52) *rhipe* (Gk.)—Instantly or suddenly, as in the batting of an eye.

2. Teacher Preparation

A. Prepare for today's lesson by reading the DAILY BIBLE READINGS for each day leading up to the lesson.

B. Read 1 Corinthians 15 in its entirety to get the necessary background for this lesson.

C. Closely examine the FOCAL VERSES at least twice. Be sure to use different translations for each reading and read commentaries and footnotes included in your Bibles.

3. Starting the Lesson

A. Have the students read the KEEP IN MIND verse aloud and in unison.

B. Have the students review what they know about the apostle Paul and the Corinthian church.

C. Remind the students to write their ideas in the FOLLOW THE SPIRIT and REMEMBER YOUR THOUGHTS sections.

4. Getting into the Lesson

A. Read the LESSON AIM.

B. Have the students silently read the FOCAL VERSES; then ask two or three volunteers to read the FOCAL VERSES aloud from a more contemporary Bible version.

C. Ask for a volunteer to read the BACKGROUND section.

5. Relating the Lesson to Life

A. Read THE PEOPLE, PLACES, AND TIMES.

B. Have the students break into small groups and work on the DISCUSS THE MEANING questions.

C. Have each group assign a spokesperson who will report that group's response to the entire class.

6. Arousing Action

A. Have the students read the LESSON IN OUR SOCIETY section.

B. Ask volunteers to share any thoughts they may have jotted down in the FOLLOW THE SPIRIT and REMEMBER YOUR THOUGHTS sections.

C. Ask students to give specifics about how they can complete the MAKE IT HAPPEN section.

D. Close the class with prayer, using the KEEP IN MIND verse as the focus.

WORSHIP GUIDE

For the Superintendent or Teacher
Theme: A New Body
Theme Song: "The Solid Rock"
Scripture: 1 Corinthians 15:1-11
Song: "He Lives"
Meditation: Father God, we thank You for Jesus. We thank You for His resurrection that confirms for us that death will not have the final word in our lives.
Amen.

NOV 14TH

A NEW BODY

Bible Background • 1 CORINTHIANS 15
Printed Text • 1 CORINTHIANS 15:42-57
Devotional Reading • 1 CORINTHIANS 15:1-11

LESSON AIM

By the end of the lesson, the students should be able to explain the importance of resurrection to the Christian church and the importance of this belief as it relates to their own hope of resurrection.

KEEP IN MIND

"O death, where is thy sting? O grave, where is thy victory?" (1 Corinthians 15:55).

FOCAL VERSES

1 Corinthians 15:42 So also is the resurrection of the dead. It is sown in corruption; it is raised in incorruption;

43 It is sown in dishonour; it is raised in glory; it is sown in weakness; it is raised in power:

44 It is sown in a natural body; it is raised in a spiritual body. There is a natural body, and there is a spiritual body.

45 And so it is written, The first man Adam was made a living soul; the last Adam was made a quickening spirit.

46 Howbeit that was not first which is spiritual, but that which is natural; and afterward that which is spiritual.

47 The first man is of the earth, earthy: the second man is the Lord from heaven.

48 As is the earthy, such are they also that are earthy: and as is the heavenly, such are they also that are heavenly.

49 And as we have borne the image of the earthy, we shall also bear the image of the heavenly.

LESSON OVERVIEW

LESSON AIM
KEEP IN MIND
FOCAL VERSES
IN FOCUS
THE PEOPLE, PLACES, AND TIMES
BACKGROUND
AT-A-GLANCE
IN DEPTH
SEARCH THE SCRIPTURES
DISCUSS THE MEANING
LESSON IN OUR SOCIETY
MAKE IT HAPPEN
FOLLOW THE SPIRIT
REMEMBER YOUR THOUGHTS
MORE LIGHT ON THE TEXT
DAILY BIBLE READINGS

50 Now this I say, brethren, that flesh and blood cannot inherit the kingdom of God; neither doth corruption inherit incorruption.

51 Behold, I shew you a mystery; We shall not all sleep, but we shall all be changed.

52 In a moment, in the twinkling of an eye, at the last trump: for the trumpet shall sound, and the dead shall be raised incorruptible, and we shall be changed.

53 For this corruptible must put on incorruption, and this mortal must put on immortality.

54 So when this corruptible shall have put on incorruption, and this mortal shall have put on immortality, then shall be brought to pass the saying that is written, Death is swallowed up in victory.

55 O death, where is they sting? O grave, where is thy victory?

56 The sting of death is sin; and the strength of sin is the law.

57 But thanks be to God, which giveth us the victory through our Lord Jesus Christ.

IN FOCUS

Sharon forced herself to finish dressing. She knew that if she didn't hurry, she'd be late for the funeral at the church this morning. As lead usher, she knew it was her responsibility to make sure the other ushers were in place, hand out funeral programs, and seat guests. Her hands were shaking as she combed out her hair. Fred, the 24-year-old son of one of the church's long-time members, had been killed on Saturday night. Fred and two of his friends were racing their cars when his flipped over. The two passengers in Fred's car were still hospitalized, both in critical condition. Fred had been thrown from the car and died at the scene. Sharon knew that her small church would be packed. Fred came from a large family, and he had been a popular young man in high school and at the local community college. Although Fred's parents were faithful members, she had only seen Fred in church on Mother's Day. She had run into him several times outside of church and had even invited him to come and visit more often. He had always laughed and teased that he was too young for that "church stuff."

Sharon had ushered at enough funerals to know that there would be a lot of crying; that part she didn't mind. It was the screaming and having to restrain guests from throwing themselves into the casket that bothered her. While Sharon understood that grief was natural, the funerals of young people were always chaotic. She wondered what Pastor would say during the eulogy; he couldn't possibly have known Fred that well. How, she wondered, would he comfort Fred's family and friends?

THE PEOPLE, PLACES, AND TIMES

Corinth. Located about 40 miles west of Athens, the city of Corinth is the setting for Paul's first and second epistles to the Corinthians. Corinth was one of the most prominent cities of ancient Greece. Two major harbors leading into the city guaranteed that the world's commerce flowed through the city. During Paul's writings, Corinth was a bustling commercial center renowned for its bronzeware and pottery.

Corinth was equally renowned for its sensuality and immorality. The worship of the Greek goddess Aphrodite was commonly and widely practiced. A temple, complete with priestesses or prostitutes and dedicated to her worship, sat on a hilltop overlooking the city. Sensual and hedonistic behavior was so rampant in Corinth that the expression "to Corinthianize" came to mean promiscuous conduct. In his letter or epistle to

the church at Corinth, Paul refers to some of the ungodly practices that were taking place, including incest (1 Corinthians 5:1), frequenting brothels (6:9-20), and eating meals in pagan temples (8:10).

BACKGROUND

In Paul's letter to the Corinthian church, two things are immediately clear. First, Paul loves this church. Second, it is apparent that Paul knows the Corinthian church and the issues related to this particular body of believers. In earlier chapters, Paul lovingly yet firmly teaches the Corinthians about the carnal issues that plague this particular church. He emphasizes the importance of keeping the congregation morally clean. Paul was also keenly aware of and addresses the quarrelsome factions that existed in the Corinthian church. In his letter, he directly confronts the contention created by the cliques within the church and warns them of their potential to destroy the entire body.

Similarly, Paul confronts and admonishes the church's erroneous beliefs concerning the spiritual gifts. Spiritual gifts, Paul writes, were not to be used to impose hierarchy within the church, but rather to glorify God. Paul then proceeds to teach that while gifts are wonderful, they are to be exercised in love and that love is the fruit of the Holy Spirit. Paul now begins a critical area of teaching. It is not enough that the Corinthians believe in the virgin birth, ministry, and sacrificial death of Jesus, the Christ. Paul zeros in on the key element of the Gospel: the resurrection of Jesus. Without this belief, Jesus' birth, ministry, and even His death mean absolutely nothing.

In the ancient Greek and Roman world, there were several prominent philosophies regarding death and the afterlife. In this chapter, Paul clarifies that he is not teaching a spiritual resurrection, like the Stoics who taught that following death, the soul was merged with a deity. Paul makes it clear that Jesus "was delivered over to death for our sins and was raised to life for our justification" (Romans 4:25, NIV).

IN DEPTH

1. The Relevance of the Believer's Belief (1 Corinthians 15:42-43)

Bible scholars disagree on the exact nature of the Corinthian church's doubts concerning the Resurrection. Some argue that some Corinthians held that there was no such thing as resurrection. Still others think that the Corinthians held that Jesus Himself was not resurrected. And yet others believe that the Corinthians were at odds about the status of the believers who had already died and the ability of these believers to be raised from the dead at the return of Christ.

Paul's argument seems to more clearly address the latter two theories. Paul declares, "Now if Christ be preached that he rose from the dead, how say some among you that there is no resurrection of the dead?" (1 Corinthians 15:12). Paul presses on, realizing that the stakes are enormous. If the Resurrection did not take place, then "your faith is vain; ye are yet in your sins" (1 Corinthians 15:17).

Paul is emphasizing that the Resurrection is the cornerstone, not simply a tenet, of Christian faith. If, he reasons, Christ died for their sins, but He was not resurrected, then the people have not been justified and Jesus' death was in vain. The heart of Paul's argument is that although human lives are subject to death and the body will disintegrate, decay, and decompose, that is not the end of the story. They are also subject to the will of God, who through His Son, Jesus Christ, will bring forth resurrection of the dead.

Therefore, after death there is continuity rather than a conclusion.

2. The Mystery of the Resurrection (vv. 44-54)

Next, Paul launches into the "mystery" of death that he obviously believes plagues these believers. Because of the sin of the first man, Adam, the "natural" bodies of all humankind are subject to death. However, praise be to God, because of the redemptive act of the "last Adam," Jesus Christ, believers now possess "spiritual" bodies. Paul asserts that these bodies are "incorruptible"; they are no longer subject to the laws of nature and the death penalty of sin. If believers were only subject to the inheritance of Adam, it would be fitting that we return to dust since it is through Adam's sin that mankind dies. However, through faith, believers are joined to Jesus Christ. The bodies of the believers, through their faith in Him, now bear "the image of the heavenly." It is these glorified "heavenly bodies" that are to be resurrected. Paul is clear that the nonbelievers are simply "flesh and blood" and as such "cannot inherit the kingdom of God." Part of this glorious inheritance is the resurrection!

3. Power Over Death (vv. 55-57)

Paul now addresses the opinion of some Corinthians that the believers who are "asleep," or who have died before Christ's return, have been lost. Paul explains that at the time of Christ's return, believers will be in different states: some dead, some still living. However, the result will be the same for all believers: "we shall all be changed." The change will be signaled by the sound of the "last trump" (trumpet). This signifies the final call of Christ Himself for His beloved to join Him. This image is mirrored by John when he writes, "I was in the Spirit on the Lord's day, and heard behind me a great voice, as of a trumpet" (Revelation 1:10). In that great moment when Jesus calls for the believers, the "living and the dead" will be changed to heed the trumpet call. In an instance, or the "twinkling of an eye," the resurrection will occur.

Paul reiterates that for the believer, death has no final say. Death is, at best, only a temporary state for the believers awaiting the glorious return of Jesus. At Christ's return, the believers will shed the mortal body and "put on immortality." The believer's freedom from sin (through Jesus Christ) also frees him from the penalty of sin, which is death.

Sadly, for the nonbeliever, death indeed claims the final "victory" and has the last word. Not so with the believer! Death has no "sting." It is not the final word. The victory is that the believer will have resurrected life through belief in Jesus, the Christ. Knowing this, we as believers must take more seriously and earnestly our commission to preach and teach Christ to a dying world.

SEARCH THE SCRIPTURES

Fill in the blanks.

1. "And so it is written, The first man Adam was made a _____ soul; the last Adam was made a quickening _____" (1 Corinthians 15:45).

2. "Now this I say, brethren, that _____and _____ cannot inherit the kingdom of God; neither doth corruption inherit incorruption" (v. 50).

3. "The _____of death is sin; and the _____ of sin is the law" (v. 56).

DISCUSS THE MEANING

1. In view of today's lesson, discuss whether or not you believe that mourning at funerals reflects a lack of "hope in the resurrection."

2. Discuss the difference between our "beliefs" and our "convictions."

3. What does it mean to "mourn in the hope of resurrection"?

LESSON IN OUR SOCIETY

Can you imagine knowing that one of the elevators in a 30-story office building does not work? Not only is the elevator inoperable, but when the door opens, the elevator car is missing! There is just an open shaft. Wouldn't most of us do everything possible to notify as many people as possible? Some of us would shout out warnings; others would run and place danger signs in the immediate vicinity. Some of us would even stand in front of the elevator doors, forcibly blocking the entrance so that unwitting passengers would not press the button, step forward, and drop to their deaths. In this situation, the danger is evident, and our responsibility to act quickly and decisively is clear. Why, then, do so many believers fail to act with speed and urgency when it comes to wit-

nessing to our friends and loved ones? Surely, we know that without Christ their lives will end in death. We know how to save them, yet we linger and hesitate. We concoct reasons not to use the opportunities to witness that occur regularly. We know that they will die unsaved, yet we remain quiet.

MAKE IT HAPPEN

This week, make a commitment to witness to someone about the love and saving power of Jesus Christ. No excuses! Don't concern yourself with what they will think of you. Remember that this is a life-and-death situation. Love them enough to share life with them! Perhaps you can start with a family member. Use any available opportunity to tell them about Jesus. Make it clear that without Jesus, there is no hope, only death.

FOLLOW THE SPIRIT

What God wants me to do:

_____

_____

REMEMBER YOUR THOUGHTS

Special insights I have learned:

_____

_____

MORE LIGHT ON THE TEXT

1 Corinthians 15:42-57

42 So also is the resurrection of the dead. It is sown in corruption; it is raised in incorruption.

The thrust of this section is to answer the question raised earlier in verse 35 with respect to how the dead are to be raised. Using various examples from agriculture, the animal world, and the heavenly bodies, Paul explains one central point: the resurrection body is going to be different from the present body in four significant respects. First, the present body is sown (an agricultural metaphor for death/interment) as perishable, from the Greek *phthora* (**fthor-ah**), but it will be raised imperishable. Contrary to Greek thought that regards all bodies as subject to decay, Paul says while the present body is subject to decay, the resurrection body is not going to be subject to decay though it is a body all the same.[1] Existence after resurrection is not going to be in a disembodied state.

1. Leon Morris, "1 Corinthians," *Tyndale New Testament Commentaries* (Leicester, England: Inter-Varsity Pres, 1995): 221.

43 It is sown in dishonour; it is raised in glory: it is sown in weakness; it is raised in power:

Since the present body is subject to decay, it follows naturally that it would be treated with dishonor. There is nothing honorable in the whole process of the body decaying. It is partly to reduce the dishonor that death brings to the present body that it is buried or cremated. But even this is a form of dishonor as it is actually getting rid of the body. In the Old Testament, the corpse is regarded as something capable of defiling (Numbers 19:11).[2] So people try to avoid contact with a corpse, which in itself is a dishonor to the dead body. For example, you never see an auto dealer displaying in his showroom a 20-year-old, rusty truck that no longer runs. That belongs in the junkyard. That is how we treat anything that is decaying; and the same is no less true of our present body in spite of the colossal amount we spend on cosmetics.

At resurrection the saints will assume a glorious body that is no longer subject to the dishonor of the present body because the resurrection body will not be capable of decay. All the dishonor that attends this present body will not affect the resurrection body because death will have no power over it. Instead, the resurrection body is going to be an honorable body. In this state it is going to be comparable to the glorified body of Christ after He was raised from the dead (Ephesians 3:21).[3] The resurrection is a divine act. As such it is characterized by the glory typical of such divine acts as Christ's Resurrection (Romans 6:4).

The present body is subject to weaknesses of various kinds, such as fatigue, hunger, diseases, pain, and death. In its present state this body is limited by time and space. It is not a body designed to endure for eternity or to transcend material barriers. The reality of our present body's weakness confronts us daily in our experience of pain, suffering, and death. This physical weakness will be a thing of the past as far as the resurrection body is concerned. When God raises

the saints at the resurrection of the dead, He is going to bless them with a powerful body that is no longer subject to physical weaknesses and limitations. The resurrection body will not know weariness, hunger, disease, or death. Food will be eaten not for hunger, but for pleasure and table fellowship, as was the case with Jesus (John 21:12-14).

2. Ibid., 222.

3. Albert Barnes, "1 Corinthians," *Barnes' Notes on the New Testament* (Grand Rapids, Mich. Kregel Publications, 1980): 314.

44 It is sown a natural body; it is raised a spiritual body. There is a natural body, and there is a spiritual body.

The word translated as "natural" is psuchikos (**psoo-khee-kos**). Depending on the context, it describes the immaterial, natural, or physical part of humanity. Here it contrasts with that which is spiritual and seems to refer to some quality in the material body which is able to adapt to life in the physical world.[4] The resurrection body is "spiritual" (*pneumatikos*, **pnyoo-mat-ik-os**) and refers to that quality of the resurrection body, which is able to exist in the heavenly realm. There is a realm for physical (natural) existence, and there is another for spiritual existence. Each realm has a distinct body fashioned for it, just like each season has its own clothing.

4. Morris, "1 Corinthians," 223.

45 And so it is written, The first man Adam was made a living soul; the last Adam was made a quickening spirit.

Here Paul quotes Genesis 2:7 to support his argument concerning the physical and spiritual distinctions between the present body and the resurrection body. The first Adam became a living soul and thereby represents the source of this present body that is subject to all kinds of suffering and pain. God created Adam's body directly, while the rest of humanity inherited the same kind of body through its descent from Adam. Jesus, on the other hand, is identified as the last Adam, who was made a life-giving Spirit. Jesus is not just a living Spirit, but a life-imparting Spirit.[5]

The word used to qualify "spirit" is *zoopoieo* (**dzo-op-oy-eh-o**), which, as a verb, literally means "to make alive." In contrast to the first Adam, Jesus is the life-giving source of the spiritual body in which saints are raised at the resurrection. So, just as the two sources are different, so also are the qualities of both bodies different.

5. Marvin R. Vincent, *Vincent's Word Studies in the New Testament* (Peabody, Massachusetts: Hendrickson Publishers, Inc., 1985): 284.

46 Howbeit that was not first which is spiritual, but that which is natural; and afterward that which is spiritual.

In order not to confuse the distinction between the first and last Adams, Paul further clarifies the question of what body derives from which source. This clarification is probably called for in light of Philo's misunderstanding of the creation narratives in Genesis 1 and 2. Philo was a Jewish philosopher whose teaching was current in the first century A.D. He taught that Genesis 1:27 refers to the creation of the "heavenly man," while Genesis 2:7 refers to the creation of the "earthly man." Paul, however, reverses the order and says Genesis 2:7 refers to the first Adam, who is the source of the body that is sown. Apparently for Paul, Genesis 1:27 does not refer to Christ, the last Adam. It is important not to confuse the order so Christ is not seen as the source of a body that is subject to decay and dishonor.

47 The first man is of the earth, earthy: the second man is the Lord from heaven.

This verse continues to contrast the present body with the resurrection body. The contrast here is based on the source of the substance that constitutes each body. The first man not only belongs to this world, but was also made of earthy substance. The word "earthy" (*choikos,* **kho-ik-os**) denotes that which is made from the soil or the earth and is therefore substantially of this world. The second man, however, is from heaven, and so is the substance of the body that derives from Him. We see, then, that the resurrection body is distinct from the present body by virtue of its heavenly substance as opposed to the earthly substance of our present body.

48 As is the earthy, such are they also that are earthy: and as is the heavenly, such are they also that are heavenly.

Paul is here introducing the principle of consistency in his explanation. A derivative cannot be different from its source. Since our present bodies derive from that of the first man, which was made from the soil of the earth, it follows that our bodies too will share all the characteristics of their earthly source. In the same manner, the resurrection body that awaits the saints will share all the superior qualities of its heavenly prototype borne by Christ. As Christ is in His resurrection body, so shall Christians be when they assume their resurrection body after death. In Christ we have a great hope that transcends death!

49 As we have borne the image of the earthy, we shall also bear the image of the heavenly.

Again Paul continues to highlight the principle of consistency. Just as Christians fully share all aspects of the Adamic image, so will they also share all aspects of Christ's bodily image. The word translated as "image" (*eikona,* **i-kone**) can denote, figuratively, a representation of an original, or literally, an exact replica of the original. The literal meaning seems to fit the context better. Just as we bear the exact replica of post-fall Adam in terms of his being subject to pain, suffering, and death, so shall we bear the exact replica of Christ's resurrection body in terms of its victory over pain, suffering, and death. Thus, as surely as believers bear this corruptible body with all its disadvantages, so shall they bear the incorruptible body from heaven with all its privileges.

50 Now this I say, brethren, that flesh and blood cannot inherit the kingdom of God; neither doth corruption inherit incorruption.

Paul declares here why it is essential for there to be a resurrection body. The present body, in its composition of flesh and blood, is not made for the kingdom of God. The expression "flesh and blood" figuratively refers to the entire physical part of humanity. The phrase is also used in the New Testament to emphasize the material and weak substance of which humanity is made, in contrast to the immaterial and superior makeup of angels. It was to this end that Paul warned the Ephesians that "our struggle is not against flesh and blood, but against...spiritual forces of evil in the heavenly realms" (Ephesians 6:12, NIV). Jesus describes Peter's confession of His Messiahship as from God rather than "flesh and blood," thereby suggesting the limitation of "flesh and blood" (Matthew 16:17). Given its limitations, the present body cannot inherit the kingdom of God. This present body is deemed corruptible and therefore not compatible with the eternal nature of the kingdom of God.

51 Behold, I shew you a mystery; We shall not all sleep, but we shall all be changed,

Paul makes known a mystery to his audience. A mystery (*musterion*, **moos-tay-ree-on**) in Scripture refers to a fact hidden from men until divinely revealed. The mystery here is the fact that some saints will be alive at the second coming of Christ. The bodies of both the living and dead believers are subject to decay and must be changed at the second coming of Christ. Believers will exchange their present bodies, dead or alive, for an imperishable body fitted for eternity. It is like trading an old, rickety car for a brand new model! For the believer, death is compared to sleep (*koimao*, **koy-mah-o**) from which the subject is expected to wake up. Death of the body is not the final end of man, nor annihilation of the self. It is like a comma and not a period in a sentence.

52 In a moment, in the twinkling of an eye, at the last trump: for the trumpet shall sound, and the dead shall be raised incorruptible, and we shall be changed.

The thrust here is the rapidity with which the bodies will be changed. The word "moment" is translated as the Greek word *atomos* (**at-om-os**), which refers to an atom of time—the smallest indivisible unit of time. That is to say, the change from this perishable body to the imperishable will take place in no time. It will be quite unlike the extreme makeover one sees on TV, which takes weeks. The change will be signaled by the sound of the last trumpet at Christ's Second Coming. Dead believers will be first to assume the imperishable body, and then those who are alive will

exchange their perishable body for the imperishable.

53 For this corruptible must put on incorruption, and this mortal must put on immortality.

This verse emphasizes the necessity of a change from this corruptible and mortal body to an incorruptible and immortal body. The superior quality of existence in the hereafter necessitates a body suitable for that environment. The concept of "put on" should not be misconstrued to mean the incorruptible is used only to cover the corruptible like a garment. There is going to be a total replacement of the corruptible by the incorruptible. The self is the only part of the person that will remain constant.

54 So when this corruptible shall have put on incorruption, and this mortal shall have put on immortality, then shall be brought to pass the saying that is written, Death is swallowed up in victory.

Paul shows that this change of a corruptible for an incorruptible body was anticipated in Isaiah 25:8. Its occurrence will therefore fulfill Scripture. It is in their future incorruptible bodies that believers will celebrate their ultimate victory over death; but until then, the struggle continues with physical death as an enemy of the believer. So, the believers who have died will be clothed with incorruptible bodies in which they will celebrate their final victory over death. They will have the last laugh—not death.

55 O death, where is thy sting? O grave, where is thy victory?

In a somewhat festive mood, Paul quotes Hosea 13:14 in a song. He asks rhetorically of the present sting and victory of death. These will be no more as far as the new body is concerned. Right now, this body is subject to the pain of death, and barring the coming of Christ it also faces defeat by death. But both the pain and victory of death will be done away with by the incorruptible bodies that await believers. Paul did not have to wait to put on the incorruptible body to celebrate its victory, and neither do we. While still in this corruptible body we can live in a manner that celebrates our anticipated victory over this body.

56 The sting of death is sin; and the strength of sin is the law.

In order for death to begin its deadly effect on us, it has to first sting us with sin. Once we have been poisoned with sin, we become subject to death. It is like a venomous snake that first injects its venom into its victim and then waits for it to become unconscious before consuming it. Death works its destruction in us through our sinful nature. Sin, on the order hand, is empowered to enslave us because of the Law. For sin is the transgression of the Law. Death infects us with sin; and having been infected with sin, we become sinners who sin naturally by transgressing the Law of God. Death works its destruction in us through sin and the Law.

57 But thanks be to God, which giveth us the victory through our Lord Jesus Christ.

Having described the means whereby death became victorious over us, Paul ends with thanksgiving to God, who has not abandoned us to the mercy of death, but grants us the victory over death. This victory was won on the Cross by our Lord Jesus Christ and is given to us as a gift by God. Those who accept Him as Lord are assured of victory over death through the incorruptible body that awaits them at the Second Coming of Christ.

DAILY BIBLE READINGS

M: Paul Reviews the Resurrection Tradition
1 Corinthians 15:1-11

T: Doubts Concerning Resurrection
1 Corinthians 15:12-19

W: The Significance of Christ's Resurrection
1 Corinthians 15:20-28

T: Arguments to Support Belief in Resurrection
1 Corinthians 15:29-34

F: Paul Deals With Physical Resurrection
1 Corinthians 15:35-41

S: Paul Explains the Spiritual Body
1 Corinthians 15:42-50

S: Have Confidence in the Resurrection
1 Corinthians 15:51-58

Gain a deeper understanding of 1 Corinthians 15:42-57 by contrasting the difference between perishable and imperishable using the reference tools in your *Precepts For Living* CD-ROM.

TEACHING TIPS

November 21
Bible Study Guide 12

1. Words You Should Know

A. Constraineth (2 Corinthians 5:14) *sunecho* (Gk.)—To control, bind, or hold fast; to be under the influence of.

B. Reconciled (v. 18) *katallasso* (Gk.)—God taking our sin upon Himself and establishing a relationship of peace with mankind.

2. Teacher Preparation

A. Look up the terms in the WORDS YOU SHOULD KNOW section in a Bible dictionary for further clarity.

B. As you study the lesson, take note of questions you may have, words you do not know the meaning of, and concepts that are not clear. Take time this week to find the answers to your questions. You may need to talk to someone; or if your church has a teacher's training meeting, be sure to ask your questions then.

3. Starting the Lesson

A. Ask each student to offer a sentence prayer for understanding of this lesson.

B. Ask two or three students to read the FOCAL VERSES loudly and expressively. You might also want them to read the passages again in a modern translation.

4. Getting into the Lesson

A. Read the IN FOCUS section of the lesson. Ask the students if they have ever had to be a peacemaker or do any conflict resolution. Help them to see that each day we may be challenged in that way.

B. Put the AT-A-GLANCE outline on the board and read it over.

C. Go over the WORDS YOU SHOULD KNOW, and read BACKGROUND and THE PEOPLE, PLACES, AND TIMES.

D. Allow the students to do the SEARCH THE SCRIPTURES questions on their own, and then discuss them together. Incorporate the DISCUSS THE MEANING questions into your discussion.

5. Relating the Lesson to Life

A. Read the LESSON IN OUR SOCIETY section. Ask the students how many of them set goals or make New Year's resolutions. In general, what has the outcome been—good or bad?

6. Arousing Action

A. Read the KEEP IN MIND verse.

B. Read the MAKE IT HAPPEN section. Discuss the three ways to deal with the flesh. Then give the class time to fill in what they plan to do.

WORSHIP GUIDE

For the Superintendent or Teacher
Theme: A New Creature in Christ
Theme Song: "Have Thine Own Way Lord"
Scripture: 2 Corinthians 5:11-21
Song: "Thank You Lord"
Meditation: Lord, thank You that You have made peace with us through Your Son, Jesus. And thank You for our salvation and new life in Christ and for this ministry of reconciliation. Amen.

A NEW CREATURE IN CHRIST

Bible Background • 2 CORINTHIANS 5:11-21
Printed Text • 2 CORINTHIANS 5:11-21
Devotional Reading • 2 CORINTHIANS 4:16—5:5

LESSON AIM

By the end of the lesson, the students should be better able to articulate what Paul is talking about when he says we are to be reconciled to God and become ministers of reconciliation. Also, they should be motivated to help others do the same.

KEEP IN MIND

"Therefore if any man be in Christ, he is a new creature: old things are passed away; behold, all things are become new" (2 Corinthians 5:17).

FOCAL VERSES

2 Corinthians 5:11 Knowing therefore the terror of the Lord, we persuade men; but we are made manifest unto God; and I trust also are made manifest in your consciences.

12 For we commend not ourselves again unto you, but give you occasion to glory on our behalf, that ye may have somewhat to answer them which glory in appearance, and not in heart.

13 For whether we be beside ourselves, it is to God: or whether we be sober, it is for your cause.

14 For the love of Christ constraineth us; because we thus judge, that if one died for all, then were all dead:

15 And that he died for all, that they which live should not henceforth live unto themselves, but unto him which died for them, and rose again.

16 Wherefore henceforth know we no man after the flesh: yea, though we have known Christ after the flesh, yet now henceforth know we him no more.

LESSON OVERVIEW

LESSON AIM
KEEP IN MIND
FOCAL VERSES
IN FOCUS
THE PEOPLE, PLACES, AND TIMES
BACKGROUND
AT-A-GLANCE
IN DEPTH
SEARCH THE SCRIPTURES
DISCUSS THE MEANING
LESSON IN OUR SOCIETY
MAKE IT HAPPEN
FOLLOW THE SPIRIT
REMEMBER YOUR THOUGHTS
MORE LIGHT ON THE TEXT
DAILY BIBLE READINGS

17 Therefore if any man be in Christ, he is a new creature: old things are passed away; behold, all things are become new.

18 And all things are of God, who hath reconciled us to himself by Jesus Christ, and hath given to us the ministry of reconciliation;

19 To wit, that God was in Christ, reconciling the world unto himself, not imputing their trespasses unto them; and hath committed unto us the word of reconciliation.

20 Now then we are ambassadors for Christ, as though God did beseech you by us: we pray you in Christ's stead, be ye reconciled to God.

21 For he hath made him to be sin for us, who knew no sin; that we might be made the righteousness of God in him.

IN FOCUS

Tamika, a young attractive mediator, led her colleagues from the Office of Dispute Settlement through a valley of picket signs and angry chants. The bitter strike was in its sixth month. Tamika began to ease her jittery feelings by silently reciting Psalm 23.

Once inside the factory, she offered her hand to the union leader, Mr. Dunbar—a young athletically built man. He seemed to hold her hand a few seconds too long and in an inappropriate way. She thought the verse. "I will fear no evil, for you are with me. Your rod and staff comfort me." He surprised her again after releasing her hand by briefly touching her

NOV
21ST

cheek with the tips of his fingers. Smiling, his outrageous behavior continued when he sarcastically introduced the plant owner, Mr. Goens, as the greediest man in Iowa. Tamika was taken completely off guard, and she knew her colleagues were gauging her response. She collected herself and said, "Well, we better sit down so we can get down to business."

The 12 men and women took their seats at the long, sleek negotiating table, and Tamika called to mind that her job was to help both parties get a better understanding of each other. As she took her seat at the head of the table, she thought of how she would have stacked the bargaining chips against Mr. Dunbar for his crudeness. However, recently she had strengthened her belief in her Christian walk, and her spiritual eyes let her focus on the bigger picture of the men and women on the picket line who were risking their jobs in the name of fairness.

Taking a deep breath, Tamika began to address the two adversaries at her right and left hand. "Mr. Dunbar, Mr. Goens, I assure you both that I come as an unbiased peacemaker in this dispute." Then looking directly into Mr. Dunbar's eyes she added, "I am a woman of God and believe God called me to this role." Never taking her eyes off Mr. Dunbar, she let her voice rise slightly saying, "Please govern yourselves accordingly."

Mr. Dunbar lowered his eyes and said, "I understand." With that the negotiations started.

We are to be a reconciler and an encourager of peace between men and God. This lesson examines our job description.

THE PEOPLE, PLACES, AND TIMES

False Teachers. Those who "glory in appearance, and not in heart" (2 Corinthians 5:12) were false preachers (2:17) who were concerned only about prestige in this world. They were preaching the Gospel for money, while Paul and his companions were preaching out of concern for eternity.

An Ambassador. An official representative from one country to another. As believers, we are Christ's ambassadors sent with His message of reconciliation to the world.

Life Application Study Bible. Wheaton: Tyndale House Publishers, 1997. 2036.

BACKGROUND

The apostle Paul was in Ephesus when he wrote 1 Corinthians. He expected Timothy to visit Corinth and then return to him with a full report of the activities of the Corinthian church. Timothy apparently brought Paul a report of the opposition that had developed against him in Corinth. After hearing the news, Paul made a brief and painful visit to the Corinthians. Upon returning to Ephesus, the apostle regretfully wrote the sorrowful letter of 1 Corinthians to urge the church to discipline the leaders of the opposition. Titus carried this letter.

Paul, anxious to learn the results, went to Troas and then to Macedonia to meet Titus on his return trip. Paul was greatly relieved by Titus's report that the majority of Corinthians had repented of their rebelliousness. However, a minority opposition persisted, which was led by a group of Judaizers.

While in Macedonia late in A.D. 56, Paul wrote a second letter (2 Corinthians) and sent it with Titus and another brother. Paul then made a third trip to Corinth in A.D. 58, where he wrote the letter to the Romans.

AT-A-GLANCE

1. Motivated by Christ
(2 Corinthians 5:11-13)
2. New Creatures in Christ (vv. 14-17)
3. Ambassadors for Christ (vv. 18-21)

IN DEPTH

1. Motivated by Christ (2 Corinthians 5:11-13)

The Corinthian church had been swayed by false teachers who had stirred the people against Paul. This negative campaign started after Paul wrote 1 Corinthians, which called for serious disciplinary action in the congregation. In the first part of 2 Corinthians, Paul attempts to defend his apostolic conduct and character and speaks out harshly against these false teachers.

Paul's false accusers had produced doubt toward him in the minds of the Corinthian believers. They had questioned his sincerity and his motives. Paul's response is to stress that one day he and all believers would appear before the judgment seat of Christ and give account of their actions done in the body (5:10). Paul says, "Knowing therefore the terror of the Lord, we persuade men; but we are made manifest unto God; and I trust also are made manifest in your consciences" (v. 11). Paul explained that he was not operating out of impure motives, but from a solemn sense of responsibility before God.

Paul goes on to say that he was not attempting to brag or boast. He was simply answering the lies the false teachers were spreading about him. These Judaizers wanted to enrich themselves, and they spread the Gospel for selfish gain.

2. New Creatures in Christ (vv. 14-17)

Paul wanted the congregation in Corinth to be convinced that he and his coworkers in the Gospel were motivated by their love for Christ and what He had done for them on Calvary.

Paul clearly understood that since they were identified with Christ in His death, they were now dead to their old life. The old unregenerate man no longer dominated and caused them to do wrong. Christ now controlled their decisions and behavior. Paul had no desire to please or promote himself; he had dedicated his life to pleasing Christ, who died and rose again on his behalf. His entire purpose in life was wrapped up and tied to Jesus Christ.

His desire for the Corinthian Christians, and all Christians, was that they too would revel in Christ and actualize their identity in Him. Paul wanted them to wake up in the morning and commit all of their body members (organs) to Christ and spend every moment of their day in dedication to Him. As a result of their Christ-centered thinking, Paul believed that God's children would have a different way of looking at people. Carnal or fleshly ideas and attitudes would not prevail. Instead, the overflowing love of Christ would be foremost in the person's attitude and actions toward others.

Paul states that at one time he himself used to think of Christ in a carnal, fleshly way. He thought Jesus was merely a man. But once he became a Christian, his outlook totally changed. Paul states, "If any man be in Christ, he is a new creature: old things are passed away; behold, all things are become new (v. 17). How refreshing this news must have been for Paul, a former persecutor of believers. It is also evident that he hoped this truth would give the Corinthians a new perspective.

3. Ambassadors for Christ (vv. 18-21)

A new life in Christ is only possible when He works in us. Becoming a Christian means no longer trusting in religious activities and rituals (i.e., going to church, getting baptized, being good, following the Ten Commandments, etc.). If we are Christians, we have put our confidence in what Christ did on Calvary's Cross as the basis for our entrance into heaven. We stop trying to get there by our own efforts, and we place our lives in the hands of Jesus to deliver us to heaven.

When we put our confidence in Christ for our salvation, we are reconciled (or brought back) to God. Christ blots out the believers' sins and puts us in good standing with God. We can talk to God like we talk to a good friend. He is no longer our enemy, and our sins no longer keep us separated from Him.

Once we understand these truths, God will give us a desire to share this good news with others. We become His messengers to the world so that they too can have intimate fellowship with God. He desires to "be all" within us so that we can speak out to those who do not know Him and to those (believers and unbelievers) who do not understand Him.

Paul concludes this passage with the heart of the Gospel message: "For he hath made him to be sin for us, who knew no sin; that we might be made the righteousness of God in him" (v. 21). When we place our confidence in Christ and not in self-effort for salvation, a trade is instantly made. God gives us His righteousness and takes our unrighteousness.

SEARCH THE SCRIPTURES

Answer **True** or **False**.

1. Paul was writing to the Corinthian church in response to the accusations of false teachers. _____

2. The love of money controlled Paul. _____

3. In Christ, we are new creatures. _____

4. Becoming a Christian means to attempt to be a good person, make good decisions, and treat others kindly. _____

5. Once we become Christians, we are now ambassadors for Christ. _____

6. As believers in Christ, we have exchanged our sins for God's righteousness. _____

DISCUSS THE MEANING

1. Why do you think the false teachers were trying to discredit Paul?

2. What was Paul's motivation in ministry?

3. What does it mean to be a "new creature"?

4. What is the difference between trying to make it to heaven and trusting Christ to take us to heaven?

5. How have you been Christ's ambassador since you have become a Christian?

LESSON IN OUR SOCIETY

Conflicts prevail in our society. The nightly news is filled with reports of murders in the community, domestic violence, and disagreements in the workplace. Even in the Christian community, church splits are common. It seems to be part of human nature to disagree and fail to get along with one another.

How many people realize that their conflicts with others stem from their broken relationships with God?

MAKE IT HAPPEN

Years ago, there was a Christian play called *Your Arms Too Short to Box with God*. By the time the play was over, you found yourself agreeing with the title of the play. There is no way we can win a fight with the almighty, all-powerful God. However, each person is born with the selfish tendency to fight God. We come into this world wanting to oppose Him and to have our own way. Once we become Christians, a transformation occurs. We receive a new nature like Christ and we desire to do God's will, not our own. Yet many of us still seem to have our boxing gloves on.

What are you fighting God about? Why is it necessary for you to make peace with God before you can help someone else do the same thing?

FOLLOW THE SPIRIT

What God wants me to do:

_____

_____

REMEMBER YOUR THOUGHTS

Special insights I have learned:

_____

_____

MORE LIGHT ON THE TEXT
2 Corinthians 5:11-21

Paul's second epistle to the Corinthians was written as a result of some problems within the church, including a challenge to his apostleship and his authority. The challenge to his apostolic credentials is evident in chapters 10-13, but the theme of vindication of his ministry is apparent in the first nine chapters. In chapter 4, Paul discusses Christ, the theme of his ministry (4:1-7). He talks about the sufferings and trials that are prevalent in his ministry (4:8-15) and the things that motivate him to go on, in spite of his sufferings. These motives include the reward he looks forward to at the judgment, the wonder of being in Jesus' presence forever (5:1-10), the love of Christ demonstrated by his death (5:11-16), and the message of reconciliation with which he has been entrusted (5:17-21).

11 Knowing therefore the terror of the Lord, we persuade men; but we are made manifest unto God; and I trust also are made manifest in your consciences.

Verse 11 is connected with the previous thought in verse 10, which talks about standing in the presence of the Lord for judgment, where each person will receive what he or she is due from God according to their deeds, "whether . . . good or bad." The phrase "the terror of the Lord" means the fear of the Lord. The Greek word *phobos*, which means reverence, awe, or that which causes fear, is translated as "fear" 41 times in the New Testament and as "terror" 3 times (including Romans 13:3; 1 Peter 3:14).

The knowledge that he would stand before the throne of God to give account of himself prompts Paul to persuade men. What does Paul mean by the fear (or terror) of the Lord? At first glance, one might be tempted to interpret it as being afraid of God's anger. Such interpretation would only take into consideration the negative side of the judgment. However, neglecting the positive rewards, which occupy Paul's mind and the greater part of the argument (4:13—5:10), would be out of place. These rewards motivate Paul to continue in ministry in spite of his trials and sufferings (4:8-12).

The knowledge that "the Lord is to be feared" constitutes one of the most powerful reasons for Paul's zeal to persuade people to be reconciled to God. To "persuade" is the Greek word *peitho*, meaning to convince by argument. What does Paul, with others (fellow apostles or fellow workers), try to convince the people about? They are probably trying to convince them of the truth of the Gospel and the authenticity of their ministry. Paul tells them that his motives are pure (1:12) and his credentials and conduct as an apostle are sound (3:1-6; 4:1-6). Paul's goal is also to persuade them of his integrity in order to demonstrate the integrity of the Gospel.

Whether they approve of him personally does not seem to matter so much to Paul, since the Lord knows him (and his commitment to the Gospel). Paul states, "We are made manifest unto God." To "manifest" (Gk. *phaneroo*) is to make plain or apparent. Paul's conduct, motive, and apostleship for ministry are made plain before God. However, it is necessary that the Corinthians understand his apostolic status and conduct. Paul calls upon the believer's own conscience as their witness.

12 For we commend not ourselves again unto you, but give you occasion to glory on our behalf, that ye may have somewhat to answer them which glory in appearance, and not in heart. 13 For whether we be beside ourselves, it is to God: or whether we be sober, it is for your cause.

Paul insists that what he has been saying should not be interpreted as a way of soliciting their praise. Rather, it is intended first to be a source of joy and pride for the Corinthians; they are the testimony of Paul and his other workers (3:2). Second, it is intended to be a defense of his apos-

tleship against those who take pride in outward appearance, rather than purity of the heart.

These false teachers made a superficial claim of superiority over Paul based upon their Jewish orthodoxy (11:22). They claimed to have a greater revelation and vision than Paul (12:1-7). Their aim was to discredit Paul and his coworkers. Here, Paul reminds the Corinthians that they know him better. Consequently, they can take pride in him and are able to defend the genuineness and zeal of his ministry.

Paul defends his zeal for the Gospel and explains its purpose by stating, "it is to God." Although this verse is difficult to explain, a number of explanations have been given by different scholars. First, it is proposed that Paul's critics had accused him of being "out of his mind" because of his alleged esoteric teaching (Acts 26:24 ff.), rapturous experiences, and tireless work. A second suggestion is that Paul is referring to his experience of speaking in tongues (Gk. *glossolalia*) and having visions (Acts 22:17-21), which led some to say he was "beside himself." His only answer was, "it is for God" or "it is between God and me." The third proposal is that on occasion, the Corinthians had viewed Paul as having been carried away by excessive emotion. A fourth proposal is that his self-commendation is a sign of lunacy. The final suggestion is that, in Jewish eyes, Paul's conversion experience on the Damascus road is evidence of his madness. To all of these accusations, Paul says, "whether we be beside ourselves, it is to God." In other words, "if I am mad or not, it is to God's glory." However, he continues on to say, "Whether we be sober, it is for your cause." The word "sober" (Gk. *sophroneo*) means to be of sound mind or right mind (compare Mark 5:15; Luke 8:35; Romans 12:3; Titus 2:2-6; 1 Peter 4:7). In summary, Paul's thoughts are that it does not matter what accusations come when you are working in obedience for the glory of God. It is as if he is saying, "We are in our right minds; we are just carrying out the work of God. It is for God's glory and your own good and benefit that we do what we do."

14 For the love of Christ constraineth us;

because we thus judge, that if one died for all, then were all dead: 15 And that he died for all, that they which live should not henceforth live unto themselves, but unto him which died for them, and rose again.

In verses 14 and 15, Paul states clearly that it is the love of Christ demonstrated by His death and resurrection that motivates, or compels, them to serve Christ and the Corinthians. The thought of it also constrains them to persuade men to accept the Lord (v. 11). The word "constrain" (Gk. *sunecho*) is translated as "to urge" or "to press" (Acts 18:5).

Paul attributes the love of Christ as the compelling force for his ministry and conduct. This same Greek verb is used in Luke 12:50 about the compulsion Jesus felt to accomplish his mission. Paul gives two motives for his Christian service. The first is the knowledge of accountability to Christ (v. 11), and the second is the love of Christ shown by His death. Although Christ's death is sufficient for the salvation of all, only those who respond through repentance and faith can appropriate the benefits it offers. Those who have accepted the offer of salvation are now dead with Christ. This should impel them to live for Him and "no longer live for themselves" (v. 15, NIV).

They are no longer their own; they belong to Christ (compare 1 Corinthians 6:19), who not only died, but also rose again. The New Testament almost always links the death and resurrection of Christ because without the resurrection of Christ, His death is in vain and our salvation is senseless. Writing to the Romans, Paul says that as Christ was raised, so are we raised with Him into a new life (Romans 6:4; 7:6; Colossians 3:1-2, 10). The awareness of this fact is Paul's motivation to expend himself in serving Christ through his service to others (2 Corinthians 4:11-12; 12:15; compare Philippians 2:17; 1 Thessalonians 2:8).

16 Wherefore henceforth know we no man after the flesh: yea, though we have known Christ after the flesh, yet now henceforth know we him no more. 17 Therefore if any man be in Christ, he is a new creature: old things are passed away; behold, all things are become new.

The new life in Christ has transformed Paul, has given him a new perspective, and has changed him into a new creature. He no longer regards man, and especially Christ, with a worldly perception. He now has spiritual understanding. With the use of the Greek conjunction *hoste* (translated as "so" or "therefore") in verses 16 and 17, the apostle introduces the changes that union with Christ in His death and Resurrection brings in people's lives.

Paul ceased to judge people from a "worldly point of view." He no longer based his judgment on external appearances, but on the heart (v. 12). His previous views of race and nationality had changed. He regarded individuals primarily in terms of their spiritual status, rather than their nationality. The Jew-Gentile division no longer had any bearing on his life and conduct. What mattered now for Paul was the new relationship he enjoyed with Christ (see Romans 2:28-29; 1 Corinthians 5:12-13; Galatians 3:28; 6:10; Ephesians 2:11-22, etc.). It has affected his total outlook on life—his goals and aspirations. He was no longer guided by fleshly desire, but by the Spirit (see Philippians 3:1-10).

In verse 17, Paul makes a very categorical statement: "If any man be in Christ" (when anyone is united with Christ by faith), "he is a new creature" (he is re-created). There is a radical internal change that occurs when one becomes a believer. The new creation involves new principles of living, new moral ideas, and a new way of thinking. It also changes our relationships with people and our attitudes toward life and living. This transformation is the work of the Holy Spirit and is consistent with the Lord's teaching when He told Nicodemus, "You must be born again in order to enter the kingdom of God" (John 3:5-7).

When we become new creatures, "old things are passed away." What are the old things that pass away? Paul gives a long list in Galatians 5:19-21. These things can be summed up as the behavior of the old man or old nature. They are characterized by all types of sin and sinful desires that must be eradicated (see Romans 6:6-11; Ephesians 4:22; Colossians 3:9). The phrase "behold, all things are become new" adds emphasis to the already stated fact. This statement can be interpreted as "indeed, all things have become new."

18 And all things are of God, who hath reconciled us to himself by Jesus Christ, and hath given us the ministry of reconciliation; 19 To wit, that God was in Christ, reconciling the world unto himself, not imputing their trespasses unto them; and hath committed unto us the word of reconciliation.

The phrase "all this is from God" (v. 18, NIV) refers to the new attitude and perception of life (v. 16), as well as the new creation (v. 17). Paul attributes the changes that take place in man to God. God is the Author of the second creation (new birth), just as He is of the first (compare 4:6). This new creation is what Paul calls the work of grace (see Ephesians 2:8-10). The phrase "all things are of God" takes away any notion that salvation can be earned, or achieved, through human effort. This nullifies the notion that man's destiny is within himself. Our new creation is the result of our new relationship with God and is accomplished by Christ's death and Resurrection. It is a process of reconciliation. God initiates this process and carries it out Himself. Again, it is all God without man's effort or contribution. The phrase "by (i.e., through) Jesus Christ" means that Christ is the medium and source through whom the reconciliation is accomplished.

"Reconciled" is the Greek verb *katallasso,* meaning to change mutually, and is from the noun *katallage,* meaning to exchange, to restore to (divine) favor, atonement, or reconciliation. It communicates the idea of reestablishing a broken relationship between enemies and making peace between two or more opposing parties. God is both the offended party and the arbitrator/judge; man is the offender. God decides to reconcile with man without man's playing a part in it. He did this by sending His Son to die on behalf of man for man's redemption. This reconciliation, based on the love of God, constitutes the foundation for the new creation, where old things pass away and all things become new (v. 17). Being reconciled with God is removing that which stands in the way of a right relationship between God and man and restoring the broken relationship caused by sin (cf. Isaiah 59:2).

Continuing this concept, Paul adds that God also "hath given to us the ministry of reconciliation." Not only has our relationship with God been restored, but we have been given the ministry to bring about reconciliation to the world—to those not yet reconciled. Although Paul was referring to himself and his fellow workers, it is also true for all believers. We are now God's agents of reconciliation; as Paul calls it, we are God's "ambassadors" (v. 20).

Verse 19 emphasizes the concept and explains the process further. The statement "To wit (or "namely") "that God was in Christ, reconciling the world unto himself," reinforces and emphasizes the fact that God is the One who does the reconciling. Although it is all God's doing, God uses man as an instrument to spread "the word of reconciliation."

How did God reconcile us to Himself? The answer is found in the phrase, "not imputing their trespasses unto them." The word "imputing" (Gk. *logizomai*) means to take an inventory, to reckon, to count, or to put down into one's account. Paul says that in the process of reconciliation, God did not take into account how the world sinned against Him. Nor did He allow man's sinful nature to stand in the way of mending the broken relationship between Himself and the world. Although the world had offended Him through disobedience and rejection, He forgave anyway. Paul seems to say that God overlooked (without condoning) the sin of the world and offered forgiveness by giving His Son as a ransom (see Matthew 20:28; Hebrews 9:15). Because of our faith in the finished work of Christ on our behalf, God "hath committed unto us the word (message) of reconciliation." That message is the same as Christ's commission to His disciples (see Matthew 28:18-20; Mark 16:15-20; Acts 1:8) to proclaim the Good News of reconciliation.

20 Now then we are ambassadors for Christ, as though God did beseech you by us: we pray you in Christ's stead, be ye reconciled to God. 21 For he hath made him to be sin for us, who knew no sin; that we might be made the righteousness of God in him.

As proclaimers of the Good News, the "gospel of peace" (Ephesians 6:15), Paul says, "now then (therefore) we are ambassadors (Gk. *presbeuo*) for

Christ." We are duly appointed and official messengers—representatives of Christ, acting on His behalf. Paul implies, "It is as if God Himself were pleading to you through us (by our preaching) to receive the offer of reconciliation given through Christ's death." He also offers a direct invitation to the people to accept God's offer.

Using another word for plea, "we pray you," that is, "we implore or beg you," Paul exhorts the readers, on behalf of Christ, to allow the reconciliation God offers to take effect in them. This is a call for a response from man. The offer is there, but it must be appropriated with a positive response to be effective. Using the concept of banking: The check has been issued by God, but the recipient must cash it in order to receive the benefit.

What does Paul mean by the statement "for he hath made him to be sin"? A number of suggestions have been given. The first is that Christ was treated as if He were a sinner by becoming the object of God's wrath and bore the penalty and guilt of sin. This matches in some measure Paul's statement to the Galatians: "Christ hath redeemed us from the curse of the law, being made a curse for us" (3:13). This is an allusion based on the Old Testament law carrying the idea of substitution. The second suggestion has the notion of participation. In His incarnation, Christ took on human nature "in the likeness of sinful flesh" (Romans 8:3); thus, God made Him to be sin. The third concept deals with His becoming a sacrifice for sin (i.e. a sin offering). Christ was made to be sin—an Old Testament concept of sacrifice. By dying and by paying the covenant penalty for our sin, Christ identified with sinful human nature. He took upon Himself the consequences of sin on behalf of man. The sinlessness of Christ is echoed in 1 Peter 2:22 (compare Isaiah 53:9).

The last part of verse 21 declares God's reason for making Christ "to be sin," that is, "that we might be made the righteousness of God in him." This mystery is the Good News for all. God, through His love, laid on Christ the iniquity of us all (Isaiah 53:6) so "that we might be made the righteousness of God in [Christ]." Christ is identified with man's sin, and man is identified with God's righteousness.

The word "righteousness" (Gk. *dikaiosune*, which is also translated as "justification") means to have a right standing before God. Jesus took our sin and in exchange gave us His righteousness. Based on Christ's sacrificial death, God declares the believer justified, or righteous, in His sight. This mystery, together with the knowledge of the fear of God (2 Corinthians 5:11), the love of Christ (v. 14), and the message of reconciliation, motivates Paul and his fellow workers to continue in the ministry, in spite of all hardships (4:8 ff.). What is it that motivates you or hinders you in your Christian walk?

DAILY BIBLE READINGS

M: Christ's Ministers Act Boldly
2 Corinthians 3:12-18
T: Paul Serves for God's Glory
2 Corinthians 4:1-15
W: We Must Live by Faith
2 Corinthians 4:16—5:5
T: Serve God with Confidence
2 Corinthians 5:6-10
F: Paul Serves God Faithfully
2 Corinthians 5:11-15
S: Paul's Ministry of Reconciliation
2 Corinthians 5:16-21
S: Now Is the Day of Salvation
2 Corinthians 6:1-10

Why not review what you discovered about the word *new* by using your *Precepts For Living* CD-ROM in this lesson as you did earlier (in lesson six).

TEACHING TIPS

November 28
Bible Study Guide 13

1. Words You Should Know

A. Aliens (Ephesians 2:12) *apallotrioo* (Gk.)—To be shut out from fellowship and intimacy.

B. Fellowcitizens (v. 19) *sumpolites* (Gk.)—Those possessing the same citizenship as others.

2. Teacher Preparation

A. Read the background Scripture for the lesson. After you have studied the lesson, write your own definition of God's grace.

B. Before class begins, think of two or three famous people who are well-known for their self-glorification. Ask class members how they feel about such people. Should we boast about our accomplishments here on earth? Are there times when it is necessary to boast? Are there times when it is harmful to boast?

3. Starting the Lesson

Read the IN FOCUS story about Carl and Regina. Lead the class in a discussion of the difficulty of blending two previously independent groups, whether they be families, churches, or social groups. What are some ways to foster a sense of unity and harmony?

4. Getting into the Lesson

A. Pose the following question to your class: "What would you say to God if He asked you, 'Why should I let you into heaven'?"

B. After giving the class members sufficient time to respond, remind them that eternal life is granted to us only by the grace of God. Read John 3:16 aloud. Spend some time talking about the goodness and generosity of God in giving us His Son and the gift of eternal life.

5. Relating the Lesson to Life

A. Review the information about the temple at Jerusalem and circumcision in THE PEOPLE, PLACES, AND TIMES. What traditions or rituals exist in your church that may cause division if abolished or overlooked?

B. Give students an opportunity to answer the questions in SEARCH THE SCRIPTURES.

C. DISCUSS THE MEANING deals with the importance of being good disciples and being attentive to our responsibilities. Discuss, with compassion, why the Jewish Christians must have had difficulty giving up their traditions.

D. LESSON IN OUR SOCIETY focuses on the tendency of some believers to create disharmony within the fellowship based on rituals or doctrines. Why is it important for Christians to devote our time and attention to creating harmony, not discord?

6. Arousing Action

A. Ask class members to take an honest assessment of themselves. Ask each to consider if he or she has ever looked down on another Christian or church member because that person was a new believer or new member, like the Jews looked down upon the Gentiles.

B. From the instructions given in the MAKE IT HAPPEN section, create a "job description" for a good disciple, one who is a devoted worker in good standing.

C. Give class members an opportunity to complete the FOLLOW THE SPIRIT and REMEMBER YOUR THOUGHTS sections.

WORSHIP GUIDE

For the Superintendent or Teacher
Theme: A New Relationship
Theme Song: "Come We That Love the Lord"
Scripture: John 17:1-11, 20-23
Song: "Pass Me Not, O Gentle Saviour"
Meditation: Lord, thank You for the gift of salvation. I thank You for not waiting for me to earn my salvation. Instead, You have given it to me freely out of Your love for me.

NOV 28TH

113

A NEW RELATIONSHIP

Bible Background • EPHESIANS 2:11-21
Printed Text • EPHESIANS 2:11-21
Devotional Reading • EPHESIANS 2:4-10

LESSON AIM

By the end of the lesson, the students should demonstrate a greater appreciation for the fact that salvation is God's gift to all people.

KEEP IN MIND

"Now therefore ye are no more strangers and foreigners, but fellowcitizens with the saints, and of the household of God" (Ephesians 2:19).

FOCAL VERSES

Ephesians 2:11 Wherefore remember, that ye being in time past Gentiles in the flesh, who are called Uncircumcision by that which is called the Circumcision in the flesh made by hands;

12 That at that time ye were without Christ, being aliens from the commonwealth of Israel, and strangers from the covenants of promise, having no hope, and without God in the world:

13 But now in Christ Jesus ye who sometimes were far off are made nigh by the blood of Christ.

14 For he is our peace, who hath made both one, and hath broken down the middle wall of partition between us;

15 Having abolished in his flesh the enmity, even the law of commandments contained in ordinances; for to make in himself of twain one new man, so making peace;

16 And that he might reconcile both unto God in one body by the cross, having slain the enmity thereby:

17 And came and preached peace to you which were afar off, and to them that were nigh.

18 For through him we both have access by one

LESSON OVERVIEW

LESSON AIM
KEEP IN MIND
FOCAL VERSES
IN FOCUS
THE PEOPLE, PLACES, AND TIMES
BACKGROUND
AT-A-GLANCE
IN DEPTH
SEARCH THE SCRIPTURES
DISCUSS THE MEANING
LESSON IN OUR SOCIETY
MAKE IT HAPPEN
FOLLOW THE SPIRIT
REMEMBER YOUR THOUGHTS
MORE LIGHT ON THE TEXT
DAILY BIBLE READINGS

Spirit unto the Father.

19 Now therefore ye are no more strangers and foreigners, but fellowcitizens with the saints, and of the household of God;

20 And are built upon the foundation of the apostles and prophets, Jesus Christ himself being the chief corner stone;

21 In whom all the building fitly framed together groweth unto an holy temple in the Lord:

IN FOCUS

Carl and Regina embarked on a new married life. At the altar with their preteen children, they vowed in their hearts to love each as their own.

However, the weekend visits from Carl's children filled the house with resentment and clashes. Last evening was the worst. An argument over which television program to watch escalated into a pushing match between Carl's daughter, Kari, and Regina's daughter, Nicole, that resulted in a cut over Nicole's eye.

In bed, Regina whispered softly into Carl's ear, "You are favoring your children too much when they visit."

Carl shut his eyes tighter but understood where his wife was coming from. Without moving, he whispered back, "I feel so guilty about not being with them all the time. I never knew it would be so hard to blend our families." Kari's screaming voice from earlier drenched his thoughts.

Unable to sleep, Carl went to his knees in prayer and said, "God, show me how to resolve this conflict." Carl's answer came with the rising sun. After sharing with Regina, they brought the children together. Going from eye to eye, Carl told them, "God has made us one family and we will work to respect each other and please God from now on." He continued, "Each visit will start with us praying as a family."

Our lesson today will help us understand and appreciate our oneness within the Body of Christ.

THE PEOPLE, PLACES, AND TIMES

The Temple. The Temple at Jerusalem was made up of many courts. Paul focuses on the outer court, but there were really about four different courts. First, there was the outer court, where the Gentiles had to stay. A lot of money exchanging or selling took place in the outer court. Second was the court of the Jewish women. The women could only go as far as this court. Third was the court of the Israelites, where the Israelite men would go and offer up sacrifices. Forth was the inner court, called the "Holy Place" and containing the Holy of Holies. No one could go into the Holy of Holies but the high priest, and he could go in only once a year. Before he could enter, he had to undergo a cleansing ritual. The Holy of Holies was the place where God dwelled. It was separated from the rest of the temple by a curtain. The Gospels report that when Jesus was crucified, the curtain was torn.

McCalep, Dr. George O. *Growing Up to the Head.* Lithonia: Orman Press, 1997. 87-88.

Circumcision. The act of removing the foreskin of the male sex organ. In ancient Israel, it was a sign of the covenant applied to male children of natives, servants, and aliens on the eighth day of life. In the Jewish faith, it signified cleanliness. For adults, it was to be an external symbol of one's total and complete allegiance and devotion to Yahweh.

Initially, circumcision was performed by the father using a flint knife. In later times, specialists were employed among the Jewish people to carry out the act.

Controversy arose in the early church about whether Gentile converts to Christianity needed to be circumcised (Acts 15:1-29). Jews of the first century A.D. frowned upon noncircumcision among Christians. The apostle Paul played a crucial role in settling the dispute. He, along with other leaders of the Jerusalem council, determined that physical circumcision was not essential to Christian faith and fellowship. Circumcision of the heart through repentance and faith were the only requirements of the faith for non-Jewish Christians.

Butler, Trent, gen. ed. *Holman Bible Dictionary.* Nashville: Broadman & Holman Publishers, 1991. 262.

BACKGROUND

Many barriers divided the Jews and the Gentiles in the ancient world. Paul devotes much of his attention in this portion of the letter to the essential oneness of the church.

For the Jews, Paul did away with the law as a requirement for salvation. Christ is the fulfillment of the law, making it complete. Salvation cannot be earned through works or by strict adherence to the law. Nevertheless, we are not absolved of our responsibility to do what is right. No one has the right to boast about personal goodness. Salvation by grace through faith leads to good works. There was no need for Jews and Gentiles to be divided based on Mosaic Law. Jesus Christ is the Peace of all believers. Therefore, there is no need for division and discord.

By lessening the significance of ethnic and cultural identity, both Jews and Gentiles gained something far better and greater.

AT-A-GLANCE

**1. Christ, Our Hope
(Ephesians 2:11-13)
2. Christ, Our Peace
(vv. 14-18)
3. Christ, Our Cornerstone
(vv. 19-21)**

IN DEPTH

1. Christ, Our Hope (Ephesians 2:11-13)

Paul reminds his readers that before they were converted, they were Gentiles by birth and therefore considered outcasts by the Jews. They were despised and called the "Uncircumcision."

The Jews regarded their circumcised state with snobbery. They referred to themselves as the "Circumcision." Paul corrects their sense of superiority by clearly stating that their circumcision was done in the body by human hands. What was really important, he told them, was circumcision of the heart.

While the Jews held on to a false sense of superiority, the Gentiles were without a Saviour altogether. Isaiah foretold that the blessing of the Messiah, which was promised to the Jews, would flow to all nations. Christ was sent "unto the lost sheep of the house of Israel" (Matthew 15:24).

The Gentiles were "aliens from the commonwealth of Israel" (Ephesians 2:12). They were strangers to God's covenant promises to the Jews. For all practical purposes, the Gentiles stood on the outside looking in—without hope.

But because of God's love, the former division was done away with. When Gentiles receive Jesus Christ as Lord and Saviour, God places them in Christ and accepts them through Him. Jesus Christ has broken down the barriers that separate all people.

Jesus enabled the Gentiles to be brought near to God. Until the time of Christ, the world was divided into two camps: Jews and Gentiles. Now the Saviour had introduced a new corporate body—His Church—which united all believers in Him as one.

2. Christ, Our Peace (vv. 14-18)

In the first part of chapter two, Paul traced the salvation of both Jews and Gentiles. The two groups held different perceptions of what it meant to be saved.

Here, Paul moves forward to dissolve their nationalistic and cultural biases to create unity in Christ and explain the necessity for unity. Through His shed blood, Christ broke down "the middle wall of partition between us" (Ephesians 2:14). The barriers that divided Jews and Gentiles are now gone. Where there were two, there is now one. There is but one Christ for both the mighty and powerful and the lowly and powerless. For every race and culture, there is only one Saviour.

Paul describes Christ as our Peace. When Christ came to us, He "preached peace" (v. 17) to those near and far. In this instance, those who were near were the Jews. They had already received the promise. Those who were far were the Gentiles, who had no covenant relationship with God; they held no assurance of His presence or promise. The Jews were to be a "light to the Gentiles" (Isaiah 49:6), but they failed. Instead, they became snobbish and arrogant concerning their status as God's people. We, as Christians, are just as culpable when we fail to take the Great Commission (Matthew 28:18-20) seriously.

Peace was needed to unify two groups who were alienated from each other. As our Peace, Christ has created a new race, free from the limitations of imposed human bondage such as culture, nationality, gender, education, or social or economic standing. All believers now have access to the presence of God at any time. This was in stark contrast to the Old Testament, when only the high priest could go into the Holy of Holies, the place where God dwelled.

While Jesus was being crucified, the temple curtain that separated humanity from the Holy of Holies was split wide open. Now, all believers have free access to the Father through the great Intercessor Himself, Jesus Christ. Because of Christ, we also now know God as Father through prayer, a greater blessing than in the Old Covenant. In fact, all three Persons of the Trinity are directly involved in the prayers of even the most humble believer. We pray to the Father, approaching Him through our Lord Jesus Christ, in the power of the Holy Spirit.

3. Christ, Our Cornerstone (vv. 19-21)

Paul often uses the words "now therefore" when making a conclusion. He concludes that the Gentiles were in no way inferior to the Jews. Christ had discredited that concept.

The apostle lists some of the many great benefits available to all believing Gentiles, as they are no longer strangers and foreigners. Never again will they be looked upon as less than others or as outsiders. Now they are fellow citizens and equal heirs to the inheritance. Christians of Jewish ancestry have no advantage over the believing

Gentiles. All believers are first-class citizens in the kingdom of heaven.

As they are now a part of the Church, they have become stones, or building blocks in the construction of a holy temple. This new temple will also have a foundation, with Christ as the "chief corner stone" that bonds the temple together. This new temple, the Church, is built on the foundation of the apostles and prophets. They are not the foundation; Christ is. The apostles and prophets taught about the Person and work of Christ.

Christ is more than the foundation of the Church. He is also the chief cornerstone, joining the two walls that were once separated: Jews and Gentiles. In this new temple that Christ has created, everyone will have an equal place.

When Jesus established the New Covenant, He brought forth a new people. They were no longer Jews and Gentiles, but one body, one faith, one baptism, and one hope, in the "unity of the Spirit" (Ephesians 4:3-6).

Paul compares the Church to a building or structure, using terms that are familiar in construction. The Church is also a living organism which takes its shape with the guidance of the Holy Spirit. Like any other structure or living organism, the Church must be tended to and maintained to operate as Christ intended. God expects the church to grow. The church must continue to bring new stones to be fitted into the building. The added stones will be all types, shapes, and sizes. Some will be so dirty we may not want to touch them. Our job as workers is not to judge the fitness of the stones. Our job is simply to bring them to the Church, to continue to add to the magnificent structure God has already built.

SEARCH THE SCRIPTURES

1. What were the Gentiles called (Ephesians 2:11)?

2. How did the Jews refer to themselves (v. 11)?

3. How were the Gentiles looked upon (v. 12)?

4. How were those who were far away from the promise of the Messiah drawn near to Him (v. 13)?

5. What barrier did Christ break down (v. 14)?

6. For what reason did Christ make one new man (vv. 15-16)?

7. What did Christ preach (v. 17)?

8. What do we have because of Christ (v. 18)?

9. What is Christ in relation to the Church as a building (v. 20)?

DISCUSS THE MEANING

1. Since it is our responsibility to care for the Church of Christ and to invite others to become new stones, in what ways have we neglected our duties, both to the universal Church and in the local church?

2. There were great barriers separating Jews and Gentiles in the early Church. Why was it so difficult, especially for the Jews, to let go of long-held traditions in favor of unity among all believers in the Church?

LESSON IN OUR SOCIETY

No matter how plainly the Bible reads, there are some believers who are determined to create barriers within the body of Christ. Many arguments and divisions have arisen over petty issues of doctrine. Some Christian faith groups have attacked other Christians as being unsaved because they do not adhere to their particular beliefs.

In the early church, the issue of circumcision was no less significant to many Jewish believers. Paul reminded them that the matter was a human act and, therefore, could only serve a limited purpose in the faith. Instead, he placed emphasis on unity within the body.

All believers should be careful in their attempt not to ostracize others and create division based on human preferences. Christ desires that true believers engage themselves in activities which draw them closer to Him and to one another.

MAKE IT HAPPEN

Think about your role in your home, in your church, in your job, and in the community. Why is it important that you have good standing in all of these areas? Do you work hard and devote yourself to maintaining your role as a spouse or parent? As an employee, manager, or business owner? As a church member? As a member of your community?

Now think about your status as a child of God. Do you devote yourself equally to maintaining your status as a follower of Christ (not merely a church member)? Do you try to hold yourself responsible to do what Christ desires of you?

Think of at least one action or step you can take to show that it is important to you to continue to live as a disciple "in good standing."

FOLLOW THE SPIRIT

What God wants me to do:

_____

_____

REMEMBER YOUR THOUGHTS

Special insights I have learned:

_____

_____

MORE LIGHT ON THE TEXT
Ephesians 2:11-21

In Ephesians 2, after the eulogy for God's unspeakable blessings, Paul prays that God will open our eyes to fully understand the magnitude of the blessing He has given to us. He asks that God might reveal to us the hope and richness of our calling (1:18-19), the greatness of God's power and authority that He has given to the Church (1:20-23), and the efficacy of the death and resurrection of Jesus Christ (2:1-10).

11 Wherefore remember, that ye being in time past Gentiles in the flesh, who are called Uncircumcision by that which is called the Circumcision in the flesh made by hands;

Paul for the first time identifies those whom he is addressing in verse 11: the Gentiles. He reminds them who they were before they received Christ. He uses different terms to describe their position before their union with Christ. First, they were "Gentiles in the flesh." That is to say, they were *ethnos,* i.e., heathen, non-Jewish nations by birth, whom the Jews (the Circumcision) disrespectfully called the Uncircumcision.

God had instructed Abraham in Genesis to circumcise every male in his household, including his servants (Genesis 17:11). This practice became a visible, physical sign of the covenant between the Lord and His people. Any Jewish male who was not circumcised was to be cut off from his people (Genesis 17:14) and regarded as

a covenant-breaker. The Jewish people took great pride in circumcision, and it became a badge of pride. Devout Jews practiced circumcision in the New Testament period. Both John the Baptist (Luke 1:59) and Jesus (Luke 2:21) were circumcised in accordance with the Jewish rite. The practice raised a spirit of exclusivity and resentment between Jews and Gentiles and later brought discord into the fellowship of the first-century Church (Acts 15:1ff; see Paul's letter to the Galatians). An exaggerated importance was placed on the rite, and each side called the other names.

Paul (especially in Galatians) seems to deemphasize the physical rite, and he says that the so-called Jewish circumcision is only in the flesh (a purely physical mark) and something made by human hands, rather than spiritual. Here, Paul in essence says that the true motive behind the circumcision of the flesh is a circumcision of the heart that is spiritual rather than physical. That kind of circumcision is needed and available to both Jews and Gentiles alike (Romans 2:28-29; Colossians 2:11-13). Writing to the Philippian Christians (both Jews and Gentiles), Paul says, "For we are the true circumcision, who worship in the Spirit of God and glory in Christ Jesus and put no confidence in the flesh" (Philippians 3:3, NASB).

12 That at that time ye were without Christ, being aliens from the commonwealth of Israel and strangers from the covenants of promise, having no hope, and without God in the world:

Paul calls attention to their spiritual and physical alienation. First, they are to remember that during that time ("in time past," Ephesians 2:11) they were alienated from Christ ("ye were without Christ," v. 12). The word "Christ" is probably used here in the general sense of *Messiah,* which means they did not share in the Jews' Messianic hope for the future. This Messianic hope was included in Israel's privileges listed in Romans 9:4-5. The Gentiles were alienated from the commonwealth of Israel. Therefore, they were strangers from (and to) the covenants of promise. The word "commonwealth" (Gk. *politeia*) means "citizenship." Therefore, Gentiles, by the fact of their birth, were deprived of the privileges of Israel and excluded from participation in their national rights, hopes, and promises. We know from the Old Testament that this covenant is the very heart of Israel's relationship with God, in which God solemnly pledged to be their God and they would be called His people (Leviticus 26:12). According to the Jews, to partake in the covenant relationship, one had to be born a Jewish male and circumcised according to the Law of Moses. As far as the Jews were concerned, the Gentiles were excluded from the Old Covenant.

As people separated from the Messianic hope (without Christ), estranged from the commonwealth of Israel and its privileges, and excluded from the covenant of promise as God's people, the Gentiles had "no hope, and were without God in the world." It is like a chain reaction. One thing leads to another. The ultimate result was that they were without God and hopeless in the world. This described their position in their disbelief before they became Christians. Their lifestyle was evidence of this, as they "walked according to the course of this world, according to the prince of the power of the air, the spirit that now worketh in the children of disobedience" (Ephesians 2:2). They had no knowledge of God's laws (Psalm 147:20), nor did they have fellowship with him. This was the position of all of us before we received Christ: We were without Christ, outside the covenant promise of God, and without hope. However, the death and resurrection of Christ changed it all. Through Christ, we have been accepted into God's new family as adopted children (Ephesians 1:5-6) with all the privileges that pertain to sonship. Now, we have God as our Father. We can approach God with confidence through the Spirit, and therefore we hope to be with Him forever. Paul explains that through Christ we have access to God the Father (2:18). Paul therefore calls on non-Jewish believers to remember the past (v. 11) in order to appreciate the present and have hope for the future.

13 But now in Christ Jesus ye who sometimes were far off are made nigh by the blood of Christ. 14 For he is our peace, who hath made both one, and hath broken down the middle wall of partition between us;

After describing the apparently gloomy and hopeless situation of the Gentiles before they became Christians, Paul now moves to the present positive state brought about by their new relationship in Christ. He says, "you who once were far off have been brought near." That means that they were no more aliens and strangers to the covenant promises of God; they were no more regarded as people without God and without hope (v. 12). They now have the same close relationship with God. "Far off" describes how separated the Gentiles were from God compared with His nearness to Israel. Moses said, "For what great nation is there that has God so near to it, as the LORD our God is to us" (Deuteronomy 4:7, NKJV). The psalmist called them "a people near unto him" (Psalm 148:14).

The alienation of the Gentiles from God and from Israel is symbolized in the construction of the temple in Jerusalem. There were partitions between the outer and inner courts. The Gentiles were only allowed entrance to the outer court; hence, it was named Court of the Gentiles. The inner court, which was closer to the court of the priests and the Holy of Holies (representing the presence of God), was reserved for Jews. It is said that notices in different languages stated that death was the punishment for any non-Jew caught entering the inner court. This segregation was analogous to the far-off position of the Gentiles from God.

However, God also promised to bring peace to all people both far and near (Isaiah 57:19). This is done in Christ Jesus. Through Christ and because of their new relationship with Him, Gentiles are brought into the fold. They are engrafted into the new family of God by the blood of Christ.

The reference to the blood of Christ refers to the sacrificial and atoning death of Christ—on the—Cross. Through this atonement, all believers are reconciled to God and to each other. The Gentiles, through their faith in the sacrificial death of Christ, have become members of the people of God together with the Jews who have received Jesus as Messiah and Saviour. Apart from symbolizing alienation from God and Israel, the partition was also a symbol of hostility between the Jews and the Gentiles. The Cross is the uniting force that binds the two sides into one community.

Paul makes the unification of the two groups clear in the next verse through a profound declaration: "He is our peace" (v. 14). The use of the pronoun "he" (*autos*) is emphatic, which means "He Himself" or "He and He alone" is our peace. This echoes the prophecy of Isaiah (9:6), where Christ is given the title "Prince of Peace" because of His mission on earth. Christ is peace personified, because through Him and Him alone are believers reconciled to God and each other—He has made both one. Not only has He unified the two sides into one entity, He has also broken down the middle wall of partition that separates them. As we mentioned earlier, this probably refers to the literal partitioning wall that separates the courts in the temple.

15 Having abolished in his flesh the enmity, even the law of commandments contained in ordinances; for to make in himself of twain one new man, so making peace;

In addition to the separating walls of the temple, the Jews always endeavored to live separate from the rest of the world. They always wanted a river or wall between them and their Gentile neighbors. Their laws and customs also separated them from the rest of the world, like the physical walls in the temple. These were points of hostility between the two. Christ, through His sacrificial death, abolished the Law with its commandments and regulations, provided a new covenant that is inclusive for both Jews and Gentiles, and made them one. He brings everyone to the same level. This breakdown was literally demonstrated when the curtain of the temple was ripped from top to bottom. It indicated that the way into the Holy of Holies is left open and accessible to all—Jews and Gentiles alike.

The abolition of the law raises some questions. What does Paul mean by abolishing the law in relation to Christ's words in Matthew 5:17? There, Christ teaches that He has come, not to abolish, but rather to fulfill the law. Is this then a contradiction in Scripture? In what sense was either used? The difference seems to lie in the two types of law: the moral law and the ceremonial law. Christ requires from His followers a more radical

obedience to the moral law compared with the Pharisees' own standards (Matthew 5:18ff). Paul refers to Christ's abolishment of the ceremonial law, which includes the physical ritual of circumcision (Ephesians 2:11), rather than the spiritual circumcision of the heart. This also includes some of the dietary regulations in Colossians 2:11 and 16-21. These constitute barriers between the Jews and the Gentiles. Jesus has abolished these regulations through His death on the Cross. He has made the two one in Himself, making peace between them.

The unification of all believers in Christ, as we shall see later in the book, includes the abolition of the gender, social, and racial distinctions, which have led to hostility between different peoples of the earth. The change does not mean amalgamation of all races, change of skin color, or physical gender change. It refers to a change of attitude toward one another and the acceptance of each other as equals. When we have this attitude, the peace that Christ died for on the Cross will be realized.

16 And that he might reconcile both unto God in one body by the cross, having slain the enmity thereby: 17 And came and preached peace to you which were afar off, and to them that were nigh.

Verses 16 and 17 speak to the same theme using different terms. These terms further describe what Christ has done through His blood—He has reconciled both (Jews and Gentiles) unto God in one body by the Cross. In verse 15, we see that the Law which brought about the enmity is abolished (*katargeo*, or done away with, rendered idle, or destroyed); but in verse 16, the enmity that is caused by the Law is slain (*apokteino*), or killed. This speaks of total annihilation. In the one single act of sacrifice on the Cross, Christ first abolished the ceremonial law, which for centuries had separated humanity from each other and from their Creator. Second, He created a new humanity where everyone was equal, thereby making peace between them—figuratively, slaying the enmity. Third, by this act of sacrifice, Christ reconciled this new society to God, their Creator. In many of Paul's writings, reconciliation is associated with the Cross

Through Jesus, believers are reconciled to one another and to God.

(Romans 5:6-11; 2 Corinthians 5:17-21; Colossians 1:21-22).

He continued the theme of Christ's activity—bringing near those far away, reconciling the two entities, and uniting them into "one new man" by abolishing the ceremonial law. Paul describes this same activity in a different way in Ephesians 2:1-17. While in verse 14 Christ "is our peace" (i.e., the object of peace), here he preaches "peace to you which were afar off" (the Gentiles) as well as "to them that were nigh" (the Jews). He "came and preached peace" probably refers to Christ's earthly mission and the ministry of the early Church. The word "preached" is the same as the Greek word *euaggelizo*, translated as "preach the good news" in Luke 4:17ff, where Jesus announced His mission in fulfillment of Isaiah's prophecy (cf. Isaiah 61:1-2). Here, Paul says that Jesus came and then declared the Good News of peace to those who were afar off and to those who were nigh. Those "afar off" here would include the undesirables—the poor, the sick, the tax collectors, and sinners. He ministered to Gentiles as well, e.g., the Samaritan woman, the Roman centurion, the Samaritan leper, and the Syrophoenician woman. Apart from Christ's ministry, the preaching of the Good News by His disciples might also be referred to here as if Christ preached through them (2 Corinthians 5:20).

18 For through him we both have access by one Spirit unto the Father. 19 Now therefore ye are no more strangers and foreigners, but fellowcitizens with the saints, and of the household of God;

Ephesians 2:18-19 states the affect of Christ's preaching. Through Him, Jews and Gentiles are now reconciled to one another and to God. Consequently, by Him they both can approach God the Father in one Spirit. It is noteworthy to recognize a deliberate reference to the Trinity here, which proves the distinctiveness of the three persons in the Godhead (cf. 1 John 5:7). The word "access" (*prosagoge*) speaks of the freedom we have to approach God as our Father with boldness and assurance—that we are acceptable to Him and shall not be turned down. Paul writes in Romans 5:2, "By whom also we have access by faith into this grace wherein we stand, and rejoice in hope of the glory of God." The access we have is because of Christ's work of reconciliation, which brought us into peace with God. This is what Paul calls "justification," using the court language in Romans 5:1. But here in Ephesians 2:17, he uses evangelistic language—"preached peace." Both result in peace with God the Father. The Spirit activates the free approach to the Father. **Therefore, He regards us equally as His sons and daughters.** To the Galatians (4:6), Paul writes, "And because ye are sons, God hath sent forth the Spirit of his Son into your hearts, crying, Abba, Father." Being sons, we are no more bound or barred by fear from approaching God (Romans 8:15).

This relationship with our Heavenly Father is comparable to our relationship with our earthly parents (vis-á-vis sons and daughters). We can have free access to them any time, unless there is a serious relationship breakdown in the family. In such a situation, access to the parents is difficult or impossible until the situation is resolved and peace is restored. This was the case between us (both Jews and Gentiles) and God in the past, but through Christ and by the Holy Spirit, the barrier is now removed. Moreover, we are now members of the same family, with the same rights and privileges, claiming the same citizenship.

In Ephesians 2:19, there is a shift in Paul's use of metaphor, from membership in a family unit to citizenship nationhood. In verse 12, the Gentiles are said to be outside of the commonwealth (*politeia*) of Israel, strangers without hope and without God. Now they are no more strangers (*xenos*) and foreigners (*paroikos*); these terms are synonymous and refer to one who lives in a place without the right of citizenship. Israel claimed the right of being the people of God and regarded all Gentile nations as excluded from their number. Gentiles were treated as strangers or foreigners. They were not allowed to integrate into the community of God's people. They remained as resident aliens. It is the equivalent of aliens residing in the U.S. or Canada who have no citizen's rights whatsoever. As a foreigner, one is denied access to jobs, medical privileges, or voting rights. If one is

a foreign student, he or she is charged almost double the tuition paid by those who are citizens. There are many other privileges one enjoys as a U.S. or Canadian citizen. The same applies in other countries as well. However, when one becomes a U.S. or Canadian citizen by choice, all the privileges are made accessible (at least theoretically) to him or her. Here, Paul reminds the Gentiles that through Christ, they have become fellow citizens (*sumpolitai*) with the saints (Israel) in God's own kingdom. Paul again moves back to the use of the more intimate metaphor, the family portrait, which he alluded to in verse 18 (cf. 1:5; 3:14-15; 4:6). Believers become members of God's household, which is the Church, the body of Christ (5:23), God's new community.

20 And are built upon the foundation of the apostles and prophets, Jesus Christ himself being the chief corner stone;

Paul now moves from speaking of the Church as God's family, or community, to referring to it as a building (house) whose foundation is laid upon what the apostles and prophets taught. He refers to Christ here as the builder. Jesus called the apostles and gifted the prophets, charging them to bear the Good News to all nations (Matthew 28:19-20). The word "apostles" refers to the 12 disciples (see our discussion of the word *apostolos* in the last study) and includes Paul himself. Some scholars feel that the word "prophet" here refers to the Old Testament prophets. However, in other passages Paul places the offices of apostles and prophets side by side as God's gift to the Church (1 Corinthians 12:28-29; Ephesians 3:5; 4:11).

Christ is not only the builder; He is also the chief cornerstone (*akrogoniaios*). Peter also refers to Christ as the cornerstone (1 Peter 2:6), using the same Greek word. The stability of a house or building depends upon its foundation. Therefore, the most important part of a building is its foundation. A house without a solid foundation will not stand the test of time. Christ's parable of the two builders in the Beatitudes emphasizes the need for a strong foundation laid on a rock. Here, Paul says that Jesus is "the chief (main) corner stone" that holds together the whole building and keeps the rest of the foundation in place, while the apostles and prophets are parts of the foundation. What does Paul mean by referring to the apostles and prophets as the foundation on which Christ has built His church? This is a question for group discussion.

21 In whom all the building fitly framed together groweth unto an holy temple in the Lord:

Paul goes on to elaborate on the structural makeup of the building. As we have seen, the structural stability of a building depends on its foundation; so just the stability of the Church is dependent upon none other than the One who is both builder and the chief cornerstone: Christ. Jesus says to Peter and the rest of the disciples "Upon this rock I will build my church; and the gates of hell shall not prevail against it" (Matthew 16:18), referring to Peter's earlier confession that Jesus was "the Christ, the Son of the living God" (Matthew 16:16).

A building does not stop at the foundation. It needs some fittings and other structures before it can be called a building. Paul moves his picture of the whole structure to the individual stones that are used to erect a building. Peter also uses the picture of a building or temple to describe the Church. In the same picture where he refers to Christ as the chief cornerstone (1 Peter 2:6), he describes the individual members as "a living stone...built up a spiritual house, an holy priesthood" (1 Peter 2:4-5). Paul's picture here also portrays the members of the Church as the stones, which the master builder (Christ) masterfully and meticulously fits together upon the chief foundation (Christ) into a magnificent edifice unto a holy temple in the Lord.

We know from Scripture that God is so great that even the whole earth cannot contain Him— not even Solomon's magnificent temple, nor the one rebuilt by Herod. God does not dwell in man-made houses (1 Kings 8:27; Acts 7:48-49; 17:24),

nor in homes built with earthly materials. However, He manifested His glory and presence in the temple. He also makes His abode in the hearts of men. In other places, Paul refers to Christians as temples of the living God (1 Corinthians 3:16-19; 6:16; 2 Corinthians 6:16), where God dwells by the Holy Spirit. Instead of the Old Testament temple in which God manifested His presence through His glory, the Church (the individual Christian, the local church, and the universal Church) becomes the New Testament temple in which God manifests Himself through the Holy Spirit.

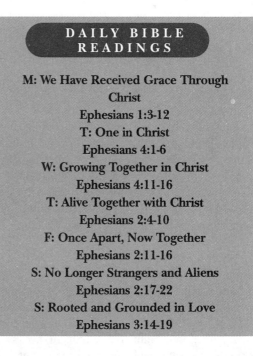

DAILY BIBLE READINGS

M: We Have Received Grace Through Christ
Ephesians 1:3-12

T: One in Christ
Ephesians 4:1-6

W: Growing Together in Christ
Ephesians 4:11-16

T: Alive Together with Christ
Ephesians 2:4-10

F: Once Apart, Now Together
Ephesians 2:11-16

S: No Longer Strangers and Aliens
Ephesians 2:17-22

S: Rooted and Grounded in Love
Ephesians 3:14-19

You can easily search through past *Precepts For Living* lessons for relevant information within seconds, by using your *Precepts For Living* CD-ROM. Why not make use of this excellent feature!

DECEMBER 2004
QUARTER AT-A-GLANCE
Called to be God's People

This quarter focuses on God's various calls to numerous people. God recognizes our differences, and His divine appointments are based upon His call to each individual.

UNIT 1. GOD CALLS A PEOPLE

In the first lesson, Abram is called by God to leave his comfortable home to live in a land that would someday belong to his descendants. In the second lesson, God calls Samuel to appoint a king of Israel. Samuel almost appointed the wrong son until he realized that God's choices were not according to appearances. The third lesson, the Christmas lesson, presents the call to Mary and Joseph to be the earthly parents of Jesus. In the fourth lesson, Mary and Joseph take Baby Jesus to the temple where Simeon and Anna bless Him.

LESSON 1: December 5
A Call to Follow God
Genesis 11:27—12:9

God called Abram to follow Him to a new land; so Abram left all that was familiar and comfortable: his family, his country, his culture, and his home. God promised to make Abram into a great nation, to make his name great, to bless him, to bless those who blessed him, to curse those who cursed him, and to bless all the people of the earth through him.

LESSON 2: December 12
A Call to Lead Faithfully
1 Samuel 16:1-4, 6-13

Samuel was called of God to anoint the future king of Israel. This task required courage and spiritual perception. Samuel was hesitant because he feared that King Saul would hear about it. Then Samuel assumed that Jesse's oldest son was the one to be anointed. God said no. God rejected every son except David, who was the youngest and was out tending sheep. God taught Samuel to judge people by the heart, not by outward appearance.

LESSON 3: December 19
A Call to Respond
Matthew 1:17-25

Mary and Joseph had the most precious call upon their lives. Mary was called to be the mother of our Saviour, and Joseph functioned as the stepfather of our Lord. Joseph was shocked when he found out that his bride-to-be was pregnant. But this was no ordinary pregnancy. This was to be a virgin birth.

LESSON 4: December 26
A Call to Hope
Luke 2:22-38

Forty days after the birth of Jesus, Mary and Joseph took Him to the temple to dedicate Him to God. At the temple, Simeon and Anna, the prophetess, blessed Him. Simeon had been promised by God that he should live to see the Messiah. The Holy Spirit witnessed to him that Jesus was the Christ, the anointed One. Simeon took Baby Jesus in his arms and praised God for Him. He prophesied that Mary and Jesus would both experience anguish. Then Anna gave public thanks for Jesus.

UNIT 2. THE CALL OF JESUS AND HIS FOLLOWERS

This unit is based upon Scriptures taken from the Gospel according to Mark. It begins with the call of Jesus and then moves on to the calling of His disciples. The last two lessons focus on Jesus' call to His followers to total commitment and true greatness.

LESSON 5: January 2
Jesus Begins His Ministry
Mark 1:14-28

Jesus began His ministry by calling disciples to follow Him. First, He called Simon and Andrew, the fishermen. Then He called their cousins, James and John. Jesus and His disciples entered the village of Capernaum where Jesus cast out an evil spirit. People were amazed that Jesus displayed such power and authority.

LESSON 6: January 9
Jesus Calls Levi (Matthew)
Mark 2:13-17

Jesus called Levi (Matthew) to follow Him. Matthew was a tax collector, a profession that the Pharisees considered sinful. Matthew followed Jesus immediately and invited his friends to dine with Jesus. This shocked the Pharisees, who could hardly believe that Jesus would eat with these "sinners." Jesus said that He came to call those who recognized their own sinfulness.

LESSON 7: January 16
Jesus Sends Out the Twelve
Mark 3:13-19; 6:6-13

Jesus called 12 disciples to follow Him. Then He sent them out two by two. The disciples were commissioned to have power over evil spirits. They were to take nothing for their journey except staffs—no money, no extra clothing. They were dependent upon the hospitality of the people to whom they were sent.

LESSON 8: January 23
Jesus Calls for Total Commitment
Mark 8:27-38

In this passage, Peter goes from being inspired by God to being inspired by Satan. First, he testifies that Jesus is the Christ. Then he tells Jesus that He must not speak of suffering and dying. Jesus uses this occasion to tell the disciples of His coming death on the Cross.

LESSON 9: January 30
Jesus Defines True Greatness
Mark 10:32-45

Jesus again predicted His death, but the disciples hardly seemed to hear what He was saying. James and John asked Jesus for special seats next to Him in the kingdom. Jesus taught them that true greatness is in serving others.

UNIT 3. WHOSOEVER WILL—COME!

In this unit, four people are challenged to overcome obstacles to following the Lord. Ruth was challenged to overcome grief; Naaman—pride; Nicodemus—uncertainty; and the Samaritan woman—prejudice. When following Christ, we all face obstacles that we must overcome.

LESSON 10: February 6
Overcoming Grief
Ruth 1:3-8, 14-18

Ruth faced a number of obstacles. First, her husband died. Then Naomi, her mother-in-law, decided to return to Israel. Ruth loved her mother-in-law and was determined to follow her and her God. Ruth overcame her grief to follow the right path.

LESSON 11: February 13
Overcoming Pride
2 Kings 5:1-5, 9-15

Naaman was a proud man in charge of the army of Aram, which he had led to success in battle, but he had leprosy. His wife had a young servant girl from Israel. This young girl advised her mistress that Elisha, the prophet in Israel, would be able to heal Naaman. So Naaman made a journey to see Elisha. He expected that Elisha would wave his arm over the spot to cure him. Instead, Elisha told Naaman to wash himself seven times in the muddy Jordan River. Naaman resisted doing so, but his servants talked him into obeying the word of God through the prophet Elisha. Immediately his skin was as pure as a young child's.

LESSON 12: February 20
Overcoming Uncertainty
John 3:1-16

Nicodemus was uncertain about who Jesus was, but he was determined to find out. He came to see Jesus at night, perhaps because he feared being associated with Jesus, or because he wanted to have a one-on-one conversation with the Lord. Jesus told him that he must be born again.

LESSON 13: February 27
Overcoming Prejudice
John 4:7-10, 19-26

Since Samaritans and Jews avoided having anything to do with each other, the Samaritan woman was surprised that Jesus spoke with her. But she soon was drinking in all that Jesus had to tell her. Jesus said that the day was coming when true worshipers would worship Him in spirit and in truth. Then Jesus announced to the woman that He was the Christ.

CALLED TO BE GOD'S PEOPLE

by C. M. Taylor

By tradition, getting "the call" from God means going into ministry, usually pastoral. However, if we look at God's call to various people in the Bible, we discover that His call is never a single call to a single mission but rather a series, or progression, of calls throughout the believer's life.

The nature of the call can include, but is not limited to, a personal or public call; a specific task; a definite time frame; specific people; a relationship; and/or a long-term ministry. Abraham is a perfect example of a man of faith who was given a series, or progression, of calls. The first call was to separate himself from his family and country to move to unknown territory. Today we might consider this the call to salvation and entrance into the family of God.

Abraham was called simultaneously to believe that God would make a great nation of him and that it would be blessed above all other nations of the earth. Abraham was called by an invisible God to leave his homeland of Ur and household idols and go to a not yet visible land. God often calls us *away* from people and things that present obstacles to His plan and purpose as much as He calls us *to* Himself.

What if at some point I do not wish to respond to the call of God? Does my refusal to cooperate bring God's plan to a halt? Certainly not! Ask King Saul, the first king of Israel. At first a reluctant monarch, Saul proceeded to assume responsibilities that were not in his job description, including offering up sacrifices when he thought the prophet Samuel was too slow in arriving. Saul also presumed to know better than God what was appropriate in settling the spoils of battle. He was replaced by young David, who became a direct ancestor of Jesus Christ. As for Saul, not only was the kingdom taken away, but the consequences of his refusal to cooperate with God caused suffering to the innocent, including his son Jonathan, who died an untimely death. Jonathan would have inherited the throne.

After the call to salvation, the second call is to live holy and righteous lives daily, letting our lights shine for the world to see. In other words, we are simply called to *live*. We are called to rise and shine—go to school, work, church, the mall, PTA meetings, etc. And *while* we are going about our daily business, infusing every aspect of our daily living with the essence of Christ, we are called to be sensitive to the divine prompting of God to "step out" of our normal routine for what author Bruce Wilkerson calls a "divine appointment." This divine appointment can be anything from sensing the need to give a homeless person five dollars (instead of our usual quarter or fifty cents) to striking up a conversation in the airport waiting area that leads to the salvation of the person in the seat next to us. When the divine appointment is concluded, we step back into daily routine without missing a beat and joyfully anticipate the next appointment God sets up for us. Simeon and Anna had such an appointment, spending years in the temple waiting for the birth of the Messiah. Jesus called together and equipped His disciples for such an appointment, sending them out two by two on a short-term mission.

Every believer is called to be a witness to the existence, sovereignty, power, and love of God in season and out of season. While we freely acknowledge and share Jesus Christ, we must also understand that the very act of doing so elicits from us a commitment to:

Deny ourselves and pick up our crosses (Mark 8:34).

Decrease while Christ increases (John 3:30).

Count all things as "dung" in order to gain Christ (Philippians 3:8-9).

The call of God places the believer in the position of servant, specifically a "bond servant." If a servant was given his or her freedom but did not wish to leave the master, an awl was used to pierce the ear of the servant. This was done by hammering the awl through the servant's earlobe into the door of the master's home. Thus, the piercing of a servant's ear might be considered a type of blood covenant. This servant was now bound by choice as a servant for life.

In the race for ministerial fame, some forget that the very word *minister* means to serve. While we honor church leaders, we remember that they are servants as are all God's people. We also recognize that the more we serve, the greater we become in the eyes of God (see Matthew 28:11-12).

After I have responded to God's first call to salvation, and after I have responded to God's call to holy and righteous living, exactly what is it that qualifies me to respond to any other call or divine appointment in my life? It is God Himself who qualifies. Every nook, cranny, and corner of our lives, especially those traits and tragedies we think totally unusable by God, are training grounds for the things that God will call us to do. Consider the experience of Ruth and Naomi. Neither of them would say she heard a "call" from God, or that God revealed His ultimate purpose, but God took the cacophony of poverty and widowhood and turned their lives into a well-orchestrated, joyous symphony. The tragedy of widowhood compelled Ruth and Naomi to cling to one another for support, and compassion from Boaz, which placed them in the line of direct ancestors of King David and Jesus Christ.

If God wants me to answer His call and qualifies me, why does He call me when I do not consider myself ready to answer? God is the resource center for all that responding to the call requires. Our only concern is the willingness to say "yes" when we are called. Often, the solution to our own problems is found in responding to God's call. Are you filled with pride? You may be called to serve in a soup kitchen. Are you filled with doubt about the afterlife? You may be called to share Christ with hospice patients. Are you a free spirit? You may be called to care for a disabled parent. Are you impatient? You may be called to work in children's ministry.

What if I'm not sure whether God is calling me to a particular task? We must ask Him for proof. Let's check our Bibles. Is there a precedent set therein? Will God be glorified? The call of God does not break up families. The call of God does not neglect parental duty in the name of "ministry." The call of God never involves lying, cheating, stealing, and backbiting. The call of God does not reduce us to begging except in prayer as we plead for souls.

Will God's call bring me embarrassment and humiliation? Ask Naaman the leper. Ask Nicodemus. Ask the Samaritan woman Jesus met at the well. God called Naaman to know Him through healing. Naaman's pride as a Philistine commander almost prevented him from responding to God's call. How embarrassed do you suppose Naaman was as he dipped into common waters of the Jordan River seven times? What were his troops grinning and mumbling about among themselves? With each dip, he may have thought, "If nothing happens, what a fool I shall have been!" Though perhaps at times humbling, God's call never leads to failure—unless we say "no." The seventh time up, Naaman's leprosy was healed. Now who do you think was laughing out loud?

Nicodemus's response to God's call was cloaked by the darkness of night to prevent the reproach of his colleagues. The evidence of his response is seen later as he accompanies Joseph of Arimathea to the burial of Jesus. It is Nicodemus who supplies 75 pounds of spices to wrap the body of Christ. Both were secret disciples who answered the call to see to the burial of God's Son (John 19:38-42).

Another example of God's call is found in the story of the woman at the well. The Jews had no dealings with the Samaritans, and men did not approach women in public. Jesus was Jewish and He was a man. The woman at the well had no reason to socialize with Jesus. Married five times (looking for Mr. Right in all the wrong places) and presently shacking up, she was at the well alone—that spoke volumes.

At the well, she encounters what she thinks is a Jewish man—a prophet—who calls her to living water. She may have been temporarily embarrassed that Jesus knew her business, but she responds to His call. Then she runs to tell others about the Messiah. Was there embarrassment and humiliation in God's call? "What do you mean, woman? Everybody knows your business!" When we respond to God's call to receive salvation and to share the Gospel of Jesus Christ with others, others might be surprised. However, like the Samaritan woman, we cannot be put off by what others know about our past. Instead, we move on as she did, and people will come to Christ.

So, we see the call to be God's people is the umbrella under which a variety of subsequent calls await us. Only one thing should concern us: How shall we respond?

Connie M. Taylor is the Editor for UMIs *J.A.M. Jesus And Me®*. She is a schoolteacher and lifelong educator.

EXAMINING THE MINISTRY OF JESUS FOR THE POSTMODERN ERA

by Rukeia Draw, M.A.C.E.

The American church is amid a cultural shift that is turning the modern world upside down! Tony Jones (2001) says that in modernity, science; reason; individuality; and analysis reigned. The church attempted to transform this paradigm by uniting faith and reason but instead became wed to it. Consequently, the church is very uneasy about postmodernity.

Another valid explanation for the church's refusal to embrace postmodernity is the latter's rejection of absolutes and universals. Postmodernists don't believe that ultimate reality, truth, and morality can be found in any single essence. Instead, communities are said to construct them (Downey 1998). Therefore, the Bible isn't accepted as the universal story of God's redemptive work in human history. Rather, it's considered the unifying myth that shapes the world of the Christian community, who, in turn, use that myth to construct what is ultimately real, true, and moral for them.

While acknowledging all that stands to keep Christianity and postmodernism at odds, the church should constructively engage postmodernism. Bridges between the two are identified in the gospel of Matthew, a book that portrays Jesus as a teacher and preacher, according to Elwell and Yarbrough (1998). The text reveals that the postmodern values of community, holism, and spirituality are in harmony with Jesus' educational philosophy and methodology (Slattery 1995). How these themes fit into postmodern culture will be discussed, and illus-trations of how they are guiding principles for Jesus will be provided.

Jesus, the Master Teacher (Matthew 23:10), demonstrates how educators with a marginalized voice can creatively engage learners in a context of religious pluralism. Creative teaching hasn't been clearly defined by scholars and so is best described metaphorically. Creative teaching is like a religious pilgrimage! Let's use the exodus story as an example. When the Israelites set out for Canaan, they knew their destination and what awaited them there. However, reaching their destination required the pilgrims to undertake a journey filled with challenge and uncertainty. Similarly, creative teaching carries this paradox. Education is about far more than the destination, although it is the destination that determines the course or curriculum. The journey is a risky endeavor because it deals with the particulars of the educational process. It takes into account what the learners will encounter along the way as well as how and when these experiences occur.

POSTMODERNISM AND HOLISM

Holism is an ecological perspective that sees the world as thoroughly interconnected. A "big picture" view is necessary to understand how all these web-like connections affect individuals, communities, and environments. Therefore, education should influence the whole person in the totality of his or her experience. Jesus left no part of a learner's being or life untouched or untapped.

AUTHENTICITY

"Keeping it real" is a popular slogan that is truly a sign of the times. This call for authenticity may manifest itself as genuineness, consistency, paradox, ambiguity, or even mystery. Jesus could teach creatively because He was authentic!

Jesus didn't avoid the complexity of life. Instead, He often highlighted or reconciled seemingly contradictory realities. For example, Jesus told the disciples they would have to lose their lives in order to save them (Matthew 16:25). His teaching ministry allowed for mystery and ambiguity as well. Jesus was confident enough to release Himself from the pressure to know everything and give oversimplified answers. For instance, when the disciples inquired about His Second Coming, He responded that they should keep watch and be ready at any time because the hour was unknown (Matthew 24:42-44).

Jesus often addressed the need for consistency in His teaching. One of the most obvious of these occasions is when Jesus accuses the teachers of the law and the Pharisees of hypocrisy in Matthew 23. He warns His hearers to obey the teachings of the religious leaders but not to follow their practices, for the two lacked congruency.

However, Jesus Himself is the epitome of authenticity. He embodies His teachings and perfectly models consistency, paradox, and mystery. Jesus consistently lives out the reality that the kingdom of God is at hand, through His healing, preaching, and teaching. He personifies paradox by having the fullness of both divinity and humanity coexist in His being and by introducing life through His death. Jesus also embodies the mysteries of the incarnation, resurrection, and Godhead.

Jesus consistently lives out the reality of the kingdom of God being at hand through His healing, preaching, and teaching.

EXPERIENTIAL

Dewey (1938) proposed an intimate connection between experience and education. Experience-based learning is active, learner-centered, and values practical engagement whereby there is direct interaction with what is being learned. Debriefing and reflection are essential; experience alone is not educative. The learner's relevant experience is acknowledged and employed. The teacher demonstrates trust, respect, validation, and concern. These four components, which Andersen et al. (2000) described as essential to experience-based education, are evident in the creative teaching of Jesus.

Jesus teaches Peter a powerful lesson by drawing on his past experience and expertise as a fisherman. Jesus could have simply explained the irony of a temple tax for the Son of God and the certainty of God's provision, but He stimulated Peter's thinking with questions and then invited him to participate in his own education by retrieving money from the fish's mouth (Matthew 17:24-27).

POSTMODERNISM AND COMMUNITY

For postmodernists, everyone is connected in a global sense, but their world(s) are constructed in communities. This means learning cannot truly take place outside of community. Jesus emphasized the communal in His teaching ministry, which is characterized by interdependent relationships and collaborative learning.

RELATIONAL EDUCATION

Jesus' methodology is relational. He invites the disciples on a journey to follow Him (Matthew 4:18-22; 9:9). The intensity of the connection between them is illustrated when Jesus asks, "'Who is my mother, and who are my brothers?' Pointing to His disciples, he said, 'Here are my mother and my brothers. For whoever does the will of my Father in heaven is my brother and sister and mother'" (Matthew 12:48-50, NIV). There are few bonds that surpass that of kinship, but that is the type of connection Jesus had with the disciples.

COLLABORATIVE LEARNING

Not only did the disciples sit at Jesus' feet, but also their interaction with one another was educationally valuable. For example, on one occasion the disciples forgot to bring bread on one of their journeys. Jesus instructed them to be on guard against the yeast of the Pharisees and Sadducees. Upon hearing this, they discussed it among themselves and concluded Jesus was referring to their forgetfulness. Aware of their conversation, Jesus used this teachable moment and further assessed their level of understanding (Matthew 16:5-12).

POSTMODERNISM AND SPIRITUALITY

There is a search for more intimate connection and relationship in the postmodern era. O'Gorman (2001) defines postmodern spirituality as a way of life in which one is in relationship with self, others, the cosmos as a whole, and God. Jesus was primarily concerned with spirituality in His teaching.

As Jesus sent out the Twelve, He instructed them to preach, "The kingdom of heaven is near" (Matthew 10:7, NIV). In His teachings on the kingdom of heaven, He sought to help the listener discern authentic relationship with God and to explain the implications of an "already" and "not yet" eschatological reality of the ruling presence of God (Ladd 1998).

There are few bonds that surpass that of kinship, but that is the type of connection Jesus had with the disciples.

Bibliography

Andersen, Lee, David Boud, and Ruth Cohen. "Experience-Based Learning." *Understanding Adult Education and Training.* 2nd ed. Edited by G. Foley. Sydney: Allen & Unwin, 2000.

Dewey, John. *Education and Experience.* New York: McMillan Company, 1938.

Downey, John K. "Postmodernity and Pedagogy: Connecting the Dots." *Horizons* 25 (1998): 238-257.

Elwell, Walter A., and Robert W. Yarbrough. *Encountering the New Testament.* Grand Rapids, Mich.: Baker Books, 1998.

Jones, Tony. *Postmodern Youth Ministry.* Grand Rapids, Mich.: Zondervan, 2001.

Ladd, George E. *A Theology of the New Testament.* Edited by Donald A. Hagner. Grand Rapids, Mich.: Eerdmans, 1993.

O'Gorman, Robert T. "Effect of Theological Orientation on Christian Education in Spiritual Formation: Toward a Postmodern Model of Spirituality." *Review and Expositor.* 98 (2001): 351-368.

Slattery, Patrick. *Curriculum Development in the Postmodern Era.* New York: Garland, 1995.

Rukeia Draw is an adjunct instructor at Trinity Evangelical Divinity School. She is pursuing a Ph.D. in Educational Studies from Trinity International University in Deerfield, Illinois.

GOD'S DIVINE CALL ON ORDINARY LIVES

by Pastor Philip Rodman

There are many people in churches around the world who have never understood the call of God upon their lives. They may say things like, "I don't know what God has called me to do," or "I'm not called to preach God's Word. After all, that's what we pay the pastor to do." But the Bible is very clear—every member of the body of Christ has a divine call from God. In fact, here is the principle: God calls no one (for service) until He first puts a call upon their lives (for salvation and eternal life). No matter how ill-equipped or insignificant we may feel, God has placed a call upon our lives to serve Him and others (Ephesians 3:7-4:16).

What is the call of God? According to the New Testament Greek language, the word "call" is *kaleo*. In the active voice, *kaleo* has a personal objective and signifies one who is called or invited to respond to God's personal invitation as well as the blessings of redemption. In the passive voice, *kaleo* means to call someone to a specific destination or vocation. Thus, every believer has been called by God to follow Him and assist the Lord in the work of His kingdom (see Matthew 28:18-20; Mark 16:15-20).

There is an interesting passage of Scripture that gives us a clearer picture of God's divine call (see Matthew 16:13-20). After feeding four thousand people and castigating the Pharisees, Jesus, along with His disciples, entered Caesarea Philippi, a city located about 25 miles northeast of the sea of Galilee on the southern slope of Mount Hermon. Once they arrived in the city, Jesus turned to His disciples and asked them to share any comments they may have heard about Him from others. Immediately, the disciples responded: "Some say that thou art John the Baptist: some, Elias; and others, Jeremias, or one of the prophets" (Matthew 16:14).

Certainly, the common people had heard Jesus' teaching (see Matthew 5—7), saw Him heal the sick (Matthew 8—9), and feed multitudes of people with very little resources (see Matthew 14:13-21; 15:32-39). They were also eyewitnesses of Jesus' rebuke of the religious leaders. The people knew their history, and they knew that, according to the law and prophets, no one could do these things unless they were called and empowered by Jehovah God. That is why they assumed Jesus was one of the Old Testament prophets. Certainly, they had been taught the law that Moses shared with the people of Israel: "The LORD thy God will raise up unto thee a Prophet from the midst of thee, of thy brethren, like unto me; unto him ye shall hearken. ...I will raise them up a Prophet from among their brethren, like unto thee, and will put my words in his mouth; and he shall speak unto them all that I shall command him" (Deuteronomy 18:15, 18).

From the people's perspective, it was clear that

> *No matter how ill-equipped or insignificant we may feel, God has placed a call upon our lives to serve Him.*

Jesus was a Prophet sent from God. However, Jesus was more interested in what the disciples had learned after being with Him and seeing His ministry firsthand. Jesus wanted to know the disciples' personal assessment of Him.

It is one thing for the world to identify Jesus ("He's a good teacher," "He's the man upstairs," "He's no different than Buddha, Muhammed, or Confucius"), but it's another for the church to *know* Him. In the Bible, the word "know" is always defined as experiential or intimate knowledge of a person or thing. What Jesus was saying to His disciples was, "I want you to have more than just head knowledge of who I am. You must truly understand My call and its impact on your life."

The body of Christ must understand this same principle. There are many people who have only "head knowledge" of Jesus Christ. Perhaps this is one reason why people have difficulty fully understanding the call of God upon their lives. They will not allow themselves to become intimately acquainted with the Saviour. Then they justify their distant relationship ("I may have to give up too much if I get close to Jesus"). We can never be fulfilled and understand our divine destiny by staying on the periphery of religion. We must let go and let Jesus change us, even as Jesus desired to change His disciples.

Matthew states that only Peter responded to Jesus' question: "Thou art the Christ, the Son of the living God" (from Matthew 16:16). Jesus knew that Peter's statement didn't come from Peter! In fact, Jesus made it clear that Peter had received *revelation knowledge* directly from God Himself. The significance of Peter's statement is threefold. First, it clearly revealed who Jesus is. The word "Christ" is *Christos* in Greek, and it designates Jesus as the Anointed One. In the Old Testament, the priest was anointed with the holy oil of consecration (see Leviticus 8:12, 30-36), signaling his special relationship as mediator between the peo-

We are God's called out people with a divine call upon our lives.

ple and God. In the New Testament, Jesus is the Great High Priest anointed by God the Father to be the true mediator for all who put their trust in Him (see 1 Timothy 2:5). The writer of Hebrews calls Jesus "that great shepherd of the sheep" and indicates that it is "through the blood of the everlasting covenant" that we have a special relationship with the Father (13:20). After the birth of the church, Peter and John were brought before the religious leaders, who demanded that they stop preaching in the name of Jesus. But Peter makes a bold declaration about Jesus that is still relevant for the church today: "Neither is there salvation in any other: for there is none other name under heaven given among men, whereby we must be saved [than Jesus Christ]" (Acts 4:12). Jesus is not just some great prophet, teacher, or religious figure. Paul helps us better understand the Person and work of Jesus when he says that Jesus "is the image of the invisible God, the firstborn of every creature: For by him were all things created, that are in heaven, and that are in earth, visible and invisible, whether they be thrones, or dominions, or principalities, or powers: all things were created by him, and for him: And he is before all things, and by him all things consist. And he is the head of the body, the church: who is the beginning, the firstborn from the dead; that in all things he might have the preeminence" (Colossians 1:15-18). Indeed, the Church has been purchased by the blood of Jesus Christ, the Son of the Living God.

Second, Peter's confession signifies the foundation on which God's Church is established. Paul tells the Gentile believers that we are "built upon the foundation of the apostles and prophets, Jesus Christ himself being the chief corner stone; In whom all the building fitly framed together groweth unto an holy temple in the Lord: in whom ye also are builded together for an habitation of God through the Spirit" (Ephesians 2:19-22). Even the psalmist refers to Jesus as the foundation of the Church when he affirms: "The stone which the builders refused is become the head stone of the corner. This is the LORD's doing; it is marvellous in our eyes" (Psalm 118:22-23).

For years, the church of Rome has taught that Peter is the foundation. But if we carefully examine the text and the response that Jesus gives to Peter—"thou art Peter [petros—rock or stone], and upon this rock I will build my church" (from Matthew 16:18)—we can see that the Saviour was specifically referring to the statement Peter made about Him. After all, it would be impossible to "build" the Church on a human being. Like so many people today, Peter was impetuous, impatient, impertinent, and immature. He needed "seasoning" and a greater understanding of the call of God upon his own life.

There are thousands of church congregations that have been established by family members, denominations, and even schools. While their work is to be commended, we must never forget that the foundation of the Church is Jesus Christ. When people understand this principle, church bickering and church splits will cease. The Scriptures make it clear that "The earth [and every church congregation and building within it] is the LORD's, and the fulness thereof; the world, and they that dwell therein. For he hath founded it upon the seas, and established it upon the floods" (Psalm 24:1-2). We have no right to try to "control" the church. We are called to follow the Lord Jesus so that He can be glorified in our local congregations.

Finally, Peter's faith-filled statement about the identity of Jesus Christ has a continuing effect upon the Church today. The Church of Jesus Christ is not a monolithic institution, but a living organism built on the promise of God the Father, God the Son, and God the Holy Spirit. "For God so loved the world, that he gave his only begotten Son, that whosoever believeth in him should not perish, but have everlasting life" (John 3:16). Indeed, Peter had no idea just how profound his words were when he answered Jesus, "Thou art the Christ, the Son of the living God" (from Matthew 16:16). Because of Jesus Christ of Nazareth, this "rock of revelation" has been used by God to establish a peculiar people destined for greatness (see 1 Peter 2:9-10).

The word Jesus uses for "church" is the Greek word ekklesia and means the assembly of the called out ones who have a calling upon their lives. Thus, the "call" of God is two-fold: (1) the call of salvation, deliverance, and eternal life; and (2) the call to serve the Lord in a specific area of ministry. No one is called just to sit in a building and soak up information. Instead, God's people, the Church, are called to go into the world to open the eyes of the blind, unstop deaf ears, and share God's unending love with those who are lost; so that they, too, can become a part of this living organism (see 2 Corinthians 4:3-5). The Church's only agenda is to make Christ known to the world so people can be saved and become a part of the true and living Church where Jesus is Lord.

We are God's called out people with a divine call upon our lives; therefore, no one is insignificant or unimportant in the body of Christ. In fact, in the apostle Paul's teaching about the human body's similarity to the Church, he reminds us that God places His call and purpose upon the lives of ordinary people (see 1 Corinthians 12:12-31). When every member of the body understands their calling and fulfills God's will, the Church can become a powerful weapon in the hands of our Lord. We can then say, like Jesus, that the gates of hell *shall not* prevail against God's Church (cf. Matthew 16:18).

Do you know God's divine call upon your life?

Pastor Philip Rodman is a former editor for UMI and is presently the senior pastor of Refreshing Spring Church in Jefferson City, Missouri.

DR. MARTIN LUTHER KING, JR.

(1929-1968) • *Civil Rights Leader*

It would be interesting to know what inspired the name *Martin Luther* for the King men when they were born. Martin Luther of the famed "95 Theses" and Protestant Reformation certainly led a hard life for what he believed. Like the 16th-century Martin Luther, Martin Luther King, Jr. was destined to break the mold and cause an ever-expanding ripple of change to eventually encompass the globe.

Martin Luther King, Jr. was born January 15, 1929 in Atlanta, Georgia to Baptist minister Martin Luther King, Sr. and his wife, Alberta. King, Jr. was ordained into the ministry at age 18. Like other Black boys, King attended segregated schools in the South; unlike many, he excelled at his studies, graduating at 15 and heading to Morehouse College, where President Benjamin Mays shaped King's perspective on racial equality. King went on to Crozer Theological Seminary and Boston University, where he earned his Ph.D. in systematic theology in 1955. It was during his time in Boston that King met Coretta Scott, who would become his wife, the mother of his four children, and his partner in the Civil Rights Movement.

It was during his first pastorate in Montgomery, Alabama, that King was brought to the forefront when Rosa Parks ignited the Montgomery bus boycott by refusing to relinquish her seat to a White person. Being new in Montgomery, King was thought to be the ideal person to lead the boycott, which lasted more than a year, was successful, and resulted in desegregation of the bus system there. His passion for racial justice inflamed, King became one of the founding fathers of the Southern Christian Leadership Conference (SCLC), setting up marches, demonstrations, and boycotts, which often landed him and his followers in jail. It was in jail that his famous "Letter from Birmingham City Jail" was penned, calling for responsible disobedience to unjust laws.

King's cause was drawing influential, material, and financial support of people in every arena and race. Along with other Black leaders, King organized the 1963 March on Washington for economic and civil justice. It was there he made his legendary "I Have A Dream" speech. As a result, the Civil Rights Act was passed and King was awarded the Nobel Peace Prize. Later (1965), national attention was focused on Selma, Alabama, as King and his followers marched for voting rights. Police violence against marchers was televised in a national broadcast. This violence is now known as "Bloody Sunday" but acted as a catalyst to the passage of the Voting Rights Act of 1965.

As major issues appeared to have been addressed, King turned his attention to protesting the Vietnam War and working for economic empowerment, which sparked no little dissent among Civil Rights activists. King was assassinated on April 4, 1968 in Memphis, Tennessee, while supporting striking sanitation workers. Rather than quell the storms of change, King's death made him a martyr and sparked more engagement in securing Civil Rights. In 1983, the Congress of the United States designated the third Monday in January a national holiday—a day to honor Dr. Martin Luther King, Jr. It is a day to pick up shards from the mold he broke and run on with the vision.

Connie M. Taylor is the Editor for UMIs *J.A.M. Jesus And Me*®. She is a schoolteacher and lifelong educator.

TEACHING TIPS

December 5
Bible Study Guide 1

1. Words You Should Know

A. Kindred (Genesis 12:1) *mowledeth* (Heb.)—Relatives or family members.

B. Moreh (v. 6) *Mowreh* (Heb.)—The name of the first place where Abraham set up camp.

2. Teacher Preparation

A. Read the BIBLE BACKGROUND for today's lesson so that you can see how God's work in humankind becomes personal through His covenant with Abraham.

B. Ask your pastor or another person who has had a strong sense of calling from the Lord to write down that experience in a few brief paragraphs. If you have the biography or autobiography of a well-known religious leader, you may choose instead to read that person's experience of being called into ministry.

3. Starting the Lesson

A. Read today's IN FOCUS story about Alfredia's invitation to enter a new vocation after retiring from a totally different vocation.

B. Discuss how we must always be open to the Lord's invitation to do a new thing. Sometimes that call comes directly from the Lord; at other times, it may come indirectly through another servant or messenger of the Lord. No matter how the call comes, we must stay in constant prayer so that we can have the assurance that it is indeed God calling us to serve Him.

4. Getting into the Lesson

A. After reviewing today's lesson, read the portions that related to Abram's call. What are some distinguishing features of his call from God?

B. Determine whether there are any similarities between the call of Abram and the call experience you shared at the beginning of the lesson.

5. Relating the Lesson to Life

A. Today's DISCUSS THE MEANING section focuses on obedience and faith. Discuss how it is often difficult for us to have complete faith and trust in the Lord, without questions or reservations about following His lead.

B. The LESSON IN OUR SOCIETY section addresses the fact that oftentimes our plans for our lives may be leading us in a direction quite different from, and even directly opposite to, God's plans for us. How can Christians make plans for their future and still leave themselves open to the will of God? Should we not make plans for our future? How do we respond when God calls us to a new thing?

6. Arousing Action

A. Ask the students to complete the MAKE IT HAPPEN exercise in today's lesson. Remind them to look at the criteria for a call that you have identified and to use these criteria to help them clarify whether God has called or is calling them into a particular area of service.

B. Give class members an opportunity to complete the FOLLOW THE SPIRIT and REMEMBER YOUR THOUGHTS sections.

WORSHIP GUIDE

For the Superintendent or Teacher
Theme: A Call to Follow God
Theme Song: "Where He Leads Me"
Scripture: Hebrews 11:8-12
Song: "Close to Thee"
Meditation: Lord, teach me to be open to Your will so that I may hear Your voice whenever You call me.

A CALL TO FOLLOW GOD

Bible Background • GENESIS 11:27—12:9
Printed Text • GENESIS 11:27—12:9
Devotional Reading • JEREMIAH 1:4-10

LESSON AIM

By the end of the lesson, the students will develop an openness and begin to explore ways in which God may be calling them to a special work. Also, they can discover an appropriate faithful response to that call.

KEEP IN MIND

"Now the LORD had said unto Abram, Get thee out of thy country, and from thy kindred, and from thy father's house, unto a land that I will shew thee" (Genesis 12:1).

FOCAL VERSES

Genesis 11:27 Now these are the generations of Terah: Terah begat Abram, Nahor, and Haran; and Haran begat Lot.

28 And Haran died before his father Terah in the land of his nativity, in Ur of the Chaldees.

29 And Abram and Nahor took them wives: the name of Abram's wife was Sarai; and the name of Nahor's wife, Milcah, the daughter of Haran, the father of Milcah, and the father of Iscah.

30 But Sarai was barren; she had no child.

31 And Terah took Abram his son, and Lot the son of Haran his son's son, and Sarai his daughter in law, his son Abram's wife; and they went forth with them from Ur of the Chaldees, to go into the land of Canaan; and they came unto Haran, and dwelt there.

32 And the days of Terah were two hundred and five years: and Terah died in Haran.

12:1 Now the LORD had said unto Abram, Get thee out of thy country, and from thy kindred, and from thy father's house, unto a land that I will shew thee:

LESSON OVERVIEW

LESSON AIM
KEEP IN MIND
FOCAL VERSES
IN FOCUS
THE PEOPLE, PLACES,
AND TIMES
BACKGROUND
AT-A-GLANCE
IN DEPTH
SEARCH THE SCRIPTURES
DISCUSS THE MEANING
LESSON IN OUR SOCIETY
MAKE IT HAPPEN
FOLLOW THE SPIRIT
REMEMBER YOUR THOUGHTS
MORE LIGHT ON THE TEXT
DAILY BIBLE READINGS

2 And I will make of thee a great nation, and I will bless thee, and make thy name great; and thou shalt be a blessing:

3 And I will bless them that bless thee, and curse him that curseth thee: and in thee shall all families of the earth be blessed.

4 So Abram departed, as the LORD had spoken unto him; and Lot went with him: and Abram was seventy and five years old when he departed out of Haran.

5 And Abram took Sarai his wife, and Lot his brother's son, and all their substance that they had gathered, and the souls that they had gotten in Haran; and they went forth to go into the land of Canaan; and into the land of Canaan they came.

6 And Abram passed through the land unto the place of Sichem, unto the plain of Moreh. And the Canaanite was then in the land.

7 And the LORD appeared unto Abram, and said, Unto thy seed will I give this land: and there builded he an altar unto the LORD, who appeared unto him.

8 And he removed from thence unto a mountain on the east of Bethel, and pitched his tent, having Bethel on the west, and Hai on the east: and there he builded an altar unto the LORD, and called upon the name of the LORD.

9 And Abram journeyed, going on still toward the south.

IN FOCUS

Alfredia had replayed her conversation with

Pastor Reese for what seemed like the 100th time that day. He was asking her to serve as director of the church's ministry to the homeless.

Alfredia had never been the leader of anything. Now that she had retired from the post office, being in charge of something had not even crossed her mind! If she took the position, she would have to take a couple of training classes.

"I'm too old to be going to some class to study something new," she thought. As she continued to come up with reasons not to accept Pastor Reese's offer, she remembered that God puts no age limit on service.

"As long as God gives me health and strength," she reasoned, "I ought to be able to give something back." She prayed that she was making the right decision.

After her prayer time, Alfredia opened a book that contained a chapter about how people often have several careers in a lifetime, even after retiring from a "first" job.

Then she turned to her Bible. In the Old Testament, Alfredia found the names of many people who had continued to serve the Lord, even after reaching what many would term "old age."

One of the people she read about was Abram, who was 75 years old when God called him. After reading this, Alfredia decided that she was not going to let her age, or anything else, stand in the way of serving God. She called Pastor Reese and gladly accepted the position.

THE PEOPLE, PLACES, AND TIMES

Lot. When Abraham left his homeland in obedience to God, his nephew, Lot, also began the journey with him. Later, they parted company and Lot went to Sodom.

Abram. God began a new thing through Abram, carrying out His purpose through this one man. Through him, all the nations of the world would be blessed. The Lord called Abram into an adventure. He told Abram to leave his country, his family, and his home. God regularly invites men and women to participate in His great plans. Like Abram, many of us accept the invitation; others, like the rich, young ruler (Matthew 19:16-22) are unwilling to leave behind what they already have for fear of losing it.

Abraham. When Abram was 90 years old, God appeared to him and established an everlasting covenant with him and his descendants. At this time, God changed his name from Abram, meaning "great father," to Abraham, meaning "father of many nations" (Genesis 17:1-7).

Although 25 years passed before the son God promised to Abraham and Sarai was born, God did not forget His word. In those years of waiting, the couple continued on their faith journey with the Lord.

BACKGROUND

The call of Abram highlights God's relationship to His people and represents a significant new development in God's dealings with humanity. Through His covenant relationship with Abram and his descendants, God set in motion His plan to work with a people, not just individuals.

The progression from Abram to Abraham is a model of how God's providence and grace sustain us as we are molded into position to follow His plan. Far from perfect, Abraham was not different from any person who believes in God. Over time, he grew closer to the Lord through his experiences with Him.

Abraham did not always follow God's plan as God had intended. On occasion, he and Sarai both seemed to have an urge to give God a helping hand. At other times, the two acted out of cowardice, instead of faith, in the God who called them.

From the time of his call, Abraham had no knowledge of where he would be going. He stepped out on the word of God. He never stopped believing in God's purpose, even when it seemed that everything was working against him.

AT-A-GLANCE

1. Abram's Family (Genesis 11:27-32)
2. God Calls Abram (Genesis 12:1-3)
3. Abram in Canaan (vv. 4-9)

IN DEPTH

1. Abram's Family (Genesis 11:27-32)

Terah was Abram's father. Nahor and Haran were Abram's brothers. Haran was the father of Lot, Abram's nephew. Sometime after Lot was born, Haran (his father) died. Terah decided to take his son Abram, his grandson Lot, and his daughter-in-law Sarai and move to Canaan. However, when they reached Haran, they settled there.

It is not really known why Terah moved his family away from the land where he had raised his children. Perhaps it was part of the great migration taking place at the time. When the family began their journey away from Ur, Terah, the patriarch, was already an old man. Though he died long before reaching Canaan, God clearly used Terah to start Abram on his journey.

Abram's call began in Ur (Genesis 11:31). He may have actually encouraged his elderly father to journey with him to a foreign land—Canaan. Abram's call was apparently renewed more clearly when Terah's clan did not reach Canaan, but settled in Haran instead. A move to Canaan might have been too much for the patriarch to bear.

2. God Calls Abram (Genesis 12:1-3)

Throughout history, people have been known to run from the call of the Lord—and for good reason. The Lord often calls us out of our comfort zone and into an arena that is unknown to us. It is through our venture into the unknown that we learn to rely on Him and trust in His promises.

Sometimes the place to which we have been called is a lonely place. We may even feel as though no one understands—and usually, no one else does. Only the one who is given the call can hear the call.

The Lord's call to Abram was a great challenge, but it was also filled with great promise. The Talmudic rabbis taught that God's promise to Abram consisted of seven components:

(1) God promised that Abram would be the father of a great nation. This was a great test of Abram's faith because he was already 75 years old and had no children.

(2) God promised to bless Abram within his own lifetime. This meant that Abram would enjoy divine protection from harm and divine favor in ways he could probably not imagine.

(3) Abram's name would be great as he would become a person known and celebrated around the world.

(4) Abram would be a blessing to others. God intended to bless Abram so that he, in turn, could be a blessing to others. God was calling Abram to a high level of responsibility, not merely a life of privilege and personal pleasure.

(5) Those who blessed Abram and treated him well would be blessed by God. All those who received Abram would be showing their willingness to receive his God.

(6) Those who rejected or cursed Abram would be cursed by God. Their rejection of him would be an act of rejection of God's work in him.

(7) Abram would be a man of worldwide influence. Through him, blessings would come to many, many others.

3. Abram in Canaan (vv. 4-9)

Abram did not choose God; God chose him to fulfill His purposes. Abram's positive response to God's challenge gives insight into the depth of his faith. He prepared his family to depart on an unknown, but not uncertain, journey with God. He could not foresee the end of his journey, but he possessed courage and restlessness in his spirit that allowed him to take the first step.

It cannot be known precisely why Lot accompanied Abram, as no divine call was extended to Lot. Abram may have taken his nephew out of a sense of family obligation. The Lord had specifically stated, however, that Abram was to: "Leave your country, your people and your father's household" (Genesis 12:1, NIV). It is just as likely that Lot invited himself along for the trip, possibly having nowhere else to go and perhaps even intrigued by his uncle's adventure. Later, however, Abram did have to part ways with Lot in order to continue his journey with the Lord.

Apparently, Lot was not the only one inspired to follow Abram's cause. "And the souls that they had gotten in Haran" indicates that Abram already had the beginnings of a community of faith (12:5). It is unlikely that the "souls" mentioned were slaves, as they would have been included in the general category of "substance that they had gathered," or possessions (v. 5).

Abram worshiped God wherever he went. At Sichem, Abram built an altar and worshiped the Lord. Abram built altars out of gratitude for the Lord's promise to him. These alters also symbolized Abram's recognition of God.

When Abram reached Sichem, the Lord appeared and informed him that he had reached the land that would be given to his descendants. Interestingly, Abram was not told the land was his until he had walked on it. This calls into question the possible outcome if Abram had not gone where the Lord told him or if he had stopped short of God's directive.

Abram's faith was being tested when the Lord promised him a land that another group of people already occupied. How could it become his? The process would take centuries before God would give the land to Abram's descendants. This required Abram to trust God.

Obedience to God is sometimes costly but is never in vain. As with Abram, God very often calls us away from all that we hold near and dear. God may call us out of the very thing into which He has previously called us. He may call us out of the familiar and friendly and into the unexplored and unknown.

We can never reach our fullest potential in the Lord if we desire what the world has to offer more than God's promises. Fortunately for Abram, his sense of happiness and well-being were not derived from worldly pleasures. Instead, his pleasure emerged from his sense of purpose, which had its origin beyond this world. He found the call of God more intriguing than the comfort of family, the security of homeland, and the lure of riches.

SEARCH THE SCRIPTURES

1. Who went along with Terah on the journey from Ur (Genesis 11:31)?

2. How old was Terah when he died (v. 32)?

3. What did the LORD tell Abram to do (12:1)?

4. What did God promise Abram (vv. 2-4)?

5. How did Abram respond to the Lord's call (v. 4)?

6. Who went with Abram on his journey (v. 5)?

7. Where did Abram stop for a time (v. 6)?

8. What did Abram do while he was there (v. 8)?

DISCUSS THE MEANING

1. God did not give Abram any information about where he was going. Name some qualities Abram must have possessed in order to follow God's call and leading without question or reservation.

2. Wherever he went, Abram built an altar as a sign of faith, discipleship, and thanksgiving. Although building altars is not practical for us in modern times, what steps can we take in order to "mark" our journey with the Lord as Abram did?

LESSON IN OUR SOCIETY

It is said that the most successful people in this world have a written plan of action for their lives, and they follow that plan. God's call may run contrary to human plans. The question then becomes: Where do we put our trust: in human planning mechanisms, or in God? If God has called us to do a work that defies human logic or planning, what do we do? Do we follow God? Do we dismiss taking a step of faith, determining that such a move is illogical?

Our world applauds planning and shuns that which cannot be proven or seen—otherwise known as faith. It is essential that the one whom God calls be willing to block out the voices of human reasoning in order to clearly hear the Master's call.

MAKE IT HAPPEN

Many people believe that, like Joseph, God gives us goals or dreams to strive for in life. Are there some things that you have told yourself are too late to accomplish? List things that have gone undone in your life, like finishing your education and getting a degree, changing careers, taking on a new hobby, or joining a new organization.

After making your list, write down obstacles to completing these tasks or unfulfilled dreams. As you complete your list, remember that God has wonderful things in store for you at any age if you are willing to live by faith and not by human sight, reasoning, or understanding.

FOLLOW THE SPIRIT
What God wants me to do:

_____

_____

REMEMBER YOUR THOUGHTS
Special insights I have learned:

_____

_____

MORE LIGHT ON THE TEXT
Genesis 11:27—12:9

11:27 Now these are the generations of Terah: Terah begat Abram, Nahor, and Haran; and Haran begat Lot. 28 And Haran died before his father Terah in the land of his nativity, in Ur of the Chaldees. 29 And Abram and Nahor took them wives: the name of Abram's wife was Sarai; and the name of Nahor's wife, Milcah, the daughter of Haran, the father of Milcah, and the father of Iscah. 30 But Sarai was barren; she had no child. 31 And Terah took Abram his son, and Lot the son of Haran his son's son, and Sarai his daughter in law, his son Abram's wife; and they went forth with them from Ur of the Chaldees, to go into the land of Canaan; and they came unto Haran, and dwelt there. 32 And the days of Terah were two hundred and five years: and Terah died in Haran.

Genesis 11:27-32 introduces the narrative about Abram. Three major religions claim Abram as their progenitor: Judaism, Christianity, and Islam. However, the true children of Abram are those who share his faith—those who are in his "seed," namely, Jesus Christ (John 8:56; Galatians 3:16). Here we read of Terah, who took his family and left the mountains of Chaldees. The Old Testament does not tell us why this man decided to move his family.

Though this passage does not state so explicitly, something seems to have happened to Terah. Here we find grace working in the heart of the one whose children were going to inherit the Land of Promise and serve as instruments of God, bringing the promised seed into the world. Terah must have done something right as a father. He was the father of three sons: Haran, Nahor, and Abram. The descendants of Nahor and Abram combined to form the line of Israel, for all the wives of Isaac and Jacob came from the line of Nahor.

When Terah left Ur, he took his extended family with him. This example is vital to people of African descent, for we have always been people who value the extended family. In the old days, grandparents took their grandchildren in if their children died before them. Haran, Terah's son and the father of Lot, died before Terah. This could have been the reason for leaving; as in most ancient culture, they considered this a bad sign. God may have been speaking to the family through Abram to leave, but they did not leave until Haran died.

We read here of Abram's departure from Ur of the Chaldees with his father Terah, his nephew Lot, and the rest of his family in obedience to the call of God. "Went forth" suggests that they departed carrying with them all their belongings. There is a certain sense in which this means they condemned the place of their departure. It can also mean they were drawn forth by a power beyond themselves. It is possible that they were trying to escape or get away from some kind of bondage. The fact that they "went forth" may suggest they were looking for a place to grow. They stopped halfway between Ur and Canaan. They were not far from the Promised Land, yet they never proceeded to it. They dwelt in Haran until the death of Terah. The name of this place is similar to the name of Terah's first son. Could it be that this place was named for him? This was a halfway house that fell short of their goal to reach Canaan.

Why did the family stop in Haran? It may have been because of Terah's age. No matter what their reason may have been, we must remember that they stopped short of the goal that God had for them. They made their abode there and applied the words of God's promise to the place because it felt comfortable. They found employment and proceeded to enter into relationships with the people of the place. It took a tragedy for Abram to leave Haran and head to the place where God had directed him.

12:1 Now the LORD had said unto Abram, Get thee out of thy country, and from thy kindred, and from thy father's house, unto a land that I will shew thee:

The death of his father and the fact that Abram may have felt comfortable in Haran did not change Abram's calling. While it is good that Abram respected his father, a time comes when children must take the vision of their parents further. Respect for his father was not to stand in the way of God's command. The fact that this verse begins with, "Now the LORD had said unto Abram" is very important (v. 1). The use of the word "now" serves as a reminder of what God had said to Abram. "Had said" suggests that this was not the first time that God had spoken to Abram. They left Ur of the Chaldees because God had spoken to them. It could also mean that while Abram was in Ur wondering and asking what to do, especially in response to their religious orientation, God had answered him. In this response, God appoints a place for Abram. In that response, God challenged and charged Abram. It could also mean that God entered into a relationship with Abram and communed with him.

God's words were "get thee out" (v. 1). This phrase was directed to three very important levels of Abram's life. The first was the sentiment of national attachment. "Country" and "land" are translated as *'erets* (**eh'rets**) in Hebrew. Ancients defined themselves by a radical connection to their own parcel of earth. Relating to this attachment to earth or land may be hard for people in America today; for people of the African world, this was once considered the ultimate attachment. This was Abram's world. Along with a requirement to abandon sentiments of national attachment comes the requirement to deny other gods. For many ancients, their god was tied to their land. So what Yahweh was asking Abram to do was radical. One can understand, then, why Abram and his family stopped at Haran. Staying at Haran gave them a sense of being among their own people.

Second, the phrase "get thee out" was directed toward Abram's extended family connection. It seems that God went from the remote to the very personal. "Kindred" comes from the root *mowledeth* (**mo-leh'-deth**), which speaks to the lineage of Abram. Abram was not someone who was leaving because he had nothing good or worth-while to do; he probably was the offspring of a well-to-do extended family. So it would seem that God was asking Abram to go from where everyone knew and respected him to a place where he would be the constant object of other people's jealousy and envy.

The third direction of the divine instruction to "get thee out" or "leave" was toward Abram's father's house. The word translated as "house" in Hebrew is *bayith* (**bah'-yith**) and refers to a family. God could be saying to Abram, "As great as your father's house may be, you need to get out."

Though God was giving Abram a command to leave these three important attachments, He was not sending Abram without a guiding light. Abram was not to wander alone in the wilderness. The command "get thee out" had a positive direction. God said, "Go to a land that I will show you." God was indicating that He was moving toward something great and wanted Abram to be more than a quiet spectator. There was within this command the implication that God was in charge—that God was with him in a very specific way.

God was going to "shew" (show) Abram a land. The Hebrew word used here is *ra'ah* (**raw-aw'**). It comes from a primitive root meaning to see literally and figuratively. God is saying to Abram here that if he would obey, then it would appear to him what God was doing. Abram would also enjoy the place that God would show him. The word can also mean that God would "mark" the land. In that land, God would be near and Abram will perceive the presence of God, who was now calling him to this radical act of faith. This call is full of implications for the relationship that would develop between Abram and the Lord God. God would have regard and respect for Abram and cause him to see sights never thought of by others.

2 And I will make of thee a great nation, and I will bless thee, and make thy name great; and thou shalt be a blessing: 3 And I will bless them that bless thee, and curse him that curseth thee: and in thee shall all families of the earth be blessed.

In verses 2-3, we see God's promises to Abram.

There are three explicit "I wills" and four implied "I wills." The first "I will" is a promise directed to Abram's posterity. God says, "I will make of thee a great nation." Here, God is clear that upon Abram He will bestow greatness. God will bring forth that which He has charged and committed to Abram. What was God going to make? God says, "a great nation" (v. 2). The word "great" is from the Hebrew word *gadowl* (**gaw-dole'**), which means "important in all ways." The term used for "nation" is the Hebrew word *gowy* (**go'ee**), which is rarely used to refer to Israel. This is one of the few times this word is used to refer to the true children of Abram. This term comes from the same root as the Hebrew word that means a massive troop of soldiers or animals. This literally means that God will fashion a nation from Abram as a potter fashions pottery. More than just fashioning a nation, God will fulfill His purpose for that nation and furnish her with all that she needs to be His nation. God was intent on working for the emergence of a great people through Abram.

The second "I will" is a promise directed to Abram as a person. It reads, "I will bless thee" (v. 2). God knows that human beings need immediate blessing. God understands that as much as Abram would love to have a great posterity, he also desires to be blessed in his lifetime. The use of the Hebrew word *barak* (**baw-rak'**) means that Abram was going to be one who kneels to the true God. He would bless God through acts of adoration. It also means that he will be a man who benefits from his relationship with God. God will personally congratulate Abram for whatever Abram does for His sake.

The third "I will" is implied, not stated explicitly. This "I will" is directed to Abram's name. The idea here is that Abram will occupy a definite and conspicuous position in the history of humankind. The Hebrew word for "name" (*shem*, **shame**) denotes a mark of memorial placed where everyone who passes by can see. Abram's name will be recognized wherever it is named, because Abram will be a man of honor and authority.

The fourth "I will" is also implied and is where God adds, "And thou shalt be a blessing" (v. 2).

Many of us know people who are blessed but fail to bless others. We also may have met people who are renowned but whose presence has not been a blessing. Just because someone is great does not mean that they will bless others.

Abram, on the other hand, is told by God that he will be a blessing. The word for blessing is *berakah* (**ber-aw-kaw**). It implies that Abram will make others prosper by his relationship with God. Many will share in the pool of treasures that God will store up for Abram.

The fifth "I will" is found in verse 3 and speaks to what God will do for those who bless Abram: "I will bless them that bless thee." God will prepare a blessing for those who bless Abram. This could mean that God will say thanks to those who reach out to Abram and to his children. This promise is very important, particularly given the fact that Abram will live out his life as a stranger in a strange land. The unwritten rule of the ancient world and in African cultures is that those who minister to strangers or pilgrims were in fact ministering to God. They shall be blessed by God.

The sixth "I will" (implied) from God to Abram is related to people's treatment of Abram and Sarai in their pilgrimage: "and curse him that curseth thee" (v. 3). "Curse," translated from the Hebrew *'arar* (**aw-rar'**), tells us what God will do. The word is from the primitive root that means to abhor or to hate. God, then, will hate and attack those who curse Abram. It also means that God will censure or condemn them. What God is saying here is that those who mistreat this pilgrim will be despised and scorned; they shall receive the bitter medicine of their own curse.

The seventh "I will" is implied also: "in thee shall all families of the earth be blessed" (v. 3). God's final "I will" to Abram was a universal promise. This blessing includes all human beings. The Hebrew word *mishpachah* (**mish-paw-khaw'**), translated as "families," can mean family. The way it is used here can also mean all classes of people. It can also refer to the whole race or humanity as a species. In the final word, Abram's call is for the blessing of all tribes, people, and kindred.

4 So Abram departed, as the LORD had spoken unto him; and Lot went with him: and Abram was seventy and five years old when he departed out of Haran. 5 And Abram took Sarai his wife, and Lot his brother's son, and all their substance that they had gathered, and the souls that they had gotten in Haran; and they went forth to go into the land of Canaan; and into the land of Canaan they came.

In verse 4, Abram begins his second journey to Canaan. Abram brought out the various properties that he had acquired in Haran. He was now assured that God would be with him through thick and thin. Abram probably carried his family and escaped in secret as his brother and his relatives may have tried to stop him from leaving. His going away from Haran was in obedience to God's word.

We are also told that he was 75 years old when he left Haran. One is never too old to strike out on a new venture for the Lord. As an old man of 75, Abram followed the commandment to go forth into a new area and spread his wings. Though it may have been the "winter" of life in human eyes, God's command caused Abram to stand up and step out for God and for the blessing of humanity.

After hearing the seven "I wills" from God, Abram was surely ready to take God's word into the land of promise. Any time is a good time to obey the Lord; any age is a good age.

Abram ran with the promise. The three persons who left Haran for the second journey to Canaan were Abram, Lot, and Abram's wife Sarai.

This verse also points out that Abram had prospered in Haran. God's blessing was already upon him, but it was not yet the perfect blessing that God promised. They departed with "all their substance" (v. 5). The Hebrew word *rekvwsh* implies riches gathered through hard work blessed by God. They also took with them "the souls that they had gotten in Haran" (v. 5). The word for "souls" in Hebrew is *nephesh* (**neh'-fesh**). It is an indication that Abram was not mainly concerned about gathering material property. He also gathered people around him and had animals. He sought not only his own

personal pleasure, but that of other souls also. Abram, by this action, began to fulfill God's promise to bless the whole world through him. Abram and Sarai, in obedience to the word of God, came into Canaan.

6 And Abram passed through the land unto the place of Sichem, unto the plain of Moreh. And the Canaanite was then in the land. 7 And the LORD appeared unto Abram, and said, Unto thy seed will I give this land: and there builded he an altar unto the LORD, who appeared unto him.

Abram's first activity was to survey the land. The Hebrew word `abar (**aw-bar'**) means to cross over or to make a transition from one place to another. This implies a thorough overview. He entered the land to claim it according to the promise of God. It could also mean that he went through it to sanctify it. In this passage, Abram and Sarai came to "the place of Sichem." This refers to a place that offers good conditions for the body and mind. It could mean that Abram found a place where he could feel safe.

Another way to look at it is that Abram came to an open place, or room, that provided enough space for his caravan. It was in the north central part of Canaan, which means that, as he came from Chaldea, this was among the first sites that Abram would have encountered. This place of Abram's first stop became an important city for the northern kingdom of Israel and for the whole nation. It was a city built on one side of the mountains of Ephraim. Sichem was a favorite spot for ancient travelers. African travelers from Egypt speak of it as an important city, and the patriarchs after Abram came back to this spot again and again. When Jacob returned from Paddan-aram, he made his first home here at Sichem (Genesis 33:18-19). When Israel came into Canaan, their first place of worship was Sichem, where Joshua erected an altar; and there the people renewed their covenant written in the Law of Moses (Joshua 8:30-35; compare Deuteronomy 27:12-13).

Abram's second stop was "the plain of Moreh." The Hebrew word for "plain" is the word `elown (**ay-lone'**), which means an oak grove. Moreh, or *Mowreh,* means the place of instruction. This also was a place where several important events occurred in the lives of the patriarchs and the nation of Israel. The oak tree served as a religious site for ancients. In the absence of a temple, people used the oak grove as a place of worship.

Here is the place where Abram builds his first altar in the land of Canaan. Abram had taken a step of faith into the land, and he had built an altar in acknowledgment of the God whose power had led him thus far. Then God appeared to him. This appearance of God meant that God caused Abram to know the direction he should go. God advised Abram that He approved his actions and allowed him to behold His glory. In a certain way, it implies that God considered and enjoyed the company of Abram. Abram's obedience now gives an experience of the divine. It was not until Solomon built the temple that the people were advised to stop worshiping under oak trees. We read when Abram entered the land of Canaan, the Canaanites were still there. In the process of his obeying the word of God, the Lord appeared to Abram. It is also significant to note that God did not appear to Abram until he had worshiped.

God appeared with some words for His friend. The words were, "Unto thy seed will I give this land" (v. 7). Abram's call was to see the land, to have a clear vision of the land, and to lay the ground for the future generations to inherit the land. How important it is for the older generation to have a clear vision of God's will and be willing to do what it takes to prepare the way for future generations. Abram will see the land, and his seed will inherit the land.

8 And he removed from thence unto a mountain on the east of Bethel, and pitched his tent, having Bethel on the west, and Hai on the east:

and there he builded an altar unto the LORD, and called upon the name of the LORD. 9 And Abram journeyed, going on still toward the south.

This verse continues to describe Abram's movement across the land. His second major stop was near Bethel. Bethel simply means the house of El, or the house of God. In this location, Abram built his second altar. This points to the fact that he will obtain that which has been promised to him.

DAILY BIBLE READINGS

M: God Calls Isaiah
Isaiah 6:1-8
T: God Calls Jeremiah
Jeremiah 1:4-10
W: Jesus Calls the First Disciple
Luke 5:4-11
T: God Calls Saul
Acts 9:1-9
F: Abram and Sarai Live in Haran
Genesis 11:27-32
S: God Calls Abram
Genesis 12:1-9
S: God Makes a Covenant with Abram
Genesis 15:1-6

Find out more about the meaning of the word *follow* by using the *Strong's* reference materials on your *Precepts For Living* CD-ROM.

TEACHING TIPS

December 12
Bible Study Guide 2

1. Words You Should Know

A. Anointed (1 Samuel 16:3, 12-13) *mashach* (Heb.)—To rub with oil, to smear, or to consecrate. A very important part of Jewish ceremony.

B. Countenance (vv. 7, 12) *mar'eh* (Heb.)—The outward appearance, the face, or the part of a person visible to the eye.

2. Teacher Preparation

A. Familiarize yourself with the BIBLE BACKGROUND and DEVOTIONAL READING for the lesson.

B. Next, study the FOCAL VERSES, paying particular attention to the KEEP IN MIND verse.

C. Read MORE LIGHT ON THE TEXT. Write down any questions you may have as you read the biblical content.

D. Materials needed: pencils or pens, Bible, maps of Israel and Judah.

3. Starting the Lesson

A. Before the students arrive, write the AT-A-GLANCE outline on the chalkboard, along with the names Samuel and David.

B. After the students arrive, assign three to read the FOCAL VERSES according to the AT-A-GLANCE outline. Be sure the students have paper and pencils or pens to take notes.

C. Now assign several students to answer the SEARCH THE SCRIPTURES and DISCUSS THE MEANING questions later in the class time.

D. Have a student pray, using the LESSON AIM as the foundation of the prayer.

4. Getting into the Lesson

A. Have a student read the IN FOCUS story. Ask the students to comment on how it relates to today's lesson.

B. Ask a volunteer to read the BIBLE BACKGROUND. Briefly review last week's lesson to see how it relates to today's lesson.

C. Direct the students' attention to the names of Samuel and David on the chalkboard. Have the students comment on how today's lesson relates to both men, and write their comments under each name on the board.

D. After the students have finished reading the IN DEPTH section, ask the students to give the answers to the SEARCH THE SCRIPTURES and DISCUSS THE MEANING questions.

5. Relating the Lesson to Life

A. Have a student read the KEEP IN MIND verse.

B. Have the students give brief comments on why God selected David. Also have them comment on whether or not David was qualified to be king.

C. Read the LESSON IN OUR SOCIETY. Give the students an opportunity to brainstorm ideas for implementation.

6. Arousing Action

A. Ask the students to come up with a specific plan on how they intend to complete the MAKE IT HAPPEN assignment.

B. Remind the students to read the DAILY BIBLE READINGS for the week, which will help them grow in their walk with the Lord.

C. Close the class with prayer.

WORSHIP GUIDE

For the Superintendent or Teacher
Theme: A Call to Lead Faithfully
Theme Song: "I Say Yes, Lord"
Scripture: Psalm 23:1-6
Song: "I'll Go All the Way"
Meditation: Lord, help me to follow You no matter the cost. Keep me from rejecting or preferring others based on their looks. Help me to see and love others the way You see and love me. In Jesus' name. Amen.

A CALL TO LEAD FAITHFULLY

Bible Background • 1 SAMUEL 16:1-4, 6-13; 2 SAMUEL 7:8-16
Printed Text • 1 SAMUEL 16:1-4, 6-13
Devotional Reading • 2 SAMUEL 7:18-29

LESSON AIM

By the end of the lesson, the students should be able to explain why David was anointed to be king, affirm God's process of selecting leaders, and commit to obeying God's directions no matter the cost.

KEEP IN MIND

"The Lord seeth not as man seeth; for man looketh on the outward appearance, but the LORD looketh on the heart" (from 1 Samuel 16:7).

FOCAL VERSES

1 Samuel 16:1 And the LORD said unto Samuel, How long wilt thou mourn for Saul, seeing I have rejected him from reigning over Israel? fill thine horn with oil, and go, I will send thee to Jesse the Bethlehemite: for I have provided me a king among his sons.

2 And Samuel said, How can I go? if Saul hear it, he will kill me. And the LORD said, Take an heifer with thee, and say, I am come to sacrifice to the LORD.

3 And call Jesse to the sacrifice, and I will shew thee what thou shalt do: and thou shalt anoint unto me him whom I name unto thee.

4 And Samuel did that which the LORD spake, and came to Bethlehem. And the elders of the town trembled at his coming, and said, Comest thou peaceably?

16:6 And it came to pass, when they were come, that he looked on Eliab, and said, Surely the LORD's anointed is before him.

7 But the LORD said unto Samuel, Look not on his countenance, or on the height of his stature; because I have refused him: for the LORD seeth not as man seeth; for man looketh on the outward appearance, but the LORD looketh on the heart.

8 Then Jesse called Abinadab and made him pass before Samuel. And he said, neither hath the LORD chosen this.

9 Then Jesse made Shammah to pass by. And he said, Neither hath the LORD chosen this.

10 Again, Jesse made seven of his sons to pass before Samuel. And Samuel said unto Jesse, The LORD hath not chosen these.

11 And Samuel said unto Jesse, Are here all thy children? And he said, There remaineth yet the youngest, and, behold, he keepeth the sheep. And Samuel said unto Jesse, Send and fetch him: for we will not sit down till he come hither.

12 And he sent, and brought him in. Now he was ruddy, and withal of a beautiful countenance, and goodly to look to. And the LORD said, Arise, anoint him: for this is he.

13 Then Samuel took the horn of oil, and anointed him in the midst of his brethren: and the Spirit of the LORD came upon David from that day forward. So Samuel rose up, and went to Ramah.

LESSON OVERVIEW

LESSON AIM
KEEP IN MIND
FOCAL VERSES
IN FOCUS
THE PEOPLE, PLACES, AND TIMES
BACKGROUND
AT-A-GLANCE
IN DEPTH
SEARCH THE SCRIPTURES
DISCUSS THE MEANING
LESSON IN OUR SOCIETY
MAKE IT HAPPEN
FOLLOW THE SPIRIT
REMEMBER YOUR THOUGHTS
MORE LIGHT ON THE TEXT
DAILY BIBLE READINGS

IN FOCUS

The Bradshaw administration was extremely nervous when they discovered that the African American community had selected one of their own to oppose the mayor in the general election. Having taken the Black vote for granted for years, Mayor Bradshaw knew that he would have to visit many of the Black churches in the city if he expected to win another term as mayor.

However, this time the mayor's platitudes, one-liners, and broken promises did not win the people over. In the end, Mayor Bradshaw was ousted from office and a young businessman was voted in. When asked why the change occurred, many in the Black community stated that not only was it a rejection of Bradshaw, but also a rejection of his policies and the promise of good things to come with mayor-elect Peters.

Sometimes change is important, especially when policies fail and people's lives are at stake. The idea of "out with the old and in with the new" should apply when corrupt leaders are more intent on following their own agenda rather than doing what is best for all. In today's lesson, we will get a clear understanding of this principle when Saul is rejected and David is anointed as the new king of Israel.

THE PEOPLE, PLACES, AND TIMES

Bethlehem. This Hebrew word literally means "house of bread." Bethlehem was a small town of approximately 15,000 inhabitants, about five miles south of Jerusalem, but now forming part of the modern Jerusalem-Bethlehem network of communities. Perched 2,460 feet above sea level on the north-south ridge road along the central highlands, the city of Bethlehem faces westward to the fertile cultivated slopes around Beit Jala and eastward to the desolate wilderness of Judah.

Bethlehem was first mentioned in one of the Armana letters written to Egyptian pharaohs by local kings of Palestine and Syria prior to 1250 B.C. Prior to the period of the Israelite monarchy, Bethlehem was the home of the Levite who went to act as priest for a man named Micah in Ephraim (Judges 17:7-13) and of the unfortunate concubine, whose murder caused the tragic massacre of the people of Gibeah (Judges 19—20).

After the division of the Hebrew kingdom into Israel and Judah following Solomon's death, Bethlehem was one of the 15 cities in Benjamin and Judah fortified by Rehoboam (2 Chronicles 11:5-12).

The great importance of Bethlehem for Christians throughout the centuries is that the Gospels record the birth of Jesus Christ as having taken place there in fulfillment of Bible prophecy (Micah 5:2).

Bethlehem was destroyed by the emperor Hadrian in the second century A.D.; but in about 325, after the empire had become Christian, Queen Helena, the mother of Constantine, promoted the building of a great church there. Badly damaged during the Samaritan revolt of 521-528, the church was rebuilt in the sixth century in very much its present form by the emperor Justinian. It was spared during the savage Persian invasion of 614 because the soldiers saw the mosaic portrayal of the Magi in Persian costume.

Achtemeier, Paul J., gen. ed. *The Harper Bible Dictionary.* San Francisco: Harper and Row Publishing Co., 1984. 106-107.

BACKGROUND

As the Israelites adjusted to life under the monarchy, it became increasingly clear that they were not in God's perfect will. What Samuel had prophesied began to take shape (see 1 Samuel 8:10-19). Not only did King Saul lack godly leadership, but he also sinned against God, making him unfit to lead Israel (see 1 Samuel 13:11-14).

The final strike against Saul was that he was more concerned about people's opinions than obeying God. After Saul failed to obey in a pivotal time in the life of Israel (see 1 Samuel 15:10-35), God replaced him. The new king would be someone who had a heart to be faithful to God no matter what.

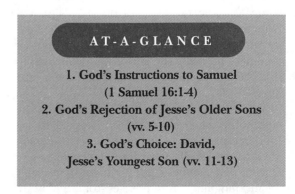

AT-A-GLANCE

**1. God's Instructions to Samuel
(1 Samuel 16:1-4)
2. God's Rejection of Jesse's Older Sons
(vv. 5-10)
3. God's Choice: David,
Jesse's Youngest Son (vv. 11-13)**

IN DEPTH

1. God's Instructions to Samuel (1 Samuel 16:1-4)

Though King Saul had twice disobeyed God's word spoken through Samuel, it is clear that Samuel deeply admired Saul. Once God rejected Saul as king, Samuel returned to his home in Ramah to mourn (1 Samuel 15:34-35). Perhaps Samuel mourned because Saul's potential to be a great king was lost. Maybe the prophet mourned because he knew the effect God's rejection of Saul would have on Israel. Whatever the reason, God had enough of Samuel's gloom and doom. It was time for Samuel to be about the Father's work. There was still a nation to look after, God was still in control, and He had already chosen the next king for Israel. So, as Samuel continued mourning in Ramah, God visited him and gave the prophet specific instructions for his next assignment.

Samuel was told to go to Bethlehem, a city approximately 15 miles south of Ramah, with a horn full of oil to see a man named Jesse, the father of eight sons. Among the eight, Samuel would not only discover God's choice for Israel's next king, but would also be the one to anoint him, just as he had Saul. Samuel immediately balked at God's command since Bethlehem was not a part of his circuit (1 Samuel 8:16). The prophet reasoned that Saul would find out why he was going to Bethlehem and have him killed.

To relieve his fears, God told Samuel to take with him a sacrificial animal and invite Jesse and his sons to the sacrifice as they worshiped the Lord in the city. That way, if Saul found out Samuel was in Bethlehem, the king would conclude that the prophet was on an assignment from the Lord—which he was. Realizing the futility of arguing with God, Samuel got himself together and made the journey to Bethlehem to find the man God had chosen to be Israel's next king.

When the prophet arrived in Bethlehem, the city fathers were surprised and shocked to see him. Because Samuel had shut himself in Ramah after Saul's rebellious actions, the elders were fearful that Samuel's arrival in town probably meant judgment and rebuke from the Lord.

Therefore, they wanted to know whether or not Samuel's visit was a peaceful one.

When God gives us an assignment, we need to obey Him, even when we are misunderstood by others. Our responsibility is to do what He has called us to do and let Him take care of the outcome and response of other people.

2. God's Rejection of Jesse's Older Sons (vv. 5-10)

Samuel informed the elders that he had come to Bethlehem in peace—to perform a sacrificial service unto the Lord. Samuel invited Jesse and seven of his sons to join him in the service. As the service progressed, Samuel looked at all of Jesse's sons trying to discern the right one to anoint as king. However, Samuel forgot that it wasn't his responsibility to choose the man, it was God's.

The first person Samuel saw was Eliab, the oldest of Jesse's sons. Scripture does not give us a complete description of Eliab, but we can surmise that he was a tall, strong, and handsome man who greatly impressed Samuel (see vv. 6-7). Samuel probably thought, *This isn't a hard job after all. The first son must be the one God has chosen. After all, look how handsome he is.*

Samuel was about to call it a day when he suddenly heard the Lord speak to him. In essence, God said, "Hold on, Samuel. Eliab may be good-looking, strong, and able, but I have not chosen him. In fact, I don't choose people based on the way they look. I choose people whose hearts are right before Me—those who are willing to follow My commands, no matter how good-looking or gifted they may be," (vv. 6-7, paraphrased). As if to emphasize this point, Jesse called his second son, Abinadab, his third son, Shammah, and his other sons to pass before Samuel, but none of them was chosen by God to become king.

So many churches are guilty of choosing leaders based on looks, financial contributions, political influences, social standing, or other characteristics that are not in line with God's Word. However, if we are to be faithful to God, we must choose for leadership positions only those people whose hearts are in tune with God's calling.

3. God's Choice: David, Jesse's Youngest Son (vv. 11-13)

Having been rebuked by God, Samuel wondered whether or not Israel's next king was among Jesse's seven sons who had come to the sacrifice. Had he truly heard from God? Was there another son nearby?

Jesse told the prophet that he did have a younger son, but that he was out in the field taking care of the sheep. Since none of the other sons were chosen by God, Samuel concluded that whoever he was, the younger son must be God's choice. Therefore, Samuel made it clear that no one would partake of the sacrificial meal until he had seen all of Jesse's sons.

When David arrived at the service, Samuel looked at him and noticed two things: (1) he was ruddy—the word literally means "red" or "to show blood in the face." It is clear from this verse that David was not a White man; and (2) like King Saul, he was a very handsome young man. Perhaps he was more handsome than all of his other brothers.

To eliminate any doubts Samuel may have had about David, God spoke to the prophet and told him to get up and anoint David as Israel's next king. God wanted David's brothers to see him being anointed with the horn of oil for several reasons: (1) the Bible affirms that the last will be first. David's work in the field did not eliminate him from being chosen as God's man. We must learn that God can choose us for His work no matter where we are; and (2) only from the Davidic line would come the Messiah of the world. Thus, David's choice as king was not only to replace Saul, but also to fulfill biblical prophecy. Because David was willing to be out in the field tending his father's sheep, God knew He could trust this young man with His "sheep."

Once Samuel poured the oil on David's head, God's anointing came upon the young man for the rest of his life. Having successfully completed his assignment, Samuel returned to his home in Ramah.

SEARCH THE SCRIPTURES

1. What was the Lord's command to Samuel (1 Samuel 16:1)?

2. Why didn't Samuel want to obey the Lord (v. 2)?

3. When Samuel arrived in Bethlehem, how did the elders respond (v. 4)?

4. How did Samuel respond when he met Eliab, Jesse's oldest son (v. 6)?

5. Whom did the Lord tell Samuel to anoint as Israel's next king (vv. 12-13)?

DISCUSS THE MEANING

1. How important is it for believers to follow God's Word even when we may not understand every detail?

2. What does it mean that the Lord "looks on the heart of man"? Discuss.

3. What is the significance of David's being anointed with oil? Does anointing with oil have any significance for believers today?

4. Can we be chosen by God for a specific work without being in the right place at the right time? Discuss.

LESSON IN OUR SOCIETY

We live in a class-conscious society where people are chosen for success based on good looks, financial influence, or race. How can we help the people who have been left out feel more accepted by our society regardless of their looks, economic status, or race? Explain.

MAKE IT HAPPEN

This week, ask the Lord to help you see people as He sees them. Perhaps spend a day or two at a homeless shelter or missions center, volunteering to help the less fortunate in our society. Report on your activities next week.

FOLLOW THE SPIRIT

What God wants me to do:

_____

_____

REMEMBER YOUR THOUGHTS

Special insights I have learned:

_____

_____

MORE LIGHT ON THE TEXT

1 Samuel 16:1-4, 6-13

When Saul becomes the King of Israel, the

David, the new anointed and appointed king of Israel, praises God, his Source.

prophet Samuel no longer serves in the public political arena. He now devotes his time solely to instructing and training the sons of prophets. Samuel knows that Saul had been rejected because of his disobedience to God. In this passage, we learn that obedience to God is better than sacrifice; obedience to God is better than duty or works (1 Samuel 15:22). The passage speaks of the tendency that we as human beings sometimes have to choose to please people instead of God. It was this course of action that led God to reject Saul as Israel's king. We also see Samuel, the man of God, as he mourns for Saul.

1 And the LORD said unto Samuel, How long wilt thou mourn for Saul, seeing I have rejected him from reigning over Israel? fill thine horn with oil, and go, I will send thee to Jesse the Bethlehemite: for I have provided me a king among his sons.

This verse begins with the proper Hebrew name for God—*Yahweh*, derived from the Hebrew word *hayah*, meaning "to be." Whenever this word is used, it is meant to affirm the belief in the God of Israel as the self-existent, Eternal One. This puts a clear distinction between the Lord and idols created by man or idols connected with nature (in the Hebrew culture, nature is a created organism and as such is not self-existent). It is this self-existent God who spoke to Samuel.

The Hebrew word used here for "said" is *'amar* (**aw-mar'**) and is used to distinguish God from idols that cannot speak or hear. This relates to the communicative nature of God, showing further that God is a being on whom one can call and receive an answer. Moreover, it speaks to the issue of God as One who considers action and who does not deal rashly with human beings. In Hebrew, Samuel (*Shemuw'el*) means heard of God, to hear with intelligence, or with the intent of acting on what has been heard. God heard Samuel and answered him. But the response was in the form of a question: "How long will you mourn for Saul?" The word "mourn" in Hebrew is *'abal* (**aw-bal'**), meaning "to lament." Samuel seems to have cried for Saul so long that it took God to comfort him.

We read further: "Seeing I have rejected him" (v. 1). We could interpret this as "you have been wailing until now because I have rejected him." The Hebrew word for "reject" is *ma'ac* (**maw-as'**), indicating that God had spurned Saul. Indeed, God now abhors him and is casting him away. Saul's actions have caused God to look at him with contempt and disdain, thereby causing God to loathe him. God not only rejects Saul but stops him from reigning over Israel. The Hebrew translation of the word "reigning" is *malak* (**maw-lak'**). When used in conjunction with the word "rejection," it means that Saul can no longer ascend the throne.

God instructs Samuel, "Fill thine horn with oil, and go, I will send thee to Jesse the Bethlehemite: for I have provided me a king among his sons" (v. 1). He was to consecrate oil and fill the horn. The Hebrew word *qeren* (**keh'-ren**) suggests a horn, but it could also mean an elephant's ivory. The horn represented power; it was usually filled with oil. The Hebrew word *shemen* (**sheh'-men**) refers to liquid from the olive; it symbolized the richness of fruitfulness expected from the person being anointed. Samuel was to walk to Bethlehem. The word "send" (Heb. *shalach*, **shaw-lakh'**) suggests that he was to make an appointment; he was to stop whatever else he was doing and go there. He was to go to Jesse, whose name in Hebrew is *Yishay*, meaning "a man of God," and to a place called *Beyth Lechem* (Bethlehem), the Hebrew word for "house of bread." God tells Samuel, "I have provided me a king" (v. 1). The word "provide," or *ra'ah* in Hebrew, means to see or to have a vision. God may be saying to Samuel that once he arrives in Bethlehem, He will give him a vision of whom the king will be.

2 And Samuel said, How can I go? if Saul hear it, he will kill me. And the LORD said, Take an heifer with thee, and say, I am come to sacrifice to the LORD.

Samuel's apprehension concerning Saul is valid. Will Saul indeed kill him? This fear is possibly derived from the fact that he had informed Saul of his dethronement. From that moment on, Saul grew more intolerant of the people around him.

Samuel has reason to fear Saul's rage. Samuel asks God, "How can I go?" The Hebrew translation reads, *Eglat baaqaar tiqach byaadekaa*. In actuality the phrase translates, "How *do* I go?" In other words, Samuel was asking for directions and a strategy for going to Bethlehem: "What is the best way to go so that I do not get killed?" The phrase can also be read: "How do I carry myself?" It was a question dealing with his behavior. Immediately Samuel gave his reason for this question: "If Saul hears about it, he will kill me." If Saul heard that Samuel was gone, he would have had witnesses against him and tried him for treason. The word for "kill" is not the word used for accident or manslaughter; instead, the Hebrew word *harag* (**haw-rag'**) is used here, meaning Saul will personally strike him down with deadly intent. Saul was not beyond committing murder, even the murder of a prophet. There is also the implication that Saul would slaughter anyone connected with this. Here we see that God did not dismiss Samuel's fear. Rather, the Lord gave Samuel a strategy to allay suspicion. God instructs Samuel to take a heifer with him as a sacrifice unto the Lord. This sacrifice was probably long overdue since Samuel was in mourning for Saul. Samuel would be asked why he was there. He was to say that he came to offer a sacrifice.

3 And call Jesse to the sacrifice, and I will shew thee what thou shalt do: and thou shalt anoint unto me him whom I name unto thee.

God's explicit instructions continue: Invite Jesse and his family to the sacrifice, wait for further instructions, then anoint the one whom God names.

Those who go about doing God's work in God's way shall be directed step by step. Some adults prudently plan the best means of accomplishing their goals. Often, when God calls us to do something, we proceed without receiving explicit instructions. Yet God's plans are not necessarily our plans. When God calls us for a purpose, He gives explicit instructions to accomplish His work. The word "call" (Heb. *qara'*, **kaw-raw'**), as used here, implies that Samuel would encounter Jesse. He was to properly address Jesse by name, as Jesse was going to be the father of the future king of Israel. This invitation was to be proclaimed and published. The Lord returns to His word: "I will shew thee what thou shalt do" (v. 3). Samuel would receive further revelation as he went. By using the word *yada`* (**yaw-dah'**), translated as "show," the Lord is saying "you will know." Conversely, Samuel will gain understanding of God's intent when he gets there.

It is only after Samuel has received this revelation that he can anoint. The Hebrew word for "anoint" is *mashach* (**maw-shakh'**) meaning to rub with oil and thus consecrate whomever or whatever has been rubbed. The implication is that the act of anointing is as though one is painting a portrait. It is from this word that the word

"Messiah" is derived, meaning one who is anointed. Not only will God show Samuel the person to anoint, but He says that the person shall be named. Samuel may not like the person God chooses. He may not think of him as kingly material; but if this person has been named by God, the anointing oil must fall on him.

4 And Samuel did that which the LORD spake, and came to Bethlehem. And the elders of the town trembled at his coming, and said, Comest thou peaceably?

In this verse we see Samuel obeying God by going to Bethlehem. He takes the heifer to sacrifice. Samuel demonstrates obedience to God even though he feels uncomfortable. We must always obey God even if it makes us feel uncomfortable. Obedience is better than sacrifice (1 Samuel 15:22). God wants loyal actions, not lip service.

We read, "And Samuel did that which the LORD spake, and came to Bethlehem" (v. 4). The key word in this phrase is "did" (Heb. *'asah*, **aw-saw'**). Broadly translated, "do" or "make" implies a sense of accomplishment, advancement of a cause, or the keeping of an appointment. This directly relates to Samuel's ability to follow the Lord's instruction. He had fulfilled the word of the Lord. Here is a man who is industrious in his service to God, even when it may cost him his life.

16:6 And it came to pass, when they were come, that he looked on Eliab, and said, Surely the LORD's anointed is before him.

Eliab was tall and physically strong. Because Samuel was aware of the appearance of the first king, he assumes that Eliab is the one to be anointed as Saul's successor. Sometimes people make choices based on past experiences and/or incorrect judgments. Samuel looks at Eliab's outer appearance; because he looks like Saul, Samuel automatically jumps to his own conclusion and assumes that Eliab is God's choice.

A key phrase here is, "that he looked on Eliab" (v. 6). The name Eliab (**el-ee-awb'**) is translated as "my God is father." The word "looked," as it is used here, is the Hebrew word *ra'ah* (**raw-aw'**), inferring that Samuel's literal sight took over his visionary insight and he approved of what he saw. The use of the word "surely," or *'ak* (**ak**) in Hebrew, is similar to the English definition of the word *truly*. By stating "surely the LORD's anointed," Samuel implies that God's choice is limited to Eliab only (v. 6). The word for "anointed" here is the direct translation of the word for "Messiah." Therefore, this phrase literally says, "Look! The Lord's Messiah." The Hebrew word *neged* (**neh'-ghed**) means before him, in front of someone, or counterpart of one who represents. Thus Samuel is saying, "This is the one, the Lord's Messiah."

7 But the LORD said unto Samuel, Look not on his countenance, or on the height of his stature; because I have refused him: for the Lord seeth not as man seeth; for man looketh on the outward appearance, but the LORD looketh on the heart. 8 Then Jesse called Abinadab, and made him pass before Samuel. And he said, Neither hath the LORD chosen this. 9 Then Jesse made Shammah to pass by. And he said, Neither hath the LORD chosen this. 10 Again, Jesse made seven of his sons to pass before Samuel. And Samuel said unto Jesse, The LORD hath not chosen these.

God quickly corrects Samuel's mistake. God responds that outward appearances do not matter to God. Some people are swayed by outward appearances, but God does not show favoritism. God does not care about a person's gender, ethnicity, age, weight, height, or status; God is concerned about a person's heart. God knows the hearts of people and sees their thoughts and intents. God judges people by their hearts. Some people affirm that "it's what's inside a person" that matters. They know that there is more to a person than meets the eye.

God's word to Samuel is a word of challenge. God tells Samuel to stop looking at the outward appearance. He tells Samuel that He has rejected Eliab. At this time Samuel is thoroughly confused because every nation wants a good-looking king. God takes the opportunity to give Samuel a lesson in theology. First, God does not look at things the same way humans do. How do human beings see? God says that human knowledge is based in physical sight. Human beings have a truncated vision

of reality. The Lord closes the conversation by stating how He sees. God sees beyond the physical appearance; He sees the heart.

11 And Samuel said unto Jesse, Are here all thy children? And he said, There remaineth yet the youngest, and, behold, he keepeth the sheep. And Samuel said unto Jesse, Send and fetch him: for we will not sit down till he come hither.

After all seven of Jesse's eldest sons' rejections, Samuel asks if they are all there and is told that the youngest son is keeping sheep. Notice that David is left alone in the fields, even when there is a sacrifice going on in his father's house. Even David's father, who should have known the character of his own children, did not suggest that David be brought home to participate in the sacrificial ceremony. Samuel, now frustrated with God's rejection of every eligible candidate, turned to Jesse. Samuel asks, "Are all your children here?" The Hebrew term *tamam* (**tawmam'**), translated as "all," means complete. So we could read Samuel's question as, "Does this complete the number of your children?" Jesse responds that "There is still the youngest." In Hebrew, the word *na`ar* (**nah'-ar**) refers to a boy from the age of infancy to adolescence. By implication this word can also mean a servant and is probably derived from the custom of the younger serving the elder as in African society. This servant heart may also be the reason that God chose David to represent the Messiah, the true servant of Yahweh. Jesse adds, "but he is tending the sheep." Samuel sends someone to fetch him and tells them, "We will not sit down to eat until he comes." This may have hinted to David's parents that he was the guest of honor.

12 And he sent, and brought him in. Now he was ruddy, and withal of a beautiful countenance, and goodly to look to. And the LORD said, Arise, anoint him: for this is he.

The youngest son does not have the appearance of height and physical strength. He is "ruddy," translated as a redhead or someone with a red complexion. Derived from the Hebrew word *admoniy* (**ad-mo-nee'**), "ruddy" also means something from earth, i.e., "adam," or earthen in color. When David appears, Samuel is instructed by God to anoint him as the king. David is also handsome, goodly, and pleasant in his outward appearance. Samuel confirms and decrees him the new king.

Only God knows the beginning and the end; He sees what we cannot see. We must allow God to lead us in our decision-making efforts. Then, we must act in obedience to God's Word and His will.

13 Then Samuel took the horn of oil, and anointed him in the midst of his brethren: and the Spirit of the LORD came upon David from that day forward. So Samuel rose up, and went to Ramah.

Samuel anoints David, the youngest son of Jesse, on God's command in the presence of his brothers. In spite of David's youth, his lack of education, and his lack of respect from his family, Samuel acquiesces in obedience to God. The anointing of the oil signifies royal power and communication of God's gifts and graces. The Spirit of God comes mightily on David from this day forward. He finds himself growing inwardly wise, courageous, and concerned for the people.

After the anointing, the Spirit of the Lord came upon David. The word *ruwach* (**roo'-akh**) means "wind." Figuratively, it means that life came upon David. The word *tsalach* (**tsaw-lakh'**) means to push forward. Therefore, one could say that, from that day forward, the Spirit of the Lord propelled David forward. His ascent to the throne was a gradual process. Scholars estimate David's age at this time to be 20 or 25; his trouble with Saul lasted either 10 or 15 years.

Samuel returns to Ramah, and we don't read of him again until his death (1 Samuel 19:18). *Matthew Henry's Commentary* tells us that "the best evidence of our being predestined to the king-dom of glory is our being sealed with the Spirit of promise, and our experience of a work of grace in our own heart." Often, when God calls us for a purpose, the manifestation does not occur instantly. Verse 13 of 1 Samuel 16 is the beginning of the Messianic promises to David. Jews recognized that the Messiah, the Christ, the Anointed One, would come from David's descendants. This was also Samuel's final act as a prophet.

Matthew Henry's Commentary. Nashville: Thomas Nelson Publishers, 1997. 278.

DAILY BIBLE READINGS

M: God Will Protect
Psalm 3
T: God Makes the Way Straight
Psalm 5:1-8
W: God Is a Rock and Fortress
Psalm 18:1-6
T: God Rejects Saul as King
1 Samuel 15:10-19
F: Samuel Visits Jesse and His Sons
1 Samuel 16:1-5
S: David Is Anointed King
1 Samuel 16:5-13
S: David Joins Saul's Court
1 Samuel 16:14-23

With your *Precepts For Living* CD-ROM you can quickly find out how many times the words *heart* and *appearance* are used in the Bible. Which word do you think is used more frequently?

TEACHING TIPS

December 19
Bible Study Guide 3

1. Words You Should Know

A. Just (Matthew 1:19) *dikaios* (Gk.)—The biblical concept denoting what is right; proper judgment.

B. Emmanuel (v. 23) *Emmanouel* (Gk.)—The prophetic announcement of the virgin birth of Christ. It means "God with us."

2. Teacher Preparation

A. To gain a better understanding of why humankind needed a Saviour, read the story of Adam and Eve's sin in Genesis 3:1-19. You will see how humankind fell from grace through the first Adam and needed a second Adam to restore us. This could only be done through the shed blood of Jesus Christ for the remission of our sins.

B. Next, study the FOCAL VERSES. Understand what kind of man Joseph was, and why God used him to be Jesus' legal and earthly father. Also, examine the times in which they lived and how becoming pregnant before marriage had grave implications for Mary.

C. Write down the answers to the SEARCH THE SCRIPTURES and DISCUSS THE MEANING questions.

D. Materials needed: Bibles, a chalkboard, chalk.

3. Starting the Lesson

A. Before the students arrive, write the title of the lesson and the AT-A-GLANCE outline on the board.

B. After the students are seated and settled, ask for prayer requests, and start your session with prayer by taking the requests before God and concentrating on the LESSON AIM. Then, ask them to define the words *just* and *Emmanuel* in the context of today's lesson.

C. Read the IN FOCUS story.

4. Getting into the Lesson

A. Have volunteers read the BACKGROUND information and THE PEOPLE, PLACES, AND TIMES section. You may want to explain some of the significant points found in these sections.

B. Ask for volunteers to read the FOCAL VERSES according to the AT-A-GLANCE outline.

C. You may want to explain and discuss each verse after it is read or have an overall discussion after the entire passage is read.

5. Relating the Lesson to Life

A. Direct the students' attention to the LESSON IN OUR SOCIETY section and encourage discussion.

B. Review and discuss the DISCUSS THE MEANING questions. Help the students to see how the lesson applies to their own lives.

6. Arousing Action

A. Direct the students to the MAKE IT HAPPEN section, and challenge them to put the suggestion into practice during the week.

B. Encourage them to read the DAILY BIBLE READINGS.

C. Finally, pray and ask God to prepare your hearts.

DEC 19TH

WORSHIP GUIDE

For the Superintendent or Teacher
Theme: A Call to Respond
Theme Song: "Go Tell It on the Mountain"
Scripture: Matthew 1:1-6, 18-25
Song: "O Holy Night"
Meditation: May our Lord and Saviour Jesus Christ become so real in our hearts, that we will know without a doubt that He is truly the Son of God, who came to die for us so that we might have eternal life.

A CALL TO RESPOND

Bible Background • MATTHEW 1
Printed Text • MATTHEW 1:17-25
Devotional Reading • LUKE 1:26-32

LESSON AIM

By the end of the lesson, the students should know without a doubt that Jesus is the one and only Son of God, and that He came into the world for one purpose—to die for the salvation of all believers. They should know that Jesus is God-man; He is God, who lived as a man. They should more fully trust the Christ who understands all our experiences and struggles.

KEEP IN MIND

"Then Joseph being raised from sleep did as the angel of the Lord had bidden him, and took unto him his wife" (Matthew 1:24).

FOCAL VERSES

Matthew 1:17 So all the generations from Abraham to David are fourteen generations; and from David until the carrying away into Babylon are fourteen generations; and from the carrying away into Babylon unto Christ are fourteen generations.

18 Now the birth of Jesus Christ was on this wise: When as his mother Mary was espoused to Joseph, before they came together, she was found with child of the Holy Ghost.

19 Then Joseph her husband, being a just man, and not willing to make her a publick example, was minded to put her away privily.

20 But while he thought on these things, behold, the angel of the Lord appeared unto him in a dream, saying, Joseph, thou son of David, fear not to take unto thee Mary thy wife: for that which is conceived in her is of the Holy Ghost.

LESSON OVERVIEW

LESSON AIM
KEEP IN MIND
FOCAL VERSES
IN FOCUS
THE PEOPLE, PLACES, AND TIMES
BACKGROUND
AT-A-GLANCE
IN DEPTH
SEARCH THE SCRIPTURES
DISCUSS THE MEANING
LESSON IN OUR SOCIETY
MAKE IT HAPPEN
FOLLOW THE SPIRIT
REMEMBER YOUR THOUGHTS
MORE LIGHT ON THE TEXT
DAILY BIBLE READINGS

21 And she shall bring forth a son, and thou shalt call his name JESUS: for he shall save his people from their sins.

22 Now all this was done, that it might be fulfilled which was spoken of the Lord by the prophet, saying,

23 Behold, a virgin shall be with child, and shall bring forth a son, and they shall call his name Emmanuel, which being interpreted is, God with us.

24 Then Joseph being raised from sleep did as the angel of the Lord had bidden him, and took unto him his wife:

25 And knew her not till she had brought forth her firstborn son: and he called his name JESUS.

IN FOCUS

Marva raised her son, George, in the church environment. In fact, as a very small tyke, he went to Sunday School, children's church, revivals, Vacation Bible School, and later, Youth Fellowship. However, when George got into junior high and especially into high school, Marva noticed a drastic change in George's behavior. He was on a negative downturn. Peer pressure was more pronounced, and George was having a hard time saying no to some of his peers' demands.

Marva had always prayed for George—prayed that God would save him, keep him, and cover him with the blood of Jesus. She knew she had trained him in the way he should go, but Satan was definitely attacking her child.

Not only did Marva continue to pray, but she began to fast and she had others do so as well. They prayed that God would give George a change of heart, and that the Holy Spirit would remind him of God's Word and point him back to God's righteousness.

Years passed; George was a junior in college and Marva found herself still praying . . . still claiming George's salvation. One Sunday as Marva sat in church worshiping God, she looked up and saw George walking into church. He seemed focused, purposeful, and determined.

When the pastor gave the altar call, George went to the altar and gave his heart to the Lord. Indeed, it was a time of rejoicing! Jesus Christ was born in George's heart. The prayers of the righteous had availed much; they had won a soul to Christ.

THE PEOPLE, PLACES, AND TIMES

Joseph. A descendant of King David. He was Jesus' earthly and legal father, who was engaged to Mary (Jesus' mother) when Jesus was conceived by the Holy Ghost. The Word calls him a man of integrity and shows that he believed God's Word. Joseph was not swayed from his stand by public opinion, but stood firm on the Word and did what was right. He had spiritual discernment and was sensitive to the guidance of the Lord, regardless of the consequences.

Mary. A poor young woman who lived in Nazareth. She was chosen by God to conceive Jesus, a child born without sin. Her cousin was Elizabeth, the mother of John the Baptist. John was the forerunner of Jesus. Mary was engaged to Joseph when she conceived by the Holy Spirit. Later, Mary and Joseph were married but did not come together until after the birth of Jesus. Mary was also a descendant of King David and later had other children.

BACKGROUND

Matthew wrote his Gospel to the Jews especially to prove that Jesus was indeed the long-awaited Messiah. He wrote to show that the prophecies of the Old Testament had been fulfilled in the New Testament. The promised Saviour, the promised Deliverer was Jesus Christ Himself.

It had been more than 400 years since the last Old Testament prophets had told of Christ's coming. Now the Jews were oppressed by Roman rule. Therefore, they looked for a king who would set up his kingdom here on earth. That king would then establish justice in his kingdom.

Jesus came as a suffering Saviour, not as the expected political and military leader. When He was accused by the religious leaders, tried, convicted, and crucified, many Jews rejected Him as Messiah. Jesus came talking about a heavenly kingdom established in the hearts of those who put their trust in Him and receive salvation. He came serving rather than being served.

AT-A-GLANCE

1. From Abraham to Jesus
(Matthew 1:17)
2. From Confusion to Divine Clarity
(vv. 18-23)
3. From Divine Clarity to Human
Obedience (vv. 24-25)

IN DEPTH

1. From Abraham to Jesus (Matthew 1:17)

Matthew began his Gospel with Jesus' genealogy to show the royal lineage of Jesus. One's family background was very important in Israel. To the Jews, this bloodline proved whether or not a person was one of God's chosen people. The Messiah needed to be Jewish in all respects. To appeal to the people of Israel, He needed to meet the genealogical criteria, and Matthew set out to prove that He did.

Matthew's task was not so much to prove that the Messiah was divine, but to show that He was connected to God's covenant promise to Abraham. Israelites believed that the Messiah must be genealogically traceable to Abraham, Isaac, and Jacob. But more significantly, He must be traceable to the beloved king David. As divine, the Messiah is intimately connected to God. But as a human, He is intimately connected to the best of the spiritual and prophetic tradition of

Israel. Therefore, it is easy to understand why Matthew takes this Davidic connection so seriously.

2. From Confusion to Divine Clarity (vv. 18-23)

How did the particular process leading to the birth of the Messiah begin? Having laid out the background of the Messiah's birth, Matthew introduces something else. When he says, "Mary was espoused [engaged] to Joseph," his Jewish audience would have nodded their heads in affirmation. When Matthew says that "before they came together, she was found with child of the Holy Ghost," he introduces a problem to the Jewish mind—for to them the Messiah was nothing more than a human being. By stating it this way, Matthew sets the stage to argue that this human being was and indeed is equal to the Eternal One of Israel. This would have posed a great intellectual and theological problem for Jewish people of the first century A.D.

This problem is exemplified in the way God deals with Joseph. First, Joseph is described as a righteous man. This righteousness exceeded the letter of the law. Unlike the Pharisees, who would show themselves unwilling to be compassionate, Joseph understood the compassion of the Lord. Since Mary was now thought to be unfaithful, a marriage to her would have been a tacit admission of his own guilt. Confused, Joseph decided to break the engagement (divorce her).

Fully applying the letter of the law might have led to Mary being stoned to death. However, Joseph was unwilling to expose her to the disgrace of public divorce. He therefore chose a quiet divorce before two witnesses as permitted by the law of Moses (Numbers 5:11-31). Thus Joseph would satisfy the requirement of the law and fulfill his sense of covenant righteousness and his compassion.

God sent an angel to dispel Joseph's confusion. Note also that in all of Israel's history, whenever a great one was to be born who would impact the direction of the nation—Isaac, Jacob, Samson, Samuel—there was divine manifestation. God spoke to Joseph in connection with the divine acts in history. By calling Joseph a "son of David," God intended for Joseph to consider several things. First, Joseph needs to consider what God

has done in history as it relates to His people. Second, God sought to help Joseph look at the situation from a broader perspective rather than concentrate on the shame which he and Mary would endure. Third, God wanted to take away the spirit of fear that had overtaken Joseph because of his confusion. God said, "fear not to take unto thee Mary thy wife." These words from God clarified the relationship that Joseph was to have with his spouse. They also clarified what his perception of the child should be. Furthermore, they helped to clarify the event to the Jews, who for so long had awaited deliverance from the Lord. Now Joseph must see this child as God's Child, and this event as a God-event. When God speaks into our situation, He wipes away all the confusion we face as we seek to do His will. We see more clearly and our relationships are put in the right perspective.

God also clarifies the situation by pointing us back to the Scripture. Here Matthew says all this can be related to what God had said. This reference to the past may seem to us like a mere appendage, but for the Jews this was of great significance. This prophetic utterance helps to point out to Joseph and to those of us who believe that we are not living within human wishful thinking. Rather our faith as well as Joseph's acceptance of Mary is grounded in the prophetic insight that comes directly from the Lord God. If Joseph understood Isaiah 7:14, his heart would have leaped. He would have thought, "Look, the very One who takes away our human confusion is in my house. The wisdom of God, the insight of the holy, the light that chases the human night is in my house. There is no need to be afraid." Can you envision the angel calling to this confused brother and saying, "A virgin shall conceive and bear a son"? Can you envision the angel saying, "And they shall call his name Emmanuel" (v. 23), which means "God with us"? Can you imagine how the clouds were lifted from his befuddled mind? Can you see him as he literally wakes up, wipes his eyes, and says, "Now I see"?

3. From Divine Clarity to Human Obedience (vv. 24-25)

Once God clarifies the events to Joseph and

reveals that this was God's work, Joseph set aside his personal feelings. He now worked with respect to the clarified Word spoken to him. Divine clarification must lead to practical application of God's Word. God reveals things to us so that we might act in concert with the movement of His Spirit in the world. Insights are not given to us so that we harbor them and hoard them for self-promotion, but to create within ourselves a motion to action. But not just any action; such clarifications ought to lead to action that is consistent with the character of God. God can use us to unfold this divine will, just as He did with Joseph. All we need to do is listen to the divine voice that speaks to us in the Word of God.

Too many of us spend time fighting with God when we should take our lesson from Joseph and stop worrying about who agrees or disagrees with how God guides us. God would only command us to do something that is consistent with His Word. After God told Joseph what to do, human opinion no longer mattered. Instead he chose to please the One who was in charge of his life. God's approval meant more to him than man's. We can thank God that Joseph trusted God to clarify his vision as it relates to the birth of the Saviour.

SEARCH THE SCRIPTURES

1. Why did the angel of the Lord appear to Joseph (Matthew 1:20)?

2. Why was Joseph instructed to name his son Jesus (v. 21)?

3. In times past, God had given His message through whom (v. 22)?

4. Why is the prophesied name *Emmanuel* important (v. 23)?

DISCUSS THE MEANING

1. Jesus came into the world fulfilling prophecy and God's plan of salvation. What is His plan?

2. God knew the stigma in the Jewish society of a woman having a baby before she was married. Why do you think God chose to use Mary to conceive Jesus?

LESSON IN OUR SOCIETY

You and I cannot save ourselves from our own sins. This truth is evident in the direction of our society today. The crime, drug usage, alcohol usage, rise in unwanted pregnancies, abortions, teens putting their babies in trash cans, and wars tell us that people are in desperate situations and are feeling hopeless. Government programs and laws have not remedied these situations.

In many of our cities, there are churches on every corner; yet the ills of humankind have become even more grave. People are spiritually lost. They have either heard the Good News and have become discontented or disillusioned by church leaders who only lead to be served instead of serving God's people, or they have not heard the Good News of salvation at all. Indeed, the fields are ready for harvest, but the laborers are few.

We each need to believe on the Lord Jesus Christ as our personal Saviour and be saved, not only from sin, but from ourselves as well. God's Word tells us that God knows how to direct and guide our lives better than we do. Only God can forgive us and cleanse us from sin. Only Jesus can set us free from the power and guilt of sin. We can be forgiven through believing that Jesus is the Son of God and trusting what He did for us when He laid down His life as a sacrifice for our sins. The living God wants us to turn from our sins and believe the Good News!

MAKE IT HAPPEN

There are so many people who do not understand the Good News of salvation and what it means for them. Their eyes are on people and their missteps and mistakes instead of on Jesus Christ. Let these people see Jesus in you this day and every day. Pray and ask God to help you walk the walk as well as talk the talk of a Christian because you are saved. Witness to someone this week.

FOLLOW THE SPIRIT

What God wants me to do:

_____

_____

REMEMBER YOUR THOUGHTS

Special insights I have learned:

_____

_____

MORE LIGHT ON THE TEXT
Matthew 1:17-25

17 So all the generations from Abraham to David are fourteen generations; and from David until the carrying away into Babylon are fourteen generations; and from the carrying away into Babylon unto Christ are fourteen generations.

In recording this account of the genealogy of Jesus, Matthew attempts to show Jesus as the "Christ," the one who is the "Son of David" and the "Son of Abraham." This is meant to identify Jesus, who was born to Mary and Joseph, as the One who will fulfill the covenant promise made to Abraham and David.

The genealogy begins with Abraham, to whom the promise of blessing to all nations was made. The importance of Abraham to the life of the Messiah cannot be overstated. He was declared by God to be the father of a multitude and called by God for the specific purpose of blessing the world (Genesis 12:2-3, 7). The promise made to him was both immediate and perpetual—material and spiritual. The heart of his call and blessing was that he would be the ancestor of the great Deliverer, whose coming had been declared by God in Genesis 15:3. Abraham's part in the genealogy of the Messiah is exemplified by the fact that he, himself, had one son of promise—Isaac—whom he offered to God as a sacrifice on Mount Moriah. As the ancestor of Messiah in the flesh, Abraham exemplified faith that stands the test of circumstances and time (Hebrews 11:17-19).

"David" is a personal name meaning "favorite," or "beloved." David was the first king to unite Israel and Judah and the first to receive the promise of a royal Messiah in his lineage. David was pictured as the ideal king of God's people. He ruled from about 1005 to 965 B.C.

The list of generations from Abraham to David was given to prove that Jesus Christ was indeed of the lineage from which the Messiah was to arise. New Testament Scripture confirms that Christ is the long-awaited seed of Abraham and of David, and that He is the Messiah and Saviour of the world (John 7:42; Romans 1:3; Galatians 3:16, 29; 2 Timothy 2:8).

18 Now the birth of Jesus Christ was on this wise: When as his mother Mary was espoused to Joseph, before they came together, she was found with child of the Holy Ghost.

The phraseologies here suggest that the author is about to change the direction of his thought. It is almost like saying "be that as it may." The word "now" (Gk. *de*) tells us that the writer is about to recommence with a broken thought. The beginning of this verse resumes the story announced in Matthew 1:1. The second half of this verse introduces Mary and Joseph, who are the main characters in the narrative to follow. It also presents the plot of the story: Mary is engaged to Joseph. They have not engaged in premarital sexual relations; yet, Mary is pregnant by the Holy Ghost. The writer tells us, in the Greek, that this section is about the genesis of Jesus Christ. The use of the word "birth" (Gk. *gennesis*) speaks directly to the present condition of natal revelation, not to Christ's ancestry.

The King James Version of the Bible includes the phrase, "was on this wise," meaning "it was like this." Note the use of the Greek word *houto* **(hoo'-to),** which means "in this way" or "in this manner." Matthew's goal here seems to be to show the uniqueness of the birth of Jesus.

The writer proceeds to tell us the condition in which Mary found herself. The Greek word translated as "espoused" is *mnesteuo* **(mnace-tyoo'-o),** which means the act of giving a woman over to a man to be his wife. It really refers to something precious that is given at the time of one's engagement. The word *mnaomai* points to the idea of fixing one's mind or mentally grasping something or someone. In this case, Mary was fixed in the mind of Joseph; she was precious in the mind of another.

Having described the mental connection between Mary and Joseph, the writer now adds, "before they came together," which in the Greek reads, *prin sunelthein autous.* This phrase means more than coming together in the same vicinity. The Greek word translated here as "come together" is *sunerchomai* **(soon-er'-khom-ahee),** which means "to convene," such as the gathering that takes place at wedding parties. In this case, the phrase could mean, "before Mary departed into

Mary brings forth the Messiah-King, and calls Him, "Jesus"!

the company of her husband to be associates," or "before there was any conjugal cohabitation." Matthew says all this to prepare us for the uniqueness of this birth.

We read further that Mary was "found" (Gk. *heurisko,* **hyoo-ris'-ko).** The use of this word suggests that it may have been a while before she was "found." What was Mary found with? She literally is seen as one who, according to the Greek, was *en gastri.* Simply stated, she was found "with the stomach," or "with belly," a euphemism for being with child, or pregnant. However, Matthew does not stop there. He states that Mary's being with

child is not a result of an act of Joseph, but from the Holy Spirit. The Greek word *hagios* (**hag'-ee-os**), translated as "holy," means that the condition of being pregnant resulted from something sacred, physically pure, morally blameless, religiously righteous, and ceremonially clean.

It would have been simple for Matthew to stop there. However, he says it was not merely something ceremonially clean that caused Mary's condition, but rather the *pneuma* (**pnyoo'-mah**), or Holy Ghost. Thus, he insists, that which is currently in the womb of this "found" woman is the breath of God, the very breeze of holiness. This child was the result of a vital principle and mental disposition of something superhuman. In the Jewish context, this being could only be God.

19 Then Joseph her husband, being a just man, and not willing to make her a public example, was minded to put her away privily.

Note here that Joseph is referred to as the husband of Mary—nothing less, nothing more. The word "husband" (Gk. *aner,* **an'-ayr**) primarily refers to an individual male—specifically, the husband. In truth, since Mary was to be Joseph's wife, Jewish tradition demanded that she should be killed for conceiving a child by another person. But we read that Joseph is a just man. However, unlike the King James Version of the Bible, the Greek does not say "just man." Rather, the Greek simply reads, "being righteous" (Gk. *own dikaios*). It means that Joseph was equitable in character and practice. It implies that he was innocent and holy. Of course, here we are dealing with relative innocence. The fact that he was "a just man" could mean that he lived by the laws of God.

Mary was pregnant, and her conception was by the Holy Spirit; but Joseph did not know this. By law, he had the right to divorce her or to have her stoned to death. Yet, he decided to privately dissolve the engagement. We read further that Joseph was "not willing to make her a publick example" (Gk. *mee theloon autees deigmatisan*). His just nature would not allow him to act in a certain way. This again will throw light on the word translated as "just." It does not mean justice in terms of giving someone what they deserve, but connotes a sense of mercy and compassion. What made Joseph "just" was the fact that he was determined to take a different position from that of the crowd. Rather than let the sanction of the law take its course, he chose the mercy of the law. To "will" something is to be inclined or glad to do a thing. In the Greek language, the concept of "will" (*thelo,* **thel'-o**) is tied to having delight in some thing or action. "Just" people do not delight or desire to see others hurt, even when they are wronged.

The Greek word translated into the phrase "make her a publick example" is *paradeigmatizo* (**par-ad-igue-mat-id'-zo**) and means to show to the public or to expose to infamy. It also means to put to open shame. We also read in the same verse that he "was minded to put her away privily" (Gk. *eboulethe lathra apolusai aute*). The Greek word *boulomai* (**boo'-lom-ahee**) is translated as "minded," which denotes a reflective disposition. It is comparable to the word used in the first part of the verse translated as "willing" (i.e., "not willing to expose her to public shame"). Again we see Joseph not only as an innocent man, but as a deeply religious man whose profound reflection on divine things led him to act in ways that set him apart from his generation.

20 But while he thought on these things, behold, the angel of the Lord appeared unto him in a dream, saying, Joseph, thou son of David, fear not to take unto thee Mary thy wife: for that which is conceived in her is of the Holy Ghost.

The line of thought we have followed from verse 19 that reflects the character of Joseph is further confirmed in verse 20 as we encounter the Greek word *enthumeomai* (**en-thoo-meh'-om-ahee**) in the phrase "while he thought." This word is a combination of the Greek terms *en* and *thumos*, which together mean "to be inspired" or "to ponder by spiritual animation." So here we see how deeply Joseph's thoughts went. Here was a man whose sense of justice did not blind his ability to think. His contemplation paid off, for in the next phrase we read, "behold, the angel of the Lord appeared unto him in a dream." This phrase reflects Matthew's Hebraism of the Old Testament. We find a divine messenger bringing tidings to many of God's people in times of confusion. In Joseph's confusion, he went into contemplation, and in the middle of his contemplation, a heavenly messenger was sent. This messenger is meant to lead him into the proper way to act. God sent this messenger to bring clarity and drive away the confusion.

We are told that the angel of the Lord "appeared." The use of the Greek word *phaino* (**fah'-ee-no**) shows that in the midst of Joseph's confusion came a light to show him the way—to effect a transition literally and figuratively from ignorance and confusion to wisdom and understanding. The appearance of the angel is revelation.

Next we read, "Joseph thou son of David." The first revelation was to remind Joseph of who he really is. Joseph's connection with David immediately reminded him of the covenant promise given to his ancestor David regarding the coming Messiah. We read further, "fear not to take unto thee Mary thy wife." The angel then addresses the issue at hand. The angel speaks to the psychological condition of fear that was keeping Joseph from doing what he knew was right. In addressing the present situation, the angel did not avoid the fact that Mary was pregnant, but assured Joseph that the child was divine.

21 And she shall bring forth a son, and thou shalt call his name JESUS: for he shall save his people from their sins.

In this verse, the angel announces to Joseph that the child is to be named Jesus. After having an angel put his life in historical perspective and explain what was going on in the present, Joseph was probably left with the question: What is the purpose of all this? First, the angel dealt with the immediate future—the child will be a son. Second, the child shall be named Jesus, which probably reminded Joseph of the great warrior conqueror who, by the power of God, delivered the Children of Israel from their enemies. Finally, the angel connects the name of the child with the future act of the child: "He shall save his people from their sins." "Jesus" (Gk. *Iesous,* **Yea-soos**) is the Greek form of "Joshua" (Heb. *Yehosua,* **Ye-shoo-ah**), which means "Yahweh is salvation." The use of the word "save" (Gk. *sozo,* **sode'-zo**) addresses the salvific view held by the Jews. In fact, living in the midst of oppression, Joseph would have understood this term in relation to deliverance and protection. "Save" also implies healing and preservation. In this period of "Israel's pain," this term also spoke to the Jews' need for well-being and wholeness.

22 Now all this was done, that it might be fulfilled which was spoken of the Lord by the prophet, saying,

Here again we see Matthew's deep entrenchment in Israel's prophetic tradition as he points us back to the Old Testament. He tells us that everything that is happening here has been prophesied by the prophets. Isaiah prophesied, in a message to King Ahaz, about a virgin birth and a child who would save the people of God (Isaiah 7:10-16). A key term here is "fulfill" (Gk. *pleroo,* **play-ro'-o**), which means to make replete, to make level a hollow or a valley. Thus, this experience furnishes Joseph with an explanation of the text in the Old Testament. In a sense, God inspired the word of the prophet with meaning for the reader. It also means that what has been promised is now being executed.

23 Behold, a virgin shall be with child, and shall bring forth a son, and they shall call his name Emmanuel, which being interpreted is, God with us.

Matthew affirms that Jesus is the One whom the prophet Isaiah spoke about in Isaiah 7:14. Jesus is Emmanuel, meaning "God with us"—the Promised Deliverer. Again, in Matthew 1:23, we are told that his mother was a virgin. The word for "virgin" that is used here is the Greek word *parthenos* (**par-then'-os**), which, as far as can be determined by scholars, means a maiden and by usage implies an unmarried daughter. In biblical times, females married at a very early age and the bride was expected to be a virgin. Any interpretation must take into consideration that Mary did not know a man sexually. In fact, the Hebrew word `*almah* (**al-maw'**) is the feminine form for a young person. Here it denotes the one who is still governed by parental authority or one who is veiled. It also means a damsel or virgin. It must be remembered that the law regarding virginity was strictly enforced in Israel, and breaking it resulted in death. So all interpretations of this passage must include the absence of a sexual relationship. What was at stake here was not only that Mary was a virgin, but that she was found with child. The context in which this prophecy occurs in Isaiah shows the Lord challenging the people and calling them to see God do a new thing.

Verse 23 continues with the phrase, "and they shall call his name Emmanuel." Here the name itself explains the nature of the child who is to be born. Emmanuel is the combination of the Hebrew *im*, which means "with" or "equal with," and the Hebrew *el,* which is the singular form of *Elohim.* This term is often used to mean something that accompanies or something before or beside another. Here it can mean that He, Emmanuel, is the reason for which Elohim, the Creator of the universe, has come among us.

24 Then Joseph being raised from sleep did as the angel of the Lord had bidden him, and took unto him his wife:

The phrase "being raised from sleep" has deep spiritual significance. Remember, Joseph was dreaming until this verse. Here, the phrase "being raised" implies that someone raised Joseph. The word translated as "raise" is the Greek word *diegeiro* (**dee-eg-i-ro**), which is a combination of the two Greek words *dia* and *egeiro* means to be fully awake. It can also mean to arise, awake, or stir up oneself.

We then read that Joseph "did as the angel of the Lord had bidden him." The word for "did" is the Greek word *poieo* (**poy-eh'-o**), meaning to make or do. It means to make application of ideas directly to life. It can also mean that Joseph agreed to the solution that the angel had purposed. It also implies that Joseph committed himself to continue to exercise himself fully in the Word of God revealed to him. What God had ordained was now going to be his purpose. His reason for rising up was not to transgress the law, but to live out the revelation.

25 And knew her not till she had brought forth her firstborn son: and he called his name JESUS.

The phrase "knew her not" in the Greek reads *ouk eginosken autee* and suggests the absolute absence of knowledge. One possible meaning is that one is unaware of, or lacks, certain expressive feelings. In other words, one is resolved not to understand. In this case, the phrase means that Joseph had absolutely no sexual relationship with her. The next word "till" suggests that Joseph continued in a state of abstinence until, or for as long as, Mary was pregnant. Actually he remained abstinent until she gave birth. The Greek word *tikto* (**tik'-to**) means to produce something from seed or to bring forth as a mother. What did Mary bring forth? The Greek use the word *prototokos* (**pro-tot-ok'-os**) to describe this event. It comes from the word *protos* and another form of the word *tikto,* or firstborn. Note that this word is different from the word *monogenes,* used to describe the relation between God the Father and the Son in John 3:16. Joseph names the child Jesus as the angel instructs him to, which incorporated Jesus into the Davidic line.

DAILY BIBLE READINGS

M: Our God Is a Powerful God
Isaiah 40:3-11
T: A Sign of Reassurance
Isaiah 7:10-17
W: An Angel Speaks to Mary
Luke 1:26-38
T: Jesus Is a Descendant of Abraham
Matthew 1:1-6a
F: Jesus Is a Descendant of David
Matthew 1:6b-11
S: Jesus' Ancestry Is Traced Through Joseph
Matthew 1:12-16
S: Jesus Is Born and Named
Matthew 1:17-25

Do you need personal encouragement? The *Precepts For Living* CD-ROM has devotional books to help you in your daily Bible reading.

TEACHING TIPS

December 26
Bible Study Guide 4

1. Words You Should Know

A. Blessed (Luke 2:28, 34) *eulogeo* (Gk.)—To celebrate with praises; to invoke blessings; to acknowledge God's goodness for His glory.

B. Peace (v. 29) *eirene* (Gk.)—The tranquil soul assured of salvation through Christ, fearing nothing, and content with life.

C. Salvation (v. 30) *soterion* (Gk.)—Saving; He who embodies salvation, or the One through whom God will achieve it.

2. Teacher Preparation

A. Read Luke 2:22-38 throughout the week. Try studying from the *Precepts For Living* CD-ROM.

B. Read Psalm 71:1-8. Focus on: refuge, fortress, cruelty, hope, and trust.

C. Study and take notes. Read the MORE LIGHT ON THE TEXT section. Does this information help to bring the Scripture to life for you?

3. Starting the Lesson

A. Discuss the title of this lesson, A CALL TO HOPE.

B. Read and discuss the questions in the DISCUSS THE MEANING section. Ask a student to read the FOCAL VERSES aloud.

C. Review the LESSON AIM. Ask the students to note any ideas that come to them throughout the class.

D. While your students rotate out, invite those who remain to share personal stories of hope. Ask if they have an idea that would bring hope to others.

4. Getting into the Lesson

A. Read the KEEP IN MIND verse. Talk about the IN FOCUS story. Encourage your students to read these sections before class to become better prepared for the discussion.

B. Use the AT-A-GLANCE outline to review the FOCAL VERSES. Ask the students to discuss the roles of Joseph, Mary, Simeon, and Anna in God's plan of salvation.

C. Answer the SEARCH THE SCRIPTURES questions together as a review.

5. Relating the Lesson to Life

A. Read Jeremiah 29:11 aloud. Then ask how we can encourage others without telling them what to do. How can telling others what to do be harmful?

DEC 26TH

B. Then ask: How do we know God's will for *our* lives? How do we become available?

6. Arousing Action

A. Explain that we all go through negative situations, tragedies, or trials. How can we (judiciously) turn tragedy, or poor choices, into a message of hope for others? How do we regain hope? Allow time for the students to discuss each point.

B. Close in prayer based on needs shared.

WORSHIP GUIDE

For the Superintendent or Teacher
Theme: A Call to Hope
Theme Song: "Great Is Thy Faithfulness"
Scripture: Psalm 71:4-5
Song: "Trust and Obey"
Meditation: Dear faithful Heavenly Father, You have given us refuge, rescued us from both danger and folly, and answered prayers we didn't even know how to pray. Father, help us to remember Your faithfulness in times of doubt.
Amen.

A CALL TO HOPE

Bible Background • LUKE 2:22-38
Printed Text • LUKE 2:22-38
Devotional Reading • PSALM 71:1-8

LESSON AIM

By the end of the lesson, the students will explore the importance of hope and expectation in realizing God's promises, and they will list simple ways to help others rediscover hope.

KEEP IN MIND

"For mine eyes have seen thy salvation, Which thou hast prepared before the face of all people" (Luke 2:30-31).

FOCAL VERSES

Luke 2:22 And when the days of her purification according to the law of Moses were accomplished, they brought him to Jerusalem, to present him to the Lord;

23 (As it is written in the law of the Lord, Every male that openeth the womb shall be called holy to the Lord;)

24 And to offer a sacrifice according to that which is said in the law of the Lord, A pair of turtledoves, or two young pigeons.

25 And, behold, there was a man in Jerusalem, whose name was Simeon; and the same man was just and devout, waiting for the consolation of Israel: and the Holy Ghost was upon him.

26 And it was revealed unto him by the Holy Ghost, that he should not see death, before he had seen the Lord's Christ.

27 And he came by the Spirit into the temple: and when the parents brought in the child Jesus, to do for him after the custom of the law,

28 Then took he him up in his arms, and blessed God, and said,

29 Lord, now lettest thou thy servant depart in

LESSON OVERVIEW

LESSON AIM
KEEP IN MIND
FOCAL VERSES
IN FOCUS
THE PEOPLE, PLACES, AND TIMES
BACKGROUND
AT-A-GLANCE
IN DEPTH
SEARCH THE SCRIPTURES
DISCUSS THE MEANING
LESSON IN OUR SOCIETY
MAKE IT HAPPEN
FOLLOW THE SPIRIT
REMEMBER YOUR THOUGHTS
MORE LIGHT ON THE TEXT
DAILY BIBLE READINGS

many hearts may be revealed.

36 And there was one Anna, a prophetess, the daughter of Phanuel, of the tribe of Aser: she was of a great age, and had lived with an husband seven years from her virginity;

37 And she was a widow of about fourscore and four years, which departed not from the temple, but served God with fastings and prayers night and day.

38 And she coming in that instant gave thanks likewise unto the Lord, and spake of him to all them that looked for redemption in Jerusalem.

peace, according to thy word:

30 For mine eyes have seen thy salvation,

31 Which thou hast prepared before the face of all people;

32 A light to lighten the Gentiles, and the glory of thy people Israel.

33 And Joseph and his mother marvelled at those things which were spoken of him.

34 And Simeon blessed them, and said unto Mary his mother, Behold, this child is set for the fall and rising again of many in Israel; and for a sign which shall be spoken against;

35 (Yea, a sword shall pierce through thy own soul also,) that the thoughts of

IN FOCUS

Maria made a point of going to all of the Christmas parties she was invited to. She bought and wrapped piles of thoughtfully selected presents. She went caroling with her church, she led the children's choir at her church during this season, and she delivered turkeys to the needy.

At first Maria involved herself so heavily in Christmas activities because she wanted to fight the Christmas blues. The season had been particularly rough for her since her husband's unexpected death five years ago. But when she thought about the meaning of Christmas, she found renewed hope. All of the activities and gifts reminded her of the hope Christ brought into the world.

Jesus Christ represents hope. And just as Anna and Simeon hoped and trusted in the promise of a Saviour in today's lesson, we can hope and trust in the promises of the abundant and eternal life made possible through the gift of Jesus.

THE PEOPLE, PLACES, AND TIMES

Days of Purification. Under Jewish law, it took 40 days for purification after the birth of a male child (Leviticus 12:2, 6). In observance of the law, Mary waited until this period of time was complete before she appeared in public worship and brought Jesus to the temple.

Offering a Sacrifice. When they did come to the temple, Mary and Joseph offered the required sacrifice: "a pair of turtledoves." At that time, neither mother nor child would be considered under the Lord's covenant (under divine protection) until this was done. The fact that Mary and Joseph were not required to bring a lamb—the offering of the rich—is further testimony that the family was not wealthy. Jesus became poor that we might become rich (2 Corinthians 8:9).

Simeon. He was, perhaps, a descendant of Hillel—a man revered as the most brilliant doctor and philosopher since Moses. It is thought that Simeon was also the president of the grand Sanhedrin. Whatever his position or heritage, he took his walk with God seriously and weighed each decision with God's law and direction. He was known as a rare man, both pious of heart and righteous in behavior.

Anna. She was known as a prophetess—a holy woman with great knowledge and experience in God's ways. As defined in 1 Corinthians 14:3, her role was to edify, instruct, and comfort others—a commitment she kept throughout most of her adult life.

Anna married as a young virgin, but her husband lived only seven years. From his death until we meet Anna at age 84, Anna "departed not from the temple, but served God with fastings and prayers night and day" (Luke 2:37). Consequently, nearly all of Anna's life was devoted to service in God's temple and to God's people.

Her life experience in following the Holy Spirit was critical. She knew the exact moment to arrive and find Simeon holding the Messiah. Further, a lifetime of service and learning prepared her to share the Gospel with all who would hear.

BACKGROUND

The birth of Christ is detailed in only two books of the New Testament: Luke and Matthew. The story of Anna and Simeon is told only in Luke. As Mary and Joseph fulfilled their covenant obligations, it was inevitable that they would cross paths with these two faithful servants of God. It was after the shepherds, Simeon, and Anna are given their revelations of the birth of the Messiah that the Magi visit Jesus.

These events—from the humble offerings at the temple signifying Mary and Joseph's relative poverty, to the revelation of the Messiah to women, shepherds, and the faithful aged—clearly show God's people are important to Him. Status with God is not defined as the Pharisees would have the Jews believe. It is seen within the faithfulness and love of regular people.

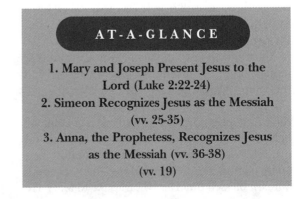

AT-A-GLANCE

1. Mary and Joseph Present Jesus to the Lord (Luke 2:22-24)
2. Simeon Recognizes Jesus as the Messiah (vv. 25-35)
3. Anna, the Prophetess, Recognizes Jesus as the Messiah (vv. 36-38)
(vv. 19)

IN DEPTH

1. Mary and Joseph Present Jesus to the Lord (Luke 2:22-24)

Mary and Joseph followed the laws of their faith and traveled to Jerusalem to present Jesus to the Lord. Even though Mary and Joseph had distinct knowledge about the Christ Child from both angels and divine revelations, they never felt "too good for" or "above" obeying the terms of the covenant. Joseph and Mary's personal decisions about their baby were critical to the fulfillment of God's Word and the fulfillment of Christ's future in God's world.

2. Simeon Recognizes Jesus as the Messiah (vv. 25-35)

Simeon, a rare and godly man, was divinely inspired and protected by the power and influence of God. He was informed by the Holy Ghost that he would live until he actually *saw* the hope of Israel—the Messiah, the Lord's Christ. He had prepared, both in his heart and in his behavior, for the grand blessing he was about to experience. At the appropriate time, the Holy Spirit led Simeon to the Temple. In this holy, public place of worship, Simeon's expectations were rewarded and the prophecy of the Hope of Israel—the Coming of Christ—was fulfilled.

Simeon recognized Jesus as the Messiah and said, "Lord, now lettest thou thy servant depart in peace, according to thy word."

Simeon's peace and assurance is for all of us—not just for him. Because our hope is in Jesus Christ, death has lost its hopeless state. Through faith in Christ we can be assured of eternal life with God.

The promised Messiah has been "prepared before the face of all people." Simeon called Jesus "a light to lighten the Gentiles, and the glory of thy people Israel."

Mary and Joseph stood nearby as this revered, pious man pronounced their son to be a Light to the world. Certainly, they "marveled" at the significance of all they had experienced so far. With the trials of a virgin birth in a small village not far behind them, Simeon's outburst of blessings and prophecy must have been both a comfort and confirmation of the revelations they received. Simeon blessed them and then spoke to Mary. He prophesied that her baby boy would be "for a sign"—a metaphor taken from archers meaning a mark to be shot at. Simeon also told Mary that a "sword shall pierce" her very soul—she will suffer searing, slicing pain when her son is tortured upon the Cross. She will be there and her heart will be pierced as she sees Jesus martyred to save the world.

3. Anna, the Prophetess, Recognizes Jesus as the Messiah (vv. 36-38)

Like Simeon, Anna knew this baby was the Messiah, and she gave immediate thanks to God.

Mary and Joseph returned to Nazareth, where Jesus grew and became strong. He learned life's most basic lessons of love, wisdom, strength, and family—with "the grace of God" upon Him (Luke 2:40). Anna immediately began her own, fantastic journey. She spoke of Jesus "to all them that looked for redemption in Jerusalem." The awaited Messiah—our salvation—had arrived.

SEARCH THE SCRIPTURES

1. Why did Mary and Joseph take Jesus to the temple (Luke 2:22)?

2. What does their sacrifice tell us about Joseph's social status (v. 24)?

3. What does Simeon say God's salvation entails (vv. 30-32)?

4. What is Simeon's prophecy for Mary (v. 35)?

DISCUSS THE MEANING

We are each called to different purposes in God's world. Consider the "search for hope." Consider God's promises. What is God calling you to do? How do you prepare, each day, to fulfill God's call on your life? If you don't know yet, or are in a stage of expectation or waiting, what can you do to prepare and train?

LESSON IN OUR SOCIETY

God fulfilled a promise of hope to Simeon and Anna. They, in turn, shared their joy and comfort with Mary.

Sharing, reaching out, and even building new traditions that fit our current conditions are tools that help fight depression. List several ways that

Simeon beholds the Hope of Israel and all mankind—Jesus Christ, the Lord!

we can help ourselves and others find hope, strength, and motivation for the new year.

MAKE IT HAPPEN

Over the next week, pray for a need God would have you meet. At the top of next week's lesson, place a reminder of your commitment to share God's hope and salvation with the hurting.

If you experience a loss of hope, remember that it is not a "weakness" and that it takes time to overcome this loss. Vow to reach out to a safe source. Next year, you'll be able to use your experience to help others. You might even save a life.

FOLLOW THE SPIRIT

What God wants me to do:

_____

_____

REMEMBER YOUR THOUGHTS

Special insights I have learned:

_____

_____

MORE LIGHT ON THE TEXT

Luke 2:22-38

22 And when the days of her purification according to the law of Moses were accomplished, they brought him to Jerusalem, to present him to the Lord; 23 (As it is written in the law of the Lord, Every male that openeth the womb shall be called holy to the Lord;) 24 And to offer a sacrifice according to that which is said in the law of the Lord, A pair of turtledoves, or two young pigeons.

Some manuscripts render the phrase "days of her purification" (Gk. *hemerai tou katharismou*

169

auton) referring either to Mary and the child or to Mary and Joseph. According to Levitical laws, the mother of a male child remains ceremonially unclean for 40 days (Leviticus 12:1-8). Furthermore, in recognition of Israel's deliverance from bondage, the firstborn child is consecrated unto the Lord (Exodus 13:2f). Because Jesus was "made under the law" (Galatians 4:4), the requirement for ceremonial purification needed to be fulfilled. Thus, Mary and Joseph brought Jesus to Jerusalem "to present him to the Lord" (Gk. *parastesai toi Kurioi*). They brought for the sacrifice "a pair of turtledoves, or two young pigeons." This was an indication of Jesus' household's limited means (cf. Leviticus 12:8).

25 And, behold, there was a man in Jerusalem, whose name was Simeon; and the same man was just and devout, waiting for the consolation of Israel: and the Holy Ghost was upon him.

Simeon was "just and devout" (Gk. *dikaios kai eulabes*). The Greek word *eulabes*, translated as "devout," means "carefully taking hold." Simeon was called by God to be a witness. So he devoted his life to "waiting for the consolation of Israel" (Gk. *prosdechomenos paraklesin tou Israel*). At a time of national despair and spiritual deadness, Simeon's Messianic hope was kept alive because the Holy Spirit was "upon him" (Gk. *ep' auton*).

26 And it was revealed unto him by the Holy Ghost, that he should not see death, before he had seen the Lord's Christ. 27 And he came by the Spirit into the temple: and when the parents brought in the child Jesus, to do for him after the custom of the law,

The coming of the Messiah was "revealed unto him by the Holy Ghost." The construction of *kechrematismenon*, translated as "was revealed" (or having been warned, advised, or commanded), makes the Holy Spirit the "Agent" and hints of His personhood.

At this time, Simeon was advanced in age. But by the Spirit he was given a special insight to recognize the Messiah. Having assured Simeon that he would see the Christ before he slept in death, God now fulfilled His word in the fullness of time. Simeon was directed into the temple at the pre-

cise moment that Jesus' parents came to present Him to the Lord. God watches over His Word to perform it!

28 Then took he him up in his arms, and blessed God, and said, 29 Lord, now lettest thou thy servant depart in peace, according to thy word: 30 For mine eyes have seen thy salvation, 31 Which thou hast prepared before the face of all people; 32 A light to lighten the Gentiles, and the glory of thy people Israel.

Simeon took the child Jesus in his "arms" (Gk. *agkale*), meaning the inner angle of his arm, and blessed the Lord. In taking the child in his arms, it was as if Simeon was grasping hold of the salvation that he had been waiting for through the years.

Verse 29 in the Greek is *nun apolueis ton doulon sou, despota,* which translates literally as, "now loose off (or release) the slave of you, Master." Simeon here calls himself *doulos* (a servant), contrasting himself with Despota (the Lord or Master, from which our English word "despot" is derived). Simeon desires to be released, having seen the "salvation" (Gk. *soterion*) of the Master. What more is there to wait for?

The Lord's salvation is "prepared before all peoples," a "light to lighten the Gentiles," and the "glory of thy people." The Greek word translated as "Gentiles" is *ethnos* (eth'nos), from which our English word "ethnic" is derived. In New Testament usage, it often refers to people other than the Jews. In contrast, the people (Gk. *loas*) usually refers to the Jews. Clearly, the worldwide mission of the Messiah is indicated here. Christ is God's revelation to all ethno-linguistic people— Jews and Gentiles.

33 And Joseph and his mother marveled at those things which were spoken of him. 34 And Simeon blessed them, and said unto Mary his mother, Behold, this child is set for the fall and rising again of many in Israel; and for a sign which shall be spoken against; 35 (Yea, a sword shall pierce through thy own soul also,) that the thoughts of many hearts may be revealed.

Jesus' parents "marveled" (Gk. *thaumazo*) at what Simeon was saying. Not only was Simeon confirming what they had heard from Gabriel (Luke 1:31-33), Elisabeth (1:42), and the shepherds (2:16-19), but he goes beyond it with astonishing details. Simeon "blessed" (Gk. *euloge,* **yoo-log-eh'-o**) both parents but directed some specific prophetic words to Mary: "Behold, this child is set for the fall and rising again of many in Israel." Jesus is a rock of offense—a stumbling block—to all who will choose unbelief, but a rising unto glory for those who will choose to believe. With great opportunity comes great responsibility. Just as Mary was "blessed...among women" (Luke 1:28), so will her "soul" (Gk. *psuche*) be pierced with a large "sword" (Gk. *rhomphaia*)—probably a cryptic reference to the agony of the Cross. God's purpose is that the "thoughts" (Gk. *dialogismos*) of human hearts will be "revealed" (Gk. *apokalupto*) so that they will be compelled to take a stand for or against Christ. People's decisions about Christ are a good mirror by which the thoughts of their hearts are made manifest.

36 And there was one Anna, a prophetess, the daughter of Phanuel, of the tribe of Aser: she was of a great age, and had lived with an husband seven years from her virginity; 37 And she was a widow of about fourscore and four years, which departed not from the temple, but served God with fastings and prayers night and day.

"Anna, a prophetess" (Gk. *prophetis*), was the second witness to the coming of the Messiah. Her pedigree goes back to Asher—one of the 12 sons of Jacob. She was well advanced in age—84 years of widowhood after living with her husband for only seven years of marriage. Her credentials included faithfulness; she "departed not from the temple" but "served God with fastings and prayers night and day." What a godly woman! No wonder she was found worthy of witnessing and heralding the first coming of the Messiah.

38 And she coming in that instant gave thanks likewise unto the Lord, and spake of him to all them that looked for redemption in Jerusalem.

The phrase "coming in" (Gk. *ephistemi*) literally translates as "having stood on." On this occasion, Anna's routine service in the temple took a dramatic turn. On hearing Simeon's prophetic utterances she "gave thanks" in agreement, and began to speak "to all them that looked for redemption in Jerusalem." Some authorities suggest Anna's immediate audience was a band of old saints who met together with her at the temple in prayer and expectation of Messianic redemption. Anna says to them and to us that the expectation of all mankind was wrapped up in that Babe.

DAILY BIBLE READINGS

M: You, O Lord, Are My Hope
Psalm 71:1-8

T: New Things I Now Declare
Isaiah 42:1-9

W: Jesus Is Born
Luke 2:1-7

T: Angels Appear to the Shepherds
Luke 2:8-14

F: The Shepherds See Jesus
Luke 2:15-20

S: Jesus Is Taken to the Temple
Luke 2:22-26

S: Simeon and Anna Praise God
Luke 2:27-38

Gain a deeper understanding of the word *salvation* by doing a cross-reference search of Luke 2:30 using your *Precepts For Living* CD-ROM.

TEACHING TIPS

January 2
Bible Study Guide 5

1. Words You Should Know

A. Gospel (Mark 1:14) *euaggelion* (Gk.)—Glad tidings of the kingdom of God, preached by Jesus.

B. Fishers of men (v. 17) *halieus* (Gk.)—A term that implies that disciples of Jesus are to be ready for evangelistic activity.

C. Amazed (v. 27) *thambeo* (Gk.)—Everyone was astonished at Jesus' power.

2. Teacher Preparation

A. Read the first chapter of Mark, as well as commentaries that deal with the passage we are studying.

B. Try to imagine Mark's gospel as good news to oppressed people.

C. Imagine what oppressed people would call "good news," and remind students of the historical and sociological context of the gospel of Mark.

3. Starting the Lesson

A. Open the session with prayer. Then ask students to explain what it means to be a disciple. Challenge students to identify a person in their life they have followed and share why they followed that person and how it has made a difference in their lives.

B. Ask the students about the meaning of purpose and passion in life. Remind them that Jesus was a man of purpose and passion. Challenge them to discover purpose and passion in their lives. Explain that what separates history-makers from history-watchers is purpose and passion.

4. Getting into the Lesson

A. Have the students read the LESSON AIM in unison.

B. Have each student read one verse of the FOCAL VERSES.

C. Explore possible feelings of fear, inadequacy, or honor the early disciples must have felt at being given the weighty invitation, "Come and follow me."

5. Relating the Lesson to Life

A. Challenge them to introspection with the question, "Are you a real disciple?"

B. Ask the students if they have truly made a commitment to Christ and whether they are willing to make sacrifices in order to live for Him.

6. Arousing Action

A. Ask each student to point out one thing the newly-called disciples did and strive to emulate it.

B. Challenge students to make an intentional effort to study the life of Jesus using the Bible as the primary source but also by reading supplemental books on the life of Jesus.

WORSHIP GUIDE

For the Superintendent or Teacher
Theme: Jesus Begins His Ministry
Theme Song: "Must Jesus Bear the Cross Alone?"
Scripture: Mark 8:34-38
Theme Song: "Follow Me"
Meditation: God, help all of us to be authentic in our Christianity by following the example of Jesus the Christ. Help us to deny ourselves, pick up our own crosses, and follow Jesus no matter where He leads us. You have not given us a Spirit of fear but of power, love, and a sound mind. Amen.

JESUS BEGINS HIS MINISTRY

Bible Background • MARK 1:14-28
Printed Text • MARK 1:14-28
Devotional Reading • MATTHEW 4:18-25

LESSON AIM

By the end of the lesson, the students should understand the sacrifice of true discipleship and the partnership disciples have in spreading the Good News of Jesus.

KEEP IN MIND

"And Jesus said unto them, Come ye after me, and I will make you to become fishers of men" (Mark 1:17).

FOCAL VERSES

Mark 1:14 Now after that John was put in prison, Jesus came into Galilee, preaching the gospel of the kingdom of God,

15 And saying, The time is fulfilled, and the kingdom of God is at hand: repent ye, and believe the gospel.

16 Now as he walked by the sea of Galilee, he saw Simon and Andrew his brother casting a net into the sea: for they were fishers.

17 And Jesus said unto them, Come ye after me, and I will make you to become fishers of men.

18 And straightway they forsook their nets, and followed him.

19 And when he had gone a little further thence, he saw James the son of Zebedee, and John his brother, who also were in the ship mending their nets.

20 And straightway he called them: and they left their father Zebedee in the ship with the hired servants, and went after him.

21 And they went into Capernaum; and straightway on the sabbath day he entered into the synagogue, and taught.

22 And they were astonished at his doctrine: for he taught them as one that had authority, and not as the scribes.

23 And there was in their synagogue a man with an unclean spirit; and he cried out,

JAN 2ND

24 Saying, Let us alone; what have we to do with thee, thou Jesus of Nazareth? art thou come to destroy us? I know thee who thou art, the Holy One of God.

25 And Jesus rebuked him, saying, Hold thy peace, and come out of him.

26 And when the unclean spirit had torn him, and cried with a loud voice, he came out of him.

27 And they were all amazed, insomuch that they questioned among themselves, saying, What thing is this? what new doctrine is this? for with authority commandeth he even the unclean spirits, and they do obey him.

28 And immediately his fame spread abroad throughout all the region round about Galilee.

IN FOCUS

Carl was a young man in high school when he began attending church on a regular basis. He fell in love with the church and attended Sunday School, Bible study, and Sunday morning worship. He developed a hunger for the Word of God. One day, while in one of his high school classes, Carl heard a voice in his head say, "Preach My Word. Preach My Word. Preach My Word." He heard this phrase repeated six times. He could not shake it out of his mind; but as fast as he heard it, it was soon gone.

Carl did not think much about it until one Sunday while in church, he felt the Lord tug at his heart all morning. He had a strange feeling that something weird was going to happen to him today. At the end of the worship service, his pastor "opened the doors of the church," and Carl found himself walking up to the front. The pastor gave him the microphone, and Carl astounded everyone by announcing that God had called him to preach at the tender age of 16. Carl didn't realize what he had said. He had accepted his call to ministry at such a young age at a time when he had so many other career options.

At first, he tried to fight the "calling" by telling others he wanted to become a lawyer and preach only on the weekends. He seriously thought that he could have his own secular career and a sacred career in ministry at the same time. Soon, the Lord showed him that pastoral ministry is a full-time job that needed his undivided attention. Carl realized that when he had accepted Jesus' invitation to preach, he had accepted a lifelong, life-altering commitment. He had to make a choice to follow Jesus wholeheartedly, holding nothing back.

After years of trying to decide what to do, Carl finally surrendered totally to the Lord's will and is now a successful pastor of a medium-sized church in California. He looks back over his young life and thanks God for guiding him in the right direction even though he didn't know what direction he was going in. Carl realized that when God calls you to ministry, He knows what He is doing. He will never leave you nor forsake you, and He will bless you beyond your wildest expectations.

Carl also learned one other important lesson: When Jesus calls you to ministry, it is a lifetime commitment of selfless service, which involves surrendering your will to His will on a daily basis. Like Carl, we each have to trust God with our lives and answer His call to follow Him and share the Good News with others.

THE PEOPLE, PLACES, AND TIMES

John the Baptist. A prophet held in high regard who led a revival in Judea that prepared the people to receive Jesus' message. The gospel of Luke records that John the Baptist was Jesus' cousin. John was a holy and righteous man who was wrongly executed by the state. His life was characterized by the graces of self-denial, humility, and holy courage. In his humility, he declined the honors that an admiring crowd wanted to confer upon him and declared himself to be no one, merely a voice calling people to repent because the kingdom of God was near.

Capernaum. The residence of Jesus and His apostles, and the scene of many miracles and discourses. Jesus spent His childhood at Nazareth, but Capernaum was His ministry headquarters.

BACKGROUND

The nation of Israel was well aware that for 400 years the voice of prophecy had been silent. They were waiting for some authentic word from God. In John the Baptist, they heard it. The Jews had a saying that "if Israel would only keep the law of God perfectly for one day the kingdom of God would come." When John summoned men to repentance, he was confronting them with a decision that they knew in their heart of hearts they ought to make. Despite John the Baptist's success at getting many of the Jews to repent and turn back to God, he himself knew that he was not the Messiah. When asked if he was the Messiah, John replied, "There cometh one mightier than I after me, the latchet of whose shoes I am not worthy to stoop down and unloose. I indeed have baptized you with water: but he shall baptize you with the Holy Ghost" (Mark 1:7-8). He reminded the crowds that followed him that he was preparing the way for the real Messiah.

In our lesson today, John finishes his divine assignment and is arrested. Fresh from His baptism and testing in the desert, Jesus is ready to fulfill His destiny as the Redeemer and Saviour of the world. Jesus steps onto the world stage proclaiming a message of repentance, for the kingdom of God has now come. He preaches Good News to the poor and the powerless. He also enlists four fishermen to be His students (disciples) and to help Him spread the Good News. Just as He called them into His service, He calls us today to reach others with the powerful message of the Gospel.

AT-A-GLANCE

1. Called to Repent (Mark 1:14-15)
2. Called to Serve (vv. 16-20)
3. Called to Be Victorious Over Evil
(vv. 21-28)

IN DEPTH

1. Called to Repent (Mark 1:14-15)

Jesus comes preaching the Gospel of the kingdom of God, saying that the time is fulfilled and the kingdom of God has arrived. It was time to repent and believe the Gospel. The word "repent" comes from the Greek word *metanoeo*, and it literally means to change one's mind. Jesus preached change to His audiences. He understood that if the nation of Israel was going to undergo a radical transformation from disobedience to obedience to God's Word, they would have to change their minds about God. They would also have to change their minds about how they viewed themselves. Change in action is preceded by a change in one's attitude. External change indicates an internal change. In order for the kingdom of God to become a reality in the minds of the Jews, Jesus motivated them to change from self-centeredness to God-centeredness. Jesus said, "The time is fulfilled," meaning change should not be put off. Now is the acceptable day of the Lord. Now is the time for change. Jesus proclaims that the reign of God, with justice and love, equality and abundance, wholeness and unity, is dawning. Jesus proclaims that the only way the people can embrace it, and at the same time recognize it, is through a change of mind (repentance).

Along with salvation, there must be transformation; some change must take place in you before some change takes place in the world. As we approach Black History Month, we recognize that our heroes challenged America to change her views toward her children of African descent if she wanted to "save" herself. From Sojourner

Truth to Malcolm X, they called on America to change her mind. After much bloodshed, sweat, and tears, change has come slowly and at a great price. Repentance is no easy subject, yet it is powerful once actualized in godly people.

2. Called to Serve (vv. 16-20)

Jesus called working men in the midst of their labor to a life of labor of a different sort. The objective of their first career of fishing was to feed their families and make money. However, when Jesus called them to become "fishers of men" He called them to a labor that was not about making money but about remaking the world. Jesus invited them to invest their lives not in man-centered careers but in a God-centered one. He called them to proclaim the Good News of the Kingdom and to sabotage evil in the world. He called them to follow His example of selfless love to the highest degree. He wanted them to understand that the kingdom of God meant people being transformed by the message of the Gospel—that Jesus had come to give them holistic salvation in every aspect of life. The Good News is that every believer can have victory over sin, Satan, and evil systems of oppression.

God is in the business of providing for His people. Over 2000 years ago, the call to discipleship was not based on human ability, but on the grace of God. The disciple's main focus was to live a life completely dedicated to the glory of God—a life of service to the world for the sake of God's kingdom. Today, Jesus is still looking for men, women, and children who are willing to completely yield themselves to Him and follow wherever He leads.

3. Called to Be Victorious Over Evil (vv. 21-28)

After Jesus invites the fishermen to a life of sacrificial service, He attends the synagogue, where He teaches like no one else has ever done. His audience marvels at His authority, style, and power. He is then heckled by a man with an evil spirit. Jesus does not run from confrontation with the evil spirit; rather, He rebukes it and casts it out of the man. This demonstrates Jesus' power over evil spiritual forces that undergird oppressive forms of religious thought and practice. Such false concepts were exemplified by Jesus' antagonists among the Pharisees, Sadducees, and the scribes.

Jesus calls for victory over any unclean spirit—especially in the house of God. In casting out the unclean spirit, Jesus gives every believer a responsibility to confront every evil spirit they encounter. The church should not allow evil spirits, evil agendas, evil systems of power and control, or evil attitudes to rule in the house of God. Accepting the call to follow Jesus and spread the Gospel is also a call to work toward the destruction of evil in every sphere of human life, and particularly in the church.

SEARCH THE SCRIPTURES

1. Why was it necessary for Jesus to announce His ministry (Mark 1:14-15)?

2. What was it about the background of the fishermen that made them attractive to Jesus (vv. 16-17)?

3. How long did it take the fishermen to accept Jesus' invitation (vv. 18, 20)?

4. When we confront evil in the church, what should be our response (v. 25)?

DISCUSS THE MEANING

1. If Jesus preached a message of change for His audience, what message should be preached by the church today? Has the Black Church drifted away from the core message of Jesus? Explain.

2. Discuss the sacrificial aspects of following Jesus in your current context. What does it mean to deny yourself, pick up a cross, and follow Him?

3. According to Jesus' example, should we tolerate or confront evil? Discuss the reasons and results.

LESSON IN OUR SOCIETY

It is time for the church to stand up and take their call to discipleship seriously. In the movie *X: An Autobiography on Malcolm X*, there was a powerful quote by Malcolm X to Brother Baines. Malcolm said, "God's work ain't no hustle!" The real disciples of Jesus must usher in the kingdom of God with power and authority for the kingdom's sake and not for any selfish gain. The church has a dying world to save, and it is time to confront evil with the Gospel that Jesus saves.

Jesus needs authentic disciples to carry on His mission. If the church does not do it, then who will?

MAKE IT HAPPEN

In order to truly follow Jesus, you have to do more than talk; you have to pray consistently. You have to read and study the Word of God in order to follow Him. Adopt a lifestyle of love, mercy, compassion, nonviolence, justice, truth, and sense of urgency to transform your reality. Finally, learn and become comfortable with communicating the Gospel with others. Articulating the truth of God's Word is difficult at first, but once you start doing it, it will get easier. It is not enough just to hear the Gospel; you have to be able to share it also. This week, share the Gospel with someone who does not know Jesus.

FOLLOW THE SPIRIT

What God wants me to do:

_____

_____

REMEMBER YOUR THOUGHTS

Special insights I have learned:

_____

_____

MORE LIGHT ON THE TEXT

Mark 1:14-28

14 Now after that John was put in prison, Jesus came into Galilee, preaching the gospel of the kingdom of God, 15 And saying, The time is fulfilled, and the kingdom of God is at hand: repent ye, and believe the gospel.

Mark's account of the beginnings of Jesus' active public ministry was marked by two significant events: the incarceration of John for his fearless preaching and the call of Jesus' disciples. John was imprisoned and later killed by Herod Antipas, tetrarch of Galilee and Perea, for speaking out against his unlawful marital relationship with Herodias (Luke 3:19; Matthew 14:9). Notwithstanding, Jesus came into Galilee, "preaching the gospel of the kingdom of God." Jesus' message was twofold: "repent" (Gk. *metanoeo*, **met-an-o-eh'-o**), i.e., experience a change of mind and "believe" (Gk. *pisteuo*, **pist-yoo-o**) i.e., trust in the Good News.

16 Now as he walked by the sea of Galilee, he saw Simon and Andrew his brother casting a net into the sea: for they were fishers. 17 And Jesus said unto them, Come ye after me, and I will make you to become fishers of men. 18 And straightway they forsook their nets, and followed him.

Mark's picturesque description of Jesus' actions indicates the vividness of an eyewitness. Literally Mark says, "And leading along the sea of Galilee he saw Simon and Andrew." There is a strong indication in Mark's construction of this scene that Jesus watched these brothers with extended interest before speaking to them. He had greater purpose for them than catching fish. "Come ye after me," He summoned, "and I will make you to become fishers of men." The use of the word *ginomai* suggests a process of becoming. Jesus (not His followers) initiates the call and undertakes the task of fashioning them into what only He can make them. "Straightway" (Gk. *eutheos*), or immediately, they relinquished their nets and followed the Lord. Great ministers are made of ordinary people who are willing to obey the Lord's voice and take on service for Christ.

19 And when he had gone a little further thence, he saw James the son of Zebedee, and John his brother, who also were in the ship mending their nets. 20 And straightway he called them: and they left their father Zebedee in the ship with the hired servants, and went after him.

Going a little further, the Lord summons the Zebedee brothers to become His permanent followers. This detail, included only in Mark, indicates proximity between Simon and Andrew and the Zebedee brothers. Leaving their fishing business and their father with the "hired servants" (Gk. *misthotos*), they follow Jesus. The Greek word *misthos* (one hired for wages) suggests that the Zebedees' was a fairly large fishing business. Simon (Peter) and Andrew left their fishing occupation, but John and his brother (James) left their father as well as their occupation. Discipleship, or the call to ministry, often means

Jesus is tenderly calling fishers of men!

sacrifices that include leaving our former ways of life and former ties.

21 And they went into Capernaum; and straightway on the sabbath day he entered into the synagogue, and taught. 22 And they were astonished at his doctrine: for he taught them as one that had authority, and not as the scribes.

These verses summarize Jesus' teaching and set the stage and location of His encounter with evil spirits. Jesus had moved His headquarters to Capernaum after the rejection in his hometown of Nazareth (cf. Matthew 4:13; Luke 4:16-31). In the Capernaum synagogue, He was teaching on the Sabbath. Jesus both "taught" (Gk. *didasko*) and "preached" (Gk. *kerusso*), but Mark gives prominence to Jesus the Teacher and His teaching. Jesus' teaching (*Gk. didaskalia*) literally struck the people out of their senses—"they were astonished" (Gk. *ekplesso*)—and contrasts sharply with the teaching of the scribes. He struck a note not found in the teaching of the rabbis, who thought of their function as quoting other rabbis and expounding their traditions. But Jesus was teaching "as one that had authority" (Gk. *exousia*), and it resonated with the deep longings of the people's thirsty souls.

23 And there was in their synagogue a man with an unclean spirit; and he cried out,

Jesus did not teach only with words; He also

demonstrated the power of God. In the synagogue was one "with an unclean spirit," literally translated as, "in spirit unclean" (Gk. *en pneumati akathartoi*). This person was under the power of some unclean spirits or demons, and he "cried out" (Gk. *anakrazo*). The reality of demons and demonic activity is implied here. It is as dangerous to be fixated on demons as it is to be ignorant of their presence and activities. Jesus took Satan and his demons seriously.

24 Saying, Let us alone; what have we to do with thee, thou Jesus of Nazareth? art thou come to destroy us? I know thee who thou art, the Holy One of God. 25 And Jesus rebuked him, saying, Hold thy peace, and come out of him. 26 And when the unclean spirit had torn him, and cried with a loud voice, he came out of him.

"What have we to do with thee?" (Gk. *ti hemin kai soi?*) The term "we" indicates either the presence of more than one demon or that the man is speaking for himself and the demon. In either case, we have an incident of multiple personalities. Note the singular construction in the phrase "I know" (Gk. *oida*), possibly indicating an interchange between the man and the demon. The demon[s] recognize Jesus as "the Holy One of God" (Gk. *ho hagios tou theou*) and indicate that His presence will "destroy" (Gk. *apollumi*), i.e., ruin their well-being. The phrase "Hold thy peace," literally, "be muzzled" or "shut up" (Gk. *phimotheti*), indicates that our Lord would not dialogue or negotiate with demons; instead, He expelled them. The phrase "torn him" indicates a convulsion like a spasm (Gk. *sparaxan auton*). At Jesus' command, the demon had to come out of the man. The phrase "a loud voice" translates literally as "a great sounding of the voice" (Gk. *phonei megalei*).

27 And they were all amazed, insomuch that they questioned among themselves, saying, What thing is this? what new doctrine is this? for with authority commandeth he even the unclean spirits, and they do obey him. 28 And immediately his fame spread abroad throughout all the region round about Galilee.

The combined effect of our Lord's teaching and miracle produced widespread amazement— they were all "amazed" (Gk. *thambeo*). There was excitement in the air. They "questioned" (Gk. *suzeteo*), or disputed, among themselves. Who is this? His teaching was original and fresh. What "new doctrine," (Gk. *didache*) or new teaching, was this? He orders unclean spirits, and they obey Him! Here was One who did not make use of magical formulae like the Jewish exorcists the people were used to. Here was Someone with inherent authority! Like wildfire on the prairie, His "fame" (Gk. *akoe*) was spreading "throughout all the region," or all places throughout the Galilean region.

DAILY BIBLE READINGS

M: John Proclaims That Jesus Is Coming
Mark 1:1-8

T: Jesus Prepares for His Ministry
Mark 1:9-13

W: Jesus Preaches and Calls Disciples
Mark 1:14-20

T: Jesus Teaches and Performs a Miracle
Mark 1:21-28

F: Jesus Heals Many People
Mark 1:29-34

S: Jesus Preaches in Galilee
Mark 1:35-39

S: Jesus Proclaims Good News
Matthew 4:16-25

Use the resources in your *Precepts For Living* CD-ROM to study the ways the word *call* is used in Scripture.

TEACHING TIPS

January 9
Bible Study Guide 6

1. Words You Should Know

A. Publicans (Mark 2:15) *telones* (Gk.)—There were two types. First, tax farmers oversaw collection of the major land taxes and tributes. Next, there were toll collectors who handled the myriad of local transportation taxes and tariffs.

B. Sinners (v. 15) *harmatolos* (Gk.)—The word "sinner" described someone who broke the moral law. However, it also meant a person who did not observe the scribal law either. Jesus spoke of sin as sickness (Mark 2:17) and sometimes as folly (Luke 12:20). Nevertheless, Jesus declared that sinners can be cured with God's help (Mark 6:36-50).

C. Pharisees (v. 16) *Pharisaios* (Gk.)—A religious sect active in Palestine during the New Testament period. The Pharisees are depicted in the Gospels as Jesus' antagonists, yet some followed Christ (e.g. John 19:38-39). It was commonly thought that the Pharisees represented mainstream Judaism early in the first century despite their negative depiction in the Gospels.

2. Teacher Preparation

A. Study the DEVOTIONAL READING and pray for your students.

B. Read BIBLE STUDY GUIDE 6 at least twice and record any insights you want to share.

C. Read all of Mark 6 and consult a Bible commentary to help you understand it better.

3. Starting the Lesson

A. Before the students arrive, write the AT-A-GLANCE outline on the board.

B. Write your significant observations underneath the AT-A-GLANCE subheadings. Use these observations as discussion material.

C. Read and discuss the IN FOCUS story.

4. Getting into the Lesson

A. Pray with the students that God will reveal to them the need to extend His hospitality to everyone, including those they do not like.

B. Read and discuss THE PEOPLE, PLACES, AND TIMES and BACKGROUND sections.

C. Ask the students to read the FOCAL VERSES and the corresponding IN-DEPTH section.

5. Relating the Lesson to Life

A. Ask the students to discuss ways they can welcome an unchurched person to their church.

B. Discuss how and why sinners may be discouraged from attending church.

C. Read and discuss the LESSON IN OUR SOCIETY section.

6. Arousing Action

A. Ask the students to record their reflections on the lesson in the FOLLOW THE SPIRIT and REMEMBER YOUR THOUGHTS sections.

B. Encourage the students to become like Jesus by receiving into the church those whom society rejects, such as gangbangers, drug dealers, and AIDS sufferers.

C. Close the class with a prayer that is centered on becoming as inclusive as Jesus was.

WORSHIP GUIDE

For the Superintendent or Teacher
Theme: Jesus Calls Levi (Matthew)
Theme Song: "Amazing Grace"
Scripture: John 3:16-17
Song: "There Is a Balm in Gilead"
Meditation: Dear God, please give us a love like Jesus had for all humanity regardless of the sin in their lives. Help us not to judge one another but to love one another. Give us a love like Jesus and help us to spread that love. In Jesus' name we pray. Amen.

JESUS CALLS LEVI (MATTHEW)

Bible Background • MARK 2:13-17
Printed Text • MARK 2:13-17
Devotional Reading • EPHESIANS 4:25-32

LESSON AIM

By the end of the lesson, the students will recognize the inclusive nature of God's love, understand that the mission of Jesus Christ was to heal those who were spiritually sick, and elect to make that their mission as well as disciples of Jesus Christ.

KEEP IN MIND

"I came not to call the righteous, but sinners to repentance" (from Mark 2:17).

FOCAL VERSES

Mark 2:13 And he went forth again by the sea side; and all the multitude resorted unto him, and he taught them.

14 And as he passed by, he saw Levi the son of Alphaeus sitting at the receipt of custom, and said unto him, Follow me. And he arose and followed him.

15 And it came to pass, that, as Jesus sat at meat in his house, many publicans and sinners sat also together with Jesus and his disciples: for there were many, and they followed him.

16 And when the scribes and Pharisees saw him eat with publicans and sinners, they said unto his disciples, How is it that he eateth and drinketh with publicans and sinners?

17 When Jesus heard it, he saith unto them, They that are whole have no need of the physician, but they that are sick: I came not to call the righteous, but sinners to repentance.

IN FOCUS

Curtis was a good kid who grew up in the wrong

LESSON OVERVIEW

LESSON AIM
KEEP IN MIND
FOCAL VERSES
IN FOCUS
THE PEOPLE, PLACES, AND TIMES
BACKGROUND
AT-A-GLANCE
IN DEPTH
SEARCH THE SCRIPTURES
DISCUSS THE MEANING
LESSON IN OUR SOCIETY
MAKE IT HAPPEN
FOLLOW THE SPIRIT
REMEMBER YOUR THOUGHTS
MORE LIGHT ON THE TEXT
DAILY BIBLE READINGS

environment. Many of his relatives were charter members of a local street gang that was notorious for intimidation, violence, and drug trafficking. Curtis was socialized around this "gang and drug culture" all of his life. In fact, since it was all he knew, as he grew older he rose up in the gang as a well-respected and feared leader.

Everyone in the community knew what kind of *activity* Curtis was involved in. He had notoriety and street credibility from young and old. However, one fateful day would change his life forever. He was in the midst of a drug deal and someone shot him six times. He was rushed to the hospital and underwent hours of surgery to repair the damage caused by the bullets. Curtis survived that gun battle. During surgery, he told friends and family that he had a vision that Jesus was telling him to turn his life around and to use his street smarts for the good of God's kingdom rather than for the destruction of God's kingdom. In the vision, he remembered saying yes to Jesus and vowing to do what he could to end the gang violence and drug trafficking in his community. He remembered making a promise to Jesus to use his "street credibility" to steer other gang members to the Lord. He was tired of the life he was living, and he desired to make a change.

After weeks of recovery and rehabilitation, Curtis was released from the hospital and was ready to live for Christ. He went to the church he had joined and been baptized in as a youth. As soon as he walked into the church, everybody that knew him in his "former vocation" began to stare and whisper under their breath, "What is he doing here?" "He sold out the community by selling drugs and being in a gang." Curtis was aware that many negative comments were being made about him, but he just ignored them. Nothing was going to deter him from fulfilling his promise to Jesus. In fact, he had called the pastor of the church while he was in the hospital and told him about his vision. The pastor had already warned him about the backlash from people who had known him when he was a gang member.

During the service, when the pastor saw Curtis sitting in the front row, he called him up to the front of the church and announced to the congregation, "Curtis, in spite of his past, has finally come home! Curtis is a child of God just like you!"

All of us have sinned and fallen short of the glory of God. We are all saved by grace through faith. God loves us all. If God can forgive us, then we should be able to forgive others. Today's lesson gives an example of God's acceptance and forgiveness. Jesus welcomes all who will accept His invitation, including the "Levis" of the world!

THE PEOPLE, PLACES, AND TIMES

The Pharisees. Before the destruction of the temple, this religious group was primarily a society devoted to teaching and table fellowship. The dietary, ritual, and legal orientation focused largely on this table fellowship, which was the high point of their life as a group. Jesus unmasks the Pharisees for what they truly were: a religious sect that was more interested in preserving their own privileged status than in extending holiness to all of Israel. Oftentimes, the Pharisees were more interested in keeping rigid rules in place for their own benefit. Jesus would show His adversaries and acquaintances that in God's kingdom there were no rigid social boundaries between "the righteous" and "the sinner." John 3:16-17 says, "For God so loved the world, that he gave his only begotten Son, that whosoever believeth in him should not perish, but have everlasting life. For God sent not his Son into the world to condemn the world; but that the world through him might be saved."

Jesus' mission was to restore people and not to ignore them. It was profound and revolutionary for Jesus, a rabbi, to sit at a table with Levi (Matthew), a known sinner.

BACKGROUND

Jesus was intentional in breaking the social codes that oppressed rather than liberated the common folk and other ostracized groups within Israel. He chose to upset the status quo religiosity of the Pharisaic class by associating with known sinners. Why? To demonstrate that no one was outside the realm of God's grace and love. The followers of Jesus, other than His 12 disciples, were mostly comprised of the lower class, poor, uneducated—hence, those outside of mainstream Judaism. Jesus, the Son of God, identifies Himself with those who are rejected by the mainstream. How revolutionary! Jesus was comfortable with calling the outcast and the sinner.

How was Levi singled out? At some point, Jesus finished His teaching to the crowds and began walking along the seashore. As He walked along, He passed by the tax booth that had been set up to collect the taxes owed by incoming ships. Then Jesus saw Levi, the publican (tax collector) in charge of the tax station. All publicans were considered traitors, outcasts, and sinners in the minds of Jewish society. They were bitterly hated and ostracized. They were looked upon as having sold their souls to the Roman authorities. According to most accounts, the vast majority were thieves, cheats, and extortionists—always adding to the legal fee in order to fill their own pockets. Most publicans were wealthy, and the fact that Levi had a house large enough to accommodate a large party indicates that he may have been rich (Mark 2:14-17; Luke 5:27-32). Despite the "spiritual and cultural baggage" Levi had, Jesus still invited him to become His disciple.

AT-A-GLANCE

1. Jesus Engages a Sinner (Mark 2:13-14)
2. Jesus Eats with Sinners (vv. 15-16)
3. Jesus Enunciates His Mission (v. 17)

IN DEPTH

1. Jesus Engages a Sinner (Mark 2:13-14)

Jesus had a preoccupation with sinners and social outcasts. Jesus invites a social outcast named Levi to become one of His disciples. It was a powerful symbolic act on His part. The unusual invitation let His audience know that His mission was truly reconciliation for the sinner and social outcast. The tax collectors' widespread reputation for dishonesty, and the fact that they were bureaucratic representatives of the oppressive political-economic order, caused them to be shunned.

While the Pharisees, Sadducees, and scribes ignored the needs of the sinners and the social outcasts, Jesus did not. In fact, he did just the opposite by embracing them and including them in His ministry. His mission was to preach Good News to the poor, heal the brokenhearted, open the eyes of the blind, set the captives free, and proclaim the acceptable year of the Lord (Luke 4:18).

We need to truly embrace the inclusive nature of the Gospel. Those who were not accepted and ostracized, Jesus accepted and invited to become His disciples. Jesus loved people regardless of what they had done. He hates the sin but loves the sinner. In Jesus' eyes no one is hopeless or beyond the reach of His transforming grace. If Jesus changed you, surely Jesus can change someone else. As Christians and followers of Christ, it is our mission to invite others to receive Jesus as Lord over every area of life and to yield themselves to Him as instruments to change the world. Are we inviting sinners to become disciples of Jesus Christ?

2. Jesus Eats with Sinners (vv. 15-16)

It appears that many Christians have forgotten a long lost secret: Jesus knew how to draw lost sinners to Himself! Jesus was surrounded by social outcasts and misfits. There were many of them, and they were together with Jesus in Levi's house enjoying a wonderful meal. What a strange scene! Publicans were hated because of what they did—collect foreign taxes—and the sinners were hated for what they did not do—observe the Mosaic Law! But here was Jesus, in table fellowship with them and enjoying their company. It was scandalous for Jesus to be in the presence of such people, but He engaged, accepted, and welcomed such people. Jesus knew that they could be translated into and accepted as participants in the kingdom of God.

The modern counterparts of publicans and sinners do not come to our churches in great numbers. They feel uncomfortable being there and church folk are uncomfortable having them there. However, Jesus was spiritually social. In other words, He was so spiritual that He could interact with sinners and not compromise who He was! His mission was to the people with much sin in their lives, and that is who He welcomed. He preached "repentance" to them—the same message He preached to everyone else. But He also had three secret weapons: love, mercy, and compassion.

We need to emulate the love, mercy, and compassion of Jesus. When we are instruments of God's love, others will be attracted to Jesus and His transforming grace. We must actively seek out the lost and lovingly share the Gospel. Since "it is the power of God for the salvation of everyone who believes," it will produce a change in their heart and character (Romasn 1:16, NIV). Love has the greatest power to draw people to Jesus Christ.

3. Jesus Enunciates His Mission (v. 17)

Jesus announced His mission to reclaim the sinners who were rejected by mainstream Judaism. His evangelistic focus was on people who felt excluded from temple and synagogue worship and Jewish life. The Pharisees objected to Jesus, eating with outsiders and violators of their traditions, but Jesus was not deterred by what they thought.

For the sake of salvation and restoration of a fractured community, Jesus reached out to two ostracized groups of individuals: publicans and sinners. He gave them a glimpse of the limitless power of God's love to smash the traditional and cultural boundaries set up to exclude them from the mainstream. Using a bit of sarcasm, Jesus answered His critics with the following words, "I came not to call the righteous, but sinners to

Jesus demonstrates that even hated tax collectors like Matthew can repent and be saved.

repentance" (v. 17). Jesus was on a reclamation project. His critics, like their modern-day counterparts, did not understand His methodology for redeeming publicans and sinners. They did not understand that He loved humanity so much that He would risk reputation and social status to save just one of them. His love for the sinner is expressed in Luke 15:1-32, commonly referred to as the "chapter of the lost and found."

Jesus' activity reminds us that He was on a serious mission. His mission was salvaging broken brothers and sisters in need of reconciliation, identity, love, forgiveness, acceptance, and a sense of purpose. His mission was focused on people and not prestige, money, or any other selfish

endeavors. We must remember that the church exists to seek and save the lost. The church, the body of Christ, must become an agent of healing in the same spirit of Jesus. We must do all we can to heal the breach between the righteous and the sinners. The Church is called by Christ to bear witness to His power to save and transform sinners into saints. Like Christ, the Church is called to break down all divisive and destructive boundaries that separate us from one another. All Christians need to hear and obey Jesus' pronouncement, "I came not to call the righteous, but sinners to repentance" (Mark 2:17).

Decide today to be concerned about your unsaved brothers and sisters who need Jesus.

Make the decision to invite them to be a part of the family of God. As disciples, we are all doctors of the soul. Let us go and bring God's healing to a world full of sin.

SEARCH THE SCRIPTURES

1. Where did Jesus find Levi (Mark 2:13)?

2. What was Levi's response to Jesus' invitation to follow Him (v. 14)?

3. What was Jesus doing at Levi's house with other publicans and sinners (v. 15)?

4. Did Jesus have more followers than His 12 disciples? If yes, then how many followers did He have (v. 15)?

5. Why did the scribes and Pharisees criticize Jesus (v. 16)?

6. How did Jesus silence his critics (v. 17)?

7. What was Jesus' mission? What is the mission of Jesus' followers today (v. 17)?

DISCUSS THE MEANING

1. What does it mean to follow Jesus? Explore all possible meanings.

2. Jesus came not to call the righteous but sinners to repentance. Can you truly be a Christian and not associate with sinners? Why or why not?

3. Can we make disciples of the unsaved if we don't go where they are or do not have any contact with them? Discuss how far we should go to associate with and witness to unbelievers. How can we wisely follow Jesus' example today?

LESSON IN OUR SOCIETY

As Christians, our lives should serve as our ministries. The ministry of the church is found outside the four walls of the church, and we should strive for our light to shine in the darkness. Jesus had an inner circle of disciples and significant relationships with sinners. He associated with them to transform them, and Christians must do the same.

MAKE IT HAPPEN

Reach out to the unchurched in your community to bring them into the knowledge of Jesus Christ. If your community is going to be healthy, safe, and nurturing, then you as the church must help by engaging those who feel left out, dispossessed, and disenfranchised by empowering them with the Good News of Jesus Christ. The term *Christian* means to be Christlike; it is more than just a title, it is a lifestyle!

FOLLOW THE SPIRIT

What God wants me to do:

_____

_____

REMEMBER YOUR THOUGHTS

Special insights I have learned:

_____

_____

MORE LIGHT ON THE TEXT
Mark 2:13-17

13 And he went forth again by the sea side; and all the multitude resorted unto him, and he taught them.

Jesus' teachings and miracles continued to attract larger and larger crowds. But He would not be diverted or distracted by His popularity. He withdrew for solitary prayer (Mark 1:35) and took time to get away from the crowd for a walk along the seaside. He "went forth" (Gk. *exelthen*) again "by the sea" side (Gk. *para ten thalassan*), but it would not be long before "all the multitude resorted unto him" or "all the crowd was coming to Him" (Gk. *pas ho ochlos echeto pros auton*) and He was teaching them (Gk. *edidasken autous*).

14 And as he passed by, he saw Levi the son of Alphaeus sitting at the receipt of custom, and said unto him, Follow me. And he arose and followed him.

As he "passed by," Jesus saw Levi at the tax collector's booth or "the receipt of custom" (Gk. *telonion*). Levi (Matthew) collected tolls for Herod Antipas. Because publicans (tax collectors) worked for the hated Roman occupation authorities and collected money from their own people for the Romans, they were despised by the Jews. Therefore, Matthew was an unlikely candidate for the ministry. However, Jesus called Matthew to follow Him, and he promptly obeyed and followed Jesus.

15 And it came to pass, that, as Jesus sat at meat in his house, many publicans and sinners sat also together with Jesus and his disciples: for there were many, and they followed him.

The same Greek word *telonai* is translated as "tax collectors" and "publicans." The Jews classified the publicans with "sinners" (Gk. *hamartoloi*). The association of publicans and sinners here may refer to their immoral lifestyles or to the dishonesty and defilement associated with their jobs. At any rate, Matthew had arranged a banquet in Jesus' honor to celebrate his call to discipleship. Naturally, he invited his friends and colleagues, many of whom were also considered to be "sinners." Jesus feasted with these kinds of people and a growing crowd of "many" (*polloi*).

16 And when the scribes and Pharisees saw him eat with publicans and sinners, they said unto his disciples, How is it that he eateth and drinketh with publicans and sinners?

The "Pharisees" (*Pharisaios*) were a separatist movement within Jewish society. Their focus was on doing and teaching the Law of Moses in everyday life—inner and outer separation according to the law. The ideal of everyday sanctification according to the law led them to develop a "hedge" around the law. In turn, over time this process evolved into multiple layers of "tradition of elders." By Jesus' time, the Pharisees had become one of the leading Jewish religious parties, along with the Sadducees and Essenes. Their strict emphases on details of the law (which often abrogated its demands) and legalistic separation from the people fueled their opposition to Jesus. On this occasion, Jesus' mingling and eating with the *undesirable* people rattled the religious sensitivities of "the scribes and the Pharisees" (*hoi gram mateis ton Pharisaion*). They could not understand how Jesus could risk ritual defilement and moral contamination by bonding with these "sinners."

17 When Jesus heard it, he saith unto them, They that are whole have no need of the physician, but they that are sick: I came not to call the righteous, but sinners to repentance.

In response, Jesus declares that He came "not to call the righteous, but sinners" (*ouk dikaious alla hamartolous*). In focusing on the strict requirements of the letter of the law, the Pharisees had obscured the purpose of the law. God's purpose is to bring wholeness to those afflicted by the disease of sin. The law is good, but legalism is unfruitful. Jesus came to offer spiritual life to sinners estranged from God by announcing the coming of God's kingdom, and He calls all to respond. Although all who have received spiritual life in Christ separate themselves from sin, mere separation from sin does not cure the internal disease of human sinfulness. All who come to God must come through Christ.

DAILY BIBLE READINGS

M: Jesus Heals a Leper
Mark 1:40-45

T: Jesus Forgives a Paralytic
Mark 2:1-5

W: The Paralytic Stands Up and Walks
Mark 2:6-12

T: I Have Come to Call Sinners
Mark 2:13-17

F: Love and Live in the Light
1 John 2:9-17

S: Love One Another
1 John 4:7-21

S: We Are Members of One Another
Ephesians 4:25-32

You may find it interesting to see how the words *sin* and *sinner* are used in Scripture by doing a cross-reference check on Matthew 2:15 using your *Precepts For Living* CD-ROM.

TEACHING TIPS

January 16
Bible Study Guide 7

1. Words You Should Know

A. Mountain (Mark 3:13) *oros* (Gk.)—The symbol of the mountain was powerful in Jewish religious thought in the time of Moses. Mountain imagery is prevalent throughout the Gospels, especially in Matthew and Mark.

B. The Twelve (v. 14) *Idodeka* (Gk.)—The twelve disciples who comprised Jesus' inner circle. They would later move from discipleship to apostleship and be entrusted with the mission of establishing the universal church.

C. Oil (6:13) *elaion* (Gk.)—In the ancient world, olive oil was regarded as a healing agent. Oil was used for cooking, for anointing the body, for medicinal purposes, for anointing kings and priests, and in religious offerings.

2. Teacher Preparation

A. Read Mark 3 and 6.

B. Read the entire lesson, including MORE LIGHT ON THE TEXT.

3. Starting the Lesson

A. Before the students arrive in class, write the lesson title, AT-A-GLANCE outline, and the headings from the IN DEPTH section on the chalkboard or on poster board.

B. Have a student open the class with prayer, using the LESSON AIM as a guide for the prayer.

C. Have the students read the FOCAL VERSES and answer the SEARCH THE SCRIPTURES questions.

D. Be sure the students understand the context of the lesson by reminding them that the subject matter is the calling and commissioning of the disciples.

4. Getting into the Lesson

A. Generate a discussion on how the mission of the church today compares to the mission of the disciples in today's text. Compare and contrast the similarities and differences.

B. Using the outline on the board and the information from the IN DEPTH section, take students through the lesson, focusing on the evangelism and the social outreach of the 12 disciples.

5. Relating the Lesson to Life

A. Impress upon the students the necessity to move beyond the four walls of the church building in order to build the kingdom of God.

B. Jesus sent the Twelve out to interact with and invest in the lives of others. Remind the students that one of the requirements of discipleship is to invest in the lives of people and not just in church property.

6. Arousing Action

A. Have the students share how they can apply the truths from today's lesson to become followers of Christ who interact with unsaved people.

B. Challenge the students to read the DAILY BIBLE READINGS throughout the week.

WORSHIP GUIDE

For the Superintendent or Teacher
Theme: Jesus Sends Out the Twelve
Theme Song: "Lift Him Up"
Scripture: Matthew 28:19-20
Song: "Go, Tell It On the Mountain"
Meditation: Dear Lord, help us to be authentic disciples who move beyond the four walls of the church to deliver the Gospel to the downtrodden, the helpless, and the hopeless. Open our eyes to the needs within our community so that we can transform our community. In Jesus' name we pray. Amen.

JESUS SENDS OUT THE TWELVE

Bible Background • MARK 3:13-19; 6:6-13
Printed Text • MARK 3:13-19; 6:6-13
Devotional Reading • LUKE 9:1-6

LESSON AIM

By the end of the lesson, the students will know that discipleship means engaging the world in order to transform it, preaching repentance to a world in need of change, and becoming agents of healing and reconciliation.

KEEP IN MIND

"And he ordained twelve, that they should be with him, and that he might send them forth to preach" (Mark 3:14).

FOCAL VERSES

Mark 3:13 And he goeth up into a mountain, and calleth unto him whom he would: and they came unto him.

14 And he ordained twelve, that they should be with him, and that he might send them forth to preach,

15 And to have power to heal sicknesses, and to cast out devils:

16 And Simon he surnamed Peter;

17 And James the son of Zebedee, and John the brother of James; and he surnamed them Boanerges, which is, The sons of thunder:

18 And Andrew, and Philip, and Bartholomew, and Matthew, and Thomas, and James the son of Alphaeus, and Thaddaeus, and Simon the Canaanite,

19 And Judas Iscariot, which also betrayed him: and they went into an house.

6:6 And he went round about the villages, teaching.

7 And he called unto him the twelve, and began to send them forth by two and two; and gave them

LESSON OVERVIEW

LESSON AIM
KEEP IN MIND
FOCAL VERSES
IN FOCUS
THE PEOPLE, PLACES,
AND TIMES
BACKGROUND
AT-A-GLANCE
IN DEPTH
SEARCH THE SCRIPTURES
DISCUSS THE MEANING
LESSON IN OUR SOCIETY
MAKE IT HAPPEN
FOLLOW THE SPIRIT
REMEMBER YOUR THOUGHTS
MORE LIGHT ON THE TEXT
DAILY BIBLE READINGS

power over unclean spirits;

8 And commanded them that they should take nothing for their journey, save a staff only; no scrip, no bread, no money in their purse:

9 But be shod with sandals; and not put on two coats.

10 And he said unto them, In what place soever ye enter into an house, there abide till ye depart from that place.

11 And whosoever shall not receive you, nor hear you, when ye depart thence, shake off the dust under your feet for a testimony against them. Verily I say unto you, It shall be more tolerable for Sodom and Gomorrha in the day of judgment, than for that city.

JAN 16TH

12 And they went out, and preached that men should repent.

13 And they cast out many devils, and anointed with oil many that were sick, and healed them.

IN FOCUS

One day a preacher and his teenage son were taking a walk. The son turned to his father and asked him, "Dad, if there are so many churches in our community, why aren't our people doing better? I am sick of seeing people walking listlessly down streets and alleys doing nothing with their lives or only looking for their next drug high. I wish our church would do more for the people in the community."

His father turned to him and said, "You know, son, the church just last year decided to reach out more to the community. We decided that we were going to invest more time, talents, and tithes into the lives of the people in the community. We decided ...."

Just then his son interrupted him and said, "Dad, let me tell you a story I heard yesterday. Five frogs were sitting on a log. Four decided to jump off. How many remain?"

His father answered, "One."

His son shot back, "No, Dad, five remained! Why? Because deciding and doing are two different things! Our church has got to stop deciding to do the work of Jesus and start doing it! Then, and only then, can we save our community!"

His father looked at him, amazed at his wisdom, and said, "Amen!"

Is it time for you to stop "deciding" to take action and just "take action"? Today's lesson relates how Jesus called, appointed, and equipped the 12 disciples to take action.

THE PEOPLE, PLACES, AND TIMES

Nazareth. A village in the Roman province of Galilee and the home of Jesus. Always small and isolated, Nazareth is not mentioned in the Old Testament. In the time of Jesus, Nazareth, along with the entire region of South Galilee, lay outside the mainstream of Jewish life, providing the reason for Nathaniel's disparaging remark to Philip, "Can anything good come from there?" (John 1:46, NIV).

Sodom and Gomorrah. Two of the "cities of the plain" referred to in Genesis 13:12. There were five cities: Sodom, Gomorrah, Adonah, Zeboim, and Bela or Zoar—all situated in the valley of Siddim (i.e., the Salt Sea). Sodom and Gomorrah became known in biblical literature as the supreme example of a wicked city and its destruction (Genesis 19:24). It was also used as a warning of God's judgment in other biblical writings. The people of Sodom were arrogant, overfed, and unconcerned about the poor and needy (Ezekiel 16:49). The city was known as a place of sexual perversion, especially promiscuity and homosexuality.

BACKGROUND

Jesus was disrespected in His hometown. It appears that the name that Jesus was making for Himself scandalized the neighborhood and upset the status quo. Without their cooperative faith, Jesus could not perform any mighty works there. Jesus was not only rejected by His native townspeople, but also by His immediate family and relatives. However, He does not resign Himself to rejection, but takes His message to the remote parts of the region. Jesus gathers His own "community," the 12 disciples, to assist Him with spreading the Good News of the Gospel. This is where today's lesson begins.

AT-A-GLANCE

1. Jesus Sends Out the Twelve with Power (Mark 3:13-19; 6:6-7)
2. Jesus Sends Out the Twelve with Provision (vv. 8-11)
3. Jesus Sends Out the Twelve with a Plan (vv. 12-13)

IN DEPTH

1. Jesus Sends Out the Twelve with Power (Mark 3:13-19; 6:6-7)

The first Mark passage deals with Jesus' calling of the 12 disciples. After He taught them, He sent out the 12 disciples in groups of two. He gave them power and authority over unclean spirits. They were given power to impact the villages they would enter for the good of the kingdom. As Christians we have been called and commissioned to impact our world, but many are not "walking" in their calling. We have to remember that the church is not the building but the faithful who occupy the building. Each of us is called to minister beyond the four walls of our church buildings so that people can experience God's salvation. It is time to get involved in the communities that we serve in order to become the authentic church of Jesus the Christ.

2. Jesus Sends Out the Twelve with Provision (vv. 8-11)

Jesus sends out the disciples with the necessary yet unconventional provisions. In doing so, Jesus intended for His disciples to depend upon God to provide for their needs. In contrast to other religious professionals of the day, the disciples were to go about giving and not getting. We can see this in the beginning of the Christian movement; the mark of the Christian disciple was to be utter simplicity, complete trust, and the generosity that causes one to give and never demand. Jesus commissions His community of disciples to begin their missionary journey with basic supplies. It was rabbinic law that when a man entered the temple courts, he must remove his staff, shoes, and money girdle. All ordinary things were to be set aside when entering the sacred place. It may be that Jesus was thinking of this, and that He intended His disciples to see that the humble homes they were to enter were every bit as sacred as the temple courts.

If the disciples experienced rejection from anyone, Jesus instructed them to shake the dust off their sandals and keep moving. The rabbinic law said that the dust of a Gentile country was defiled, and that when a man entered Palestine from another country, he must shake off every particle of dust of the unclean land. It was as if Jesus was telling His disciples, "If they refuse to listen to you, there can be no fellowship between you and them."

Jesus prepared the Twelve for the success of their apostolic mission and for their rejection. The key theme in these verses is that when we actively engage people with the Gospel, we must completely trust God with the results. Additionally, we must realize that when people reject the Gospel, we should not take it personally. No matter how people respond to our efforts, we must keep on preaching the Good News! The provision that Jesus gives us today is the power to preach to the unsaved while "shaking off" the dust of rejection when it arises. We have a mission to complete: to make disciples for Jesus the Christ. Our earthly desire for material possessions, fame, and notoriety have to decrease so

Jesus empowers the apostles to live and preach the transforming Good News.

that the agenda of God's kingdom can increase. We have divine orders to go into our communities as change agents. Jesus dispatched His disciples to the streets with the transforming "Good News." The church must do the same.

3. Jesus Sends Out the Twelve with a Plan (vv. 12-13)

The disciples brought the message of repentance to the people. "Repentance" is a fancy word for "a change of heart and action." It is bound to disturb because it means a complete reversal of life. It requires moving from self-centeredness to Christ-centeredness. The message of repentance involves revolutionary change and not just remorse for one's sins. It creates a sense of community among people divided by class, gender, and geographical region.

Procrastination is the grave where opportunity is buried. Drastic change is needed, and the Church must initiate such change. When we move from self-centeredness to Christ-centeredness, we will manifest the kingdom of God in our present reality.

SEARCH THE SCRIPTURES

1. How did Jesus react to the unbelief of His hometown friends and family (Mark 6:6b)?

2. Why did Jesus enlist the disciples to help Him spread the Gospel (v. 7)?

3. How were the disciples told to deal with rejection (v. 11)?

4. What message did the disciples preach and why (v. 12)?

5. What else did the disciples do besides preach (v. 13)?

DISCUSS THE MEANING

1. Discuss ways in which the church can "take action" to alleviate the plethora of problems facing African American communities nationwide.

2. Jesus called ordinary people with few skills to be His disciples and then empowered them to do extraordinary things. Does He do the same today? Give examples.

3. Name the skills needed in order to be equipped for the tasks of discipleship.

4. Ask the students to list various forms of ministry in which they serve.

LESSON IN OUR SOCIETY

We have more Black churches than any other African American institution in America. It is important to remember that as Christians we work for Jesus and not for our personal gain. The church should serve as a training ground to prepare people for service and discipleship throughout the community. Discuss the viability of this statement: "The Church must become the vehicle for the salvation and liberation of the unsaved. In order to do so, we have to move out into the world just as Jesus sent His disciples into the world."

MAKE IT HAPPEN

Choose this day to view the church not just as a place to gather every Sunday morning but also as a community of the faithful that has the power to make a difference in the lives of people. Get involved in a ministry at your church that reaches out to the community. Use your available resources to help a child go to school with a new school uniform, new shoes, and good school supplies. Decide to deny yourself, take up a cross of service, and follow Jesus into the community to serve.

FOLLOW THE SPIRIT

What God wants me to do:

_____

_____

REMEMBER YOUR THOUGHTS

Special insights I have learned:

_____

_____

MORE LIGHT ON THE TEXT
Mark 3:13-19; 6:6-13

3:13 And he goeth up into a mountain, and calleth unto him whom he would: and they came unto him. 14 And he ordained twelve, that they should be with him, and that he might send them forth to preach, 15 And to have power to heal sicknesses, and to cast out devils: 16 And Simon he surnamed Peter; 17 And James the son of Zebedee, and John the brother of James; and he surnamed them Boanerges, which is, The sons of thunder: 18 And Andrew, and Philip, and Bartholomew, and Matthew, and Thomas, and James the son of Alphaeus, and Thaddaeus, and Simon the Canaanite, 19 And Judas Iscariot, which also betrayed him: and they went into an house.

6b And he went round about the villages, teaching. 7 And he called unto him the twelve, and began to send them forth by two and two; and gave them power over unclean spirits;

Jesus resumes His role as an itinerant teacher. He called "the twelve" (*tous dodeka*) and began "to send" (*apostellein*), or delegate, them out in twos. Sending them in pairs provided mutual support and encouragement during this period of training. But this instruction might also have been founded on the Jewish legal practice of establishing the credibility of evidence by the witness of more than one person (Deuteronomy 17:6; 19:15). To the Twelve, our Lord was giving power over (*exousian*) unclean spirits. The construction of *edidou* points to His continuous giving of authority. The Twelve were to preach and heal, but here the task of casting out unclean spirits is the one that is mentioned at the outset.

8 And commanded them that they should take nothing for their journey, save a staff only; no scrip, no bread, no money in their purse: 9 But be shod with sandals; and not put on two coats.

Jesus then told them what to take for the journey—actually, what not to take. No "bread" (*arton*) or provisions for eating, no bag (*peran*) for collecting stuff along the way, and no "money" (*chalkon*) in their belt or purse—and not even a change of clothing! The messenger must travel light, taking nothing "save a staff only" (*ei me rabdon monon*). The rigorous list and simplicity commanded by the Lord removes any sense of self-sufficiency. The laborer being worthy of hire must depend entirely on his Master for sustenance.

10 And he said unto them, In what place soever ye enter into an house, there abide till ye depart from that place. 11 And whosoever shall not receive you, nor hear you, when ye depart thence, shake off the dust under your feet for a testimony against them. Verily I say unto you, It shall be more tolerable for Sodom and Gomorrha in the day of judgment, than for that city.

Speaking directly, Jesus continues to instruct them about their stay in any given place. Wherever they were welcomed they would "there abide" (*ekei menete*) rather than move about. They were to avoid a restless and dissatisfied disposition. Also, He tells the disciples how they should respond to a place that rejects them and their message. As a symbolic gesture, the disciples were to "shake off" (*ektinaxate*) the dust under their feet. They would have absolved themselves from the blood of those who would not receive their message. As a "testimony against them" (*marturion outois*), this action might also awaken the rejecters' conscience to the dire consequences of their unbelief.

12 And they went out, and preached that men should repent. 13 And they cast out many devils, and anointed with oil many that were sick, and healed them.

The disciples' ministry consisted of three distinct elements: they "preached (announced) that [people] should repent" or change their minds (*ekerusan hina metanoosin*); they "cast out many devils" (*daimonia polla exeballon*), i.e., exorcism; and they "healed" (*etherapeuon*) the sick by anointing them with oil (*eleiphon elaioi*). Consequently, the Twelve were not only invited to be with Jesus but also to share actively in His ministry. They were called and sent to preach and exercise authority over demons. Their commission to preach repentance, to cast out demons, to heal, and to teach covers the spectrum of Jesus' ministry. It corresponds with their apostolic mandate as authorized representatives of Jesus.

DAILY BIBLE READINGS

M: Jesus Appoints the Twelve
Mark 3:13-19
T: Jesus Sends the Twelve with Instructions
Mark 6:6b-13
W: The Twelve Have a Mission
Matthew 10:5-15
T: The Twelve Have Power and Authority
Luke 9:1-6
F: Have the Mind of Christ
Philippians 2:1-11
S: Press On Toward the Goal
Philippians 3:12—4:1
S: Rejoice in the Lord Always
Philippians 4:4-9

Discover a deeper meaning to the word *authority* by looking in the Greek and Hebrew dictionary included as a study resource in your *Precepts For Living* CD-ROM.

TEACHING TIPS

January 23
Bible Study Guide 8

1. Words You Should Know

A. Rejected (Mark 8:31) *apodokimazo* (Gk.)—To spurn or disallow as a result of examination and disapproval.

B. Deny (v. 34) *aparneomai* (Gk.)—Disregarding one's own interest in favor of another's.

C. Life (v. 35) *psuche* (Gk.)—The natural life that may be preserved to resurrection life; the present natural vitality that is lost at death.

2. Teacher Preparation

A. Begin preparing for this lesson by studying the DEVOTIONAL READING (Matthew 16:24-28).

B. Carefully read the FOCAL VERSES for this lesson. Try to determine where the action takes place. Who are the major characters? What commands are given? What is the eternal truth of the passage?

3. Starting the Lesson

A. Before the students arrive, write the title of today's lesson and the AT-A-GLANCE outline on the chalkboard or poster board.

B. To help focus the students' attention, ask each student what adjective they would use to describe themselves. Explain that this is similar to what Jesus asked His disciples on their way to Caesarea Philippi.

C. Read the IN FOCUS story, and open the class in prayer.

4. Getting into the Lesson

A. To help the students gain a better understanding of the context for today's lesson, ask for a volunteer to read the BACKGROUND section and another to read THE PEOPLE, PLACES, AND TIMES section.

B. Next assign three students to read the IN DEPTH commentary according to the AT-A-GLANCE outline. After each section, review the appropriate SEARCH THE SCRIPTURES question.

5. Relating the Lesson to Life

A. To help the students see how the lesson applies to our modern-day society, direct them to read and discuss the LESSON IN OUR SOCIETY section.

B. Ask the students to share any insights they may have received from today's lesson.

6. Arousing Action

A. Direct the students to the MAKE IT HAPPEN section, and ask them to share ways they could help someone else carry a heavy burden. Make a list of their suggestions on the board. Challenge the students to choose one idea from the board and put it into practice this week. Tell them to be prepared to share their experiences with the class next week.

B. Encourage the students to use the DAILY BIBLE READINGS as a part of their daily devotions.

C. Close the class in prayer.

WORSHIP GUIDE

For the Superintendent or Teacher
Theme: Jesus Calls for Total Commitment
Theme Song: "I Know Whom I Have Believed"
Scripture: Psalm 118:19-29
Song: "The Unveiled Christ"
Meditation: Precious Lord, I thank You for revealing Your Son to me. Help me to follow in His footsteps and to bear my cross.

JESUS CALLS FOR TOTAL COMMITMENT

Bible Background • MARK 8:27-38
Printed Text • MARK 8:27-38
Devotional Reading • MATTHEW 16:24-28

LESSON AIM

By the end of the lesson, the students will understand what it means to identify with Christ in His suffering, death, and Resurrection; be able to explain the requirements of discipleship; and determine to follow Jesus through all of life's trials and temptations.

KEEP IN MIND

"And when he had called the people unto him with his disciples also, he said unto them, Whosoever will come after me, let him deny himself, and take up his cross, and follow me" (Mark 8:34).

FOCAL VERSES

Mark 8:27 And Jesus went out, and his disciples, into the towns of Caesarea Philippi: and by the way he asked his disciples, saying unto them, Whom do men say that I am?

28 And they answered, John the Baptist: but some say, Elias; and others, One of the prophets.

29 And he saith unto them, But whom say ye that I am? And Peter answereth and saith unto him, Thou art the Christ.

30 And he charged them that they should tell no man of him.

31 And he began to teach them, that the Son of man must suffer many things, and be rejected of the elders, and of the chief priests, and scribes, and be killed, and after three days rise again.

32 And he spake that saying openly. And Peter took him, and began to rebuke him.

LESSON OVERVIEW

LESSON AIM
KEEP IN MIND
FOCAL VERSES
IN FOCUS
THE PEOPLE, PLACES, AND TIMES
BACKGROUND
AT-A-GLANCE
IN DEPTH
SEARCH THE SCRIPTURES
DISCUSS THE MEANING
LESSON IN OUR SOCIETY
MAKE IT HAPPEN
FOLLOW THE SPIRIT
REMEMBER YOUR THOUGHTS
MORE LIGHT ON THE TEXT
DAILY BIBLE READINGS

33 But when he had turned about and looked on his disciples, he rebuked Peter, saying, Get thee behind me, Satan: for thou savourest not the things that be of God, but the things that be of men.

34 And when he had called the people unto him with his disciples also, he said unto them, Whosoever will come after me, let him deny himself, and take up his cross, and follow me.

35 For whosoever will save his life shall lose it; but whosoever shall lose his life for my sake and the gospel's, the same shall save it.

JAN 23RD

36 For what shall it profit a man, if he shall gain the whole world, and lose his own soul?

37 Or what shall a man give in exchange for his soul?

38 Whosoever therefore shall be ashamed of me and of my words in this adulterous and sinful generation; of him also shall the Son of man be ashamed, when he cometh in the glory of his Father with the holy angels.

IN FOCUS

A minister was talking to his son who was about to go off to college. The young man planned to major in business in the hopes of becoming rich and famous. The father asked his son to take a ride with him, and they drove out to the cemetery. The son was confused. "Dad, why did you take me to the graveyard? I'm about to leave home and begin a new life, and you bring me to the place where life ends."

The father smiled. "Son, you're beginning to get the point. Don't ever begin anything without thinking about how it ends." He told the young man to look around the cemetery and tell him what he saw.

The young man looked around. "I see green grass, multicolored flowers, headstones, and a few people visiting grave sites."

The older man smiled again. "Son, the point I'm trying to make is this: The one thing you will never see in a graveyard is a Brinks truck. All that the world has to offer ends when you reach this place."

The young man was now even more confused. "Dad, are you saying that it's wrong for me to try to achieve success in life?"

"No, son," the father replied, "that's not what I'm saying. I just want you to keep everything in perspective. Always remember that it's not what you acquire that defines who you are, it's what you give. Give your life to Christ, your best effort to the Gospel, and your heart to heaven. Everything else will fall into place."

At the end of His Galilean ministry, Jesus took His disciples aside and taught them the ultimate truth of His person, His mission, and the cost of discipleship. He wanted them to have all the facts so they could make a practical decision about following Him. Today's lesson examines who Christ is and what He expects of His followers.

THE PEOPLE, PLACES, AND TIMES

Titles of Jesus Christ. A title is a designation that describes or refers to some particular function or status of a person and, hence, may indicate the honor ascribed to the Person.

The name *Jesus* is not strictly a title for the Person who bore it. It is, however, a name with a meaning, being the Greek form of Joshua, which means "Yahweh is salvation." The name therefore indicated the function which was ascribed to Jesus.

Jesus was also known as "the Master" (Mark 5:35), which means "the rabbi." Jewish teachers were regularly addressed as "rabbi" (literally, "my great one") as a mark of respect.

Jesus is most widely known as "the Christ" (Mark 8:29). This is the Greek translation of the word *Messiah*, which means "Anointed One." "Anointed one" was originally used to describe a prophet, priest, or king, but during the intertestamental period it came to refer specifically to the anticipated agent of God.

Jesus' favorite title for Himself was "Son of man." The significance of this phrase is derived from Daniel 7:13; the term refers to the glorious sovereign ruler whose domain will never end (Mark 13:26; 14:62).

Just as these titles express the function of Jesus, His status and relationship to God find expression in the title "Son of God." The title expresses Jesus' particular relationship to God, whom He addresses by the intimate title "Abba," meaning "Dad" (Mark 14:36).

BACKGROUND

Chapter 8 brings us to the high point of Mark's gospel. The pivotal moment occurs when Peter announces that Jesus is the Christ. In the very first sentence of Mark's account, the apostle designates Jesus as the Christ (Messiah). Yet between Mark 1:1 and Mark 8:29 there is no human recognition of this fact.

Up to this point, Jesus' extraordinary power and teaching had provoked many questions regarding His authority and wisdom, but His true identity remained unrecognized. Even though demons recognized and identified Him (Mark 1:23-24; 3:11; 5:2-7), the religious leaders insisted that Jesus' power came from Satan. On at least one occasion, the disciples questioned Jesus' identity (4:41), but their hearts were not prepared to accept the truth of His deity.

All the miracles and wonders recorded by Mark thus far point to the central question of the universe—who is Jesus? At one point, Jesus appeared to become disappointed with the lack of understanding among His disciples—"How is it that ye do not understand?" (8:21). Finally, we reach the high point of Mark's narrative with Peter's confession of faith. Peter's confession marks the midpoint of the Gospel and the turning point in Jesus' ministry. A new theme is introduced: rejection and suffering. Jesus responds to

Peter's confession with a declaration of His impending suffering and then announces the requirements of discipleship. He then heads to Jerusalem and the ultimate fulfillment of His mission.

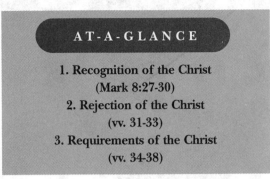

AT-A-GLANCE

1. Recognition of the Christ
(Mark 8:27-30)
2. Rejection of the Christ
(vv. 31-33)
3. Requirements of the Christ
(vv. 34-38)

IN DEPTH

1. Recognition of the Christ (Mark 8:27-30)

After leaving Bethsaida, where He healed a blind man, Jesus and His followers set out for Caesarea Philippi, a city located about 35 miles north of Bethsaida. Caesarea Philippi was the capital of the district of Iturea, and the home of Herod Philip (see Mark 6:17). The city was renowned for its magnificent temples devoted to the Greek god Pan, and its citizens were proud to affirm Caesar as Lord. This pagan stronghold was a fitting place for Jesus' disciples to recognize Him as the Son of God.

Shortly before reaching the city, Jesus gave His disciples a pop quiz—"Whom do men say that I am?" (8:27). Jesus knew that the general population was impressed with Him because He had met their physical needs. He fed them (6:30-44), healed them, and delivered them from demons (1:32-34). The people were confused and voiced many different opinions about Jesus (John 10:19-21). The disciples repeated to Jesus what they had heard from the people. Like John the Baptist, Jesus preached repentance, and many people, including Herod (Matthew 14:1-2), believed that He was John the Baptist returned to life. Jesus performed miracles like Elijah. Malachi had predicted that Elijah would return before the last days, so some thought Jesus was Elijah. Others felt that Jesus was one of the prophets. All the people seemed to believe that Jesus was the one who would prepare the way for the Messiah. No one saw Him as the "Anointed One" they had been waiting for.

After hearing their responses, Jesus asked the disciples the crucial question—one that every person must answer for themselves: "Whom say ye that I am?" No one can make an accurate decision about Christ based on the opinions of others. The important thing is not what others say, but who Jesus is to each of us personally.

Mark's account of this discussion provides only the bare bones of the conversation, but Matthew fills in more details. As spokesman for the group, Peter responds to Jesus' question by declaring, "Thou art the Christ [Messiah], the Son of the living God" (Matthew 16:16). Peter's bold announcement was not the result of his own thought processes. The revelation came as a gracious act of God, who had hidden the truth from the worldly wise and revealed it to His children (Matthew 11:25). Jesus confirmed this by telling Peter, "Flesh and blood hath not revealed it unto thee, but my Father which is in heaven" (16:17).

Acknowledging the identity of Christ is more than mentally agreeing that He is the Son of God. It means totally surrendering ourselves to His Lordship and trusting His sacrifice as the ultimate payment for our sins.

2. Rejection of the Christ (vv. 31-33)

Although Peter's understanding of Jesus' identity is correct, His understanding of Jesus' mission is flawed. The Jews of Jesus' time expected the Messiah to immediately establish an eternal kingdom that would rule over all the nations of the earth (Daniel 7:13-14). But rather than announcing His eternal rule, Jesus made the first prediction of His death and Resurrection. "The Son of man must suffer many things, and be rejected of the elders, and of the chief priests, and scribes, and be killed, and after three days rise again" (Mark 8:31).

The idea of a suffering Saviour was completely alien to Jewish thought. And Jesus knew it was crucial that He warn His disciples that He was not going to Jerusalem to conquer, but to die. This open and frank discussion of Jesus' death was too much for Peter to bear. The distraught disciple pulled Jesus to the side and rebuked Him. "Be it far from thee, Lord," he said. "This shall not be unto thee" (Matthew 16:22).

Peter was both a devoted friend and disciple of Jesus, and he wanted to protect Jesus from all harm and danger. However, Satan had once promised to give Jesus all the kingdoms of the world and their splendor without going to the Cross (Matthew 4:8-9). So when Peter spoke, Jesus recognized the true source of Peter's words. The Lord turned and looked directly at Peter. The presence of the other disciples, who probably all agreed with Peter, necessitated a sharp and open rebuke. He said, "Get thee behind me, Satan: for thou savourest not the things that be of God, but the things that be of men" (from Mark 8:33). Jesus was not addressing Peter as Satan; He was commanding Satan to stop influencing the thoughts of Peter. God had ordained that Jesus would achieve victory over the forces of evil by means of the Cross. Any suggestion that He do otherwise was satanically inspired.

Many times when believers are faced with trials and suffering, we react like Peter because we cannot see the complete picture. It is often impossible for us to see the glory that can result from apparent evil. We must learn to trust God in times of joy as well as suffering.

Jesus explains His mission and what it means to be a follower of Christ.

3. Requirements of the Christ (vv. 34-38)

Jesus would not allow anything or anyone to dissuade Him from His mission. He knew what awaited Him in Jerusalem, yet He was determined to go there. The Lord wanted all those who would follow Him to know that discipleship would cost them. Many people had followed Jesus because of the miracles and healing He performed. It was important for the people to understand that following Him meant sacrifice.

Jesus and His disciples had discussed His identity in private, but the crowds were not too far away. The truth He was about to reveal was not a secret between Himself and the Twelve, but an eternal truth to be followed by all believers. He summoned the crowd and told them, "Whosoever will come after me, let him deny himself, and take up his cross, and follow me" (v. 34). In this mes-

sage, Jesus set three important conditions of discipleship. Deny yourself—this is much more than simple self-denial. It is a continuous willingness to say no to our own self-interest, abandoning ourselves to the will of God. Take up your cross—condemned prisoners were forced to carry their own crosses to the place of crucifixion. This brutal practice demonstrated the prisoner's total submission to Rome's power. Jesus used this metaphor to illustrate that believers must submit themselves completely to God. Follow Christ—this means absolute obedience to God's will and Word. True Christianity is not concerned with what one may be able to gain, but how much one is willing to sacrifice.

Believers should be easy to identify by their willingness to deny themselves for the benefit of others, their ability to bear up under undeserved persecution, and their determination to follow Jesus' example in all situations.

The Lord wants us to follow Him rather than chase after sin and self-satisfaction. We must willingly surrender control of our lives and destinies to Him. "For whosoever will save his life shall lose it; but whosoever shall lose his life for my sake and the gospel's, the same shall save it" (v. 35). To illustrate His point, Jesus asks His audience a rhetorical question using words taken from the business world: *profit, loss, gain,* and *exchange.* The word *soul* in this case means "life."

Jesus is asking His audience to make a practical decision about following Him in the same way they make decisions about purchasing products. In this case, the product to be gained is world approval through the denial of Christ and the Gospel. The cost of this approval is one's life—not just ordinary physical life, but eternal life. The riches and approval of the world are temporary (Matthew 6:19), but the rewards of Christ are eternal and absolute.

Many people waste their lives chasing worldly success and public acknowledgment. Jesus wants us to invest our lives in eternal opportunities, so that we will have something to show for our lives when we stand before God. Jesus speaks of the evil world's system as an "adulterous and sinful generation" (Mark 8:38). If we shamefully deny Christ to gain the pleasures of this sinful generation, then He will deny us when He returns.

Jesus taught His disciples about His office (v. 29); His suffering, death, and Resurrection (v. 31); and His return (v. 38). He explained humanity's ultimate decision—Christ or the world?

SEARCH THE SCRIPTURES

1. What three answers did the disciples give when Jesus asked them who the people said He was (Mark 8:28)?

2. Jesus was rejected by the ruling religious body of Israel. Name the three groups that made up the ruling body (v. 31).

3. How did Jesus respond to Peter after Peter had rebuked Him (v. 33)?

4. What three things does Jesus demand that His disciples do (v. 34)?

5. When Jesus returns, how will He treat those people who have been ashamed to acknowledge Him (v. 38)?

DISCUSS THE MEANING

1. How would you explain to someone what Jesus meant when He told believers to deny themselves, take up their crosses, and follow Him?

2. If you could gain the whole world, what things would you be sure to acquire? How important are these things when compared to spending eternity with God?

3. Why is Jesus' question, "Whom say ye that I am?" (Mark 8:29) so important to both believers and nonbelievers?

LESSON IN OUR SOCIETY

Today, Christians are not hung on crosses to die in defense of their faith in Christ. However, God is still calling Christians to be identified with Christ and His kingdom, and to deny the ways of the world. Many times, when a person leaves a family religion, such as Judaism, Hinduism, Muslim, or even the Jehovah's Witnesses, they lose their family inheritance and are considered as dead or nonexistent to their family and community. Still others who are born in a so-called Christian society appear not to suffer at all for the cause of Christ. Should all Christians experience suffering for the cause of Jesus Christ? If this is so, name and discuss some ways in which contemporary Christians suffer.

MAKE IT HAPPEN

When Jesus carried His cross to Calvary, it was not because of His sin, but ours. Taking up one's cross means a willingness to bear the burdens of others. What are some ways that believers can "take up the cross" for those less fortunate in our communities? Think of how you may be able to help someone bear their burdens; then do it. Be prepared to share your experiences with the class next week.

FOLLOW THE SPIRIT

What God wants me to do:

_____

_____

REMEMBER YOUR THOUGHTS
Special insights I have learned:

_____

_____

MORE LIGHT ON THE TEXT
Mark 8:27-38
27 And Jesus went out, and his disciples, into the towns of Caesarea Philippi: and by the way he asked his disciples, saying unto them, Whom do men say that I am? 28 And they answered, John the Baptist: but some say, Elias; and others, One of the prophets.

Jesus and His "disciples" (Gk. *mathetes*) went out "into the towns of Caesarea Philippi" (Gk. *Kaisereia Philippoi*). This city, north of the Sea of Galilee near the slopes of Mount Hermon, is to be distinguished from the city of Caesarea down on the Mediterranean Sea. Here, Jesus would have the opportunity to give the disciples special teaching concerning the crucifixion. Jesus opened by asking, "Whom do men [people] say that I am?" It was time for the disciples to reveal the extent to which they understood Jesus. Was their understanding influenced by their environment or by direct contact with Christ? The popular view about Jesus was that He was a very prominent messenger from God—not unlike today's view of Him. But in spite of popular opinion, Jesus wants those who follow Him to be clear about His true identity and purpose.

29 And he saith unto them, But whom say ye that I am? And Peter answereth and saith unto him, Thou art the Christ.

With emphasis, Jesus turns to the Twelve and asks directly: "But whom say ye that I am?" Opinions, no matter how widespread, will not suffice. "Thou art the Christ." The Greek word *Christos* (Christ) is the equivalent of the Hebrew word *Messiah*, which means "Anointed One." It may seem that in saying what "some say" the disciples had given their opinions about Him. But it is more likely that Peter was representing the conviction of the Twelve when he uttered those immortal words.

30 And he charged them that they should tell no man of him. 31 And he began to teach them, that the Son of man must suffer many things, and
be rejected of the elders, and of the chief priests, and scribes, and be killed, and after three days rise again.

At the appropriate time, Jesus' identity will be revealed to all. In the meantime, they were "to tell no [one] of him." Their confession of faith indicates that the time was ripe for them to be told about His approaching death.

"The Son of man" was the most common title Jesus used for Himself. Popular Jewish notions of the Messiah had become largely political and national. Consequently, Christ seldom used the term *Messiah* to refer to Himself. Jesus explained that He would suffer and die at the hands of the "elders, and of the chief priests (Gk. *archiereus*) and scribes." But there would be resurrection; He would rise again "after three days."

32 And he spake that saying openly. And Peter took him, and began to rebuke him.

Jesus held nothing back. He spoke frankly and emphatically, or "openly" (Gk. *parrhesia*), about His imminent Passion. Peter took Him aside and began "to rebuke" (Gk. *epitimao*) Jesus for teaching what seemed not only inconceivable but terribly wrong. In the prevailing Jewish thought, the very idea of messiahship excluded suffering and execution. Still today, the Cross of Christ is a stumbling block for many. But anyone who seeks to follow Jesus as example must embrace Him as the Lord and Saviour who by His voluntary and vicarious death saves His people from their sin and brings them to glory.

33 But when he had turned about and looked on his disciples, he rebuked Peter, saying, Get thee behind me, Satan: for thou savourest not the things that be of God, but the things that be of men.

Apparently, Peter's rebuke was having an affect on the other disciples. After Jesus "had turned about and looked on His disciples," He severely rebuked Peter. It is even possible that they shared Peter's views and were watching the effect of his rebuke of Jesus. By the response, "Get thee behind me, Satan" (Gk. *satanas*), we see that Christ fully realized that behind Peter stood Satan himself, who through Peter was trying again to turn His attention away from the cross. Satan's ally was Peter's human frame of mind, which "savourest not the things that be of God." From the human point of view, being subjected to discomfort, suffering, or death is unacceptable. But from God's point of view, the cross is the way to glory.

34 And when he had called the people unto him with his disciples also, he said unto them, Whosoever will come after me, let him deny himself, and take up his cross, and follow me.

What better occasion than this for Christ to explain and contrast His philosophy of life and death with that of the world. He "called the people unto him with the disciples." This point of discourse had significance for all, not just His disciples. Jesus presents self-denial as key to discipleship. The Greek phrase *aparnesastho eauton* literally means, "let (him) thoroughly deny himself." In other words, let those who would follow Christ say no to themselves and give up all reliance on whatever they are by nature. A disciple takes up his cross, voluntarily and decisively accepting the pain and suffering—even death—resulting from his trust in and loyalty to Christ.

35 For whosoever will save his life shall lose it; but whosoever shall lose his life for my sake and the gospel's, the same shall save it.

Whoever will wish to save "his life" (Gk. *psuche*) "shall lose" (Gk. *apollumi*) it. Physical life may be "saved" by denying Christ, but eternal life will be lost. The one who wishes to obtain salvation by any means other than the regenerating grace of God will destroy it. On the other hand, the one who loses his life in full devotion to Christ and His kingdom saves it.

36 For what shall it profit a man, if he shall gain the whole world, and lose his own soul? 37 Or what shall a man give in exchange for his soul?

It is a very poor bargain to exchange eternal life for this present life. The phrase "the whole world" means all the things that could possibly be achieved or acquired in this life. Earthly goods, fame, and power lack permanence. Only Christ and what is done in His name remains eternally.

38 Whosoever therefore shall be ashamed of me and of my words in this adulterous and sinful generation; of him also shall the Son of man be ashamed, when he cometh in the glory of his Father with the holy angels.

To "be ashamed" (Gk. *epaischunomai*) of Him means to be so proud that one wants to have nothing to do with Jesus. People's attitude and conduct in the present will determine their future state when He comes "in the glory of his Father with the holy angels." There is clear prediction of the final eschatological coming of Christ. Those who are ashamed of Jesus "in this adulterous and sinful generation" will find that He is going to be ashamed of them. One who is more concerned about fitting into and pleasing the world than about following and pleasing Christ will have no part in God's kingdom.

DAILY BIBLE READINGS

M: Whoever Believes Has Eternal Life
John 6:41-51

T: Eat My Flesh, Drink My Blood
John 6:52-59

W: This Teaching Is Difficult
John 6:60-69

T: Who Do You Say I Am?
Matthew 16:13-20

F: Let Them Deny Themselves
Matthew 16:24-28

S: You Are the Messiah
Mark 8:27-30

S: Take Up Your Cross, Follow Me
Mark 8:31-38

Contrast the striking differences between the words *save* and *lose* by looking at the ways they are used in Scripture. You can use your *Precepts For Living* CD-ROM to find definitions and do cross-reference checks.

TEACHING TIPS

January 30
Bible Study Guide 9

1. Words You Should Know

A. Scourge (Mark 10:34) *mastigoo* (Gk.)—To chastise; punish severely with physical pain.

B. Lordship (v. 42) *katakurieuo* (Gk.)—To bring under one's power; to be master of.

C. Servant (v. 44) *doulos* (Gk.)—The term in the days of the early church referred to one being obedient to Christ. Christ commanded and the early disciples obeyed.

2. Teacher Preparation

A. Read Mark 10 in its entirety.

B. Ask yourself how the world's definition of greatness and success compares to Jesus' definition.

C. Answer the SEARCH THE SCRIPTURES and the DISCUSS THE MEANING questions. This will help you prepare for the class discussion.

3. Starting the Lesson

A. Open the session with prayer. Start the lesson by reminding the students that Jesus called 12 men to comprise His inner circle, but He had many more disciples that followed Him along with the Twelve.

B. Ask the students to imagine what it must have been like to be a disciple.

C. Remind students that Jesus was a servant-leader. Ask the students to define a servant-leader.

4. Getting into the Lesson

A. Have the students read aloud the FOCAL VERSES.

B. After reading the Scriptures, ask two students to role-play the ambitious James and John, while the rest of the class plays the indignant disciples who were offended at the brothers' request.

5. Relating the Lesson to Life

A. Divide the students into two groups and have them answer the DISCUSS THE MEANING questions.

B. Ask each student whether it is good to have ambition as a disciple of Jesus Christ. Differentiate between what is proper ambition for a Christian and what is not.

C. Challenge them to remember the great heroes of our tradition, such as Richard Allen, Henry Highland Garnett, Harriet Tubman, and Dr. Martin Luther King, Jr. Remind them that wealth and status was not their goal in life, but serving their fellow man. Encourage the students to become servant-leaders like Jesus and our African American heroes.

6. Arousing Action

A. Encourage the students to get involved in a service project in their community such as tutoring or reading to younger children at a library. This will teach them the value of service for the good of the community.

B. Remind the students that a call to discipleship is a lifelong commitment to service. Help them find ways they can provide service in the church as well as the community.

C. Close the class with prayer.

WORSHIP GUIDE

For the Superintendent or Teacher
Theme: Jesus Defines True Greatness
Theme Song: "Glad to Be in the Service"
Scripture: Philippians 2:5-16
Song: "This Little Light of Mine"
Meditation: Lord, help all of us, from the pulpit and the pew, to become better servants of Jesus the Christ. When we serve, we can all become great. If anyone desires distinction, let him or her distinguish himself or herself through serving the less fortunate and those in need. In Jesus' name we pray. Amen.

JESUS DEFINES TRUE GREATNESS

Bible Background • MARK 10:13-45
Printed Text • MARK 10:32-45
Devotional Reading • MATTHEW 20:20-28

LESSON AIM

By the end of the lesson, the students will be able to understand the servant-leadership role of Jesus, know the difference between the world's definition of greatness and Jesus' definition, and embrace the concept of service as the way to distinction in the kingdom.

KEEP IN MIND

"Whosoever will be great among you, shall be your minister: And whosoever of you will be the chiefest, shall be servant of all" (Mark 10:43b-44).

FOCAL VERSES

Mark 10:32 And they were in the way going up to Jerusalem; and Jesus went before them: and they were amazed; and as they followed, they were afraid. And he took again the twelve, and began to tell them what things should happen unto him,

33 Saying, Behold, we go up to Jerusalem; and the Son of man shall be delivered unto the chief priests, and unto the scribes; and they shall condemn him to death, and shall deliver him to the Gentiles:

34 And they shall mock him, and shall scourge him, and shall spit upon him, and shall kill him: and the third day he shall rise again.

35 And James and John, the sons of Zebedee, come unto him, saying, Master, we would that thou shouldest do for us whatsoever we shall desire.

36 And he said unto them, What would ye that

LESSON OVERVIEW

LESSON AIM
KEEP IN MIND
FOCAL VERSES
IN FOCUS
THE PEOPLE, PLACES, AND TIMES
BACKGROUND
AT-A-GLANCE
IN DEPTH
SEARCH THE SCRIPTURES
DISCUSS THE MEANING
LESSON IN OUR SOCIETY
MAKE IT HAPPEN
FOLLOW THE SPIRIT
REMEMBER YOUR THOUGHTS
MORE LIGHT ON THE TEXT
DAILY BIBLE READINGS

I should do for you?

37 They said unto him, Grant unto us that we may sit, one on thy right hand, and the other on thy left hand, in thy glory.

38 But Jesus said unto them, Ye know not what ye ask: can ye drink of the cup that I drink of? and be baptized with the baptism that I am baptized with?

39 And they said unto him, We can. And Jesus said unto them, Ye shall indeed drink of the cup that I drink of; and with the baptism that I am baptized withal shall ye be baptized:

40 But to sit on my right hand and on my left hand is not mine to give; but it shall be given to them for whom it is prepared.

41 And when the ten heard it, they began to be much displeased with James and John.

42 But Jesus called them to him, and saith unto them, Ye know that they which are accounted to rule over the Gentiles exercise lordship over them; and their great ones exercise authority upon them.

43 But so shall it not be among you: but whosoever will be great among you, shall be your minister:

44 And whosoever of you will be the chiefest, shall be servant of all.

45 For even the Son of man came not to be ministered unto, but to minister, and to give his life a ransom for many.

JAN 30TH

IN FOCUS

In his sermon entitled "The Drum Major Instinct," Rev. Dr. Martin Luther King, Jr. talked about man's innate desire to be great and to have some distinction from his peers. Dr. King suggested that the desire for distinction could be aptly called the "Drum Major Instinct." Persons have the desire to be first, to lead the "parade," to be the only one to accomplish something, or to be the one out in front. Dr. King condemned this type of thinking as counterproductive. Ambition is not bad, but it must be harnessed and directed in the proper way. Dr. King quoted Jesus by saying, "Whoever wants to become great among you must be your servant, and whoever wants to be first must be slave of all" (Mark 10:43-44). King was suggesting that if a person wants to be a "drum major," then let him be a drum major for justice, peace, love, mercy, and truth. If a person wants to be a drum major, let him be a drum major for a cause that will benefit the community. There are many ways for each of us to become great and do something to improve our communities. The road to greatness is paved with the bricks of service.

THE PEOPLE, PLACES, AND TIMES

James and John. Brothers who were fishermen by trade. They were always in the center of things with Jesus, along with Simon Peter. Because of their attachment to Jesus, they attained a place of primacy among the disciples. They were present at the Mount of Transfiguration (Mark 9:2), and also when Jairus' daughter was raised (Mark 5:37). Jesus gave James and John the nickname *Boanerges,* or "sons of thunder" (Mark 3:17), when He rebuked them for impetuous speech and missing the purpose of His coming.

The Cup. A Jewish metaphor that Jesus used to indicate His suffering on the Cross. It was the custom at a royal banquet for the king to hand the cup to his guests. The cup therefore became a metaphor for the life and experience that God handed out to men. "My cup runneth over," said the psalmist (Psalm 23:5), when he spoke of a life and experience of happiness given to him by God. The cup of judgment is often referred to in

the Old Testament. "In the hand of the LORD there is a cup," said the psalmist (Psalm 75:8), regarding the fate in store for the wicked and the disobedient. Isaiah describes the disasters that had come upon the people of Israel as having "drunk at the hand of the LORD the cup of his wrath" (Isaiah 51:17).

BACKGROUND

Jesus is on His way to Jerusalem for the final time. Therefore, He is constantly giving His disciples final instructions in order to prepare them for His departure. While on the way, Jesus deals with a number of subjects. First, the Pharisees confront Him about the volatile issue of divorce. Jesus tells them that from its inception marriage was to be permanent, but because of the hardness of men's hearts Moses allowed them to divorce their wives using a bill of divorcement. While in the house of his disciples, Jesus goes on to highlight the primacy of marriage by explaining that whoever divorces their spouse forces the divorcee to commit adultery. He also deals with the issue of access by children. Children, along with women, were treated as second-class citizens in Jesus' day. Jesus rewrites the social script by allowing children to have access to Him. He embraced them and blessed them.

Next, a rich young ruler comes to Jesus asking for the secret to attaining eternal life. Jesus tells him to obey the commandments of Moses. The young man says that he has obeyed the Mosaic Law since childhood. Jesus then tells him to sell all of his possessions, give the proceeds to the poor, and follow Him. The rich young ruler went away very sad because he had many possessions. When instructing His disciples, Jesus later said that if anybody would truly follow Him they would have to forsake everything for the sake of the Gospel. Nothing could stand in the way of their total obedience to the Christ. Nothing could get in the way of their allegiance, not even ambition.

James and John were ambitious disciples. This character trait could have been a holdover from their profession as fishermen. Maybe they had ambition to become the wealthiest fishermen in all of Galilee before they accepted Jesus' invitation to ministry. They were in search of distinction among the disciples. Jesus noticed their attitude and had to clear up this misunderstanding before He left them. Jesus reminded them that His definition of greatness and honor was antithetical to the world's definition of greatness and honor. Human nature discloses that many of us, if not all of us, want to be considered great or to stand out for selfish reasons. In this lesson, Jesus explains how to look at greatness according to God's way.

AT-A-GLANCE

1. James and John Request Greatness
(Mark 10:32-37)

2. Jesus Responds to the Request for Greatness (vv. 38-40)

3. Jesus Redefines True Greatness
(vv. 41-45)

IN DEPTH

1. James and John Request Greatness (Mark 10:32-37)

The brothers, James and John, make an unusual request of Jesus. They ask for places of honor when Jesus comes into His kingdom. They show a level of ambition that none of the other disciples displays. It appears that even Jesus is surprised at their request. The brothers wanted Jesus to grant them whatever they asked Him. Jesus should never be asked to fit into our plans in order to make things convenient for us. In addition, the disciples' prayer should always be, "Thy kingdom come. Thy will be done in earth, as it is in heaven" (Matthew 6:10). James and John were not concerned with God's will for their lives; they were only concerned about themselves. Their ambitious request was that they would hold the top two positions in the kingdom of God. To sit on the right and left of Jesus in His glory symbolized positions of special honor.

The Bible says, "Let your light so shine before men that they may see your good works, and glorify your Father which is in heaven" (Matthew 5:16). Jesus did stress the need for His disciples to be bold and unwavering in their witness. Jesus

called His disciples to be dedicated to disseminating the Gospel. The difference may be that Jesus looked for ambition to promote the Gospel and not self. James and John's request did not promote the Gospel or the Christian community.

Jesus told His disciples, "Whosoever will come after me, let him deny himself, and take up his cross, and follow me" (Mark 8:34). Ambition to be the best for Christ and to do one's best is good, whether you are a preacher or a parishioner. However, it is wrong and counterproductive to have ambition to seek places of honor just for the sake of your ego.

If we have "James and John" complexes, we have to repent. We need to do what is best for the body of Christ and not just ourselves. We may have to deny fame and notoriety to pick up our crosses of ministry and follow Jesus. Our God, who sees and hears all, will justly reward us for whatever we do in His name. Ambition that is directed for the good of spreading the Gospel of Jesus the Christ benefits the entire church.

2. Jesus Responds to the Request for Greatness (vv. 38-40)

Jesus does not grant their request, but challenges them with a series of questions to test their sincerity. First, He states that they don't know what they are asking for. Usually, in a person's quest for greatness, he or she does not really know what it takes to become great. Greatness does not occur overnight or by chance. Usually, a heavy price is paid for greatness. Historically, the people we call great often risked their lives for something greater than themselves. Dr. King and Malcolm X are popular heroes, but the price they paid for fame was a life of service and sacrifice, for which they were eventually assassinated. When a person seeks greatness today, he must ask himself if he is willing to pay the high price of greatness.

Second, Jesus challenges their sincerity with the use of the metaphors of a cup and baptism. He asks them, "Can ye drink of the cup that I drink of and be baptized with the baptism that I am baptized with?" (Mark 10:38). The cup was a metaphor for the life and experience that God handed out to people. Jesus asked them if they could emulate His lifestyle and wholeheartedly obey the will of God regardless of the consequences. In other words, "Can you bear to go through the terrible experience that I have to go through? Can you face being submerged in hatred, pain, and death, as I have to be?" He was telling the two brothers that fame is not all it's cracked up to be. It comes at a high price that few are willing to pay. The standard of greatness in the kingdom is the standard of the Cross.

Truthfully, Jesus tells James and John that they will share in the life experiences and the pain of ministry with Him. However, to sit on His right and left is not in His power to decide; it shall be given to them for whom it is prepared. Jesus alludes to the salient reminder that greatness in the kingdom is assigned by God's favor and not by one's fortitude. People are called by a great God to do great things, not by their own choosing. A number of great African Americans were pushed into the land of greatness under God's providence.

We don't choose greatness but greatness chooses us. From Frederick Douglass, the great abolitionist and statesman, to former Virginia Governor Douglas Wilder, the nation's first Black governor, the circumstances of the day demanded that some men step up and meet the challenges of life head on. Jesus' last statement is powerful: "But it shall be given to them for whom it is prepared." Under divine providence, men and women are being prepared for places of honor. Are you being prepared for greatness? Through your service you will find out just how God intends to use your gifts. As the people of God, we must always remember that we exist to glorify God through service in Jesus' name.

3. Jesus Redefines True Greatness (vv. 41-45)

Jesus had to do some damage control once the other 10 disciples heard about James and John's request. He called them all together and gave a true description of greatness. Jesus reminded them that they were not to resemble the worldly systems of hierarchy and domination. Their community would be based upon selfless service to those in need, not upon titles or power. Jesus made it quite clear that the standards of greatness

in His kingdom are radically different from those of the world's kingdoms. While the kingdoms of the world define greatness based upon how many people or how much wealth one controls, in God's kingdom greatness is defined as one's capacity and ability to serve and not to be served. Greatness consists of humbling oneself to serve others. Many of us have forgotten that Jesus said, "For even the Son of man came not to be ministered unto, but to minister, and to give his life a ransom for many." Jesus defined true greatness as the willingness, ability, determination, and desire to minister to a dying humanity. It is we who provide the service and God who bestows the honor and the greatness.

SEARCH THE SCRIPTURES

1. What was so important to James and John that they needed a private meeting with Jesus (Mark 10: 37)?

2. What was Jesus' response to their ambitious request (v. 38)?

3. What final answer does Jesus give James and John (v. 40)?

4. What emotions did the other 10 disciples display toward the brothers because of their request (v. 41)?

5. How does Jesus handle the dissension among the disciples (v. 42)?

6. How does Jesus redefine greatness (v. 43)?

7. How does Jesus define His ministry (v. 45)?

DISCUSS THE MEANING

1. Does greatness have a role in the church? If so, what role does it have?

2. Is it wrong to want to be the best disciple or the best church among others? Lead a discussion on modern society's criteria for greatness.

3. Discuss various kinds of service the Church can employ to help resurrect and restore the community it serves.

4. Explain the difference between "church service" and "service to the world."

5. What steps can we take to achieve greatness in God's kingdom?

LESSON IN OUR SOCIETY

During the symposium called "The State of

Black America: The Black Church," hosted by Tavis Smiley and Tom Joyner two years ago, Dr. James Cone argued that the Black Church has not lived up to the mission of Jesus the Christ because it has adopted the world's definition of success rather than adhere to Jesus' definition of success. Dr. Cone argued that the mission of the Black Church is not "success," but fidelity to the mission and message of Jesus. If the Black Church loses its life for Jesus, it will find its life again. It exists to serve God and humanity by spreading the Good News of Jesus Christ to all.

MAKE IT HAPPEN

Service actually begins outside of the four walls of the church. Jesus gave the Great Commission in Matthew 28:19, saying, "Go ye therefore, and teach all nations, baptizing them in the name of the Father, and of the Son, and of the Holy Ghost." The command is to reach out to others in Jesus' name with the Good News of the Gospel, which is able to save and transform individuals and institutions. In the week ahead, think of ways you can serve God by serving those who do not come to church.

FOLLOW THE SPIRIT

What God wants me to do:

_____

_____

REMEMBER YOUR THOUGHTS

Special insights I have learned:

_____

_____

MORE LIGHT ON THE TEXT
Mark 10:32-45

In this brief verse from Mark 10, the entire Gospel is neatly summed up: "For even the Son of man came not to be ministered unto, but to minister" (Mark 10:45a). Jesus is making His journey to Calvary by way of Jerusalem. Yet, He pauses to ease tension and present the men closest to Him with one important teaching. "Greatness," Jesus declares, "is achieved through servanthood!" Jesus turns the popular notion of authority on its head when He teaches that greatness is inextrica-

bly linked, not with power, but with selfless service and loving sacrifice.

32 And they were in the way going up to Jerusalem; and Jesus went before them: and they were amazed; and as they followed, they were afraid. And he took again the twelve, and began to tell them what things should happen unto him.

Mark presents Jesus' final departure from Galilee. Jesus and His followers have entered the borders of Judaea into a region known as Perea, located on the east side of the Jordan River. The crowds are still following Jesus, and, as was His custom, Jesus continued to minister to them and to teach them.

Jesus is heading toward persecution and death; yet, He is walking ahead of the others. As Jesus leads His disciples along the dusty Palestinian road, we are told that the disciples were "amazed." The Greek word used here is *thambeo* (**tham-beh'-o**), suggesting that the disciples were following in an astounded daze. Their astonishment is legitimate and understandable. Jerusalem has been prophesied as the place of betrayal, arrest, trial, ignominy, and crucifixion. The "City of God" and home of the temple is also ground zero for those who hate Jesus. The disciples know that Jerusalem is the home turf of the reactionary Pharisees who have despised Jesus' scathing exposure of their hypocrisy. It is also home to the aristocratic Sadducees whose power under the Romans is threatened by Jesus' teachings about a "new kingdom."

The disciples watch as Jesus trudges resolutely into enemy territory. Jesus certainly knows that a cross awaits Him, yet because of His love for His followers (including us), He boldly presses forward and leads the way. The disciples stagger behind Jesus, amazed and "afraid." This should not surprise us. Knowing that their Master was going to be killed had to make them wonder about their own fates. Jesus had told them of the "persecutions" they would face (v. 30).

Jesus' taking "the twelve" aside indicates that the group following Jesus included more than the 12 disciples. While the 12 hand-selected disciples were the inner circle, others often accompanied Jesus and were instructed by Him. The larger group of disciples (or students) included women, most notably Mary of Magdalene. However, it is the 12 disciples whom Jesus now isolates from the others, not only to teach them, but to emphasize His mission.

33 Saying, Behold, we go up to Jerusalem; and the Son of man shall be delivered unto the chief priests, and unto the scribes; and they shall condemn him to death, and shall deliver him to the Gentiles:

Sensing their fear, Jesus does nothing to dispel it. Instead, with brutal frankness He prepares them for what awaits Him in Jerusalem. According to Mark's gospel, this is the third time that Jesus has predicted His impending death, burial, and Resurrection (Mark 8:31). Jesus adds more details when He again tells them that the Son of Man would be delivered into the hands of men, killed, and resurrected (9:31).

The first time Jesus told His disciples what he would suffer, Peter "rebuked" Him. The second time Jesus told them of His death, the disciples didn't fully understand. They "were afraid" to ask Jesus for clarification. In this verse, Jesus reveals the identity of those who would make up Jesus' persecutors—the chief priests, the scribes, and the Gentiles. They all would have a hand in Jesus' death. Rejection and execution of the Messiah would have universal participation and implications.

Modern Christians should not then be surprised that many in this society view Christianity as offensive and are committed to its eradication from our culture. The world condemned Christ and is still openly hostile to His followers.

34 And they shall mock him, and shall scourge him, and shall spit upon him, and shall kill him: and the third day he shall rise again.

The tension of the journey is certainly heightened as Jesus vividly describes the humiliation and suffering that awaits Him in Jerusalem. Jesus would undergo mocking and scourging.

The Greek verb for "scourge" is *mastigoo* (**mas-tig-o'-o**). This word is closely related to *mastix* (**mis'-tix**), which literally means beaten by one who bears a rod or whip. During this time, the Romans frequently used an instrument known as the "flagellum" for scourging. This insidious device featured a handle into which leather thongs were attached. The thongs were weighted with jagged pieces of bone or metal that ripped the victim's flesh, thus rendering each blow more bloody and painful. Jesus' harrowing prediction that His flesh would be torn and disfigured by scourging mirrors the prophecy of Isaiah that foretold that it was with "his stripes we are healed" (Isaiah 53:5).

35 And James and John, the sons of Zebedee, come unto him, saying, Master, we would that thou shouldest do for us whatsoever we shall desire. 36 And he said unto them, What would ye that I should do for you? 37 They said unto him, Grant unto us that we may sit, one on thy right hand, and the other on thy left hand, in thy glory.

It is important to note that on this occasion Jesus tells the apostles that He would rise from the dead "on the third day." Although sin would prevail on Friday evening, salvation would reign on Sunday morning! However, it appears that at least two of the Twelve did not fully appreciate the plain teaching Jesus had just put before them.

James and John are referred to here as "the sons of Zebedee." Earlier, Jesus referred to these brothers as *Boanerges,* or "the sons of thunder" (Mark 3:17). This surname probably refers to the youthful enthusiasm and energetic nature displayed by these two men. We might recall that it was James and his younger brother John who suggested that Jesus give them permission to "command fire to come down from heaven and consume" the Samaritan villagers who were inhospitable to Jesus (Luke 9:54).

Scripture is clear that James and John, along with Simon Peter, shared a particular intimacy with Jesus. They were the only disciples present with Jesus on the mountain when He was transfigured (Matthew 17:1-2), the only ones allowed into Jairus' house to witness the resurrection of his daughter (Luke 8:51), and the men who were closest to Jesus in the garden of Gethsemane while He prayed (Mark 14:32-34).

James and John use this relationship to attempt to further their personal ambitions.

James and John clearly believe that Jesus' present situation is going to change. The expression "in thy glory" indicates that eventually Jesus will take on what they believe to be the majesty of a sovereign king. The Greek word rendered here as "glory" is *doxa* (**dox'-ah**) and means "dignity" or "honor." In short, they ask Jesus to grant them prominent positions in His kingdom. That the two men would even ask this question speaks to their belief that Jesus was indeed the Messiah. Obviously, James and John expected that Jesus would one day establish a great kingdom here on earth. Their selfish presumption was that they should assume places of prominence in that kingdom: one sitting on His right hand and the other sitting on His left. Their request is a pertinent lesson for present-day Christians. We should be careful to question the motivation behind our desires. Do we really wish to serve the Lord, or are we looking to be exalted?

38 But Jesus said unto them, Ye know not what ye ask: can ye drink of the cup that I drink of? and be baptized with the baptism that I am baptized with?

How disheartening and galling this request must have been to Jesus. On an earlier occasion, the disciples had argued about who was greater than whom. Jesus had taught that if anyone wanted to be first, he must be the servant to all (Mark 9:35). Now, on the heels of Jesus' clear prediction of His betrayal, death, and Resurrection, the sons of Zebedee seek political patronage. The message of His suffering is lost on James and John as they seek to secure top positions in His kingdom. Nonetheless, Jesus patiently points out their lack of understanding.

The expression "know not" is crucial to this verse. Jesus is pointing out a lack of knowledge on the part of James and John. Jesus answers their question with a question in order to address their "intent." While verses 35 and 36 provide the "desire" of James and John, their heart's "intent" has not yet been verbalized. To do this, Jesus invokes two very powerful symbols well known to the disciples (the cup and the baptism) to teach James and John. Having listened to what they want, Jesus now asks them if they are willing to do what it takes. Are they willing to "drink of the cup"?

The cup is often used in the Old Testament as a symbol of trouble and suffering (Psalm 75:8; Isaiah 51:17). Here, its use symbolizes Jesus' death and the shedding of His blood on the Cross to pay the price of mankind's redemption. Later, when Jesus prays in the garden of Gethsemane, He will pray that "this cup" might pass from Him (Mark 14:36).

Jesus also wants to know if the two men are willing to "be baptized with the baptism that I am baptized with." The baptism spoken of here signifies identification. When Jesus is crucified, He is forever identified with our sin. God's wrath against sinful humanity is poured out on Jesus as He hangs on the Cross. In short, Jesus is asking the brothers if they are willing to partake of the experience of suffering and death.

The wrongful desire of James and John to be exalted motivated their foolish request. Modern Christians should be aware that wrongful desire will make us agree to things we don't understand. We are told: "When you ask, you do not receive, because you ask with wrong motives, that you may spend what you get on your pleasures" (James 4:3, NIV). Spiritual knowledge is essential to effective prayer. James and John's request was erroneously based on a worldly perspective and their limited understanding of power. Knowledge of God and His Word makes us pray less selfishly and causes us to pray about things according to God's will.

39 And they said unto him, We can. And Jesus said unto them, Ye shall indeed drink of the cup that I drink of; and with the baptism that I am baptized withal shall ye be baptized:

The fiery, and sometimes unthinking, impetuousness of the Sons of Zebedee is evidenced in their response to Jesus. They foolishly claim that they can share in the cup and baptism. Jesus, in His omnipotence, already knows that if the brothers truly understood, they would be begging to be spared. Also Jesus knows that after He is arrested, these two, along with the others, will desert Him. However, after being filled with the Spirit at Pentecost, their true testing period would occur and the Sons of Zebedee would indeed come through. For now, Jesus simply and lovingly states the irony of their request. He tells them that they will indeed share in his suffering. James will become the first apostle to be martyred, and his brother John will have his share of sufferings, including exile on the Isle of Patmos.

40 But to sit on my right hand and on my left hand is not mine to give; but it shall be given to them for whom it is prepared.

Jesus does not tell the two that there are no places of honor on His right and left hand in glory. Rather, He explains that the appointments of these seats of honor are not His to give. These decisions are the sole prerogative of His Father. It was useless for the two apostles to try to advance themselves in glory. Just as Jesus had been prepared as our sacrifice, positions in the kingdom would be assigned only to those who had been prepared to receive them.

James and John had incorrectly assumed that the kingdom order operated in the same way as the world order. The disciples were aware that earthly positions of authority were frequently bestowed on those who were born into the right families or could be obtained through the currying of favors. Jesus is adamant that this is not to be the case in His Father's kingdom. Heaven is a prepared place for prepared people. Honor will be bestowed on those who prepare themselves and not those who selfishly seek honor.

41 And when the ten heard it, they began to be much displeased with James and John.

While the Scripture does not tell us how the other 10 disciples become aware of this private conversation, the displeasure of the others indicates that there may have been some hostile feelings. It is unclear whether the others were outraged at the selfishness of James and John or jealous that the brothers had beat them to the punch. In either case, it is important to note that the others' displeasure is not sinful in itself. Instead, it is the implication of strife among the believers that is problematic. The body of Christ ought to govern itself through the Word of God and the Holy Spirit. Luke records that on one occasion, "a dispute arose among them as to

which of them was considered to be greatest" (Luke 22:24, NIV). This leads some of us to believe that there may have been a tendency for this group to become quarrelsome. While Jesus tolerates the individuality of the 12 disciples, He clearly promotes the unity of the body and teaches them about godly service.

42 But Jesus called them to him, and saith unto them, Ye know that they which are accounted to rule over the Gentiles exercise lordship over them; and their great ones exercise authority upon them. 43 But so shall it not be among you: but whosoever will be great among you, shall be your minister: 44 And whosoever of you will be the chiefest, shall be servant of all.

Jesus reminds the disciples that man's way is not God's way. He recounts that in the world of power and authority are all too often forces of oppression. Among the Gentiles, it is expected that those in control will use their power to advance their own personal causes. This was an easy concept for the Twelve to understand. They were living in a world where the Romans had authority over the Jews and exercised it with ruthless precision. Pride and selfish ambition were the hallmarks of Gentile power and authority. Even within the Jewish population, the disciples had witnessed how those in power—the chief priests and Pharisees, greedy publicans, and others— exercised their authority over those who were powerless.

In the ancient world, rulers were not elected. The officials were often born or appointed to their offices. All too frequently these rulers demonstrated how much power they had by exercising their superiority over those they controlled in cruel and oppressive ways, including excessive taxation, the unfair seizure of land or property, and even physical brutality. Jesus often spoke out against such ungodly exercises of power, especially when practiced by Jews against others Jews. He called such Jewish leaders fools and "vipers" (Matthew 23).

Jesus never intended for His disciples to model the world's standards of power and authority. Instead, He intends for them to use kingdom standards. When He says "it shall not be so among you," Jesus is clearly looking toward the future, when He is no longer walking daily among the disciples. In preparation for that time, Jesus is teaching that they demonstrate a new paradigm of leadership, one that He has modeled for them for the last three years.

The idea of Christian service is still confusing to many present-day saints. We mistakenly confuse worship or church attendance with service. Service always has a recipient. If our action only benefits us, then it is not service!

It is important to note that Jesus was not teaching that His disciples regard themselves as worthless. He was teaching them instead to honor others above themselves. It is this type of loving and sacrificial service that demonstrates the kingdom of God. Rather than status and glory, true leadership is evidenced by humility and service. In the kingdom of God, if one desires to lead, one must be willing to be a servant.

45 For even the Son of man came not to be ministered unto, but to minister, and to give his life a ransom for many.

For the second time in this passage, Jesus refers to Himself as "the Son of man." In the New Testament, this expression occurs almost 80 times. In most instances, Jesus is referring to Himself. The expression identifies Jesus as the ultimate Kinsman Redeemer. Here, Jesus uses this title to make a point to His disciples. Even He, the Son of God, did not come to lord it over mankind, but to serve mankind. The expression "ministered to" is more accurately rendered "serve" in other translations. Similarly, the word "minister" is the Greek word *diakoneo* (**dee-ak'-on-os**), which means "servant."

In Jesus' day, the disciples were quite familiar with the idea of ransom, particularly as it relates to slavery, which was still common practice. In the New Testament, there are three words used to describe ransom or redemption. The first Greek word is *agorazo* (**ag-or-ad'zo**) meaning "to buy" or "purchase." During this time, one could go to the marketplace or the Agora to purchase a slave. The second Greek word is *ixagorazo* (**ex-ag-or-ad'zo**). This comes from the same root word as *agorazo,* with the addition of the prefix that means "out." Essentially the word means "to buy out." It literally means purchasing the slave and then bringing him out of the market. The third and final word that is used here is *lutron* (**loo'tron**), the Greek word for "ransom." It means to go to the marketplace, purchase the slave, take him or her out of the marketplace, and then set the slave free. This is exactly what Jesus has done for us. Jesus entered this sinful world and paid for our salvation and freedom. His sacrifice on the Cross and shed blood is the payment for our release, or our ransom.

DAILY BIBLE READINGS

M: Servant of All
Mark 9:33-37

T: Jesus Surprises His Hearers
Mark 10:13-22

W: Jesus Perplexes the Disciples
Mark 10:23-27

T: First Will Be Last, Last First
Mark 10:28-31

F: Whoever Is Great Shall Be Servant
Mark 10:35-45

S: I Came to Serve
Matthew 20:20-28

S: The Exalted Will Be Humbled
Matthew 23:1-12

Why not do a cross-reference check of Mark 10:45 to discover all the places the word *serve* is used in Scripture by using your *Precepts For Living* CD-ROM. You will also find helpful definitions in the Greek and Hebrew dictionary.

TEACHING TIPS

February 6
Bible Study Guide 10

1. Words You Should Know

A. Visited (Ruth 1:6) *paqad* (Heb.)—Here, the word refers to an action by God that produces a beneficial result for His people.

B. Intreat (v. 16) *paga* (Heb.)—To encounter or entreat, or to cause to entreat.

2. Teacher Preparation

A. Familiarize yourself with the unit by reviewing the QUARTER AT-A-GLANCE.

B. During the week, prayerfully read the entire book of Ruth using a different Bible version. Next, study chapter 1. Ask yourself these questions as you review the chapter: Who are the major characters in the story? When does the story take place? Where does the story take place? What action is taking place? How does the action affect the main characters?

3. Starting the Lesson

A. During the week, become familiar with the IN FOCUS story. In class, after the students have settled in, use the IN FOCUS story as an opening devotional.

B. After the devotional, lead the class in prayer. Thank God for His loving care throughout the week. Ask Him to help you teach the class and to bless the students with understanding.

C. Take a few minutes to review the highlights of last week's lesson, especially the MAKE IT HAPPEN suggestion. Ask for volunteers to share their experiences with the class.

4. Getting into the Lesson

A. To help the students focus on today's lesson, ask for a volunteer to read the BACKGROUND section.

B. Ask for two volunteers to read the FOCAL VERSES according to the AT-A-GLANCE outline. After each section is read, ask the students to silently read the corresponding IN DEPTH section. After the students have finished reading, ask the appropriate SEARCH THE SCRIPTURES questions.

5. Relating the Lesson to Life

A. After you have completed all the reading and answered the SEARCH THE SCRIPTURES questions, review the DISCUSS THE MEANING questions. Allow time for open discussion of the questions.

B. Ask the students what meaning today's lesson has for their personal lives.

6. Arousing Action

A. Reserve some time at the end of class to cover the LESSON IN OUR SOCIETY and the MAKE IT HAPPEN sections. Ask the students to suggest ways that they can demonstrate mature, godly love in their homes and communities. Challenge the students to follow up on their suggestions this week.

B. Close the class in prayer.

WORSHIP GUIDE

For the Superintendent or Teacher
Theme: Overcoming Grief
Theme Song: "Just a Closer Walk"
Scripture: 1 Corinthians 13
Song: "Look What the Lord Has Done"
Meditation: Father, Your Word teaches us that we are to love You first and foremost, then to love others as we love ourselves. We realize that love is not governed by our emotions but by our will. We thank You for equipping us to love as You love.

OVERCOMING GRIEF

Bible Background • RUTH 1
Printed Text • RUTH 1:3-8, 14-18
Devotional Reading • PSALM 31:9-15

LESSON AIM

By the end of the lesson, the students will understand that living outside of God's will only brings misfortune, while faithful devotion results in godly reward. Students will also be able to explain the basis of real love and determine to live in obedience to God and demonstrate His love to others.

KEEP IN MIND

"And Ruth said, Intreat me not to leave thee, or to return from following after thee: for whither thou goest, I will go; and where thou lodgest, I will lodge: thy people shall be my people, and thy God my God" (Ruth 1:16).

FOCAL VERSES

Ruth 1:3 And Elimelech Naomi's husband died; and she was left, and her two sons.

4 And they took them wives of the women of Moab; the name of the one was Orpah, and the name of the other Ruth: and they dwelled there about ten years.

5 And Mahlon and Chilion died also both of them; and the woman was left of her two sons and her husband.

6 Then she arose with her daughters in law, that she might return from the country of Moab: for she had heard in the country of Moab how that the LORD had visited his people in giving them bread.

7 Wherefore she went forth out of the place where she was, and her two daughters in law with her; and they went on the way to return unto the land of Judah.

LESSON OVERVIEW

LESSON AIM
KEEP IN MIND
FOCAL VERSES
IN FOCUS
THE PEOPLE, PLACES, AND TIMES
BACKGROUND
AT-A-GLANCE
IN DEPTH
SEARCH THE SCRIPTURES
DISCUSS THE MEANING
LESSON IN OUR SOCIETY
MAKE IT HAPPEN
FOLLOW THE SPIRIT
REMEMBER YOUR THOUGHTS
MORE LIGHT ON THE TEXT
DAILY BIBLE READINGS

8 And Naomi said unto her two daughters in law, Go, return each to her mother's house: the LORD deal kindly with you, as ye have dealt with the dead, and with me.

1:14 And they lifted up their voice, and wept again: and Orpah kissed her mother in law; but Ruth clave unto her.

15 And she said, Behold, thy sister in law is gone back unto her people, and unto her gods: return thou after thy sister in law.

16 And Ruth said, Intreat me not to leave thee, or to return from following after thee: for whither thou goest, I will go; and where thou lodgest, I will lodge: thy people shall be my people, and thy God my God:

17 Where thou diest, will I die, and there will I be buried: the LORD do so to me, and more also, if ought but death part thee and me.

18 When she saw that she was stedfastly minded to go with her, then she left speaking unto her.

FEB 6TH

IN FOCUS

There is a story told about Benjamin Franklin when he was the United States Ambassador to France. Old Ben occasionally attended the meetings of an organization called the Infidel's Club, a group that spent most of its time searching for and reading literary masterpieces; however, they didn't care for the Bible. On one occasion, Franklin read the book of Ruth to the members of the club when they gathered together, but changed the names of the characters so it would not be recognized as a book of the Bible.

When he finished, the members of the Infidel's Club were unanimous in their praise. They said it was one of the most beautiful short stories that they had ever heard, and they demanded that he tell them where he had run across such a remarkable literary masterpiece.

With great delight Ben told them that the story was from the Bible, which they professed to regard with scorn and derision, and in which they felt there was nothing good.

The book of Ruth truly is a literary masterpiece. It is a beautiful story of love and devotion that inflames the imagination and is entwined throughout with love and romance. However, it is the story behind the story—its meaning and significance—that is most fascinating. The book of Ruth is one of those beautiful Old Testament pictures that illustrate the dramatic truths of the Christian faith expounded in the New Testament. It is a word picture illustrative of God's grace and divine plan in action.

Today's lesson relates the story of an Israelite family who moved away from the will and the protection of God. Yet when they returned, God was there to bless them and to bless others through them.

THE PEOPLE, PLACES, AND TIMES

Moabites. Those who were descendants of Lot. Moab was the son of Lot and his older daughter. (Ammon was the son of Lot and his younger daughter—hence the Ammonites.)

When the Israelites came up from Egypt, they approached Moab from the southeast, outside the bordering circle of hills. God forbade them to disturb the Moabites in their enjoyment of the land, which they had taken from the Emim (Deuteronomy 2:9-11). So the Israelites applied for permission to pass through their territory. The Moabites refused their request, so the Israelites went around its borders.

The Moabites did not physically wage war against Israel while they were neighbors for more than 300 years. However, they engaged in spiritual warfare against the Israelites. While Israel was approaching the land of Canaan, King Balak of Moab formed a coalition with the Midianites and hired the prophet Balaam to curse Israel (Numbers 22-24). Moab and Midian were kin by virtue of their common descent from Terah—Moab through Lot from Haran and Midian from Abraham by Keturah (Genesis 11:27; 19:37; 25:2).

When Balaam failed to curse Israel, the Moabites sent their daughters to entice Israelite men to abandon God by participating in the perverted, sexually centered worship of Baal (Numbers 25:1-2).

The result of all this was the exclusion of Moabites and Ammonites from the congregation of the Lord to the tenth generation (Deuteronomy 23:4). However, there was no direct prohibition against marriage to Moabites, as long as they were faithful to the covenant.

After the conquest of Canaan, Moab oppressed Israel for 18 years. It is significant, however, that "the LORD gave Eglon king of Moab power over Israel. Getting the Ammonites and Amalekites to join him, Eglon came and attacked Israel" (Judges 3:12, 13, NIV). The Moabite conquest ended with the assassination of Eglon by the judge Ehud.

BACKGROUND

The story of Ruth the Moabitess is a story of love, devotion, and redemption. It is fitting that this little book is situated between Judges and 1 Samuel. The book of Judges chronicles the Israelites' failure to be faithful to the covenant God established with them. The book ends with immorality (Judges 19:1-30), civil war (20:1-48), murder (21:8-15), and kidnaping (21:16-25). The complete rebellion of the Children of Israel is summed up in the final verse: "In those days there was no king in Israel: every man did that which was right in his own eyes" (21:25).

However, God always has a righteous remnant who remain faithful to God. Ruth and Boaz are beautiful examples of this truth. Ruth was a virtuous woman who lived above the immorality and rebellion of her time (Ruth 3:11). She demonstrated loyalty and love during a time of rebellion and selfishness.

1. The Tragedy of Moab (Ruth 1:3-5)
2. The Road to Bethlehem (vv. 6-7)
3. The Statement of Love (vv. 8, 14-18)

IN DEPTH

1. The Tragedy of Moab (Ruth 1:3-5)

The book of Ruth takes place during the time when judges ruled Israel (1375-1050 B.C.). During this period, apostasy, immorality, and anarchy were widespread.

During a famine, Elimelech moved his family from their home in Bethlehem, meaning "city of bread," to a neighboring country called Moab. Elimelech and both his sons died in the foreign land, leaving their wives alone and destitute. Famine in the ancient Middle East was not uncommon, but for Israel it was sometimes seen as a sign of God's judgment and His call to repentance. Elimelech attempted to escape the famine by moving his family to another country. The country he chose was only 30 miles from Bethlehem in actual distance but an infinite distance away in its relationship to God.

Because of Moab's actions toward Israel when Moses led the Israelites during the exodus, God had commanded the Israelites not to have anything to do with the Moabites. "No Ammonite or Moabite or any of his descendants may enter the assembly of the LORD, even down to the tenth generation" (Deuteronomy 23:3, NIV).

Instead of moving back to Bethlehem, his family continued to stay in the land for another 10 years. Elimelech's sons continued in the land and married Moabite women. Eventually, both sons died, leaving their widows destitute and their mother alone in a foreign land.

Although Naomi, Elimelech's wife, was a godly woman, she experienced great difficulty. She suffered famine (Ruth 1:1), she lost her husband (v. 3), and then she lost her two sons (v. 5). In fact, Naomi not only faced the loss of loved ones; as a widow without sons to care for her, she also experienced the loss of economic status. Even believers will experience the loss of loved ones, health,

jobs, or economic status. During these times, we must remember that God can sustain us through any kind of loss (see Romans 8:35-39).

2. The Road to Bethlehem (vv. 6-7)

For foreigners living in Moab, life was difficult. They could not own their own land and were forced to work for meager wages. Widows and orphans in Moab were at the bottom of the economic ladder. Things were especially hard for Naomi. The poor widow had a family and was alone in a pagan land, separated from God's people and God's blessings. On top of all this, she was left with two widowed daughters-in-law to care for. In the midst of her trials, Naomi's mind turned to God and to home.

Word reached Naomi of "how that the LORD had visited his people in giving them bread" (v. 6). God was again blessing Israel with abundant crops, and Naomi began to see the hand of God in her misfortunes (v. 13b). She made up her mind to return to Bethlehem.

Naomi and her two daughters-in-law, Ruth (meaning "friendly") and Orpah, left Moab and set out on the road to Judah. Naomi's return to Bethlehem of Judah would result in blessings for herself and for generations who would come after her. Ultimately, her return to God would bless all humanity through her descendant, Jesus Christ.

3. The Statement of Love (vv. 8, 14-18)

It is a testimony to Naomi's character that both her daughters-in-law were willing to leave their country and follow her to Bethlehem. As these three women made the three-day journey to Bethlehem, Naomi's mind probably turned to the futures of these young women. She knew that they would be treated as outcasts in Bethlehem. Their prospects for marriage were nonexistent, and even if she were able to bear more sons for them to marry, they would be too old by the time the sons reached marriageable age.

Suddenly, the older woman stopped: "And Naomi said unto her two daughters in law, Go, return each to her mother's house: the LORD deal kindly with you, as ye have dealt with the dead, and with me" (Ruth 1:8). Naomi's love for the young women was mature and selfless.

Although it would be much safer for three women to travel together than for one old woman to travel alone, Naomi considered the young women's welfare ahead of her own.

Both Orpah and Ruth protested and expressed their desire to stay with Naomi. The older woman then explained to the young women what she had been thinking, and her arguments were persuasive (vv. 11-13).

Orpah considered Naomi's words and agreed that the cost of following Naomi was too high. The young widow bid Naomi farewell and headed back to Moab and her gods. Ruth also counted the cost, but she loved Naomi too much to leave her. Ruth's love for Naomi was self-sacrificing, and she put Naomi's welfare above her own. With one stunning statement, Ruth separated herself from her home, her people, and her pagan gods forever.

"Intreat me not to leave thee, or to return from following after thee" (Ruth 1:16)—Ruth was almost begging Naomi to allow her to continue with her. "Whither thou goest, I will go" (v. 16)—neither of the women knew what fate lay ahead of her, but Ruth was faithful to Naomi even when facing the unknown. "Where thou lodgest, I will lodge" (v. 16)—there was no home for Naomi to return to, but Ruth was willing to stay with her even if it meant living in the street. "Thy people shall be my people, and thy God my God" (v. 16)—the faithful young widow was willing to forsake both her people and her gods to stay with Naomi. "Where thou diest, will I die, and there will I be buried" (v. 17)—the young woman would gladly face death in an unknown place, separated from all she knew, for the opportunity to be buried in the same place as Naomi. She backed up her words with a solemn oath: "The LORD do so to me, and more also, if ought but death part thee and me" (v. 17). Ruth's confession of faithfulness convinced Naomi of the young woman's determination to continue on with her. She started off to Bethlehem and never brought up the subject again (v. 18).

Ruth's statement is a beautiful example of the self-sacrificing love that believers should have for Christ. We should be willing to give up everything for the cause of Christ and live to please Him in all our ways. The statement is also evidence that Naomi had imparted her faith in God to her daughters-in-law. Naomi's faithfulness to God was rewarded by Ruth's faithfulness to her. The tragedies in Moab awakened Ruth to the spiritual reality of God. When she was faced with a difficult choice, she declared her love for Naomi and her submission to God.

Sometimes, God uses the tragedies of others to draw people to Himself. When we experience adversity in our lives, we should not only pray for deliverance, but also for the ultimate purposes of God to be fulfilled. When others are experiencing grief, like Ruth, we should willingly go out of our way to show comfort and support to them. God may use our actions to help strengthen their faith.

SEARCH THE SCRIPTURES

1. After the death of Elimelech, his sons married Moabite women. How long did the family live in Moab (Ruth 1:4)?

2. After the death of her husband and sons, Naomi decided to move back to Bethlehem. What brought about this decision (v. 6)?

3. On the journey home, Naomi thinks about the future of her two Moabite daughters-in-law. What advice did Naomi give to them (v. 8)?

4. Orpah saw the worldly wisdom in Naomi's words and decided to return to her people. Ruth insisted on staying with Naomi. How did Naomi respond after hearing Ruth's vow of loyalty (v. 18)?

DISCUSS THE MEANING

When her situation was most hopeless, Naomi turned her thoughts back to God and home. Therefore, she decided to return to Bethlehem and the people of God.

LESSON IN OUR SOCIETY

Psychologists tell us that love progresses through four distinct stages from infant to adult. During the first three stages, a person's sense of love stems from what is being done for them. It is self-centered and dependent on others. The fourth stage is others-centered and seeks the greatest good for the person loved. What effect do you think it would have on our cities if everyone reached this fourth stage of love?

MAKE IT HAPPEN

It has often been said that love makes the world go 'round, but in fact there is very little real love demonstrated in our society. Love is demonstrated by what we are willing to sacrifice for the good of others. You can demonstrate your love by working in a soup kitchen or by volunteering time in a hospital or senior's home. This week, look for ways that you can demonstrate the love of God for others.

FOLLOW THE SPIRIT

What God wants me to do:

_____

_____

REMEMBER YOUR THOUGHTS

Special insights I have learned:

_____

_____

MORE LIGHT ON THE TEXT
Ruth 1:3-8, 14-18

Various writers and scholars have described the story of Ruth in many different ways. Some writers describe its theme as "from emptiness to fullness," "from poverty to riches," or "from tragedy to triumph." All these describe the plight of the chief characters of the story, especially Naomi and Ruth. It is a story that begins with having nothing and ends with abundance; it goes from penury to prosperity and from tragedy of death to triumph of life. Indeed, the best way to view the story of Ruth is to see it through the lens of God's providential intervention in the affairs of His people. The story illustrates the act of God in rewarding the faithfulness of those who put their trust in Him. It also demonstrates "unconditional love" and how God rewards such love through His providential care. No matter how one looks at this story, one thing is certain: God has made His grace available to all of His creation from the beginning of time.

The book of Ruth has been classified as one of the best-structured narratives of the Old Testament. It is one of the most delightful and interesting stories in all of Scripture. The narrative gives an account of a Jewish family, namely Elimelech, Naomi, and their two sons, Mahlon and Chilion, who are forced to migrate to Moab because of famine in their homeland, Bethlehem in Judah.

3 And Elimelech Naomi's husband died; and she was left, and her two sons. 4 And they took them wives of the women of Moab; the name of the one was Orpah, and the name of the other Ruth: and they dwelled there about ten years. 5 And Mahlon and Chilion died also both of them; and the woman was left of her two sons and her husband.

Verses 3-5 tell of the tragedy that came upon the family: the death of Naomi's husband Elimelech and their sons: Mahlon and Chilion. Elimelech died first, leaving Naomi with her two sons. We are not told how long it was after their arrival in Moab that Elimelech died. What we do know is that after his death, his children took as wives two Moabites, "and they dwelled there about ten years."

The author does not give any hint as to why the tragedy befell the family or the famine fell upon Israel. There is no suggestion of any blame attached for moving to Moab and marrying Moabite women. There is also nothing to suggest that this tragedy was the result of the family's having forsaken their people in time of trouble. Indeed, these reasons have been proposed by a number of interpreters and preachers. Many of them have taught that the famine was a punishment for Israel's sin and that the family's tragedy was retribution for deserting their people, traveling to an idolatrous nation, and marrying there. These explanations are only speculative or the result of reading meaning into the story and are an attempt to "spiritualize" the story. We read from the Scriptures that there were times both before and during the monarchy in Israel when a friendly relationship existed between Moab and Israel (see Deuteronomy 2:8-9, 28-29; 1 Samuel 22:3-5). The author does not deem it necessary to give the details or reasons why the events occurred; therefore, we should not read meaning into the story based on our knowledge of Moab or of God's dealings with His people from other passages (e.g., Deuteronomy 23:3-6).

After the death of Elimelech, his two sons married Orpah and Ruth. We shall learn later in 4:10 that Mahlon married Ruth. The clause, "and they dwelled there (i.e., in Moab) about ten years" seems to be significant to the rest of the story. There is ambiguity in the time period. Do the 10 years represent the total amount of time the family stayed in Moab? Or is it the length of time between the boys' marriages and the time when Naomi and Ruth returned to Bethlehem? If the latter is the case, it may mean that they lived in Moab 10 years after their marriages. The significance of this time period becomes clear in chapter 4 with the question of heirship, which is a dominant motif of the book (see the womens' compliment to Naomi in 4:14). The narrator must have inserted this clause intentionally to stress the providential act of God in doing the impossible.

The importance of the 10-year period is implied in the mention of the death of Mahlon and Chilion in verse 5, especially in the clause, "and the woman was left of her two sons and her husband." That is, Naomi was "left" alone (Heb. *sha'ar*), or left behind, without her sons or her husband. Here we have a picture of a widow left alone with two sons (v. 3) who is given temporary relief and hope for a possible continuation of her family by her sons' marriage to two Moabite women (v. 4a).

However, this hope, first postponed by 10 years without offspring, ends dramatically in the death of both her sons. The word "left" highlights the seriousness of the tragedy. The woman is stripped of all that made her and gave her an identity: her husband and children. In the Jewish (male-dominated) culture, as in other cultures, a woman's family—her husband and children, especially male children—determined her worth. The story of Hannah and her husband Elkanah (1 Samuel 1:1-8) succinctly illustrates this point. In some African cultures, a widow has a low status in the community, especially if she has no children; hence the Igbo (of Nigeria) adage, *Ugwu nwanyi bu di ya,* which means, "the glory or honor of a

woman is in her husband." In most cases, if a woman was young and of childbearing age, and her husband died before they had children, she would leave her marital home and return to her paternal family to remarry.

This sets the stage for the dialog between Naomi and her daughters-in-law (Ruth 1:8-18). It also focuses our attention on the major players in the story and the problem in the story, which reaches a climax at the birth of Obed (4:13ff.). Verse 5 also brings the introductory part of the story to a climax—and effectively leaves us with the emotional component of the story by closing with the clause, "the woman was left of her two sons and her husband." One commentary describes Naomi's situation as thus:

"From wife to widow, from mother to no mother, this female is stripped of all identity. The security of husband, which a male-dominated culture affords its women, is hers no longer. The definition of worth, by which it values the female, applies to her no more. The blessings of old age, which it gives through progeny, are there no longer. Stranger in a foreign land, this woman is a victim of death—and of life."

Bush, Frederic W., et al. "Ruth/Esther." *Word Biblical Commentary.* Vol. 9. Nashville: Word Publishing, 1996. 68.

6 Then she arose with her daughters in law, that she might return from the country of Moab: for she had heard in the country of Moab how that the LORD had visited his people in giving them bread.

Verse 6 serves as a transition; it concludes the introductory part and sets the stage for what follows. The author seems to give a glimmer of hope amidst the rather grim and tragic circumstances that have so far dominated the first part of the story. He does this by relating the news that "the LORD had visited his people in giving them bread," which prompted Naomi to decide to go back to Bethlehem, her homeland. Naomi does not hope for a bright future beyond her present bitter situation; she decides to return home.

The phrase "then she arose" (Heb. *quwm,* **koom**) means "to stand up" or "to arise." Naomi had made up her mind to venture home. This construction is similar to the construction found in Christ's New Testament parable of the prodigal son. After being stripped of all his belongings and becoming hungry and empty, the prodigal son determines to return to his family. He said, "I will arise and go to my father . . . . And he arose, and came to his father" (Luke 15:18, 20). "Arise" (or its past tense form, "arose") is the Greek word *anistemi* (**an-is'-tay-mee**), which has the same meaning as its Hebrew equivalent used in this passage in Ruth. Just as the verb in the parable conveys a sense of determined action by the prodigal son to get up and go home in spite of the potential difficulties and shame he would face there, the verb seems to convey the same idea here.

Therefore, the reason for Naomi's decision to return to Bethlehem is that "she had heard in the country of Moab how that the LORD had visited his people in giving them bread." How did she hear this news? The narrator does not tell us. **There are a number of speculations about how she got the news.** Some think that an angel told her. If that were true, the author would have said so. Others think that some of her relatives had sent her a message about the change in Bethlehem. The tone of the rest of the story defeats this hypothesis since it seems that when the family left for Moab, all ties between them and the rest of the community were cut. The third theory is that she heard the news through rumor. This is the most likely means. Genesis 42:1 says that Jacob heard there was food in Egypt and sent his sons to buy, without saying how he heard. The writers in both instances do not deem it necessary to reveal how Jacob or Naomi got the news. However, it is not unusual for people in desperate circumstances to learn about things that would help them, especially in the case of a catastrophe such as famine. Their minds and ears would be open to learn or hear essential information that would help resolve their problem. Moreover, with her situation in a foreign land, Naomi was anxious to hear news about her home country.

The news is "that the LORD had visited his people (i.e., Bethlehem of Judah) in giving them bread." The verb "visited" (Heb. *paqad*) is used in a number of ways in the Old Testament and means "to attend to, muster, reckon, punish, or

care for." This word is translated as "visit" 60 times in the Bible and points to action that produces a great change in the position of the subject, either for good or ill will (e.g., the case of the butler and the baker in Genesis 40:13, 19). Here, as in many other instances (e.g., Genesis 50:24-25; 1 Samuel 2:21; Psalm 8:4; Jeremiah 15:15; 29:10), the visitation produces a beneficial or good result for the subject. The good result is the return of "bread," or *lechem* (**lekh'-em**), which means food in general, to the land of Judah.

7 Wherefore she went forth out of the place where she was, and her two daughters in law with her; and they went on the way to return unto the land of Judah. 8 And Naomi said unto her two daughters in law, Go, return each to her mother's house: the LORD deal kindly with you, as ye have dealt with the dead, and with me.

The statement, "Wherefore she went forth out of the place where she was, and her two daughters in law with her," simply means that she, along with her two daughters-in-law, set out from Moab where she was living. The second clause, "they went on the way to return unto the land of Judah," implies that they went toward Judah. Although we know Naomi's destination from verse 6, the first part of verse 7 does not reveal that. Probably as they set out, her daughters-in-law were not aware of where Naomi was heading. She might have decided not to tell them until they started toward Judah. This prompts the long dialog that occupies the rest of this section (Ruth 1:8-18). We can picture Naomi getting up early one morning with nothing and heading eastward. Her daughters-in-law, ignorant of where she is going, accompany her. As they turn on to the road that leads to Judah (probably at the border between Moab and Judah in the Jordan Valley), Naomi turns to them and asks them to go back to Moab, their country of origin. She blesses them and says to them, "[May] the LORD deal kindly with you, as ye have dealt with the dead, and with me; [May] the LORD grant you that ye may find rest, each of you in the house of her husband" (vv. 8-9). (For a good detailed summary and analysis of the dialog that ensued between Naomi and her two daughters-in-law, see Bush, p. 72 ff.)

The expression "Go, return each to her mother's house" is difficult to understand. Why did Naomi instruct the daughters-in-law to return each to her "mother's house" rather than to her father's house, which is normally to be expected from a Jewish woman? (see Genesis 38:11; Leviticus 22:13; Numbers 30:16; Deuteronomy 22:21; Judges 19:2-3). A number of explanations have been proposed. One explanation is that the Moabites (like the Israelites) were a polygamous community in which the men generally married more than one wife. Each wife had her own house built within the bigger family in which she raised her children. Therefore, asking the girls to return each to her mother's house is to be understood in this light. This is the most acceptable explanation and is consistent with many African traditions. This, however, does not imply that their mothers' house is different from their fathers' house. By telling the girls to return to their mother's, Naomi probably had the emotional needs of the girls in mind. Who would understand their plight better than their mothers? One could also argue that the girls' mothers may well have been widows or divorced, and therefore they had to return to their mothers. Naomi, however, might also have used the phrase "mother's house" in a generic or general sense to mean their homeland of Moab. Her statement to Ruth in verse 15 supports this theory: "Behold, thy sister in law is gone back unto her people."

1:14 And they lifted up their voice, and wept again: and Orpah kissed her mother in law; but Ruth clave unto her. 15 And she said, Behold, thy sister in law is gone back unto her people, and unto her gods: return thou after thy sister in law. 16 And Ruth said, Intreat me not to leave thee, or to return from following after thee: for whither thou goest, I will go; and where thou lodgest, I will lodge: thy people shall be my people, and thy God my God: 17 Where thou diest, will I die, and there will I be buried: the LORD do so to me, and more also, if ought but death part thee and me. 18 When she saw that she was stedfastly minded to go with her, then she left speaking unto her.

After listening to a long, persuasive plea and a convincing argument by Naomi for her daugh-ters-in-law to return to their people, Orpah goes back, "but Ruth clave unto her." Then Naomi goes through another passionate plea for Ruth to return with her sister-in-law (v. 15), but Ruth determinedly commits herself to go with Naomi back to Judah. She does this through one of the most beautiful and poignant statements of human loyalty and commitment in all of Scripture and indeed "in world literature," as one writer puts it.

The English translation of the phrase "and Ruth said" does not seem to bring out the force and emotion of the statement that follows. "Said" (*'amar*) is used over 5,000 times in the Old Testament with a variety of meanings. It is some-times used to mean "promise," as in God's promise to David for a perpetual dynasty (2 Kings 8:19); God's promise to Israel to possess the land of promise (Nehemiah 9:15); or Haman's promise to Xerxes (Ahasuerus) to pay the king for the opportunity to destroy all the Jews in his domain (Esther 4:7). Other meanings of this verb include "command," as in God's command to Joshua (Joshua 11:9) and Xerxes' command through letters to reverse the edict to slaughter the Jews by hanging Haman and his sons (Esther 9:25). The most interesting use is to mean "avow" or "pledge" (e.g., Moses' closing remarks remind-ing Israel that they had vowed to have God as their own in Deuteronomy 26:17-18). Instead of the Hebrew verb "said" being used here, a verb meaning "answered" would have been more appropriate since Ruth was responding to what Naomi had just said to her. In her reply, Ruth asks Naomi: "Intreat me not to leave thee, or to return from following after thee," which in simple English means, "do not ask me or urge me to leave you." The word translated as "intreat" (KJV) or "urge" (NASB, NIV) is the Hebrew word *paga'*, often meaning "to meet, intercede, urge, or encounter." In this case, it means "to encounter with a request." It seems to be a gentle but deter-mined objection to Naomi's effort to dissuade Ruth from following her to Judah. This objection translates into an absolute committed loyalty, which Ruth expresses in a beautiful poetic form that runs something like this:

A—"Intreat me not to leave thee, or to return from following after thee:"

B—"For whither thou goest, I will go; and where thou lodgest, I will lodge:"

C—"Thy people shall be my people, and thy God my God:"

B2—"Where thou diest, will I die, and there will I be buried:"

A2— "The LORD do so to me, and more also, if ought but death part thee and me."

Bush, Frederic W., et al. "Ruth/Esther. " *Word Biblical Commentary.* Vol. 9. Nashville: Word Publishing, 1996. 74.

Ruth's commitment and allegiance to Naomi extends beyond a commitment to one individual; it transcends the boundaries of nationality and ethnic religion. Her resolve to follow Naomi to the end is expressed as a matter of both life and death by statements B and B2. In many cultures, especially in Africa and in the Igbo culture in particular (as in the Jewish culture), people may decide to live among another tribe or people, but at death they always want to be buried in their homeland, among their people. For example, consider Jacob's request to Joseph that his body be taken to his homeland (Genesis 47:29ff.; 48:21; 50:5) and Joseph's instruction to his brothers to carry his bones to the Promised Land (Genesis 50:25; Exodus 13:19; Joshua 24:32). By these statements (B and B2), Ruth implicitly declares her allegiance to the Jewish community, culture, and religion. This she explicitly declares by the statements in C: "Thy people shall be my people, and thy God my God." She invokes God's covenant name and seals this declaration with an oath (A2). In it, she pronounces a curse on herself if she fails to keep this promise or fails to do what she has pledged to do. In Hebrew, it literally means, "May the Yahweh deal with me, be it ever so severely," a formula found about 12 times in the Old Testament (cf. 1 Samuel 3:17; 14:44;

20:13; 25:22; 2 Samuel 3:9, 35; 19:13; 1 Kings 2:23; 2 Kings 6:31, etc.). In B2, Ruth says that not even death would be able to separate her from Naomi. In A2, she says that the only thing that could keep her from fulfilling her vow to Naomi was if she died first. A covenant oath of this nature in Hebrew is taken very seriously and is binding, especially when the name Yahweh is invoked.

Naomi understands the degree of Ruth's commitment and determination to go with her, and she entreats her no longer (Ruth 1:18). When she saw that she was determined to go with her, she stopped urging her to return to Moab. The rest of the chapter summarizes their return to Bethlehem and the reception given to Naomi by the women (vv. 19-22).

DAILY BIBLE READINGS

M: I Am Weary with Weeping
Psalm 6:1-7

T: My Life Is Spent with Sorrow
Psalm 31:9-15

W: My Soul Refuses to Be Comforted
Psalm 77:1-10

T: Naomi Loses Her Husband and Sons
Ruth 1:1-5

F: Go Back to Your Home
Ruth 1:6-11

S: Orpah Goes, Ruth Stays
Ruth 1:12-17

S: Naomi and Ruth Travel to Bethlehem
Ruth 1:18-22

Ruth determined to *go* and *stay* with her mother-in-law (Ruth 1:15). Find out the deeper meanings of these words by looking in the Greek and Hebrew dictionary and doing a cross-reference check. These are just a few of the types of research you can do using your *Precepts For Living* CD-ROM!

TEACHING TIPS

February 13
Bible Study Guide 11

1. Words You Should Know

A. Leprosy (2 Kings 5:3) *tsarath* (Heb.)—A contagious disease characterized by an eruption of rough, scaly patches, or ulcers of the skin, bone, and muscles leading to loss of feeling, paralysis, gangrene, and deformity.

B. Wroth (v. 11) *qatsaph* (Heb.)—To be very angry; hot anger.

2. Teacher Preparation

A. Begin preparing for this lesson by reading the DAILY BIBLE READINGS throughout the week as a part of your daily devotions. Then read 2 Kings 5.

B. Study the FOCAL VERSES and the commentary in the BIBLE STUDY GUIDE.

3. Starting the Lesson

A. Before the students arrive, write the lesson title and the AT-A-GLANCE outline on the board.

B. Write the word *leprosy* on the board. Ask the class to share what they know about the disease.

C. Read the IN FOCUS story and open the class in prayer, concentrating on the LESSON AIM.

4. Getting into the Lesson

A. Have a student read the BACKGROUND section, and another student read THE PEOPLE, PLACES, AND TIMES section to help the students gain a better understanding of the context for today's lesson.

B. Assign three students to read the IN DEPTH commentary according to the AT-A-GLANCE outline. Discuss it together.

C. Answer the SEARCH THE SCRIPTURES and DISCUSS THE MEANING questions together as a class.

5. Relating the Lesson to Life

A. To help the students see how the lesson applies to our modern society, direct them to the LESSON IN OUR SOCIETY. Allow them to read the section silently and briefly discuss their thoughts and opinions.

B. Ask the students to share other insights they have received from today's lesson.

6. Arousing Action

A. Guide the students through the activity in MAKE IT HAPPEN. Read the suggested Scripture together; then give them adequate time to meditate on the question and suggested prayer.

B. Close the class in prayer.

WORSHIP GUIDE

For the Superintendent or Teacher
Theme: Overcoming Pride
Theme Song: "Here Am I, Send Me"
Scripture: 2 Kings 5:1-19
Song: "Guide Me, O Thou Great Jehovah"
Meditation: Jehovah God, thank You for giving instructions for life and godliness in Your Word. Help me to lay aside my pride and opinions to obey Your Word and do all that I can to give You glory.

OVERCOMING PRIDE

Bible Background • 2 KINGS 5
Printed Text • 2 KINGS 5:1-5, 9-15
Devotional Reading • MARK 7:17-23

LESSON AIM

By the end of the lesson, the students will consider how pride and prejudice can cause us to miss God's blessings, rejoice that God works through people for His glory, and individually resolve to seek to work for God's glory.

KEEP IN MIND

"And his servants came near, and spake unto him, and said, My father, if the prophet had bid thee do some great thing, wouldest thou not have done it? How much rather then, when he saith to thee, Wash, and be clean? Then went he down, and dipped himself seven times in Jordan, according to the saying of the man of God: and his flesh came again like unto the flesh of a little child, and he was clean" (2 Kings 5:13-14).

FOCAL VERSES

2 Kings 5:1 Now Naaman, captain of the host of the king of Syria, was a great man with his master, and honourable, because by him the LORD had given deliverance unto Syria: he was also a mighty man in valour, but he was a leper.

2 And the Syrians had gone out by companies, and had brought away captive out of the land of Israel a little maid; and she waited on Naaman's wife.

3 And she said unto her mistress, Would God my lord were with the prophet that is in Samaria! for he would recover him of his leprosy.

4 And one went in, and told his lord, saying, Thus and thus said the maid that is of the land of Israel.

LESSON OVERVIEW

LESSON AIM
KEEP IN MIND
FOCAL VERSES
IN FOCUS
THE PEOPLE, PLACES, AND TIMES
BACKGROUND
AT-A-GLANCE
IN DEPTH
SEARCH THE SCRIPTURES
DISCUSS THE MEANING
LESSON IN OUR SOCIETY
MAKE IT HAPPEN
FOLLOW THE SPIRIT
REMEMBER YOUR THOUGHTS
MORE LIGHT ON THE TEXT
DAILY BIBLE READINGS

5 And the king of Syria said, Go to, go, and I will send a letter unto the king of Israel. And he departed, and took with him ten talents of silver, and six thousand pieces of gold, and ten changes of raiment.

5:9 So Naaman came with his horses and with his chariot, and stood at the door of the house of Elisha.

10 And Elisha sent a messenger unto him, saying, Go and wash in Jordan seven times, and thy flesh shall come again to thee, and thou shalt be clean.

11 But Naaman was wroth, and went away, and said, Behold, I thought, He will surely come out to me, and stand, and call on the name of the LORD his God, and strike his hand over the place, and recover the leper.

12 Are not Abana and Pharpar, rivers of Damascus, better than all the waters of Israel? may I not wash in them, and be clean? So he turned and went away in a rage.

13 And his servants came near, and spake unto him, and said, My father, if the prophet had bid thee do some great thing, wouldest thou not have done it? how much rather then, when he saith to thee, Wash, and be clean?

14 Then went he down, and dipped himself seven times in Jordan, according to the saying of the man of God: and his flesh came again like unto the flesh of a little child, and he was clean.

15 And he returned to the man of God, he and all his company, and came, and stood before him: and he said, Behold, now I know that there is no God in all the earth, but in Israel.

FEB
13TH

IN FOCUS

Shelle worked for the toughest and most unappreciative boss possible. Despite her boss, Shelle, a faithful Christian, worked very hard. She arrived at work each day before 8 a.m., and she gladly stayed past 5 p.m. whenever her boss needed extra help. But her boss never thanked her or commended her for extraordinary service. In fact, she gave Shelle only an average rating on her last performance review.

One day, Shelle's boss looked more unpleasant and unhappy than usual. A concerned Shelle asked what was wrong. Her boss, happy to have someone to talk with, told Shelle about a personal problem.

Shelle empathized with her, and she immediately thought of a place where her boss could get help. Just as Shelle was about to open her mouth to share the information, she started having flashbacks about how mean her boss had been to her. She thought about the average rating she unjustly received on her last performance review and about the hassle her boss gave her when she asked for a personal day last month.

Shelle returned to her desk without saying a word about the information, but she didn't feel right. Then she remembered how she had prayed for God to use her. She thought perhaps He was answering her prayer. He could use her to help her boss.

She quickly wrote down a name and number and went into her boss' office to give her the information.

Our lesson narrates how a high-ranking official named Naaman discovered the importance of humility and obedience when he followed the instructions of a Hebrew servant girl and the prophet Elisha in order to be healed by God.

THE PEOPLE, PLACES, AND TIMES

Aramaeans (Syrians). The Aramaeans are usually called "Syrians" in the English Old Testament. After leaving Ur, the patriarchs first settled in "Arm-naharaim" in the upper Mesopotamian area (see Genesis 11:28-32). Part of the family (Nahor, Bethuel, Laban) stayed there and became known as the Aramaeans. Part of the Old Testament was written in the Aramaic language (e.g., Daniel 2-7; Ezra 4:8-6:18), the international trade language during the sixth century B.C.

Elisha. Elisha was a 9th-century prophet of Israel. His name means "God is salvation." Information about Elisha's background is recorded in 1 Kings 19:16, 19-21. His ministry extended over 50 years and under six kings. Narratives of his ministry are recorded in 1 and 2 Kings and comprise some 18 episodes. Elisha was very much like Samuel, with gifts of knowledge, foresight, and a capacity to work miracles.

Naaman. Naaman was the army commander for Aram (Syria). The Aramaeans' king at this time (860-841 B.C.) was Ben-Hadad II. Earlier, in 1 Kings 11:23-25, God had raised up the Aramaeans' king and his army to be one of King Solomon's adversaries. Therefore, there had been a long history of hostility between the Aramaeans and Israel. God gave victory to the Aramaeans in their battles with Israel. It was under Naaman's leadership that many of these victories occurred (2 Kings 5:1).

BACKGROUND

One of the many advantages of being victorious in battle was slave captivity. It was common for the winners to take captives out of their enemies' land and make them slaves in their own land. During one of the Aramaeans' victories over Israel, a girl had been captured and brought to Naaman. He gave this girl to his wife to become her maidservant.

This humble Hebrew girl served in the home of Naaman, a successful and courageous warrior. Naaman held a great position and had found great favor in the king's eyes. He also had great wealth. But Naaman was a leper. In God's sovereignty, Naaman's leprosy and the faith of this Hebrew girl would lead to an opportunity for God to be glorified through the work of his prophet Elisha.

AT-A-GLANCE

1. Naaman Desires Healing from Leprosy
(2 Kings 5:1-5)
2. Naaman Receives the Prophet Elisha's
Prescription for Healing (vv. 9-15)

IN DEPTH

1. Naaman Desires Healing from Leprosy (2 Kings 5:1-5)

Naaman's success and great military achievements were overshadowed by his leprosy, although it had not yet incapacitated him from military service. Naaman, his family, and his friends probably feared that he would succumb to his leprosy and die.

This fear probably led his wife's servant to speak to her mistress about the matter. The servant was a Hebrew girl who had been captured during one of the Aramaeans' battles with Israel. Naaman had given her to his wife as a maidservant. The Hebrew servant told her mistress, "If only my master would see the prophet who is in Samaria! He would cure him of his leprosy" (v. 3, NIV). The young Hebrew maidservant knew that God's power worked through the prophet to heal others.

Naaman's wife told her husband about the prophet, and he quickly sought the king's approval to see the prophet in Samaria (v. 4). Naaman, being in good standing with the king, not only received approval to go, but he was given a letter to assist him in his trip to Samaria. The letter was addressed to the king of Israel requesting that Naaman be cured of leprosy (v. 6).

Naaman traveled to Samaria prepared to meet the prophet and be healed. He carried the letter from the king, 10 talents (750 lbs.) of silver, 6000 shekels (150 lbs.) of gold, and 10 sets of clothing (v. 5). Naaman carried the large sum of money assuming that he would have to directly or indirectly pay for his healing. He desperately wanted to be cured.

2. Naaman Receives the Prophet Elisha's Prescription for Healing (vv. 9-15)

After taking the letter to the king of Israel, Naaman arrived at the prophet Elisha's humble home in Samaria with his horses and chariots. Naaman stood at Elisha's door with great expectation. He waited for Elisha to come out, call upon God, and heal his leprosy (v. 11).

Naaman's expectations were shattered. Elisha did not come out to meet Naaman; instead, he sent a messenger. Elisha, no doubt, was not impressed with Naaman's status and wealth. Elisha's messenger gave Naaman this simple prescription for his healing: "Go and wash in Jordan seven times, and thy flesh shall come again to thee, and thou shalt be clean" (v. 10). Not only were Naaman's expectations shattered, but he was angry.

Naaman's anger stemmed from both the apparent lack of respect he received from Elisha and the seemingly ridiculous prescription for his healing. Why would Elisha tell Naaman to travel 20 miles to the Jordan River? Upon Naaman's arrival at the Jordan, he was to remove his clothes and wash himself seven times in the water. Of course, the cure did not lay in the water of the Jordan, but in Naaman's obedient faith. This prescription was to test his faith in God working through His prophet.

Naaman failed the first test. He was not only filled with rage, but he questioned the prescription given to him. Naaman asked, "Are not Abana and Pharpar, rivers of Damascus, better than all the waters of Israel? may I not wash in them, and be clean?" (v. 12) The rivers of Damascus were streams of great freshness and beauty, while the Jordan River was muddy and lacked beauty. The water of Jordan was inferior to the rivers in his hometown. Why would there be a cure at the river Jordan?

But the faith of Naaman's humble servants prevailed over Naaman's lack of obedient faith. The servants tenderly approached him with an astounding question: "My father, if the prophet had told you to do some great thing, would you not have done it? How much more, then, when he tells you, 'Wash and be cleansed'!" (v. 13, NIV). The servants challenged Naaman's actions. What harm would there be in obeying Elisha's simple prescription for healing? The servants' faith and reasoning were inarguable.

Naaman put aside his pride and acted upon his servants' faith and reasoning. He went down to the Jordan River and obeyed Elisha's prescription (v. 14a). As a result, Naaman was cleansed of leprosy. His flesh became soft and tender like a boy's. He then returned to the prophet Elisha. Before the man of God and "all his company," Naaman testified to the glory of God (v. 15a). Naaman's healing occurred as a result of his putting aside his pride, acting in obedient faith in God, and following God's instructions as given.

SEARCH THE SCRIPTURES

Read 2 Kings 5:1-5, 9-15 and match the action with the character who performed it.

1. He wrote a letter on Naaman's behalf to the king of Israel.

2. They challenged Naaman's response to Elisha's prescription for healing.

3. He was known as a prophet of God.

4. She told Naaman's wife about Elisha.

5. He was a great army commander with leprosy.

a. Elisha
b. King of Syria
c. Hebrew girl
d. Naaman
e. Naaman's servants

DISCUSS THE MEANING

1. What circumstance(s) could have led the Hebrew girl to speak of the prophet Elisha in Samaria at this time (2 Kings 5:2-3)? Discuss the importance of Naaman's obedience to the suggestion of a Hebrew servant girl.

2. What did Naaman take with him as he traveled to meet Elisha (vv. 5-6)? Did he equip himself with everything necessary for healing by the prophet? Why are faith, humility, and obedience to God's Word important to receive the blessings of God?

3. Do you think that Elisha's prescription for Naaman to wash himself "seven times" has a significant meaning (v. 10)? Discus the importance of Naaman's obedience to the instructions given by the prophet Elisha.

LESSON IN OUR SOCIETY

Healing services are often bursting at the seams with people expecting God to work through His servant to heal them. Despite the results of some healing services, Christians should demonstrate that our faith is in God for healing. When and if God chooses to use His servants to heal others, it's His choice, not man's choice. When God chooses to use human beings as His agents in physically, mentally, emotionally, or spiritually healing others, it's always for His glory.

MAKE IT HAPPEN

Read Isaiah 6:1-10. Consider Isaiah's response to being in God's presence. He responded in humility and was available to be used by God. Are you willing to humble yourself before God and say, "Here am I, God. Use me for Your glory"?

Start each day this coming week with this prayer to God: "Lord God, I'm not worthy to be used by You, but here I am; use me today for Your glory." Then be sensitive to God's leading throughout the day. At the end of the week, briefly write down the various ways God used you in the lives of others to glorify God.

FOLLOW THE SPIRIT

What God wants me to do:

_____

_____

REMEMBER YOUR THOUGHTS

Special insights I have learned:

_____

_____

MORE LIGHT ON THE TEXT
2 Kings 5:1-5, 9-15

The focus of the book of 2 Kings centers largely on the lives and activities of two of the most prominent prophets, Elijah and Elisha, under the rule of ungodly kings in Israel. Chapters 1 and 2 record the conclusion of Elijah's ministry and the beginning of Elisha's ministry. The book records the various miracles God performed through the ministry of the prophet Elisha. Among them is the healing of Naaman in chapter 5, which forms the basis for our study.

As we study this passage, we will see how faith and trust in God are rewarded and how vanity and arrogance are barriers to God's blessings. We will also see how simple obedience to the Word of God is the catalyst to receiving God's blessings and changing one's life.

1 Now Naaman, captain of the host of the king of Syria, was a great man with his master, and honourable, because by him the LORD had given deliverance unto Syria: he was also a mighty man in valour, but he was a leper.

Second Kings chapter 5 starts by introducing one of the major characters of the passage, Naaman. He is the commander, or captain, of the Syrian army under Ben-hadad the king (8:7). To understand Naaman's position in relation to the king, one might consider the Armed Forces Chief of Staff in relation to the U.S. President. Naaman occupied a very important position in the Syrian army and government.

The author of this book uses different adjectives to describe how important Naaman is to the king. He is the "captain of the host (army) of the king" (v. 1), which simply means that he is the commander of the armed forces. He is "a great (Heb. *gadowl*) man with his master," i.e., he is important. This greatness could also mean that Naaman and the king had a good relationship or that he was obedient to his king. It could also mean that Naaman was honorable and highly regarded in the country because of his achievements. Through Naaman, the Lord had given victory to Syria. As if all these honors were not enough, the author says that he was also a "valiant soldier" (v. 1, NIV). What the author seems to infer here is that all of these honors were not merely conferred on Naaman; he earned them. He was both strong in character and in physical strength—a good soldier.

Verse 1 ends with the phrase, "but he was a leper." The word "but" is important to the whole story. It brings to anti-climax the qualities of this man, Naaman, and places emphasis upon the story. It calls our attention to the word "leper". . . to what follows. The author is saying, "Although Naaman has all these qualities and attributes, he has a very serious flaw: He is a leper." A study of the disease will help us to understand its implication to the story.

The Hebrew word *tsara'ath* is used for various skin diseases. It is translated here as "leper" to identify the most dreadful disease one could have because it was contagious and incurable. Therefore, people with this disease were usually quarantined and isolated from society as a medical precaution. One of the symptoms of leprosy is the eating away of parts of the flesh, such as fingers and toes (see Numbers 12:12). A person with leprosy was to be identified by their torn clothes and the announcement of being "unclean" when he/she was in the streets. Having leprosy, therefore, was a very humiliating experience. That is why the author uses the word "but" to bring a contrast between this highly celebrated army "general" and his condition as a leper.

2 And the Syrians had gone out by companies, and had brought away captive out of the land of Israel a little maid; and she waited on Naaman's wife. 3 And she said to her mistress, Would God my Lord were with the prophet that is in Samaria! for he would recover him of his leprosy.

Verse 1 introduces us to Naaman, a notable and highly respected person. Verse 2, in contrast, introduces us to a "less important" person, but one who is an important character to the story. Namely, a "captive...little maid." She is so insignificant, according to human standards, that she is not even mentioned by name. She is only identified as a war captive, a slave girl, which places her in the lowest group of society.

Second, she is a "little maid," or "young girl" (NIV), which means she should be seen and not heard. In other words, her opinions, or suggestions, do not count. She does not even have the freedom or right to speak of matters of importance, especially related to the health of the "general." To wait on a commander's wife is a rare opportunity, and it is a position of honor and trust. To be a maid is on the one hand debasing, but to serve the wife of an army official is an elevation.

The girl speaks to her mistress about her master's illness. How she knew that he had this disease is not given in this story. It seems probable that the leprosy is still in the early stages of development but has progressed enough to be of great concern to Naaman's household. Maybe it had started to appear outwardly. It may have been rumored within the family and she heard about it, and everyone was concerned that it would soon come out in the open. At this time, it seems that

Naaman's servant girl has faith in the God of
Israel to heal her master.

the situation is grave. Naaman is in such a desperate position that he is ready to do anything.

This little girl, although a slave, has a good relationship with her masters and is treated well. She, therefore, wants to return the favor shown her. However, the greatest motivation is her confidence in Elisha and her faith in God. She must have heard of or seen the wonderful miracles performed by both Elijah and Elisha. She confidently says, "Would God my Lord were with the prophet that is in Samaria," i.e., "If only my master would see the prophet who is in Samaria" (NIV). The New American Standard Bible (NASB) translates it as, "I wish that my master were with the prophet who is in Samaria!" The phrase "Would God my Lord (master)" is a plea that could be read as, "I wish in the name of the Lord that my master would go before the prophet who is in Samaria." No matter the translation, what we see here is confidence and trust.

The word "with" literally means "before" and indicates that her master would appear before (or go to) the prophet in Samaria. The next phrase, "for he would recover him of his leprosy," qualifies this confidence and faith. The word "would" denotes assurance. Although she is confident in what the Lord can do, the choice is Naaman's. She is so sure of what God can do that she never

thinks that it might fail. Failure, of course, might mean danger for her. What she expresses is simple faith in the God of Israel. This is what God requires of us. Having heard of the miracles Elijah and Elisha performed previously, the little girl assures her mistress that Naaman's leprosy would be cured.

4 And one went in, and told his Lord, saying, Thus and thus said the maid that is of the land of Israel. 5 And the king of Syria said, Go to, go, and I will send a letter unto the king of Israel. And he departed, and took with him ten talents of silver, and six thousand pieces of gold, and ten changes of raiment.

The little girl's faith must have been persuasive—either that or Naaman is so desperate that he acts on the servant's advice. We suggest that both are the case. "And one went in, and told his Lord" refers to Naaman. He goes and reports to the king all that the girl from Israel says. Without hesitation, the king sends him to the king of Israel with a written note. The king's response, "Go to, go," or "By all means" (NIV), shows the urgency of the situation and how readily the king approves his mission. Apart from the relationship between the two as discussed above, Naaman's healing would be advantageous to the king. Losing him would affect the king's position, and other nations might take advantage of this.

Naaman departs for Israel armed with the king's letter and gifts for the king of Israel. The Bible records the amount: 10 talents of silver, 6,000 pieces of gold, and 10 changes of clothes. While it may be impossible to give a correct estimate of these gifts in today's currency given the changing inflation rate, suffice it to say the gifts were worth very much—between one and two million dollars in today's market.

5:9 So Naaman came with his horses and with his chariot, and stood at the door of the house of Elisha. 10 And Elisha sent a messenger unto him, saying, Go and wash in Jordan seven times, and thy flesh shall come again to thee, and thou shalt be clean.

Naaman, fully dressed in his military regalia, pompously arrives at the door of the house of

Elisha the prophet. He was accompanied by his bodyguards, horsemen and chariots, and a caravan loaded with presents. He is probably expecting a rousing fanfare to welcome him. He thinks that on hearing of his arrival, Elisha would hurry out to welcome him. This does not happen. Instead, he stands at the door and waits. The word "stood" in Hebrew is 'amad, which means "to stand, remain, or endure." That means that when Naaman arrives at the door (or probably at the gate), he waits there for a period of time. How long he has to wait is not revealed to us. He must have waited long enough to become upset (v. 11).

Elisha does not show the courtesy of going out to meet Naaman or inviting him in. Rather he sends a messenger to tell him to go down to the river Jordan and wash himself seven times (v. 10). It is significant to note here that he sends a messenger and not his servant Gehazi, whom we shall assume is his apprentice. The message to Naaman is simple and clear: "Go, wash yourself seven times in the Jordan, and your flesh will be restored and you will be cleansed" (NIV).

Is Elisha trying to humiliate Naaman? Or is Elisha so confident in the Lord he serves that he thinks it is unnecessary to go out to him? By not going out to Naaman, is Elisha trying to avoid receiving praise for himself, wanting rather, the glory to go to God? Is Elisha just following the leading of the Lord? The answers to the above questions are in the affirmative.

11 But Naaman was wroth, and went away, and said, Behold, I thought, He will surely come out to me, and stand, and call on the name of the LORD his God, and strike his hand over the place, and recover the leper. 12 Are not Abana and Pharpar, rivers of Damascus, better than all the waters of Israel? may I not wash in them, and be clean? So he turned and went away in a rage.

This treatment does not go well with Naaman. Disappointed that he is neither welcomed into the house nor met by Elisha at the gate, Naaman gets angry. He thinks that he is such a great man (as commander of the whole Syrian Army) that it would be an honor for Elisha to come out to him, lay hands on him, and pray; but Elisha thinks differently. As a man of God, Elisha follows the direction of the Lord.

In this account, the Lord is not only teaching the lesson of humility to Naaman, He is teaching people of all ages that He does not regard human prestige. He wants every human being to learn that His thoughts are not our thoughts and His ways are not our ways (see Isaiah 55:8-9), and that "God resisteth the proud, and giveth grace to the humble" (see 1 Peter 5:5; compare Proverbs 3:34). The word "wroth" (Heb. qatsaph) meaning "to be displeased" or "to fret oneself," is used to describe Naaman's disposition. He is so upset with what he sees as the disrespectful treatment he receives from Elisha that he decides to return home. Fuming with rage, he either talks aloud to himself or complains to his servants as he turns to go home. To him, it is better to remain leprous than receive such an insult. The use of the words "behold" and "surely" show how disappointed Naaman is that Elisha never bothered to see him. Note his expectations were that Elisha would definitely come out to him, stand before him, call on his God, lay his hand on him, and halt the disease. To add insult to injury, not only does Elisha fail to come out to see him and send a messenger to tell him what to do; he orders him to go and wash in the Jordan River. This is another blow to his ego.

Again, it does not make sense to him to have come all the way from Syria only to be asked to go and wash in the muddy Jordan River. He might as well have gone to Abana and Pharpar (rivers in Damascus, a province in Syria), which were better than all the rivers in Israel, or at least they were nearer to home. The more he thinks about it, the angrier he becomes. So he turns and goes away in "a rage" (Heb. chemah), i.e., furious, indignant wrath. Naaman's high hopes of showing off his riches and enriching whoever heals him are destroyed by the treatment he receives. Finally, he is humiliated in front of his servants who have great respect for him. No wonder he is in a great fever of rage and decides to return home.

13 And his servants came near, and spake unto him, and said, My father, if the prophet had bid thee do some great thing, wouldest thou not have done it? how much rather then, when he saith to thee, Wash, and be clean?

We note here the better judgment and wise counsel of his servants. They reason with him. His servants simply point out to him that if the prophet had asked him to do something greater, he would have done so peacefully; now see how much easier it is to dip seven times into the river and be clean. They must have asked, "Are you going away in anger without even trying what the prophet says would make you clean?" Going home, after taking the long trip from the north, without trying what he is asked to do, did not make sense. Their use of the term "father" shows the respect they have for him and implies a persuasive appeal for him to consider their suggestion. A look at the map would show that they would cross the Jordan River on their way home.

14 Then went he down, and dipped himself seven times in Jordan, according to the saying of the man of God: and his flesh came again like unto the flesh of a little child, and he was clean. 15 And he returned to the man of God, he and all his company, and came, and stood before him: and he said, Behold, now I know that there is no God in all the earth, but in Israel:

The servants' counsel pacifies the captain, and he decides to take their advice. Finally, and perhaps grudgingly, he obeys the man of God. He goes down to Jordan and washes seven times, according to the word of Elisha. He comes out clean, a changed man physically and emotionally.

Naaman's physical transformation was evident by the restoration of his skin: "his flesh came again like unto the flesh of a little child, and he was clean." Naaman's spiritual transformation was evident when he came and stood before Elisha and those who were with him and proclaimed in faith and humility, "Now I know that there is no God in all the world except in Israel" (v. 15a, NIV).

Obedience is the key that opens the door to the treasure of God's blessings. By simply obeying God's Word, we receive from Him all the things He has in store for us. God uses the foolish things of this world to confound the wise and chooses the weak things of this world to shame the strong (1 Corinthians 1:27, paraphrased NIV). Sometimes God may ask us to do things that make no sense, humanly speaking. All we need to do is exercise simple faith and humble obedience.

DAILY BIBLE READINGS

M: These Evil Things Defile a Person
Mark 7:17-23

T: Trap My Enemies in Their Pride
Psalm 59:10-17

W: God Will End Arrogant People's Pride
Isaiah 13:9-13

T: Naaman Hopes for a Cure
2 Kings 5:1-5a

F: Elisha Tells Naaman What to Do
2 Kings 5:5b-10

S: Naaman Is Cured
2 Kings 5:11-14

S: Naaman Accepts the God of Israel
2 Kings 5:15-19

Use the reference materials available in your *Precepts For Living* CD-ROM to find out more about the serious nature of leprosy.

TEACHING TIPS

February 20
Bible Study Guide 12

1. Words You Should Know

A. Born (Again) (John 3:3) *gennao* (Gk.)—Refers to the gracious act of God in conferring the nature and disposition of the children of God upon those who believe.

B. Spirit (v. 5) *pneuma* (Gk.)—This word primarily denotes the wind and is often used to refer to the Holy Spirit, which, like the wind, is invisible, non-material, and powerful.

2. Teacher Preparation

A. Pray for your students, especially those who have not accepted Christ as Saviour.

B. Read the BIBLE BACKGROUND and the DEVOTIONAL READING.

C. Study the FOCAL VERSES, IN DEPTH, and MORE LIGHT ON THE TEXT.

3. Starting the Lesson

Before the students enter the classroom, write the lesson title and the AT-A-GLANCE outline on the board.

4. Getting into the Lesson

A. Open the class with prayer. Thank God for His loving care this past week, and then focus on the LESSON AIM.

B. Pass out index cards or paper. Ask the students to write one paragraph explaining what it means to be born again.

C. Review the SEARCH THE SCRIPTURES questions.

D. Explain that in today's lesson you will encounter religious people who did not seek the Lord, and others who left everything to seek Him.

E. Assign three students to read the FOCAL VERSES according to the AT-A-GLANCE outline, another to read the BACKGROUND section, and another to read THE PEOPLE, PLACES, AND TIMES.

5. Relating the Lesson to Life

A. Call on students to answer the SEARCH THE SCRIPTURES questions. This will help reinforce the reading from the FOCAL VERSES.

B. Use the DISCUSS THE MEANING questions to help the students think through and apply the truths they have learned today.

C. Use the LESSON IN OUR SOCIETY section to help the students grasp the wider implications of these truths.

6. Arousing Action

A. Review the MAKE IT HAPPEN section. Ask your students to give their suggestions, then challenge the students to put them into practice.

B. Assign the DAILY BIBLE READINGS as homework for the next week.

C. Ask the students if they have any prayer requests they would like to share with the class.

WORSHIP GUIDE

For the Superintendent or Teacher
Theme: Overcoming Uncertainty
Theme Song: "Born Again"
Scripture: Psalm 91:1-6
Song:" You Have a Gift from God"
Meditation: Father, I thank You for loving me so much that You would sacrifice Your only begotten Son for my salvation. Help me to live worthy of Your sacrifice.

FEB 20TH

OVERCOMING UNCERTAINTY

Bible Background • JOHN 3:1-21
Printed Text • JOHN 3:1-16
Devotional Reading • JOHN 3:17-21

LESSON AIM

By the end of the lesson, the students will be able to relate the story of Nicodemus' visit with Jesus; understand that the initial step in restoring our relationship with God is based on faith, and determine to accept Christ's work on the Cross as payment for their sins or renew their commitment of faith in Christ.

KEEP IN MIND

"Jesus answered, Verily, verily, I say unto thee, Except a man be born of water and of the Spirit, he cannot enter into the kingdom of God. That which is born of the flesh is flesh; and that which is born of the Spirit is spirit" (John 3:5-6).

LESSON OVERVIEW

LESSON AIM
KEEP IN MIND
FOCAL VERSES
IN FOCUS
THE PEOPLE, PLACES, AND TIMES
BACKGROUND
AT-A-GLANCE
IN DEPTH
SEARCH THE SCRIPTURES
DISCUSS THE MEANING
LESSON IN OUR SOCIETY
MAKE IT HAPPEN
FOLLOW THE SPIRIT
REMEMBER YOUR THOUGHTS
MORE LIGHT ON THE TEXT
DAILY BIBLE READINGS

FOCAL VERSES

John 3:1 There was a man of the Pharisees, named Nicodemus, a ruler of the Jews:

2 The same came to Jesus by night, and said unto him, Rabbi, we know that thou art a teacher come from God: for no man can do these miracles that thou doest, except God be with him.

3 Jesus answered and said unto him, Verily, verily, I say unto thee, Except a man be born again, he cannot see the kingdom of God.

4 Nicodemus saith unto him, How can a man be born when he is old? can he enter the second time into his mother's womb, and be born?

5 Jesus answered, Verily, verily, I say unto thee, Except a man be born of water and of the Spirit, he cannot enter into the kingdom of God.

6 That which is born of the flesh is flesh; and that which is born of the Spirit is spirit.

7 Marvel not that I said unto thee, Ye must be born again.

8 The wind bloweth where it listeth, and thou hearest the sound thereof, but canst not tell whence it cometh, and whither it goeth: so is every one that is born of the Spirit.

9 Nicodemus answered and said unto him, How can these things be?

10 Jesus answered and said unto him, Art thou a master of Israel, and knowest not these things?

11 Verily, verily, I say unto thee, We speak that we do know, and testify that we have seen; and ye receive not our witness.

12 If I have told you earthly things, and ye believe not, how shall ye believe, if I tell you of heavenly things?

13 And no man hath ascended up to heaven, but he that came down from heaven, even the Son of man which is in heaven.

14 And as Moses lifted up the serpent in the wilderness, even so must the Son of man be lifted up:

15 That whosoever believeth in him should not perish, but have eternal life.

16 For God so loved the world, that he gave his only begotten Son, that whosoever believeth in him should not perish, but have everlasting life.

IN FOCUS

Brother Williams is a gifted Christian who

serves on his church's Board of Trustees and teaches a Sunday School class. He and his family hardly ever miss a church service and love to entertain in their home. Brother Williams' love and respect for his wife is evident to all who meet them. However, this was not always the case.

Brother Williams is a recovering alcoholic who used to frequently beat his wife and children. He also considered himself somewhat of a ladies' man, frequently neglected his family, and squandered his paycheck while partying with other women. He would sometimes be absent from home for days at a time while engaging in indecent activities.

After years of tolerating her husband's behavior, Mrs. Williams had finally had enough. One weekend, Mr. Williams arrived home drunk as usual and found his wife, children, and all their possessions gone. When he found out where his family had gone, he demanded that they return. When this failed, he pleaded with his wife to come back, promising that he would turn over a new leaf. Still, Mrs. Williams refused to come home and filed for divorce.

Mr. Williams was miserable without his family. He began to drink even more than before. One of his coworkers noticed his downward spiral and invited him out to lunch. Over lunch, the two men discussed Bro. Williams' problem. He confessed to being unable to turn his life around and did not know where he could find help.

His coworker, a devoted Christian, told him about the drug habit he used to have. Like Mr. Williams, his life had also spun out of control. Then Mr. Williams asked him how he managed to turn things around. He told him about the life-changing relationship he had with Jesus. When he had finished his story, he asked Mr. Williams if he would like to become a new person in Christ. Brother Williams jumped at the opportunity and right there in the restaurant he gave his life to Christ. He no longer drinks; he and his family are reunited and happy.

Brother Williams did not just turn over a "new leaf." He actually became a new person in Christ. In today's lesson, Jesus explains to a religious scholar named Nicodemus what it means to be born again.

THE PEOPLE, PLACES, AND TIMES

Nicodemus. Nicodemus' name means "victory of the people." He was a wealthy Pharisee and a member of the Sanhedrin, Israel's ruling religious body (John 3:1-9; 7:50; 19:39). There had been no direct voice from God in Israel since the prophet Malachi hundreds of years ago. Nicodemus, a man of spiritual perception, sought out Jesus because he realized Jesus was sent from God. He may have had such a hunger for the truth that he decided not to wait until morning but came to visit Jesus at his first opportunity.

BACKGROUND

At the beginning of Jesus' ministry, John presents two events that reveal the changing and cleansing power Jesus offers to the world. The first event was a wedding in the small village of Cana. Jesus, His mother, and His disciples were present at the celebration. During the wedding, the hosts ran out of wine for the guests. Mary, Jesus' mother, asked her son to help out, and He replied that "mine hour is not yet come" (John 2:4). John repeats this phrase several times throughout his narrative (7:6, 30; 8:20). On the day of His death, Jesus prayed to His Father and the phrase then became, "Father the hour is come."

Jesus agreed to Mary's request and changed water into wine. This is the first miracle of Jesus' ministry. The fact that it took place at a wedding is striking because the intimate relationship between God and His people is often portrayed as a marriage (Jeremiah 3:14) and the final act of human history is the marriage between Christ, the Lamb, and His bride, the Church. After the first miracle, Jesus performed many other miracles in Cana that revealed various aspects of His person. The purpose of these "signs" was to encourage the faith of His disciples.

Sometime after the wedding feast, Jesus moved His headquarters to Capernaum. However, shortly after arriving in the city the time of the Passover came, and Jesus and His followers made the pilgrimage to Jerusalem. The Passover, which celebrates the Israelites' deliverance from Egyptian bondage, is Israel's greatest festival. Every adult male within a 15-mile radius of Jerusalem was required by law to come to Jerusalem for the holy day.

After arriving in Jerusalem, Jesus went to the temple to worship. The temple was the central place of worship for the Jews, and its ground was considered sacred. Yet the temple priest allowed merchants to turn the outer court, where Gentiles were allowed to worship, into a loud, competitive marketplace. Passion for His Father's house welled up in Jesus and He struck out in anger, turning over tables and driving the merchants from the temple with a whip. This act of cleansing would occur again near the end of Jesus' life on earth.

The Jewish religious leaders recognized the outburst as a messianic act, and they demanded a sign to verify His authority. Jesus responded to their request with His first prophecy of His death: "Destroy this temple, and in three days I will raise it up" (John 2:19). After this, Jesus performed many miracles in Jerusalem, and many believed in Him. The new kingdom age had been demonstrated in two public celebrations—a small-town wedding and a national holy day. To gain entrance into this new kingdom, one must be changed through new birth and cleansed through the water of God's Word and the Holy Spirit.

AT-A-GLANCE

1. Question One: What Must I Do?
(John 3:1-3)
2. Question Two: Can a Man Be Reborn?
(vv. 4-8)
3. Question Three: How Can This Be?
(vv. 9-16)

IN DEPTH

1. Question One: What Must I Do? (John 3:1-3)

One of the people impressed by Jesus' acts was a Pharisee named Nicodemus. John describes Nicodemus as a Pharisee, or "separated one." The Pharisees were an elitist religious group who constantly studied Scripture and tried to live out every detail of the law. As a "ruler of the Jews" (John 3:1), Nicodemus was a member of the Sanhedrin, the

religious body that controlled the religious life of Israel.

Nicodemus waited until after dark to approach Jesus. This may be because he was afraid of what the Pharisees would think about his visit to Jesus. Or, perhaps it was because there were too many people clamoring for Jesus' attention during the day. Or, as one observer has noted, it was customary to visit busy people very early in the morning before daybreak. Whatever the reason, Nicodemus must be given credit for his bold visit. Because he was a Pharisee and a member of the Sanhedrin, this open conversation with the upstart Jesus would be frowned upon by his peers.

Nicodemus initiated the conversation by addressing Jesus as "Rabbi" (v. 2), a title of deep respect. This learned man would only use this title if he actually believed he could learn something from this new teacher. Then he acknowledged Jesus' divine calling as a teacher: "We know that thou art a teacher come from God" (v. 2). The use of the word *we* may imply that Nicodemus was speaking for others who may or may not have been present. Nicodemus based his assumption about Jesus' divine calling on the miracles Jesus had performed.

Jesus knew the question that compelled Nicodemus to seek Him out (see John 2:24-25). Before Nicodemus could give voice to his question, Jesus answered him: "Verily, verily, I say unto thee, Except a man be born again, he cannot see the kingdom of God" (v. 3). The phrase "born again" can also be translated as "cometh from above" (see 3:31). This description makes it evident that spiritual regeneration is a birth from God.

New birth, or regeneration, is one of the fundamental doctrines of Christian faith. The new birth involves a re-creation and transformation of the person. Those who are "born again" are set free from the bondage of sin and no longer make sin a habitual practice in their lives. Without this new birth, no one can enter the kingdom of God, that is, receive eternal life and salvation through Jesus Christ.

2. Question Two: Can a Man Be Reborn? (vv. 4-8)

Nicodemus clearly thought Jesus was referring

to a physical process since he asks Jesus, "How can a man be born when he is old?" (v. 4). However, Jesus was speaking of spiritual matters, and Nicodemus was thinking in earthly terms. The poor man was completely baffled by Jesus' answer, so he continued: "Can he enter the second time into his mother's womb, and be born?" (v. 4). Although Nicodemus was well-versed in Old Testament Scripture, his thoughts were limited to the physical world. Nicodemus imagined new birth from a physical perspective, and Jesus' response made no earthly sense to him.

Jesus made it clear to Nicodemus that He was not speaking of physical rebirth. "Except a man be born of water and of the Spirit, he cannot enter into the kingdom of God" (v. 5). Many interpretations have been suggested for the meaning of water in this verse. Some believe it refers to baptism as a requirement for salvation. However, this interpretation contradicts many other passages, such as Ephesians 2:8-9. Others believe that it refers to natural birth, meaning a person must be born a first time physically by water, and a second time spiritually. Many believe the water means the Word of God, as in John 15:3. Still others believe the water is symbolic of the Holy Spirit. Whatever interpretation one prefers, one thing is clear: New birth is from God through Christ, by the Holy Spirit.

To drive His point home, Jesus told the bewildered Pharisee, "That which is born of the flesh is flesh; and that which is born of the Spirit is spirit" (John 3:6). Understanding that Nicodemus still did not fully understand His teaching, Jesus used a common element to explain a spiritual truth. In His metaphor, Jesus compared the new birth to the wind. The Greek word *pneuma* means both wind and Spirit. Jesus explained that just as we cannot completely explain or control the wind, the ways of the Holy Spirit are beyond our complete comprehension and control. The unseen wind is identified by its activity; likewise, the Holy Spirit is also identified by His activity in the lives of believers.

Adam became a living creature when God breathed into his nostrils the breath (*pneuma*) of life (see Genesis 2:7). In that same way, believers become "new creatures" when God infuses us

with His Spirit (*pneuma*). Our old lives are passed away as if they never existed (see 2 Corinthians 5:17). We are not reformed or rehabilitated; we are re-created. Believers have not merely turned over a new leaf; we have a completely new beginning. We serve a new master, and we live a new lifestyle.

In response to Nicodemus' questions, Jesus told him specifically and directly, "Ye must be born again" (John 3:7). The call of Jesus comes to each of us in the same way, specifically and directly. Surrendering one's life to Christ is a personal choice that each individual must make.

3. Question Three: How Can This Be? (vv. 9-16)

The apostle Paul once said, "The man without the Spirit does not accept the things that come from the Spirit of God, for they are foolishness to him, and he cannot understand them, because they are spiritually discerned" (1 Corinthians 2:14, NIV). Perhaps this helps to explain the difficulty Nicodemus was having in understanding and accepting Jesus' teaching. Nicodemus now understood that the new birth Christ was talking about came from God, but he could not accept what Jesus told him. He asked, "How can these things be?" (John 3:9).

Here, one can almost detect a note of sadness in Jesus' reply to Nicodemus' question. Nicodemus was a learned scholar who had dedicated his life to the study of Scripture. He was a teacher of the people, yet he could not grasp this basic doctrine of the faith.

Jesus mildly rebuked Nicodemus for doubt. He assured the Pharisee that "we speak [what] we do know, and testify [to what] we have seen." Perhaps Jesus included the disciples by the use of the word *we*. Then Jesus asked Nicodemus a rhetorical question: "If I have told you earthly things, and ye believe not, how shall ye believe, if I tell you of heavenly things?" (v. 12). If Nicodemus could not accept the basic teaching of redemption, he would never be able to understand the deeper mysteries of God.

To prove His point, Jesus made an astounding statement: "And no man hath ascended up to heaven, but he that came down from heaven, even the Son of man which is in heaven" (v. 13). Jesus is saying that no man has been to heaven except the Son of man who came down from heaven. Here Jesus is openly declaring that He came down from heaven to reveal heavenly truths (1:14).

To clarify His identity and explain the meaning of His coming down from heaven, Jesus referred to an incident that Nicodemus was certainly aware of. Shortly before the Israelites entered the Promised Land, they again complained about their situation. The Lord sent venomous snakes among them that bit the people, and many died. Then the Israelites repented of their sin. God then commanded Moses to fashion a bronze serpent and put it on a pole. Anyone who looked up to the serpent would be saved by this simple act of faith (see Numbers 21:4-9). In that same way, Jesus came down from heaven to be lifted up on a pole (cross). Whoever will look to the Cross and accept Jesus' sacrifice as an act of faith will be saved.

Nicodemus had spent his life studying and strictly trying to observe the most minute details of the law. Now Jesus was telling him that entrance into God's kingdom was not earned through works. Jesus' explanation of God's loving-kindness is the most well-known and cherished verse in all of Scripture: "For God so loved the world, that he gave his only begotten Son, that whosoever believeth in him should not perish, but have everlasting life" (John 3:16).

This verse reveals God's heart and His purpose. It explains the "breadth, and length, and depth, and height" of God's love (Ephesians 3:18). God's love is so wide that it embraces all persons in "the world." It is so long that it reaches out to "whosoever." The depth of His love is shown by what He was willing to sacrifice in our behalf—His "only begotten Son." His love lifts His people to new heights, granting us "everlasting life" in heaven and more abundant life on earth.

The story of Jesus' conversation with Nicodemus explains that Jesus did not leave heaven and come to earth to condemn lost souls. He came to save the world. However, those who fail to accept the person and work of Christ condemn themselves. It is often difficult for unbelievers to accept the teachings of Christ. The ways of God

are impossible to grasp unless the Holy Spirit reveals them. Taking the first step to spiritual rebirth is not an intellectual decision; it must be based on faith.

SEARCH THE SCRIPTURES

1. What religious party did Nicodemus belong to, and what religious body was he a part of (John 3:1)?

2. What convinced Nicodemus that Jesus was a teacher sent from God (v. 2)?

3. What are the two elements necessary to enter the kingdom of heaven (v. 5)?

4. Jesus used an analogy to explain the new birth to Nicodemus. To what earthly element did He compare the Holy Spirit (v. 8)?

5. What precious gift did God give to humanity that demonstrates the depth of His love for us (v. 16)?

DISCUSS THE MEANING

1. Nicodemus could have sent assistants to question Jesus, but instead he made a personal visit to learn the truth from Jesus Himself. Does this say anything about the importance of our personal time of devotion, Bible study, and prayer?

2. Jesus compared His ministry to the serpent that Moses raised up for the Israelites during their desert wanderings. What is the spiritual relationship between Jesus' ministry and the events of Numbers 21?

3. Jesus said that "the Son of Man [must] be lifted up: that whosoever believeth in him should not perish, but have eternal life" (John 3:14b-15). Describe the importance of our faith in Jesus Christ.

LESSON IN OUR SOCIETY

According to several recent surveys, most citizens consider America to be a Christian nation. Most Americans profess a belief in God and in His Son, Jesus Christ. Yet this nation is one of the most morally corrupt nations on the earth. How do we reconcile our belief in God and Christ with our deeds? Many people think that belief is nothing more than intellectual agreement. How can true believers demonstrate to the masses that true belief means to place one's complete trust and confidence in Christ and to give Him absolute control over our present plans and eternal destiny?

MAKE IT HAPPEN

We must come to God in faith, especially when we have questions or are uncertain. Hebrews 11:6 says, "But without faith it is impossible to please him: for he that cometh to God must believe that he is, and that he is a rewarder of them that diligently seek him." This week, seek out the answers to some questions that you may have as you study God's Word. Remember that God rewards those who seek Him.

FOLLOW THE SPIRIT

What God wants me to do:

_____

_____

REMEMBER YOUR THOUGHTS

Special insights I have learned:

_____

_____

MORE LIGHT ON THE TEXT

John 3:1-16

1 There was a man of the Pharisees, named Nicodemus, a ruler of the Jews:

The Pharisees were regarded as the most devout keepers of the law among the Jews. Thus, they sought to guard the standards and judge the actions of the Jewish community. By the first century A.D., the Pharisees were the most popular of the three main Jewish sects. The other two sects were the Essenes and the Sadducees. Although Pharisees were extremely detailed in all matters of the law, their religion was often an outward show based on self-righteousness. Throughout Jesus' ministry, the Pharisees were bitter enemies of our Lord and sought to destroy His influence among the people.

The phrase "ruler of the Jews" means that Nicodemus also served on the Sanhedrin Council, which was composed of seventy priests, elders, scribes, and the high priest. Thus Nicodemus was a very powerful and educated man.

2 The same came to Jesus by night, and said unto him, Rabbi, we know that thou art a teacher come from God: for no man can do these miracles that thou doest, except God be with him.

Under the cover of darkness, this man of religious authority sought Jesus out. He addressed Jesus as "Rabbi," a title of honor used by the Jews to address doctors of the law and distinguished religious teachers. By using this title, Nicodemus was giving honor and recognition to the divine authority of Jesus' teachings and signs that He was performing.

The "we" whom Nicodemus speaks for is unclear. It would appear that he was speaking for the Pharisees and/or the Sanhedrin Council. But the behavior of the Pharisees would seem to oppose any notion that they sincerely believed Jesus' work was God-inspired. Nicodemus was more likely referring to a group of Pharisees who were beginning to believe in Jesus. It is difficult to judge the sincerity of Nicodemus' statement.

Some have suggested that this could have been just a method of entrapment, as described by the other Gospel writers when referring to the Pharisees. If so, Nicodemus's heart was melted as he dialogued with the Master Teacher.

3 Jesus answered, and said unto him, Verily, verily, I say unto thee, Except a man be born again, he cannot see the kingdom of God.

Verse 3 begins with the words: "Jesus answered." The Greek word translated as "answered" (*apokrinomai*, **ap-ok-ree'-nom-ahee**) means to answer a question or to speak in response to something that is said or done. Nicodemus had not yet asked a question; however, something caused Jesus to give an answer. It may have been Nicodemus' statement of faith, "we know that thou art a teacher come from God," or it may have been that Jesus understood the true question that was in his heart. In either case, Jesus gives the following answer: "I tell you the truth, no one can see the kingdom of God unless he is born again" (v. 3, NIV).

The phrase "kingdom of God" denotes Christ's authority and rule, and all of the blessings and advantages available to those who are subjects of God's kingdom through faith in Christ. This truth was a radically new concept. Many thought that being a Jew by birth was to be born into the kingdom because of God's covenant with Moses and the Children of Israel. But what is born of physical heritage is physical, and what is born of the Spirit is spiritual (cf. v. 6; see also Galatians 3:26-29).

4 Nicodemus saith unto him, How can a man be born when he is old? can he enter the second time into his mother's womb, and be born?

Nicodemus has come to Jesus to learn more about His doctrines; however, the Lord answers him with a statement about the necessity of new birth. Nicodemus' response was a natural and logical response. How else is anyone born, except through their mother's womb? And it is certainly not possible to enter there again, especially as an old man! So Nicodemus asks his first question. The word "how" is the Greek word *pos,* which means "by what means," "after what manner," or "in what way."

5 Jesus answered, Verily, verily, I say unto thee, Except a man be born of water and of the Spirit, he cannot enter into the kingdom of God.

To enter God's kingdom requires a new beginning, which Jesus describes as new birth. The metaphor of birth is used here to signal the beginning of life. Therefore, to be "born again" indicates the beginning of new (eternal) life from above.

To be born of water is the natural birth. The birth of the child is preceded by a rush of water, as the water sac, which nourished and protected it from its beginning, bursts forth. It is the way of all humans. To be born of the Spirit was a different matter. This has to come from heaven. But Jesus did not say how this was to be done. Perhaps one must look back to John's statement in 1:12-13: "to them gave he power to become the sons of God. . .Which were born, not of blood, nor of the will of the flesh, nor of the will of man, but of God." This new birth by the Spirit of God gives us membership in the family of God and entrance to His kingdom.

6 That which is born of the flesh is flesh; and that which is born of the Spirit is spirit.

The Greek word for "flesh" (*sarx*) denotes fallen human nature apart from divine influence.

Nicodemus questions Jesus on the new birth.

This word is also translated as "carnal" (see 1 Corinthians 3:3). The Bible teaches that the flesh is prone to sin and selfishness and is therefore in opposition to the Spirit of God (Romans 8:5-9). Being "in the flesh" means being unrenewed; to live "according to the flesh" is to live and act sinfully (Romans 6:9; 7:5; Ephesians 2:3).

Flesh cannot enter into the kingdom of God. The flesh belongs to the kingdom of this world, but the spirit belongs to heaven. Flesh and spirit do not share the same realm; one is temporal, the other eternal (see 1 Corinthians 15:50).

7 Marvel not that I said unto thee, Ye must be born again.

In Psalm 51:5, David acknowledges, "Behold, I was shapen in iniquity; and in sin did my mother conceive me." In verse 10, he asks: "Create in me a clean heart, O God; and renew a right spirit within me." Like David, we each have inherited a sin nature from Adam (cf. Romans 5:12). Similarly, in John 3:7 it is as if Jesus is saying to Nicodemus, "Do not be surprised that something drastic must happen to transform the human nature."

The word "must" (Gk. *dei*) indicates that the new birth is an absolute necessity. Our God represents holiness in the highest sense (cf. Isaiah 6:3; Revelation 15:4). To enter His kingdom and become His children, we must be radically transformed (see 1 Peter 1:16; Hebrews 12:14)—we, who have been "born of the flesh," must be "born of the Spirit" (John 3:6-8).

8 The wind bloweth where it listeth, and thou hearest the sound thereof, but canst not tell whence it cometh, and whither it goeth: so is every one that is born of the Spirit.

In Greek as well as in Hebrew, the same word (*pneuma*) is used for both "spirit" and "wind." The wind cannot be controlled because God directs it. Though the source of the wind is invisible, the effect, or evidence, of its activity is plain. So it is with everyone born of the Spirit.

9 Nicodemus answered and said unto him, How can these things be?

Perhaps Nicodemus was questioning how one can become born of the Spirit. Jesus did not explain how this might be achieved, only that it is a requirement for entering the kingdom of God. Another possibility is that Nicodemus, as a Pharisee, who regulated Israel's worship standards, was concerned about the apparent freedom of those born of the Spirit. How could such freedom be permitted? Unregulated lives and worship practices might endanger the established religious system. After all, their history was full of such apostasies.

10 Jesus answered and said unto him, Art thou a master of Israel, and knowest not these things?

Here, Jesus uses the word "master" (Gk. *didaskalos*, **did-as'-kal-os**) to describe Nicodemus as one who is expertly qualified to teach, or who thinks that he is. The *New International Version* renders this verse as Jesus saying to him, "You are Israel's teacher and you do not understand these things?"

How could Nicodemus teach what he does not understand himself? He could not. Thus the people would never find out this crucial truth from the teachings of the Pharisees.

11 Verily, verily, I say unto thee, We speak that we do know, and testify that we have seen; and ye receive not our witness.

Nicodemus—a prominent Pharisee, a member of the Sanhedrin Council, a doctor of the Jewish law, and a spiritual leader—did not know these things. However, Jesus makes it clear that He and His followers know the truth through firsthand experience (John 7:16; 8:38; 1 John 1:3). Yet Nicodemus and the Jewish authorities refused to believe them.

12 If I have told you earthly things, and ye believe not, how shall ye believe, if I tell you of heavenly things?

What was Jesus referring to when He talked about "earthly things" (Gk. *epigeios*, **ep-ig'-i-os**), meaning the things that occur on earth? It is likely that Jesus is speaking of His analogies related to birth, wind, and water. The phrase "heavenly things" (Gk. *epouranios*, **ep-oo-ran'-ee-os**) refers to things that exist or take place in heaven.

The word "believe" (Gk. *pisteuo*, **pist-yoo'-o**) means to think or be persuaded that something is true; to place confidence, conviction, and trust in something or someone. This word is used in John 3:12, 15, and 16 to identify a critical requirement. If Nicodemus would not believe, trust, or rely on Jesus' explanation of mere earthly things, how could he possibly believe, trust, and rely upon the truth about the more important heavenly things associated with the kingdom of God?

13 And no man hath ascended up to heaven, but he that came down from heaven, even the Son of man which is in heaven.

Jesus is more than qualified to reveal the truth about heavenly things because He alone "came down from heaven," has "ascended up to heaven," and "is in heaven" (see John 6:38; 16-28; Mark 16:19; Ephesians 4:10).

The phrase "Son of man" appears in the Old Testament primarily to specify a member of humanity (cf. Psalm 8:4). It was also used to refer to the prophet in the book of Ezekiel. Later in the apocalyptic book of Daniel, one sees a new development in the use of the phrase. The "Son of man" takes on the character of a divine agent who will carry out judgment and deliverance (see Daniel 7:13).

In the New Testament, John the Baptist testified

that Jesus is the Son of God (John 1:34). Also, he stated that this "Son" was the Word become flesh (1:14). Moreover, this Word was in the beginning with God, and was God (1:1). Therefore, Jesus is the Word of God, who became flesh and dwelt in the world as a man, the "Son of man." The Word of God is the Son of God who became the Son of man, our Lord Jesus Christ.

14 And as Moses lifted up the serpent in the wilderness, even so must the Son of man be lifted up: 15 That whosoever believeth in him should not perish, but have eternal life.

In the wilderness when the Israelites murmured against God, God sent fiery (poisonous) serpents among the people to bite them, and many Israelites died. When the people repented, the Lord told Moses to make a bronze serpent and set it upon a pole. Then if anyone who was bitten would look at that bronze serpent, they would live (Numbers 21).

Our just and merciful God provided a means of salvation for a disobedient people so that they might survive divine judgment.

The phrase "lifted up" is translated from the Greek word *hupsoo* (**hoop-so'-o**), which means "to lift up on high" or "to exalt"; both definitions apply in this verse. Jesus was lifted up on the Cross of Calvary to become the source of salvation for all who will look to Him in faith (John 12:32). In addition, Jesus Christ should be exalted as Saviour and Lord in the heart and life of every believer (2 Peter 3:18), and He will ultimately be exalted in all the earth (Philippians 2:8-11). The One who suffered death for us is the source of life for all who believe.

16 For God so loved the world, that he gave his only begotten Son, that whosoever believeth in him should not perish, but have everlasting life.

John 3:16 is one of the most beloved verses in all of Scripture. However, in this study, we must also remember that it is found in the context of a conversation between Jesus and Nicodemus.

Out of the darkness of night, under the shadow of uncertainty, Nicodemus came to Jesus, the Light of the world. It is in John 3:16 that Nicodemus (and each of us) finds the answer: God takes away our sins and grants us new birth, or "everlasting life," because of His unmerited love for us, which is manifested by the sacrifice of His Son and our Saviour Jesus Christ.

DAILY BIBLE READINGS

M: You Have Been Born Anew
1 Peter 1:18-23
T: Born of God, Children of God
1 John 2:29—3:5
W: Born of God, Conquer the World
1 John 5:1-5
T: How Can I Be Born Again?
John 3:1-5
F: How Can These Things Be?
John 3:6-10
S: God So Loved the World
John 3:11-16
S: Jesus Came to Save the World
John 3:17-21

Find out more about the meaning of the word *believe* by using the resources on your *Precepts For Living* CD-ROM.

TEACHING TIPS

February 27
Bible Study Guide 13

1. Words You Should Know

A. Samaria (John 4:7) *Samariea* (Gk.)—Home to the 10 tribes of Israel before their dispersion by the Assyrians.

B. Prophet (v. 19) *prophetes* (Gk.)—One specially commissioned by God to make known His will to humankind or one who has God's "words in his mouth" (Deuteronomy 18:18).

2. Teacher Preparation

A. Pray for the students in your class, asking God to open their hearts to today's lesson.

B. Read and study the FOCAL VERSES, paying attention to the Lord's approach to the woman at the well.

C. Carefully review the Bible Study Guide, making notes for clarification.

D. Share a personal thought with the class about an encounter with racism. How did it make you feel?

3. Starting the Lesson

A. Before the class arrives, write the words *Samaria* and *prophet* on the board.

B. After the students arrive and are settled, lead the class in prayer. Pray specifically for godly insights on the lesson and blessings on the lives of the students.

4. Getting into the Lesson

A. Ask volunteers to read IN FOCUS and then spend time in discussion about what the story means.

B. Ask volunteers to read THE PEOPLE, PLACES, AND TIMES and BACKGROUND sections.

C. Ask the students to read the FOCAL VERSES together and then have a student read the corresponding IN DEPTH section. Allow time for discussion between each section.

5. Relating the Lesson to Life

A. Spend time answering the questions in the DISCUSS THE MEANING section.

B. Ask if any student has an insight that he/she would like to share regarding today's lesson.

6. Arousing Action

A. Read the LESSON IN OUR SOCIETY section to the class. Ask the class to share their personal encounters with racism.

B. Direct the students to the MAKE IT HAPPEN section and discuss it in class.

C. As a review, tell the students to complete the FOLLOW THE SPIRIT and REMEMBER YOUR THOUGHTS sections during the week.

D. End the class with prayer.

WORSHIP GUIDE

For the Superintendent or Teacher
Theme: Overcoming Prejudice
Theme Song: "He Looked Beyond My Faults"
Scripture: Galatians 3:28
Song: "What a Friend We Have in Jesus"
Meditation: Holy Father, You created us in Your image that we might one day shine brighter than the sun. Thank You for bringing us all together through the blood of Your Son—Jesus Christ.

FEB 27TH

OVERCOMING PREJUDICE

Bible Background • JOHN 4:1-42
Printed Text • JOHN 4:7-10, 19-26
Devotional Reading • JOHN 4:35-42

LESSON AIM

By the end of the lesson, the students will understand that God is no respecter of persons, and that He will go to great lengths to affirm the worth and dignity of each individual.

KEEP IN MIND

"There is neither Jew nor Greek, there is neither bond nor free, there is neither male nor female: for ye are all one in Christ Jesus" (Galatians 3:28).

FOCAL VERSES

John 4:7 There cometh a woman of Samaria to draw water: Jesus saith unto her, Give me to drink.

8 (For his disciples were gone away unto the city to buy meat.)

9 Then saith the woman of Samaria unto him, How is it that thou, being a Jew, askest drink of me, which am a woman of Samaria? for the Jews have no dealings with the Samaritans.

10 Jesus answered and said unto her, If thou knewest the gift of God, and who it is that saith to thee, Give me to drink; thou wouldest have asked of him, and he would have given thee living water.

4:19 The woman saith unto him, Sir, I perceive that thou art a prophet.

20 Our fathers worshipped in this mountain; and ye say, that in Jerusalem is the place where men ought to worship.

LESSON OVERVIEW

LESSON AIM
KEEP IN MIND
FOCAL VERSES
IN FOCUS
THE PEOPLE, PLACES, AND TIMES
BACKGROUND
AT-A-GLANCE
IN DEPTH
SEARCH THE SCRIPTURES
DISCUSS THE MEANING
LESSON IN OUR SOCIETY
MAKE IT HAPPEN
FOLLOW THE SPIRIT
REMEMBER YOUR THOUGHTS
MORE LIGHT ON THE TEXT
DAILY BIBLE READINGS

21 Jesus saith unto her, Woman, believe me, the hour cometh, when ye shall neither in this mountain, nor yet at Jerusalem, worship the Father.

22 Ye worship ye know not what: we know what we worship: for salvation is of the Jews.

23 But the hour cometh, and now is, when the true worshippers shall worship the Father in spirit and in truth: for the Father seeketh such to worship him.

24 God is a Spirit: and they that worship him must worship him in spirit and in truth.

25 The woman saith unto him, I know that Messias cometh, which is called Christ: when he is come, he will tell us all things.

26 Jesus saith unto her, I that speak unto thee am he.

IN FOCUS

Rasheeda marveled at her best friend Trina's ability to get along with people of all races. She had close friends from just about every race. Rasheeda didn't consider herself prejudiced, but she didn't feel comfortable "hanging" with people of other races and cultures. She preferred to be with her own.

One day, Rasheeda asked Trina how she was able to get along with others from various cultures so well. Trina told her friend that she realized that all people were children of God and that Christ had died for everyone. She tried to see people as Jesus sees them, not according to color or culture.

Just as prejudice is a problem today, it was a problem in Jesus' day. The story of how Jesus dealt with the Samaritan woman at the well offers hope for those of us who seek to overcome the evil of prejudice.

THE PEOPLE, PLACES, AND TIMES

The Samaritan woman. Little is known of this woman except the fact that she had married and divorced five times. At the time of this meeting with Jesus, she was living with a man to whom she was not married. The fact that she was drawing water alone in the hottest part of the day speaks to the fact that she was probably ridiculed by the other women of her community.

Samaria. Located north of Judea and west of the Jordan River, Samaria was home to the 10 tribes of Israel. They were conquered by Assyria in 722 B.C. All but the poorest Israelites were deported, and captives from other countries were resettled in the land. These new residents mixed their pagan religion with what was left of Baal worship and the worship of God, producing a confusing religion (2 Kings 17:24-41). Over the decades, the foreign captives intermarried with remaining Israelites from the region and produced a nation of mixed blood. As a result, by the first century A.D. Jews hated the Samaritans for racial and religious reasons.

BACKGROUND

After a very successful evangelism campaign in Judea, where the Lord preached and His disciples baptized, Jesus decided to leave the area and move His ministry to Galilee. There were reports that the Pharisees were unhappy with His activity. Usually, the Jews traveled to Galilee by crossing east of the Jordan River. This was done so that they would not have to travel through Samaria. However, Jesus informed His disciples that it was necessary for Him to go through Samaria. By this time, the disciples had learned not to question such decisions by the Lord.

AT-A-GLANCE

1. A Deliberate Encounter (John 4:7-8)
2. An Invitation to Eternity (vv. 9-10)
3. Correcting a Past Error (vv. 19-25)
4. The Revelation (v. 26)

IN DEPTH

1. A Deliberate Encounter (John 4:7-8)

In John 4:4, it was declared that Jesus "must needs go through Samaria." This is a curious statement unless one considers that Jesus wanted to make an intentional statement about prejudice. He arrived at Jacob's well at about noon, which would have been the hottest part of the day, and there He found a Samaritan woman coming to get water.

The woman knew that other women would not be present at the well during this time and was seeking to avoid an unpleasant encounter.

Jesus startled the woman by asking her for a favor. It was unusual for a Jew to speak to a Samaritan and even more unusual for an unaccompanied male to speak to an unaccompanied female. Jesus deliberately violated both taboos in an effort to enter into conversation with the woman at the well.

2. An Invitation to Eternity (vv. 9-10)

Since she was well aware of the taboos, she may have been probing to see if Jesus might have something other than a drink of water on His mind; in fact, He did. Jesus was seeking to help her reach beyond her gender and her experiences as a part of a despised group. The Lord established a common connection with the woman, the human need for water, and guided her toward eternal considerations.

3. Correcting a Past Error (vv. 19-25)

The woman was now thinking beyond earthly ambitions and beginning to perceive that Jesus was more than an ordinary man. She asked the Lord a spiritual question that would test the depth of His prejudice as a Jew. Her life to this point did not reveal any deep religious inclinations, so it is doubtful that she really cared on which mountain worship of God should occur. However, she knew that no strict Jew would ever acknowledge that God could be worshiped in a mountain of Samaria.

Jesus recognized what she was attempting and once again helped her to lift her thinking beyond the frame of reference that she had received from her culture and experiences. The Lord wanted her to understand that the worship of God could not be confined to a place. God is Spirit, and his worshipers must worship in spirit and in truth. Not understanding this truth was the error that the Lord ventured into Samaria to correct. The error had persisted among the Samarians since the time of the Assyrian occupation when they worshiped God along with the idol gods of the nations around them (2 Kings 17:24-41). At this point, the woman at the well revealed to Jesus probably what was the deepest longing of her heart—that of her hope in the coming Messiah who would tell them all things.

4. The Revelation (v. 26)

The woman's greatest hope is realized when Jesus revealed that He is, in fact, the long-anticipated Messiah. Though the Samaritans existed as a hated and subjugated people, the Messiah would be the source through which salvation would come to all humankind. Jesus wanted them to understand that no one was beyond the reach of God's grace.

SEARCH THE SCRIPTURES

1. In what way did Jesus seek to establish common ground with the Samaritan woman (John 4:7)?

2. Who did the woman believe Jesus to be (v. 19)?

3. How will true worshipers worship the Father (v. 23)?

DISCUSS THE MEANING

1. Why do you think the Samaritan woman questioned the Lord's request for a drink?

2. Why is it significant that the woman believed that Jesus was a prophet?

3. How did Jesus correct the woman's misunderstanding of how to worship God? Why did He correct this misunderstanding?

LESSON IN OUR SOCIETY

Many in our society have tried firsthand to understand the nature of the racial prejudice that so affects us all. John Howard Griffith is one White man who is well-known for his effort to try to understand. Through a combination of pills and suntan, he was able to turn his skin dark enough to pass for a Black American. You can read about his experiences in the book, *Black Like Me*. Do you think America would be different if everyone attempted to understand what it is like to live as a member of a different race the way John Howard Griffith did?

MAKE IT HAPPEN

Do racial or gender prejudices hinder you from being all that God desires? Do you know how to approach someone who is different from yourself and suffering under the pains of prejudice? Why not develop a skit and act out the conversation between Jesus and the woman at the well.

FOLLOW THE SPIRIT

What God wants me to do:

_____

_____

REMEMBER YOUR THOUGHTS

Special insights I have learned:

_____

_____

MORE LIGHT ON THE TEXT

John 4:7-10, 19-26

7 There cometh a woman of Samaria to draw water: Jesus saith unto her, Give me to drink. 8 (For his disciples were gone away unto the city to buy meat.)

Drawing water was customarily one of the tasks performed by women. It was usually done in the early morning before the heat of the day. The fact that this woman came to the well during the hottest part of the day was a clear indication that she was not held in high regard by other women in her community.

Thirst is common to all human beings. In asking the woman for a drink, Jesus was connecting with her at one of the most basic of human levels. In a desert environment like Samaria, to deny anyone water was unthinkable. Fatigue is also a common human condition. Jesus was weary from the long journey and needed water and rest. The writer of John's gospel is making an intentional effort to show the Lord's humanity.

9 Then saith the woman of Samaria unto him, How is it that thou, being a Jew, askest drink of me, which am a woman of Samaria? for the Jews have no dealings with the Samaritans.

The antagonism between the Jews and the Samaritans was more than 500 years old and went back to the time when Israel, the northern kingdom, was conquered and exiled by the Assyrians (see 2 Kings 17:28-41). The woman knew that Jesus was a Jew just from His appearance, and therefore did not expect for Him to enter into any type of conversation with her. This probably would have suited her just fine. She came out to get water under the hot sun so that she could avoid conversation.

When Jesus did speak to the woman, it surprised her and she questioned his intentions. Was He trying to come on to her? Did He really just want water? That she would think this is not surprising. Historically, the Jews felt themselves to be superior to the Samaritans, and men were held in higher regard than women. She also knew to drink from a cup used by a Samaritan would have rendered Jesus unclean. So the woman at the well was both cautious and curious as she responded to the Lord's inquiry.

Surprisingly, the woman did not shy away from entering into conversation with the Lord. She was very used to interacting with men and probably prepared to handle any direction the conversation might have gone.

10 Jesus answered and said unto her, If thou knewest the gift of God, and who it is that saith to thee, Give me to drink; thou wouldest have asked of him, and he would have given thee living water.

Jesus encounters the Samaritan woman and offers her "living water."

The Lord is speaking here of flowing or running "water" (Gk. *hudor*) which comes from outside of man. In the Old Testament, this phrase is used to describe the divine activity of giving life to man (Jeremiah 2:13; Zechariah 14:8).

The woman did not grasp what the Lord was saying to her. She failed to think in spiritual terms. However, Jesus intentionally puts the woman at ease and turns the conversation in a spiritual direction. Jesus wanted her to understand that only the gift of God could satisfy the deeper longings of her heart. By referencing "living water," Jesus was pointing the woman to a source of life outside of herself. We know that this source of life was, in fact, Christ Himself (John 1:4).

4:19 The woman saith unto him, Sir, I perceive that thou art a prophet.

The direction the conversation had taken was not what she had anticipated from this man. Historically, the Samaritans did not recognize the authority of Jewish prophets after Moses. So it is remarkable that she would confess that Jesus was a prophet (Gk. *prophetes*, **prof-ay-tace**).

Not ready to deal with the issues in her own life, the woman again tries to divert the conversation. If this is a true prophet, then perhaps He can settle the age-old dispute: On which mountain should the worship of God take place?

20 Our fathers worshipped in this mountain; and ye say, that in Jerusalem is the place where men ought to worship.

The Samaritans built a temple on Mount Gerizim that rivaled the temple in Jerusalem and declared that God had chosen to put His name there. Their declaration was based on the fact that Moses commanded the Levites to stand in the valley and read the Law to the people there. Half the people would respond from Mount Gerizim by pronouncing the covenant blessings. The other half would respond from Mount Ebal by pronouncing the covenant curses (Deuteronomy 27:12-13; Joshua 8:33).

This, of course, only added to the animosity that existed between the Jews and the Samaritans since the Jews believed that they had the true primacy with God, who had chosen to reside in Jerusalem.

21 Jesus saith unto her, Woman, believe me, the hour cometh, when ye shall neither in this mountain, nor yet at Jerusalem, worship the Father. 22 Ye worship ye know not what: we know what we worship: for salvation is of the Jews.

The Son of God was born a Jew and would be the source through which salvation would come to mankind (see Acts 4:12). Because the Samaritans did not know Him, Jesus asserted that their worship was misdirected.

23 But the hour cometh, and now is, when the true worshippers shall worship the Father in spirit and in truth: for the Father seeketh such to worship him. 24 God is a Spirit: and they that worship him must worship him in spirit and in truth.

Jesus wanted the woman to understand that God is not like man. He is "Spirit" (Gk. *pneuma*, **pnyoo-mah**) and therefore is beyond notions of gender, race, or prejudice.

Worship is the highest form of praise. It flows from the true essence of what man is and cannot be faked. All men were created in God's image. This truth provides the common ground upon which humanity should stand to oppose anything that would counsel that one human being is above another.

25 The woman saith unto him, I know that Messias cometh, which is called Christ: when he is come, he will tell us all things. 26 Jesus saith unto her, I that speak unto thee am he.

The Samaritans held a hope for a coming Messiah. In His conversation with the woman, Jesus confirmed that their hope was not in vain. This was Jesus' first declaration of His messianic identity that is recorded in the Gospels.

DAILY BIBLE READINGS

M: Christ Is All and in All
Colossians 3:11-17

T: Jesus Travels to a Samaritan City
John 4:1-6

W: Jesus Speaks About Living Water
John 4:7-12

T: The Samaritan Woman Wants Living Water
John 4:13-18

F: I Am the Messiah
John 4:19-26

S: Come and See the Man
John 4:27-34

S: Many Samaritans Believed Jesus' Word
John 4:35-42

Do you have a personal testimony of how God has refreshed you with His living water? Why not share that in the *Precepts* Discussion Groups located on your *Precepts For Living* CD-ROM.

MARCH 2005
QUARTER AT-A-GLANCE
God's Project: Effective Christians

The first two units of this quarter focus on the book of Romans, and the third unit focuses on Galatians. The lessons center on what it means to be a Christian, from salvation through spiritual growth. The key word for this quarter is *covenant*.

UNIT 1. SAVED BY GOD

The first lesson tells us that we have all sinned and need to come to Christ for salvation. Our conviction as sinners is just, whether we are judged by the law or by our consciences. Our justification, which comes by faith, is made possible through Christ's death on the Cross. Our old selves are crucified with Christ, but our new selves are resurrected with Him.

LESSON 1: March 6
All Have Sinned
Romans 1:16-20; 3:9-20

The reason we need to be saved is that we all have sinned. We must recognize our sinfulness in order to come to God for salvation. But salvation is available to us only through the power of the Lord Jesus. Paul says that he is not ashamed of the Gospel because it is the power of God for salvation to everyone who believes.

LESSON 2: March 13
God's Judgment Is Just
Romans 2:1-16

God judges those under the law by the law. He judges those not under the law by the law written on their hearts—their consciences. Some people are judgmental of others' lack of obedience, but they fall short of the same laws by which they judge others. God's law is given to lead us to repentance, not judgmental attitudes toward others.

LESSON 3: March 20
We Are Justified by Faith
Romans 5:1-11, 18-21

Justification comes through faith, and with this justification comes a relationship of peace with God. This relationship sustains us when we go through suf-

fering, and the suffering causes us to grow spiritually. Our justification and reconciliation with God is made possible through Christ's death on the Cross and His blood shed for us.

LESSON 4: March 27
We Have Victory in Christ
John 20:1-10; Romans 6:1-11, 13

The first passage gives us John's eyewitness account of the Resurrection. First, we read that Mary Magdalene came to the tomb and found it empty. Then Peter and John, the beloved disciple, looked inside the tomb. When he saw the burial cloth, John was convinced that Jesus had risen from the dead. The second passage teaches us that as believers our old selves are buried with Christ, and we also arise with Him in newness of life.

UNIT 2. THE CHRISTIAN LIFE

Paul has much to say about how to live the Christian life. The Spirit-filled life is condemnation free and begins with salvation. Salvation is received through faith in Christ, expressed with the mouth, and experienced in the heart. The Christian is to commit his or her entire being to Christ, which is reasonable since Christ gave His life for us. In this life, Christians will have differences of opinion on what is permissible. Stronger believers will have more freedom than weaker Christians, but such issues should not cause disunity.

LESSON 5: April 3
Life in the Spirit
Romans 8:1-16

Life is different with Jesus. There is no condemnation, no guilt over past sins. Jesus has set the believer free from legalism. The believer lives by the Spirit. The Holy Spirit makes the righteous life possible. Jesus Christ died to condemn sin in order to fulfill the law. The sinful nature leads to death. The mind controlled by the Spirit has life and peace.

LESSON 6: April 10
Salvation in Christ
Romans 10:5-17

Salvation is the gift of God to those who call upon the name of Christ. If we confess with our mouths that Jesus is Lord and believe with our hearts that God raised Him from the dead, we are saved. Being saved does not require amazing feats such as ascending up into heaven or descending in the deep, but salvation is received by faith in Christ. We are called to proclaim the Good News of salvation so that others may believe.

LESSON 7: April 17
Mark of the True Christian
Romans 12:1-2, 9-21

We are to commit our entire beings to God, which is reasonable since He gave us His Son. We are to turn our backs on the worldly system of values and evil desires. God wants our wills and thoughts committed to Him. This commitment is a process, not a one-time act. Then Paul describes what this Christian life will look like. It begins with sincere love and is manifested in deeds of love.

LESSON 8: April 24
Don't Judge One Another
Romans 14:1-13; 15:5-6

Christians have different opinions on minor issues. Each one must answer to God and do as his or her conscience dictates. The stronger Christian has more freedom. The weaker Christian must be more careful in what he or she does. The important thing is that a spirit of unity be preserved.

UNIT 3. SET FREE (GALATIANS)

This last unit is based upon Scripture passages from the epistle to the Galatians. The theme of the book of Galatians is freedom through Christ. Certain Judaizers had come to tell the Gentile believers that they must be circumcised and obey the whole law. Paul warned the Galatians that just as they were saved by grace, they must live by grace. The law could never save anyone. Salvation is by grace through faith in Christ alone. The purpose of the law is to show us our sinful human natures. Such realization should show us our need for salvation. The believer's freedom from the law does not mean moral license. The Spirit-led life is a demonstration of the attributes of obedience and love.

LESSON 9: May 1
No Other Gospel
Galatians 1:1-12

Paul is defending the Gospel from those who would pervert it. Judaizers came to tell Gentile converts that they must follow the whole Old Testament law. Paul warned them to stay with the Gospel of Christ that was preached to them.

LESSON 10: May 8
All Saved by Faith
Galatians 2:15—3:5

If we could have achieved righteousness through the law, then Christ need not have been crucified. Our justification is obtained through the finished work of Christ. We who believe have been crucified with Christ, and Christ lives in us. The way we live this present physical life is dictated by our faith in the Son of God.

LESSON 11: May 15
The Purpose of the Law
Galatians 3:19-29; 4:4-7

The purpose of the law was to show us our sins. When we see how sinful we are, we know we need God's grace; thus, the law leads us to Christ. At just the right time, God sent Jesus to redeem those who were under the law. Those of us who have come to Christ by faith are His children. There is no distinction between us; we are one in Christ Jesus.

LESSON 12: May 22
Christian Freedom
Galatians 5:1-15

Grace and law are opposites. With grace, the believer trusts in the work of Christ. The follower of the law is seeking to earn his or her own salvation, which is impossible. But the freedom that grace affords is not moral license. This is freedom that is summed up in love for one another.

LESSON 13: May 29
Living Out Covenant with One Another
Galatians 5:22—6:10

This passage begins with a list of the fruit of the Spirit. The freedom of grace does not produce moral licentiousness, but these Spirit-filled attributes. Paul then gives specific situations and shows how each is lived out in love.

GOD'S PROJECT: EFFECTIVE CHRISTIANS

by Katara A. Washington

This quarter's theme poses an intriguing concept: God has a project, and it is to make Christians effective. As we picture God, the master Creator and Artist, pulling out the tools needed to begin the project of shaping humans into effective disciples of Christ, we may wonder what's involved in this project and what responsibility we have to participate in the effective Christian-making process. While God is the ultimate conductor of the symphony of life, we also play a key part in following our leader. Just as the violinist or bass player has to follow the conductor, we too have to follow our God's leading and direction to become effective Christians.

In order to begin the work of becoming effective Christians, we have to understand our agreement, or covenant, with God. Our relationship to God has been made possible through the saving grace and sacrifice of Jesus Christ, who instituted the new covenant of grace. Because of Christ, we have a relationship with God. Without Christ, we would not have an advocate and we would not have access to our holy God.

Understanding as well as consistently reflecting on our relationship with God through Christ are important steps in our journey to become effective Christians. We need to constantly thank God for saving grace. A thorough study of the book of Romans can aid in helping us to reflect on and remember the awesomeness of our new covenant through Christ. The book of Romans is considered to be a theological masterpiece and the centerpiece of Pauline writing. Scholars believe Paul wrote the letter to the Romans in preparation for his visit to them to establish them as his base of operations in the West. If we are to be God's base—the ones God depends on to spread the truth and effectively minister to others about God's awesomeness and power—we too may want to take heed to the teachings of the letter to the Romans.

The epistle describes and highlights key elements of our faith, such as God's righteousness and our justification and redemption. It also teaches on reconciliation and peace, which are basic conditions that we need to become effective Christians. The letter makes clear the sinfulness of humans and the grace of God through Christ. Remembering what God has done for us through Christ keeps us humble, keeps us grateful, and keeps us willing and ready to live as witnesses for Christ and to become effective Christians. We can never thank God enough for the blood sacrifice of Jesus. Reviewing the Gospel message should always bring us back to Calvary and prompt us to become better servants of our Lord.

While continually remembering our gift of salvation is one of the most important stimulants to becoming effective Christians, we also need to reflect upon and consider other benefits of our relationship with God through Christ. One of the major benefits of salvation and the acceptance of Christ is the victory we have to overcome evil. The power we have is comparable to the power that God used to raise Jesus from the grave (Ephesians 1:19-20). As we study and reflect upon the Easter story this season, we should not only thank God for Jesus' Resurrection and the promise of our resurrection, but we should remember that the same power that could raise a dead Jesus is available to those of us who believe. Now that's power. As Christians we have power to conquer evil, to resist temptation, and to live victorious lives for Christ.

However, before we begin to boast about this great power available to us, we should not forget the source of our amazing power (Acts 1:8). Our power is available to us through God's Holy Spirit, which is promised to every believer (John 7:38-39). God's Holy Spirit not only gives us resurrection power, but guides us, teaches us, and comforts us (John 14:26).

According to the book of Romans, the effective Christian is guided first and foremost by the Holy Spirit. This gift from God is the source for Christian living. Nothing is done without the leading of the Holy Spirit; nothing is said without the prompting of our guide. We are no longer driven by our own desires; instead, we yield to God's Spirit, realizing that it is from the master we choose to please. After all, Jesus is Lord of our life. We have confessed Him with our mouths (Romans 10:9), and we are working to allow our actions to demonstrate Jesus' lordship in our lives. If we are to be effective Christians, we have got to be in tune with God's Spirit, we have to feed our spirit through God's Word, and we have to honor instead of grieving God's Spirit. Our minds should be set on the desires of the Spirit (Romans 8:5).

Because we know our relationship to God is through the grace and gift of Christ and we recognize our power comes directly from the Holy Spirit, our guide, we live according to certain standards. We're not caught up in the rules and regulations of the law, for we know that the law does not save us (Galatians 2:21). However, we follow God's standards because we want to please God; we want to say "thank you" through our actions for all God has done for us in Christ and all God continues to do for us.

Therefore, the effective Christian—the one controlled by the Holy Spirit and driven by reflections of saving grace—seeks to live a life that bears the fruit of the Spirit. The effective Christian exhibits patience, kindness, goodness, faithfulness, gentleness, and self-control (Galatians 5:22). The effective Christian also carries the burdens of others (Galatians 6:2). The effective Christian realizes that tests and trials come and can be used to sharpen his/her faith. While effective Christians endure pain and sorrow—just as others do—the way we view our trials is different. Our faith shows us that truly all things work together for good—even when things don't look and feel good (Romans 8:28). Our faith reminds us that Jesus said, "In the world ye shall have tribulation: but be of good cheer; I have overcome the world" (from John 16:33). As effective Christians we exercise our faith regularly, believing those things that we cannot see and believing in the omnipotence of the Power Source that overcomes the world.

"God's Project: Effective Christians" means that God desires for us to be effective and will continually mold and shape us so that we can be the vessels our Lord desires to use. We can do our part by reflecting on God's awesomeness, yielding to God's power, and living to please the Spirit rather than our flesh. Then we will be more effective as God's instruments, God's tools to draw others to Him. God will get the glory, and we will be blessed.

Katara A. Washington is the Director of the Editorial Department at UMI (Urban Ministries, Inc.). Her position combines her passions for God, youth, and publishing. She has a Master of Divinity degree from Garrett-Evangelical Theological Seminary, a Master of Journalism degree from Northwestern University, and a Bachelor of Arts degree from Dillard University.

WHY DO WE ATTEND CHURCH?

by Aja M. Carr

For hundreds of years, millions of people all over the world have attended some form of church service. It seems that in general, people and Christians, in particular, believe that Sunday mornings mark a time of reflection and acknowledgment of Jesus Christ as Lord. Among African Americans and in the inner city, it appears that it is good to "Remember the sabbath day, to keep it holy" (Exodus 20:8). However, our philosophies about church should border on this cliché: Anything worth practicing, and anything valued enough to perform in a repetitive fashion, is worth understanding. We must become comfortable enough in our relationship with God and in our endeavor to practice good Christian values to question our practices and beliefs. Thus, we become comfortable enough to seek the answer to one pressing question in particular: Why do we attend church? Many would argue that the Bible commands it. Hebrews 10:25 admonishes us to "not [forsake] the assembling of ourselves together," meaning that we should often afford ourselves the opportunity to join with other Christian men and women. Some Christians agree with that notion and some do not; however, it is relatively easy to conclude that many of us attend church because it is a part of our familial upbringing, or because of what the church represents to our society and our communities.

I believe the truth about our theology as churchgoers is deeply rooted in our upbringing. It is a part of our familial matrix. We attend church because our parents attended or because our families have been members of a particular church for years. It represents a place where we all come together in fellowship and worship. One could survey any given church and interview countless parishioners capable of testifying about the positive experiences afforded to their families because of their commitment to attending service. Throughout history, we can point to the church as a place that has allowed all of God's children to be a family. Even during slavery, the church represented the one place where the slave family might be allowed to go together. Slaves attended the church of his or her master, and as long as the family worked on the same plantation, they could almost be assured that Sundays represented a small space in time where they could be with their families and be encouraged through some scriptural interpretation.

"What better way is there to view the ministry of churches in inner-city areas than as agents that both prolong life and help to avoid decay in communities where almost every other business and institution has abandoned the area? In some respects, churches are among the very few institutions that have remained in the inner city. A drive through any of America's inner-city communities will reveal that barbershops and beauty salons, bars (and liquor stores), and a wide assortment of small businesses and churches of various sizes occupy almost every corner, amid a sea of vacant lots and abandoned buildings. This flight from the inner cities has resulted in the loss of a tax base, the rapid decline in the size of the middle-class remaining in the cities. Almost everything that inner city residents need in order to have a meaningful life is located outside of their community, ranging from medical care to adequate shopping facilities to employment beyond minimum wage jobs at fast-food restaurants."[1] The city of Chicago, for instance, is home to several megachurches. Still and all, these churches are primarily located in the inner city in predominately African American neighborhoods. For example, the Salem Baptist Church of Chicago, which boasts some 15,000+ members, sits in the heart of the Roseland community (largely African American and partially Latino). The Apostolic Church of God, pastored by Dr. Arthur M. Brazier, and The Trinity United Church of Christ, pastored by Rev. Jeremiah A. Wright Jr., are both situated on the South Side of the inner city and are predominantly African American. The African American church is the only inner-city community presence that has not uprooted itself from the community. While the quality of life for many of the parishioners *has* improved—allowing them to relocate to suburban areas—the church *has not* relocated. I believe many African Americans continue to attend churches in our community for that reason. The church has always been there (as a part of the community) and is viewed as an entity that will remain. It is a prototype of the nature of Christ in the community; its presence will remain steadfast and unmovable.

As we have changed and grown, so have our churches. The emergence of the African American middle-class brought with it the emergence of the African American megachurch. Many scholars committed to the study of church growth and trends would argue that the birth of the megamall brought with it an influx of megachurches. However, I would argue that the expansion of the African American middle-class and their ability to participate as valuable consumers in society (meaning that we could now shop at the megamalls) also gave us the affluence to support and become a part of larger church ministries. Thus, this supports the claim that some of us continue to attend church because its complexion has changed to represent the color of society as a whole. And, every time society "upgrades," we have watched the church "upgrade," creating social constructs in the church. We subscribed to cable television because it was new and exciting; it offered us more channels and more programs. Likewise, the church began to embrace the insurgence of cable markets. Now, we see church services broadcasted on cable television. The African American church has aligned itself with the culture of our society, and we continue to attend because we can relate to that.

The argument about the theology of church-goers exists: We attend church because it has conformed itself to a changing society, but we also attend church to be rescued (emotionally) from that very same society. Moreover, the argument exists regarding the role of the church. The church has been a steadfast and unchanging part of our community, but the economic incline of the parishioners and the rise of mega-entities have caused the church to change (and we can relate to the fluctuation). Because these arguments are easily debated, they do not carry as much weight as the proceeding argument: We attend church because of our love for Jesus Christ. Countless theologians have harvested mounds of information regarding church membership, trends in church growth, and the theology of churchgoers, but none can easily refute that many Christians simply love the Lord, and that is why they attend church services. Church represents the one place in society where we can worship and praise God in our own way and with few inhibitions. While we might acknowledge the role of our families in our relationship with God and might identify with the consistent and conversely changing roles of the church, it is beyond debate that Jesus is the number one reason why Christians attend church.

[1]Marvin McMickle and Gardner C. Taylor, *Preaching to the Black Middle Class: Words of Challenge, Words of Hope* (Valley Forge, Pa. Judson Press, 2000). 57-58.

Aja M. Carr is a freelance Christian writer and aspiring author. She holds a Bachelor of Arts degree in history from the University of Illinois at Urbana-Champaign and is currently pursuing a Masters in Theological Studies at the Garrett-Evangelical Theological Seminary.

EFFECTIVE CHRISTIANITY: AVOIDING SHORTCUTS TO MATURITY

by Lisa Crayton

Shortcuts work—sometimes. Often, however, the shortest path to accomplishing a goal results in a dream deferred. Countless scholastic objectives, home improvement projects, and weight loss/exercise programs are abandoned each day simply because goal seekers take shortcuts that promise quick and easy paths to success. The result? Broken focus and shipwrecked ambitions.

Similarly, spiritual shortcuts that appear to be fast tracks to growth and maturity are usually detours to destruction. While not always easy to detect, these can by identified by their overemphasis on works, self-confidence, personal gain, and/or abilities. These sharply contrast, respectively, with the Bible's teachings about grace, faith, service (to God and mankind), and spiritual gifts. Jesus warned of spiritual shortcuts when he advised, "Enter ye in at the strait gate: for wide is the gate, and broad is the way, that leadeth to destruction, and many there be which go in thereat: Because strait is the gate, and narrow is the way, which leadeth unto life, and few there be that find it" (Matthew 7:13-14). Effective Christians will seek that narrow way, embracing a foolproof covenant with God that overflows to self and others.

An Enduring Covenant

A covenant is a fully enforceable, binding agreement. Like a legal contract, it affords privileges and responsibilities to each party. Knowing contract provisions makes it easier to adhere to them and avoid forfeiture of contractual promises. Ignorance, on the other hand, hinders a party's ability to fulfill contractual obligations and may result in forfeiture. Whether you're the policyholder or beneficiary, it is necessary for you to understand and adhere to the contracts to which you are a party.

Covenant with God

When it comes to covenant with God, effective Christians can easily understand their rights and responsibilities by turning to a trusted source: the Bible. From it we understand that recognizing one's sin nature is a necessary first step to making peace with God (Romans 5:1). Accepting, by faith, the atoning sacrifice of Jesus is a second. "For by grace are ye saved through faith; and that not of yourselves: it is the gift of God: Not of works, lest any man should boast" (Ephesians 2:8-9). "And Jesus is the propitiation for our sins: and not for ours only, but also for the sins of the whole world" (1 John 2:2). Conforming to biblical definitions of godly behavior is a third. "For the grace of God that bringeth salvation hath appeared to all men, Teaching us that, denying ungodliness and worldly lusts, we should live soberly, righteously, and godly, in this present world" (Titus 2:11-12).

It would be impossible to live such a life if not for the example of Jesus Christ. He modeled godly behavior while on earth, and then sent the Holy Spirit to give us the power to do the same. Nonetheless, if a spiritual shortcut exists, it will likely manifest during that third step. And it will be subtly encouraged by friends, family, coworkers, and others who resent the effective Christian's Christlike behavior.

Like the serpent that wooed Eve, those seemingly caring individuals will question, "Did God really say that?" Translated in modern vernacular: "Who says you can't do this or that?" "Why can't you go (to such a place)?" "Why must you tithe, attend church regularly, serve others, etc.?" But, the biggest temptation usually comes in the form of, "You used to be more fun (caring, sharing, forgiving, etc.) before you were a Christian." That's the one that usually hurts the most, as it questions whether we're self-righteous or spiritual. And it often compels otherwise effective Christians to water down the Word of God in their lives to become more acceptable to others.

Covenant with Self

The cure for that ailment is to acknowledge that our covenant with God spurs self-improvement. No matter how good we think we are before coming to Christ, we're reminded that, "All have sinned, and come short of the glory of God; Being justified freely by his grace through the redemption that is in Christ Jesus" (Romans 3:23-24). But, warns the apostle James, "Be ye doers of the word, and not hearers only, deceiving your own selves" (James 1:22).

Heeding James' admonition, effective Christians actively seek to know the written and Living Word (Jesus). Thus, prayer, Bible reading and study, and regular church attendance become vehicles through which knowledge is gleaned, retained, and acted upon. The goal is not learning for learning's sake, but for life application and obedience. The effective Christian asks daily, "What would Jesus do, say, and teach others by example?" Living under a microscope is never easy. But it's possible when we remember that we are not perfect, although we strive for perfection. Our bodies, after all, have not been redeemed, so we'll continually grapple with some of the same appetites, attitudes, and actions that we once enjoyed. The good news? "Ye are of God, little children, and have overcome them: because greater is he that is in you, than he that is in the world" (1 John 4:4-5).

Spiritual health is only one aspect of our self-covenant. The other is physical health. As living "temple[s] of God" (1 Corinthians 3:16), effective Christians take care of their bodies by fueling them with proper nutrition, rest, and—yes—exercise. Proper medical care also becomes essential, especially regular annual examinations as one ages.

Covenant with Others

Serving others is also an integral right and responsibility of our covenant with God. Leading others to follow Christ, or grow up in Him, is also a great privilege. From sharing the Gospel, to treating our enemies with kindness, to helping those less fortunate, we become instruments of grace, peace, and hope as we reach out to others. More so, embracing a global perspective of the term *neighbor* opens doors for us to be more effective as we adapt to changing societal needs in times of peace and war. Whether that's through personal, church, or business outreaches, we can show others the truth of John 3:16. Doing so keeps us on the right track, while also helping others avoid spiritual shortcuts that undermine faith and growth.

Long-Term Effectiveness

Spiritual effectiveness is a worthy goal, but it won't happen overnight. That's why shortcuts won't work. They'll compel you to focus on short-term achievement garnered by either physical, mental, or emotional power. Admonishing the Galatians' reliance on a similar shortcut, the apostle Paul queried, "Are ye so foolish? having begun in the Spirit, are ye now made perfect by the flesh?" (Galatians 3:3).

The apostle Paul's question is appropriate for self-reflection as we address the issue of effectiveness this quarter. As we move from unit to unit, keep in mind that God never fails, and neither will His covenant. And, like the apostle Paul, we can be "confident of this very thing, that he which hath begun a good work in you will perform it until the day of Jesus Christ" (Philippians 1:6).

Lisa Crayton is an award-winning, internationally published freelance writer and the editor of *Spirit-Led Writer,* an online magazine for Christian writers. Lisa is also an ordained licensed minister.

MARIAN WRIGHT EDELMAN

Founder and President of the Children's Defense Fund

Marian Wright Edelman continues to demonstrate God's command to love and care for our neighbors as we love and care for ourselves. Edelman is recognized throughout the world for her advocacy work for children, especially children who are poor, minorities, and/or disabled.

Edelman founded the Children's Defense Fund (CDF) in 1973. The CDF is an advocacy organization for children as well as a research center that documents the problems of and solutions for the nation's children. Edelman has served as a public speaker, lobbyist in Congress, and the president of the CDF. In an effort to remain independent, the organization accepts only private funds. In 1996, Edelman also founded Stand For Children, an organization that unites children's rights advocates.

Marian was born in Bennettsville, South Carolina in 1939. Her father was a Baptist preacher. He taught Marian and her siblings that service to the world was a key component of Christianity.

This children's advocate attended Spelman College in Atlanta. While in college, she studied abroad, and when she returned to Spelman she became active in the Civil Rights Movement. Her involvement with the movement prompted her to change career plans and enter law school at Yale University in New Haven, Connecticut. At Yale, she worked on a project to help register Black voters in Mississippi.

After graduating from law school, Marian worked for the NAACP Legal and Defense Fund in New York and later in Mississippi, where she became the first Black woman to be admitted to the bar in that state. She worked on racial justice issues, as well as helped start one of the country's largest Head Start programs in her community.

When Marian met her husband, Peter, who was working as an assistant to Senator Robert Kennedy, she moved to Washington, D.C. In the nation's capital, she helped start the Poor People's Campaign with Dr. Martin Luther King, Jr. and began focusing on child development and poverty.

Under Edelman's direction, the CDF has also lobbied for improvements in pregnancy prevention, child care funding, health care funding, prenatal care, parental responsibility, the amount of violent images presented to children, and selective gun control. The organization's mission is to "Leave No Child Behind" and to "ensure every child a Healthy Start, a Head Start, a Fair Start, a Safe Start, and a Moral Start in life with the support of caring families and communities."

Edelman has receive numerous honors and awards. She received a MacArthur Fellowship; a Presidential Medal of Freedom, which is the nation's highest civilian award; and the Robert F. Kennedy Lifetime Achievement Award. She has written seven books, including several prayer books for children and those who work with them. In her reflections on success in an article at Black Collegian Online, she lists "faith in God" and finding out what "God has placed you in the world to do" as keys to true success.

Edelman and her husband have three sons.

Katara A. Washington is the Director of the Editorial Department at UMI (Urban Ministries, Inc.). She has a Master of Divinity degree from Garrett-Evangelical Theological Seminary, a Master of Journalism degree from Northwestern University, and a Bachelor of Arts degree from Dillard University.

TEACHING TIPS

March 6
Bible Study Guide 1

1. Words You Should Know

A. Righteousness (Romans 1:17) *dikaiosune* (Gk.)—Addresses the divine moral character and justice of God.

B. Faith (v. 17) *pistis* (Gk.)—The conviction, persuasion, or belief in the truth or reality of a person or concept.

C. Justified (3:20) *dikaioo* (Gk.)—Shown, declared, and demonstrated that one is righteous or just.

2. Teacher Preparation

A. Familiarize yourself with the upcoming lessons by reading the MARCH 2005 QUARTER AT-A-GLANCE and the THEMATIC ESSAY.

B. Read Romans 1—3 to get the setting of today's lesson and be better prepared to answer questions from your students.

C. Read outside materials and study guides to obtain as much information as you can about Paul's letter to the Romans.

3. Starting the Lesson

A. Read the LESSON AIM aloud and open the class with a prayer focusing on the KEEP IN MIND Scripture.

B. Ask the students to share an experience when they did what they thought was "right" without praying about it or seeking any godly counsel. Give them time to discuss what the results were and what they learned from these experiences.

C. Remind the students to write their ideas in the FOLLOW THE SPIRIT and REMEMBER YOUR THOUGHTS sections.

4. Getting into the Lesson

A. Ask the students to share what they know about the book of Romans.

B. Have volunteers read the FOCAL VERSES.

C. Divide the class into four groups. Have each group read and discuss a section from IN DEPTH and present a three- or four-sentence summary to the entire class. Give them about 15 minutes to complete this exercise.

5. Relating the Lesson to Life

A. Have the students break into small groups and work on the DISCUSS THE MEANING questions.

B. Have each group assign a spokesperson who will report that group's response to the entire class.

6. Arousing Action

A. Have the students read the IN FOCUS story and discuss Jawanna's response.

B. Ask volunteers to share any thoughts they may have jotted down in the FOLLOW THE SPIRIT or REMEMBER YOUR THOUGHTS sections.

C. Ask one of the students to close the class with prayer.

WORSHIP GUIDE

For the Superintendent or Teacher
Theme: All Have Sinned
Theme Song: "Oh, I Want to See Him"
Scripture: Psalm 59:1-5
Song: "Jesus, Lover of My Soul"
Meditation: Lord Jesus, thank You for continuing to love us just as we are. Lord, we know that all week long we have, in some way, failed to live righteously. We thank You this morning for another opportunity to try to do what You would have us do and live in a way that is pleasing to You. Amen.

ALL HAVE SINNED

Bible Background • ROMANS 1:16-20; 3:9-20
Printed Text • ROMANS 1:16-20; 3:9-20
Devotional Reading • PSALM 59:1-5

LESSON AIM

By the end of the lesson, the students should understand that neither their intellect nor their deeds are responsible for their salvation; it is only by redeeming grace that they are saved.

KEEP IN MIND

"There is none righteous, no, not one" (Romans 3:10).

FOCAL VERSES

Romans 1:16 For I am not ashamed of the gospel of Christ: for it is the power of God unto salvation to every one that believeth; to the Jew first, and also to the Greek.

17 For therein is the righteousness of God revealed from faith to faith: as it is written, The just shall live by faith.

18 For the wrath of God is revealed from heaven against all ungodliness and unrighteousness of men, who hold the truth in unrighteousness;

19 Because that which may be known of God is manifest in them; for God hath shewed it unto them.

20 For the invisible things of him from the creation of the world are clearly seen, being understood by the things that are made, even his eternal power and Godhead; so that they are without excuse:

3:9 What then? are we better than they? No, in no wise: for we have before proved both Jews and Gentiles, that they are all under sin;

10 As it is written, There is none righteous, no, not one:

11 There is none that understandeth, there is none that seeketh after God.

LESSON OVERVIEW

**LESSON AIM
KEEP IN MIND
FOCAL VERSES
IN FOCUS
THE PEOPLE, PLACES,
AND TIMES
BACKGROUND
AT-A-GLANCE
IN DEPTH
SEARCH THE SCRIPTURES
DISCUSS THE MEANING
LESSON IN OUR SOCIETY
MAKE IT HAPPEN
FOLLOW THE SPIRIT
REMEMBER YOUR THOUGHTS
MORE LIGHT ON THE TEXT
DAILY BIBLE READINGS**

12 They are all gone out of the way, they are together become unprofitable; there is none that doeth good, no, not one.

13 Their throat is an open sepulchre; with their tongues they have used deceit; the poison of asps is under their lips:

14 Whose mouth is full of cursing and bitterness:

15 Their feet are swift to shed blood:

16 Destruction and misery are in their ways:

17 And the way of peace have they not known:

18 There is no fear of God before their eyes.

19 Now we know that what things soever the law saith, it saith to them who are under the law: that every mouth may be stopped, and all the world may become guilty before God.

20 Therefore by the deeds of the law there shall no flesh be justified in his sight: for by the law is the knowledge of sin.

IN FOCUS

Jawanda, a member of her church since childhood, prayed for guidance concerning a meeting with her pastor later that day. Usually her devotion left her with beautiful feelings about her relationship with God. This morning, Jawanda felt she was on the wrong side of God's love.

By the time she reached the pastor's office, a thin veil of anger clouded her thoughts. The pastor had asked her to step down as chairperson of the Annual Women's Day Committee and serve as cochair under Sadie, who had been a member for only six months. Her first thought was that it was because Sadie was so young and attractive. However, she shook off that notion. Her eyes were moist as she sat next to the pastor and relayed her anxiety.

"I have tithed and served faithfully in our church my entire adult life. Never have I been asked to step down from a leadership role. Why now?"

The pastor's lips turned down as he began to speak. "Jawanda, this is not about you. This is about Sadie and her Christian walk."

Jawanda pulled a hand over her face and spoke in a muffled voice. "Please, pastor, don't ask me to serve under this young girl. Less than a year ago by her own testimony, she was using heavy drugs and living wildly. How do you expect me to respect her decisions?"

"Listen to me." The pastor gently pulled Jawanda's hands away from her face. "The role I'm asking you to play is not a demotion; it is a promotion. If you stand as co-chair, your humility and support will be an instrument of deliverance for God's salvation plan for this young woman. Remember, Jawanda, all Christians have been delivered from sin." It was the pastor's last words that released her anger as she recalled the redeeming grace Christ had given her.

THE PEOPLE, PLACES, AND TIMES

Paul's Roman Citizenship. The apostle Paul was clearly proud of his Jewish heritage. He boasts of being "circumcised on the eighth day, of the people of Israel, of the tribe of Benjamin, a Hebrew of Hebrews" (from Philippians 3:5, NIV). Yet Paul was also a citizen of Rome from birth. Paul was from the city of Tarsus, a thriving center of commerce that had been granted the status of *libera civitas* (a free city and hence, a part of a Roman province) by Mark Antony in 42 B.C. Paul's Roman citizenship is evident in Acts when he successfully challenges the legality of his being publicly flogged on the grounds that he is a Roman citizen (Acts 22:22-28). Paul's declaration that he was "born free" implies that his father was also a citizen of Rome. Roman citizenship could be purchased or given as a reward for some special service. However Paul obtained it, Roman cit-

izenship earned him certain rights and privileges not extended to non-Roman Jews. As a Roman citizen, for instance, Paul was exempt from certain forms of punishment such as whippings and crucifixion. While many assume that Paul's name was changed from Saul to Paul at his conversion on the Damascus Road, in reality it was the common practice of the day for Jews who were citizens of Rome to have both a Hebrew and a Roman name assigned at birth. Paul's almost exclusive use of his Roman name after his conversion is probably best explained by the fact that his commission from God was to preach to non-Jews (Acts 9:15).

Packer, J. I., and M. C. Tenney, eds. *Illustrated Manners and Customs of the Bible.* Nashville: Thomas Nelson Publishers, 1980. 547-558.

BACKGROUND

Paul's letter to the Roman church was probably written in Corinth sometime around A.D. 56. Although he and the apostle Peter would be executed there, it seems clear that neither of them had the opportunity to go to the capital of the Roman Empire at the time this epistle was written. Paul explains, "I planned many times to come to you (but have been prevented from doing so until now) in order that I might have a harvest among you" (Romans 1:13, NIV). In spite of this, Paul is aware of the conditions and issues that face the Roman church, possibly through his good friends and fellow co-laborers in the Gospel, Priscilla and Aquila.

He knew, for instance, that the Roman church contained both Jews and Gentiles. This mix often gave way to harsh feelings between the two groups. While there is no indication that this particular issue had gotten out of hand the way it had in the Galatian church, Paul was still aware that concerns surrounding ethnic differences could be divisive and destructive to this church if left unchecked. As a Jew, Paul was acutely aware that some Jewish Christians insisted that Gentile Christians should be circumcised and required to observe the regulations of the Mosaic Law. More importantly, Paul was aware that many of the Jewish Christians felt their Jewish legacy made them superior to their Gentile brothers and sisters.

In this letter, Paul explains that righteousness

is not a result of ancestry or adherence to the Law. Rather, he lovingly explains that it is only through God's grace and faith in Jesus Christ that both Jewish and Gentile Christians obtain salvation.

AT-A-GLANCE

1. Confidence in the Gospel
(Romans 1:16-20)
2. Jews and Gentiles Equal Under Sin
(Romans 3:9-10)
3. The Impossibility of Righteousness
(vv. 11-18)
4. Impotence of the Law (vv. 19-20)

IN DEPTH

1. Confidence in the Gospel (Romans 1:16-20)

Earlier in the letter, Paul expressed his desire to come to Rome. This major world capital and center of international commerce in the center of the Roman empire made it an ideal evangelistic outpost. While he had not been there, his greetings in subsequent chapters indicate that Paul had a large number of close friends and relatives in Rome (Romans 16:3-15). It is worth noting that a number of women are included in Paul's greeting, indicating the dedication of the female workers. According to Paul, the faith of the Roman congregation had been "spoken of throughout the whole world" (Romans 1:8). Paul not only prays for the church, but he is anxious to come to Rome so that "you and I may be mutually encouraged by each other's faith" (Romans 1:12, NIV). How much more effective would our congregations be today, if we only understood how important it is for believers to constantly encourage one another's faith? Paul goes on to boldly declare that he "is not ashamed of the gospel" (v. 16). This is a sentiment that should be echoed by every believer. Paul's confidence is based, no doubt, on his understanding of what the Gospel means in his life and in the lives of the Roman believers to whom he is writing. At first glance it may seem curious that Paul would even imply that anyone would be "ashamed of the gospel." This is more clearly understood when we take into consideration that at the heart of the Gospel is the acknowledgment that Jesus was crucified. To the people of this time, this was a shameful and humiliating form of capital punishment. Yet, to Paul, there is no shame in it, for it is the key to man's justification before his God.

Paul's confidence in the Gospel is twofold. Firstly, he acknowledges that the Gospel is the "power," or the energizing force, of God Almighty Himself for the "salvation to every one that believeth" (v. 16). Secondly, Paul writes "in the gospel a righteousness from God is revealed" (v. 17, NIV). Here, Paul is declaring that the only way to salvation is shown or revealed through the Gospel. This revelation is, as Paul writes, only for those who "believe." Our automobiles will not start just because we get in, shut the door, and sit there. We must access the car's power, or engine, by using the key to turn the ignition. So it is with our salvation. It is through faith in the Gospel that we tap into the power of God's saving grace. Although Jesus and the apostles offered salvation to "the Jew" first, Paul reminds the readers that his Jewish brethren rejected it. The Gospel was then given to the Gentiles.

2. Jews and Gentiles Equal Under Sin (Romans 3:9-10)

Paul is clear that because the Gospel was given to the Gentiles, there is no hierarchy. The Jewish Christian is not better in the eyes of God than his Gentile brother. All men are sinners. In this, Jews and Gentiles are equals. Both Jews and Gentiles were created by God and made in His image. Through His loving-kindness and through the provision of His only begotten Son, Jesus Christ, they are equally welcomed as full partakers in salvation. In chapter three, the reader sees Paul's diplomacy at its best. Paul knows that by declaring that the Jew and the Gentile are equal, he is ruffling ethnic feathers, especially those of the Jewish believers who are so proud of their heritage. Paul delicately mediates this, yet fully maintains the integrity of the message of justification. He maintains that all of mankind is guilty of sin. Jew and Gentile alike are unrighteous. Nor are than the Jewish and Gentile converts inherently better than the Jewish and Gentile non-believers: they simply are the recipients of God's unmerited favor. Paul declares that "Jews and Gentiles alike are all under sin" (Romans 3:9, NIV). As such, all are equally in need of a saviour.

3. The Impossibility of Righteousness (vv. 11-18)

Paul writes to the Romans, "There is none that seeketh after God" (Romans 3:11). Here, Paul is arguing that the very desire or longing for godliness is not present in man. To further explain the lack of any inherent righteousness, Paul outlines the sinful and willful behavior of man. When he writes, "Their throat is an open sepulchre," Paul is addressing the cruelty men inflict upon one another through their words (v. 13). The apostle compares the deceitfulness that comes out of their mouths with the venom of an asp, a small but deadly snake. This analogy of a deadly tongue is repeated in verse 14. The word "bitterness" is the Greek word *pikria* (**pik-ree'-ah**), which means "poisonous." Having demonstrated the unrighteous speech of men, Paul now turns his attention to man's unrighteous behavior. Taking the life of their brother, Paul implies, comes easily to man. The yoke of sin is so heavy that man's companions are destruction and misery. These attributes are the antithesis of peace and mercy! Because of man's unrighteousness, the propensity toward destruction and misery are constantly present. In verse 18, Paul presents the strongest evidence of man's unrighteousness: "There is no fear of God before their eyes." The sinful nature of man results in his failure to recognize God's sovereignty and governance in his life. Lacking fear of God results in wickedness and corruption. We must be careful to always remember: where God does not rule, sin will always reign.

4. Impotence of the Law (vv. 19-20)

The Law, Paul emphasizes, is not enough to legislate such a dire situation. Man has no fear or reverence of God. Without this reverence, God and man are separated and alienated. The Law is not enough to reconcile a righteous God to unrighteous mankind. This reconciliation could only be brought about through justification. That is, man had to be declared "not guilty" in the eyes of God. The Law had no power to do this. Paul turns his attention to the Jewish Christians. Yes, Paul admits, the Law may mean something to the Jews who allow themselves to live "under the Law," but it does not provide for man's reconciliation to God's holiness (Romans 3:19, NIV). Paul acknowledges that the Law was useful. The Law had two essential purposes. Firstly, the Law accused, or pointed out the sin. The Law did provide a name for the sin, and in some cases, it even prescribed a punishment. Secondly, the Law provided a moral compass, or a standard of godly behavior for man to emulate. The Law did not and could not remove the guilt of man's sin. The Law simply pointed mankind to what he needed—Jesus the Christ.

SEARCH THE SCRIPTURES

Fill in the blanks without referring to the printed text.

1. "For I am not ashamed of the _____ of Christ: for it is the _____ of God unto salvation to every one that _____; to the Jew first, and also to the _____" (Romans 1:16).

2. "For the _____ of God is revealed from heaven against all _____ and unrighteousness of men, who hold the _____ in unrighteousness" (v. 18).

3. "Therefore by the deeds of the _____ there shall no flesh be _____ in his sight: for by the law is the _____ of sin" (3:20).

DISCUSS THE MEANING

1. Paul is clearly addressing the issue of ethnic differences in today's lesson. How effective is the African American church in evangelizing to other ethnic groups? What are the reasons for the success or lack of success in this endeavor?

2. It has been said that the African American expression of and perspective on Christianity are uniquely different from those of Euro-Americans. Do you agree or disagree with this? If you agree, do you think it is a help or a hindrance in the evangelism efforts of Blacks and/or Whites?

3. Do you think that it is true that "Sunday morning" is the most segregated time in

Let us thank God for His plan of salvation.

America? Why do you think this might be true? What, if anything, can we do to change it?

LESSON IN OUR SOCIETY

Magazine covers are graced with the faces and bodies of women with flawless complexions and svelte, toned bodies. Olympic gold medals are reserved for athletes who routinely score a perfect 10. Special openings are reserved in Ivy League colleges and the leading universities for students whose parents were alumni, and they are provided admittance to these schools by virtue of their "lineage." Coveted partnerships in many firms are the province of the junior members who quickly become rainmakers, or of employees who know how to consistently bring in large monetary contracts or land prestigious clients. It's sad to say, but there are churches where only the choir members with outstanding vocal abilities are allowed to lead solos during Sunday morning services, while those with less than stellar voices are consigned to the chorus. In a world that privileges perfection, it is sometimes difficult for Christians to maintain a more balanced biblical perspective. What a joy it is to know that our salvation is not based in any part on our talents, abilities, or even goodness. Rather, it is only the grace, or unmerited favor, of God and our faith that secures our covenant relationship with Jesus Christ.

MAKE IT HAPPEN

Make a commitment to memorize Romans 1:16-17 this week. Write the Scripture on three 3 x 5" index cards. Place one card in your wallet or purse. Tape one copy to the bathroom mirror. Place the final card on your desk (if you work) or in your notebook (if you are a student). Read the Scripture at least three times during each day. In the evening—before bedtime—practice reciting it without looking at the card. By the end of the week you will have memorized it.

FOLLOW THE SPIRIT
What God wants me to do:

_____

_____

REMEMBER YOUR THOUGHTS
Special insights I have learned:

_____

_____

MORE LIGHT ON THE TEXT
Romans 1:16-20; 3:9-20

16 For I am not ashamed of the gospel of Christ: for it is the power of God unto salvation to every one that believeth; to the Jew first, and also to the Greek.

The apostle Paul penned these remarkable words to the church at Rome because he wanted to help all Christians understand the great kindness God was showing to all who believed in His Son, Jesus Christ. Earlier Paul had declared that he was debtor to all because of the past life he had lived (v.14). After his conversion experience on the Damascus Road and some training by the Holy Spirit, he would declare himself ready to preach (v. 15). Finally, here in verse 16, Paul would declare his confidence in God's work for humanity through His beloved Son. The word "gospel" (Gk. *euaggelion,* **u-ang-gel-lee-on**) means "good news." The story of Christ's coming to earth, dying for humanity's sins as a substitute, and then being raised from the dead by God the Father is good news for everyone who believes.

Salvation (Gk. *soterion,* **so-tear-ee-on**) is God's gift to all who believe on His Son, Jesus Christ. With salvation comes the promise of eternal life (John 3:16). Salvation has three aspects: All who receive Christ as Lord and Saviour are saved from the guilt and penalty of their past sins (Luke 7:50). They are also being saved daily from the guilt and penalty of present sins (Romans 6:14). Finally, all believers will be saved from the guilt and penalty of future sins as they allow the Holy Spirit to work with them to remove the presence of sin from their nature (Romans 13:11). We are not able to accomplish this by ourselves. For that reason, we are encouraged to function within a community of believers who will help us to see the sins of which we are not aware.

17 For therein is the righteousness of God revealed from faith to faith: as it is written, The just shall live by faith.

God chose faith in the finished work of His Son Jesus Christ as the means by which He would restore a right relationship between Himself and man. "Faith" (Gk. *pistis,* **pie-is-tis**) in relation to righteousness and salvation is believing that what God says is indeed true even before we can see that it is true. God uses faith to help us to learn that we can trust Him and His love for us, even when we cannot point to something that we've seen or touched as proof. His desire is that we learn to walk by faith each day of our lives (Habakkuk 2:4).

18 For the wrath of God is revealed from heaven against all ungodliness and unrighteousness of men, who hold the truth in unrighteousness: 19 Because that which may be known of God is manifest in them; for God hath shewed it unto them. 20 For the invisible things of him from the creation of the world are clearly seen, being understood by the things that are made, even his eternal power and Godhead; so that they are without excuse:

Creation speaks to the fact that God exists and provides us with a sense of His divine nature. God has placed something inside each of us that helps us to know that He is holy and just. Men, however, continue to suppress and reject this truth and earn for themselves God's anger. Because we know the truth about God and deliberately choose to ignore it, He will not accept any excuse from us when we stand before Him.

3:9 What then? are we better than they? No, in no wise: for we have before proved both Jews and Gentiles, that they are all under sin;

The good news of God was first delivered to the Jews because they were the nation chosen to receive it and then communicate it to the rest of the world. However, as a nation they rejected the good news of Christ coming into the world and continued to prove themselves, along with the Gentile nations, guilty before God. Like the Gentiles, the Jews missed the mark that God had set for them. This was done willfully by the Jews and is the essence of sin. We should not gloat because our sin nature causes each of us to miss the mark God has set for us.

10 As it is written, There is none righteous, no, not one. 11 There is none that understandeth, there is none that seeketh after God. 12 They are all gone out of the way, they are together become unprofitable; there is none that doeth good, no, not one. 13 Their throat is an open sepulchre; with their tongues they have used deceit; the poison of asps is under their lips: 14 Whose mouth is full of cursing and bitterness: 15 Their feet are swift to shed blood: 16 Destruction and misery are in their ways: 17 And the way of peace have they not known: 18 There is no fear of God before their eyes.

Paraphrasing various Old Testament passages so that his words have the authority of Scripture, the writer of Romans shares God's indictment of humanity. This indictment reveals that no one is worthy of God's love. Even the various parts of the body that God fashioned are used in such a way that God is dishonored. By our very actions, we prove that what we deserve is God's anger (see Isaiah 53:6). But because He has chosen to love us instead of destroying us, God is slow to anger and works patiently with us, giving us the opportunity to turn from our sin and embrace His love.

19 Now we know that what things soever the law saith, it saith to them who are under the law: that every mouth may be stopped, and all the world may become guilty before God. 20 Therefore by the deeds of the law there shall no flesh be justified in his sight: for by the law is the knowledge of sin.

A famous comedian, Flip Wilson, used to thrill America each week by performing a skit in which he deliberately did wrong and, once confronted with what he had done, would proclaim for all, "The devil made me do it." In similar fashion, we try to blame God's law for our wrong actions. However, the law's function is to show us our wrong. It is not the cause of that wrong; it is simply a mirror that helps us see what we are. Our desire to do wrong flows from the sin nature that is part of each of us. We must acknowledge that we cannot truly please God without changing that inherent sin nature. Neither should we believe that we have the ability to obey God's law and save ourselves. We cannot. God's law is perfect and was given to us to help us see our need for a Saviour. Without the Saviour, humanity has no hope of having its broken relationship with God restored.

DAILY BIBLE READINGS

M: No One Does Good
Psalm 14:1-6

T: The Wicked Won't Turn to God
Psalm 10:1-6

W: Sinners Can't Accuse Others
John 8:1-9

T: The Gospel Has Saving Power
Romans 1:16-20

F: We Are All Sinful
Romans 3:9-14

S: We Are All Guilty
Romans 3:15-20

S: We Have All Sinned
1 John 1:5-10

Do people around you seem confused in regard to God's definition of sin? Find out more about what the Bible has to say on this subject by using the Bible Cross-Reference Tool within your *Precepts for Living* CD-ROM.

TEACHING TIPS

March 13
Bible Study Guide 2

1. Words You Should Know

A. Longsuffering (Romans 2:4) *makrothumia* (Gk.)—A Christian virtue; a fruit of the Spirit that manifests in Christian behavior and character.

B. Wrath (vv. 5, 8) *orge* (Gk.)—Strong anger or indignation.

2. Teacher Preparation

A. To prepare for today's lesson, read the BIBLE BACKGROUND and THE PEOPLE, PLACES, AND TIMES section.

B. Study the FOCAL VERSES. Use several Bible translations to help you understand the meaning of the verses. Take pertinent notes to help you explain the verses to the class.

C. Write down the answers to the SEARCH THE SCRIPTURES and DISCUSS THE MEANING questions and study them.

D. Read and reflect on the DEVOTIONAL READING.

3. Starting the Lesson

A. Open the class with prayer.

B. Share the WORDS YOU SHOULD KNOW with the students.

C. Read the FOCAL VERSES and the KEEP IN MIND verse together in class. Ask each student to read two paragraphs of the IN DEPTH section and explain the verses.

4. Getting into the Lesson

A. To help the students focus on today's lesson, ask for a volunteer to read THE PEOPLE, PLACES, AND TIMES and BACKGROUND sections. Discuss briefly.

B. Ask the students to answer the appropriate SEARCH THE SCRIPTURES questions.

C. Allow time for an open discussion for the DISCUSS THE MEANING questions for further understanding of the lesson.

5. Relating the Lesson to Life

A. Spend as much time as possible with the LESSON IN OUR SOCIETY section.

B. Ask the students to share any insights they may have received from today's lesson.

6. Arousing Action

A. Call the students' attention to the MAKE IT HAPPEN section, and encourage them to practice the suggestions this week.

B. Challenge the students to read the DAILY BIBLE READINGS for the week.

C. Remind the students to use the FOLLOW THE SPIRIT and REMEMBER YOUR THOUGHTS sections. This will help them stay focused on what they've learned from today's lesson.

D. Ask if there are any prayer concerns and then end the session with prayer.

WORSHIP GUIDE

For the Superintendent or Teacher
Theme: God's Judgment Is Just
Theme Song: "Great is the Lord"
Scripture: Romans 2:1-16
Song: "I Worship You, Almighty God"
Meditation: Lord Jesus, thank You for having patience with me. Teach me to be honest before You and reveal to me those things I need to change and grant me strength to change them. In Jesus' name I pray. Amen.

GOD'S JUDGMENT IS JUST

MAR 13TH

Bible Background • ROMANS 2:1-16
Printed Text • ROMANS 2:1-16
Devotional Reading • PSALM 50:1-15

LESSON AIM

By the end of the lesson, the students will learn that God is impartial and just in judging the actions of all people. Students will learn why it is important to ask God to expose sin in their lives and the consequences of an unrepentant heart.

KEEP IN MIND

"God shall judge the secrets of men by Jesus Christ according to my gospel" (from Romans 2:16).

FOCAL VERSES

Romans 2:1 Therefore thou art inexcusable, O man, whosoever thou art that judgest: for wherein thou judgest another, thou condemnest thyself; for thou that judgest doest the same things.

2 But we are sure that the judgment of God is according to truth against them which commit such things.

3 And thinkest thou this, O man, that judgest them which do such things, and doest the same, that thou shalt escape the judgment of God?

4 Or despisest thou the riches of his goodness and forbearance and longsuffering; not knowing that the goodness of God leadeth thee to repentance?

5 But after thy hardness and impenitent heart treasurest up unto thyself wrath against the day of wrath and revelation of the righteous judgment of God;

6 Who will render to every man according to his deeds:

LESSON OVERVIEW

LESSON AIM
KEEP IN MIND
FOCAL VERSES
IN FOCUS
THE PEOPLE, PLACES, AND TIMES
BACKGROUND
AT-A-GLANCE
IN DEPTH
SEARCH THE SCRIPTURES
DISCUSS THE MEANING
LESSON IN OUR SOCIETY
MAKE IT HAPPEN
FOLLOW THE SPIRIT
REMEMBER YOUR THOUGHTS
MORE LIGHT ON THE TEXT
DAILY BIBLE READINGS

7 To them who by patient continuance in well doing seek for glory and honour and immortality, eternal life:

8 But unto them that are contentious, and do not obey the truth, but obey unrighteousness, indignation and wrath,

9 Tribulation and anguish, upon every soul of man that doeth evil, of the Jew first, and also of the Gentile;

10 But glory, honour, and peace, to every man that worketh good, to the Jew first, and also to the Gentile:

11 For there is no respect of persons with God.

12 For as many as have sinned without law shall also perish without law: and as many as have sinned in the law shall be judged by the law;

13 (For not the hearers of the law are just before God; but the doers of the law shall be justified.

14 For when the Gentiles, which have not the law, do by nature the things contained in the law, these, having not the law, are a law unto themselves:

15 Which shew the work of the law written in their hearts, their conscience also bearing witness, and their thoughts the mean while accusing or else excusing one another;)

16 In the day when God shall judge the secrets of men by Jesus Christ according to my gospel.

IN FOCUS

Mike admired his new car. He housed it safely in

his parents' garage. Over the summer, he worked long hours to save money to purchase his beautiful used Ford Mustang. His younger brother, Josh, would frequently hint around to Mike that he wanted to take the car for a joyride. Mike insisted the car was not to be moved or driven by his younger brother. One evening, Mike accidentally left the garage door unlocked and a kid from down the street walked in and stole his car. The next morning, Mike noticed the car was missing and accused Josh of stealing his car. Josh repeatedly denied having anything to do with Mike's missing car; nonetheless, after their parents called the police to report the car missing, Josh was unfairly punished. Two weeks later, the police came to the house and reported that the car had been confiscated. The perpetrator who stole the car had been arrested and was in police custody. Mike and his parents realized they had accused Josh unjustly and apologized. Josh's feelings were hurt; however, he forgave them.

Human beings have a tendency to judge too quickly, and our hasty conclusions hurt other people. How often have you jumped to the wrong conclusion regarding a particular situation? Are you overly critical of others? Does the punishment fit the crime? In this lesson, we will learn that God is the only fair assessor of human behavior. His calculations are never wrong, and He is just in His distribution of rewards and punishment. In addition to this, we will learn that the only behavior we should regularly observe is our own!

THE PEOPLE, PLACES, AND TIMES

Gentile. This name is given to any ethnic group other than the Jewish race. The Jews looked down upon other races as barbarous and unclean. In the Old Testament, Jews referred to themselves as "God's chosen people" or "God's elect." In the New Testament, salvation is offered to Jews and Gentiles alike.

The Law (also referred to as the Law of Moses) is the authoritative rule of conduct spelled out in the Ten Commandments and the Pentateuch (the books of Genesis, Exodus, Leviticus, Numbers, and Deuteronomy). The Lord revealed this code to Moses on Mt. Sinai (Deuteronomy 5:1-2). While many of the regulations are ceremonial and procedural in nature, the moral law embodied in the Law of Moses is eternal, unchangeable (Romans 7:7-12), and fulfilled through Jesus Christ (Matthew 5:17-18)

BACKGROUND

The apostle Paul is writing to the church in Rome. The congregation consists of Jewish and Gentile believers. Paul and the other apostles had heard of the church in Rome but had never been there. It is believed that Jewish believers who were present on the Day of Pentecost established the church. These believers were among the 3,000 that were added to the church and took the Gospel to Rome. Paul's comment in his letter shows evidence that the Gospel had gone out to the Gentiles and that their presence was visible in the Roman church (Romans 1:13-15). During New Testament times, Rome was the capital of the Roman Empire. It was a "cultural center," experiencing prosperity along with literary and artistic advancement. Yet it was surrounded by moral decay. Roman citizens worshiped idols and practiced acts of perversion. In the prior chapter (Romans 1:18-32), Paul goes into great detail describing the depth of man's depravity and the evil acts committed against God; these acts include: violence, greed, envy, murder, strife, malice, arrogance, boastfulness, disobedience, and every form of ungodly behavior imaginable to man. Because of man's wretched condition and his refusal to acknowledge and obey God's commandments, God gave man over to his depraved mind. Paul goes on to say in Romans 2:1-16 that believers are without an excuse for disobeying God. Paul explains how God's long-suffering is purposeful, allowing plenty of time for human repentance and giving mankind time to draw closer to God. Nevertheless, man's tendency is to take God's grace for granted. In his letter, Paul makes a strong case for repentance by unfolding the consequences of sin and the inevitable destruction of those who continue to do evil. In this lesson we will learn why God's punishment for sin is just, impartial, and inevitable.

**1. God's Judgment Is Just
(Romans 2:1-4)
2. God's Judgment Is Impartial
(vv. 5-11)
3. God's Judgment Is Inevitable
(vv. 12-16)**

IN DEPTH

1. God's Judgment Is Just (Romans 2:1-4)

The Word of God says, "You, therefore, have no excuse, you who pass judgment on someone else, for at whatever point you judge the other, you are condemning yourself, because you who pass judgment do the same things" (Romans 2:1, NIV). What an incredible statement! It is amazing how quickly we can recognize and magnify the sin in someone else's life while scrutinizing our own sin through rose-colored glasses.

Before Paul made this powerful statement, he had already discussed the sinful ways of the ungodly in chapter 1. Now in chapter 2, he shifts his criticism toward the believer. He proclaims Christians are guilty of committing the same sins against God!

Paul explains why believers are guilty and sternly cautions the believer! He warns us to be careful how we judge others, especially when we become justifiably angry at someone else's sin, because the sin that we recognize in the lives of others may be the same sin operating in our own lives. For example, people who gossip have a tendency to become extremely irritated when others talk behind their backs, and individuals who are self-promoting tend to be very critical of others who seek the spotlight. God's Word reveals to us the necessity of examining our own behavior, not against the conduct of others, but against the Word of God—adjusting our lifestyles so that they line up with His perfect will.

Paul is not suggesting that everyone who judges the sinner is actively involved in the same sin. Moreover, what Paul is saying is those who point an accusatory finger—for instance, at the adulterer—may be involved in a similar sin, but one deemed more "socially acceptable." For example, one might cruise the Internet for pornographic material, watch X-rated movies in the privacy of their own home, or read books or watch sitcoms with sexually explicit stories centered around adultery. The point here is that sin is sin, and the Bible tells us that anyone who looks at a woman lustfully "has committed adultery with her in his heart already" (Matthew 5:28). Sin begins in our minds and hearts. It is important to bathe our minds on a daily basis with the Word of God. What we see, think, and meditate on will eventually become visible through our actions. God's Word must transform us, cleansing our hearts and minds of all impurities.

Paul goes on to say that God's judgment against individuals who commit evil is based on truth (Romans 2:2). The infallible Word of God will condemn and destroy the wicked. Paul is not saying believers should condone or not judge sin. What he is saying is that we should hate sin but love the sinner. We should pray and ask God to save the ungodly. Our response toward others should be one filled with humility, compassion, and love, recognizing that we all are sinners saved by the grace of God (Ephesians 2:8-10).

We are obligated to obey God's commands. So when we pass judgment on others and do the same things, God does not turn a deaf ear or blind eye to our sinful behavior (Romans 2:3). God is holy, just, and faithful to His Word. God does not lie. He will correct and chastise His children, molding us to the likeness of His Son, Jesus Christ.

Paul warns believers not to take lightly the riches of God's kindness, tolerance, and patience (v. 4). It is God's loving grace and our faith in His Son, Jesus Christ, that provides access to His holy throne. It is a huge mistake to take God's grace for granted or to use our freedom in Christ as a license to sin. God's delay in correcting our misconduct is not a stamp of approval to keep on living wrongly. God is waiting with open arms for all His children to come "naked" before Him, confessing our sins to the Lord. God gives us ample time for repentance.

2. God's Judgment Is Impartial (vv. 5-11)

When we purposely continue to sin against God, we are storing up wrath against ourselves (v. 5). How can a believer store up wrath? By possessing an unrepentant and hardened heart. A hardened heart can be filled with unforgiveness, envy, jealousy, anger, bitterness, and other sinful attitudes. These hindrances make it difficult for God's Word to grow and mature in our hearts. As we pray and meditate on God's Word, our hearts can be restored. When we ask God to forgive us, His redemptive Word heals our brokenness and restores our hearts to a purified condition. It is God's will that we serve Him with a clean heart, which allows us to rest in knowing we have security and eternal life with Him.

God will give to each person according to what he has done in the flesh (v. 6). God will grant immortality, blessings, and eternal life to every believer who seeks to serve the Lord and do His will (vv. 7, 10). At this point, I must interject that our good works do not lead to eternal life. It is our faith in Christ Jesus that provides eternal life. Our desire to please our Lord and Savior results in our performing good deeds.

We all stand guilty before God. Paul's letter gives us a clear indication of the importance of godly obedience. Tribulation, anger, and wrath are the future reality for those who insist on living ungodly lives (vv. 8, 9). God makes no distinction between Jew and Gentile; all are subject to His penetrating eye. Every human being will be judged accordingly. God is fair and accurate in His assessment of human behavior (v. 11).

3. God's Judgment Is Inevitable (vv. 12-16)

Most people know the difference between right and wrong. Even people who live in the most remote areas of the world and have never seen a Bible or heard the Gospel have an instinctive moral sense, which is given to us by God. In every culture, moral laws are created to govern human behavior. And in every society these same laws are broken. For example, in most cultures murder is considered a crime and punishable by law. Regardless of the law, murder continues to be a repeated offense. Lying, stealing, and adultery are also considered moral laws, which are constantly violated by the human will. As human beings, we tend to fall short of maintaining our own laws, let alone the laws of Almighty God!

In short, human beings will not be judged according to what they do not know but according to what they know and what they do with the information. By His Word, God will judge those of us who have been exposed to His truths and laws. He will judge others according to the moral laws they make and fail to keep. The bottom line is that no one can escape the impartial judgment of God (vv. 12-16).

SEARCH THE SCRIPTURES

1. What will be the reward for those who are patient in doing good (Romans 2:7, 10)?

2. What will be the reward for those who are contentious and unrighteous (vv. 8, 9)?

3. What is meant by, "For there is no respect of persons with God" (v. 11)?

4. "But glory, honour, and peace to every man that worketh good, to the _____first, and also to the _____" (v. 10).

5. "In the day when God shall _____ the _____ of men by Jesus Christ according to my gospel" (v. 16).

DISCUSS THE MEANING

1. The Bible says that God will judge man's secrets. What does this tell us about the things we try to keep secret from God?

2. After reading this lesson, we've learned that God's judgment is inevitable. Knowing this, what can we do to help spread the Good News of the Gospel to other people?

3. Explain in your own words what the following Scripture means to you: "Who will render to every man according to his deeds" (Romans 2:6).

LESSON IN OUR SOCIETY

The September 11, 2001 tragedy in New York brought many Americans to their knees in prayer. It was a sobering time. Families mourned the death of loved ones, friends, and coworkers. People from all around the world took the time to pray and ask God for His comforting mercy. The president of this great nation called for a National Day of Prayer, and, for a brief moment, children were allowed to pray in schools again. The people who lost their lives in the World Trade Center tragedy came from all walks of life. They were innocent victims, unsuspecting prey of a calculated terrorist attack. After the terrible event, people came up with their own explanation for why it happened. Some blamed God, while others blamed innocent people. Who did you blame? How did you view this horrendous catastrophe? Did you judge the victims? The perpetrators? How did you feel about God when it happened? And why do you think God allows things like this to happen in our society?

MAKE IT HAPPEN

This week spend quality time in prayer and ask God to examine your heart. Ask God to reveal to you hidden or overt sin in your life. Ask the Lord a series of questions; for example, "What things do I need to change in my life? Do I judge others unfairly?" Write down the things the Lord reveals to you. Submit yourself to God and allow the Lord to minister to you. Do whatever the Lord instructs you to do. Be prepared to share your experiences with the class next week.

FOLLOW THE SPIRIT

What God wants me to do:

_____

_____

REMEMBER YOUR THOUGHTS

Special insights I have learned:

_____

_____

MORE LIGHT ON THE TEXT

Romans 2:1-16

1 Therefore thou art inexcusable, O man, whosoever thou art that judgest: for wherein thou judgest another, thou condemnest thyself; for thou that judgest doest the same things.

How easy it is to fall into the habit of judging others. We live in a society that encourages competition, and this reality makes it easy for people to develop the habit of judging others. God is perfectly holy and wants us to understand that all human beings are flawed and damaged because

of sin. For that reason, we should not judge anyone without subjecting ourselves to the same standard. To do so only causes us to condemn ourselves, because even if we don't commit the same sin as someone else, we still are guilty of our own sin and God will hold us accountable.

2 But we are sure that the judgment of God is according to truth against them which commit such things. 3 And thinkest thou this, O man, that judgest them which do such things, and doest the same, that thou shalt escape the judgment of God?

This Scripture passage should cause each one of us to pause and consider the things we permit ourselves to embrace. Unlike sinful human beings, there is no falsehood in God. He is the very essence of truth (see John 14:3; Titus 1:2). Therefore, we should not expect Him to see our actions and activities in the same fashion as we do. God formed us; He knows every part of us— our desires, our intentions, even the thoughts that motivate us. None of us can deceive Him, nor should we expect to avoid standing before Him in judgment.

4 Or despisest thou the riches of his goodness and forbearance and longsuffering; not knowing that the goodness of God leadeth thee to repentance? 5 But after thy hardness and impenitent heart treasurest up unto thyself wrath against the day of wrath and revelation of the righteous judgment of God;

Our desire to live for ourselves and satisfy our sin natures result in our rejecting God's kindness toward us. We don't want to believe that God is good and that He loves us despite the fact that we don't know how to love ourselves most of the time. God doesn't desire to be angry with us; that's why He is long-suffering.

6 Who will render to every man according to his deeds:

There does come a point when God will accept a person's rejection and deal with that person in righteous judgment. Each person will stand before God to review the life he or she lived. When the examination of his or her life is ended,

God judges the motives of our hearts in giving and well-doing.

the person who has rejected God's saving grace will understand that he or she never came close to meeting the standard that would please God. It is impossible for any human without Christ to do so.

7 To them who by patient continuance in well doing seek for glory and honor and immortality, eternal life: 8 But unto them that are contentious, and do not obey the truth, but obey unrighteousness, indignation and wrath,

God rewards those godly attributes that He has established in those He loves. These rewards include glory, honor, and eternal life. It is not possible for a person to earn these things; our sin nature ensures that we will always fall short of God's standard. Rather, these rewards are gifts from God (see Ephesians 2:8-9) given in recognition of the changes occurring in one's life. By the same token, those individuals who are contentious and do not obey God will receive His wrath and indignation.

9 Tribulation and anguish, upon every soul of man that doeth evil, of the Jew first, and also of the Gentile; 10 But glory, honour, and peace, to every man that worketh good, to the Jew first, and also to the Gentile:

It has been suggested that with great privilege comes great responsibility. The Jews are a living example of what happens when people, even those specially chosen and set apart by God, fail to live up to their God-given privileges. The Jewish nation's rejection of God's Son, Jesus Christ, as their Messiah resulted in God's rejection of them as His corporate people. Now, the privilege of being God's chosen people is offered to all of humanity. However, each of us must respond by either accepting God's offer and allowing the Holy Spirit to guide us into good works, or rejecting it and incurring God's great anger.

11 For there is no respect of persons with God. 12 For as many as have sinned without law shall also perish without law: and as many as have sinned in the law shall be judged by the law;

God's does not "respect" (Gk. *prosopolepsia*, **pros-o-pol-ape-see'-ah**), or favor, one person or nation above another. We are all the same in His eyes. Because we are all the same, we can expect that His judgments will be fair and impartial. God shows no concern for the outward appearance or circumstances when considering the deeds of human beings. Instead, it is God's grace that prevails when He considers the sins of man.

The Mosaic Law was given to the Jews by Moses. In verse 12, Paul is saying that the Gentiles who sin will perish but the Law of Moses will not be used as a standard of judgment against them. However, the Jews, who were given the law, will be judged by the law.

13 (For not the hearers of the law are just before God, but the doers of the law shall be justified.

Often when the question of the rightness or wrongness of an action occurs, a quiet little voice guides us toward doing what is right. By listening to that voice and doing what is right, we avoid sin. However, we should not be deceived into thinking that just doing right is sufficient for earning God's favor.

In this verse, the word "hearers" is translated as *akroates* in Greek (**ak-ro-at-ace**), and means "to listen intensely." The Jews were always "hearers" of the law. However, it will take more than just hearing the Word of God to be considered justified in God's sight; one must be a "doer"(Gk. *poietes*, **poy-ay-tace**) of God's Word to be found righteous.

14 For when the Gentiles, which have not the law, do by nature the things contained in the law, these, having not the law, are a law unto themselves: 15 Which shew the work of the law written in their hearts, their conscience also bearing witness, and their thoughts the mean while accusing or else excusing one another;)

Written on every man's heart is the knowledge of right and wrong. No matter how good we think we are or how many good deeds we do, it will never be enough to remove the taint and stain of the sin we all possess and which alienates us from God.

16 In the day when God shall judge the secrets of men by Jesus Christ according to my gospel.

On that Day of Judgment, even the most intimate and secret things will be revealed. Fortunately for us, we don't have to rely on our own goodness or deeds. Anyone who trusts Jesus Christ for salvation and forgiveness of sins is given God's righteousness. No longer are we judged for our own deeds, but Christ's righteousness is substituted (2 Corinthians 5:21). For that reason, while we live in this earth, we who belong to Christ and are clothed in righteousness have a responsibility to do good continually (Ephesians 2:10).

DAILY BIBLE READINGS

M: God Is a Righteous Judge
Psalm 7:6-17

T: God Himself Is Judge
Psalm 50:1-5

W: Do Not Judge Others
Romans 2:1-5

T: God Will Judge All
Romans 2:6-11

F: Doers of the Law Are Justified
Romans 2:12-16

S: Do Jews Follow the Law?
Romans 2:17-24

S: Real Jews Obey the Law
Romans 2:25-29

Use your *Precepts For Living* CD-ROM to do an in-depth study of the word *law*. You will find the *Strong's Concordance* and the *Strong's Greek and Hebrew Dictionary* especially helpful.

TEACHING TIPS

March 20
Bible Study Guide 3

1. Words You Should Know

A. Peace (Romans 5:1) *eirene* (Gk.)—Refers to the absence of war and hostilities, metaphorically, the tranquility of mind that arises from reconciliation with God and a sense of divine favor.

B. Access (v. 2) *prosagoge* (Gk.)—The term is commonly used for the audience or right of approach granted to someone by high officials or kings.

C. Offence (v. 18) *paraptoma* (Gk.)—Implies fault, mistake, or wrongdoing.

2. Teacher Preparation

Begin preparing for this lesson by reading Romans 5. Then prayerfully study the FOCAL VERSES for this week's lesson.

3. Starting the Lesson

A. Have a student read the IN FOCUS story as a devotional. Open in prayer. Ask God to reveal through this lesson how Christ is our living hope of resurrection.

B. Before beginning this lesson, briefly review the highlights of last week's lesson. Then ask for volunteers to share their experiences from last week's MAKE IT HAPPEN section.

C. Write on the chalkboard in large letters the word *HOPE*. Then ask the students to share some incident where someone they had hope for or trust in disappointed them. After the discussion, explain that the hope we place in God will not disappoint us or make us ashamed.

4. Getting into the Lesson

A. Have a student read the BACKGROUND section and another read THE PEOPLE, PLACES, AND TIMES section.

B. Assign three students to read the FOCAL VERSES according to the division of AT-A-GLANCE.

C. After the students read the IN DEPTH section, ask them to answer the corresponding SEARCH THE SCRIPTURES questions for each section.

5. Relating the Lesson to Life

A. Use the DISCUSS THE MEANING questions to help the students understand how these truths relate to their lives.

B. Instruct the students to read the LESSON IN OUR SOCIETY section.

C. Have the students share the most significant point they have learned from today's lesson and how they plan to use it during the week.

6. Arousing Action

A. Have the students read the KEEP IN MIND verse in unison.

B. Read the MAKE IT HAPPEN assignment. Challenge the students to apply it to their lives this week.

C. Remind the students to use the DAILY BIBLE READINGS, the REMEMBER YOUR THOUGHTS, and FOLLOW THE SPIRIT sections.

D. Close in prayer.

WORSHIP GUIDE

For the Superintendent or Teacher
Theme: We Are Justified by Faith
Theme Song: "Lamb of God"
Scripture: John 3:16-21
Song: "Amazing Grace"
Meditation: God and Father of our Lord Jesus Christ, thank You for loving me so much that You offered up your only begotten Son to die in my place. I now enter boldly into Your presence, having gained access by faith in the completed work of my Saviour, Jesus Christ.

WE ARE JUSTIFIED BY FAITH

Bible Background • ROMANS 5:1-11, 18-21
Printed Text • ROMANS 5:1-11, 18-21
Devotional Reading • 2 CORINTHIANS 3:4-11

MAR 20TH

LESSON AIM

By the end of the lesson, the students should understand what it means to have peace with God, be able to describe several of the blessings that result from justification, and determine to involve themselves in the ministration of reconciliation by inviting others to get right with God.

KEEP IN MIND

"Therefore being justified by faith, we have peace with God through our Lord Jesus Christ" (Romans 5:1).

FOCAL VERSES

Romans 5:1 Therefore being justified by faith, we have peace with God through our Lord Jesus Christ:

2 By whom also we have access by faith into this grace wherein we stand, and rejoice in hope of the glory of God.

3 And not only so, but we glory in tribulations also: knowing that tribulation worketh patience;

4 And patience, experience; and experience, hope:

5 And hope maketh not ashamed; because the love of God is shed abroad in our hearts by the Holy Ghost which is given unto us.

6 For when we were yet without strength, in due time Christ died for the ungodly.

7 For scarcely for a righteous man will one die: yet peradventure for a good man some would even dare to die.

8 But God commendeth his love toward us, in that, while we were yet sinners, Christ died for us.

9 Much more then, being now justified by his blood, we shall be saved from wrath through him.

LESSON OVERVIEW

LESSON AIM
KEEP IN MIND
FOCAL VERSES
IN FOCUS
THE PEOPLE, PLACES, AND TIMES
BACKGROUND
AT-A-GLANCE
IN DEPTH
SEARCH THE SCRIPTURES
DISCUSS THE MEANING
LESSON IN OUR SOCIETY
MAKE IT HAPPEN
FOLLOW THE SPIRIT
REMEMBER YOUR THOUGHTS
MORE LIGHT ON THE TEXT
DAILY BIBLE READINGS

10 For if, when we were enemies, we were reconciled to God by the death of his Son, much more, being reconciled, we shall be saved by his life.

11 And not only so, but we also joy in God through our Lord Jesus Christ, by whom we have now received the atonement.

5:18 Therefore as by the offence of one judgment came upon all men to condemnation; even so by the righteousness of one the free gift came upon all men unto justification of life.

19 For as by one man's disobedience many were made sinners, so by the obedience of one shall many be made righteous.

20 Moreover the law entered, that the offence might abound. But where sin abounded, grace did much more abound:

21 That as sin hath reigned unto death, even so might grace reign through righteousness unto eternal life by Jesus Christ our Lord.

IN FOCUS

The day after he gave his life to Christ, Tyrone was driving in heavy traffic listening to a Christian radio station. Tyrone turned up the volume when the newscaster announced that one of his favorite comedians, John Ritter, the star of the TV show "Three's Company," had died suddenly of a heart attack at the age of 54. Turning off the radio, Tyrone wondered if John Ritter had accepted God's gift of eternal life. Changing lanes, Tyrone noticed a bumper sticker on the car ahead of him that read: "Many people wait until the 11th hour to seek Jesus' salvation. Unfortunately, many die at 10:59."

Suddenly out of the driver's side window, Tyrone caught a quick glimpse of the huge grill on a speeding truck as it smashed into his car broadside. The impact knocked him unconscious as the truck rolled over his car and drug his vehicle down the middle of the expressway. Tyrone woke an hour later, dazed and struggling for breath, watching the firefighters still working to free him from the mangled car. The pain in his back and head seemed unbearable, but at the same time, a great peace and comfort came over him.

Lying in the hospital bed the next day, he wondered about his feelings of peace and comfort in the midst of something so terrible. Sharing the feeling with his wife, he realized that he had pressed the fragile membrane between life, death, and life beyond. He also realized the peace he received came from his acceptance of God's grace. Tyrone resolved that he would invite as many as he could to get right with God so that they, too, could share that peace and comfort of the promise of eternal life.

In today's lesson, the apostle Paul explains the blessing that comes from God to all those who have been justified by faith.

THE PEOPLE, PLACES, AND TIMES

Reconciliation. Reconciliation is at the heart of Pauline theology. The word *reconciliation* was not used in a religious sense by the other religions of Paul's time. Reconciliation is roughly the same as justification but is broader and includes the aspect of forgiveness. The same God who judges also reconciles, so through reconciliation the sinner's guilt is removed.

Reconciliation comes from God's initiative. The apostle summarizes God's initiative in 2 Corinthians 5:17-19 (NIV): "Therefore, if anyone is in Christ, he is a new creation; the old has gone, the new has come! All this is from God, who reconciled us to himself through Christ and gave us the ministry of reconciliation: [telling others] that God was reconciling the world to himself in Christ, not counting men's sins against them."

Christians are brand-new people. The Holy Spirit gives us new life, and we are not the same

anymore. We are re-created and live in union with Christ (Colossians 2:6). God brings us back to Himself by blotting out our sins and declaring us righteous. Because we have been reconciled to God, we have the privilege of leading others to do the same. This is our ministry of reconciliation.

BACKGROUND

In chapter 5, Paul almost sings with the joy of his confidence in God. Accepting God at His Word has accomplished what human effort could not; it has given believers peace with God. Before Jesus came, no one could ever be intimate with God.

In presenting his case, Paul has proved that all humanity stands guilty before God. He has clearly shown that no one can ever be saved through deeds such as circumcision or obedience to the law. He has used Abraham as an example of how anyone can achieve right standing with God through faith. Even if Paul's readers stopped reading at this point, they would know that they needed salvation and that it was available to them.

In chapter 4, the apostle Paul established that Abraham is the father of the family of faith, not just the Hebrews. All who believe that God raised up Jesus from the dead and receive Him as Lord and Saviour are Abraham's spiritual seed. In verse 25, Paul makes a transitional statement concerning Christ being raised for our justification. Paul is now finished with his discussion of Abraham.

Justification is the first blessing of the Christian life and carries with it many other blessings. When believers are justified, they receive everything God has to give. In chapter 5, Paul explains the blessing of our salvation: Justification brings us peace with God and access to Him by faith, and Christ is the basis of our justification.

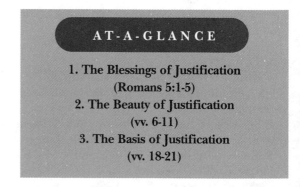

AT-A-GLANCE

1. The Blessings of Justification
(Romans 5:1-5)
2. The Beauty of Justification
(vv. 6-11)
3. The Basis of Justification
(vv. 18-21)

IN DEPTH

1. The Blessings of Justification
(Romans 5:1-5)

Paul opens the chapter with the word *therefore.* This word is used often by Paul to mark points of transition (see Romans 3:20; 8:1; 12:1). "Therefore" looks back at what has gone before and uses it as a basis to present the next phase of Paul's teaching.

Because believers are justified by faith, we are abundantly blessed, and Paul explains some of these blessings to us. The key word of this chapter is "we." Paul uses this word to describe all believers and explain the blessing we all have through our justification.

We have peace with God because we are justified. Trusting faith has given us what working to keep the law could never give us—peace with God. "There is no peace," says the LORD, "for the wicked" (Isaiah 48:22, NIV). Every sinner is God's enemy "because the carnal mind is enmity against God" (Romans 8:7). When we are justified, the animosity between God and us is taken away. As the prophet Isaiah explained of Christ, "But he was pierced for our transgressions, he was crushed for our iniquities; the punishment that brought us peace was upon him, and by his wounds we are healed" (Isaiah 53:5, NIV). Christ paid the price for our rebellion and brought about the end of hostilities between the creature and the Creator. Everyone who rejects God's offer of reconciliation through Christ chooses to remain God's enemy.

Because we are justified, we have "access by faith" (Romans 5:2). The Jewish tabernacle contained an inner room called the Holy of Holies. This place symbolized the presence of God. The high priest was the only person ever allowed into the Most Holy Place, and he could only enter once a year on the Day of Atonement. When Christ died on Calvary, the curtain separating the Most Holy Place from the rest of the temple was split in two from top to bottom.

The ripping of the curtain signified the acceptance by God of all His faithful to the throne of grace. In contrast to the limited access the Jews had, believers have unlimited access to God. "Therefore, brothers, since we have confidence to enter the Most Holy Place by the blood of Jesus, by a new and living way opened for us through the curtain, that is, his body" (Hebrews 10:19-20, NIV).

Because we are justified, we have a new standing with God. Notice the apostle's reference to "this grace wherein we stand" (Romans 5:2). The psalmist David once asked the question, "If thou, LORD, shouldest mark iniquities, O Lord, who shall stand?" (Psalm 130:3). The angel who opens the sixth seal of judgment at the end of time repeats this question: "For the great day of his wrath is come; and who shall be able to stand?" (Revelation 6:17). The answer is, of course, no one could stand the scrutiny of God if and when He begins to pick out the iniquities of the sinful.

Thank God that our justification gives us a right standing before Him. We shall stand, and in fact do stand, before God in Christ. In union with Christ is the only way anyone will ever be able to stand before God. Being in Christ means that we are identified with His death, burial, and Resurrection (Romans 6:1-8)—a concept we will cover in greater depth in our next lesson. Because of our identification with Christ, we now stand in the place of highest privilege. Not only has God declared us not guilty, but He has drawn us nearer to Himself; instead of being enemies, we are friends. That is why we can boldly proclaim, "Christ in you, the hope of glory" (Colossians 1:27).

Because we are justified, "We rejoice in the hope of the glory of God" (Romans 5:2). Faith, hope, and love are foundational to the Christian experience (1 Corinthians 13:13). We have a heavenly hope that someday we will share the glory of God, and because of this hope we rejoice! The glory of God is His likeness, His character. Hebrews 1:3 says that Christ is the brightness of God's glory. Paul says, "For those God foreknew he also predestined to be conformed to the likeness of his Son" (Romans 8:29a, NIV). Since Christ is the brightness of God's glory and we will be conformed to the image of Christ, then we shall also share the brightness of God's glory! Who could hope for more?

Because we are justified, "We glory in tribulations" (Romans 5:3). The word *glory* in this case means to rejoice. This is something unbelievers will never be able to do. As believers, we can rejoice in time of suffering because of our faith in the power and presence of God. We know that nothing ever touches us that has not been filtered through God's loving fingers. And we know that no matter what happens in this world, our God has the power to see us through and make it work out for our good (see Romans 8). Tribulation in the believer's life produces patience as we learn to wait on God without losing hope. This patience gives us tested experience of the faithfulness and power of God and proves we are children of God. Because of our past experiences, we view new troubles with hope. That is, we learn to look past immediate circumstances to our ultimate deliverance or victory.

"And hope maketh us not ashamed; because the love of God is shed abroad in our hearts by the Holy Ghost which is given unto us" (Romans 5:5). Most of us have at some time placed our hope in something or someone who disappointed us or made us ashamed. However, the hope that Paul is talking about is a definite hope. Christian hope will never fail; disappoint, or make us ashamed, because our hope is not in some frail, mortal, or economic bright idea. It is not in our homes or our husbands, wives, or children. All of these things and people can and will let us down. They will disappoint us and make us ashamed for believing so strongly in them. Christian hope does not fail, because our hope is in God—and one thing God can never do is fail!

When the Holy Spirit permeates the life of a believer, He opens our spiritual eyes to the wonders of God's love. He shows us that our lives are now ruled by God's love and that all future circumstances will be related to His loving purposes. This knowledge of God's love and purposes empowers believers to rejoice during the most difficult of trials.

2. The Beauty of Justification (vv. 6-11)

After discussing the blessing that results from justification, Paul moves on to discuss the depths of God's love. "For when we were yet without strength, in due time Christ died for the ungodly" (5:6). Here the apostle highlights the absolute inability of humans to deliver themselves from the grip of sin. The phrase "without strength" literally means weak, sick, infirmed, and helpless. We were completely unable to free ourselves from the bondage of sin and death. We needed a rescuer, and our God sent one from heaven.

"Ungodly" refers to those who live impious, wicked, and sinful lives—people with little regard for God in their minds and hearts. Christ offered Himself up as a sacrifice on the Cross to do for weak, sinful people what they could never do for themselves. What a thought: the godly dying for the ungodly!

The phrase "in due time" shows that God has always been involved in human history. Nothing catches Him by surprise. The good Lord had always planned to send Christ to die for us; He made the initial announcement after humanity's fall from grace (Genesis 3:15). Then, at just the right time, He sent His only begotten Son to teach, minister, and die for the sinful. Whenever we think things in our lives are running out of control, we can remember that God always moves "in due time."

Now Paul pens one of the most beloved sentences ever written: "But God commendeth his love toward us, in that, while we were yet sinners, Christ died for us" (Romans 5:8). Christ's death is a clear demonstration of divine love in action. This is what Christ means when He commands us to love our enemies (Matthew 5:44). Humanity was in flat-out rebellion against God. We were servants of the evil one and demonstrated our contempt for God by our lifestyles. Yet God loved us so much that He sent His Son from the glories of heaven to the filth of earth. God clothed holiness in sinful flesh and sent Christ to the Cross on our behalf. No greater expression of love has ever, or will ever, be made.

Because of Christ's death and Resurrection, all who put their faith in Him are "justified by his blood" (v. 9). The consequences of sin lead to the certain expectation of divine judgment. God's justification flows from His love for us. If God justified us through loving grace, how much more shall we be saved from God's wrath? "For if, when we were enemies, we were reconciled to God by the death of his Son, much more, being reconciled, we shall be saved by his life" (v. 10). Our salvation lies in Christ's shed blood. Christ paid the price for our rebellion; so now we who believe in Christ are forgiven and restored to a right relationship with God. This is the initial salvation experience.

Our status with God was changed from enemy to friend, but God's grace does not end there. Something more is needed if we are to grow in our newfound relationship with our Creator. Not only must our status change, but our state must also be changed. This change occurs when the living Christ takes residence within us. The living Christ empowers us to turn away from our sinful selves and live righteously. Our change in status is called "justification." Our change in state is called "sanctification." In sanctification, the salvation process continues throughout our lives.

We are reconciled to God by Christ's death, and we are saved by His life. Because of God's love, we have been "saved from wrath through him" (v. 9).

3. The Basis of Justification (vv. 18-21)

The apostle goes on to examine the eternal effect two men have had on the human condition. The first man, Adam, brought a death sentence on humanity by disobedience. Adam walked and talked with God; he knew Him intimately. Yet sin and death entered the world through his disobedience.

However, by one man, Jesus Christ, came the wonderful grace of God and eternal life. "For if by one man's offence death reigned by one; much more they which receive abundance of grace and of the gift of righteousness shall reign in life by one, Jesus Christ" (v. 17). God's gift of righteousness has been given to us through Jesus Christ. Adam's sin brought condemnation; Christ's obedience brings justification. Adam fell into sin; Christ laid down His life for our forgiveness. Adam's sin brought death; Christ's resurrection brings life.

"Therefore as by the offence of one judgment came upon all men to condemnation; even so by the righteousness of one the free gift came upon all men unto justification of life" (v. 18). Adam's sin resulted in condemnation for all who came

after him. This condemnation becomes real for each person as he or she rejects God and His Word (cf. 2:12-16). Likewise, justification through Christ "came to all men" who chose to accept it. This justification becomes real at the point of salvation when we believe in Christ and receive God's grace, mercy, and righteousness through Jesus Christ.

Paul now closes his discussion on reconcilement by returning to the subject of the law: "For as by one man's disobedience many were made sinners, so by the obedience of one shall many be made righteous. Moreover the law entered, that the offence might abound. But where sin abounded, grace did much more abound" (vv. 19-20). Those who are separated from God see the law as a means of getting close to God. People have repeatedly used the law to try to gain intimacy with God, but they will always come up short.

What they fail to see is Jesus standing right before them with His arms open wide, beckoning them to come to Him and allow Him to take them directly to God. Once Christ brings us into God's presence, we are free to obey God's law out of love for Him. And not only that, but He now supplies us with the power to live righteously. The law becomes our guide, alerting us when we stumble. And when we do stumble, we simply turn to the Giver of grace for more grace.

Even though we rebel against God's righteous laws, one man's gift is able to bring us back into friendship with God. Through Adam's disobedience, death rules over humanity. Now, through the obedience of Christ, we have an abundance of spiritual life and natural provision. Through our faith in Jesus, we enjoy a rich, beautiful quality of life that will continue into eternity. Thank God that one man who was sent from the Father has passed life on to us.

SEARCH THE SCRIPTURES

1. What result does our justification have on our relationship with God (Romans 5:1)?

2. Since we have peace with God, what should our emotional response be in times of difficulty and sorrow (vv. 2-3)?

3. How did God demonstrate His love for us beyond any doubt (v. 8)?

4. From what does our justification through Christ's shed blood save us (v. 9)?

5. Because of sin we were separated from God and considered His enemies. How are we reconciled back to the Father (v. 10)?

DISCUSS THE MEANING

1. What enables believers to rejoice in good times or bad? How can one really be happy when facing difficult trials or tragedy? Does our rejoicing mean that we never feel sad or lonely?

2. Explain how unbelievers are condemned through the disobedience of Adam. Explain how believers are declared righteous through the obedience of Christ.

3. Why does Paul emphasize humanity's weakness and our inability to change ourselves? Do you believe that all unsaved people are God's enemies? If so, why? If not, why not?

LESSON IN OUR SOCIETY

Our lesson today emphasizes how death and destruction entered the world through one man, and how God's love and grace entered through another. Many people in our society believe that the problems we face are so big that one person cannot make a difference. They feel that their one vote will not make a difference in an election and their presence at a PTA meeting will not amount to anything. After studying today's lesson, how would you respond to a person who claims one person cannot make a difference?

MAKE IT HAPPEN

Share the eternal truths of today's lesson with at least two people this week. Explain how Christ's death not only reconciles us to God, but also empowers us to live godly lives. Record the reactions of the people you share this Good News with and be prepared to share your experiences with the class next week.

FOLLOW THE SPIRIT

What God wants me to do:

_____

_____

REMEMBER YOUR THOUGHTS

Special insights I have learned:

_____

_____

MORE LIGHT ON THE TEXT
Romans 5:1-11, 18-21

1 Therefore being justified by faith, we have peace with God through our Lord Jesus Christ:

With the close of the fourth chapter, Paul completes his teaching on how God justifies a person. Justification is the initial blessing of salvation, but carries with it all the other blessings of Christian life.

In chapter 5, Paul launches into an explanation of eight attendant blessings of justification by faith. Because we are justified by faith, we have "peace with God" (v. 1); "access" to God's presence and a standing in grace, joy, and "hope" (v. 2); and "the love of God" and "the Holy Ghost" (v. 5); we are also "saved from wrath" (v. 9), and "saved by his life" (v. 10).

Another literal translation of verse 1 is, "Since we have been justified by faith, let us have peace with God." "Justified" is in the Greek past tense and points to an accomplished fact. This illustrates that justification is not a process, but rather an instantaneous act that takes place at the moment a sinner receives Christ as Lord.

The phrase "we have peace with God" could also be translated as "let us have peace with God." The "let us" is from the Greek present tense verb *echomen*, which means to keep on having or enjoying our peace with God. It is the privilege of those who are justified to "have peace with God," and Paul is encouraging believers to both realize this privilege and to enjoy it. As believers, we must never allow doubt or fear to rob us of what is rightfully ours. This "peace," translated from the Greek word *eirene*, is first a change in God's relationship to us. Then, as the natural consequence of God's changed relationship to us, we change in our relationship to Him. Because of our fallen nature, humanity is in a state of hostility toward God. In other words, sinners are God's enemies (see v. 10). When we are justified, that hostility is removed and we have "peace with God." Awareness of our peace with God brings a sense of peace to our souls.

2 By whom also we have access by faith into this grace wherein we stand, and rejoice in hope of the glory of God. 3 And not only so, but we glory in tribulations also: knowing that tribulation worketh patience; 4 And patience, experience; and experience, hope:

Not only does Christ remove the hostility that existed between God and sinners; He also gives us "access" into the very presence of God. *Prosagoge* (**pros-ag-ogue-ay**) is the Greek word translated as "access," and it means "the act of bringing to." In the Hebrew temple, the presence of God was in a room called the Holy of Holies. A huge veil or curtain separated this room from the rest of the temple, and only the high priest was allowed past the veil once a year to offer sacrifices for the sins of the people. This curtain represented the separation of sinful humanity from God. When Christ died on the Cross, the curtain that led to the Holy of Holies ripped down the middle (Matthew 27:51). We believe the ripped curtain represented the elimination of the separation so that all believers now have access to God. Christ's eternal sacrifice in our behalf "brings" us into the presence of God and allows us to have continuous access to Him.

Being justified by faith also brings us into a new permanent standing with God where we enjoy His divine favor. The basis of our new standing is obtained by grace. No one can stand before God by his own deeds, character, or righteousness. Our new standing is totally the result of God's undeserved favor.

And we rejoice "in hope of the glory of God." The glory spoken of here is twofold. First, we hope to experience the Divine presence in heaven. Second, it is to bring glory to God through our tribulations. Therefore, we "glory" or "rejoice" in tribulation because we realize that tribulation is heaven's way of teaching us patience. Patience is the confident endurance of things hoped for or difficulties we wish removed. The fruit of patience (see Galatians 5:12) is humble endurance of all because of the realization that nothing comes against us that has not been allowed by God.

And "tribulation worketh patience," or better, "perseverance," steady persistence in spite of difficulties, obstacles, or discouragement. Believers enter periods of tribulation and patiently endure. Our patient endurance is rewarded with eventual victory over our circumstances, and our victorious experience proves the faithfulness of God to deliver us from future trials. Testings prove or establish one's character made evident through patient endurance.

Experience brings us back to "hope." We have hope in two distinct ways and at two successive stages of the Christian life. First, immediately upon believing, along with the sense of peace and abiding access to God, we have hope in our new relationship. Next, hope grows after the reality of our faith has been "proved" by the patient endurance of trials sent to test it. Our hope comes from looking away from ourselves to the Cross of Christ. Then we look to ourselves as being transformed into the image of Christ. In the first case, our hope is based on faith, and in the second, by experience.

5 And hope maketh not ashamed; because the love of God is shed abroad in our hearts by the Holy Ghost which is given unto us.

Our hope of heaven, which presupposes faith, is the confident expectation of future good. Our faith assures us that heaven will be ours, and our hope expectantly anticipates it. This hope in the glory of God will never make us ashamed (like empty hopes do) because it is based on "the love of God"—not our love of God, but God's love of us that is "shed abroad," or literally, "poured forth." God's love for us is seen in the indwelling presence of the Holy Spirit.

6 For when we were yet without strength, in due time Christ died for the ungodly.

At the appointed time, Christ offered Himself as our eternal sacrifice "when we were yet without strength"—that is, when we were powerless to deliver ourselves and therefore ready to perish. Christ's death reveals three properties of God's love. First, "the ungodly" are those whose character and sinful nature are repulsive in the eyes of God. Second, He did this when they were "without strength"—nothing stood between humanity and damnation but divine compassion. Third, He did this "in due time" when it was most appropriate that it should take place.

7 For scarcely for a righteous man will one die: yet peradventure for a good man some would even dare to die. 8 But God commendeth his love toward us, in that, while we were yet sinners, Christ died for us.

The apostle now proceeds to illustrate God's compassion. Few, if any, people would be willing to sacrifice their lives for a "righteous man" of exceptional character. A few more might be willing to die for a man who, besides being exceptional, is also distinguished for goodness or a benefactor to society. "But God" displayed His love, in glorious contrast to what men might do for each other, "while we were yet sinners"—that is, in a state of absolute rebellion—"Christ died for us."

9 Much more then, being now justified by his blood, we shall be saved from wrath through him. 10 For if, when we were enemies, we were reconciled to God by the death of his Son, much more, being reconciled, we shall be saved by his life.

Having been "justified by his blood," we shall be saved from wrath through the sacrifice of Christ. Christ's death restored our relationship with God while we were in open rebellion against God. "Being now," or "having now been," reconciled, we shall be saved by His life.

To be "saved from wrath through him" refers to the entire work of salvation—from the moment of justification to the great judgment (Revelation 20), when the wrath of God shall be revealed to all who ignore the Gospel of our Lord Jesus Christ. The apostle Jude best described Christ's continuing work of salvation when he said that He "is able to keep you from falling, and to present you faultless before the presence of his glory with exceeding joy" (Jude 24).

11 And not only so, but we also joy in God through our Lord Jesus Christ, by whom we have now received the atonement.

"And not only so" refers back to the blessing Paul mentioned previously. We not only find joy in our newfound peace, access, standing, hope, love, indwelling, and salvation, but we rejoice in

God Himself. We find joy in our God, not only for what He has done, but also for who He is.

Our joy proceeds from our union with Christ, who brought about our atonement. "Atonement" (Gk. *katallage*) is a translation of the Hebrew noun meaning "covering." Atonement is the gracious act by which God restores a relationship of harmony and unity between Himself and believers. The word can be broken into three parts that express this great truth in simple but profound terms: "at-one-ment." Through God's atoning grace and forgiveness, we are reinstated to a relationship of "at-one-ment" with God.

5:18 Therefore as by the offence of one judgment came upon all men to condemnation; even so by the righteousness of one the free gift came upon all men unto justification of life.

All humanity is related to Adam, and we all inherited Adam's sinful nature (tendency to sin) and God's wrath. One man's single act of disobedience brought separation from God and death to all the generations that followed him. Likewise Christ's single act of righteousness (on the Cross) brings justification and life to all who believe. We can trade in our sin for Christ's righteousness.

19 For as by one man's disobedience many were made sinners, so by the obedience of one shall many be made righteous.

A clearer translation is: "For as by the one man's disobedience the many were made sinners, even so by the obedience of the One shall the many be made righteous." The "obedience" of Christ that Paul speaks of here is Christ's active obedience, as distinguished from His sufferings and death. The reference is to the entire work of Christ in its obedient character.

The key word of this verse is "made," which appears twice. The word is a translation of the Greek verb *kathistemi* (**kath-is-tay-mee**), which literally means to "set down" and so to set in order, appoint, or make. In this case, the word expresses a judicial act that holds all humanity as sinners by virtue of their connection with Adam, and as righteous in connection with Christ. This is what many theologians call "federal headship."

Note the change in tense from the past to the

future: "through Adam we *were* made sinners, so through Christ we *shall be* made righteous." The change in tense expresses the enduring nature of Christ's act, in contrast with the forever past ruin of those lost in Adam.

The word "many" in this verse and the phrase "all men" in verse 18 refer to the same group, though under slightly different terms. In verse 15, the contrast is between the "one" (Adam/Christ) and the human race, affected for death/life, respectively, by the actions of that "one." Similarly in this verse, the contrast is between the "one" representative (Adam/Christ) and the "many" whom he represented. In the latter case, it is the redeemed family of man in view; it was lost in Adam, but now is saved in Christ.

20 Moreover the law entered, that the offence might abound. But where sin abounded, grace did much more abound: 21 That as sin hath reigned unto death, even so might grace reign through righteousness unto eternal life by Jesus Christ our Lord.

One might argue that since the divine purpose of God toward humanity is centered in Adam and Christ, what part does the law play? Paul's answer is that "the law entered" so that sin might increase. In other words, when the law was given to the Israelites at Sinai, the primary purpose was to more fully reveal the evil brought about by Adam and the need for and glory of the remedy given by Christ.

"But where sin abounded" (or was multiplied), "grace did much more abound" (or did exceedingly abound). The comparison here is between the multiplication of one offense into countless transgressions, and the awesome overflow of grace that more than meets the need. The law "entered" to show people how great their sin was and thus their need for a Saviour. The law does not make a person a sinner; it proves him a sinner.

As guilty sinners, we were subject to death and were condemned in Adam. Even as death reigned through sin, so now grace reigns through righteousness (v. 14). The result is that we receive "abundance of grace and of the gift of righteousness" (Romans 5:17) through not *our* but certainly *His* "obedience" (v. 19), meaning Christ's entire work of mediation. His absolute obedience is the righteous medium through which God's grace reaches out to believers and results in "eternal life," which is salvation in its highest form and fullest development.

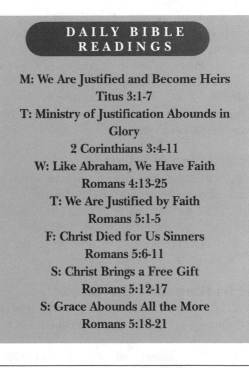

DAILY BIBLE READINGS

M: We Are Justified and Become Heirs
Titus 3:1-7
T: Ministry of Justification Abounds in Glory
2 Corinthians 3:4-11
W: Like Abraham, We Have Faith
Romans 4:13-25
T: We Are Justified by Faith
Romans 5:1-5
F: Christ Died for Us Sinners
Romans 5:6-11
S: Christ Brings a Free Gift
Romans 5:12-17
S: Grace Abounds All the More
Romans 5:18-21

Do you want to increase your faith and grow in your devotional life? Take a few moments to read the daily devotional on your *Precepts For Living* CD-ROM.

TEACHING TIPS

March 27
Bible Study Guide 4

1. Words You Should Know

A. Sin (Romans 6:1) *hamartia* (Gk.)—Disobedience to the will of God.

B. Death (v. 3) *thanatos* (Gk.)—The absence of life; also, eternal separation from the loving presence of God. This alienation from God finds its ultimate expression in the "lake of fire" (Revelation 20:14-15).

C. Resurrection (v. 5) *anastasis* (Gk.)—The act of having life restored after death.

2. Teacher Preparation

A. Pray for the students in your class, asking God to open their hearts to today's lesson.

B. Read and study the FOCAL VERSES, paying attention to the disciples' reaction upon finding the tomb empty.

C. Carefully review the entire BIBLE STUDY GUIDE, making notes for clarification.

D. Share a personal thought with the class about a personal loss due to death and your hope because of Christ's triumph.

3. Starting the Lesson

A. Before the class arrives, write the words *sin, death,* and *resurrection* on the chalkboard.

B. Lead the class in prayer after the students arrive and are settled. Pray specifically for godly insights into the lesson and blessings on the lives of the students.

4. Getting into the Lesson

A. Ask volunteers to read the IN FOCUS section and then spend time in discussion about what the story means.

B. Ask volunteers to read THE PEOPLE, PLACES, AND TIMES and the BACKGROUND section.

C. Ask the students to read the FOCAL VERSES together and then have the students read the corresponding IN DEPTH section. Allow time for discussion between each section.

5. Relating the Lesson to Life

A. Spend time answering the questions in DISCUSS THE MEANING.

B. Ask if any student has an insight that they would like to share regarding today's lesson.

6. Arousing Action

A. Read LESSON IN OUR SOCIETY to the class. Tell your class that during the Easter season they are each to plant some seeds in a pot and then tend the plant until life comes. Direct the students to the MAKE IT HAPPEN section and discuss it in class.

B. Tell the students to complete the SEARCH THE SCRIPTURES questions during the week as a review.

C. End the class with prayer.

WORSHIP GUIDE

For the Superintendent or Teacher
Theme: We Have Victory in Christ
Theme Song: "Moment by Moment"
Scripture: Romans 6:9
Song: "God Can Do Anything But Fail"
Meditation: Holy Father, in Your love and by Your power You raised Jesus from the dead and counted my sins pardoned through the blood He shed. Thank you for Your Son, Jesus, and for Your gift of life. Amen.

WE HAVE VICTORY IN CHRIST

Bible Background • JOHN 20:1-10; ROMANS 6:1-14
Printed Text • JOHN 20:1-10; ROMANS 6:1-11, 13
Devotional Reading • ROMANS 6:15-23

LESSON AIM

By the end of the lesson, the students will understand the importance of Christ's death and the victory His death secured at Calvary. Because of His triumph, death no longer has a claim over those who believe in Him and subject themselves to His authority.

KEEP IN MIND

"Knowing that Christ being raised from the dead, dieth no more; death hath no more dominion over him" (Romans 6:9).

FOCAL VERSES

John 20:1 The first day of the week cometh Mary Magdalene early, when it was yet dark, unto the sepulchre, and seeth the stone taken away from the sepulchre.

2 Then she runneth, and cometh to Simon Peter, and to the other disciple, whom Jesus loved, and saith unto them, They have taken away the Lord out of the sepulchre, and we know not where they have laid him.

3 Peter therefore went forth, and that other disciple, and came to the sepulchre.

4 So they ran both together: and the other disciple did outrun Peter, and came first to the sepulchre.

5 And he stooping down, and looking in, saw the linen clothes lying; yet went he not in.

6 Then cometh Simon Peter following him, and went into the sepulchre, and seeth the linen clothes lie,

7 And the napkin, that was about his head, not

lying with the linen clothes, but wrapped together in a place by itself.

8 Then went in also that other disciple, which came first to the sepulchre, and he saw, and believed.

MAR 27TH

9 For as yet they knew not the scripture, that he must rise again from the dead.

10 Then the disciples went away again unto their own home.

Romans 6:1 What shall we say then? Shall we continue in sin, that grace may abound?

2 God forbid. How shall we, that are dead to sin, live any longer therein?

3 Know ye not, that so many of us as were baptized into Jesus Christ were baptized into his death?

4 Therefore we are buried with him by baptism into death: that like as Christ was raised up from the dead by the glory of the Father, even so we also should walk in newness of life.

5 For if we have been planted together in the likeness of his death, we shall be also in the likeness of his resurrection:

6 Knowing this, that our old man is crucified with him, that the body of sin might be destroyed, that henceforth we should not serve sin.

7 For he that is dead is freed from sin.

8 Now if we be dead with Christ, we believe that we shall also live with him:

9 Knowing that Christ being raised from the dead dieth no more; death hath no more dominion over him.

10 For in that he died, he died unto sin once:

but in that he liveth, he liveth unto God.

11 Likewise reckon ye also yourselves to be dead indeed unto sin, but alive unto God through Jesus Christ our Lord.

13 Neither yield ye your members as instruments of unrighteousness unto sin: but yield yourselves unto God, as those that are alive from the dead, and your members as instruments of righteousness unto God.

IN FOCUS

The story was told: there once lived a little boy who loved ants. He loved ants so much that each day after school he would dash home, throw his books onto a table, make a quick sandwich, grab his radio, and exit to the back steps, where he would sit for hours listening to his favorite music while watching the ants as they worked and played.

One afternoon as he sat watching the ants, the announcer interrupted the music with an urgent announcement. "Beware, beware," he warned, "an aardvark has escaped from the local zoo." The boy became terrified. He knew that the zoo was only a few blocks from his home and the ants were in great danger. Excitedly, he began to jump up and down on the ground while shouting at the ants. "Beware, beware; you are in danger!" No matter how hard he made the ground vibrate or how loud he shouted at the ants, they did not seem to know that he existed. The boy grew more frantic and finally went into the house to share his dilemma with his father. "Dad, no matter what I do, they just ignore me. If only I could become one of them, I could go down there and warn them."

Miraculously, the boy got his wish and became an ant. He made his way to the highest place he could find and began to shout his warning to all the other ants. Soon he began to attract a large crowd that listened intently to what he was saying. Before long, they began to whisper to one another. "Who is this and where did he come from? What does he mean, 'Get into your colony, you're in danger'? What's an aardvark?" The crowd grew impatient with the strange ant in their midst and had their leadership drive him to the edge of their camp, where they beat him until he died.

The apostle John tells us that Jesus was in the world and the world was made by Him. He goes on to inform us that Jesus came unto His own and most did not receive Him because they did not know Him. But to everyone who received Him, He gave the power to become the sons of God.

THE PEOPLE, PLACES, AND TIMES

Mary Magdalene. She was first introduced to us by Luke, the physician (Luke 8:2-3), as one of the women from whom Jesus cast demons. Mary had been delivered from seven demons and apparently spent her days joining the other women who devoted themselves to ministering to Jesus.

Simon Peter. He served as the head of the band of disciples. The other disciples recognized Peter's authority after the Lord entrusted him with the keys of the kingdom. It is not surprising, therefore, that Mary and John would defer to his leadership upon seeing the empty tomb.

The Other Disciple. This is the apostle John, also identified in Scripture as the disciple whom Jesus loved. While hanging from the Cross, Jesus would instruct John to care for His mother. John would later be confined to the Isle of Patmos, where he would receive the vision that became our book of Revelation.

Jerusalem. It is a mountain city that sits on the edge of one of the highest tablelands in Palestine. Under Kings David and Solomon, Jerusalem became the capital of the kingdoms of Israel and Judah. Though called "the City of Peace," Jerusalem has known very little peace throughout its history. At the time of Jesus, the city had fallen under the authority of King Herod and the Roman Empire.

BACKGROUND

For three years Jesus walked the earth, teaching His disciples and demonstrating before the Jewish religious authorities that He was their long-awaited Messiah. Finally, in an ultimate show of rejection and contempt, the religious authorities conspired with the Roman government and the Jewish populace to kill the Lord. The Roman form of capital punishment was chosen, and Jesus was hung on a Cross until He died. After all were certain of His death, Jesus' disciples were permitted to take His body down from the Cross and lay it in an unused grave. On the first day of the week, Mary Magdalene was returning to the grave to tend to the body of the Lord when she discovered that the stone covering the tomb's opening had been rolled away and the body was no longer there.

AT-A-GLANCE

1. The Discovery (John 20:1-7)
2. The Illumination (vv. 8-10)
3. Our Response (Romans 6:1-11, 13)

IN DEPTH

1. The Discovery (John 20:1-7)

After Roman soldiers were certain that Jesus was dead, and intervention was made with Pontius Pilate, loving hands were permitted to lower Him from the Cross, wrap His body in a shroud with spices, and place it in a borrowed grave. On the first day of the week, Mary Magdalene arrived at the tomb only to discover that its stone covering had been rolled away and the body of Jesus was gone. She promptly returned to the city, where she informed John and Peter of her discovery. The two disciples began running toward the site where they knew that Jesus had been buried. Because he was younger, John outran Peter and arrived at the tomb first, but out of respect for Peter's position as the leader of the disciples, he did not enter. Rather, John waited until Peter arrived and then followed him into the grave.

2. The Illumination (vv. 8-10)

Peter didn't hesitate before entering the Lord's tomb. The same eagerness and impulsiveness that characterized his life before the Lord's death remained. Once inside, Peter could observe that the burial cloth (napkin), which had been used to cover the Lord's face, was neatly folded together in a place separate from the other grave clothes. John, after following Peter into the cave, was also able to observe the empty cloth. Scripture does not record Peter's response to what he observed. However, John saw, and because of what he saw, he believed.

John's faith was bolstered by the physical evidence of the empty grave clothes and he was able to believe what he did not understand. In time, Peter would believe as well. Perhaps his exposure to the empty tomb and to John's faith helped him.

3. The Response (Romans 6:1-11, 13)

Grace has been said to be an acronym for "God's Riches At Christ's Expense." The riches that Christ secured for us included the right to share in His victory over death. Death is defined as eternal separation from both the presence and influence of God, so when Christ's sacrifice on Calvary was accepted by God—as evidenced by God raising Him from the dead—Christ extended that acceptance to each of us. For that reason, anyone who is in Christ need no longer fear death—separation from God.

The only condition upon our acceptance by God is that we receive Christ and seek to live our lives in a fashion worthy of His sacrifice. God's grace is a gift offered to us through Christ.

SEARCH THE SCRIPTURES

1. What was John's response upon entering the tomb and seeing the shroud (John 20:8)? *saw & believed*

2. Where was the napkin that had covered the Lord's face (v. 7)? *wrapped in a place by itself*

3. Why does the Scripture say we are dead to sin (Romans 6:2)? *we do not live any longer Roman 6:4 therein*

DISCUSS THE MEANING

1. Why do you think Mary was returning to the tomb before daybreak? Do you think she was alone?

2. Why do you suppose Mary did not enter the tomb with the disciples?

3. What is the significance of the fact that the linen clothes were still present in the tomb?

4. What does it mean that "anyone who has died has been freed from sin" (Romans 6:7, NIV)? What kind of death are we freed from?

LESSON IN OUR SOCIETY

Movies, videotapes, and books have all conspired together to condition our response to the notion of death. We see it as a terrible realm inhabited by demons, zombies, and the like. However, when we lose a loved one to death, our response to that realm is completely different. Our fear gives way to a hope that they have gone to a place of light, rest, and peace. How does the way we live our life in this world temper the way we view death? Which would you prefer to have: the popularity and wealth of this world, or the assurance that death would find you in a realm of light, rest, and peace?

MAKE IT HAPPEN

Jesus, by living a life pleasing to God, broke the bonds of death over humanity. God confirmed this by raising Jesus from the dead. Write a litany celebrating the victory of Christ over death.

FOLLOW THE SPIRIT

What God wants me to do:

_____

_____

REMEMBER YOUR THOUGHTS

Special insights I have learned:

_____

_____

MORE LIGHT ON THE TEXT

John 20:1-10; Romans 6:1-11, 13

1 The first day of the week cometh Mary Magdalene early, when it was yet dark, unto the sepulchre, and seeth the stone taken away from the sepulchre.

Mary Magdalene's association with Jesus most likely begins when He cures her and other women of demon possession (Luke 8:2) sometime during the second year of His ministry. Prior to that time, there is no mention of her. Her name indicates that she either came from or was a resident of the town of Magdala, situated on the western shore of the Sea of Galilee. The identification of Mary Magdalene as a prostitute is widely believed, especially by American Catholics and also in many western European countries where

homes for unwed mothers are routinely named "Magdalene" homes. This notion is, however, unfounded and has no scriptural evidence to support it.

There is, however, plenty of evidence to show that from the time of Mary's deliverance at the hands of Jesus, all of the Gospel writers acknowledge her as a constant presence in the life and ministry of Jesus. Her miraculous cure by Jesus earned Him her untiring faith and devotion. Mary Magdalene appears to have been a woman of substantial means, as it seems she ministered to the needs of Jesus and the other disciples with her own money (Luke 8:1-3). Interestingly, the account of the sepulchre visitation differs ever so slightly between the Gospel writers. Matthew reports that Mary Magdalene was accompanied by the "other Mary" (Matthew 28:1). Mark records the presence of three women: Mary Magdalene; Mary, the mother of James; and Salome (Mark 16:1). Luke records the greatest number of women. He writes, "It was Mary Magdalene, and Joanna, and Mary the mother of James, and other women that were with them" (from Luke 24:10). John only bothers to mention Mary Magdalene visiting the tomb. The fact that her name is always mentioned first when listed with a group of women indicates that she was obviously a leader in the female circle of disciples. (Matthew 27:56; Mark 16:1; Luke 24:10). The only exception is at the foot of the Cross, when Jesus' female family members' names are listed first (John 19:25).

Faithful to Jesus even after His death, Mary is described by John as rising early and going to Jesus' tomb to anoint His body with precious ointments and spices as was the custom of the day. Both Mark (15:47) and Luke (23:55) record that Mary and the other women had watched Jesus' burial and the sealing of the tomb. So, while we are not surprised that Mary could locate the tomb in the dark of the early morning hours, it is not clear how she expected to remove the huge stone placed at the entrance of the tomb. Perhaps she expected the Roman soldiers who were guarding the tomb to roll away the stone for her. In any case, when Mary Magdalene arrives at the burial site, the giant stone has already been removed.

Mary Magdalene discovers that Jesus' tomb has been opened and He is not there.

selves (28:2-6). The narratives of both Mark and Luke indicate that the women enter the tomb and encounter an angel, who announces that Jesus has risen. John's difference does not imply any disharmony in the Gospels. Instead, it suggests a differing view of the more significant points of the account. We must also remember that of the four Gospel writers, John is the only writer who was actually an eyewitness to this event. It is quite possible that he prioritized the notification of Peter and himself and simply chose to leave out details that occurred before his arrival at the grave site. This is logical in light of the fact that his Gospel is written after the other three; he knows they have already included this detail. The fact that Mary announces that the body is missing implies that she has indeed entered the sepulchre.

Interesting, too, is the fact that John does not name the other disciple, the one "whom Jesus loved." There is no doubt that it can only be the writer of the Gospel, John, the brother of James. John never identifies himself in his own Gospel, choosing instead to refer to himself only as the son of Zebedee or, as he does in this account, the one Jesus loved.

2 Then she runneth, and cometh to Simon Peter, and to the other disciple, whom Jesus loved, and saith unto them, They have taken away the Lord out of the sepulchre, and we know not where they have laid him. 3 Peter therefore went forth, and that other disciple, and came to the sepulchre.

At this point in John's narrative, Mary Magdalene runs to tell Peter and the other disciples that Jesus' body is missing. John does not tell us that Mary has yet to even enter the interior of the tomb. In John's account, Mary does not enter the tomb until after she notifies the men (20:11-12). Matthew's account tells of a "great earthquake" and has the angel rolling back the stone, making the announcement to the women, and inviting them inside the tomb to see for them-

4 So they ran both together: and the other disciple did outrun Peter, and came first to the sepulchre.

Only John's gospel records that the "other disciple" outran Peter to the sepulchre. Again, this does not indicate disharmony, but rather the emphasizing of certain details by the writer, who also happens to be a central character. Here, John is relating the sense of excitement he surely must have felt at that time. He was younger than Peter and certainly would have been able to outdistance the older man as they raced to the tomb.

5 And he stooping down, and looking in, saw the linen clothes lying; yet went he not in.

Although John outruns Peter and arrives at the sepulchre first, he does not go in. Some have argued that perhaps John was afraid to enter the tomb alone. A more likely reason is that he simply defers to the older apostle. It is probably out of respect for Peter's position as leader of the apostles that John allows Peter to enter the tomb first.

6 Then cometh Simon Peter following him, and went into the sepulchre, and seeth the linen clothes lie, 7 And the napkin, that was about his head, not lying with the linen clothes, but wrapped together in a place by itself.

Here John seems to emphasize the supernatural implications concerning the burial linens. Also, since Jesus was no longer dead and had conquered death by His Resurrection, He no longer had need of burial clothing. The linen grave clothes were for the dead; those who had not risen could not, and had not, conquered death. Only the Son of the One and Only God could win and seal the victory over sin and death, therefore, securing our own salvation.

8 Then went in also the other disciple, which came first to the sepulchre, and he saw, and believed.

John's gospel alone records that upon seeing the empty grave and the discarded grave clothes John "believed." This is understandable since the writer, better than anyone else, would know this to be a fact. It is interesting to note that in Luke's account, Peter, upon seeing the discarded burial clothing, "wonder[ed] in himself at that which was come to pass" (Luke 24:12).

While Peter, the elder statesman, puzzles over the occurrence, the younger disciple believes. Here John uses the Greek word *pisteuo* (**pist-yoo'-o**), which means to have faith or conviction.

9 For as yet they knew not the scripture, that he must rise again from the dead. 10 Then the disciples went away again unto their own home.

Verse 9 offers a fuller explanation for Peter's puzzlement and John's subsequent belief by emphasizing how unexpected these events were to both he and Peter. Although the two of them were closer to Jesus than any of the other apostles, these events still take these men by surprise. It had only been days earlier when Jesus had spoken to His disciples, telling them, "A little while, and ye shall not see me: and again, a little while, and ye shall see me" (John 16:19). The apostles were unsure of what Jesus meant. That He would defy the laws of nature and be physically raised from the dead had not occurred to them. Therefore, in verse 10, they simply went to their homes again, pondering all that they had seen and heard.

Romans 6:1 What shall we say then? Shall we continue in sin, that grace may abound?

In the previous chapter, Paul, writing to the church in Rome, underscores that grace is the supreme example of God's unmerited and certainly undeserved favor toward unrighteous mankind. Paul has previously argued that in the absence of reverence for God, sin reigns in the life of man. While the Mosaic Law pointed out man's sin and provided a guideline for godly behavior, the Law did not have the power to save mankind from the ultimate penalty of sin: death. No, the Law was not enough. Man was justified, or made clean in the eyes of God, through the sacrificial death of an innocent Jesus Christ on the Cross and through the power of His resurrection from the dead. At the heart of Paul's argument is that strict and unfailing adherence to the Law is impossible. However, through grace, man has already been justified. Man is not saved through the Law, but by grace through faith (Ephesians 2:8-9). Knowing this would raise the inevitable question, "Why then should man even bother trying to obey the Law since man is no longer under the Law?" Paul raises the question rhetorically.

2 God forbid. How shall we, that are dead to sin, live any longer therein?

Continue to live in our sin? Certainly not, Paul answers. Through Jesus' death, we died to sin. We cannot continue to live in something that has died. We are different now.

3 Know ye not, that so many of us as were baptized into Jesus Christ were baptized into his death?

Paul now uses the symbolism of baptism to explain the change in life that should be evident in the lives of the Christians. His Roman readers were familiar with the rite of baptism. The Greek word for "baptized" is *baptizo* (**bap-tid'-zo**) meaning "to wash." When being baptized (washed), a person is identified with the death, burial, and resurrection of Christ. This signifies that the person is a new creation. Old things, or the old way of living, has passed away. All things were now new as the born-again believer could begin life anew, fresh, with a clean slate (2 Corinthians 5:17).

4 Therefore we are buried with him by baptism into death: that like as Christ was raised up from the dead by the glory of the Father, even so we also should walk in newness of life.

The baptism of a group to their leader was a recognizable possibility that Paul had addressed earlier in his writings to the Corinthian church. Paul had described how the Children of Israel "were all baptized unto Moses in the cloud and in the sea" (1 Corinthians 10:2). The protective cloud, provided by God, had accompanied and protected the Israelites as they were symbolically buried between the walls of the Red Sea that hovered on either side of them. The symbolic connection between death, Resurrection, and water baptism was pointed out by Jesus Himself. From the beginning of His earthly ministry, Jesus was aware that His prepared body had to be put to death, buried, and raised (resurrected) by His Father on the third day. Jesus had, in fact, already told His disciples, "I have a baptism to be baptized with" (Luke 12:50). He had also told His disciples that they, too, would have to undergo a baptism unto death (Mark 10:39). It is by faith in the risen Lord, Jesus Christ, that the believer becomes an integral part of that death, burial, and Resurrection. This is the baptism that grace provides for all believers, that they may be fully united with Jesus Christ.

5 For if we have been planted together in the likeness of his death, we shall be also in the likeness of his resurrection:

This spiritual union with Jesus Christ is made clearer in this verse by the use of the Greek word for "planted," *sumphutos* (**soom'-foo-tos**), and the word for "likeness," *homoioma* (**hom-oy'-o-mah**). *Sumphutos* means "to be closely united to," while *homoioma* means "made like." Paul, then, is stating that if we have been united with Jesus in His death, then we will also experience a resurrection similar to His. In short, like Jesus, we will conquer the power of sin and the penalty of sin: death.

6 Knowing this, that our old man is crucified with him, that the body of sin might be destroyed, that henceforth we should not serve sin. 7 For he that is dead is freed from sin.

Here Paul points out the sacrificial nature of Jesus' death. As He hung on the Cross, and at the very hour of His death, the sins of the world were taken on by Him. Because Jesus had stepped out of His glory and had assumed the prepared body of flesh and blood, He could offer that body to His Father as a perfect and final sacrifice for the sins of the world.

The literal translation of verse six is, "Knowing this, that our old man was crucified with (Him) that the body of sin might be done away, so that we no longer serve sin." Paul is asserting that our sinful nature is slain so that the yoke of sin is destroyed. Once released from the enslavement, man is free to love God and enjoy fellowship with our liberator, Jesus Christ. More specifically, man is now free to pursue righteous rather than sinful acts.

8 Now if we be dead with Christ, we believe that we shall also live with him:

"Dead with Christ" refers to our dying (figuratively) to our old sinful nature. Through faith, we believe that just as our former sinful nature was destroyed by Jesus' death, our new life was started with His Resurrection. In both death and resurrection, we are one with Christ.

9 Knowing that Christ being raised from the dead dieth no more; death hath no more dominion over him. 10 For in that he died, he died unto sin once: but in that he liveth, he liveth unto God.

When Jesus' body died on the Cross, the collective sins of those living, and those yet to be born, died with Him. The bottom line of justification is that when Jesus died, in the eyes of God the sinful nature—"the old man"—died, too. The sin that was created in the flesh was destroyed in the flesh. This act of justification was singular; it was done once for all! Sin is dead, and the "new man" is free to enjoy a new life of fellowship in Jesus Christ.

11 Likewise reckon ye also yourselves to be dead indeed unto sin, but alive unto God through Jesus Christ our Lord.

Jesus took our sins upon His shoulders on the Cross at Calvary. When He died, so did the former hold of sin on our lives. Sin was dead. When Jesus arose on the third day, He arose with power and glory. The sin remained dead. Through faith in Jesus Christ, the Christian acknowledges that his sin was crucified on the Cross. When He arose, He was no longer enslaved to sin. The new Adam (Jesus Christ) has fully and finally paid for the sin of the first Adam.

Mankind is only able to serve one master. If indeed we recognize that we have been blood bought, redeemed, and justified, then we are obligated to renounce any former hold sin may have had in our lives. Through the baptism of the Holy Spirit, we are empowered to have dominion over ungodly thoughts and deeds. Because Jesus paid the price, Christians are free to choose to live righteously.

13 Neither yield ye your members as instruments of unrighteousness unto sin: but yield yourselves unto God, as those that are alive from the dead, and your members as instruments of righteousness unto God.

Here, Paul makes it painfully clear that though the penalty of death has been removed from the lives of believers, sin still exists and must be guarded against. In other words, we no longer live in sin, but sin still lives in us. The literal Greek translation of the words for "yield" (*paristemi,* **par-is'-tay-mee**) and "instruments" (*hoplon,* **hop'-lon**)

sheds some interesting insight on this verse. *Paristemi* means "to stand beside." Similarly, the word "instrument" is literally translated to mean "weapons." Thus, we can read the verse this way: "Don't stand beside your members (or body parts) as weapons to sin." The implication is that the body does not rule man; rather, man rules the body. The next clause, "as those that are alive from the dead," makes it clear that this empowerment over the will of the sinful nature is given to the believer through his faith. "Alive" alludes to the new life we have through our faith in the Lord Jesus Christ. This new life is one of power and dominion, rather than helplessness and subjection. Instead, the Scripture tells us, we are to stand beside the body, including the thoughts, as weapons to God for His use and purpose.

DAILY BIBLE READINGS

M: Walk in Newness of Life
Romans 6:1-5

T: Not Under Law, But Under Grace
Romans 6:6-14

W: Be Slaves of Righteousness
Romans 6:15-23

T: Jesus Rises to New Life
Luke 24:1-9

F: The Resurrection of Jesus
John 20:1-10

S: Jesus Appears to Mary
John 20:11-18

S: Jesus Appears to the Disciples
John 20:19-23

Find out how many times the word *dead* is used in relation to spiritual concepts by using your *Precepts For Living* CD-ROM to cross-reference Romans 6:11.

TEACHING TIPS

April 3
Bible Study Guide 5

1. Words You Should Know

A. Condemnation (Romans 8:1) *katakrima* (Gk.)—Means an adverse sentence (the verdict). It is a word used to declare a sinner guilty and deserving of punishment.

B. Abba (v. 15) *abba* (Gk.)—An affectionate word for "father" in Aramaic. It is equivalent to "Dad" or "Daddy." "Abba" was used by Jesus in Gethsemane (Mark 14:32, 36) and used by the apostle Paul to express the Christian's relationship with God.

2. Teacher Preparation

A. Pray for the students in your class, asking God to open their hearts to today's lesson.

B. Study the FOCAL VERSES.

C. Read BACKGROUND and THE PEOPLE, PLACES, AND TIMES section. •

D. Write the answers to the SEARCH THE SCRIPTURES and DISCUSS THE MEANING questions and study them.

3. Starting the Lesson

A. Before the students arrive to class, write the LESSON AIM on the board.

B. Ask one student to lead the class in prayer.

C. Read the FOCAL VERSES and KEEP IN MIND verse together in class. Ask for volunteers to read the IN DEPTH section and explain the verses.

4. Getting into the Lesson

A. To help the students focus on today's lesson, ask for a volunteer to read BACKGROUND and THE PEOPLE, PLACES, AND TIMES section. Discuss the sections briefly.

B. Have volunteers read, and then solicit responses to, the SEARCH THE SCRIPTURES questions.

C. Ask a student to read the DISCUSS THE MEANING questions, and generate a thorough discussion around class responses.

5. Relating the Lesson to Life

A. Have the students read the LESSON IN OUR SOCIETY exercise. Ask the students to give examples of how the flesh can act as a "bully" in their lives.

B. Ask the students to share any insights they may have received from today's lesson.

6. Arousing Action

A. Direct the students' attention to the MAKE IT HAPPEN section, and encourage them to practice it this week.

B. Remind the students to read the DAILY BIBLE READINGS and to complete the REMEMBER YOUR THOUGHTS and FOLLOW THE SPIRIT sections for the week.

C. Ask if there are any particular prayer requests, and end the lesson with prayer.

APRIL 3RD

WORSHIP GUIDE

For the Superintendent or Teacher
Theme: Life in the Spirit
Theme Song: "Spirit of the Living God"
Scripture: Romans 8:1-17
Song: "Holy Spirit, We Welcome You"
Meditation: Lord Jesus, we thank You
for redeeming us. We honor and praise
Your holy name. Help us to live in accordance with Your Spirit, and guide us in all
righteousness. In Jesus' name we pray.
Amen.

LIFE IN THE SPIRIT

Bible Background • ROMANS 8:1-17
Printed Text • ROMANS 8:1-16
Devotional Reading • ROMANS 7:1-6

LESSON AIM

By the end of the lesson, the students will understand the difference between living in accordance with the sinful nature or with the Spirit of God. Students will also learn why those who are in Christ Jesus are not condemned.

KEEP IN MIND

"For as many as are led by the Spirit of God, they are sons of God" (Romans 8:14).

FOCAL VERSES

Romans 8:1 There is therefore now no condemnation to them which are in Christ Jesus, who walk not after the flesh, but after the Spirit.

2 For the law of the Spirit of life in Christ Jesus hath made me free from the law of sin and death.

3 For what the law could not do, in that it was weak through the flesh, God sending his own Son in the likeness of sinful flesh, and for sin, condemned sin in the flesh:

4 That the righteousness of the law might be fulfilled in us, who walk not after the flesh, but after the Spirit.

5 For they that are after the flesh do mind the things of the flesh; but they that are after the Spirit the things of the Spirit.

6 For to be carnally minded is death; but to be spiritually minded is life and peace.

7 Because the carnal mind is enmity against God: for it is not subject to the law of God, neither indeed can be.

8 So then they that are in the flesh cannot please God.

LESSON OVERVIEW

LESSON AIM
KEEP IN MIND
FOCAL VERSES
IN FOCUS
THE PEOPLE, PLACES,
AND TIMES
BACKGROUND
AT-A-GLANCE
IN DEPTH
SEARCH THE SCRIPTURES
DISCUSS THE MEANING
LESSON IN OUR SOCIETY
MAKE IT HAPPEN
FOLLOW THE SPIRIT
REMEMBER YOUR THOUGHTS
MORE LIGHT ON THE TEXT
DAILY BIBLE READINGS

9 But ye are not in the flesh, but in the Spirit, if so be that the Spirit of God dwell in you. Now if any man have not the Spirit of Christ, he is none of his.

10 And if Christ be in you, the body is dead because of sin; but the Spirit is life because of righteousness.

11 But if the Spirit of him that raised up Jesus from the dead dwell in you, he that raised up Christ from the dead shall also quicken your mortal bodies by his Spirit that dwelleth in you.

12 Therefore, brethren, we are debtors, not to the flesh, to live after the flesh.

13 For if ye live after the flesh, ye shall die: but if ye through the Spirit do mortify the deeds of the body, ye shall live.

14 For as many as are led by the Spirit of God, they are the sons of God.

15 For ye have not received the spirit of bondage again to fear; but ye have received the Spirit of adoption, whereby we cry, Abba, Father.

16 The Spirit itself beareth witness with our spirit, that we are the children of God:

IN FOCUS

Little Marshall, only 12 years old, had the title of school bully. Every day he would post himself outside the schoolyard fence and demand a 25-cent toll from those students he could intimidate. Jake was one of his favorite classmates to hit or put in a headlock if he would not kneel on the ground and give him a quarter. One day, Jake finally had enough. Little Marshall ordered him in front of a large circle of students.

"Get down on your knees and give me my money, and you won't get hurt."

Jake went down on one knee with the quarter squeezed in his fist. Something in Little Marshall's voice and the laughter of his class-mates hit Jake harder than any punch he had taken from the bully. In that second, Jake's spirit of fear subsided. He flew at Little Marshall swinging wildly and blindly; this time, Little Marshall had no time to get in the first blow. A looping openhanded wallop caused the quarter in Jake's hand to clip the bully in the eye. The unexpected pain was too much for Little Marshall. He fell to his knees crying. Jake was surprised that he had bested the bully and surprised himself again by saying, "I will never let you hurt me again." Little Marshall never did.

Believers have a Spirit in them, the Holy Spirit, who will fight our battles and help us overcome the bullying tactics of the flesh. Through the power of the Holy Spirit, we can live victoriously over our sinful nature.

THE PEOPLE, PLACES, AND TIMES

The law of the Spirit. Represents the authority that is exercised by the Holy Spirit, a principle of law.

The Spirit of life. This term is used to describe the Holy Spirit. He brings into the believer the essence of life, for He is the Spirit of Life.

The law of sin and death. Represents our unsaved and condemned state before sanctification in Christ Jesus. "It is the authority that sin had over our old nature, ending in complete severance of fellowship with God. That new nature could not break the shackles at all. Only the coming of a higher authority and power could accomplish this, namely, the Holy Spirit. The Holy Spirit operates upon the new nature, which is vitally joined to the life of Christ."

McGee, J. Vernon. "Thru the Bible Commentary." *Precepts For Living, The Annual Sunday School Lesson Commentary.* Chicago: UMI, 2002. CD-ROM.

BACKGROUND

In the previous chapter, the apostle Paul talks about the Law of God and how our sinful nature wars against God's Law. It is the Law of God that reveals our guilt and sin. It is against the Law of God that we see the wretchedness of man, his frailty, his depravity, and his natural inability to keep the commandments of God's perfect will. Paul meticulously breaks down man's natural horrid condition and explains why it was necessary for a divine intervention from God; for without God's Spirit, man is completely lost and unable to live this Christian life. Even with the Spirit of God living on the inside of us, every believer must continuously fight this ongoing battle between the Spirit of God and the sinful nature. The Spirit of God resides in an imperfect body, and it is within this earthly tent that a spiritual war is waged! However, God has given us complete victory over sin through our Lord and Saviour Christ Jesus. Victory is achieved by surrendering our will to the Spirit of God. This involves submitting to God's Word and allowing God's Spirit to control every aspect of life, spiritual and physical.

In chapter 8, Paul continues to speak on the topic of spiritual victory over the sinful nature (the flesh). The power of God's Spirit dwells on the inside of those who are in Christ Jesus. Christians are not doomed or weakened by the sinful nature. We have the potential to live victoriously over sin. We are alive in Christ Jesus, and our bodies, although active and living, are "dead" to the sinful nature. The same "resurrection power" that raised Jesus from the dead resides on the inside of us. This is a powerful chapter, for it makes a believer question his or her walk with God. It also helps the believer examine his or her relationship with God. What kind of lifestyle do you demonstrate? Are you walking according to the sinful nature or the Spirit of God?

AT-A-GLANCE

1. God Redeems Us (Romans 8:1-4)
2. God Regenerates Us (vv. 5-9)
3. God Reminds Us (vv. 10-13)
4. God Reconciles Us (vv. 14-16)

IN DEPTH
↘ 1. God Redeems Us (Romans 8:1-4)

Jesus' death at Calvary reconciled us back into a right fellowship with God. Jesus took our place on the Cross and broke the power of "the law of sin and death" in our lives. The "law of sin and death" refers to man's fallen condition. The penalty for man's rebellion against God was spiritual and physical death. We humans in our sinful condition cannot uphold the righteous laws of God. So God sent His Son Jesus Christ to do what we could not do for ourselves. He totally fulfilled every aspect of the law by living a perfect life, thus earning all the blessings of God. He also exhausted all God's condemnation (curses) for sin on the Cross. What was impossible to achieve through our flesh was accomplished through our Lord and Saviour Jesus Christ. In Him we have credit for having kept all the law's requirements and suffered all the law's punishments. Therefore, there is now no condemnation for those who are in Christ Jesus (Romans 8:1, NIV). We are free!

Before He returned to heaven, Jesus promised His followers He would never leave them to face the troubles of this world alone. He told them He would always be with them, even to the end of the age. Jesus also promised to send a Comforter, the Holy Spirit (Spirit of life), who would empower them and lead them into the truth of God's Word. Jesus kept His promise. If we are believers, we have access to the Holy Spirit, who dwells on the inside of us and enables us to live this Christian life.

2. God Regenerates Us (vv. 5-9)

The man without God's Spirit is powerless to follow God. There is nothing in him that summons a need to follow or respond to God. Even on our very best day, the sinful nature will always fall short of meeting God's standards. A worldly-minded person seeks to please his or her sinful nature. A worldly-minded person is "dead" to the things of God and "alive" to his/her sinful nature. The Spirit of God does not lead worldly-minded people. Worldly-minded people serve themselves, not God. If we are not serving God and glorifying His name, then we are exalting and glorifying ourselves. Self-glorification leads to "spiritual death." The term "spiritual death" describes someone who is spiritually disconnected from God. Those who are in Christ Jesus are spiritually connected to God. They are "alive" to the things of God and "dead" to the sinful nature.

Peace with God grants us security in knowing that after physical death we will receive eternal life with God. The carnal mind is inept and cannot comprehend or experience the peace of God. Because of sin, the worldly mind is hostile toward God. What God requires of our minds is in contrast to the desires of our sinful nature. Only the infallible Word of God and the power of the Holy Spirit can change a worldly mind. Anyone operating from a worldly and sinful existence cannot please God. His faith is not rooted in God, nor does he have the Holy Spirit to lead or instruct him in the things of God. And without faith it is impossible to please God.

3. God Reminds Us (vv. 10-13)

As children of God, we are given the precious gift of the Holy Spirit. Some religious denominations believe this gift is given to us when we are saved; others believe it is given to us when we are baptized; and still others believe it is something we ask God to give us. In any case, it is the Holy Spirit that enables the believer to live a Spirit-filled life. The Holy Spirit reminds us of the Word of God. With the Holy Spirit working on the inside of us, we should demonstrate God's Word through our actions, speech, and attitudes.

The blood of Jesus Christ is the cleansing power that redeems the man without the Spirit. When the child of God sins, he or she is convicted by the Holy Spirit. The convicting power of the Holy Spirit troubles a believer, making the believer uncomfortable with sin, which leads to confession and repentance. On the contrary, the unbeliever doesn't operate from this premise. An unbeliever is deceived into thinking his or her piety controls the sinful nature. All of us have met self-righteous people who delight in their accomplishments and idolize their concept of "goodness." They are deceived and believe their "good deeds" have earned God's favor. Unfortunately these individuals have no knowledge of the cleansing and healing power of Jesus Christ (1 John 1:7). The unbeliever is oblivious to human depravity. This powerful delusion is one of Satan's most popular tricks. He convinces the unbeliever that he doesn't need God. The truth is, we all need God.

As Christians, we must examine our faith and ourselves. Are we in the faith? Do we pay more attention to the fleshly sinful nature or to the Spirit? We do not owe the sinful nature our time, love, or attention. We are dead to its unrelenting demands and are not obligated to serve it. If we serve the Lord and are led by His Spirit, our worldly ways should diminish and we will seek to please the Lord.

The sinful mind goes to great lengths to accomplish its goals. It is relentless, yet with the power of the Holy Spirit, believers can overcome its persistent efforts! How many victories have you had over your sinful nature lately? Are you saved? If not, now is a perfect time to ask the Lord to come into your life. He is ready!

4. God Reconciles Us (vv. 14-16)

What does it mean to be a son (or daughter) of God? It means we have complete security in Christ Jesus! It means God owns us! He declares us as His children (v. 14)! As children of God, we walk in confidence, acknowledging our true inheritance—eternal life. This tremendous change in our legal status makes God our Father! This is a difficult concept to grasp, but it is true! When we receive Jesus Christ as Lord and Saviour, God becomes our spiritual "Dad" [or Abba] (v. 15).

When we become children of God, the Spirit of God bears witness with our spirit (v. 16). What this means is that our spirit is connected to God. There is something about being connected to God that only a child of God can understand. It is more than a feeling; it is a confirmation within our spirit that tells us that Christ lives in us. It is an affirmation we get when we read His Word, it is the evidence we see in answered prayers, and it is the faith we have when we intercede on behalf of our loved ones.

As God's precious sons and daughters, we have legal rights to His promises. All the promises of God are "yes" and "amen" in Christ (2 Corinthians 1:20). God is faithful, and we can rest in His promises and know that He loves us.

SEARCH THE SCRIPTURES

1. Why is there no condemnation for those who are in Christ Jesus (Romans 8:1)?

2. What is the difference between a carnally-minded person and a spiritually-minded person (vv. 6, 7)?

3. What does it mean to be a son (or daughter) of God (vv. 14-16)?

DISCUSS THE MEANING

1. Describe the lifestyle of someone who lives in accordance with the flesh.

2. Describe the lifestyle of someone who lives in accordance with the Spirit.

3. Why are carnally-minded people hostile toward God?

LESSON IN OUR SOCIETY

Many churches have developed outreach ministries that deal with addiction. Saints who suffer from alcohol and drug abuse can join these ministries to seek godly assistance and counsel. These ministries have helped thousands abstain from substance or alcohol abuse. Most of us might not belong to a particular ministry that deals with addiction. However, if the truth be told, many saints suffer from old compulsive habits or less conventional addictive behavior, which interferes with our living in accordance with God's Spirit. Some examples of this behavior, are gossiping, overspending (which leads to debt), lying, promiscuity, overeating, gambling, procrastination, slothfulness, negative thinking, talkativeness, and compulsive exercising, just to name a few. What compulsive habits or addictive behavior do you suffer from?

MAKE IT HAPPEN

Think about your own behavior. Pray and ask God to reveal to you whether you are living a carnal or Spirit-filled life. Ask God to identify those old fleshly habits in your life. Write down His response. God will lead you in what to do and help you in conquering this habit and/or attitude. Take action today!

FOLLOW THE SPIRIT

What God wants me to do:

_____

_____

REMEMBER YOUR THOUGHTS
Special insights I have learned:

_____

_____

MORE LIGHT ON THE TEXT
Romans 8:1-16

Here in chapter eight, Paul preaches power! Paul argues that the power of the Holy Spirit changes the believer through his faith in Jesus Christ. In previous chapters, Paul has introduced the power of sin. Now he turns his attention to the solution: the power of the Holy Spirit over sin. The indwelling power of the Holy Spirit offers man triumph rather than struggle. Through the "law of the Spirit of life" (Romans 8:2), the believer's faith will give him the power to become the new creature God has declared him to be.

1 There is therefore now no condemnation to them which are in Christ Jesus, who walk not after the flesh, but after the Spirit.

In this chapter, Paul's theme is centered on power in the life of the believer. The New Testament writers, in general, and Paul, in particular, write of two specific types of power: *exousia* (Gk. **ex-oo-see'-ah**) and *dunamis* (Gk. **doo'-nam-is**). The first, *exousia*, is the power equated with divine authority. It is the *exousia* that Jesus refers to when He declared to His apostles that "all power is given unto me in heaven and in earth" (Matthew 28:18). The second power, or *dunamis,* describes the dynamic strength or wonder-working power exercised through the Holy Spirit by the believer. This is the power that is referred to when Jesus instructs His disciples that "ye shall receive power, after that the Holy Ghost is come upon you" (Acts 1:8). It is this latter power, this gift of the Holy Spirit, which emboldens and enables believers to live a Christian life.

Paul personalizes this very important teaching by addressing the Roman church in the first person. He has already emphasized the stronghold of sin, in general, and sinful nature, in particular: "For what I want to do I do not do, but what I hate I do" (Romans 7:15, NIV). There is, he points out, a constant battle to subdue the sinful nature and bring it into submission. The Law, Paul explains, only seems to make him more aware of how far he is from righteousness. Paul concludes that there are two laws at work: God's law and the law of sin. He admits that in his mind, he is "a slave to God's law, but in the sinful nature a slave to the law of sin" (v. 25b, NIV).

Moving forward, Paul is adamant that there is "no condemnation to them which are in Christ Jesus." To be sure, the first-century Roman believers, to whom this letter is addressed, had an immediate understanding of the concept of "condemnation." Many of the Hebrew Christians were not citizens of Rome and enjoyed none of its privileges or protections. These Hebrew Christians were under constant and oppressive scrutiny by the Roman government. They would have been painfully aware that the tiniest infraction could result in their immediate condemnation by the Roman authorities. Being found guilty of any breach of Roman laws (i.e., failing to show the proper deference to the emperor or some other authority figure) could subject them to loss of property, beatings, or imprisonment.

Similarly, we should recall that even the strictest adherence to the Mosaic Law did not have the power to free man from sin. In fact, everything about the Law condemned the sinful nature. The Law could only offer a standard for righteousness. At best, it served to demonstrate how far afield humanity was from righteousness. Man's salvation was accomplished only through Jesus' redemptive death on the Cross. Thus, through Jesus Christ, we are free to live under grace and not the Law. Similarly, Jesus' death and Resurrection justified man, or made us guiltless before God. Through Jesus Christ, man was brought out of sin and returned to sonship with God. It is only through our faith and belief that Jesus died, was buried, and rose to save us from our sins that the penalty is forever removed from the lives of believers.

2 For the law of the Spirit of life in Christ Jesus hath made me free from the law of sin and death.

The Spirit Paul refers to in this verse must be understood to be *pneuma* (**pnyoo'-mah**), the Holy Spirit. We should understand the Holy Spirit to be a distinct personality of the triune God and a significant influence in the lives of believers. He is the same Spirit Jesus referred to when he told Nicodemus, "Except a man be born of water and of the Spirit, he cannot enter into the kingdom of God" (John 3:5).

3 For what the law could not do, in that it was weak through the flesh, God sending his own Son in the likeness of sinful flesh, and for sin, condemned sin in the flesh:

In this verse, Paul again refers to the inadequacy of the Law. The Law held only the power to condemn. It had no power to renew or change man's desire to live godly. This renewal was accomplished though the Resurrection of Jesus Christ. God, Paul explains, fashioned his only Son in the form of a man in order to sacrifice Him for the sins of man. Jesus, in flesh, died for the flesh. It is the power of sin to condemn us to death that has been nullified. God will no longer condemn us to death for our sins as the Law once did.

Here again, the reader must appreciate Paul's candor. He makes it clear that the struggle between "the sinful nature or the flesh" and righteousness is always present in his life (i.e., the life of every believer). It is obvious that he knows the Roman believers are struggling as he has been struggling. He wants to make it clear that God does not condemn or reject the believer for the struggle. Through Jesus Christ, we are members of God's family, and He does not kick us out because of our failures. This security was blood bought!

4 That the righteousness of the law might be fulfilled in us, who walk not after the flesh, but after the Spirit.

It is important to note that neither our salvation nor our justification eliminated sin itself. Sin still exists. Man still wrestles against sin. Paul acknowledges this constant struggle, as every believer should. Some believers mistakenly believe that upon their confession of faith, God removes sin and temptation. Paul posits that the desire, or temptation, to "walk...after the flesh" will abate only after the believer understands and believes that in Christ he has been made a new creature. Through the power of the Holy Spirit, believers will want to walk in righteousness rather

than in the sinful nature. That which the Law was unable to legislate—the will to live righteously—the Holy Spirit empowers the believer to do.

5 For they that are after the flesh do mind the things of the flesh; but they that are after the Spirit the things of the Spirit.

The Holy Spirit does not mysteriously hover over the heads of believers, suddenly swoop down on them, bring a short period of deliverance, and then simply vanish. The Holy Spirit is not an "act." Rather, the Holy Spirit is the operative that empowers and enables the believer to live a godly life. While the Holy Spirit indwells every believer, the believer must choose to access that power. This, Paul makes clear, is an all-or-nothing proposition. The old self cannot be permitted to live, because God has declared that it must die.

6 For to be carnally minded is death; but to be spiritually minded is life and peace.

Paul has already established that the worldly ("carnal") people cannot please God, and that through the Holy Spirit, the believer is empowered to live righteously. The notion of "carnal" and "flesh" immediately bring to mind sins of a sexual nature. We should note, however, that as "carnally minded" is used here, it does not mean only the body. More specifically, Paul is addressing sins that take root in our bodies. Hence "carnally minded" certainly includes lying, jealousy, obscene and lustful thoughts, selfish ambitions, ungodly conversation, hostile and bitter feelings toward others, and, perhaps the most dangerous of all, arrogance. All are an abomination to God. The carnal or worldly must die so that the Spirit can reign in the life of the believer. Here, Paul makes it clear that the mind that longs for the carnal will end in death. Similarly, the spiritually minded, that is, the mind of the believer that is, empowered by the Holy Spirit, ends in life and peace.

7 Because the carnal mind is enmity against God: for it is not subject to the law of God, neither indeed can be.

Here, Paul pauses to provide the reason for the opposition he presented in verse six. The answer lies in the Greek translation for the word "enmity," *echthra* (**ekh'-thrah**) meaning "hatred." Paul is saying that the carnal mind hates God! Jesus Himself had taught that "No man can serve two masters: for either he will hate the one, and love the other; or else he will hold to the one, and despise the other" (Matthew 6:24). The believer, now free to choose, must decide between the old master—the sinful nature or the new master—a Spirit-filled life in Jesus Christ.

8 So then they that are in the flesh cannot please God.

All of the previous verses are wrapped up neatly in this one simple sentence. A sinful man cannot please God! This is at odds with the condition of the believer, who longs to please his Creator. This verse echoes a similar teaching for the Galatian church: "For the sinful nature desires what is contrary to the Spirit...They are in conflict with each other" (from Galatians 5:17, NIV).

9 But ye are not in the flesh, but in the Spirit, if so be that the Spirit of God dwell in you. Now if any man have not the Spirit of Christ, he is none of his.

Now that Paul has drawn the line in the sand, he reminds the readers that they are not in the flesh. Through the grace of God, which provided the means of our salvation, and through our justification in Jesus, our minds are renewed by the constant indwelling of the Holy Spirit.

10 And if Christ be in you, the body is dead because of sin; but the Spirit is life because of righteousness.

The conditional clause "and if Christ" at the beginning of this verse indicates that the verse is clarifying Paul's previous point. It also serves to protect the integrity of Paul's gospel against those who would attempt to weaken it by saying, "If you're in Christ, and the penalty of sin is gone, then you can do anything you want." Here Paul argues that this is impossible since the Holy Spirit is at work in the life of each believer.

The preposition "in" carries tremendous weight in this context. The Greek word *en* (**en**) functions to describe the Holy Spirit at rest and in

a fixed position within us. The believer, then, is possessed by God, who resides at the center of our being. The dependent clause that follows—"the body is dead"—is ironic. How can the believer be dead and alive at the same time? The Greek word for "rendered dead" is *nekros* (**nek-ros'**) and describes a life that is spiritually destitute of God. Paul is using it here to support the affirmation of believers being dead to the body that would otherwise condemn us. Instead, Paul argues that our life is now a possession of the Spirit.

The Greek word for "righteousness," *dikaiosune* (**dik-ah-yos-oo'-nay**), describes a condition acceptable to God. It implies correct thinking, purity of life, virtue, and integrity from God's perspective. Paul is teaching that unless the believer embraces righteousness as given by the Spirit, he or she is left with only self-righteousness.

"Righteousness" is an important word in Scripture. It is especially significant to Paul, who uses it 38 times in the book of Romans alone. It is used more in this epistle than any other time in the entire New Testament.

11 But if the Spirit of him that raised up Jesus from the dead dwell in you, he that raised up Christ from the dead shall also quicken your mortal bodies by his Spirit that dwelleth in you.

Paul is repeating the theme of Spirit possession here. Paul stresses that the "quickening" is the power that raised Christ from the dead and is the same Holy Spirit power residing in each believer. This quickening revives us from the flesh to godly living.

12 Therefore, brethren, we are debtors, not to the flesh, to live after the flesh. 13 For if ye live after the flesh, ye shall die: but if ye through the Spirit do mortify the deeds of the body, ye shall live.

The use of the word "therefore" indicates that Paul is now concluding the previous thought. This conclusion appears to be a call to action for believers. Knowing that we are redeemed (a result of God's unmerited favor on our behalf), knowing the price of that redemption (the intentional sacrifice of His beloved Son), and knowing the benefit of our redemption (kinship with the Father, Son, and Holy Spirit), what are we prepared to do? Paul declares that we are free to live, through the Holy Spirit, for God that we might one day live and reign with Him.

14 For as many as are led by the Spirit of God, they are the sons of God.

It is interesting to note the similarity and continuity of theme in this verse and John 1:12: "But as many as received him, to them gave he power to become the sons of God." Here and in John, the emphasis is on "the power" and the title, "sons of God." John offers that the believer is endowed with the power and the title upon his entry, or acceptance, into Christ. Here in Romans, Paul emphasizes that as the believer progresses and pursues God's plan, he affirms his right to assume both the power and the sonship of God.

15 For ye have not received the spirit of bondage again to fear; but ye have received the Spirit of adoption, whereby we cry, Abba, Father.

Through the Holy Spirit, the creation (man) now shares in the most intimate of relationships with our Creator. We, like His beloved Son, Jesus, are freed from the sinful nature and are able to come before Him as His children in full sonship with Jesus to cry Abba. "Abba" is a tender modification, appealing to both the love and compassion of the Father. This is the term of endearment Jesus Himself used in the Garden of Gethsemane when he lay on the ground agonizing over His impending crucifixion and praying "Abba, Father" (Mark 14:36).

16 The Spirit itself beareth witness with our spirit, that we are the children of God:

The chapter concludes with a glorious affirmation. Paul declares that the evidence of our salvation is known subjectively. He describes the Spirit of God bearing witness, or in direct communication with, our spirit. While our faith affirms that

we belong to Christ Jesus, the Holy Spirit confirms that we belong and are in covenant relationship with Him. When the Holy Spirit is operating in the life of the believer, there is a change. Both believers and others will see a discernable difference. The indwelling of the Holy Spirit manifests itself by the visibility of the fruit of the Spirit in our lives. The sinful works of the sinful nature will be replaced by "love, joy, peace, patience, kindness, goodness, faithfulness, gentleness and self-control" (Galatians 5:22-23, NIV).

DAILY BIBLE READINGS

M: New Life in the Spirit
Romans 7:1-6

T: Sin Brings Death
Romans 7:7-13

W: The Struggle with Sin
Romans 7:14-19

T: Captive to the Law of Sin
Romans 7:20-25

F: Living According to the Spirit
Romans 8:1-5

S: You Are in the Spirit
Romans 8:6-11

S: Led by the Spirit
Romans 8:12-16

Utilize your *Precepts For Living* CD-ROM to search through past *Precepts For Living* lessons for additional insights on the person and work of the Holy Spirit.

TEACHING TIPS

April 10
Bible Study Guide 6

1. Words You Should Know

A. Heart (Romans 10:6, 8-10) *kardia* (Gk.)—The center of one's physical and spiritual life.

B. Deep (v. 7) *abussos* (Gk.)—A pit of an immeasurable depth used to hold the dead.

C. Report (v. 16) *akoe* (Gk.)—An instruction, hearsay, or rumor. It refers here to the preaching of the Gospel.

2. Teacher Preparation

A. Read the BIBLE BACKGROUND and the FOCAL VERSES.

B. Read Mark 7:1-14 and Romans 10—11 for an understanding of the Israelites' misplaced zeal and God's plan for their restoration.

C. Think about a time when you were zealous about a cause based on incomplete knowledge. Be prepared to share how receiving additional information rounded out your knowledge and either positively or negatively impacted your zeal.

D. Be prepared to share definitions of *Lord* and *Saviour,* and how a person's behavior is based on correct knowledge of the two.

3. Starting the Lesson

A. Begin the class with prayer, thanking God for the assurance of a zealous faith based on accurate knowledge of salvation through Jesus Christ.

B. Share your "zealous cause" story.

C. Ask volunteers to read KEEP IN MIND.

D. Discuss the question: "If accepting salvation is so easy, why does it appear to be so difficult?"

4. Getting into the Lesson

A. Ask a volunteer to read the FOCAL VERSES.

B. Write the words *Lord* and *Saviour* on the board; ask for definitions of both. Discuss what it means to live as a Christian, focusing on definitions provided by students, and a person's behavioral responses to those definitions.

5. Relating the Lesson to Life

A. Have the students write a brief, one-paragraph "affirmation" of faith, including the year in which they were born again, what they did to receive Christ, and how He is both Lord and Saviour in their lives.

B. Have a few volunteers read their affirmations.

C. Encourage them to examine their affirmations in light of the discussions and Romans 10:9.

6. Arousing Action

A. Some of your students may have made Christ their Saviour, but have difficulty trusting Him as Lord. Others may never have received Christ. If any are willing to share their fears, or challenges, allow them to do so.

B. Conclude with prayer. If any students desire the new birth, pray with them to receive Christ. Pray that all students will affirm Christ as Lord and Saviour, with corresponding zeal.

WORSHIP GUIDE

For the Superintendent or Teacher
Theme: Salvation in Christ
Theme Song: "Pass Me Not O Gentle Saviour"
Scripture: Romans 10:9
Song: "Is Your All on the Altar?"
Meditation: Dear Lord, thank You that You do not want anyone to be lost, and that Your salvation includes even me. I trust You as Saviour. Always let me trust You as Lord. Amen.

SALVATION IN CHRIST

Bible Background • ROMANS 10:5-21
Printed Text • ROMANS 10:5-17
Devotional Reading • HEBREWS 5:5-10

LESSON AIM

By the end of the lesson, the students will understand that while salvation is offered to everyone, knowledge plays a key role in one's ability to affirm Christ as Lord and live a faith-based, rather than works-driven, Christian life.

KEEP IN MIND

"That thou shalt confess with thy mouth the Lord Jesus, and shalt believe in thine heart that God hath raised him from the dead, thou shalt be saved" (Romans 10:9).

FOCAL VERSES

Romans 10:5 For Moses describeth the righteousness which is of the law, That the man which doeth those things shall live by them.

6 But the righteousness which is of faith speaketh on this wise, Say not in thine heart, Who shall ascend into heaven? (that is, to bring Christ down from above:)

7 Or, Who shall descend into the deep? (that is, to bring up Christ again from the dead.)

8 But what saith it? The word is nigh thee, even in thy mouth, and in thy heart: that is, the word of faith, which we preach;

9 That if thou shalt confess with thy mouth the Lord Jesus, and shalt believe in thine heart that God hath raised him from the dead, thou shalt be saved.

10 For with the heart man believeth unto righteousness; and with the mouth confession is made unto salvation.

LESSON OVERVIEW

LESSON AIM
KEEP IN MIND
FOCAL VERSES
IN FOCUS
THE PEOPLE, PLACES, AND TIMES
BACKGROUND
AT-A-GLANCE
IN DEPTH
SEARCH THE SCRIPTURES
DISCUSS THE MEANING
LESSON IN OUR SOCIETY
MAKE IT HAPPEN
FOLLOW THE SPIRIT
REMEMBER YOUR THOUGHTS
MORE LIGHT ON THE TEXT
DAILY BIBLE READINGS

---

11 For the scripture saith, Whosoever believeth on him shall not be ashamed.

12 For there is no difference between the Jew and the Greek: for the same Lord over all is rich unto all that call upon him.

13 For whosoever shall call upon the name of the Lord shall be saved.

APRIL 10TH

14 How then shall they call on him in whom they have not believed? and how shall they believe in him of whom they have not heard? and how shall they hear without a preacher?

15 And how shall they preach, except they be sent? as it is written, How beautiful are the feet of them that preach the gospel of peace, and bring glad tidings of good things!

16 But they have not all obeyed the gospel. For Esaias saith, Lord, who hath believed our report?

17 So then faith cometh by hearing, and hearing by the word of God.

IN FOCUS

"I believe my dog is my dead grandmother," said the contestant on a television pet talent show before beginning their routine. The woman's words stumped this writer's second grade son. "That's stupid," he said, "a dog can't be a person." Agreeing, I patiently explained that the person wasn't stupid, just ignorant of Scripture's teaching on death and the afterlife. I also explained that after a loved one's death, some people without

Christ seek solace from the occult, or by believing a pet (or something else) is their lost loved one. Hearing the Gospel could possibly lead them to recognize the truth of mankind's mortality, and accept Christ. Doing so can bring the needed comfort during bereavement.

It's been said that knowledge is power. In today's lesson, we'll see just how powerful knowledge can be in transforming one's belief systems.

THE PEOPLE, PLACES, AND TIMES

Romans. The church at Rome, recipients of the apostle Paul's letter, primarily comprised of non-Jewish (Gentile) believers.

Word of Faith. The apostle's letter reaffirms the basic doctrine of salvation by faith—(not works)—available to Jews and Gentiles alike. He also affirms that preaching as a form of word-of-mouth promotion continues to be a primary way to spread the Gospel, and to build a foundation of faith necessary to desire and receive salvation.

BACKGROUND

Born a Jew, Paul was highly educated in the Jewish faith and understood the doctrine, teaching, and workings of the Law. His education, training, and love for the Law contributed to his zealous opposition of Christians and their teachings. As a former persecutor of Christians, therefore, he understood how zeal for a cause could turn a person into a murderous opponent.

After his dramatic conversion while traveling to Damascus to detain and imprison Christians (Acts 9), Paul (also called Saul) became a defender of the faith he had, up to then, despised. More so, he became the Apostle to the Gentiles and the one directly called to reach his former enemies.

In addressing the believers of the church at Rome, Paul confesses his fervent prayer that his Jewish brothers would be saved. He relates that he can "bear record" of their zeal without knowledge, referring to his former anti-Christian activities.

Finally, he makes it clear that the church at Rome should not become cocky in their position in Christ, because God's plan is to restore a remnant of Israel. The following chapter more thoroughly addresses this, admonishing Gentile

believers not to get conceited about their faith in light of Israel's present disobedience.

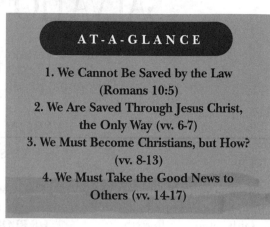

AT-A-GLANCE

1. We Cannot Be Saved by the Law (Romans 10:5)
2. We Are Saved Through Jesus Christ, the Only Way (vv. 6-7)
3. We Must Become Christians, but How? (vv. 8-13)
4. We Must Take the Good News to Others (vv. 14-17)

IN DEPTH

1. We Cannot Be Saved by the Law (Romans 10:5)

Even though Paul had not started the church at Rome, he had heard a great deal about it. In this letter to them, after having introduced himself in earlier chapters, he championed the real message of the Good News of salvation. He enlightened these Gentile and Jewish believers about the futility of trying to be saved by the Law. He showed them, and us today, that no one can meet such high standards set by the Law and be saved. After all, we are all sinners. He wanted us to appreciate that in order to be saved by the Law, a person would have to live a perfect life, and no one but Jesus Christ Himself could do that. Sinning even one time would mean that we would be lost.

Paul explained further that God gave the Law, not to save us, but to show us how guilty we are before a holy God; to show us our lostness, our dilemma. The sacrificial system of the Law educated people of their need for a lamb without blemish. That lamb is Jesus Christ (Hebrews 10:1-4). This system of ceremonial Laws was to be fulfilled in Christ. The Law, therefore, pointed to Christ. This was the reason for all those animal sacrifices before He came. Even though the animals had to be without blemish as spelled out in Deuteronomy 15:21, oftentimes the rules were broken by Israel because of their own rebellion against God.

2. We Are Saved Through Jesus Christ, the Only Way (vv. 6-7)

Jesus is the "end of the law." With His death, burial, and Resurrection, He fulfilled the purpose and goal of the Law (Matthew 5:17). Unlike Jesus Christ, however, the Law cannot save anyone. Nothing can bridge the gap between a holy God and sinful man. Receiving Jesus Christ as Lord and Saviour is the only way. Therefore, God's salvation is right in front of us, and we have to choose Jesus if we want eternal or everlasting life. The salvation that God offers is a gift, and we need to respond and receive it or be lost forever.

Through Jesus, we can stand before a holy God justified, as though we had never sinned. Otherwise, we will stand before Him guilty and have to take the punishment for our sins. Instead of grace and mercy, we will receive condemnation. Therefore, mankind should be grateful that God loved us so much that "He sent His only begotten Son, that whosoever believeth in him should not perish, but have everlasting life" (John 3:16).

What makes Jesus' coming even more awesome is the fact that God sent His Son when we were yet sinners, when we did not love Him in return. This showed God's limitless unconditional love for mankind.

Furthermore, Paul wanted us to know that this great salvation is available to all regardless of who we are, where we come from, or what we have done or have not done in life. We are saved by God's grace (unmerited and undeserved favor). We receive this grace by putting our complete trust in Jesus—in His death and Resurrection. His Resurrection meant that our atonement for sin was finished. He had conquered both sin and death. The first Adam brought sin and death into the world. The second Adam, Jesus, defeated them both and brought victory to all believers.

3. We Must Become Christians, but How? (vv. 8-13)

Sin has cut us off from God, but Paul explains in verses 8-13 how to get back to God and be *saved*. It is not a complicated process, but based on a simple faith in the finished work of Jesus on the Cross. God said that if we confess with our mouths that Jesus is Lord, and believe in our hearts that God Himself raised Jesus from the dead; then we are saved (v. 9). This profession can be made by both Jews and Gentiles alike (v. 12) because with God there is no favoritism when it comes to salvation (Romans 2:11). This stipulation is very important to both the Jews and Gentiles, because oftentimes disputes arose over salvation, traditions, and Jewish customs such as circumcision or eating the right foods. Some Jews wanted to add to God's plan of salvation, but these additional things were not included by Him. Therefore, they wanted confession of sin, believing on the Lord Jesus Christ, plus circumcision or eating the right foods for the Gentiles to be saved. Also because they thought they were chosen by God because they were Jews, they often felt superior to the non-Jewish Christians. Paul, however, explained that it's God's plan by itself that saves, and nothing is added, or subtracted from it.

Paul wanted both Jews and Gentiles to know in this letter that our sins point out our need for a Saviour. We need to be cleansed and made whole—and only Jesus can do that.

4. We Must Take the Good News to Others (vv. 14-17)

Because there is no favoritism with God, He desires that none be lost. God wants everyone to have the opportunity to confess and receive Jesus as Saviour and Lord. Therefore, motivated by God's glory, God's love, and our own love for mankind, we must take the Good News to our family, neighbors, and others who cross our paths, so that they can hear and believe as well. God is calling us to bring the Good News of salvation to others.

God has decreed that witnessing and preaching to the lost will be our role. Through our Christian living, loving, teaching, and preaching, they will know that we follow Christ. We are to "let our lights so shine before men that they may see our good works, and glorify our Father which is in heaven" (Matthew 5:16). If God's Spirit is indeed in us, we will obey this command. If this is not true of us, then we need to examine ourselves, because God's Word says, "You, however, are

It is the Cross that reconciles sinful humans with Holy God.

controlled not by the sinful nature but by the Spirit, if the Spirit of God lives in you. And if anyone does not have the Spirit of Christ, he does not belong to Christ" (Romans 8:9, NIV). God's Spirit operating in us will certainly obey God's Word to carry the Good News to the ends of the earth.

Scripture notes that we are "ministers of reconciliation" (2 Corinthians 5:18) and "ambassadors of Christ" (v. 20). Our "preaching" is usually in the form of sharing our testimony as we proclaim the power of the Gospel to change lives. In order to demonstrate faith in Jesus Christ, Paul mentions "preaching" as a means of spreading the word of faith. In today's multimedia environment, "preaching" goes beyond pulpit ministry. It includes messages shared during telecasts and broadcasts, in books, videos, CDs, DVDs, and websites. Regardless of the technology, however, verbally proclaiming the Gospel will always remain an integral part of evangelistic endeavors, as word-of-mouth promotion is often the most effective way to share Good News.

SEARCH THE SCRIPTURES

1. Who described the righteousness that is of the law (Romans 10:5)?

2. What must a person believe about God and Jesus (v. 9)?
3. Who can be saved (vv. 11, 13)?
4. How does God use the preacher (v. 14)?
5. Can just anyone be a preacher (v. 15)?
6. How does faith come (v. 17)?

DISCUSS THE MEANING

1. Why is it so hard for some people to accept God's Plan of Salvation?
2. What might happen if God allowed man to decide who would be saved or lost?

LESSON IN OUR SOCIETY

God surely has a sense of humor. Religious, racial, and economic barriers separate people and fuel hatred and discord. But just when we think we know it all and are better than everyone else, God provides a Damascus Road experience to shed light on our own unrighteousness and neediness. Our perceived enemies today may be our mission fields tomorrow. Jesus died and was resurrected because of God's love for all persons. How does knowing this make it easier to share your faith with nonbelievers?

MAKE IT HAPPEN

There are people all around you who need to hear the Good News of salvation. Determine in your heart and carry out the plan of witnessing to someone in your family, on your job, or in your community. Pray first and ask God to show you someone who is in need of a Saviour and to help you find the right time, place, and words to obey His command.

FOLLOW THE SPIRIT

What God wants me to do:

_____

_____

REMEMBER YOUR THOUGHTS

Special insights I have learned:

_____

_____

MORE LIGHT ON THE TEXT
Romans 10:5-17

Paul's letter to the church in Rome is written to speak to both Jewish and Gentile Christians. It is overflowing with the theme of "salvation through faith in Christ, and not of works." Paul is addressing Jewish and Gentile Christians, creating an environment of peace and unity rooted in faith in Christ.

5 For Moses describeth the righteousness which is of the law, That the man which doeth those things shall live by them.

The description the apostle Paul gives of the righteousness of the Law is written in Leviticus 18:5. Paul is speaking of God's command to the people to observe and keep the moral law. The word "righteousness" comes from the Greek word *dikaiosune* (**dik-ah-yos-oo'-nay**), which means "to be in a condition acceptable to God." Righteousness by the Law is directly related to human works, both external and internal. In the Law, the emphasis is placed on human activity, and righteousness is based on one's actions and deeds. The Law required perfect obedience, something impossible for fallen mankind.

6 But the righteousness which is of faith speaketh on this wise, Say not in thine heart, Who shall ascend into heaven? (that is, to bring Christ down from above:) 7 Or, Who shall descend into the deep? (that is, to bring up Christ again from the dead.)

Paul moves his reader from the righteousness of the Law to the righteousness of faith. Paul uses phrases taken from Deuteronomy 30:12-13. Just as Moses left the Children of Israel without an excuse, Paul is leaving both his original audience and his modern-day readers without an excuse. The righteousness of faith is not a mystery. It is not hidden in the heavens, nor is it buried in the deep. The righteousness of faith is not attainable by human actions. It is not necessary or possible for any person to go to heaven or to launch into the deep to bring Christ and have Him revealed. Christ has done all the work necessary for humans to obtain right standing with God. Christ descended from heaven, took on human form, and fulfilled all the righteousness of the Law by living a life free of sin. He bore the penalty of sin, suffered on the Cross, died, and rose again in order that we might be declared righteous, regardless of the sins we have committed.

8 But what saith it? The word is nigh thee, even in thy mouth, and in thy heart: that is, the word of faith, which we preach;

Unlike in Deuteronomy 30:14, Paul uses this verse to remind us that the word is near us, in our mouth and heart; it is not based on what we will or will not do, but is based solely on faith. It is not what we must do, but what we must believe. The mystery of salvation, the righteousness of faith, has been revealed in Christ. "Word" comes from the Greek word *rhema* (**hray'-mah**) and means that which is or has been uttered by the living voice, the spoken word. The word is the message here. The way of righteousness has come to you. It is not in the Law, works, deeds, or behaviors; it is in your mouth and in your heart. The word of faith—righteousness based on faith—is what the apostle Paul is proclaiming. Paul's message to the church in Rome is equally relevant to the modern Christian regardless of location. We should not focus on outward deeds as a measuring tool for inward righteousness. Our focus on "works" righteousness will prevent us from seeing Christ (Romans 9:32). The message is to believe that God exists, that He is the Creator, and that He provides salvation and right standing to His creation through Jesus Christ. This is the message that transcends time and supercedes context and culture. Our justification and righteousness are rooted in our proclamation with our mouth and our belief in our heart that Jesus is Lord.

9 That if thou shalt confess with thy mouth the Lord Jesus, and shalt believe in thine heart that God hath raised him from the dead, thou shalt be saved.

The Greek word for "saved" is *sozo* (**sode'-zo**)

meaning "to save a suffering one from perishing." Notice the difference between the conditions of the Law and the righteousness of faith. The requirements of the Law were impossible. Yet salvation by faith is simple and easily attainable by anyone willing to confess with their mouth that Jesus is Lord and believe in their heart in His Resurrection from the dead. This inward belief and outward confession speaks to both Jesus as man and Jesus as God.

While we recognize that we are not saved by works, when we confess Jesus as Lord we must allow Him to reign over us in total. The proclamation that Jesus is Lord speaks of His triumph over sin, death, and the grave. However, it should also speak of our ability, through Christ, to live a life that represents Christ on the inside of us. Our outward life should be a testimony of our inward faith. While we are not perfect, let us continue to press toward perfection in Christ Jesus (Philippians 3:14).

10 For with the heart man believeth unto righteousness; and with the mouth confession is made unto salvation.

Righteousness begins in the heart. It is belief with all your heart that Jesus took on human nature, walked among mankind, lived a life free of sin, died on the Cross, and was resurrected from the dead. This belief in our heart is confirmed and reaffirmed by the confession of our mouth. The mouth speaks what is in the heart (Matthew 12:34).

"Salvation" comes from the Greek word *soteria* (**so-tay-ree'-ah**) meaning deliverance and preservation. Salvation, then, comes from God through Christ and is not based on one's works of righteousness, but on believing in the heart and confessing with the mouth. We must refrain from any attempt to add to the requirements of salvation. Notice it does not say that you must not do this or stop doing that. Salvation is simple and easy and is accessible to even a small child with limited understanding. The belief in the heart and the confession of the mouth provide the Christian with redemption from the wages of sin and preservation

from eternal damnation. The salvation of the Christian is in both the present and the future. The Christian is called to live victoriously and abundantly in this life and in the life to come.

11 For the scripture saith, Whosoever believeth on him shall not be ashamed. 12 For there is no difference between the Jew and the Greek: for the same Lord over all is rich unto all that call upon him. 13 For whosoever shall call upon the name of the Lord shall be saved.

Verses 11 through 13 show the inclusiveness of the Gospel of Jesus Christ. *Whosoever* does not omit anyone willing to believe in their heart and confess with their mouth the Lordship of Jesus Christ. The "whosoever" is not contingent upon race, gender, economic status, educational achievements, or human accolades. The "whosoever" bridges the gap between those who "have" and those who "have not." Paul speaks to both the Jewish and Gentile Christians. Christ is the common denominator and liberates us from the keeping of the Law. Christ moves beyond the Law of Moses and Jewish custom and opens the door for all to access the covenant blessings of God.

Christ will not dishonor, disgrace, or put you to shame. He is the ultimate example of God's impartiality toward His creation and His desire to see all mankind redeemed. God is ready to pour out His abundance upon all those who call upon Him. Verse 13 is taken from Joel 2:32 and is used to show that God is rich in mercy and is ready to dispense grace and salvation to all who ask. "Everyone who calls on the name of the Lord will be saved"—delivered from the penalty of judgment. We call on the Lord. Salvation through faith in Jesus Christ moved beyond Jewish custom and cultural practices. In the same manner, we are unable to earn our salvation through good works, church culture, and tradition. Christians must be careful not to judge one another based on outward actions. We must also strive to live a life that represents Christ and the power of the Holy Spirit to operate as Lord in and over our life. A life in Christ should differ markedly from a life void of Christ.

14 How then shall they call on him in whom they have not believed? and how shall they believe in him of whom they have not heard? and how shall they hear without a preacher? 15 And how shall they preach, except they be sent? as it is written, How beautiful are the feet of them that preach the gospel of peace, and bring glad tidings of good things!

Salvation comes through faith in Jesus Christ and the Resurrection. In order to believe, you must first hear the Gospel. In order to hear the Gospel, it must be preached. Who will preach the Good News for all to hear? Paul's charge to preach should be embraced by every Christian. Who will be sent to preach, proclaim, and share the Gospel? Anyone willing to go. "The harvest truly is plenteous, but the laborers are few" (from Matthew 9:37). You don't have to be a pastor, minister, or special person to share the Gospel. Be willing to share your testimony of salvation through faith in Jesus Christ to all who will listen. Preaching the Gospel is not limited to the Sunday preachers, for they are able to reach only those few who will come into the church. But every Christian has a responsibility to share Sunday's message with the friends, family, and coworkers they encounter throughout the week. For the only sermon that some will hear will be the one you preach. The only Bible that some will read will be the life you live.

16 But they have not all obeyed the gospel. For Esaias saith, Lord, who hath believed our report?

Not all Jews who heard the message of Jesus Christ embraced it and believed unto salvation; neither did all the Gentiles. However, that did not keep Paul and others from preaching the Good News that Jesus the Messiah had come, died, and risen from the grave. The same is true today. Not everyone who hears the message of Jesus Christ will accept the invitation to salvation. However,

that does not relieve us of our responsibility to preach to all we can. For we have a commission to spread the Gospel throughout the world (Mark 16:15). Our commission to preach the Good News is independent of the hearer's response to the message preached.

17 So then faith cometh by hearing, and hearing by the word of God.

Therefore, if people are going to have faith in God, the message of Jesus Christ must be preached. It is impossible to believe in what you have never heard. It is the hearing of the Word of God that ignites our faith. It is not always a one-time hearing, but it is a continuous hearing of the Word of God that feeds our faith. Whether you are a new convert or a seasoned Christian, it is imperative that your faith be continuously fed by the Word of God and that you be strengthened on this spiritual journey.

DAILY BIBLE READINGS

M: Christ, the Source of Eternal Salvation
Hebrews 5:5-10
T: On Your Lips, in Your Heart
Romans 10:1-8
W: Christ Is Lord of All
Romans 10:9-13
T: Faith Comes Through Christ's Word
Romans 10:14-21
F: Israel Is Not Lost to Christ
Romans 11:1-6
S: Gentiles Also Receive Salvation
Romans 11:13-18
S: All Will Be Grafted Together
Romans 11:19-23

Would you like to encourage and be encouraged by other believers? Why not share the testimony of how you became a Christian with the *Precepts* Discussion Group contacted through your *Precepts For Living* CD-ROM. You will be encouraged by the testimonies others have shared.

TEACHING TIPS

April 17
Bible Study Guide 7

1. Words You Should Know

A. Beseech (Romans 12:1) *parakaleo* (Gk.)—To beg urgently; to entreat.

B. Bless (v. 14) *eulogeo* (Gk.)—To speak well of by expressing good wishes upon another.

2. Teacher Preparation

A. Read through the BIBLE STUDY GUIDE and focus on the FOCAL VERSES.

B. Study the IN DEPTH section and make notes to discuss in class.

3. Starting the Lesson

A. Review last week's lesson with the students.

B. Role-play the IN FOCUS story. Next give the students the opportunity to talk about times when they experienced compromising situations and how they were able to overcome them.

C. Have a student lead the class in prayer, using the LESSON AIM as the foundation.

4. Getting into the Lesson

A. Divide the class into groups according to the AT-A-GLANCE outline. Give the students ample time to read through the FOCAL VERSES so they will be able to answer the SEARCH THE SCRIPTURES questions at the end of the study period.

B. Ask your students what it means to be "a living sacrifice." Discuss their responses during the question and answer session.

C. Read THE PEOPLE, PLACES, AND TIMES section and ask the students to comment on what it must have been like to live in Rome during the time of Paul's writings.

5. Relating the Lesson to Life

Scripture says that we are *in* the world, but *not of* the world. In other words, there should be a distinction between believers and unbelievers. We must remember that we have the Holy Spirit living inside of us so that we can live according to God's Word. The world needs to see believers who refuse to compromise, are consecrated, and are committed to Jesus Christ.

6. Arousing Action

A. Allow your students to answer the DISCUSS THE MEANING questions as a group.

B. Next, have the students brainstorm on how they plan to accomplish the LESSON IN OUR SOCIETY exercise.

C. Challenge the students to complete the MAKE IT HAPPEN assignment.

D. Close the class with prayer, using the meditation below.

> *"Let love be without dissimulation. Abhor that which is evil; cleave to that which is good. Be kindly affectioned one to another with brotherly love; in honour preferring one another"* (Romans 12:9-10).

MARKS OF THE TRUE CHRISTIAN

Bible Background • ROMANS 12:1-21
Printed Text • ROMANS 12:1-2, 9-21
Devotional Reading • ROMANS 12:3-8

LESSON AIM

By the end of the lesson, the students will better understand how God's Word empowers them to live consecrated lives, they will commit to living transformed lives, and determine to apply brotherly love to their daily living.

KEEP IN MIND

"Let love be without dissimulation. Abhor that which is evil; cleave to that which is good. Be kindly affectioned one to another with brotherly love; in honour preferring one another" (Romans 12:9-10).

FOCAL VERSES

Romans 12:1 I beseech you therefore, brethren, by the mercies of God, that ye present your bodies a living sacrifice, holy, acceptable unto God, which is your reasonable service.

2 And be not conformed to this world: but be ye transformed by the renewing of your mind, that ye may prove what is that good, and acceptable, and perfect, will of God.

12:9 Let love be without dissimulation. Abhor that which is evil; cleave to that which is good.

10 Be kindly affectioned one to another with brotherly love; in honour preferring one another;

11 Not slothful in business; fervent in spirit; serving the Lord;

12 Rejoicing in hope; patient in tribulation; continuing instant in prayer;

LESSON OVERVIEW

LESSON AIM
KEEP IN MIND
FOCAL VERSES
IN FOCUS
THE PEOPLE, PLACES, AND TIMES
BACKGROUND
AT-A-GLANCE
IN DEPTH
SEARCH THE SCRIPTURES
DISCUSS THE MEANING
LESSON IN OUR SOCIETY
MAKE IT HAPPEN
FOLLOW THE SPIRIT
REMEMBER YOUR THOUGHTS
MORE LIGHT ON THE TEXT
DAILY BIBLE READINGS

---

13 Distributing to the necessity of saints; given to hospitality.

14 Bless them which persecute you: bless, and curse not.

15 Rejoice with them that do rejoice, and weep with them that weep.

16 Be of the same mind one toward another. Mind not high things, but condescend to men of low estate. Be not wise in your own conceits.

17 Recompense to no man evil for evil. Provide things honest in the sight of all men.

18 If it be possible, as much as lieth in you, live peaceably with all men.

19 Dearly beloved, avenge not yourselves, but rather give place unto wrath: for it is written, vengeance is mine; I will repay, saith the Lord.

20 Therefore if thine enemy hunger, feed him; if he thirst, give him drink: for in so doing thou shalt heap coals of fire on his head.

21 Be not overcome of evil, but overcome evil with good.

IN FOCUS

Joe and Rhonda are Sunday School teachers. For the past month, they have been teaching the theme of "In the World, But Not of the World." They challenged their students to live so that others can see Jesus Christ glorified in them. The students respect Joe and Rhonda as

APRIL
17TH

Christians who are living what they teach.

One Saturday night, Joe and Rhonda decided to go to a party at an unsaved couple's home. Everyone at the party seemed to be having a good time. One of the guests started telling jokes. The crowd thought he was funny, but his jokes were filled with obscenities and they degraded both women and men. Soon, Joe and Rhonda were laughing right along with everyone else. When a new couple arrived at the party, they listened in on the jokes. They were surprised to see Joe and Rhonda, their Sunday School teachers, laughing at such jokes. The couple approached Joe and Rhonda and asked, "What on earth are you doing here? We wouldn't expect you to be enjoying this type of party."

When Joe and Rhonda looked at the couple and then at each other, they felt a surge of guilt. Had they truly been practicing what they preached?

THE PEOPLE, PLACES, AND TIMES

Jews and Christians in Rome. Roman power made itself felt in the Mediterranean world during the time between the Old and New Testaments. By the opening of the New Testament, it was the dominant power in the Mediterranean region. Because Rome was the principal city of the empire, both Christians and Jews were eventually attracted to the city.

It is difficult to know when the first Jews arrived in Rome. Their presence in other major cities of the Mediterranean world, however, would make it likely they were present for a length of time before the Christian movement reached the city. We also have no information about when the Christian faith arrived in Rome. By the time Paul wrote the epistle to the Roman church (around the mid-first century A.D.), it had already become important (Romans 1:8). About the year A.D. 49, the emperor Claudius issued an edict expelling Jews from Rome. The fact that he expelled Christians as well (see Acts 18:2) indicates that at that time Roman officials did not differentiate between Christians and Jews, perhaps because the Christian community was not large enough to be significant. Some 15 years later, however, they were numerous enough to attract the blame from Nero for a fire that devastated Rome. An early tradition puts the martyrdom of both Paul and Peter in Rome around A.D. 64.

Cornell, T., and J. Matthews, ed. *Atlas of the Roman World.* New York: Norton Publishing Co., 1982. 5-140.

BACKGROUND

The epistle to the Romans is the longest and most influential letter the apostle Paul wrote. In fact, Romans is placed first among the other New Testament books. The apostle writes this letter with his apostolic mission to the Gentile world in mind.

In Romans 15:20, Paul's affirmation that he does not consider Rome as another apostle's specific territory or mission field leads another group of scholars to suppose that the church at Rome was established by some of Paul's converts from Asia and Macedonia. However, Acts 2:10 indicates that some of the Jews and proselytes converted on the Day of Pentecost were from Rome and could also have been instrumental in establishing the church.

Paul states that he often had plans to preach the Gospel to believers in the city, but was hindered from doing so (Romans 1:13-15; 15:22). He writes this book to prepare the way for his missionary trip to Rome and his anticipated mission trip to Spain. The apostle has a twofold purpose in writing this letter: to address certain problems in the church between the Jews and Gentiles and to challenge some ungodly attitudes among them (Romans 2:1-29; 11:11-36).

AT-A-GLANCE

1. The Believer's Call to Consecration (Romans 12:1-2)
2. The Believer's Call to Love (vv. 9-12)
3. The Believer's Call to Practical Living (vv. 13-21)

IN DEPTH

1. The Believer's Call to Consecration (Romans 12:1-2)

This is a clarion call to live a consecrated life. The call is based on all that God did. The way Paul phrases the idea shows that this is no arbitrary command, but is based squarely on God's active grace toward His people. "I beseech you therefore" is a culmination of the discussion of the righteousness of God, which has brought grace to us.

Paul begins the book by pointing out what God did for us through Jesus Christ. Through Christ, God brings Good News to us. This Good News empowers us and is available for the empowerment of all people.

The fall of Adam condemns us all to death, but God sent a second Adam—Jesus. We read in Romans 5:8 that God "commendeth His love toward us, in that, while we were yet sinners, Christ died for us"—the ungodly. Thus far, Paul addresses several reasons why we should consecrate ourselves to God.

It is important to note that throughout the King James Version, there are at least two words from the original Greek that can be translated as "mercy." One is *eleeo* and the other *eleos*. Here, Paul uses *eleos*, which contains within it the sense of helping one who is afflicted or seeking aid. We are called to enter into the pain God shares for us. It means "to sympathize with someone," but here it speaks more of God's compassion. This mercy has already been evoked within God before we even thought to ask for it. On this basis, Paul urges us to live a consecrated life. First, we are to consecrate our bodies. Because of our emphasis on spirituality, we tend to downplay the physical aspect of life. In Paul's day, some thought all God wanted was our spirit. For them, the spirit was completely removed from the human body and mind. Thus, for them, no matter what happened in the body, one could still be saved. In these verses, Paul turns this view upside down.

In 1 Corinthians, Paul goes further and states that our bodies are "the temple or dwelling place" of God. What does it mean, then, to "present our bodies"? The word "present" (*paristemi*, from the root word *paristano*), means "to bring to" or "to bring near." Our bodies serve as the conduit for recommending God to the world. They are the substantiation of our belief in God. Though our treasure (money) is important, our bodies must also be presented. Your physical presence is vital for communion with God. Saying, "I am in church in spirit" is insufficient. You must present your body!

Next, Paul tells us that our body is to be a "living sacrifice." In the Old Testament, there were a variety of sacrifices. There were "killed sacrifices" and offerings which were made of living seeds and animals. These living sacrifices were to be kept to sustain the priest of God, who in turn sustained the people of God through their ministry.

A sacrifice also entails surrender. Thus, in consecration, bodies are given to sustain God's work. Our bodies are given to reproduce the work of God daily; therefore, they are no longer ours, for they have been surrendered to the work of God. Not only is our sacrifice living, it is holy and set apart for the work of God. The fact that our bodies are living sacrifices for God means that they must conform to His character. They must be holy, for God is holy. Only that sacrifice that has God's characteristics as living and holy can be truly acceptable to God. Paul closes by telling us that this demand upon our bodies is both spiritual worship (NIV) and reasonable service (KJV).

Paul's argument goes deeper. He says, "be not conformed to this world." The idea here is that even our external mode of expressing ourselves should not reflect the present age. Why? Simply because our bodies, which are the external expressions of ourselves, have been given to God. If in fact our bodies have now been yielded to God, they should not seek fulfillment in this world, which is fundamentally anti-God. This negative exhortation, "be not conformed," is another way to remind us of the body's presentation to God. Consecration doesn't just call for the presentation of our external bodies to God; it calls for transformation of our minds.

When believers are renewed and transformed, they move into a position to prove what is the good, acceptable, and perfect will of God. In essence, they will be equipped to proclaim God's truths and His righteous standards as recorded in the Bible.

2. The Believer's Call to Love (vv. 9-12)

Our consecration, based on the mercies of God, leads us into a transformation made of relating not only to God but to our brothers and sisters. The call to consecrate is also a call to love. In fact, God says the only way to identify true believers is by the love we demonstrate to each other (1 John 4:7-11).

When we experience God's love despite our failures and imperfections, we are better able to love others. Yielding our lives to the Spirit of God empowers us to love others, abhor (or hate) evil, and cling to what is good (Romans 12:9).

Out of this love for others grows an orientation toward respect, kindness, affection, and a sincere concern for the welfare of others. When the love of God is shed abroad in our hearts, we may find ourselves desiring God's best for those with whom we interact and willing to help others achieve their God-given potential.

Paul reminds us that it is this love grounded in God's transforming mercy that helps us to "prefer" one another in honor. We are to look beyond the present to the God-given possibility in others. Too often, we focus more on people's weaknesses. We are encouraged to look beyond their shortcomings and pray for their victories. Praying for others changes our attitude and effects positive change in their lives.

The dedication to love also challenges us to be industrious in business, fervent in spirit. Why? We are ambassadors for Jesus Christ. Our pursuit of excellence in everything, including our home, workplace, and also our ministry grows out of our deep love for the God who saved us. We cannot afford to be lazy or indifferent because we belong to a God who excels. When people are hopeless, we offer them hope. When we face times of testing, we patiently endure them because we know the love of God. Having presented ourselves, we know that our lives ought to give glory to God and motivate others to put their trust in Him.

3. The Believer's Call to Practical Living (vv. 13-21)

Paul entreats believers to demonstrate their Christianity in practical ways. He says, "Bless them which persecute you: bless and curse not" (v. 14).

God wants us to respond in a Christlike manner since He has given us the Holy Spirit to enable us to overlook an offense.

We should remember that the only Jesus many people will see is His life manifested in us. We should not react like the world. Instead, we must learn how to "overcome evil with good" (v. 21). We can be instrumental in bringing people who have done us wrong to the Saviour. We should bless them when they persecute us. We may have to inconvenience ourselves by doing something kind and leaving the results up to the Lord.

Paul tells us how to react when others experience a "season" of joy. We must be happy for them and rejoice with them. On the other hand, we need to learn how to identify with another's pain and sorrow and weep with them. Every believer will go through seasons of joy and pain. We should be available and sensitive to the needs of others.

There is no place in the family of God for believers to favor one over another. We must avoid cliques and "the good old boys network." Our associations in Christ should be more of sowing in another's life rather than seeing what we can get from them. When people mistreat us, our new life in Christ dispels the "I'll get even with them" mentality. Instead, we are called to be people of integrity who deal honestly with others (vv. 15-17).

Christians are called to be peacemakers since the peace of Christ resides in us through the Holy Spirit. Paul does not encourage us to compromise our Christian faith, nor does he advocate that we disobey God's Word in order to live peaceably with others. In fact, he adds "if it be possible" as an addendum (v. 18). The apostle realizes that there may be times when we may not be able to keep the peace. On the other hand, we should avoid strife since we are called to seek and pursue peace at all times (Psalm 34:14).

Finally, Paul reminds believers of our responsibilities to live out the Gospel: to feed our enemies, give them something to drink, and treat them well, "for in so doing, thou shalt heap coals of fire on his head" (v. 20). They will be ashamed of how they have mistreated us. They will be surprised that the evil they perpetuated against us did not overcome us and cause us to react in a negative way. In fact, our goodness toward evildoers may motivate them to change their lives and become believer's in Jesus Christ.

SEARCH THE SCRIPTURES

1. What is "reasonable service" for a believer (Romans 12:1)?

2. What kind of love should believers demonstrate toward other people (v. 10)?

3. Why shouldn't believers avenge themselves (v. 19)?

4. How should a believer respond to someone who has done them wrong (vv. 20-21)?

DISCUSS THE MEANING

1. Is it possible for believers to live as the apostle Paul instructs? Why or why not?

2. How important is a transformed life? Discuss.

3. What would our world be like if we had more transformed people in religion, business, government, education, and our local communities?

4. How important is it for us to model rather than preach Christianity to unbelievers?

5. Does God expect us to turn the other cheek every time another person mistreats us? Why or why not?

LESSON IN OUR SOCIETY

Today, people are looking for the "real thing" in every phase of society, including the church. We are called to be distinct and set apart from the world. What specific points in today's lesson can you use to make a difference in your life so that when you encounter unbelievers and scoffers they will know that you have a true relationship with Jesus Christ? God has given us power to overcome sin and live victoriously in Him. Let us use what He has given us, not just on Sunday, but every day of our lives.

MAKE IT HAPPEN

Make a decision to spend quality time with the Lord every day. Allow Him to speak so that you can submit every area of your life to His Lordship. Be honest with the Lord about areas in which you

struggle. Remember, He already knows. Be willing to apply what you learn about showing love toward others on your job, in your community, and in your family. Don't conform to this world, but transform and renew yourself with the power of God's Word. Be prepared to share the results with the class next week.

FOLLOW THE SPIRIT

What God wants me to do:

_____

_____

REMEMBER YOUR THOUGHTS

Special insights I have learned:

_____

_____

MORE LIGHT ON THE TEXT
Romans 12:1-2, 9-21

In this part of his letter, Paul moves from issues of doctrine to those of practical life application. Paul addresses the believer in his everyday life.

1 I beseech you therefore, brethren, by the mercies of God, that ye present your bodies a living sacrifice, holy, acceptable unto God, which is your reasonable service.

The word "beseech" is used to emphasize Paul's urgency in his request. Paul begins with a cry of the heart, a cry of love to his fellow Christians. Paul is summoning, even begging, all who read this letter to give every piece of themselves to God. The same mercy that God made available to the Christian in salvation through Jesus Christ is present, enabling believer's to give all we are and all we have to the Lord. "Body" in verse 1 includes, but is not limited to, our physical body. We are to present our entire beings to the Lord in both worship and service.

Paul calls for us to be a living sacrifice. This is a direct contrast to the sacrificial lamb giving in Old Testament Scripture. Jesus Christ, the Lamb of God, has been given; therefore, we are a living representation of the ultimate sacrifice and the operation of salvation in our life.

Paul's call to believers is not an unreasonable request, nor is it something above human achievement. Unlike the statutes of the law, Paul's admonishment to the Christians in Rome and modern-day readers falls within our capabilities. It is a request to be committed to the sanctification process. We are called to die to sin and live unto righteousness.

2 And be not conformed to this world: but be ye transformed by the renewing of your mind, that ye may prove what is that good, and acceptable, and perfect, will of God.

"Conformed" comes from the Greek word *suschematizo* (**soos-khay-mat-id'-zo**) and it means "to conform oneself (i.e., one's mind and character) to another's pattern." Therefore, Christians should not pattern their lives according to the standards of the world. We should not behave as those who do not know Christ. We should not conduct our affairs (i.e., personal, professional, etc.) based on the world's model of behavior. But we should allow the Holy Spirit to lead us according to the Word of God. If Jesus is our Saviour, He should be Lord over all of our affairs. We must be transformed into the image of Christ. "Transformed" comes from the Greek word *metamorphoo* (**met-am-or-fo'-o**). It is where we get our English word *metamorphosis*, and it means "to change into another form; to transfigure." When we are in Christ, we must allow Him to transform every area of our life, including our way of thinking. We can only be transformed from our old method of operation if we allow the Word of God to renew our mind, our intellect, and our way of thinking.

When we live according to the Word of God and structure our affairs according to God's way of doing things, we will see the will of God manifested in our lives. God's will is not always what we want initially. As a matter of fact, it may be the direct opposite of what we desire. But the apostle Paul encourages us to "prove," taken from the Greek word *dokimazo* (**dok-im-ad'-zo**), which means "to test" or "scrutinize." Live a life designed around God's Word, and you will find yourself operating in the will of God.

12:9 Let love be without dissimulation. Abhor that which is evil; cleave to that which is good.

Christian living should be marked by sincere love and kindness to one another.

10 Be kindly affectioned one to another with brotherly love; in honour preferring one another;

Paul encourages the Christians in Rome to operate in sincere love—to show sincere kindness and unconditional affection to one another. This timeless message speaks to Christians from various settings, times, and cultures. We are challenged to love God and to love our fellow man. It is not a love rooted in word only, but a love that is grounded in word and action. It is not a love based on hypocrisy—saying one thing and doing the opposite—but a love that is sincere and from the heart.

The Christian life should be centered around love—love for God and love for humanity. We must strive to live a life of good. The believer is encouraged to abhor, hate, and detest that which is evil. Evil is despicable, detestable, and an abomination to God, and we must make a conscious effort to turn away from evil—anything that is contrary to the Word of God.

However, Paul does not leave the Christian without something to hold on to. As we turn away from evil, we are urged to cleave, or be glued to, that which is good. As Christians join to God in worship, we must be fastened to His will, way, and method of operation.

As outlined in 1 Corinthians 13, love does not focus on itself but prefers its brother. Christians should not operate in jealousy or be envious of their fellow brothers and sisters. We are encouraged to speak honorably of each other and to place the needs of others above our own. It is what Christ did for us, and it is what He admonishes us to do for each other. A life in Christ is distinctively different from a life outside of Christ. Christians should show love even when love is not reciprocated. We are encouraged to always speak positively of our brothers and sisters, not engaging in gossip and negative speech about others.

11 Not slothful in business; fervent in spirit; serving the Lord;

As the media bombards us with the news of various company scandals, insider trading, and other illegal practices engaged in by trusted business executives, we are told of a different way to conduct our affairs. Whatever the career, the conduct of the believer should run parallel to the Word of God. Christians should always move forward in their profession and not allow the vicissitudes of life to wear down their spirit. And in everything, at all times and on all occasions, we should serve the Lord. All of our tasks and affairs should be done unto the Lord, giving Him glory and honor (Colossians 3:17).

12 Rejoicing in hope; patient in tribulation; continuing instant in prayer;

Notice the Christian is not told to rejoice in good, or during good times; we are told to rejoice in hope. First Thessalonians 5:18 tells us to give thanks in everything. Christians are able to rejoice in good times and bad times because their trust is not in circumstances but in a God who is Lord of all. Therefore, we rejoice in bad times because we know that trouble will not last always.

How can we be patient in tribulation? Why didn't we succumb to a nervous breakdown? Christians rest in the peace of God. Even in tribulation, God is working out events for the good of the believer. That which the devil orchestrated to destroy the believer, God knows how to change for our good and His glory—be patient in tribulation, knowing that this, too, will pass (Genesis 50:20). We rejoice in good times because we are grateful to God for His goodness and mercy. For we know that it is only because of the mercy of God that we are who we are, have what we have, and are able to do what He has called us to do. Therefore, during the good and the bad, the Christian is always in prayer. The phrase "continuing instant" reminds us that we are to live a life devoted to prayer. In good times, we acknowledge God in prayer as our source and we give thanks for His grace and mercy. In bad times, we commit to persevering in prayer and commit to never waver—for our faith in Jesus Christ carries us through the rough places in life. Prayer is the believer's communication with a God who is tangible and concerned with that which concerns His children. It is in prayer that we talk to God and He talks to us.

13 Distributing to the necessity of saints; given to hospitality. 14 Bless them which persecute you: bless, and curse not. 15 Rejoice with them that do rejoice, and weep with them that weep.

When Jesus is Lord of your life, you are willing to give of yourself in order that others may receive and have their needs met. This is the Gospel. Jesus gave His life that we might have life. How much more should we give to others that their physical, spiritual, and emotional needs may be taken care of? And we give not just to those we know, but we give as we are instructed by the Holy Spirit, to both friends and strangers. The phrase "given to hospitality" speaks to our responsibility to give to strangers. We are called to show the love of Christ to all who cross our path.

How easy it is to bless others who bless us. But Paul moves the believer beyond the limits of the law. The Christian is instructed to show Christ to those who would persecute them for their very faith in Christ. We should not be bitter or hostile toward our enemies. It is the love of Christ that draws, not bitterness, hostility, or vengeance.

The words in verse 15 speak of the Christian's ability to be concerned with the affairs of others: Don't be envious. Be glad with those who are doing exceedingly well. Don't be consumed with the events and affairs of your own life. Mourn with those who are grieving. Share in the joy of others. Participate in the grief of others.

16 Be of the same mind one toward another. Mind not high things, but condescend to men of low estate. Be not wise in your own conceits.

Unity among believers is essential. We should live in harmony with our fellow brothers and sisters. We should not think of ourselves as better than others. The love of Christ is inclusive and does not discriminate. Therefore, as Christians we should be inclusive also. As God included us and rescued us from our lowest state, we are obligated to show the same love to others. Give to others as you would want others to give to you. Treat others in the manner you would want to be treated. Regardless of your achievements, status, or accomplishments, be willing to interact with those who have achieved less and have not accomplished as much.

17 Recompense to no man evil for evil. Provide things honest in the sight of all men. 18 If it be possible, as much as lieth in you, live peaceably with all men. 19 Dearly beloved, avenge not yourselves, but rather give place unto wrath: for it is written, Vengeance is mine; I will repay, saith the Lord. 20 Therefore if thine enemy hunger, feed him; if he thirst, give him drink: for in so doing thou shalt heap coals of fire on his head. 21 Be not overcome of evil, but overcome evil with good.

Don't do evil to those who are evil to you. Always attempt to do that which is good, regardless and independent of the actions of others.

The inclusive message of the Gospel encourages us to cultivate peace with all mankind. We are able to live in peace among both saints and sinners. We must separate the behavior of the sinner from the individual. While as Christians we hate sin, we are called to love the individual. Verses 17 through 21 are an accurate picture of what a true Christian life should look like. It is a life of love, not hatred. It is a life of giving and placing the needs of others above your own. It is a life that repays evil with good. Such thoughts are contrary to this world system. It is what the world calls "killing your enemies with kindness." Enemies of the Christian are enemies of God. However, God is patient, not wanting anyone to perish but everyone to come to repentance. Therefore, it is the responsibility of Christians to exemplify Christ and to draw their enemies to the love of God.

DAILY BIBLE READINGS

M: Instructions for Living
Colossians 4:2-6

T: Live a Life Pleasing to God
1 Thessalonians 4:1-12

W: Hold Fast to What Is Good
1 Thessalonians 5:12-22

T: Do What Is Right
2 Thessalonians 3:6-13

F: Members One of Another
Romans 12:1-5

S: Marks of the True Christian
Romans 12:6-13

S: Overcome Evil with Good
Romans 12:14-21

Take a closer look at the different types of love, and find out more about the word *honor*, by using your *Precepts For Living* CD-ROM.

TEACHING TIPS

April 24
Bible Study Guide 8

1. Words You Should Know

A. Disputations (Romans 14:1) *diakrisis* (Gk.)—To separate one from another, divide, part; discerning or distinguishing a difference, dispute, or controversy.

B. Judge (v. 13) *krino* (Gk.)—To make a distinction or come to a decision; to pass sentence or give one's opinion in a private manner; to furnish matter or occasion for condemnation.

2. Teacher Preparation

A. To prepare for today's lesson, ask the Lord to reveal any area where you may be judgmental.

B. Spend at least 30 minutes a day in prayer this week to help become better prepared to teach a sensitive and delicate subject.

3. Starting the Lesson

A. Let the students share their MAKE IT HAPPEN assignment from last week and make appropriate comments as necessary.

B. Open the class with prayer, using the LESSON AIM as the foundation of the prayer.

4. Getting into the Lesson

A. Have the students read the FOCAL VERSES silently and ask them to think of times when they may have been judgmental.

B. Next, read and discuss the IN FOCUS story.

C. Then, use the AT-A-GLANCE outline to facilitate understanding of the IN DEPTH section of the lesson.

5. Relating the Lesson to Life

A. Answer the SEARCH THE SCRIPTURES and DISCUSS THE MEANING questions, and have the students write the answers on the chalkboard or a sheet of paper.

B. Ask the students to discuss the following: Based on what Paul has shared with us in Romans 14:1-13; 15:5-6, how can we unify the body of Christ when there is so much division?

6. Arousing Action

A. Read to the students the meditation in the WORSHIP GUIDE below. Then ask them to share their opinions and make comments as needed.

B. Challenge the students to make a firm commitment to complete the LESSON IN OUR SOCIETY and MAKE IT HAPPEN assignments.

C. Close the class with prayer, thanking the Lord for conviction today. Remind the students that God does not want us to be judgmental, but loving toward those whom we may not understand.

D. Take time to encourage the students before they exit for worship service today.

APRIL 24TH

WORSHIP GUIDE

For the Superintendent or Teacher
Theme: Don't Judge One Another
Theme Song: "Lord Prepare Me"
Scripture: John 3:16-17
Song: "We Are One in the Spirit"
Meditation: Lord, help me not to be judgmental or critical of others. I realize that You made people in Your image and likeness. Therefore, I need to love them as You love them. Thank You for reminding me of that truth this day. In Jesus' name. Amen.

DON'T JUDGE ONE ANOTHER

Bible Background • ROMANS 14:1-13; 15:5-6
Printed Text • ROMANS 14:1-13; 15:5-6
Devotional Reading • JAMES 4:7-12

LESSON AIM

By the end of the lesson, the students will have a better understanding of living God's way by openly accepting one another's differences. Having realized that God loves all believers despite their weaknesses and differences of opinion over personal issues, they will express love by asking forgiveness of those they have prejudged.

KEEP IN MIND

"Now the God of patience and consolation grant you to be likeminded one toward another according to Jesus Christ: That ye may with one mind and one mouth glorify God, even the Father of our Lord Jesus Christ" (Romans 15:5-6).

LESSON OVERVIEW

LESSON AIM
KEEP IN MIND
FOCAL VERSES
IN FOCUS
THE PEOPLE, PLACES, AND TIMES
BACKGROUND
AT-A-GLANCE
IN DEPTH
SEARCH THE SCRIPTURES
DISCUSS THE MEANING
LESSON IN OUR SOCIETY
MAKE IT HAPPEN
FOLLOW THE SPIRIT
REMEMBER YOUR THOUGHTS
MORE LIGHT ON THE TEXT
DAILY BIBLE READINGS

FOCAL VERSES

Romans 14:1 Him that is weak in the faith receive ye, but not to doubtful disputations.

2 For one believeth that he may eat all things: another, who is weak, eateth herbs.

3 Let not him that eateth despise him that eateth not; and let not him which eateth not judge him that eateth: for God hath received him.

4 Who art thou that judgest another man's servant? to his own master he standeth or falleth. Yea, he shall be holden up: for God is able to make him stand.

5 One man esteemeth one day above another: another esteemeth every day alike. Let every man be fully persuaded in his own mind.

6 He that regardeth the day, regardeth it unto the Lord; and he that regardeth not the day, to the Lord he doth not regard it. He that eateth, eateth to the Lord, for he giveth God thanks; and he that eateth not, to the Lord he eateth not, and giveth God thanks.

7 For none of us liveth to himself, and no man dieth to himself.

8 For whether we live, we live unto the Lord; and whether we die, we die unto the Lord: whether we live therefore, or die, we are the Lord's.

9 For to this end Christ both died, and rose, and revived, that he might be Lord both of the dead and living.

10 But why dost thou judge thy brother? or why dost thou set at nought thy brother? for we shall all stand before the judgment seat of Christ.

11 For it is written, As I live, saith the Lord, every knee shall bow to me, and every tongue shall confess to God.

12 So then every one of us shall give account of himself to God.

13 Let us not therefore judge one another any more: but judge this rather, that no man put a stumblingblock or an occasion to fall in his brother's way.

15:5 Now the God of patience and consolation grant you to be likeminded one toward another according to Christ Jesus:

6 That ye may with one mind and one mouth glorify God, even the Father of our Lord Jesus Christ.

IN FOCUS

Rebecca was born and raised in Little Rock, Arkansas. On her 24th birthday, she relocated to Washington, D.C. to take a job as an executive secretary in one of the city's most powerful law firms. Upon her arrival, Rebecca immediately looked for a new church. For several months, Rebecca visited several congregations, but finally she joined a small church that was similar to her home church in Little Rock.

The congregation had their annual picnic the second weekend after Rebecca joined the church. Rebecca was excited when asked by the pastor to assist Joanie in spearheading the activities. When she arrived at the picnic, Rebecca noticed that all the women wore slacks. As she approached the tables, several members began whispering, others laughed, and a few made unkind remarks to Rebecca because she wore a dress.

"Why would you wear a dress to a picnic? Are you that dumb and country?" asked Melissa, one of the youths. Rebecca was shocked at her comments, and for the rest of the afternoon, she felt uncomfortable around the people.

The next day, Rebecca did not attend church. The following day, Joanie called Rebecca to say that she missed her in service and wanted to apologize for the comments and behavior of the people at the picnic.

Rebecca was silent before she responded. "Maybe I joined the wrong church. You see, the church that I came from in Little Rock did not allow us to wear slacks or makeup. In fact, my pastor told us it was sinful." Joanie tried to explain to Rebecca that everyone does not have those convictions, but that did not mean they were wrong.

"Joanie, I love Jesus Christ" Rebecca informed her. "I have faithfully served Him all my life, and I would never compromise nor intentionally sin against my Saviour. I appreciate your call. May God bless you." Rebecca hung up the phone. She never returned to the church. However, after a six month search, Rebecca found a church family that loved her, accepted her, and provided her many opportunities to grow and develop in her Christian faith.

This week, we will examine the apostle Paul's warning that believers are not to pass judgment on one another. We would do well to follow his admonition so that we can help other people to develop in their faith.

THE PEOPLE, PLACES, AND TIMES

Worship. The English word is derived from the Old English word *worthship* and denotes those actions and attitudes that revere and honor the worthiness of the great God of heaven and earth. Thus, worship is God-centered. Christian worship draws us near to God to acknowledge His worthiness and to express gratitude for what He has done for us in Christ and through the Holy Spirit. It requires a faith commitment to Him and acknowledgment that He is our God and Lord.

Biblical references to worship show that Adam and Eve had fellowship regularly with God in the Garden of Eden. Abel brought acceptable offerings unto the Lord. Abraham dotted the landscape of the Promised Land with altars for burnt offerings to the Lord and talked intimately with Him.

Public worship became formalized for Israel when the tabernacle was built at Mount Sinai. Thereafter, the people performed regular daily sacrifices, especially on the Sabbath, and God established several annual religious feasts as occasions for Israelite public worship.

Worship in the early church transpired both in the Jerusalem temple and in private homes. Away from Jerusalem, Christians worshiped in the synagogues as long as they were permitted. When that was no longer allowed, they met elsewhere for worship—usually in private homes, although sometimes in public halls. Today, our Christian worship corresponds largely to the New Testament pattern for the church. Many believers desire, seek, and expect all of the elements found in the worship experience of the New Testament church.

Stamps, Donald C., gen. ed. *The Full Life Study Bible.* Grand Rapids, Mich.: Zondervan Publishing Co., 1992. 730-732.

BACKGROUND

To make a connection between Paul's theological treatise of Jesus Christ, the apostle proposes a series of practical truths that help his audience become better prepared to live the Gospel of

Jesus Christ in the midst of the Roman culture. Paul encourages the believers to submit to the legitimate authority, which has been put in position by God Himself (Romans 13:1-7). Some people question whether or not Christians are to obey the government. However, Paul makes it clear that those who serve in positions of authority are appointed by God. We are called to respect and honor these men and women, even when we don't agree with their policies. Paul does not advocate that we violate God's laws. Yet when state laws contradict God's laws, we are called to obey our Father instead (see Acts 5:29). In other words, we are to submit to authority, not to tyranny.

Paul informs Christians that we have certain responsibilities that cannot be diminished because we are believers. We must pay our bills and do all we can to stay out of debt. Paul is not saying that we cannot borrow from others if the need arises, but in doing so, we must have a Christlike attitude when the time comes to repay the debt. In essence, our borrowing habits should not be based on greed and the desire to purchase unnecessary things. Instead, the only debt that we should have is loving others. When we do, we will not sin against our neighbors—whether believers or unbelievers.

Paul helps to define the marks of a true believer. We are to love others, awaken from spiritual slumber, and cast off the works of darkness since Christ could return any day. Christians are called to imitate Jesus Christ. He is our pattern for living a life that is totally committed to the Father. We should be motivated to do all we can to emulate Christ before others so that we can bring them to a closer walk with our Saviour.

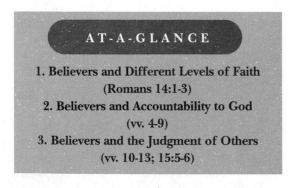

AT-A-GLANCE

1. Believers and Different Levels of Faith
(Romans 14:1-3)
2. Believers and Accountability to God
(vv. 4-9)
3. Believers and the Judgment of Others
(vv. 10-13; 15:5-6)

IN DEPTH

1. Believers and Different Levels of Faith (Romans 14:1-3)

Christians within the body of Christ are at different faith levels. The Bible affirms that we all have been given a measure of faith (Romans 12:3), but it is our responsibility to cultivate our faith. Cultivation occurs as we commit our lives to the Lord and obey His Word.

Paul addresses the Roman believers because they are divided on certain issues. Some believe they should only eat vegetables; others believe they can eat anything they want, including meat that could have been offensive to their brothers in Christ. Paul admonishes them to receive one another based on their love for Christ, not on what they did or did not eat.

Believers may differ in their opinions on trivial matters, but we should all have the following in common: (1) Jesus Christ as Lord and Saviour, (2) the Word of God as the source and final authority for daily living (3) God as our Father, and (4) the Holy Spirit as our Advocate and Helper. What believers choose to eat (or not to eat) is inconsequential. Therefore, we must be careful to avoid condemning, despising, or judging others when they don't do what we do or want them to do.

2. Believers and Accountability to God (vv. 4-9)

Paul gives a stern rebuke when he writes, "Who art thou that judges another man's servant?" We must remember that all believers are servants of the Lord and are accountable to Him. Thus, God is responsible for His servants, and He is able to correct us when appropriate to make us pleasing to Him (v. 4).

The Roman believers are debating over the special feast days that are part of Old Testament ceremonial laws. One group believes the feast days should still be observed, while another believes every day is the same. Paul addresses both groups by affirming that each should be fully persuaded in their own mind about what they feel is important to them. In essence, Paul says, "Listen, it is acceptable unto the Lord if you still want to regard these feast days as an expression of your love and devotion to Him. On the other hand, if you have no desire to observe these days, that's OK too."

In speaking of these special feast days, Paul leaves it up to the believer to decide whether to continue observing them. Paul also affirms that those who feel they can eat anything should do so as unto the Lord with thanksgiving, and the believer who has chosen not to eat certain foods should also do it as unto the Lord with thanksgiving (v. 6).

We no longer belong to ourselves, but to Christ Jesus. Therefore, whether we live or die, we are His. The choice a believer makes in this life should be based on love and devotion to the Lord. Each of us is accountable to God, so let's not waste our time judging one another on trivial matters.

3. Believers and the Judgment of Others (vv. 10-13; 15:5-6)

The reason Jesus Christ died on the Cross and rose from the grave was to be Lord over all believers, both in this life and the life to come (v. 9). Because Jesus is Lord, He deals with each of His children individually and according to God's divine plan. How God deals with one believer may be different from how He deals with another. That's why Paul says we shouldn't be so quick to judge other believers because we don't know what God is doing in their lives.

Some believers have a tendency to look down on others or refuse to fellowship with other believers based on their own convictions. God may be personally convicting and exposing certain areas of sin in one person's life that may not be a problem for someone else. If we're not careful, we may become critical and judgmental based on the assumption that we are all the same and therefore we should get the same treatment. Paul declares that each of us will have to stand before God's judgment seat for our own sins and that everything we do will be rightly judged by the Lord (vv. 10-12). All of our deeds (Matthew 12:36-37), motives (1 Corinthians 4:5), works (Ephesians 6:8), lack of love for God and others (Colossians 3:18—4:1), and attitudes (Matthew 5:22) will be exposed by the Lord. In fact, in his letter to the Corinthian church, Paul tells believ-

ers that "we must all appear before the judgment seat of Christ; that every one may receive the things done in this body, according to that he hath done, whether it be good or bad" (2 Corinthians 5:10).

In contrast, we are to expose and lovingly confront a brother or sister who is living in sin (see Luke 17:3). At times, we must exercise church discipline (see 1 Corinthians 5:12-13; 2 Thessalonians 3:6; 1 Timothy 5:20-21). On issues where God's Word is clear, there can be no compromise. We are to encourage one another to obey God's Word and to live holily (see Hebrews 10:24). We should not cause others to stumble or sin by how we live. In fact, the Bible says such behavior should be judged since we may be influential in turning someone away from the Lord.

In Romans 15:5-6, Paul gives a call for unity among those who believe in Jesus Christ. This call echoes Jesus' prayer in John 17:21-22 that believers would be one, even as He and the Father are one. Our unity is a powerful testimony that brings glory to God.

SEARCH THE SCRIPTURES

1. Why were the Roman believers divided (Romans 14:2)?

2. Why does Paul tell us not to judge others (v. 4)?

3. Christ accomplished three things for the believer. What are they (v. 9)?

4. What two things did Paul refer to that had been written (v. 11)?

5. What did Paul tell the believers to judge (v. 13)?

DISCUSS THE MEANING

1. What is the difference between judging another believer and discerning sinful behavior?

2. What can happen when our personal prejudices get in the way of our belief in Jesus Christ?

3. Can denominational differences hinder churches from coming together in the spirit of unity? Why or why not?

4. What is the best way to help a weak believer become strong in the Lord?

LESSON IN OUR SOCIETY

In our communities, there are so many churches, denominations, and people of various nationalities, cultures, and lifestyles with different personal preferences that unbelievers can become confused when someone mentions the word *church*. We must be careful that we don't allow our differences to cause us to be divided. Some people are uncomfortable when the Gospel is presented using skits, videos, dance, or film. Some churches have communion once a month, while others have it every Sunday. Our inability to accept these differences should never cause us to judge anyone without scriptural evidence. However, we need not worry since one day all will be given an equal opportunity at the judgment seat of Christ to know whether or not our worship, works, expression of love, devotion, and commitment to the Lord was pleasing to Him.

MAKE IT HAPPEN

This week, ask the Lord to expose any area in your life where you have been guilty of judging others who do not live up to your expectations. Once God has exposed your sins, ask Him to forgive you and help you to see others through the eyes of Christ. Make it a point to meet other believers who may be different in worship and style. Perhaps visit other churches and expand your horizon in Christ. Write down your activities in a journal and be prepared to share with others next week.

FOLLOW THE SPIRIT

What God wants me to do:

_____

_____

REMEMBER YOUR THOUGHTS

Special insights I have learned:

_____

_____

MORE LIGHT ON THE TEXT

Romans 14:1-13; 15:5-6

1 Him that is weak in the faith receive ye, but not to doubtful disputations.

Believers are to welcome those who are weak in

faith in regard to doubtful matters, and they should not become involved in arguments over their opinions. In verse 1, Paul suggests that those whose faith is strong should welcome their sisters and brothers whose faith is not as strong because they are not yet firm in their beliefs. We do not need to spend time in "doubtful disputations" or arguments over whose opinion is right. Their faith may be increased if they are welcomed into the body of Christ. The word "faith" (*pistis*) in the Greek means "to have conviction of the truthfulness of God." Christians have varying degrees of faith, but Paul does not see that as reason for quarreling over whose point of view is right (see Romans 15:1, 7; 1 Corinthians 8:9-11; 9:22).

2 For one believeth that he may eat all things: another, who is weak, eateth herbs. 3 Let not him that eateth despise him that eateth not; and let not him which eateth not judge him that eateth: for God hath received him. 4 Who art thou that judgest another man's servant? to his own master he standeth or falleth. Yea, he shall be holden up: for God is able to make him stand.

When believers disagree about whether they should eat meat, they should not condemn one another, because God accepts them all as servants. Believers who disagree on matters of personal preference should not condemn one another for the position they take, because God has accepted them. They are servants who are "answerable to the Lord of all" (compare Romans 14:14; 1 Corinthians 10:25; 1 Timothy 4:4; Titus 1:15).

Paul notes the difference in the choice of diets: some believe in "eating everything," while others are vegetarians ("eat herbs," v. 2). Dietary choices should not cause some to "despise" or to "judge" those who take a stance opposite from their own (see Colossians 2:16). God has received them both. The word "believeth" comes from the Greek word *pisteuo* and means "to have faith in."

Paul questions our right to pass judgment on God's servants (Gk. *oiketes*, meaning "menial" or "domestic servant"). We have no right to judge or despise other believers (see James 4:12). They are not ours, but God's. Each must stand or fall before his master (Gk. *kurios*, meaning "to have dominion

Paul explains that love should govern all our actions.

over"). The Christian's master is Christ, who is able "to make him [them] stand." The phrases "shall be holden up" and "to make him stand" have the same meaning. The Greek word *histemi* means "to abide, establish, or appoint." God, who claims those who are of weak faith, is also able to establish them in righteousness.

5 One man esteemeth one day above another: another esteemeth every day alike. Let every man be fully persuaded in his own mind. 6 He that regardeth the day, regardeth it unto the Lord; and he that regardeth not the day, to the Lord he doth not regard it. He that eateth, eateth to the Lord, for he giveth God thanks; and he that eateth not, to the Lord he eateth not, and giveth God thanks.

Believers who observe differing dietary rules and holy days are faithful if they do so in honor of and in thankfulness to God.

Paul's discussion then turns from dietary choices to special days of religious celebration. Whether it's to eat meat or not to eat meat, or to celebrate one day over another, neither is more highly esteemed than the other. Both the dietary choices and the observance of special days should be done to the honor of the Lord (1 Corinthians 6:9, 20; Galatians 2:20; 1 Thessalonians 5:19; 1 Peter 4:2). Each person should "be fully persuaded in his own mind." To be "fully persuaded" (Gk. *plerophoreo*) means "to carry out fully" or "to most fully believe." The word "mind" (Gk. *nous*) as used here refers to the intellect, thought, feeling, or will. One should understand that the choice to eat or not to eat, to celebrate the day or not to celebrate it, has no value in and of itself unless it is done to honor God—unless God gets the thanks. "Giveth God thanks" (v. 6) is translated from the Greek word *eucharisteo,* which means "to be grateful" or "to express gratitude."

7 For none of us liveth to himself, and no man dieth to himself. 8 For whether we live, we live unto the Lord; and whether we die, we die unto the Lord: whether we live therefore, or die, we are the Lord's. 9 For to this end Christ both died, and rose, and revived, that he might be Lord both of the dead and living.

All believers, whether they live or die, are

accountable to the Lord. Since God has welcomed the believer (v. 1) and is able to make us stand (v. 4), everything should be done in honor of the Lord. For we neither "live" (Gk. *zao*) nor "die" (Gk. *apothnesko*) unto ourselves, but we live or die unto the Lord because we belong to the Lord (v. 7; compare Romans 6:10-11; 2 Corinthians 5:15; and Galatians 2:19). As with eating and celebrating, we should live and die to the Lord, for we are His. Christ also lived, died, and rose for us so that He might be "Lord both of the dead and living" (v. 9).

10 But why dost thou judge thy brother? or why dost thou set at nought thy brother? for we shall all stand before the judgment seat of Christ. 11 For it is written, As I live, saith the Lord, every knee shall bow to me, and every tongue shall confess to God. 12 So then every one of us shall give account of himself to God.

Because believers are accountable to God, they are not to pass judgment or look down on others, for they are the Lord's also. The phrase "set at nought" (Gk. *exoutheneo*) means "to find contemptible or less esteemed." Paul reminds us that we, too, must stand before the "judgment seat" to be judged by Christ (see Isaiah 45:23; Philippians 2:10-11). In verse 11, it says that "every knee shall bow. . .and every tongue shall confess to God." This points out our own accountability to God (v. 12).

13 Let us not therefore judge one another any more: but judge this rather, that no man put a stumblingblock or an occasion to fall in his brother's way.

Believers are not to hinder the spiritual walk of others. When we judge others, especially those whose faith is not as strong as our own, we place a "stumblingblock" (Gk. *proskomma*) in their path. The Greek word *proskomma* can also be translated as "tempt to sin" or "enticed to apostasy." We are warned never to entice another believer to fall away from the faith or fall into sin (see 1 Corinthians 8:9, 13; 10:32).

15:5 Now the God of patience and consolation grant you to be likeminded one toward another according to Christ Jesus: 6 That ye may with one mind and one mouth glorify God, even the Father of our Lord Jesus Christ.

Believers are to worship God together in unity. We are to be "likeminded one toward another according to Christ Jesus." The word "likeminded" (Gk. *phroneo*, **fron-eh'-o.**) means "to agree together in an understanding way; to be wise and harmonious." The unity of believers is a testimony that we belong to Jesus Christ. Jesus clearly taught, "A new commandment I give unto you, That ye love one another; as I have loved you, that ye also love one another. By this shall all men know that ye are my disciples, if ye have love one to another" (John 13:34-35). As we bear with one another in love and worship the Lord together, we bring glory to God.

DAILY BIBLE READINGS

M: Speak No Evil Against One Another
James 4:7-12

T: Do Not Grumble Against One Another
James 5:7-12

W: Do Not Judge One Another
Romans 14:1-6

T: Each Will Be Accountable to God
Romans 14:7-13

F: Do Not Ruin Another Through Food
Romans 14:14-18

S: Do Not Make Another Stumble
Romans 14:19-23

S: Live in Harmony with One Another
Romans 15:1-6

In Romans 14:13 Christians are told, "Therefore let us stop passing judgment on one another. Instead, make up your mind not to put any stumbling block or obstacle in your brother's way." Why don't you take a few seconds to search for the verb *judge* and find everywhere it is used in the Bible by using your *Precepts For Living* CD-ROM!

TEACHING TIPS

May 1
Bible Study Guide 9

1. Words You Should Know

A. Apostle (Galatians 1:1) *apostolos* (Gk.)—Delegate, envoy, messenger; a group of highly honored believers who had been sent out with a special commission.

B. Gospel (vv. 6, 11) *euaggelion* (Gk.)—God's good news to humanity.

C. Preach (vv. 8-9, 11) *euaggelizo* (Gk.)—To bring or announce good news.

D. Accursed (vv. 8-9) *anathema* (Gk.)—Things devoted to evil; used in our text as a formula.

2. Teacher Preparation

A. Begin your preparation with prayer.

B. Consult the *Precepts For Living* CD-ROM for additional Bible versions of the printed text, further information on the history and culture of the apostle Paul and Galatia, dictionaries, and encyclopedias.

C. Read the BIBLE BACKGROUND, THE PEOPLE, PLACES, AND TIMES, and BACKGROUND.

3. Starting the Lesson

A. After the students arrive, ask a volunteer to pray, or lead the class in opening prayer.

B. Ask the students what they think people have to do to be saved. List their responses on the chalkboard, on poster board taped to the wall, or on an easel.

C. After they have made a list, ask them if there is anything else that they believe a person has to do to be saved. Ask them to keep the list in mind throughout the lesson.

4. Getting into the Lesson

A. Invite volunteers to read THE PEOPLE, PLACES, AND TIMES and BACKGROUND.

B. Read and discuss the IN FOCUS story with the class.

C. Read the FOCAL VERSES and the KEEP IN MIND verse. Use the IN DEPTH section to discuss the meaning of the verse in light of the background information read at the beginning of the class.

D. Divide the class into two groups and assign each group two questions from the SEARCH THE SCRIPTURES section; or, if the class is small, they can remain together and answer the questions as a group. Answer the DISCUSS THE MEANING questions as one group.

5. Relating the Lesson to Life

A. Ask the students to refer back to the list they made of what people must do to be saved.

B. Ask the students if they would make any additions or deletions to the list in light of the lesson.

6. Arousing Action

A. Invite volunteers to read the MAKE IT HAPPEN section.

B. Ask the class to complete the FOLLOW THE SPIRIT and REMEMBER YOUR THOUGHTS sections.

C. End the class in prayer.

WORSHIP GUIDE

MAY 1ST

For the Superintendent or Teacher
Theme: No Other Gospel
Theme Song: "Amazing Grace"
Scripture: Galatians 1:1-12
Song: "Worthy Is the Lamb"
Meditation: Gracious God, our Strength and our Redeemer, thank You for Your faithful witnesses throughout the ages that have brought us the Good News of Your unmerited grace. Help us to trust Your divine Word and to not be deceived by the word of others. In Jesus' name we pray.
Amen.

NO OTHER GOSPEL

Bible Background • GALATIANS 1
Printed Text • GALATIANS 1:1-12
Devotional Reading • ACTS 13:26-33

LESSON AIM

By the end of the lesson, the students will understand that they might come into contact with, or be exposed to, individuals or groups that will try to teach them the "right" way to be a Christian. However, there is only one true Gospel, and that Gospel proclaims that the only way to be saved is by believing in Jesus Christ, and not by our deeds.

KEEP IN MIND

"But I certify you, brethren, that the gospel which was preached of me is not after man" (Galatians 1:11).

FOCAL VERSES

Galatians 1:1 Paul, an apostle, (not of men, neither by man, but by Jesus Christ, and God the Father, who raised him from the dead;)

2 And all the brethren which are with me, unto the churches of Galatia:

3 Grace be to you and peace from God the Father, and from our Lord Jesus Christ,

4 Who gave himself for our sins, that he might deliver us from this present evil world, according to the will of God and our Father:

5 To whom be glory for ever and ever. Amen.

6 I marvel that ye are so soon removed from him that called you into the grace of Christ unto another gospel:

7 Which is not another; but there be some that trouble you, and would pervert the gospel of Christ.

8 But though we, or an angel from heaven,

LESSON OVERVIEW

LESSON AIM
KEEP IN MIND
FOCAL VERSES
IN FOCUS
THE PEOPLE, PLACES, AND TIMES
BACKGROUND
AT-A-GLANCE
IN DEPTH
SEARCH THE SCRIPTURES
DISCUSS THE MEANING
LESSON IN OUR SOCIETY
MAKE IT HAPPEN
FOLLOW THE SPIRIT
REMEMBER YOUR THOUGHTS
MORE LIGHT ON THE TEXT
DAILY BIBLE READINGS

preach any other gospel unto you than that which we have preached unto you, let him be accursed.

9 As we said before, so say I now again, If any man preach any other gospel unto you than that ye have received, let him be accursed.

10 For do I now persuade men, or God? or do I seek to please men? for if I yet pleased men, I should not be the servant of Christ.

11 But I certify you, brethren, that the gospel which was preached of me is not after man.

12 For I neither received it of man, neither was I taught it, but by the revelation of Jesus Christ.

IN FOCUS

Laurina's lips grew tight at the meeting of her church's Executive Council. Laurina didn't serve on the Council anymore. However, 10 years earlier she had served as committee chairperson for the drafting of the original bylaws of the Executive Council. The present Council asked if she would help support the new requirements for membership.

Silently reading the agenda, Laurina could hardly look into the faces of her circle of friends. What bothered her most was the recommendation that all new Council members must have degrees from an accredited college or university.

She felt this change would eliminate two-thirds of the congregation from ever serving on the Executive Council. She raised her hand to speak. When the pastor recognized Laurina, she rose to her feet and spoke with an emotional voice. "This change would not allow me or others that drafted the original bylaws to serve on the Council."

She went on despite knowing the pastor wanted her support. "It's not only those that have degrees who can add to the decision-making process. Just think of the other gifts needed to make good decisions, like prayer. We should think how this change might belittle some of our church members."

The pastor's eyes showed his surprise when he answered her. "Laurina, those people will be able to use their talents in the church in many other ways. Because we have grown into such a large congregation now, we need the special skills used by many big corporations."

Laurina's voice was thick and slow; she was in danger of crying when she answered with the revelation in her heart. "Pastor, when Christ comes again and if He finds Himself in our congregation, do you realize even He would not be able to serve on the Executive Council."

THE PEOPLE, PLACES, AND TIMES

Paul, the Apostle to the Gentiles. Paul was born in the first century A.D. in Tarsus, a rich cosmopolitan city located in modern-day Turkey. Jewish by birth but raised outside of Palestine, Paul learned the Scriptures from the Greek translation of the Hebrew Bible. Paul was a devout Jew and a Pharisee who strictly observed the Jewish law. Paul persecuted Jews who had converted to Christ. When Paul was converted on the road to Damascus, he was in pursuit of Jewish Christians.

Galatia. An ancient province of the Roman Empire, the Galatians were descendants of the Celts, who invaded Asia Minor in 279 B.C. at the invitation of King Nicomedes of Bithynia. The territory of Galatia included Antioch, Pisidia, Lystra, Iconium, Derbe, and Tavium. The use of the name Galatia in Paul's letter is ambiguous. He could have addressed the letter to either the inhabitants in Northern Galatia or to those in the Southern part of the province.

Schnelle, Udo, and M. Eugene Boring, trans. *The History and Theology of the New Testament Writings*. Minneapolis: Fortress Press, 998. 95-96.

Cohen, Shaye J.D., and Wayne A. Meeks, ed. *From the Maccabees to the Mishnah*. Philadelphia: Westminster Press, 1988. 50-51, 55-57.

Times. The conversion of Gentiles to Judaism is a postexilic phenomenon. Prior to the Babylonian exile, a person was Jewish by birth. The scattering of the Jews, along with those who chose to remain in Babylon after they were freed, created a situation where the Jews had to alter their understanding of who they were. Their self-identity changed from being Jewish by birth to being Jewish by religious practice. From 300 B.C. to A.D. 200, many Gentiles converted to Judaism. The conversion of Gentiles to Judaism opened the door for Gentile conversion to Christianity. Many Gentile Christians learned the Jewish Scriptures and were exposed to Jewish observances through their conversion. This led to some Gentile Christians believing that in order to be authentically Christian, they had to become Jewish.

Cohen, Shaye J.D., and Wayne A. Meeks, ed. *From the Maccabees to the Mishnah*. Philadelphia: Westminster Press, 1988. 50-51, 55-57.

BACKGROUND

Paul established the church in Galatia while recuperating from an illness. While the Galatians cared for his physical needs, Paul ministered to their spiritual needs, sharing with them the Gospel (Galatians 4:13-16). Apparently, his illness did not deter his audience, because the Galatians welcomed Paul and his Gospel message with enthusiasm. However, some time after Paul moved on to other missionary work, the Galatians accepted a version of the Gospel that was contrary to the one Paul had preached to them. Paul sent the Galatians a stern letter to defend his apostolic authority and the Gospel he had given them, and to correct their digression.

AT-A-GLANCE

1. Salutation (Galatians 1:1-5)
2. The Occasion for the Letter (vv. 6-10)
3. The Authenticity of Paul's Gospel (vv. 11-12)

IN DEPTH

1. Salutation (Galatians 1:1-5)

Paul began his letter to the churches of Galatia by presenting his credentials to them. According to Paul, he is not an apostle chosen by human beings, but rather through the appointment of Jesus Christ and God.

Paul's salutation included an early Christian confession concerning Jesus' death and Resurrection, perhaps to bring to the minds of the congregations the foundation of the Gospel message.

Paul sent the churches greetings from the believers accompanying him on his missionary journey, as well as his typical greeting of grace and peace from God the Father and the Lord Jesus Christ. Paul added to his greeting another early Christian confession regarding Jesus Christ's death on the Cross.

2. The Occasion for the Letter (vv. 6-10)

Ordinarily, an expression of thanksgiving would follow Paul's opening greetings in his letters. Instead, a thanksgiving is conspicuously absent in Paul's letter to the churches of Galatia. Rather than thanksgiving, he expressed dismay. Paul was stunned that the congregations of Galatia could so quickly desert God, who had called them into the grace of Christ, to follow after another gospel.

Our Scripture lesson does not provide the specifics about the problem, except to say that the Galatians had allowed some person or people to lead them away from the Gospel Paul preached to follow another version. However, scholars generally agree that opponents of Paul had arisen, who insisted that Gentile converts to Christianity must be circumcised (3:2; 4:21; 5:4, 18).

Many scholars have speculated about the source of the conflict. Some maintain that Paul's opponents were Jewish Christians from Jerusalem, who were following behind Paul to make certain that the Gospel he preached included observance of the law. Others have argued that the opponents came from within the congregations of Galatia and were eager to prove their fidelity to Christianity by observing the law and becoming circumcised.

Schnelle, Udo, and M. Eugene Boring, trans. *The History and Theology of the New Testament Writings.* Minneapolis: Fortress Press, 1998. 101-104.

3. The Authenticity of Paul's Gospel (vv. 11-12)

Whatever the source of the conflict may be, Paul's gospel is under attack, and Paul wrote to defend his position. The intention of his opponents might be to bring a compromising gospel acceptable to humans, but Paul argued that he did not preach a gospel for the approval of humans, but rather for the approval of Christ, and anyone who would preach otherwise should be cursed. Furthermore, Paul maintained that the gospel that he preached was not passed on to him from other humans, but was received directly as a revelation of Jesus Christ.

SEARCH THE SCRIPTURES

1. How was Paul's apostleship different from that of the other apostles (Galatians 1:1)?

2. Why was Paul upset with the churches of Galatia (vv. 6, 8-9)?

3. Did Paul preach to please the crowds (v. 10)?

4. How did Paul say that he received the Gospel preached by him (v. 12)?

DISCUSS THE MEANING

1. Paul appears to be on the defensive regarding his apostolic authority from the very beginning of the letter. Why do you think a preacher or teacher's background is or is not important for the authority of their leadership?

2. Why do you think it was so important for Paul to try to correct the Galatians' understanding of the Gospel as they tried to be faithful to the Gospel?

3. Paul denied that he tried to please human beings with his preaching of the Gospel. Why do you believe he felt it necessary to make this claim?

LESSON IN OUR SOCIETY

How often have you gone shopping with a specific purchase in mind—and a certain budget to go along with it—and the sales associate tried to convince you of all the other things you must have to go along with your purchase? Did you succumb to the temptation and return home with more items than you intended, spending money

Jesus invites all to come to Him who are "heavy laden, and [He] will give [us] rest" (Matthew 11:28).

that you had not planned to? Our faith is like this shopping excursion. God's Word teaches that all we have to do is believe in Jesus Christ to be saved, then others come along telling us that we have to follow other prescribed acts before we can be saved.

The apostle Paul encountered other believers who felt that his version of the Gospel was watered down and that the Gentiles needed to undergo certain actions before they might be saved. Paul was steadfast in preaching the Gospel Jesus Christ gave him through direct revelation. We also need to remain immovable when others tell us we must follow certain other instructions other than believing in Jesus Christ in order to be saved.

MAKE IT HAPPEN

The churches of Galatia listened to others who taught them that in order to be saved they had to be circumcised, along with believing in Jesus Christ. Whom will you believe—people who put other conditions on your salvation, or the Gospel

of Jesus Christ? Ask God to give you a spirit of wisdom to know His will from human beings, who are often sincere in their faith but misguided in their teachings.

FOLLOW THE SPIRIT

What God wants me to do:

_____

_____

REMEMBER YOUR THOUGHTS

Special insights I have learned:

_____

_____

MORE LIGHT ON THE TEXT
Galatians 1:1-12

Traditionally in the African American community and frequently today, the preacher is a significant authority figure. He or she is highly regarded and respected. To question the authority of a preacher is a serious offense. The apostle Paul encountered opposition on two fronts. On the one hand, his preaching was the center of controversy, not the man himself. Some Jewish Christian leaders believed that Paul diluted the Gospel by not requiring the Gentiles to observe the law and become circumcised. On the other hand, the Galatians were beginning to doubt Paul's authority as an apostle because he had not been one of Jesus' disciples during Jesus' earthly ministry. They had likely been exposed to Judaism and believed that circumcision was the next appropriate step in becoming Christian. Paul had a power-packed defense for both fronts.

1 Paul, an apostle, (not of men, neither by man, but by Jesus Christ, and God the Father, who raised him from the dead;) 2 And all the brethren which are with me, unto the churches of Galatia: 3 Grace be to you and peace from God the Father, and from our Lord Jesus Christ,

Paul began his letter to the churches of Galatia with a typical ancient letter-writing style which included an introduction of the writer, identification of the recipients, and a greeting. The Galatians received the letter in the same manner many enslaved Africans and newly emancipated Africans in America received it: orally. There was likely a religious leader or leaders among the churches of Galatia who assembled the congregations and read Paul's letter to them.

Paul described himself as an "apostle" and was identified by whose authority he was under: Jesus Christ and God, who raised Jesus from the dead. The word "apostle" (Gk. *apostolos*, **a-pos-to-los**) refers to an envoy, a messenger, or one sent with a commission. In the New Testament, it designated the followers commissioned by Jesus to spread the Gospel.

4 Who gave himself for our sins, that he might deliver us from this present evil world, according to the will of God and our Father: 5 To whom be glory for ever and ever. Amen.

Paul knew that evil forces were in the world and that God would conquer them. Paul taught that the events surrounding Jesus' death and Resurrection ushered in the coming age of God's reign in the world.

6 I marvel that ye are so soon removed from him that called you into the grace of Christ unto another gospel:

Paul's letters ordinarily would include words of thanksgiving following the introduction. However, Paul's letter to the Galatians is the only one among all of Paul's letters that omits a thanksgiving for the recipients, leaving the hearers to perceive that Paul is not happy with them. He gets right to the point that the churches of Galatia have abandoned the Gospel he preached to them when he was with them and have embraced another gospel. The word "gospel" (Gk. *euaggelion*, **yoo-ang-ghel'ee-on**) means "God's Good News to humanity." Similarly, the word "preach" is the Greek word *euaggelizo* (**yoo-ang-ghel-iol'-zo**), and means "to bring or announce good news."

In the African American church, the sermon is the most important element in the worship service. Everything in the worship service builds up to the moment when the preacher brings the Good News of God's saving grace to the worshipers. Since African Americans often encounter racism, joblessness, and despair throughout the week, worship is the one opportunity many look forward to in order to hear a word of comfort, joy, affirmation, and hope.

7 Which is not another; but there be some that trouble you, and would pervert the gospel of Christ.

Paul asserted there was only one true Gospel and the churches of Galatia were now following another gospel. This distorted gospel required that the Galatians be circumcised in order to be saved. In contrast, Paul preached that they could be saved through faith in Jesus Christ alone.

8 But though we, or an angel from heaven, preach any other gospel unto you than that which we have preached unto you, let him be accursed. 9 As we said before, so say I now again, If any man preach any other gospel unto you than that ye have received, let him be accursed.

Paul pronounced a curse upon himself, his comissionaries, or anyone else—even an angel from heaven—if he or she preached anything contrary to what Paul had previously preached in Galatia. The word "accursed" in Greek is *anathema* (**an-ath'-em-ah**) meaning "things devoted to evil." Curses and blessings were an aspect of the biblical covenants and were common in the ancient world. In the New Testament, anathemas were also condemnations of persons or teachings that were considered contemptible.

10 For do I now persuade men, or God? or do I seek to please men? for if I yet pleased men, I should not be the servant of Christ.

Some of Paul's opponents accused him of relaxing the requirement of circumcision to win over the Gentiles to Christianity. They wanted the Gentiles to become Jewish in order to be Christian. This was similar to the experience of many Africans and African Americans. Many Europeans required that in order to be Christian, Africans and African Americans had to become more European. Some evangelists and missionaries taught us to adopt European names and dress, sing European hymns, and adopt a European style of worship. Paul stressed that Gentiles could become Christian while remaining culturally non-Jewish. On the other hand, today we must be careful not to require Jews to become culturally Gentile in order to be saved.

The word "persuade" (Gk. *peitho*, **pi-tho**) refers to having the gift or art of persuasion or the ability to win over to one's side. In this verse, the word "persuade" could be exchanged for the word "approve." One of the attractions to an African American preaching style is the orator's gift of speech. As skilled a preacher as Paul was, he was not seeking the approval of the Galatians in his preaching. He was concerned with pleasing God.

"Please" (Gk. *aresko*, **ar-es'-ko**) means "to accommodate," as in service to someone. Paul was adamant that he was preaching the unadulterated truth in obedience to God, rather than appeasing his opponents or the Galatians. He argued that if he pleased men, then he would not be in the service of Christ.

11 But I certify you, brethren, that the gospel which was preached of me is not after man. 12 For I neither received it of man, neither was I taught it, but by the revelation of Jesus Christ.

Paul explained to the Galatians that the Gospel he preached to them was not a human gospel received from a human being. Rather, Paul maintained that his Gospel was of divine origin, received first-hand through a revelation of Jesus Christ. The Gospel and Paul's example call us to live out a divine call, rather than allow a desire for human approval to lead us to put conditions on or compromise the truth of the Gospel of Jesus Christ.

DAILY BIBLE READINGS

M: Do Not Be Led Astray
2 Corinthians 11:1-15
T: In Christ All Things Hold Together
Colossians 1:15-23
W: We Bring You the Good News
Acts 13:26-33
T: Everyone Who Believes Is Set Free
Acts 13:34-41
F: Bring Salvation to All
Acts 13:44-49
S: Do Not Turn to Another Gospel
Galatians 1:1-7
S: Only One Gospel Directly from God
Galatians: 1:8-12

Find out more about the subject, purpose, and nature of the Gospel by using the reference tools available in your *Precepts For Living* CD-ROM.

TEACHING TIPS

May 8
Bible Study Guide 10

1. Words You Should Know

A. Nature (Galatians 2:15) *phusis* (Gk.)—The way of feeling and acting that has become "normal."

B. Law (vv. 16, 19, 21; 3:2, 5) *nomos* (Gk.)—In this case, the revelation or instruction received by Moses from God found in the first five books of the Bible on how to live in right covenant relationship with God.

C. Transgressor (2:18) *parabates* (Gk.)—A person who violates a command or law; to go beyond a boundary or limit.

D. Bewitched (3:1) *baskaino* (Gk.)—To influence or affect, especially injuriously; to cast a spell over.

2. Teacher Preparation

A. Begin with prayer.

B. Read Galatians 2 and 3 from different versions of the Bible utilizing your *Precepts For Living* CD-ROM.

C. Utilize your *Precepts For Living* CD-ROM to look up terms such as Jews and Gentiles.

D. Read the LESSON AIM, keeping it in mind throughout the lesson.

3. Starting the Lesson

A. Invite one of the students to open the class with prayer.

B. Ask a volunteer to read the IN FOCUS section. Invite the class to share their insights from the story.

C. Ask for volunteers to read the FOCAL VERSES.

4. Getting into the Lesson

A. Invite the students to discuss the relationship between the FOCAL VERSES, the IN FOCUS section, and their own life experiences.

B. Answer the questions in the SEARCH THE SCRIPTURES section.

5. Relating the Lesson to Life

A. Ask volunteers to read the DISCUSS THE MEANING section. Answer the questions as a group.

B. Read the LESSON IN OUR SOCIETY section. Its focus is on accepting God's free, unconditional gift of salvation. Emphasize that some people might try to place conditions on what they must do to be incorporated into the people of God, and emphasize the importance of knowing God's Word concerning the issue.

6. Arousing Action

A. Read the MAKE IT HAPPEN section and ask the students to evaluate their beliefs and practices in light of the Bible lesson.

B. End the class with a prayer that includes the LESSON AIM.

WORSHIP GUIDE

For the Superintendent or Teacher
Theme: All Saved by Faith
Theme Song: "Since Jesus Came into My Heart"
Scripture: Galatians 2:15—3:5
Song: "Just As I Am"
Meditation: Loving God, thank You for loving us enough to send Christ to give His life for us. Help us to live as Your people and to welcome others who come just the way they are. In Jesus' name we pray. Amen.

ALL SAVED BY FAITH

Bible Background • GALATIANS 2:15—3:5
Printed Text • GALATIANS 2:15—3:5
Devotional Reading • GALATIANS 3:6-14

LESSON AIM

By the end of the lesson, the students should understand that while Christians must maintain certain standards of behavior in order to live a life pleasing to God, such principles are not conditions for salvation. Only faith in Christ assures our salvation.

KEEP IN MIND

"The life which I now live in the flesh I live by the faith of the Son of God, who loved me, and gave himself for me" (from Galatians 2:20).

FOCAL VERSES

Galatians 2:15 We who are Jews by nature, and not sinners of the Gentiles,

16 Knowing that a man is not justified by the works of the law, but by the faith of Jesus Christ, even we have believed in Jesus Christ, that we might be justified by the faith of Christ, and not by the works of the law: for by the works of the law shall no flesh be justified.

17 But if, while we seek to be justified by Christ, we ourselves also are found sinners, is therefore Christ the minister of sin? God forbid.

18 For if I build again the things which I destroyed, I make myself a transgressor.

19 For I through the law am dead to the law, that I might live unto God.

20 I am crucified with Christ: nevertheless I live; yet not I, but Christ liveth in me: and the life which I now live in the flesh I live by the faith of the Son of God, who loved me, and gave himself for me.

LESSON OVERVIEW

LESSON AIM
KEEP IN MIND
FOCAL VERSES
IN FOCUS
THE PEOPLE, PLACES, AND TIMES
BACKGROUND
AT-A-GLANCE
IN DEPTH
SEARCH THE SCRIPTURES
DISCUSS THE MEANING
LESSON IN OUR SOCIETY
MAKE IT HAPPEN
FOLLOW THE SPIRIT
REMEMBER YOUR THOUGHTS
MORE LIGHT ON THE TEXT
DAILY BIBLE READINGS

---

21 I do not frustrate the grace of God: for if righteousness come by the law, then Christ is dead in vain.

3:1 O foolish Galatians, who hath bewitched you, that ye should not obey the truth, before whose eyes Jesus Christ hath been evidently set forth, crucified among you?

2 This only would I learn of you, Received ye the Spirit by the works of the law, or by the hearing of faith?

3 Are ye so foolish? having begun in the Spirit, are ye now made perfect by the flesh?

4 Have ye suffered so many things in vain? if it be yet in vain.

5 He therefore that ministereth to you the Spirit, and worketh miracles among you, doeth he it by the works of the law, or by the hearing of faith?

IN FOCUS

Cedric was happy that his younger brother had finally accepted Christ and found a church home. For years, Eric had rejected the church as a place where rich preachers preyed on poor members. He boasted how he could get rich quickly just by setting up a church on any street corner in an impoverished neighborhood, and the people would flock to hear his message of how their heavenly eternity would someday replace their earthly hell.

Eric's cynicism changed, however, after attending church with his college roommate and being electrified by the honesty of the preacher's words concerning the poor and oppressed. The message appealed to both Eric's youth and his commitment to justice. Eventually, Eric sought a church to attend near the college campus. When he finally made the decision to become a Christian, he called his brother to invite him to his baptism and admission into the church congregation.

Cedric, who had been a Christian since he was a young boy, was overjoyed. However, his joy was tempered with caution when Eric also revealed that as part of his admission into that congregation, he would have to hyphenate his last name and add the pastor's last name. He was also required to wear an armband at all times to identify him as a member of that community. Cedric shared with Eric that although Jesus made certain demands on His followers, He did not ask them to follow a certain set of community rules or rites as a requirement for salvation, the way certain other religious communities during Jesus' life did of their new members. Jesus' message to the people was that they should repent and believe.

Cedric asked Eric to reconsider joining any congregation that would put conditions on his membership. He prayed with Eric before ending their phone conversation, thanking God for Eric's new life in Christ and asking God to show him that salvation is free and not something he can earn.

THE PEOPLE, PLACES, AND TIMES

Jewish Christians or Christian Jews. Members of a separate group within the Jewish community that continued to adhere to Jewish practices and observances, such as circumcision, attending synagogue, and dietary restrictions that included, among other things, separation from Gentiles during meals. However, they also believed in Jesus' Resurrection and His status as the Messiah. Additionally, Jewish Christians observed new rituals such as baptism and Communion. The law and its observance are central to Jewish piety, and the Jewish Christians expected the Gentiles who became Christians to observe the law as well.

Antioch. Located in Syria, Antioch was the largest city in the Roman Empire after Rome and Alexandria, and home to many Jews in Diaspora (Jews living outside of Palestine). Situated on the northeast shore of the Mediterranean, Antioch was a maritime city with its own seaport. The first intentional mission among Gentiles was in Antioch, where a group of Jewish Christians fled to escape persecution in Jerusalem. Greek-speaking Jews among them shared the Gospel with Gentiles, and many Gentiles converted. The church in Jerusalem heard of these results and sent Barnabas to investigate. Barnabas was excited by what he found and sought Paul (also known by the Greek name Saul) to return with him to Antioch. The two spent a year in Antioch teaching the new converts. Antioch is also where the disciples were first called "Christians" (Acts 11:22-26).

Strange, James F. "Antioch." *Holman Bible Dictionary.* Parsons Technology, 1994. CD-ROM, QUICKVERSE for Windows.

BACKGROUND

Paul returned to Jerusalem after 14 years to meet with the Jerusalem leaders and to present to the leaders the gospel that he preached to the Gentiles. Titus, an uncircumcised Gentile, accompanied Paul to Jerusalem, and a group separate from the leaders tried to force Titus to be circumcised as proof of his inclusion in the covenant. Paul refused and the Jerusalem leaders backed him up, affirming his mission to the Gentiles.

Upon leaving the conference in Jerusalem, Paul traveled to Antioch, a Christian community with a large Gentile affiliation. Peter (or Cephas), who had been entrusted with preaching the Gospel to the Jews outside Jerusalem, visited the church at Antioch, sharing meals with the members, even though Jewish law prohibited eating with non-Jews. Shortly after the apostles' arrival, another group of Jewish Christians joined them. Their appearance caused Peter to reverse his earlier actions and separate himself from eating with the Gentiles. The Jewish Christians of the church at Antioch did likewise. Even Barnabas, Paul's companion in the mission field, conformed. This led to a big showdown between Paul and Peter, and an impassioned speech to the Galatians by Paul that they were saved by faith through Christ, not the law.

1. Confrontation in Antioch
(Galatians 2:15-17)
2. We Live By Faith (vv. 18-21)
3. We Receive the Spirit Through the
Gospel, Not the Law (3:1-5)

IN DEPTH

1. Confrontation in Antioch
(Galatians 2:15-17)

Paul, in his letter to the Galatians, recounts a confrontation between himself and Peter. The behavior of Peter, a fellow Jew, in Antioch toward Gentile Christians was equivalent to treating them as second-class citizens in the church. In essence, the actions of Peter and the other Jewish Christians said to the Gentiles that they had to become Jewish in order to be accepted into the community. Paul argues before his fellow Jewish Christians that they should know better than to require the Gentiles to observe the law as mandatory for salvation. He further argues that if Jewish Christians know that they, who were born Jews, are saved not by works of the law but by faith in Christ, how can they demand that the Gentiles obey the law in order to be saved?

2. We Live By Faith (vv. 18-21)

Paul continued his defense that no human being can be justified before God by works of the law. He argued that he had already died to the law through baptism. Since he now shares in Christ's death and Resurrection, the law-free Gospel he shared with the Galatians is sufficient for their salvation. For him to preach otherwise would be the same as returning to the works of the law. He continued that because Jesus loved him, He died to save him, and to return to the works of the law would make Jesus' death pointless. Paul wanted the Gentiles to understand that he, a devout Jew, understood that faith in Christ was the only way he could be justified before God.

3. We Receive the Spirit Through the Gospel, Not the Law (3:1-5)

Paul finally confronted the Galatians directly concerning their retrogression. After he had brought them the Good News that salvation was theirs through faith in Christ, they began listening to the teaching that without observing the law, they would not be fully included in the covenant. The text does not make clear if any members of the churches of Galatia were actually circumcised or just publicly contemplating it. The latter appears to be the case.

Paul asked the rhetorical question, "Who cast a spell over you to make you believe such nonsense?" He was already aware who was creating confusion among the Galatians. Paul was upset with the Galatians because they were already accepted as members of God's people by receiving the Spirit, apart from observing the Jewish law. Paul inquired why they would want to be circumcised when they were already living in the Spirit, as indicated by the miracles experienced among them. He warned that they were in danger of nullifying what they had already gained through faith in Christ.

SEARCH THE SCRIPTURES

1. How does Paul say that a man or woman is justified (Galatians 2:16)?

2. If righteousness comes by the law, what then does Paul say is in vain (v. 21)?

3. According to Paul, we receive the Spirit by the hearing of faith (3:2). True or false?

4. Why does Paul call the Galatians foolish (v. 3)?

DISCUSS THE MEANING

1. Paul says that we are justified by faith in Jesus Christ, not by the works of the law. What do you think it means to be justified (living in right covenant relationship with God) (Galatians 2:16)?

2. What does Paul mean when he asks the Galatians, who are living in the Spirit, if they are now made perfect by the flesh (3:3)?

LESSON IN OUR SOCIETY

How many of us have ever heard the words, "If you loved me you would. . ."? You can fill in the blank. We have all probably heard it at one time, but some of us have even been tempted to fall for that line. We have done or said something to prove our love, fidelity, etc., only to be hurt, disappointed, or betrayed. The Galatians were in a similar situation. Unidentified Jewish Christians were challenging these Gentile Christians to prove the authenticity of their conversion by being circumcised. The Galatians wanted to demonstrate that their faith in Jesus was real, even if that meant giving in to the demands of the Jewish Christians.

What would you have done in the Galatians' situation? Have you ever been asked to choose between being accepted into God's family by faith in Christ alone and doing something to make it "more legitimate"?

MAKE IT HAPPEN

Imagine that all your life, you, your parents, and the generations before them maintained a certain tradition. One day someone you greatly respect tells your family to stop observing this long-standing tradition. This is similar to what life was like for the Jewish Christians. They were taught that salvation for the Israelites was by keeping the law. Furthermore, they would suffer if they did not keep the law. Now Paul was teaching them that they could still be saved without observing the Jewish Law. Do you think it was hard for the Jewish Christians? Would it be hard for you to let go of the tradition you had observed all your life? Think about your faith. Are there any practices or beliefs that you maintain because your family or pastor taught you that they were the right way, but are contrary to God's Word?

FOLLOW THE SPIRIT

What God wants me to do:

_____

_____

REMEMBER YOUR THOUGHTS

Special insights I have learned:

_____

_____

MORE LIGHT ON THE TEXT
Galatians 2:15—3:5

Paul's message to the Galatians explained that they did not have to become Jewish in order to be Christian. Just as observing the law did not put the Jewish Christians in right relationship with God, neither would observing the law put the Galatians in right relationship with God. Rather, both Jewish and Gentile Christians were put right or "justified" by putting their trust in Jesus Christ.

15 We who are Jews by nature, and not sinners of the Gentiles.

Paul set straight his Jewish Christian brothers and sisters who did not treat the Gentile converts as equals by teaching that the Gentiles had as much right to the covenant of God as those who were Jewish by birth. African Americans know of such discrimination in the church. In the eighteenth and nineteenth centuries, Blacks were allowed to worship with Whites in the same building but were excluded from worshiping alongside Whites; instead, they were often relegated to worshiping in the balcony. Some were even physically restrained when they attempted to join Whites in the pews. Consequently, many Blacks withdrew and formed their own churches and denominations, rather than subject themselves to mistreatment.

16 Knowing that a man is not justified by the works of the law, but by the faith of Jesus Christ, even we have believed in Jesus Christ, that we might be justified by the faith of Christ, and not by the works of the law: for by the works of the law shall no flesh be justified.

The terms translated as "justified" or "righteous" are from the Greek word *dikaiow* (**dee-KY-ow**), which means "to be acquitted," or "found blameless." In the Bible, it also means being in right covenant relationship with God. Paul argued that the Gentile converts were in right covenant relationship with God by their faith in Jesus Christ, not by observing the Jewish law. The same is true for Jewish believers.

The word "works," from the Greek word *ergon* (**er'-gon**), refers to the deeds or practices exhibited in obedience to the law—including circumcision, dietary restrictions, and sabbath observances—that set the Jewish people apart from the Gentiles. Many religions today still observe certain practices, such as not eating pork or beef, as stipulated by similar rules and regulations. Poor diets have greatly contributed to the many illnesses and diseases that affect our community. We should be better stewards of the gift from God of our earthly bodies. However, it is one thing for Christians to abstain from certain foods to maintain a healthy lifestyle and quite another to do so to try to earn God's favor.

The word "law" (Gk. *nomos*, **no'-mos**) stands for the revelation or instruction received by Moses from God that is found in the first five books of the Bible; it details how the Children of Israel were to demonstrate their covenant relationship with God. African Americans can certainly appreciate the importance of the law to the Jewish people. It was a reminder that they were once slaves in Egypt and that God had delivered them.

The law was central to Jewish piety. The Jews believed that faithful observance of the law would bring them blessings and infidelity would bring disaster upon them. It is no wonder the Jewish Christians struggled with relinquishing observance of the law as a means of justification in addition to their faith in Christ. The Greek word for "faith" is *pistis* (**pis-tis**), which means "to trust, have confidence, faith, or belief in something or someone."

17 But if, while we seek to be justified by Christ, we ourselves also are found sinners, is therefore Christ the minister of sin? God forbid.

The Jewish Christians were justified by believing in Christ, which made them equal to their Gentile counterparts in God's sight. They both had to come to God in the same way. Paul did not mean that Christ made the Jews sinners; rather, both Jews and Gentiles were sinners; saved by God's grace through faith in Christ.

18 For if I build again the things which I destroyed, I make myself a transgressor.

Paul taught the Galatians that believing in Christ could save them. Thus, submitting to Jewish circumcision would undo all that he had taught them about being accepted as Christians without observing the law. For Paul, this would be equivalent to tearing down the wall that separated Jews and Gentiles, then rebuilding it—making him wrong for destroying it in the first place.

19 For I through the law am dead to the law, that I might live unto God. 20 I am crucified with Christ: nevertheless I live; yet not I, but Christ liveth in me: and the life which I now live in the flesh I live by the faith of the Son of God, who loved me, and gave himself for me.

Paul's reference to the "flesh," *sarx* (**sarx**), has several meanings in Greek. In this verse, Paul was referring to his physical limitations as a human being. To preach a gospel that included circumcision for the Galatians would be a violation of faith in Christ. Paul figuratively died to the law when he was baptized, that he might have life in God through Christ. He could not then preach that the Galatians must follow the law when he could no longer do the same. Paul also claims that, by baptism, he died and rose with Christ, whom God raised from the dead. Because of his faith in Christ, who loved him and gave His life for him, Paul now had new life in Christ, who lived in him.

21 I do not frustrate the grace of God: for if righteousness come by the law, then Christ is dead in vain.

Paul concludes his description of his confrontation at Antioch in his letter to the Galatians by stating his final argument to his opponents: If they can be in right relationship with God by observing the law, then Christ's death on the Cross was meaningless. Instead, God's grace is sufficient for salvation.

3:1 O foolish Galatians, who hath bewitched you, that ye should not obey the truth, before whose eyes Jesus Christ hath been evidently set forth, crucified among you?

Paul uses rhetorical questions and reasoning to convince the Galatians of their foolishness. He asked who had put a spell on them to make them depart from the Gospel as they had heard it from him. He knew the answer already but wanted them to face their waywardness. The word "bewitched" (Gk. *baskainow*, **bas-KY-noh**) means to be put under a spell with a stare from one with an "evil eye." In preaching the Gospel, Paul emphasized the importance of Jesus' crucifixion and Resurrection before the Galatians.

2 This only would I learn of you, Received ye the Spirit by the works of the law, or by the hearing of faith?

The Galatians enjoyed the life of the Spirit since the profession of their faith and baptism. Paul continued his interrogation of the churches of Galatia. He asked them if they had received the Spirit by observing the law or by believing the Gospel. Once again, Paul already knew their response.

3 Are ye so foolish? having begun in the Spirit, are ye now made perfect by the flesh?

The word "flesh"(*sarx*) appears again in this passage with a different meaning. On the one hand, Paul was referring here to an earthly life in disobedience to God, as opposed to a spiritual life with God by faith in Christ. On the other hand, Paul was referring literally to circumcision, which involved the cutting of flesh. The flesh of circumcision had become an obstacle that could lead the Galatians away from a life begun in the Spirit.

Paul appealed to their rational mind with his next rhetorical question. He asked the Galatians if they were justified by faith in Jesus Christ, what was the benefit of being circumcised? It is as if Paul is asking, "Are you so foolish as to pay for something that you have already been freely given?" The Galatians already had what the Jewish Christians had, minus the obstacles.

4 Have ye suffered so many things in vain? if it be yet in vain.

Paul does not identify the source of the Galatians' suffering. It could have come from at least three sources: (1) Family. Sometimes Gentiles who converted to Judaism or Christianity were estranged from their family and friends. (2) Paul's opponents. The pressure on the Galatians to be circumcised must have placed a strain on the churches. (3) Government. There were occasional persecutions of Christians by the Roman government. Whatever the source, Paul told the Galatians that if they were circumcised, their belief in Christ would be in vain.

5 He therefore that ministereth to you the Spirit, and worketh miracles among you, doeth he it by the works of the law, or by the hearing of faith?

God's gift of the Holy Spirit to every Christian was evident in the churches of Galatia. Miracles abounded in this Gentile Christian community because of God's grace. Paul's diatribe was an attempt to force the Galatians to recognize that they received the Spirit because of their faith, and not by observing the law.

DAILY BIBLE READINGS

M: Righteousness Through Faith
Romans 3:21-26

T: Grace Given to You in Christ
1 Corinthians 1:3-9

W: Fullness of Life in Christ
Colossians 2:6-14

T: Good News for Gentiles and Jews
Galatians 2:5-10

F: We Are All Saved by Faith
Galatians 2:15-21

S: Law or Faith
Galatians 3:1-5

S: All Receive the Spirit's Promise
Galatians 3:6-14

Contrast the inadequacy of "works" with the adequacy of "faith" in bringing about salvation by using your *Precepts For Living* CD-ROM to do a search of these two words.

TEACHING TIPS

May 15
Bible Study Guide 11

1. Words You Should Know

A. Transgressions (Galatians 3:19) *parabasis* (Gk.)—A breach of an existing law.

B. Mediator (vv. 19-20) *mesites* (Gk.)—One who links two parties.

C. Redeem (4:5) *exagorazo* (Gk.)—The act of buying something from someone to initiate ownership.

2. Teacher Preparation

A. Before you begin studying this week's lesson, review last week's lesson and any special insights your class discussed. This week's lesson is a continuation from last week's.

B. Read this week's lesson from several versions of the Bible. Make notes about anything you don't understand, and underline passages you want to highlight.

C. Read the entire lesson at least twice this week. Keep track of important points you want to emphasize.

3. Starting the Lesson

A. Read the LESSON AIM aloud and open the class with a prayer focusing on the KEEP IN MIND verse.

B. Ask the students to explain what a mediator does. Ask them to give examples of mediators in their lives. Tell them that Jesus Christ serves as the mediator between God and humans.

4. Getting into the Lesson

A. Based on their reading from last week, ask the students to discuss what they think is the central theme of Galatians.

B. Read the FOCAL VERSES and ask volunteers to share their thoughts on the meaning of each verse.

C. Ask three volunteers to read the IN DEPTH section, allowing time for students to discuss and ask questions between each section.

5. Relating the Lesson to Life

A. Separate the students into three groups. One group should read the IN FOCUS section, have another answer the DISCUSS THE MEANING questions, and ask the third group to read LESSON IN OUR SOCIETY. Give each group about 10 minutes to discuss the sections and think of ways to apply them to their lives.

B. Have a spokesperson present each group's findings.

6. Arousing Action

A. Have each student take time to write their responses to the FOLLOW THE SPIRIT and REMEMBER YOUR THOUGHTS sections. You may play soft music to prompt them to reflect.

B. Ask volunteers to share what they have written.

C. Close with prayer.

WORSHIP GUIDE

MAY 15TH

For the Superintendent or Teacher
Theme: The Purpose of the Law
Theme Song: "The Only Hope"
Scripture: Romans 3:27-31
Song: "That's Love"
Meditation: Lord, thank You for adopting us into Your family. Help us to remember the special place we have in Your family.

THE PURPOSE OF THE LAW

Bible Background • GALATIANS 3:19—4:7
Printed Text • GALATIANS 3:19-29; 4:4-7
Devotional Reading • ROMANS 3:27-31

LESSON AIM

By the end of the lesson, the students should understand that they have been united with Christ and adopted as full members into the family of God through faith in Jesus Christ. Additionally, they should understand that God's family is an inclusive one, where distinctions between members do not exist.

KEEP IN MIND

"But when the fulness of the time was come, God sent forth his Son, made of a woman, made under the law, to redeem them that were under the law, that we might receive the adoption of sons. And because ye are sons, God hath sent forth the Spirit of his Son into your hearts, crying, Abba, Father. Wherefore thou art no more a servant, but a son; and if a son, then an heir of God through Christ" (Galatians 4:4-6).

FOCAL VERSES

Galatians 3:19 Wherefore then serveth the law? It was added because of transgressions, till the seed should come to whom the promise was made; and it was ordained by angels in the hand of a mediator.

20 Now a mediator is not a mediator of one, but God is one.

21 Is the law then against the promises of God? God forbid: for if there had been a law given which could have given life, verily righteousness should have been by the law.

22 But the scripture hath concluded all under sin, that the promise by faith of Jesus Christ might be given to them that believe.

LESSON OVERVIEW

LESSON AIM
KEEP IN MIND
FOCAL VERSES
IN FOCUS
THE PEOPLE, PLACES,
AND TIMES
BACKGROUND
AT-A-GLANCE
IN DEPTH
SEARCH THE SCRIPTURES
DISCUSS THE MEANING
LESSON IN OUR SOCIETY
MAKE IT HAPPEN
FOLLOW THE SPIRIT
REMEMBER YOUR THOUGHTS
MORE LIGHT ON THE TEXT
DAILY BIBLE READINGS

23 But before faith came, we were kept under the law, shut up unto the faith which should afterwards be revealed.

24 Wherefore the law was our schoolmaster to bring us unto Christ, that we might be justified by faith.

25 But after that faith is come, we are no longer under a schoolmaster. LAW

26 For ye are all the children of God by faith in Christ Jesus.

27 For as many of you as have been baptized into Christ have put on Christ.

28 There is neither Jew nor Greek, there is neither bond nor free, there is neither male nor female: for ye are all one in Christ Jesus.

29 And if ye be Christ's, then are ye Abraham's seed, and heirs according to the promise.

4:4 But when the fulness of the time was come, God sent forth his Son, made of a woman, made under the law,

5 To redeem them that were under the law, that we might receive the adoption of sons.

6 And because ye are sons, God hath sent forth the Spirit of his Son into your hearts, crying, Abba, Father.

7 Wherefore thou art no more a servant, but a son; and if a son, then an heir of God through Christ.

IN FOCUS

Hillary had wanted to be a teacher for as long as she could remember. She had always admired and respected the teachers she had had over the years, and believed that teaching would be a way to give back to the community. She had spent the past year in a special program designed to recruit teachers to urban and rural schools. The program paired Hillary and other student teachers with a more experienced master teacher, who observed them in the classroom and helped out when necessary. It also provided Hillary with professional development training that other teachers needed to advance in their profession.

Hillary tried her best over the months to be the best teacher she could be. However, the students were aware that Hillary was not the "real" teacher and caused disciplinary problems for her. The master teachers' treatment of their proteges also sometimes contributed to a feeling of inferiority, but that was about to change. Hillary was completing the program in one month and had already received a job offer. Once Hillary was hired, she would earn a salary commensurate with that of other teachers with her experience; but more importantly, Hillary would be accorded equal status with the other teachers. She would no longer be a student teacher, but would receive the same benefits and privileges as the other teachers. Hillary could not wait to sign the contract.

THE PEOPLE, PLACES, AND TIMES

Promise. The Bible contains many promises by God to His people. Significant among God's promises is His promise to bless Abraham with a son, who would become a great nation, and that all the nations of the earth would be blessed in Abraham. God also promised Abraham that his descendants would be too many to count. God's promise to Abraham is in the background as God delivered the Children of Israel from Egyptian slavery and made a covenant with them. Israel descended from Abraham through Isaac. God's presence was continually with the Israelites, who trusted in God's future salvation because of His promise to Abraham.

Slavery. Slavery was an integral part of Greco-Roman civilization. Slaves accounted for one-fifth of the population. People became slaves through various circumstances, including breeding, wars, piracy, debt, and birth to a slave mother. Slaves

were the property of their owners and had no legal rights. Slaves functioned broadly within the society, from civil service to hard labor. Household slaves were entrusted with the care of the home and child rearing. School-age children were under the moral guidance of "pedagogues," or custodians, who also looked after the children's general well-being but were not the children's teachers.

A benevolent master might grant a slave freedom in his will. The slave was freed upon the death of the master. A friend, relative, or other benefactor might also purchase a slave's freedom. "Redemption" means "to buy back," as in to purchase from slavery.

Buttrick, George A., ed. "Promise." *The Interpreters' Dictionary of the Bible*. Nashville: Abingdon Press, 1962. Vol. 3. 893-94.

Ferguson, Everett. *Backgrounds of Early Christianity*. Grand Rapids, Mich.: Eerdmans, 1987. 46-47, 84.

BACKGROUND

At this time in his letter to the Galatians, Paul had introduced God's promise to Abraham and his "seed" (descendant) into his defense of his gospel to the Gentiles. For Paul, God's promised blessing extended to all of Abraham's heirs—Jews as well as the Gentiles who shared Abraham's faith. Some Jews did not accept this teaching. Paul countered that all who live by faith in Jesus Christ, the "seed" of Abraham, are the sons of Abraham and recipients of the promise.

AT-A-GLANCE

1. Purpose of the Law (Galatians 3:19-22)
2. The Coming of Faith (vv. 23-29)
3. Slavery and Adoption (4:4-7)

IN DEPTH

1. Purpose of the Law (Galatians 3:19-22)

Paul argued throughout his letter to the Galatians that observance of the Jewish law was not a requirement for them to be accepted into the Christian community. Paul shifted to legal language to provide further evidence of why they were justified by faith, not by the works of the law. He explained that God gave the law to Israel as a codicil to the promise to help them see that sin is contrary to His will. A codicil is an addition to a will that provides further instruction or added developments. The law, Paul insisted, was a temporary system until the arrival of the promised offspring ("seed"). Furthermore, the law was compromised because Moses received it through a mediator—a go-between in the form of an angel. Abraham, on the other hand, received the promise directly from God. (The notion that God gave the law through angels is most clearly seen in the Greek version of the Old Testament translated by Jewish scholars for the Greek-speaking Jewish community.)

Paul maintained that the law did not oppose God's promise. Rather, the law could not save the people from death because it could not prevent people from sinning. The Scripture, according to Paul, concluded that the law had imprisoned the people under the power of sin. The only way to be released from the power of sin is through faith in Jesus Christ.

2. The Coming of Faith (vv. 23-29)

Paul contended that before faith came, the law was like a "pedagogue" (schoolmaster or guardian) over the Jewish people, who were as children in need of moral supervision and discipline. Now that faith had come, the people were no longer charges of the law, but had matured to the point where they were no longer in need of a custodian. They were now children of God through faith in Jesus Christ and full heirs of the promise, not by birth, but by faith expressed through baptism. Baptism into Christ clothed the Gentile with Christ and afforded him or her the status of Abraham's offspring (3:27). Baptism, unlike circumcision, was a sign of inclusion into God's covenant family for women as well as men. Social, economic, racial, and gender discrimination was erased as a part of acceptance into God's family. Native born versus non-native born was no longer an issue. They were all one in Christ Jesus, and if they were in Christ, they were Abraham's offspring and heirs to the promise.

3. Slavery and Adoption (4:4-7)

The status of children in early Christianity was only a little better than that of a slave. Although freeborn male children would someday inherit their father's property, including the slaves, children too held a subordinate position in the household. Earlier, Paul had described the Jewish people as children under the guardianship of the slave/law. However, when God's appointed hour had come, He sent Jesus into the world to redeem them from under the law and adopt them as children. Adoption was a common practice in the Greco-Roman world. A person could be adopted as an adult as well as a child. The adoptive parent gave the adopted person a new life with a new family name and status. The adopted person received all the rights and privileges of a natural-born child, including the family inheritance. The Galatians, in their faith, were in a new relationship with God. Through Christ Jesus, Gentiles were adopted into God's household with the full rights of a natural-born child with the Holy Spirit as God's witness. As children of God, they were no longer under the slave custodian, but instead, as God's children, heirs of God through Christ Jesus.

SEARCH THE SCRIPTURES

1. Paul says the law was added for what purpose (Galatians 3:19)?

2. The law is against the promises of God (v. 21). True or false?

3. Who does Paul say is the seed of Abraham and heirs of the promise (v. 29)?

4. Why did God send His Son into the world (4:4-5)?

5. Why does Paul say that we the Galatians can call God "Father" (v. 6)?

DISCUSS THE MEANING

1. The schoolmaster (or pedagogue) functioned as a custodian of minor children until they came of age. What does it mean to no longer be under a schoolmaster (Galatians 3:24-25)?

2. What does Paul mean when he says, "There is neither Jew nor Greek, there is neither bond nor free, there is neither male nor female: for ye are all one in Christ Jesus" (v. 28)?

3. Compare and contrast what it means to be naturally born versus adopted into the family of God.

LESSON IN OUR SOCIETY

When I was an adolescent, I began to hear whispers about one of my cousins not being my "real cousin." Those whispers were fueled by the revelation that my uncle was not my cousin's biological father. Learning this so-called truth about my cousin did not change our relationship, nor did my uncle love my cousin any less than his natural-born child. My cousin carries our family name and is my uncle's heir. Some of my family members were guilty of treating my cousin as some of the Jewish Christians treated the Gentiles. The Gentiles were treated as inferior because they were not natural-born Jews, and therefore were not considered by some to be the seed of Abraham. However, Paul assures us that in Christ Jesus we are all children of God through baptism, and that God does not make distinctions between Jews and Gentiles, slaves and free persons, men and women.

MAKE IT HAPPEN

How does it make you feel to know that, no matter what the circumstances were surrounding your birth, through Christ Jesus you have been adopted into God's family and made one with Christ by baptism? All your debts are paid, and you now have all the rights of a natural-born child. You share an equal inheritance with all God's children. That is good news! Create a "certificate of adoption" for yourself as an adoptive child of God.

FOLLOW THE SPIRIT

What God wants me to do:

_____

_____

REMEMBER YOUR THOUGHTS

Special insights I have learned:

_____

_____

MORE LIGHT ON THE TEXT

Galatians 3:19-29; 4:4-7

19 Wherefore then serveth the law? It was added because of transgressions, till the seed should come to whom the promise was made; and it was ordained by the angels in the hand of a mediator.

The thrust of Paul's argument is to show how the law functions to reveal sin in human nature for what it is. As the Israelites infringed upon the law, they were reminded of their sinfulness despite their covenant relationship to God. Violating the law did not make the Israelite a sinner; instead, the Israelite violated the law because he or she was a sinner. The Greek word translated as "transgressions" is *parabasis* (**par-ab-as-is**) and denotes a breach of an existing law. Before the law, it was easy for an Israelite to gloss over sin as a subjective thing; but the law shows sin to be an objective reality, a violation of God's standards (cp. Romans 7:13).

The law also stimulates faith in the promised Seed, whose coming was to fulfill the law. As the Israelites, through the law, came to terms with the reality of sin, they were pointed to the coming Messiah who would deal decisively with it. The law was interim, pending the coming of the Seed who fulfilled the promise. The law was inferior because it was given through angels and the mediatorial role of Moses. "Mediator" (Gk. *mesites*, **mes-ee-tace**) suggests one who liaises between two parties. It has been rightly observed that the involvement of a mediator points to the contractual nature of the law and implies obligations for both parties. In a land contract, for example, a mediator may be needed to facilitate the deal between the buyer and the seller and both parties assuming certain responsibilities.

20 Now a mediator is not a mediator of one, but God is one.

This verse contrasts the promise with the law by showing that the promise was solely a divine affair. Abraham was not obligated to do anything to validate the promise. Therefore, no mediator was needed. This again shows that the promise was superior to the law because its fulfillment did not depend on Israel.

All believers are God's children and joint-heirs with Jesus.

How comforting to know that the believer's status as an heir of salvation does not depend on the believer's efforts but rests solely on God's grace through Christ. It is like our relationship with our biological parent. We did absolutely nothing to merit being our mother's child.

21 Is the law then against the promises of God? God forbid: for if there had been a law given which could have given life, verily righteousness should have been by the law.

A Jewish Christian might think the law negates the promises of God. Paul very strongly rejects this notion using the expression "God forbid" (Gk. *me genoito,* **me ghin-oit-o**), which is the equivalent of an oath. The purpose of the promise was to impart life. In order for the law to replace the promise, it would have to be able to impart life too.

22 But the scripture hath concluded all under sin, that the promise by faith of Jesus Christ might be given to them that believe.

Instead of imparting life, the law of Moses condemns all humanity under sin. By using the Greek word *sugkleio* (**soong-kli-o**), meaning "to shut or enclose," Paul is personifying Scripture (the law) as a jailer who keeps the condemned secure in prison. In this country, barring a miscarriage of justice, only the guilty is imprisoned. The law has convicted all humanity as guilty of sin, so those under the law will appreciate the fact that eternal life is dependent on faith in Christ and is therefore open to all who believe.

23 But before faith came, we were kept under the law, shut up unto the faith which should afterwards be revealed.

Paul continues his personification, but this time he changes from "Scripture" (v. 22) to the "law," suggesting that both terms are used interchangeably. The phrase "shut up" (Gk. *phroureo,* **froo-reh-o**) is a military term meaning to guard a place in order to prevent an escape from inside or an invasion from outside. The law functioned like a siege, keeping those under it from escaping from the reality of their sin until Christ came. Someone has compared the law in this connection to the natural law of gravity, which pulls down anyone who tries to defy it without depending on a device.

24 Wherefore the law was our schoolmaster to bring us unto Christ, that we might be justified by faith.

Again Paul personifies the law, this time as a "schoolmaster" (Gk. *paidagogos,* **pahee-dag-o-gos**), or an escort for children as they journey to and from school. The school bus driver is the modern equivalent of an ancient pedagogue. Just as the bus driver takes the children to school to be taught by the teacher, so did the law serve to guide those under it to Christ for their justification by faith.

25 But after that faith is come, we are no longer under a schoolmaster.

Since Christ had come and fulfilled the promise, the law was no longer needed. It is like a child whose mother has just been certified to homeschool her. That child does not need the school bus driver any longer.

26 For ye are all the children of God by faith in Christ Jesus.

Special emphasis is placed on the word "all," which here includes both Jews and Gentiles. Through faith in Christ, both Jews and Gentiles have equal privileges before God as children. Faith in Christ, not obedience to the law, confers the privileges of a child of God.

27 For as many of you as have been baptized into Christ, have put on Christ.

This is the spiritual baptism by which new believers are incorporated into the body of Christ (see 1 Corinthians 12:13). This unity with Christ is tantamount to putting Christ on figuratively as a garment. The Greek verb *enduo* (**en-doo-o**) is normally used with reference to putting on a garment. It highlights the need to make visible our spiritual union with Christ.

28 There is neither Jew nor Greek, there is neither bond nor free, there is neither male nor female: for ye are all one in Christ Jesus.

Paul is not denying that these differences exist after one becomes a believer. His point is that the merits of these distinctions do not give one an edge over others as God's child. In Christ, we are all one, i.e., we are the same.

29 And if ye be Christ's then are ye Abraham's seed, and heirs according to the promise.

The person who belongs to Christ is the real seed of Abraham and the true heir of God's promise to Abraham. The contrast is clear: faith in Christ rather than obedience to the law is the way to inherit God's promise. As such, the Church (Jewish believers included) rather than the modern state of Israel represents the heirs of the promise of God today.

4:4 But when the fulness of the time was come, God sent forth his Son, made of a woman, made under the law.

At the right time, God sent His Son to redeem all humanity. The same God who made the promise to Abraham now sends His Son in fulfill-ment of the promise. The Greek word *exapostello* (**ex-ap-os-tel-lo**) means "to send forth with a commission." Christ was sent with the commission to fulfill the Father's promise of salvation through faith.

That Christ was God's "Son, made of a woman" indicates His full divinity as well as His full humanity without sin. Therefore, the Saviour could be born under the law and yet not subjected to its bondage. Thus, He identifies with the experience of those under the law, yet He is without sin.

5 To redeem them that were under the law, that we might receive the adoption of sons.

Christ came under the law to redeem those under the law. The word "redeem" (Gk. *exagora-zo,* **ex-ag-or-ad-zo**) was used to denote buying a slave out of the slave market into freedom. Those under the law were, like the rest of humanity, slaves to sin and not children of God. Slaves usually were not capable of purchasing their freedom. When Christ made redemption from the slavery of sin possible for those under the law, the result was a dramatic transformation into adopted children of God.

6 And because ye are sons, God hath sent forth the Spirit of his Son into your hearts, cry-ing, Abba, Father.

As God's children, believers receive the Spirit of Christ into their hearts, bearing witness in them of their filial relationship to God. This is a continuous witness, reassuring the believer of his/her new relationship to God. Out of respect, the Jews would not call God "Father." It was therefore a novel idea, which derives from Christ (see Mark 14:36), that believers would address God as "Father," using the very intimate and affectionate Aramaic term "Abba" (Dad). The term acknowledges the protective power,

care, and concern that God the Father shows for His children.

7 Wherefore thou art no more a servant, but a son; and if a son, then an heir of God through Christ.

With their new status as children of God comes the end of slavery to sin under the law. You can be a child and still be excluded from any inheritance by a will. Such is not the situation of God's children. Believers are not just children of God in the abstract, nominal sense without any privileges attached. To them belong the full priv-ileges of an heir. An "heir" (Gk. *kleronomos,* **klay-ron-om-os**) is one who receives an inheritance without having to work for it. That is what believ-ers have as "Abraham's seed, and heirs accord-ing to the promise" (Galatians 3:29).

DAILY BIBLE READINGS

M: God's Law Is Perfect
Psalm 19:7-14

T: Understanding the Law
1 Timothy 1:3-11

W: Jesus Fulfills the Law
Matthew 5:17-22

T: We Uphold the Law Through Faith
Romans 3:27-31

F: Why the Law?
Galatians 3:19-23

S: The Law Was Our Disciplinarian
Galatians 3:24-29

S: No Longer Slave but Heir
Galatians 4:1-7

Use your *Precepts For Living* CD-ROM to do a cross-reference check on Galatians 4:7. You'll find other places in the Bible where God's children are called "heirs."

TEACHING TIPS

May 22
Bible Study Guide 12

1. Words You Should Know

A. Liberty (Galatians 5:1) *eleutheria* (Gk.)—Freedom; not a slave, or exempt from obligation.

B. Circumcised (v. 2) *peritemno* (Gk.)—The rite of circumcision meant a man was separated from the unclean world and dedicated to God. The word is used here to denote the extinguishing of lusts and the removal of sins.

2. Teacher Preparation

A. Read BIBLE STUDY GUIDE 12 and meditate on the FOCAL VERSES.

B. Study the IN DEPTH section and make notes to discuss in class. Read the SEARCH THE SCRIPTURES and DISCUSS THE MEANING sections and answer the questions.

C. Write the LESSON AIM on the chalkboard and gear your teaching toward completing its objectives.

D. Materials needed: Bibles, pencils, pens, paper.

3. Starting the Lesson

A. Before beginning the lesson, briefly review the highlights from last week's lesson.

B. Have volunteers read the IN FOCUS section, and discuss it in detail.

C. Ask a student to lead the class in prayer, focusing on the LESSON AIM objectives.

4. Getting into the Lesson

A. Have students silently read the BACKGROUND and THE PEOPLE, PLACES, AND TIMES sections.

B. Ask for volunteers to take turns reading the FOCAL VERSES, and afterward ask the students to silently read the IN DEPTH commentary and answer the SEARCH THE SCRIPTURE questions.

C. Allow time for an open discussion using the DISCUSS THE MEANING questions as a guide.

5. Relating the Lesson to Life

Spend as much time as possible on the LESSON IN OUR SOCIETY section. Give the students time to reflect on their responsibilities as adults. Ask the students what they think it means to live free.

6. Arousing Action

A. Instruct the students to read the DAILY BIBLE READINGS for the week. This will help them stay focused on what they've learned from today's lesson.

B. Challenge the students to complete the task in the MAKE IT HAPPEN section.

C. Close the class in prayer, thanking God for understanding, knowledge, and wisdom from the day's lesson.

CHRISTIAN FREEDOM

Bible Background • GALATIANS 5:1-15
Printed Text • GALATIANS 5:1-15
Devotional Reading • 1 PETER 2:11-17

LESSON AIM

By the end of the lesson, the students will understand that God calls us to freedom in Christ Jesus to live in the Spirit. If we accept any other ritual or deed as a condition for salvation, it is the same as being enslaved to the law, and Christ's sacrifice to redeem us from sin is nullified.

KEEP IN MIND

"For, brethren, ye have been called unto liberty; only use not liberty for an occasion to the flesh, but by love serve one another" (Galatians 5:13).

FOCAL VERSES

Galatians 5:1 Stand fast therefore in the liberty wherewith Christ hath made us free, and be not entangled again with the yoke of bondage.

2 Behold, I Paul say unto you, that if ye be circumcised, Christ shall profit you nothing.

3 For I testify again to every man that is circumcised, that he is a debtor to do the whole law.

4 Christ is become of no effect unto you, whosoever of you are justified by the law; ye are fallen from grace.

5 For we through the Spirit wait for the hope of righteousness by faith.

6 For in Jesus Christ neither circumcision availeth any thing, nor uncircumcision; but faith which worketh by love.

7 Ye did run well; who did hinder you that ye should not obey the truth?

8 This persuasion cometh not of him that calleth you.

LESSON OVERVIEW

LESSON AIM
KEEP IN MIND
FOCAL VERSES
IN FOCUS
THE PEOPLE, PLACES, AND TIMES
BACKGROUND
AT-A-GLANCE
IN DEPTH
SEARCH THE SCRIPTURES
DISCUSS THE MEANING
LESSON IN OUR SOCIETY
MAKE IT HAPPEN
FOLLOW THE SPIRIT
REMEMBER YOUR THOUGHTS
MORE LIGHT ON THE TEXT
DAILY BIBLE READINGS

9 A little leaven leaveneth the whole lump.

10 I have confidence in you through the Lord, that ye will be none otherwise minded: but he that troubleth you shall bear his judgment, whosoever he be.

11 And I, brethren, if I yet preach circumcision, why do I yet suffer persecution? then is the offence of the cross ceased.

12 I would they were even cut off which trouble you.

13 For, brethren, ye have been called unto liberty; only use not liberty for an occasion to the flesh, but by love serve one another.

14 For all the law is fulfilled in one word, even in this; Thou shalt love thy neighbour as thyself.

15 But if ye bite and devour one another, take heed that ye be not consumed one of another.

IN FOCUS

Preston had been dating Paula for five months. They met during a rainstorm when Preston offered to share his umbrella with a soaking wet Paula, who was waiting for her bus to arrive. He sheltered her from the rain until her bus arrived, and before the bus pulled away from the curb, Paula called for Preston and handed him her phone number through the window. Preston called her, and they began dating shortly thereafter. Paula impressed Preston with her drive, her level head, and her love for Christ.

The two were meeting for lunch when Paula took a cigarette from a pack in her purse and began to light it. Preston had seen the recent statistics on the number of adults over 18 that began smoking cigarettes for the first time, but he was still shocked when Paula started to smoke. Preston expressed his bewilderment and frustration that Paula would do such a foolish thing. Paula told Preston he was just trying to be overprotective of her. She told him that she and all her friends had begun smoking because it made them look sophisticated and glamorous. Paula pointed to the number of celebrities that smoked on- and off-screen. Paula also claimed that smoking would help her stay slim.

Preston argued that Paula was old enough to know better than to smoke. He told her that if she kept it up, she would become a slave to nicotine. He pointed out that it only took weeks of regular smoking to become addicted. He also told her that more women die from lung cancer than from breast cancer. Paula asked Preston how he knew so much about the risks of smoking. He shared that his aunt had passed away last year from lung cancer. She had thought smoking was liberating.

Paula dismissed Preston's remarks with nervous laughter. Of course, Paula reasoned that she could stop smoking anytime she wanted. Preston was not as confident as his girlfriend. "Why," Preston asked Paula, "do you need to engage in something addictive when you are already free?" Paula pretended not to be bothered by Preston's question, but it stuck in her mind. "Why," Paula thought to herself, "when I am free indeed?"

THE PEOPLE, PLACES, AND TIMES

Free. What it means to be free was a frequent topic of discussion among early Greek thinkers. One group held that an individual was free if he was free of social and political oppression at the hands of the government. Another taught that an individual was free if he could free himself of passions and emotions, regardless of his social-political situation. Still another group maintained that man was free if he was able to free himself of the present evil age through mysterious religions that practiced such things as ascetic abstinence—

deprivation of worldly and bodily pleasures for spiritual attainment—or excessive indulgence. Paul was likely familiar with the philosophical thought popular during his time, such as that of the Stoics, who viewed freedom as self-sufficiency. He was also aware that his mostly Gentile converts were familiar with the thoughts on freedom circulating during this period. Paul took their understanding of freedom, and expanded it to conform to the Gospel's meaning of freedom. For Paul, freedom meant freedom from the law, sin, and death, and freedom in Christ to live.

Kung, Hans. *Hans Kung In The Church.* Garden City, N.Y.: Image Books, 1976. 201-2.

Roetzel, Calvin J. *The Letters of Paul: Conversations in Context.* Louisville: Westminster John Knox Press, 1998. 20-21, 27-29.

BACKGROUND

Paul evangelized the Gentiles in the territory of Galatia while recuperating from an illness there (Galatians 4:13). He preached that the Gentiles were justified before God without circumcision or observance of the Jewish law. Unnamed foes opposed Paul's gospel to the Gentiles and demanded that the converts be circumcised before they could be fully accepted as the people of God. The Gentiles could easily have been torn between Paul and his opponents because what probably drew them to the synagogue initially was their attraction to Jewish observances and practices. These Gentiles sometimes observed the Sabbath and Jewish holidays, although many avoided circumcision. They were part of a group of people called "God-fearers." Perhaps the Galatians believed that to show their fidelity to their new religion, they needed to go all the way and be circumcised.

Throughout his letter to the churches of Galatia, Paul asserts that his Gospel was the one true Gospel. He argues that if they allow themselves to be circumcised, then they are obligated to obey the whole law. Thus, Christ would be of no value to them at all. If they try to be justified by law, then they have been alienated from Christ and have fallen away from grace. They were justified by faith in Christ, not by works of the law. Their life in the Spirit was evidence of their justification. Furthermore, faith brought the fulfillment of God's promise to Abraham and his descendants. Faith in Christ freed the people from the law, and allowed acceptaance of the Gentiles as adopted children of God.

Paul made a final appeal to the Galatians to accept their freedom in Christ and left them instructions to reject those who would lead them astray before closing his letter.

AT-A-GLANCE

1. Stand Firm in Freedom
(Galatians 5:1-6)
2. True Way to Righteousness (vv. 7-12)
3. Freedom to Love (vv. 13-15)

IN DEPTH

1. Stand Firm in Freedom (Galatians 5:1-6)

The Gentile Christians of Galatia were in a quandary: Do they accept the Gospel they received from Paul, or do they believe his opponents who say the Gentiles must be circumcised and obey the law? Paul exhorted them to continue in their steadfastness and remain loyal to the Gospel, and not give in to observing the law or pagan ceremonies.

Christ had set the Galatians free for the purpose of freedom. If any of them thought that they could be in right relationship with God by circumcision or works of the law, then it was pointless to have faith in Christ. Paul explained that the Galatians could not be selective about which parts of the law they would observe. He told them that if they submitted to one rule (circumcision), they were obligated to observe all the law or die. The Spirit, on the other hand, which the Galatians had received by faith (Galatians 3:3), made them right with God and guaranteed their future with Christ at the end of time. For Paul, circumcision did not matter, but rather faith in Christ expressed in love for one another.

2. True Way to Righteousness (vv. 7-12)

Paul commended the Galatians on initially accepting his Gospel but chastised them for paying attention to those who would oppose him in the matter of circumcision. Paul declared that it was not God who had steered them in the wrong direction, but his opponents. The influence of a few troublemakers had spread throughout the congregations of Galatia, causing turmoil within the churches. Paul, however, expressed his confidence in the churches to remain obedient to the Gospel. Paul's adversaries, although unknown, descrvcd to suffcr God's judgment. There were also accusations that Paul, in his earlier exceeding zeal for the Jewish traditions, still preached circumcision. He countered that if his opponents really believed that he advocated circumcision, they would support his Gospel instead of opposing it. He instead wished that the troublemakers would castrate themselves.

3. Freedom to Love (vv. 13-15)

Finally, Paul instructed the Galatians that since they had been given freedom, they should not use their freedom for self-indulgence, but rather through love to serve each other. Paul's opponents were not as concerned that Paul preached justification by faith, as they were concerned that freedom from the law would lead to all kinds of immorality by the Gentiles. Paul taught them that the whole law was summed up in the single commandment to love one's neighbor as oneself (Leviticus 19:18; Romans 13:9). If they kept that commandment, then they would have kept the entire law. The opponents had obviously created divisions in the churches of Galatia, causing them to fight among themselves. Paul admonished them to be careful not to destroy each other. This turmoil might have been the reason for his love language.

SEARCH THE SCRIPTURES

1. How, according to Paul, might the Galatians fall from grace (Galatians 5:4)?
2. What did Paul say would happen to the troublemakers who demanded that the Galatians be circumcised (v. 10)?
3. What did Paul say was the purpose of their freedom (v. 13)?
4. According to Paul, which commandment summed up the entire law (v. 14)?

DISCUSS THE MEANING

1. What did Paul mean when he said that every man that is circumcised is a debtor to do the whole law (Galatians 5:3)?

2. Leaven is a small amount of starter bread that, when added to a batch of dough, greatly expands the batch. To what was Paul referring when he said, "A little leaven leaveneth the whole lump" (v. 9)?

LESSON IN OUR SOCIETY

In today's society, freedom for many people means absence of responsibility. We know or hear of spouses who leave their marriages because "they've got to be free." People abandon their children, quit their jobs, or practice inappropriate behavior in the name of freedom. On the other side are oppressed people in places like Africa and Brazil, whose Christian faith informs them that they have the right to freedom from social and political tyranny and freedom to self-determination. They also believe that they are free in Christ to serve one another's needs in a visible way. They worship together, study God's Word together, support each other, and address each other's social and economic needs. Paul wanted the Galatians to know that freedom from observing the law did not mean freedom to act any way they pleased, but rather that they were called to freedom to serve one another in love.

MAKE IT HAPPEN

Make a list of your future goals and divide them into three sections. Label section one "personal goals," section two "professional goals," and section three "spiritual goals." Read the key verse in the KEEP IN MIND section. At the end of your list of goals in each section, write if attainment of your goals would be freedom for self-indulgence or freedom to serve.

FOLLOW THE SPIRIT

What God wants me to do:

_____

_____

REMEMBER YOUR THOUGHTS

Special insights I have learned:

_____

_____

MORE LIGHT ON THE TEXT
Galatians 5:1-15

1 Stand fast therefore in the liberty wherewith Christ hath made us free, and be not entangled again with the yoke of bondage.

This is a connecting verse; it summarizes all that has been said and anticipates what is yet to be said. There is greater clarity of thought when this verse is read as two separate statements. First, there is a statement emphasizing the purpose of God's saving act in Christ: "It is for freedom that Christ has set us free." Second, there is a statement of entreaty, a plea or an appeal based upon the purpose of God's saving activity: "Stand firm, then, and do not let yourselves be burdened again by a yoke of slavery" (NIV).

The "yoke of bondage" was more than the yoke of the Jewish law. The Gentile Christians were never under the yoke of the Jewish law; they were under the yoke of paganism. Therefore, Paul uses the phrase "yoke of bondage" to refer to "the elements of the world" (4:3) and "the weak and beggarly elements" (4:9). Both the Jewish law and paganism were included in the elements of the world that rob people of their freedom in Christ.

The Greek word for "entangled" is *enecho* (**in-ek-ko**) meaning "to be subject to" or "to be loaded down with." Paul says that believers should not be loaded down with or subjected again to the yoke of bondage.

2 Behold, I Paul say unto you, that if ye be circumcised, Christ shall profit you nothing.

The translation "if ye be circumcised" does not do justice to the Greek. The tense of the Greek verb *peritemno* (**per-ee-TEM-no,** meaning "to cut around" or "circumcise") in this context carries the meaning: "if you should let yourselves be circumcised" or "to everyone who has himself circumcised" with the assumption that circumcision justifies, then "Christ shall profit you nothing." The inference is that the Gentile Christians had not yet submitted themselves to be circumcised

Jesus alone saves us from our sins.

but were seriously considering doing so. Paul's aim is to correct their erroneous thinking that circumcision justifies without offending the Jews for having been circumcised.

It is helpful to read this verse in conjunction with the comments in Romans 7:17-20, where

Paul makes the point that circumcision is not the issue. Rather, the issue lies in the mistaken notion that there is salvific value in circumcision.

The Greek word for "profit" is *opheleo*, which means benefit, help, use, or aid. Paul states that if we rely on works for salvation, then we benefit nothing from Christ, or our faith in Christ is negated and therefore of no use or aid. The benefits we have in Christ become void. We find ourselves back under the law.

3 For I testify again to every man that is circumcised, that he is a debtor to do the whole law.

Paul has already stated that to allow oneself to be circumcised is a confession that Christ's death has no saving value or power for Christian living. He adds that to allow oneself to be circumcised is to make oneself a "debtor" obligated to perform the duty of "the whole law."

4 Christ is become of no effect unto you, whosoever of you are justified by the law; ye are fallen from grace.

In verse 2, Paul said to put your trust in the law (circumcision) means Christ has no benefit for you. In this verse, Paul uses a different Greek word, *katargeo*, meaning to make void, powerless, or to nullify. He states that if we try to practice the law and faith in order to be saved, we have nullified what Christ has done. To think that obeying the law justifies us before God is to separate oneself from Christ. It is tantamount to falling away from the grace of God and into legalism. The choice is mutually exclusive: Choose grace and live in the power of His might, or choose legalism, forfeit grace, and try to live life in your own failing strength. There are definite and inevitable consequences that follow each choice.

5 For we through the Spirit wait for the hope of righteousness by faith.

Paul identifies with the faithful in Galatia: "For we wait rather than work for salvation," Paul says (paraphrased). "We wait for the full realization of our salvation in the faith that we already have it" (paraphrased). Thus, Paul's use of the word "hope," from the Greek verb *elpidzo* (**el-pid-zo**), means to anticipate with pleasure, certainty, and confidence that which is not yet fully realized.

There is another image that helps us to understand the full meaning of verse 5. The word "wait" is translated from the Greek word *apekdechomai* (**ap-ek-dekh-om-ahee**) and carries the meaning of waiting with patience and hope. This kind of wait-

ing does not suggest sitting around with our arms folded doing nothing. Rather, it conjures up the image of a waiter in a restaurant who is "on the case," patiently and attentively serving, discharging the expectations of the job. Likewise, Paul says, "we through the Spirit wait"; we continue to be on the job, empowered by the Spirit, patiently serving our Lord with pleasure in freedom and in anticipation of the day when God will render to every man according to his deeds (Psalm 62:12; Revelation 20:12).

6 For in Jesus Christ neither circumcision availeth any thing, nor uncircumcision; but faith which worketh by love.

Under the law, circumcision mattered; but under the freedom that comes through faith in Christ, neither circumcision nor uncircumcision matters. The circumcised Jew and the uncircumcised Gentile share equal footing in the fellowship of those who are "in Jesus Christ" expressing the "faith which worketh by love."

It is interesting that Paul does not say, "For in Jesus Christ neither circumcision availeth any thing, nor uncircumcision; but faith." Rather, he writes in terms of faith's social and communal manifestations, i.e., "but faith which worketh by love." The NIV reads, "The only thing that counts is faith expressing itself through love."

7 Ye did run well; who did hinder you that ye should not obey the truth?

Having stated his case, Paul now strings together a series of comments and questions in anticipation of a closing exhortation.

"You were running a good race. Who cut in on you and kept you from obeying the truth?" (NIV). The phrase "not obey the truth" is a translation of the Greek *peithesthai* (from the verb *peitho*, **pi-tho**), meaning "to obey, be persuaded, comply with, believe, and rely on." Paul is not simply asking, "Who hindered you from obeying?" Rather, he is asking, "Who hindered you, who cut in on you and kept you from obeying and relying on the truth by which you have already been persuaded?"

The question, "Who cut in on you?" is obviously rhetorical in nature. Paul knows it was the Judaizers. They were guilty of "cutting in," a phrase translated from the Greek word *anakopto* (**an-ak-op-to**), used to refer to those runners who come across their prescribed course and throw other participants off their prescribed course. It was also a military term used to refer to breaking up a road or erecting an obstacle to hinder or prevent the progress and advancement of an opposing army.

The Galatians were familiar with these images and therefore understood Paul's question. Paul anticipates and affirms their answer in the next verse.

8 This persuasion cometh not of him that calleth you.

Paul reminds the Galatians that God calls, and He is not the author of their confusion. It is interesting that Paul does not blame Satan for the Galatians' confusion. It appears that Paul wants to keep the focus on the false brothers who had cut in and broken up the road that the Galatians were successfully traveling on.

9 A little leaven leaveneth the whole lump.

This proverbial saying is used here as a literary technique to call further attention to the corruptive influence of the Judaizers' message.

10 I have confidence in you through the Lord, that ye will be none otherwise minded: but he that troubleth you shall bear his judgment, whosoever he be.

Paul expresses his confidence that although the Gentile converts may be considering circumcision, there is still hope that his Galatian letter will result in their recommitting to faith in Christ alone. Paul's confidence in them is "through the Lord." Paul is confident of the Lord's rule and reign in his life and the lives of the Galatians.

Paul calls the individual "he that troubleth you." Paul is not just talking about someone being a pain, but someone who is intentionally causing havoc. The Greek word for "troubleth" is *tarasso* meaning "to stir up, disturb, or throw into confusion."

Probably feeling that his letter will not change his opponents, Paul leaves their fate to the divine judgment that their false message will inevitably incur.

11 And I, brethren, if I yet preach circumcision, why do I yet suffer persecution? then is the offence of the cross ceased.

To say the least, this verse is problematic, primarily because we do not know the context of Paul's statement: "if I yet preach circumcision." It may be that he is parenthetically responding to a specific charge from his opponents. The Judaizers, for example, were not above pointing out Paul's association with Titus's circumcision in Acts 16:3. They could also reference Paul's having been circumcised. Moreover, it may be that Paul preached circumcision during his pre-Christian days. In any event, Paul refutes the suggestion that he now preaches circumcision. In fact, he adds, to do so would be an offense to the Cross of Christ.

12 I would they were even cut off which trouble you.

In this verse, the tone of the Greek is harsh. What Paul says is a terrible thing to wish on anyone: "As for those who are troubling you, O that they would go the whole way and emasculate or castrate themselves" (paraphrased). F. F. Bruce translates it as, "I wish that those who are upsetting you would complete their cutting operation—on themselves."

Bruce, F. F. *The Epistle to the Galatians: A Commentary on the Greek Text.* Grand Rapids, Mich.: Eerdmans Publishing Co., 1982. 233.

Additionally, Deuteronomy 23:1 says, "No one who has been emasculated by crushing or cutting may enter the assembly of the LORD" (NIV). It is assumed that the Galatians were familiar with this Scripture, and so would have understood Paul's harsh comment as a wish that the Judaizers remove or sever themselves from the Christian community. The harshness of Paul's language helps us to understand the depth of his disagreement with the Judaizers' message.

13 For, brethren, ye have been called unto liberty; only use not liberty for an occasion to the flesh, but by love serve one another.

Whereas Paul has been concerned about the threat of the Judaizers in verse 13, he is also concerned about the threat of the sinful nature—the

Galatians' misuse of their Christian freedom. Paul frames his concern by saying two things about the Galatian Christians: first, that they "have been called," and second, that they have been called "unto liberty." Elsewhere in Galatians (1:6 and 5:8) when Paul talks about the Galatians' "call," the emphasis is on the "call of God." The meaning of the Greek is the same here: "You have been called by God to freedom" (paraphrased).

The liberty unto which the Galatians have been called is Christian freedom. In other words, the Galatians have been called by God to be free from the elements of the world and free to live for the Lord. This call by God to live for the Lord is the essence of Christian freedom and therefore has ethical implications. In other words, Christian freedom, more than being a good end, is really a means for fulfilling God's will and lovingly serving one's neighbor. Christian freedom provides both the opportunity and possibility to serve ethical ends.

The balance of verse 13 gives focus to the ethical implications: Do not use your Christian freedom to serve your selfish, corrupt, sinful desires (i.e., the "flesh," Gk. *sarx*, **sarx**), but rather serve God by lovingly serving one another and thus—in the spirit of Jesus—fulfill the law.

Paul seems to make a distinction between trying to keep the law, as is required by those "under the law," and fulfilling the law, which is the result of living "in Christ." Those who live in the realm of Christian freedom obey, not because the law commands, but because the love of Christ compels. It is from this perspective that we are to understand verse 14.

14 For all the law is fulfilled in one word, even in this; Thou shalt love thy neighbour as thyself.

The Parable of the Good Samaritan (Luke 10:25-37) teaches that "thy neighbor" is anyone a Christian comes in contact with—including the person who lives next door.

15 But if ye bite and devour one another, take heed that ye be not consumed one of another.

Here Paul highlights the consequences of failure to make doing God's will and loving others the aim of Christian living. Paul uses a conditional clause to communicate that if you do this, consequences will follow. He warns the Church not to bite and devour one another. The Greek word for "bite" (*dakno*) is generally used to refer to the action of snakes. The Greek word for "devour" (*katesthio*) means "to eat up, consume," or "tear to pieces." This word is generally used in relation to animals. In other words, Paul warns them that they were fighting like wild animals, and if they did not stop, they would all be consumed. In contrast, the admonition in verse 14 is to love one another, thus fulfilling the law.

DAILY BIBLE READINGS

M: The Truth Will Make You Free
John 8:31-38

T: Live as Free People
1 Peter 2:11-17

W: Free in Christ
1 Corinthians 7:17-24

T: Freed from Slavery by Christ
Hebrews 2:14-18

F: Christ Has Set Us Free
Galatians 5:1-5

S: Faith Working Through Love
Galatians 5:6-10

S: Love Your Neighbor as Yourself
Galatians 5:11-15

In order to walk in the freedom Christ has purchased for you, it is important to regularly read God's Word. You will find it helpful to use your *Precepts For Living* CD-ROM to set yourself up on a systematic reading plan through the Bible.

TEACHING TIPS

May 29
Bible Study Guide 13

1. Words You Should Know

A. Gentleness (Galatians 5:22) *Chrestotes* (Gk.)—Moral goodness, or kindness.

B. Mocked (6:7) *mukterizo* (Gk.)—To turn up one's nose at someone as a gesture of ridicule, scorn, or contempt. It can also mean to outwit someone.

2. Teacher Preparation

A. Read Galatians 5:22—6:10 several times in different translations.

B. Read the DEVOTIONAL READING and pray that students will, as a result of their participation in this class, come to know more fully what it means to live by the Spirit.

C. Reread the FOCAL VERSES, then study the material under IN DEPTH.

D. Read MORE LIGHT ON THE TEXT. This will help you to better understand the FOCAL VERSES.

3. Starting the Lesson

A. Ask the students to share what they believe to be the meaning of Christian freedom. On the basis of truths and insights from the last session, help the students to clarify their responses.

B. Refer to the LESSON AIM and remind the students of the believer's commitment to live by the Spirit.

C. Read the IN FOCUS section.

4. Getting into the Lesson

A. Ask two or three volunteers to read the FOCAL VERSES. Based on the information in the BACKGROUND, IN DEPTH, and THE PEOPLE, PLACES, AND TIMES sections, help the students to understand the role of the Holy Spirit in the believer's life.

B. Use some of the DISCUSS THE MEANING questions to initiate discussion of ways in which believers can maximize the availability of the Spirit to produce the fruit of the Spirit in their lives.

5. Relating the Lesson to Life

A. Ask the students to share personal experiences of their own awareness of the Spirit's presence to help them make responsible choices and exercise their freedom in Christ.

B. Invite the students to pray about any areas of weakness in their lives, and reassure them of the sufficiency of God's grace and of the enabling power of His Spirit.

6. Arousing Action

A. Read the MAKE IT HAPPEN assignment. Challenge the students to select a day next week to put it into practice.

B. Remind the students to use the DAILY BIBLE READINGS in their times of personal devotions.

WORSHIP GUIDE

For the Superintendent or Teacher
Theme: Living Out Covenant with One Another
Theme Song: "Spirit of the Living God"
Scripture: Colossians 3:15-17
Song: "Take My Life and Let it Be"
Meditation: We thank You, O God, for the guiding presence of Your Spirit. Help us so that Your peace might rule in our hearts, and that Your Word might dwell richly within us. May Your Holy Spirit find us open and receptive to Your leading and guidance.

LIVING OUT COVENANT WITH ONE ANOTHER

Bible Background • GALATIANS 5:22—6:10
Printed Text • GALATIANS 5:22—6:10
Devotional Reading • 1 JOHN 3:14-23

LESSON AIM

By the end of the lesson, the students will understand the role and function of the Holy Spirit and acknowledge His availability to help them make decisions that will produce the fruit of the Spirit in their lives and bless the lives of others.

KEEP IN MIND

"Bear ye one another's burdens, and so fulfil the law of Christ" (Galatians 6:2).

FOCAL VERSES

Galatians 5:22 But the fruit of the Spirit is love, joy, peace, longsuffering, gentleness, goodness, faith,

23 Meekness, temperance: against such there is no law.

24 And they that are Christ's have crucified the flesh with the affections and lusts.

25 If we live in the Spirit, let us also walk in the Spirit.

26 Let us not be desirous of vain glory, provoking one another, envying one another.

6:1 Brethren, if a man be overtaken in a fault, ye which are spiritual, restore such an one in the spirit of meekness; considering thyself, lest thou also be tempted.

2 Bear ye one another's burdens, and so fulfil the law of Christ.

3 For if a man think himself to be something, when he is nothing, he deceiveth himself.

4 But let every man prove his own work, and then shall he have rejoicing in himself alone, and not in another.

5 For every man shall bear his own burden.

6 Let him that is taught in the word communicate unto him that teacheth in all good things.

7 Be not deceived; God is not mocked: for whatsoever a man soweth, that shall he also reap.

8 For he that soweth to his flesh shall of the flesh reap corruption; but he that soweth to the Spirit shall of the Spirit reap life everlasting.

9 And let us not be weary in well doing: for in due season we shall reap, if we faint not.

10 As we have therefore opportunity, let us do good unto all men, especially unto them who are of the household of faith.

LESSON OVERVIEW

LESSON AIM
KEEP IN MIND
FOCAL VERSES
IN FOCUS
THE PEOPLE, PLACES, AND TIMES
BACKGROUND
AT-A-GLANCE
IN DEPTH
SEARCH THE SCRIPTURES
DISCUSS THE MEANING
LESSON IN OUR SOCIETY
MAKE IT HAPPEN
FOLLOW THE SPIRIT
REMEMBER YOUR THOUGHTS
MORE LIGHT ON THE TEXT
DAILY BIBLE READINGS

IN FOCUS

Earlier today, before sitting down at the computer to write this lesson, this author/pastor was called to the home of a certain parish family that God has richly blessed. The husband is a recovering drug addict.

Following his participation in a rehab center and his acceptance of Jesus Christ, this young husband and father of two small children made rapid progress toward getting his life together. He was fortunate to have the support of a loving and caring wife and church family. These support systems, coupled with his desire to

MAY
29TH

make something of his life, resulted in his finishing trade school, landing a good job, and staying clean—drug free for four years now. His wife called me indicating that he was at home with her and wanted to talk with me. Sensing the distress in her voice, I responded immediately.

He confessed that he had "fallen back." "I," he said, "have messed up. I've done drugs twice during the past two weeks." At the time of this confession, he was weak and indicated that he was unable to go to work. He "did run well," but the enemy of his soul had cut in on him and broken up the road he had been traveling so faithfully (cf. Galatians 5:7)

The tragedy is that this is not an isolated situation. The lust of the flesh renders all believers vulnerable to using their Christian freedom to indulge the sinful nature. Those who refuse to walk in the Spirit will fulfill the lust of the flesh. The good news is that those who allow themselves to "be led of the Spirit" will produce the fruit of the Spirit (vv. 18, 22-23).

The need is great for believers to learn to discipline themselves to walk in the Spirit. Indeed, this is God's will concerning us!

THE PEOPLE, PLACES, AND TIMES

Walking in the Spirit. The apostle Paul challenged the believers of his day to learn what every believer today would do well to remember: The key to making progress in the realm of Christian freedom is to keep walking in the Spirit.

Paul is very much aware of the Galatians' need for a power that the law could not give. He realized from personal experience that there are some things the law cannot do (Romans 8:3). Rules and regulations can command, but they cannot empower one to do what is commanded. Rules and regulations serve as a guide or a road map, but they cannot motivate and enable one to follow the direction and guidance given.

If the Galatians were to live free from sin's power to control their lives—if they were to fulfill the law—it would be because they surrendered themselves to the enabling power of the Holy Spirit. Only those who have surrendered and who keep on surrendering themselves to the complete control of the Spirit are empowered to walk

according to the Spirit's orders. It is the power of the Holy Spirit that guides and strengthens believers to live righteously and gain victory in their warfare against the desires of the flesh (sinful nature).

BACKGROUND

Paul had just finished telling the Galatians about their freedom in Christ. They were instructed to use their freedom to make doing God's will and lovingly serving others their highest aim. Paul was not, however, unaware of the inner struggle that such freedom would bring. The desires of the sinful nature are always present to dissuade believers from fulfilling the call of God and living ethical and righteous lives.

Christian freedom requires believers to make choices. There is always the choice to serve the will of God or the desires of the sinful nature. The power to do God's will flows into the hearts of those who are now walking and who make a choice to keep walking in the Spirit.

AT-A-GLANCE

1. The Way of the Spirit Produces the Fruit of the Spirit (Galatians 5:22-26)
2. Believers Are to Rally 'Round One Another in the Spirit of Meekness (6:1-5)
3. Believers Are to Persevere in Doing Good (vv. 6-10)

IN DEPTH

1. The Way of the Spirit Produces the Fruit of the Spirit (Galatians 5:22-26)

After listing certain manifestations of the sinful nature (the flesh), Paul now mentions some of the manifestations of the Spirit. His listing of the fruit of the Spirit is not meant to be exhaustive, but rather illustrative of the kinds of qualities and behaviors produced by the Spirit.

First, it is worthy noting that Paul's list begins with love, the one quality necessary (see 1 Corinthians 13) to create the atmosphere needed for the proper functioning of all the other

We should always be compassionate, gentle, and considerate of one another.

qualities. Moreover, ending the list with temperance (i.e., self-control) is a clear indication of our Spirit-led ability to control the desires of the sinful nature.

Leon Morris offers a helpful comment about the phrase "fruit (i.e., singular) of the Spirit." Morris suggests that this is not a reference to a "series of fruits" to be distributed among believers . . . so that one believer has one and another believer has another. Rather, Paul sees "a cluster of virtuous qualities made available to each individual believer" (Morris 173). If Morris is right, then every believer, through the Spirit's grace, has access to all the fruit of the Spirit.

Therefore, while the works of the sinful nature lead to destruction, the fruit of the Spirit offers the believer the power to grow in the things of the Spirit.

Given the warfare between the sinful nature and the Spirit, what is the believer's responsibility? What should the believer do to gain victory over the desires of the sinful nature and to grow in the things of the Spirit? To this question Paul gives three specific responses. First, believers are not to undo what they have already done. What the believer has nailed to the Cross through repentance and faith is not to be removed. They that are Christ's have crucified the flesh; let the flesh remain dead! Do not bring the flesh to life again by choosing to fulfill its desires.

Second, since the Holy Spirit is the source of the believer's life in Christ, the believer is to allow the Spirit to dominate and control his or her behavior. In other words, "If we live in the Spirit, let us also walk in the Spirit" (v. 25).

Third, the believer must "not be desirous of vain glory" (v. 26). This, Paul adds, will disrupt Christian fellowship and create envy within our hearts. The implication is that the desire for vain glory works against the Spirit's desires for God's glory.

Morris, Leon. *Galatians: Paul's Charter of Christian Freedom.* Downers Grove, Ill.: InterVarsity Press, 1996. 173.

2. Believers Are to Rally 'Round One Another in the Spirit of Meekness (6:1-5)

In these verses, Paul continues to outline the responsibility and expected behavior of those who follow the Spirit's lead. Believers are to be led by the Spirit, avoid arrogance and self-deception, and rally 'round one another in the spirit of meekness, especially when another believer has been "overtaken in a fault."

Paul is not naive. He recognizes that there will be occasional instances when a believer will be guilty of missing the mark and yielding to the desires of the sinful nature. In these instances, God's plan is to involve the body of believers in the Spirit's redemptive and restorative process. This plan has no place for judging, self-deception, or arrogance. Rather, "the spirit of meekness" (Galatians 6:1a) is to characterize the congregation. Each believer is to keep in mind that he or she is vulnerable to the desires of the sinful nature (v. 1b).

In addition, believers are to "bear. . . one another's burdens" (v. 2). No believer should view himself or herself as being superior to another believer (vv. 3-5). Paul makes the point that the fruit of the Spirit is to find expression, not only through the lives of individual believers, but also through the collective life of the congregation.

3. Believers Are to Persevere in Doing Good (vv. 6-10)

In verses 6-10, Paul reminds believers to persevere in doing good. They are to remember those who teach them spiritual truths and persevere in the things of the Spirit. In contrast, he clearly states that to give place to the desires of the sinful nature has both current and eternal consequences. The consequence of pursuing the things of the Spirit is "life everlasting" (v. 8b). The consequence of yielding to the desires of the sinful nature is "corruption" (v. 8a).

Therefore, since God cannot be mocked (scornfully disregarded), believers would do well to remember that they will reap the good they have sown if they do not grow weary or give up (v. 9). In light of God's approval and external rewards, we are admonished to take advantage of opportunities to do good, especially for fellow believers in Christ.

SEARCH THE SCRIPTURES

1. How many of the fruit of the Spirit can you name (Galatians 5:22-23)?

2. If a man be overtaken in a fault, what should believers do (6:1)?

3. Why do you think that Paul makes it clear that "God is not mocked" (v. 7)?

DISCUSS THE MEANING

1. What is meant by the proverbial phrase "God is not mocked"?

2. What does it mean to "be led of the Spirit"?

3. What does it mean to "prove" one's "own work"?

√LESSON IN OUR SOCIETY

Every believer who desires to do the will of God has access to the Spirit's guiding and empowering resources. However, to do so, we must continue to walk in the Spirit. Believers have no reason to grow weary and give up. The rewards that follow those who, by the Spirit's enabling, keep choosing to do good are everlastingly beneficial. Moreover, those believers who dare to remember, and who in remembering take to heart, the truth that in love Christ died for us will find themselves increasingly compelled and constrained (2 Corinthians 5:14) to keep choosing to fulfill the desires of the Spirit by living righteously and walking in love.

MAKE IT HAPPEN

During this week, set aside a day or two to give yourself to prayer and fasting, asking God to make you more aware of the presence and leading of His Spirit. In addition to your praying and fasting, set some priorities for the week so that the pressures of your schedule will not deafen you to the Spirit's voice.

FOLLOW THE SPIRIT

What God wants me to do:

_____

_____

REMEMBER YOUR THOUGHTS

Special insights I have learned:

_____

_____

MORE LIGHT ON THE TEXT

Galatians 5:22—6:10

22 But the fruit of the Spirit is love, joy, peace, longsuffering, gentleness, goodness, faith, 23 meekness, temperance: against such there is no law. 24 And they that are Christ's have crucified the flesh with the affections and lusts.

Paul identifies the kind of qualities that will be evident in those believers who are walking in the Spirit. Paul contrasts the "fruit (singular) of the Spirit" with the aforementioned "works (plural) of the flesh (sinful nature)." The singular form of the Greek word *karpos*, meaning "fruit," is indicative of the fact that the Spirit is capable of producing this fruit in every believer. They are not fruits, but fruit.

The Spirit produces character and righteous behavior that is an outgrowth of the changed heart of the believer, thus making obedience to the law obsolete. Those who walk in the Spirit put to death the sinful nature and its desires and allow the Spirit of God to lead them and produce fruit that does not need legislation.

In other words, those who have identified themselves with Christ and belong to Christ "have crucified" or put to death everything that is in opposition to Christ and are thus free to produce through their behavior the fruit of the Spirit.

25 If we live in the Spirit, let us also walk in the Spirit.

This is a concise summary of what Paul has already said. It is a statement of what is true since "we live in the Spirit." It is also a statement that reflects the logical consequence of the reality of living in the Spirit: "let us also walk in the Spirit." Since we live in the Spirit, let us line up with the Spirit. Believers who claim to live in the Spirit must also allow their profession to find expression in behavior that is the result of the Spirit's control.

26 Let us not be desirous of vain glory, provoking one another, envying one another.

This verse seems to suggest that Paul does not want his readers to become overconfident concerning their position in Christ. To be in Christ and to be led by the Spirit does not mean that such a person will always reflect the spirit and attitude of Christ. Sometimes good behavior is carried out in ways that provoke and stir up jealousy in others. This is certainly the case when the good works are done in ways that call attention to oneself.

This is the concern that Paul telescopes in his use of the word "provoking" (Gk. *prokaleomai*, **prok-ai-eh'-om-ahee**). To illustrate the meaning of this word, F. F. Bruce cites "Philo's story of Demosthenes, who, when challenged to a slanging match" used this word to decline the challenge "because, as he said, the winner would come off worse than the loser" (Bruce 257). It is reasonable to think that Paul saw the Galatians disputing among themselves from this vantage point. Those who were right in their comments about salvation may have conducted themselves in ways that provoked others or that stirred up envy. Consequently, those who were right conducted themselves worse than those who were wrong. The implication is that believers have an obligation to manage right conduct in ways that do not tempt others to do wrong.

The spirit that seeks to prove one's "rightness" at the expense of another's spiritual well-being borders on "vain glory." This does not speak well of the Holy Spirit's leading. Therefore, "let us not be desirous of vain glory" and "let us not become conceited, provoking and envying each other" (NIV).

6:1 Brethren, if a man be overtaken in a fault, ye which are spiritual, restore such an one in the spirit of meekness; considering thyself, lest thou also be tempted.

Paul's use of the word "overtaken" (Gk. *prolambano,* **prol-am-ban'-o**) literally means "to be entrapped; to be taken, caught by surprise, or take a false step." This gives the meaning that the man "overtaken in a fault" was not intentionally doing wrong. Rather, he suddenly became aware, or it was brought to his attention, that what he was doing was wrong.

Paul counsels that believers are to handle such situations in a spirit of meekness and with a view toward restoration. In other words, do not satisfy the lust of the flesh by using the situation as occasion for gossip or for viewing oneself as superior to the one at fault. The antidote to such sinful behavior is to "consider thyself, lest thou also be tempted," or to "watch yourself, or you also may be tempted" (NIV).

2 Bear ye one another's burdens, and so fulfil the law of Christ.

Those who are led by the Spirit are called here to be willing and available to help carry one another's loads. The sense of the Greek makes this behavior a style of living in Christian fellowship with other believers. The verb "to bear" is from the Greek word *bastazo,* meaning "to take up, carry, or endure." It can also mean "to suffer or undergo."

The word for "burdens" is *baros,* meaning "weight" or "heaviness." Paul says we are to carry one another's burden. In this verse, he is referring to hardships. We are to support one another by helping to bear the weight of hardship.

Bearing one another's burdens is not an occasional act. Rather, it is a way of living and behaving in the Christian community. By so behaving, we, like Christ, will have fulfilled the law.

3 For if a man think himself to be something, when he is nothing, he deceiveth himself.

One of the expressions of the Spirit-led life is a proper and legitimate estimate of oneself.

When one connects verse 2 with verse 3, the message is clear. Those who think too highly of themselves are unlikely candidates for bearing another's burdens.

4 But let every man prove his own work, and then shall he have rejoicing in himself alone, and not in another.

Each person should evaluate his own behavior. Those who are led by the Spirit have no need to compare themselves with other believers. Proving one's own work, or testing and evaluating one's own actions in the light of God's Word, gives a basis for self-evaluation. In fact, rejoicing because one thinks that he/she is better than someone else is in opposition to our life in Christ. It is not the way of the Spirit. Given this interpretation of verse 4, verse 5 is a logical restatement.

5 For every man shall bear his own burden.

This might appear to contradict verse 2, where Paul says we should share each other's burdens." Here, Paul says, "Bear your own burden." The difference is apparent in the Greek. The Greek word for "burden" here is *phortion.* It is different from the word used in verse 2. The meaning is better conveyed by the use of the word "load," which refers to everyone pulling their own weight in relationship to their responsibilities. In other words, you should do your job and not expect someone else to do it for you. This is so that the work of ministry is shouldered by everyone and not by a few; we each have a responsibility to carry part of the load (burden). This personal responsibility is quite different from helping someone who is burdened down with problems. In this case, we come to their aid to help shoulder their pain. But nowhere in Scripture is laziness a virtue. Our Christian responsibility is to carry our own weight and help bear the misfortunes of others.

6 Let him that is taught in the word communicate unto him that teacheth in all good things.

In verse 6, Paul transitions from bearing burdens to sharing blessings. He admonishes those who hear God's Word to share all good things with their pastors and teachers.

The word translated as "communicate" comes from the Greek word *koinoneo* (**koy-no-neh'-o**), which means to enter into fellowship with, to share with, or to partner with another. The phrase "all good things" does not mean that people are to give all they have to their ministers, but that they should support them liberally and share with them the good things of this life, according to their need.

7 Be not deceived; God is not mocked: for whatsoever a man soweth, that shall he also reap. 8 For he that soweth to his flesh shall of the flesh reap corruption; but he that soweth to the Spirit shall of the Spirit reap life everlasting.

Using the metaphor of a farmer who sows and reaps the harvest, Paul says that what a believer sows determines what he or she will harvest. Put another way, our choices will determine our consequences. Whether we choose to live in the Spirit or to live in the flesh (sinful nature), consequences will follow.

9 And let us not be weary in well doing: for in due season we shall reap, if we faint not.

Believers are encouraged to sow to the Spirit and refuse to become discouraged. This explains the need for Paul's note of encouragement in verse 9. The Greek word for "weary" is *ekkakeo*, meaning "to lose heart or become tired." The word for "faint" in the Greek is *ekluo*, meaning "to give up." Paul encourages the Galatians not to get tired and give up, for there is a reward after all is said and done.

10 As we have therefore opportunity, let us do good unto all men, especially unto them who are of the household of faith.

The word "opportunity" is translated from the Greek word *kairos* (**kahee-ros'**), which means "time" or "season." In terms of sowing and reaping, we now have a seasonal opportunity to do that which is good and beneficial for others, especially to our brothers and sisters in the family of God.

DAILY BIBLE READINGS

M: A Tree and Its Fruit
Matthew 7:15-20
T: Where Two or Three Are Gathered
Matthew 18:15-20
W: Be Rich in Good Works
1 Timothy 6:11-19
T: Let Us Love One Another
1 John 3:18-24
F: The Fruit of the Spirit
Galatians 5:22-26
S: Bear One Another's Burdens
Galatians 6-1-5
S: Work for the Good of All
Galatians 6:6-10

Take a closer look at the concept of "reaping and sowing" by using your *Precepts For Living* CD-ROM to do a cross-reference check on Galatians 6:7.

JUNE 2005
QUARTER AT-A-GLANCE

JESUS' LIFE, TEACHINGS, AND MINISTRY

This quarter is based upon the Synoptic Gospels: Matthew, Mark, and Luke. These three Gospels are the most similar in content and approach to the life of Christ.

UNIT 1. JESUS' LIFE (GOSPEL OF MARK)

The month of June focuses on Jesus' life. It shows how Jesus' life and ministry drew so much criticism that it eventually led Him to the Cross. All the passages for this month are from Mark's gospel.

LESSON 1: June 5
Baptism and Temptations
Mark 1:4-13

In the first lesson, Jesus is baptized and then tempted. The story begins with people going out to be baptized by John. When John baptized Jesus, heaven opened, the Spirit descended on Him in the form of a dove, and a voice came from heaven and said, "Thou art my beloved Son, in whom I am well pleased" (Mark 1:11). Then the Spirit sent Jesus out into the wilderness for 40 days, where He was tempted by Satan. Afterward, the angels tended to Him.

LESSON 2: June 12
The Miracles
Mark 2:1-12

In this narrative, Jesus heals a paralytic. Four faithful friends of the man, determined to bring him to Jesus, made a hole in the roof of the home where Jesus was teaching. Jesus both healed the man and forgave his sins. The teachers of the law recognized that Jesus took upon Himself a prerogative of God alone. They did not believe that Jesus was God or that He could forgive sins. Therefore, Jesus demonstrated His power through healing the paralytic.

LESSON 3: June 19
The Trials and Opposition
Mark 14:53-65; 15:1-3

We find in this lesson that Jesus is arrested and questioned by Pilate. The first passage confirms that Jesus is brought before the Sanhedrin, the religious court. They brought false witnesses against Jesus, but there was no agreement among the witnesses. Then, the high priest asked Jesus, "Are you the Christ?" When Jesus answered in the affirmative, the high priest tore his clothes at what he considered a statement of blasphemy. The second passage relates the events early in the morning when Jesus was brought before Pilate. Pilate asked Him, "Are you the king of the Jews?" Jesus answered, "Yes."

LESSON 4: June 26
The Triumph
Mark 16:1-8, 12-15

This is the Resurrection narrative. Three women—Mary Magdalene; Mary, the mother of James; and Salome—took spices to the tomb to anoint the body of Jesus. They worried about rolling away the stone and did not expect Jesus to rise from the dead. However, when they arrived, they saw that the stone had been rolled away. An angel, sitting inside the tomb, announced Jesus' Resurrection and the women fled in bewilderment. Then Jesus appeared to two people who were walking in the country. They reported it to the others, but no one believed them.

UNIT 2. JESUS' MINISTRY OF TEACHING (GOSPEL OF MATTHEW)

The theme for July is "Jesus' Ministry of Teaching (Gospel of Matthew)." The first two lessons are from the Sermon on the Mount. The third lesson gives us a sample parable. The fourth lesson deals with forgiveness and the fifth with the final judgment. All the lessons for July are from Matthew's Gospel.

LESSON 5: July 3
The Beatitudes
Matthew 5:1-16

In the Sermon on the Mount, Jesus taught His disciples what we call the "Beatitudes"—principles for living that turned all the wisdom of the world upside down. The poor in spirit, those who mourn, and the meek will inherit God's kingdom. God will fill those who hunger and thirst for righteousness. He will show mercy to the merciful. He will call the peacemakers His children, and He will reserve a special place in heaven for those who are persecuted for His sake.

After the Beatitudes, Jesus spoke about the Christian's place in the world. The Christian is not to live an isolated life, but to be salt and light to the spiritually lost in society.

LESSON 6: July 10
Practices of Piety
Matthew 6:1-14

Jesus taught His followers about piety and prayers. Christians are taught to give in secret—not to make a big show of their giving so they can be seen and praised by men. It is the same with praying. Prayer should not be a big show for the eyes and ears of others, but an intimate conversation with the living and merciful God.

LESSON 7: July 17
The Purpose of the Parables
Matthew 13:9-17

This lesson discusses the parable of the sower and the seed. Jesus taught in parables so that those who truly wanted to know His teachings would pursue Him. The farmers in biblical days threw seeds from bags, and these seeds fell in a variety of soils. In the same way, Jesus' message falls on hearts in various spiritual conditions. Some people reject the Gospel, others believe but do not stick with it, and still others have hearts that hear, receive, believe, and incorporate God's Word into their lives.

LESSON 8: July 24
The Unforgiving Servant
Matthew 18:21-35

Jesus told another parable to show how important it is to forgive. A king had a servant who owed him the equivalent of millions of dollars. The king forgave the man his entire debt. Then this same man found another who owed him the equivalent of a few dollars. He had his fellow man thrown into prison. When other servants of the king saw what this unforgiving servant did, they reported him to the king. The king, in great anger, had him thrown into prison to be tortured. Jesus told this parable to show us that since He has forgiven us much—our sins—we should in turn pardon others as He has forgiven us.

LESSON 9: July 31
Final Accounting
Matthew 25:31-46

In the last lesson for July, Jesus teaches about the Great Judgment. God will reward those who fed the hungry, gave water to the thirsty, invited in the stranger, clothed the needy, looked after the sick, and visited those in prison. When we do those things for the least, it's as though we did them for Jesus Himself.

UNIT 3. JESUS' MINISTRY OF COMPASSION (GOSPEL OF LUKE)

The last unit covers the month of August and is based on passages from the gospel of Luke. The first lesson begins with Jesus' ordination sermon. The second lesson tells of one miracle of compassion interrupted by yet another. The third lesson tells the story of the Good Samaritan. The last lesson speaks of the humility and response to hospitality that Jesus demands of us.

LESSON 10: August 7
Luke's Mission Statement
Luke 4:16-24, 28-30

This passage has been referred to as Jesus' ordination sermon. Jesus went to the synagogue in Nazareth and read a passage from Isaiah 61 that described His work—preaching good news to the poor, proclaiming freedom for the prisoners, recovering sight for the blind, releasing the oppressed, and proclaiming the year of the Lord's favor. When the people of Nazareth heard these words, they did not believe. In fact, they chased Jesus from town and would have killed Him had He not miraculously walked right through the crowd.

LESSON 11: August 14
Jairus's Daughter Restored and a Woman Healed
Luke 8:40-56

Two miracles take place in this passage. First, Jairus came to Jesus and pleaded with Him to come to his home and heal his daughter. While Jesus was on His way, a crowd followed Him and pressed in against Him. One woman, who had been bleeding for 12 years, touched the edge of Jesus' cloak. Immediately, she was healed. For the good of the woman and a testimony to the crowd, Jesus inquired who touched Him. Then, someone from Jairus's home came and told him that his daughter was now dead. Jesus encouraged Jairus not to lose faith. They continued on to his home, and Jesus raised Jairus's daughter back to life.

LESSON 12: August 21
The Good Samaritan
Luke 10:25-37

A man came to Jesus and asked what he must do to inherit eternal life. He answered his own question by telling Jesus that he should love the Lord with all his heart and his neighbor as himself. Then he asked Jesus who his neighbor was.

Jesus answered with the familiar parable of the good Samaritan. This parable gave the scenario of a man who was going from Jerusalem to Jericho. On his journey, he was robbed and almost beaten to death. Both a priest and a Levite passed by without stopping to help him. Then, a Samaritan—a man from a different culture and country—came by, stopped, and helped him. The point of the parable is that all people are our neighbors and we should ameliorate or lend a hand to each one, without showing partiality.

LESSON 13: August 28
Humility and Hospitality
Luke 14:7-11, 15-24

Jesus told two parables to illustrate the kind of humility He expects of His followers. In the first, He tells of a wedding feast. Jesus reminds His listeners that if they grab the seat of honor, a person of greater honor may come later and the proud guest will have to relinquish his seat. Jesus wants His followers to take the seat of humility, thus exemplifying the servant-spirit that He—God's one and only Son—utilized.

In the second parable, Jesus speaks of the "great banquet" yet to come. An initial invitation was given, and guests said that they would come. However, when the banquet was ready to begin, they all made excuses and abdicated. Then the host, our Heavenly Father, extended the invitation to all who *would* come. We, who have responded to the Father's invitation, should remember that we are saved because of His grace extended to us. It is a gift freely given through the death and Resurrection of our Lord and Saviour, Jesus Christ.

THE SYNOPTIC GOSPELS

by Judith St.Clair Hull, Ph.D.

Matthew, Mark, and Luke are called the Synoptic Gospels because of their similarity in content, order, and statement. These three books contain the same approach to the teaching, life, death, and resurrection of Jesus. The Gospel according to John is quite different in content and approach.

Various scholars have laid out the contents to show what passages are parallel in the synoptics. Of Mark's 661 verses, all except 31 are paralleled in Matthew and Luke. Matthew has 600 verses that parallel Mark, and Luke has 350 (Styler 1993).

These similarities have caused biblical scholars to hypothesize as to the reasons for the similarities. One theory is that the Gospel writers pulled their material from the common tradition of the church. This theory has fallen out of favor in recent years, although surely the material of the Gospels was in oral form before it was written down. People heard the preaching of the apostles, and this became an informal part of their memories. Also, surely the early church had formal memorization for new members since this was the manner of learning in those days, particularly in the synagogues.

As early as St. Augustine, biblical scholars have assumed that the writers drew from each other. Which Gospel was first was a topic of much dispute. Perhaps the most common hypothesis today is that Mark was written first. Then the writers of Matthew and Luke used Mark and another source dubbed "Q." The latter source can only be hypothesized, since it no longer exists. Luke, in his Gospel, states that he drew from written materials (Luke 1:1-4).

Whenever Matthew or Luke have dissimilarities with Mark, the two do not agree with each other against Mark, and so the Q source theory has its problems. Matthew and Luke also have material not common to the other synoptics. For instance, Matthew and Luke each have birth narratives, but these are completely different from each other. Some scholars have thought that sources other than Mark and Q were available to Matthew and Luke. Whatever the theory, the early church never doubted that all four Gospels were inspired by God and were part of the New Testament canon.

Those desiring an in-depth study of Scripture will place the parallel passages side by side to see all the facets of the stories of Jesus. The different Gospels bring out different truths of the same narratives. By looking at Scripture from the different perspectives of the Gospel writers, we can gain additional insight and greater biblical understanding.

The writer of the Gospel according to Mark was identified by Papias, Bishop of Hieropolis in A.D. 130 as the "interpreter of Peter" (Hooker 1960), so he is not an eyewitness, but rather a secondhand source. His material is thought to come from the apostle Peter. First Peter 5:13 (NIV) refers to "my son Mark"; thus it is believed that this is the Mark who wrote the Gospel. Most identify Mark as John Mark of the New Testament. John Mark worked closely with Paul and Barnabas, but that does not rule out earlier mentoring by Peter.

The gospel of Mark is more concise than Matthew and Luke. The writer presents the narrative of the life of Jesus in action. "Immediately" (*eutheos*) is a word used frequently by Mark. He begins by establishing Jesus' identity through the witness of John the Baptist and then the witness of the Father and the Holy Spirit in the baptism of Jesus. In chapters 1 through 4, Jesus calls His disciples, teaches, exorcizes evil spirits, and heals. Jesus is popular with the people, although they do not recognize Him for who He truly is. However, the religious authorities sense enough of His identity to feel threatened, and they begin to conspire against Him.

In chapters 5 through 8, Jesus is busy ministering on one side of the sea of Galilee and then the other. As He performs notable miracles, the belief of a few individuals shines forth, but He mostly encounters unbelief. Through His miracles, however, Jesus demonstrates both His power and His compassion. Peter makes his grand testimony in Caesarea Philippi that Jesus is the Christ (Mark 8:29).

Beginning with Mark 8:34 through 10:52, Jesus teaches the meaning of discipleship. A disciple must take up his cross, pray intensely for God's work to be accomplished, put others first, make sacrifices to avoid sinning, come to Christ like a child, and live a life of service.

In chapters 11 through 13, Jesus reaches Jerusalem and the temple. As Jesus approached Jerusalem on Palm Sunday, the crowds cheered Him on. Yet, Jesus began showing His authority as He cleared out the temple of merchants and money changers. The hostility of the religious leaders increased as they tried to trap Him verbally, but Jesus did not tone down His message. In fact, He became more bold in His condemnation of them.

In chapters 14 and 15, we read of the passion of our Lord. These chapters cover the agony in the garden, the arrest, the trial, and the Crucifixion. Chapter 16 tells us of the Resurrection, with a postscript concluding with some of the post-Resurrection appearances.

The early church fathers were in agreement that the Gospel according to Matthew was written by Matthew, the apostle. Some scholars have argued that Matthew could not be the author of this Gospel because, as an eyewitness, he would not need to follow Mark's gospel. However, Matthew could have done so to demonstrate the unity of the apostolic message.

Matthew was uniquely qualified to write the first Gospel because as a tax collector he was able to take shorthand. Thus, he would have been able to take notes during Jesus' sermons. As a tax collector, his interest in money (Matthew 18:24; 25:15) and statistics (1:17) is shown in his writing.

Matthew's gospel was addressed chiefly to Jewish converts to Christianity. Matthew often showed how Jesus was the fulfillment of Old Testament prophecy. Jesus was the promised Messiah and was bringing about God's kingdom.

The Gospel according to Matthew is structured around five great teaching discourses. In between are narratives leading up to each. The first discourse is the Sermon on the Mount (chapters 5 through 7). The second is the Commissioning of the Twelve Disciples (chapter 10). The third is the Parables of the Kingdom (chapter 13). The fourth is the discourse on Life in the Kingdom (chapter 18). The last is the Olivet discourse concerning the End of the Age (chapters 24-25).

The Gospel according to Luke was written by Paul's dear friend, the doctor (Colossians 4:14) and fellow worker (Philemon 24). Luke addressed his book to Theophilus, whose name means "one who loves God." Theophilus was either a Roman official or at least a person of high position and wealth. However, Luke's gospel was meant for more than just Theophilus. In fact, Theophilus was expected to publish the book and see to its distribution. Being a physician, Luke was very attentive to details, especially in regard to the healing ministry of Jesus. Thus, our lessons in Luke focus on Jesus' ministry of compassion. Luke's attention to detail also made him an excellent researcher as he sought out the details of the life of Christ.

Luke's gospel can be organized into four parts. The first part, or prologue, covers the birth of John the Baptist, the birth of Christ, Jesus presented at the temple, the boy Jesus in the temple, John the Baptist's preparation of the way, the baptism and genealogy of Jesus, and the temptation of Jesus. Part two covers the events that occurred in and around Galilee (4:14—9:50), including Jesus' ordination sermon and His rejection at Nazareth, the calling of the disciples, Jesus' acts of healing, and the Sermon on the Plain. Luke 9:5—19:27 covers the events that took place in Judea and Perea: Samaritan opposition, sending out the 72 disciples, parables and teaching, visiting in the home of Martha and Mary, and healings. The last section of this book tells of Jesus' final week in Jerusalem (19:28—24:53), including the triumphal entry, the cleansing of the temple, a long day of controversy (Tuesday), the Last Supper, Jesus' prayer in Gethsemane, the arrest, the trial, the crucifixion, and the Resurrection.

Barker, Kenneth. *The NIV Study Bible, New International Version.* Grand Rapids, Mich.: Zondervan Publishing House, 1985.

Hooker, Morna D. "The Gospel According to Mark." *The International Standard Bible Encyclopedia.* Edited by James Orr. Grand Rapids, Mich.: Wm. B. Eerdmans Publishing Co., 1960.

Iverach, James. "The Synoptic Gospels." *The International Standard Bible Encyclopedia.* Edited by James Orr. Grand Rapids, Mich.: Wm. B. Eerdmans Publishing Co., 1960.

Styler, G. M. "Synoptic Problem." *The Oxford Companion to the Bible.* Edited by Michael D. Coogan and Bruce M. Metzer. New York: Oxford University Press, 1993. 724.

Judith St.Clair-Hull, Ph.D. is the Editor for *Primary Street*. She received her M.A. in Inner-Cities Studies from Northeastern Illinois University and her Ph.D. in Theological Education from Trinity Evangelical Divinity School.

THE LIFE OF CHRIST: RETURNING TO OUR BASIC PRINCIPLES

by Barbara Carr-Phillips

My pastor gives a memory verse to anyone who comes to him for counseling. He said many people show up for the second counseling session without having taken the time to memorize the verse. "Sometimes people think that memorizing a small verse from Scripture is too simplistic to solve their big problems," he said, "but the solution to any problem is each person's ability to cling to the simple fundamentals Jesus taught us by His life on earth."

The Gospels teach us the basics of Jesus' life. Jesus prayed. Jesus meditated on God's Word. Jesus served. How do we get back to the basics of living a victorious Christian life? We can begin by searching the first three books of the New Testament.

Matthew, Mark, and Luke are known as the Synoptic Gospels. "Synoptic" means "presenting the same common view"; in this case, eyewitness accounts. Each of the writers was writing for a different group: Jews, Romans, or Greeks.

The Jews were looking for the Son of God, the Messiah, in fulfillment of the Old Testament prophecies. They wanted proof that Jesus was indeed their promised King. Chapter 1 of the book of Matthew begins with the genealogy of Christ to prove that Jesus was, as prophesied, a Jew born from the royal lineage of King David. The first verse announces its purpose: "The book of the generation of Jesus Christ, the son of David, the son of Abraham" (Matthew 1:1). Also, Matthew's gospel repeatedly illustrates the connection between the prophetic Word of the Old Testament and Christ; for example, Matthew 2:23 explains, "And he came and dwelt in a city called Nazareth: that it might be fulfilled which was spoken by the prophets, He shall be called a Nazarene."

In Matthew's gospel, we find that God still meets those who patiently or diligently search for Him. God's arm reaches out through Matthew to an audience far beyond the group Matthew thought he was writing to at the time. Matthew's gospel illustrates Jesus' heart for all nations. His message is universal: "Go ye therefore, and teach all nations, baptizing them in the name of the Father, and of the Son, and of the Holy Ghost" (Matthew 28:19). Jesus continues to lead all believers, regardless of race or class, into God's kingdom.

Matthew also illustrates how God wants us to use the prayer Jesus taught His disciples as a model (Matthew 6:9-15). The world has not changed. People still look for someone who can pray in times of trouble. This was evident after the terrorist attacks on the World Trade Center on September 11, 2001—people flocked to the churches, looking for someone who could reach God for an answer. Jesus teaches us through Matthew's gospel that prayer is fundamental.

In addition to prayer, Matthew wants us to see the importance of God's Word. As the Church, we must be able to respond to Satan's lies and plans to destroy us by declaring, "It is written in the Word of God." Meditating on God's Word is a skill Jesus demonstrated for living a victorious Christian life. Even in today's world, when we know the Word of God, we have the tool to overcome any temptation.

While Matthew's gospel was written primarily

for Jews, Mark wrote to capture the attention of the Romans. Mark's gospel reveals Jesus' miracles, illustrating in great detail Jesus' power and authority over illnesses (Peter's mother-in-law, 1:30-31; the paralyzed man, 2:3-12; the woman with bleeding, 5:25-29; the deaf mute, 7:31-37), nature (calming the storm, 4:37-41; walking on water, 6:48-51; withering the fig tree, 11:12-14), and even death (raising Jairus's daughter from the dead, 5:37-39).

Unlike the Jews, the Romans were not interested in the Old Testament prophecies. As the rulers of that time period, they paid no attention to the genealogy of Jesus, whom they considered a servant. However, they were interested in hearing about the powerful miracles that would prove Jesus was the true Messiah.

Jesus came to show the way to His Father. He came to show us the principles for daily living. By His actions, He demonstrated the power of God. After He accomplished that in only a few short years, He was gone.

Many people in our churches today are like the Romans in Mark's day. New Christians are looking for a God who is relevant in their daily lives: One who can perform miracles, One who can empower them in their struggles with trials and oppositions. God can reach these people though Mark's gospel. Jesus is with us! He still heals people, He still controls nature, and because of Him, there is eternal life for all.

Luke's gospel gives us a feel for the personality of Jesus. The Greeks were looking for Christ in the form of the perfect man, and Luke presents that truth to them with a genealogy that goes all the way back to Adam, the man God created in His own image. Luke makes many references to Jesus' compassion for and interest in people who were social outcasts to show the humanity of Jesus. Luke is the only Gospel to recount an inci-dent from Jesus' childhood at the Temple of Jerusalem after the Feast of Passover. Jesus asked the scribes and Pharisees of the law, "Did you not know I must be in the things of my Father?" (2:40-52). Luke shows that even as a child, Jesus knew the reason He was living among us. Here, Jesus models yet another basic skill: a life of compassionate service.

Through Jesus, we can be examples of compassion and signs of hope to people who are hurting. Compassion is the very heart of God, and it is an effective way to bring people into His kingdom. In Luke, Jesus teaches us that compassion isn't an act of the Church or other non-profit organizations. Compassion must come from the individual, someone committed to following Christ's example of sacrificing for and investing time in someone else.

The Synoptic Gospels are not three separate biographies of Jesus' life, but three separate writings to reveal Jesus' purpose on this earth. They are three views with one purpose. Every word written in the synoptics can be applied to our lives in a practical way. God is available to talk to in prayer. We can rely on Jesus' power to reach us in our time of need. Jesus' teachings of selflessness and compassion are timeless examples of how we should conduct our daily lives. God used three different scribes to record many of the same events so that His Word would be understood in the hearts of all people. God sent Jesus to show us the basic principles for living a victorious Christian life here on earth.

Barbara Carr-Phillips is a nonfiction/inspirational writer. Her articles have been accepted by many publications including *Chicken Soup for the Soul Bible, Today's Christian Woman* magazine, and *Chocolate for a Woman's Soul II.*

WHAT IT MEANS TO FOLLOW JESUS

by Cedric McCay

Our society emphasizes and sends many messages about leadership. Seminars, workshops, colloquiums, and even national conventions have been organized around this theme. We seem to be living in a time where we are all supposed to be directing, heading, and guiding ourselves. In addition, we are also expected to manage everyone else in our lives as well! In corporations, on athletic teams—both professional and amateur—and even in volunteer and not-for-profit organizations, just to name a few, many people are maneuvering and manipulating to obtain positions of leadership—to be "number 1." It has become more than just a hip and catchy word; it is now the hypnotic standard by which one is living an enviable life—enviable in the eyes of a secular society that calls everyone to be captain of his or her own ship and to follow their own path in life.

Christians, as disciples of Jesus, are called to exercise "follower-ship"! Our lives are measured by how we pattern our hearts, minds, and lives after the Greatest Leader of them all: the One who "came not to be ministered unto, but to minister" (Matthew 20:28). Our call in life is to follow the Great Servant, Jesus Christ! God, through infinite wisdom, pardon, and grace, has given us a perfect example in Christ Jesus—the Great Shepherd who leads our flock. His leadership is without fault. Christ is the perfect Guide! As followers of Christ, we have a high privilege, honor, and duty to pattern our lives after Jesus.

As Christians, how do we actually follow Jesus? What does it really mean to be a follower of Christ? A study of Jesus' life, as recorded in the Holy Scriptures, will undoubtedly yield an infinite number of ideas, important conclusions, and helpful lessons for all Christians. Indeed, there are many parables, accounts of miracles, and even prayers that offer guidance and insight into the Christian way of life. One particular pericope in the New Testament Gospel as recorded by Saint Matthew is principally instructive for Christians seeking to follow our Saviour: the Great Commission of Jesus.

"And Jesus came and spake unto them, saying, All power is given unto me in heaven and in earth. Go ye therefore, and teach all nations, baptizing them in the name of the Father, and of the Son, and of the Holy Ghost: Teaching them to observe all things whatsoever I have commanded you: and, lo, I am with you alway, even unto the end of the world. Amen" (Matthew 28:18-20). These words, among the final ones spoken by our Saviour on earth, are directives to us all, even in this present day. This instruction is not just a guide for the disciples of that era, but it is a holy and perpetual direction for Christians throughout all ages. In following Christ's mission to the people of God, we are to baptize, teach, and remember. The life, death, and resurrection of Christ is symbolized in our baptism; His teaching is the encouragement and purpose of our faith; and the love of Christ is yet the source of our spiritual and physical energy as Christians today. As Christ's followers, we are to baptize, teach, and remember with love.

Baptizing. As a sacred ordinance of Christ, baptism is a sign and seal of the covenant of salvation. It is also a unique and unparalleled moment in the life of every Christian. Not only does it publicly signify an eternal spiritual union with God through Jesus Christ, but it also proclaims to the entire world a living fellowship with Christians and the universal church. It is the crucible of Christian identity. As followers of Christ, we have three commitments to every baptized Christian: to pray for them, to care for them, and to encourage their spiritual growth within the church family. This follows the example of Jesus, who prays for us, connects us to God, and walks with us along life's difficult and joyous journey.

In our individual and communal prayer lives, we should pray for one another, especially those new in their Christian faith walk. God does indeed hear and answer our prayers, and we should seek the blessings of God for each other. Also, we should seek every opportunity to kindly remind our fellow Christians of their special relationship to God. We are indeed of a mighty heritage! We all appreciate and enjoy encouragement; it is no different in our Christian witness. Followers of Christ should be, as Christ is, an uplifting source of support for others. Christ is a never-failing sustenance for us. We should be like Him.

Teaching. Christ is a Teacher. We, too, are to be teachers. There is a myriad of avenues for teaching in the Christian community at various occasions and levels. We are the inheritors of a great gift in the Holy Scriptures; our library is already full! Christ spoke lovingly and often in reference to the lessons of Scripture. We, too, must be enthusiastic and caring about the story of our faith. We are to be students and teachers of the Living Word. The ministry of Christ wasn't only in worship places or classrooms. Thus, we are called to teach not only in places of worship, but wherever people gather and wherever we go. Teaching involves both sharing and listening. Most teachers know that they learn at least as much from their students

as they give to them. As Christians, we are to listen as well as share our stories. We do have a powerful and persuasive story to share! We are called to keep the story of Jesus in our hearts so that we might share it with Christians and the whole world. Christ taught and preached not only to those who were already committed to following Him, but to the masses who were yet either uninformed or uncommitted. Christ did it all with love! We are to teach, listen, and share our personal journeys and the eternity-long story of God's blessing with other people. We are to do it all with love, like Christ.

Remembering with love. The ministry of Jesus is eternal. Christ stepped out of eternity onto the sands of time and returned to dwell with our eternal God. Yet, Christ has never forgotten us, not even for one second! This is the example we are to follow. We are to always remember our brothers and sisters in Christ. This means not only that we keep them in heartfelt prayers, but also present in our minds. We dwell together here on earth, and we are to, in the words of the elders, "look after one another." Remembering each other means sharing life's burdens, joys, successes, and challenges. We are to be in community, not in isolation. Christ has commanded that we should live together. His promise is that He would be with us always. Likewise, we are to be with our Christian neighbors . . . always!

Coupled with thinking about each other, we are to remember Christ. Jesus remembered our God who sent Him. Followers of Christ are commanded by the Great Commission to do as Christ did: baptize, teach, and remember in the Name of the Father, and of the Son, and of the Holy Ghost! This "follower-ship" never ends; it is a perpetual journey and joy!

Cedric McCay has a Masters of Divinity from Garrett Evangelical Seminary.

KEVIN NICHOLAS

Bible Translator

When Kevin Nicholas was just 5 years old, he and his two sisters went to visit their grandmother on the island of St. Thomas. In this Carribean setting he was introduced to Christ. He and his sister raised their hands to receive Christ, but then they went back to New York City and did not think any more about it. Kevin's father had died when he was quite young, so his mother had three young children to raise in a New York City housing project. As a teenager, Kevin had much to do to help out at home while his mother worked full-time and attended college with a full course load.

Kevin returned to St. Thomas when he was 18 years old and went to church again, this time becoming a committed believer. It took a year before he found a good church in New York, and then he was at church every time the door opened.

One day as he was praying for direction in his life, he felt the Lord calling him to the mission field. At the time he was working on his degree in computer science. He did not see how this would fit in with his call, so he thought of dropping out of the university and enrolling in a Bible school. But God had other plans, and so he finished his B.S. in computer science and then went to Bible college two years later.

While he was in Bible college he learned about the work of Wycliffe Bible Translators. He was enjoying New Testament Greek and thought about becoming a translator. In 1988 the Lord opened the door for him to go to the Philippines to be a missionary. After three months of training in Mexico, he went to the Philippines to teach in a Bible school, which he did for six years.

As he taught at the Bible school he found himself helping other missionaries with computer problems. When he came home he discovered that Wycliffe needed computer specialists to assist in translation work, and so he began the application process to become a member of Wycliffe Bible Translators. About a year later he was on his way back to the Philippines.

Computers play an important part in the work of translation today. Most translators are working with languages that have not been written down. Software helps the translators devise dictionaries and analyze the grammar structure, helps them with speech analysis, and helps them construct a phonetic alphabet for the language. Computers assist the translators in learning the language, as well as in learning how to say things and the best way to say them. Often, translators will listen to stories of the people and the computer will help transcribe the stories. Such stories help translators gain insight into how the language is used and even provide important insight into the culture of the people.

One of the benefits that Wycliffe Bible Translators provide countries in which they work is writing academic papers on the people groups with whom they are working. Computers assist translators in writing up that information.

Then as the missionaries key in the translation of the Scripture, the computer checks punctuation and spelling and makes sure all verses are included. Software helps them type in the text with appropriate page layout.

All this computer help is wonderful for the translators, but most are not computer experts and sometimes problems pop up with the best of programs. So in order to make use of computer assistance, translators often need help. This is where Kevin Nicholas used his training in computers to be of assistance to the translators.

Other computer specialists are software engineers, designing the computer software to be used in aiding all phases of translation. These specialists are seldom located in foreign fields, but also provide necessary help for the translators.

But even with all this computer help, human relationships are still extremely important. The missionary must build bridges into the culture of the people. Sometimes it is very difficult for the translator to express biblical concepts in the language of the people. But each group has within its culture ideas and ways that can be used to convey the truths of God's Word.

Kevin said regarding his work as computer support: "I faced many challenges and struggles. There were even times when I felt like quitting. But I would not change any of it for the world. Seeing the looks of appreciation when I was able to repair a computer, or restore lost data, or solve any other number of problems made it all worth it. The biggest reward though was knowing that I was a part of Bible translation as I provided support for the translators."

After working in the Philippines as a computer specialist, Kevin began providing computer assistance at the Wycliffe Bible Translators headquarters in Orlando, Florida. He was involved in setting up new computers and training staff to use their computers.

Kevin Nicholas is currently the coordinator for ethnic mobilization with Wycliffe Bible Translators. Although there are some African American Wycliffe missionaries and some missionaries of other ethnicities, Wycliffe realizes it needs to reach out to all Christians to bring God's missionary call to them. Kevin and his wife, Gertrude Nicholas (who is specifically involved in reaching the African American community), prepare videos and build bridges to churches to encourage young people to consider the foreign mission field, specifically translation work, as well as other jobs that assist with the work of translation. Needed in addition to computer specialists are teachers for the missionaries' children, literacy workers to teach nationals how to read their newly translated Scripture, web designers, artists, writers, accountants, handymen, pilots, aviation mechanics, and other support personnel.

Kevin and Gertrude are busy with travel and conferences. They are sharing the vision and letting churches know how they can be involved. They are also involved in the production of videos that feature ways that people of various ethnicities can be involved in the ministry of Wycliffe Bible Translators. A video focusing on African Americans is entitled "The Time Is Now." Other videos are being produced for Korean and Chinese churches. God is calling missionaries from all groups to bear witness cross-culturally.

Judith St.Clair Hull, Ph.D. is the Editor for *Primary Street*®. She received her M.A. in Inner Cities Studies from Northeastern Illinois University and her Ph.D. in Theological Education from Trinity Evangelical Divinity School.

TEACHING TIPS

June 5
Bible Study Guide 1

1. Words You Should Know

A. Wilderness (Mark 1:4, 12-13) *eremos* (Gk.)—Denotes a desolate, deserted, lonely, uninhabited, and uncultivated land or region.

B. Remission (v. 4) *aphesis* (Gk.)—Denotes the divine act of releasing sinful persons from their sins.

C. Latchet (v. 7) *himas* (Gk.)—The string of leather used to tie sandals to one's feet.

2. Teacher Preparation

A. A thorough review of what your church teaches about water baptism should prove helpful in preparation for teaching this lesson. One way to do this would be to schedule a conversation with your pastor.

B. Read the BIBLE BACKGROUND (Mark 1:4-13) and pray for an understanding of the Bible passage and its contemporary relevance.

C. Review the LESSON AIM. Read and digest IN FOCUS; THE PEOPLE, PLACES, AND TIMES; BACKGROUND; IN DEPTH; and MORE LIGHT ON THE TEXT.

3. Starting the Lesson

A. State the aim of today's lesson. Then have a student read aloud the FOCAL VERSES.

B. Ask for two student volunteers to share what they remember about their baptism.

4. Getting into the Lesson

A. Using the information from the BACKGROUND, IN DEPTH, and MORE LIGHT ON THE TEXT sections, call attention to the significant leadership that John provided in preparing the way for Jesus' ministry.

B. Explain that, like John, we also have a responsibility to encourage others to prepare to receive the rule of God in their lives.

C. Have the students discuss the temptations they encounter in their efforts to encourage others to receive the Gospel.

5. Relating the Lesson to Life

A. Using the LESSON AIM, SEARCH THE SCRIPTURES, LESSON IN OUR SOCIETY, and DISCUSS THE MEANING sections, remind the students that overcoming temptation is a part of living out the rule of God in one's life.

B. Discuss some of the spiritual disciplines that can help us to overcome temptation.

6. Arousing Action

A. Have the students silently identify three peers or relatives who have not accepted the rule of God in their lives. Then, lead the class in prayer asking God to give your students the resources they need to encourage their peers and relatives to accept Christ as Saviour.

B. Close the session by reminding the students that they may face some temptations while sharing their faith, but that through Bible study, prayer, and fasting they can overcome and be victorious.

WORSHIP GUIDE

For the Superintendent or Teacher
Theme: Baptism and Temptations
Theme Song: "Together We Go to Make Disciples"
Scripture: Mark 1:3
Song: "Am I a Soldier of the Cross?"
Meditation: For the presence of Your Holy Spirit, who gives us power to overcome the temptations that would thwart our sharing the Gospel with others, O God, we give You thanks. Amen.

BAPTISM AND TEMPTATIONS

Bible Background • MARK 1:4-13
Printed Text • MARK 1:4-13
Devotional Reading • MATTHEW 12:17-21

LESSON AIM

By the end of the lesson, the students will explore ways to overcome temptations and encourage others to accept the rule of God in their lives.

KEEP IN MIND

"And there came a voice from heaven, saying, Thou art my beloved Son, in whom I am well pleased" (Mark 1:11).

FOCAL VERSES

Mark 1:4 John did baptize in the wilderness, and preach the baptism of repentance for the remission of sins.

5 And there went out unto him all the land of Judaea, and they of Jerusalem, and were all baptized of him in the river of Jordan, confessing their sins.

6 And John was clothed with camel's hair, and with a girdle of a skin about his loins; and he did eat locusts and wild honey;

7 And preached, saying, There cometh one mightier than I after me, the latchet of whose shoes I am not worthy to stoop down and unloose.

8 I indeed have baptized you with water: but he shall baptize you with the Holy Ghost.

9 And it came to pass in those days, that Jesus came from Nazareth of Galilee, and was baptized of John in Jordan.

10 And straightway coming up out of the water, he saw the heavens opened, and the Spirit like a dove descending upon him:

LESSON OVERVIEW

LESSON AIM
KEEP IN MIND
FOCAL VERSES
IN FOCUS
THE PEOPLE, PLACES, AND TIMES
BACKGROUND
AT-A-GLANCE
IN DEPTH
SEARCH THE SCRIPTURES
DISCUSS THE MEANING
LESSON IN OUR SOCIETY
MAKE IT HAPPEN
FOLLOW THE SPIRIT
REMEMBER YOUR THOUGHTS
MORE LIGHT ON THE TEXT
DAILY BIBLE READINGS

11 And there came a voice from heaven, saying, Thou art my beloved Son, in whom I am well pleased.

12 And immediately the spirit driveth him into the wilderness.

13 And he was there in the wilderness forty days, tempted of Satan; and was with the wild beasts; and the angels ministered unto him.

IN FOCUS

Mark, a successful sales representative, was early for his 6:00 a.m. train for work. Before he could reach the subway station on the corner, a young man in a suit holding a Bible shuffled over to him and with direct brown eyes said, "Can I walk a little ways with you? I have something I would like to see."

Mark grinned as he quickly identified the man as a Holy Roller; they always seemed to pick him out of any crowd. Mark was ready with his usual routine to get rid of the "Bible pusher," as he called people like this man. Mark gave him a smile and said, "You're going to ask me if I know Christ, right?"

The young man's face brightened. "Absolutely!" he said.

Mark gave him his standard response. "Thanks, but no thanks. Ain't nothing you can do for me. My life is fine." Then Mark reached into his pocket for a five-dollar bill. "But here is some money you can use to help people who really need help."

The younger man chuckled. "Is that all?" he asked.

Surprised at the man's response, Mark asked, "What do you mean, 'Is that all'?"

Standing face-to-face at the stairs leading into the subway, the younger man put his hand on Mark's shoulder and said, "You don't recognize me do you?"

Mark looked more intently into the laughing eyes of the well-dressed stranger. A terrible shocked look came over his face. "You're Tony, the new V.P. of sales that was introduced at our company meeting yesterday." Mark also recalled that Tony was the youngest man to hold that position.

As Tony put the five-dollar bill back into Mark's hand, he said, "It's OK, I didn't realize who you were either until just now."

In total disbelief, Mark asked, "Tony, what are you doing walking around with a Bible this early in the morning?" Tony looked him in the eyes, still smiling broadly. "I have a ministry of winning souls for Christ. Since the day I graduated from Harvard, I approach one person each morning with the spiritual message of Jesus Christ."

Mark didn't know what to say as the two men descended into the subway station together. However, Tony said, "God has called me to be a fisher of men. You need to consider what God might be trying to do in your life."

Believers would do well to study the Gospel and encourage others with enthusiasm, with a clear, unashamed commitment to Jesus Christ.

THE PEOPLE, PLACES, AND TIMES

The Roman Setting. Most of the historical data and early church tradition supports a Roman setting for the origin of the gospel of Mark and its original audience (see Colossians 4:10; Philemon 24; 2 Timothy 4:11; 1 Peter 5:13). Concerning the ethnic background of Mark's readership, most would point to Mark's frequent explanations of Jewish customs and conclude that his readership was Gentile.

While little is known about the Christian community in Rome during the period A.D. 62-64, it is nonetheless clear that the threat of persecution was ominous. Many isolated and conflicting accounts of Jesus' ministry, teachings, and of the activities of His followers were voiced via oral tradition. Mark, like Luke (see Luke 1:1-4), wanted to set the record straight and help to meet the needs of the Christian community in Rome during a situation of intense crisis.

BACKGROUND

The opening verses of Mark link the ministry of Jesus with the history of Israel and the prophetic promises of the Old Testament. Mark combines three references from the Old Testament to show that Jesus' ministry is a fulfillment of the salvific work God initiated in the exodus from Egypt (see Exodus 23:20; Isaiah 40:3; Malachi 3:1). Three things stand out in Mark's reference to these Old Testament Scriptures: (1) the messenger, (2) the wilderness, and (3) the Lord.

Throughout the Bible, the messenger and the Lord interface with the wilderness, which seems to play a significant—but unexplained—role in salvation history. For example, the Lord sent an angel (i.e., messenger) to guard Israel "in the wilderness" (see Exodus 23:20). When running from Pharaoh for having killed the Egyptian, Moses fled to "the dry and desolate land of Midian" (see Exodus 2:11-15). When David feared that the citizens of Keilah might surrender him up to Saul, he "escaped from Keilah" and "remained in the wilderness of Ziph" (see 1 Samuel 23:7-14). When running from Jezebel, after the prophets of Baal were killed, Elijah fled to the southernmost city of Judah, Beersheba. Leaving his servant in Beersheba, Elijah "went a day's journey into the wilderness" (1 Kings 19:1-4).

In biblical thought, salvation seems always to involve, among other things, the wilderness. So in the text that follows, John the Baptist (Baptizer) and Jesus, the agent of our salvation, launch their ministries in the wilderness. Not only did Jesus launch His ministry in this barren place, but as His ministry unfolds, He is seen returning to the wilderness on numerous occasions. He is tempted in the wilderness (see Mark 1:12-13). He retreated to the wilderness (i.e., a solitary place) to pray (see Mark 1:35). When Jesus' growing popularity with the people and His increasing opposition from the Jewish leaders prevented Him from entering a town openly, He retreated to "desert places" (see Mark 1:45). He counseled His disciples to "Come...apart into a desert place," where they might "rest a while" (see Mark 6:31). Much to the surprise of His disciples, Jesus saved people from their hunger by performing miracles in the wilderness (see Mark 8:4-9).

Invariable attempts to share one's faith and to encourage others to accept the rule of God in their lives will cause the believer to meet with a variety of wilderness experiences. Often, the valley encounter comes in the form of temptation. However, it may also come in the form of maltreatment and suffering. Public humiliation or rejection cannot be ruled out either. The wilderness experience comes with the territory of being a disciple of Jesus.

AT-A-GLANCE

1. John the Baptizer Evokes a Popular Movement (Mark 1:4-5)
2. John Anticipates a More Powerful Witness (vv. 6-8)
3. Jesus Is Given Heavenly Acclaim (vv. 9-11)
4. Jesus Is Tempted by Satan in the Wilderness (vv. 12-13)

IN DEPTH

1. John the Baptizer Evokes a Popular Movement (Mark 1:4-5)

John's preaching caused great excitement. Indeed, "there went out unto him all the land of Judaea, and they of Jerusalem...." The original language suggests that the people kept going out to meet and hear John. Not only did they meet and hear him, but they were captivated by what they heard; so much so, that they confessed their sins and were baptized by John in the Jordan River.

Because the voice of the prophets had been silent for centuries, obviously, the people of that day were hungry to hear the truth. Therefore, John's voice and message were a welcome and much-needed change. While the people had heard about the prophets, they had never seen one. This, then, generated some of their excitement. The desire to see John piqued their curiosity. His words spoke to their inner hungers. Reports about John's ministry spread quickly bringing an increasing number of people to the Jordan to hear his message, to confess their sins, and to be baptized.

The walk from Jerusalem to the nearest bank of the Jordan River is about 20 miles downhill. The return trip is all uphill. Also, the walk down the dry, arid, and rocky Judean hills to the Jordan River was extremely difficult, while the hike back uphill to Jerusalem, even for the athletic, was much more arduous. Consequently, this was not a pleasure jaunt. It was the journey of a people who were hungry for a more dynamic relationship with their Creator.

John's preaching about the coming of the Messiah met the people's need and afforded them an opportunity to redirect their lives. Thus, they kept coming to hear him. There soon developed, in the wake of John's preaching, a popular movement. People are still hungry for a message that promises a hopeful future and that has the capacity to change people's lives for the better.

2. John Anticipates a More Powerful Witness (vv. 6-8)

What was the secret of the success of John's preaching ministry? It could not have been his appearance or the content of his diet. One did not have to walk the long distance from Jerusalem to the Jordan River to see an eccentric dressed in the garments of a pauper. There were eccentrics living in Jerusalem who, because of their circumstances, may not have been privileged to eat locusts and honey.

It was not John's appearance nor the appeal of his diet that attracted people to him. John's appearance and diet were eclipsed by the content of his message. John preached about the coming of the Messiah. While his hearers were turned on by his ministry, John was quick to remind them that a preacher greater than he was coming, One who would usher in the very presence of God Himself. John's preaching made it clear that however much the people may have rallied around him, he was not worthy of the One whose coming the people were urged to anticipate.

Surely the people must have asked,"Who can be greater?" John was not without an answer. He charged them to nail their hopes upon the coming Messiah and to prepare immediately for His coming arrival by repenting of their sins. Many did.

Today, while there are many conflicting voices clamoring for people's allegiance, people still respond to the call to follow Jesus. They will respond quickly when they are helped to see how Jesus can meet the deep hungers of their soul. This is without a doubt the church's greatest challenge—to overcome every temptation and every obstacle and encourage others to accept the rule of God in their lives.

3. Jesus Is Given Heavenly Acclaim (vv. 9-11)

Jesus was probably 30 years old when He began His public ministry. He "came from Nazareth of Galilee," where He grew up, "and was baptized of John in Jordan." The Bible tells us very little about Jesus' childhood and youth. All of what we know about Jesus was committed to print after His death and Resurrection. *How, then, did the early church relate its view of Jesus as being sinless with His submitting Himself to John's baptism of repentance for the remission of sins?* This also appears to have been a troublesome question for John, who, according to Matthew, was reluctant to baptize Jesus (see Matthew 3:13ff).

While Mark does not answer this question, Matthew does. In response to John's reticence to baptize Jesus, Matthew records Jesus as having said, "Suffer it to be so now: for thus it becometh us to fulfil all righteousness" (Matthew 3:15). Jesus' response helped John to understand that submitting Himself to John's baptism was part of the plan and purpose of God.

It was necessary for Jesus, at the very outset of His ministry, to identify Himself with sinful humanity. He did this when He submitted Himself to John's baptism. The apostle Paul helps us to understand this in his second letter to the church in Corinth: "For he [i.e., Jesus] hath made him to be sin for us, who knew no sin; that we might be made the righteousness of God in him" (2 Corinthians 5:21).

In view of Jesus' submission to God's plan and purpose, it is little wonder that God Himself made His presence felt at Jesus' baptism. The splitting of the heavens, the descending of the dove, and the voice from heaven—all of which Jesus saw and heard—affirmed John's witness about Jesus and launched Jesus' public ministry. What an affirming moment that must have also been for Jesus to hear God Himself, say, "You are my Son, whom I love; with you I am well pleased!"(see Mark 1:11, NIV).

One's baptism is an affirming moment and should not be taken lightly. It is a moment that garners heaven's attention. It is symbolic of one's renunciation of sin and submission to the rule of God. What a humbling thought to know that all of heaven—even God—is moved when sinful humanity repents and submits to God's Lordship.

When we think about our call to encourage others to accept the Lordship of God in their lives, we would do well to realize that we are involved in a work affirmed and ordained by God.

4. Jesus Is Tempted by Satan in the Wilderness (vv. 12-13)

When God does a great work in our lives, Satan stands somewhere in the shadows trying to figure out a way to mess up what God has set in righteous motion. We can be encouraged, however, in knowing that God is always "steps" ahead of Satan. Just as God ordained that Jesus should identify with sinful humanity, He also ordained that Jesus should identify with our struggle to overcome temptation. It was all in the plan and purpose of God. It is this perspective that helps us to understand why the Spirit sent Jesus out into the wilderness to be tempted by Satan (compare Matthew 3:1; Mark 1:12-13; Luke 4:1-2).

Jesus' struggle with temptation alerts us to the reality of our own struggles with temptation. Although it is not a part of the Scripture passage under study here, it is encouraging to know that through prayer, fasting, and a right handling of the Scriptures, Jesus proved victorious over Satan's snares (see Matthew 4:1-11; Luke 4:1-13).

Mark is brief, but he records the same results: "the angels ministered unto him" (see Mark 1:13c).

Prayer, fasting, and a right handling of the Scriptures are proven methods to overcome temptation.

SEARCH THE SCRIPTURES

1. What two themes characterized John's preaching (Mark 1:4, 7)?

2. From where did the people come to hear John preach (v. 5)?

3. What accounted for John's popularity (vv. 7-8)?

DISCUSS THE MEANING

1. How are we to interpret and understand the phrase "the baptism of repentance for the remission of sins" (Mark 1:4)?

2. Why was it necessary for Jesus to submit Himself to John's baptism (v. 9; compare Matthew 3:13-15)?

3. What was Jesus' method for overcoming temptation? And how are we to understand the phrase "and the angels ministered unto him" (Mark 1:13)?

4. In what sense is suffering a part of discipleship (vv. 3, 12-13)?

LESSON IN OUR SOCIETY

Inviting and encouraging others to accept God's rule in their lives is accompanied with many challenges and temptations. It was so for John and Jesus, and it remains so in our day.

Despite the challenges and temptations confronted by John and Jesus, they both met with success in their ministries. Their success, however, was not without struggle and suffering. Indeed, they both met with violent deaths in the course of fulfilling their ministries. Is it any wonder that we are oftentimes tempted to pursue a less difficult path?

God is not the only one who knows how much we can bear. Satan makes it his business also to see how much Jesus' followers can take. Satan, however, has no method for preventing us from remaining faithful no matter what the cost. John's commitment to his calling and Jesus' example of using prayer, fasting, and a right handling of the Scriptures are models we can imitate when Satan tempts us to take the low road.

Jesus has identified with us in our sinful humanity and in our struggle with temptation. Because He has overcome, we can overcome also. We, like John the Baptizer, can be Jesus' faithful witnesses in our communities and seek to contribute to the quality of life.

May our remembrance of our own baptism stir us to truly serve our God in the confidence that His angels will minister unto us during our times of testing.

MAKE IT HAPPEN

When was the last time you intentionally set out to invite someone to accept God's rule? What temptations did you encounter? Did you overcome them, or did you follow the lines of least resistance at the expense of compromising your witness?

People are hungry for a *word* and *message* that will give them quality of life. Get all excited about the rule of God in your own life, and go and share that excitement! Share it with your colleagues at work. Share it with your barber, your hairdresser, your dentist, your postal carrier, and the teller at your bank. Share it with your child's schoolteacher. SHARE IT! You have God's backing. This is His will for those who would follow Jesus and prepare the way for His Second Coming!

FOLLOW THE SPIRIT

What God wants me to do:

_____

_____

REMEMBER YOUR THOUGHTS

Special insights I have learned:

_____

_____

MORE LIGHT ON THE TEXT
Mark 1:4-13
4 John did baptize in the wilderness, and preach the baptism of repentance for the remission of sins.

John the Baptizer's task was to baptize people

John the Baptist: God's messenger and worship leader baptizing in the Jordan River.

We, as believers, need to be prepared to worship God during the corporate service and in private worship as well. We need to focus our hearts and minds on the Lord's goodness, mercy, and loving-kindness and consider who He is and what He is doing in our lives.

We must wisely "prepare the way of the Lord" in our hearts by disciplining ourselves to focus on God. In reality, we need to live a lifestyle of preparing our spirit to seek God, to focus on worshiping Him, and to give thanks for His provisions and blessings in our lives.

5 And there went out unto him all the land of Judaea, and they of Jerusalem, and were all baptized of him in the river of Jordan, confessing their sins.

The Spirit of God and the grace of God drew people to come to hear John the Baptizer preach. And the people came in large numbers from the region of Judea, and specifically from the city of Jerusalem, which was Israel's capital city and center of worship. These people were mostly Jewish. It is important to note that these Jews recognized an important reality. Although they were Jews, being a Jew alone was not enough to make them righteous before God. So they came to John with the goal of pursuing righteousness from God.

6 And John was clothed with camel's hair, and with a girdle of a skin about his loins; and he did eat locusts and wild honey.

John was unique. He was different. He was strange. His style, or status, was not what attracted people to come out and see this preacher. He was unusual in the way he dressed, in what he ate, and in where he lived. His wardrobe was rough and simple: He wore camel's hair and a leather belt around his waist. His clothes were similar to the clothes worn by Elijah (2 Kings 1:8). John looked like an Old Testament prophet...actually, he could be considered an Old Testament prophet because his ministry began and ended before the death, burial, and Resurrection of the Lord Jesus Christ. He ate "locusts and wild honey." A locust was a kind of insect, and the law permitted this diet (Leviticus 11:22-23). The "wild honey" was probably simply honey made by wild bees.

in the wilderness and to preach a baptism of repentance. Baptism represented a kind of washing or cleansing. By being baptized, people were seeking to receive a cleansing and thus to have their sins removed.

John the Baptist was the voice crying in the wilderness as Mark 1:3 and Isaiah 40:3 point out. He was God's messenger sent to prepare the way for Christ.

Why was a forerunner important for the coming of the Lord Jesus Christ? Well, probably for at least two reasons: First, God, in His abundant and overflowing mercy, wanted His people to be fully ready to receive the promised Messiah, the long-awaited Anointed One. The Jewish people and others who believe in God had been waiting for many years for the Messiah to come (Daniel 9:25; Deuteronomy 18:15; John 1:41; 4:25, 29, 32, 39). God did not want His people to miss Christ's coming. God wanted His people to fully recognize and receive His Son as their Saviour. Second, John the Baptizer was a kind of worship leader, as he led believers into praising and worshiping God. A worship leader encourages believers to fully receive what God longs to give us in worship.

7 And preached, saying, There cometh one mightier than I after me, the latchet of whose shoes I am not worthy to stoop down and unloose.

Just as John was simple in appearance and lifestyle, John's calling and task were simple as well. And his goal in life was simply to carry out God's will. He lived for God, period. He came to announce the Messiah who was coming, and he did it with passion and humility. His goal was not to make a name for himself in any way. His goal was to announce and prepare the way for the coming Lord and to lift up the Lord Jesus Christ (John 3:30).

8 I indeed have baptized you with water: but he shall baptize you with the Holy Ghost.

John's baptism involves washing with water. Jesus' baptism involved the washing and cleansing power of the Holy Spirit. Water can cleanse the body, but the Holy Spirit of God can cleanse an individual's heart and whole life.

9 And it came to pass in those days, that Jesus came from Nazareth of Galilee, and was baptized of John in Jordan. 10 And straightway coming up out of the water, he saw the heavens opened, and the Spirit like a dove descending upon him:

The Lord Jesus, the Messiah, now physically arrives on the scene to be baptized by John. The Lord Jesus had no sin to be washed away. He was sinless, yet His baptism was important. For Him, it was a time of new beginnings—a crucial part of His earthly ministry and the work of God that He was specifically ordained to do. It was a time of being empowered and equipped by the Holy Spirit to carry out His calling from God the Father.

11 And there came a voice from heaven, saying, Thou art my beloved Son, in whom I am well pleased.

Here, our Heavenly Father gives the voice of approval and confirmation to the Lord Jesus. This voice from heaven gives clear affirmation and encouragement to the Lord Jesus, John the Baptizer, and all others who had ears to hear: "Thou art my beloved Son, in whom I am well pleased."

12 And immediately the Spirit driveth him into the wilderness. 13 And he was there in the wilderness forty days, tempted of Satan; and was with the wild beasts; and the angels ministered unto him.

The first direction the Spirit gives the Lord Jesus after His baptism is for Him to go into the wilderness, and He obeys. The Lord Jesus now enters a time in which He is tempted by the devil in the wilderness. It was a severe time of testing. Yet the Lord Jesus did not give in to temptation. He gloriously overcomes.

DAILY BIBLE READINGS

M: You Are My Son
Psalm 2:7-12
T: Baptism for Repentance and
Forgiveness
Mark 1:4-8
W: John the Baptist's Message
Matthew 3:7-12
T: Jesus Is Baptized
Matthew 3:13-17
F: Jesus Is Baptized and Tested
Mark 1:9-13
S: Here Is My Servant
Matthew 12:17-21
S: Jesus Is Tempted by the Devil
Matthew 4:1-11

You will find it interesting to take a closer look at the word *temptation* by using the reference tools available in your *Precepts For Living* CD-ROM.

TEACHING TIPS

June 12
Bible Study Guide 2

1. Words You Should Know

A. Palsy (Mark 2:3-5, 9-10) *paralutikos* (Gk.)—A nervous affliction known as paralysis (i.e., the loss of motor power in a muscle or set of muscles).

B. Blasphemies (v. 7) *blasphemia* (Gk.)—Denotes verbal abuse; to speak with irreverence and disrespect concerning God or concerning the things that pertain to God.

C. Scribes (v. 6) *grammateus* (Gk.)—Refers to learned teachers of religion who were well versed in the law.

2. Teacher Preparation

A. The FOCAL VERSES for this lesson are also recorded in Matthew 9:2-8 and in Luke 5:18-26. Read all three accounts. Then, read them a second time from a more contemporary translation.

B. Invite a hospital chaplain to meet with the class and discuss the spiritual aspects of healing.

C. Read and familiarize yourself with all of the content in this BIBLE STUDY GUIDE.

3. Starting the Lesson

A. Introduce your special guest, the hospital chaplain, to the class and announce the LESSON AIM.

B. Take four to six minutes to consider any questions or concerns the students may have about faith and healing. List them on the chalkboard or on a flip chart.

4. Getting into the Lesson

A. Ask someone to read the FOCAL VERSES aloud.

B. Now, ask your invited guest to comment on the FOCAL VERSES and address some of the abuses and correct uses of faith in the healing process.

C. Encourage your students to ask questions and to discuss their concerns about faith and healing.

5. Relating the Lesson to Life

A. Highlight the need for believers to have a clear and biblical understanding of the role of faith in the healing process.

B. Ask the students to share stories and experiences of illness and healing in their own lives.

C. In light of today's text, what are some possible reasons why some people may be healed and others are not?

6. Arousing Action

A. Using the chalkboard or flip chart, brainstorm some things your church might do to enhance the physical and emotional health of persons in your congregation and community.

B. Remind the students that the exercise of faith involves doing what is necessary to enrich and maintain one's own health.

C. Close the session by having the students silently identify three things they can each do to enhance their own health. Pray that they might follow through on their commitments.

WORSHIP GUIDE

For the Superintendent or Teacher
Theme: The Miracles
Theme Song: "He Is Just the Same Today"
Scripture: Mark 7:32-35
Song: "Be Still and Know"
Meditation: Give us the wisdom and the courage, O God, to assume greater responsibility for our own health and well-being.
Amen.

THE MIRACLES

Bible Background • MARK 2:1-12; 3:1-6; 8:1-10
Printed Text • MARK 2:1-12
Devotional Reading • MARK 7:31-37

LESSON AIM

By the end of the lesson, the students will explore and discuss the role of faith in the healing process and identify ways to assume greater responsibility for their own health and well-being.

KEEP IN MIND

"I say unto thee, Arise, and take up thy bed, and go thy way into thine house" (Mark 2:11).

FOCAL VERSES

Mark 2:1 And again he entered into Capernaum after some days; and it was noised that he was in the house.

2 And straightway many were gathered together, insomuch that there was no room to receive them, no, not so much as about the door: and he preached the word unto them.

3 And they come unto him, bringing one sick of the palsy, which was borne of four.

4 And when they could not come nigh unto him for the press, they uncovered the roof where he was: and when they had broken it up, they let down the bed wherein the sick of the palsy lay.

5 When Jesus saw their faith, he said unto the sick of the palsy, Son, thy sins be forgiven thee.

6 But there were certain of the scribes sitting there, and reasoning in their hearts.

7 Why doth this man thus speak blasphemies? Who can forgive sins but God only?

8 And immediately when Jesus perceived in his spirit that they so reasoned within themselves, he said unto them, Why reason ye these things in your hearts?

LESSON OVERVIEW

LESSON AIM
KEEP IN MIND
FOCAL VERSES
IN FOCUS
THE PEOPLE, PLACES, AND TIMES
BACKGROUND
AT-A-GLANCE
IN DEPTH
SEARCH THE SCRIPTURES
DISCUSS THE MEANING
LESSON IN OUR SOCIETY
MAKE IT HAPPEN
FOLLOW THE SPIRIT
REMEMBER YOUR THOUGHTS
MORE LIGHT ON THE TEXT
DAILY BIBLE READINGS

9 Whether is it easier to say to the sick of the palsy, Thy sins be forgiven thee; or to say, Arise, and take up thy bed, and walk?

10 But that ye may know that the Son of man hath power on earth to forgive sins, (he saith to the sick of the palsy,)

11 I say unto thee, Arise, and take up thy bed, and go thy way into thine house.

12 And immediately he arose, took up the bed, and went forth before them all; insomuch that they were all amazed, and glorified God, saying, We never saw it on this fashion.

IN FOCUS

She was known throughout the congregation as Mother Tee. She is now deceased, but during her lifetime Mother Tee developed a personal charm that won her many friends and influenced many people. She was a joy to be around. She loved being in the company of other people. Mother Tee also loved barbecued ribs and would often comment, "Ribs don't taste good without salt."

As Mother Tee grew older, she developed a number of health complications that required her to be placed on a restricted diet. Her doctor had eliminated all pork and salt from her menu, to her regret.

I went to visit Mother Tee one afternoon following a stint in the hospital. She had been in the hospital because her blood pressure had gotten out of control. After a few days under the watchful eyes of her doctor and the hospital nurses, she was able to return home. As usual, my visit with her was an enjoyable one, but I noticed that her ankles and feet were beginning to swell. She affirmed that my observation was correct. Then I calmly asked, "Mother, how are you doing with your diet? Have you had any ribs lately?"

Immediately, her countenance communicated what her speech quickly confirmed: "Yes, Pastor, but I only had two—and they weren't very big."

"Mother," I continued to probe, "did you put any salt on them?" Rubbing the tip of her right thumb against the tip of her right forefinger, she responded coyly, "I put just a little bit of salt on them. Reverend, they just don't taste right without any salt."

"Mother," I explained tenderly, "that's why your ankles and feet are beginning to swell up again. My prayers for your healing are not going to get past the ceiling if you don't work with God to help keep your blood pressure under control. Mother, what you need is not prayer for healing, but prayer to help you stay on your diet."

What is the moral imperative of this true story? Here it is: Healing is always a work of God. Maintaining the health God allows us to have, however, is a work we must do cooperatively with God. This perspective begs for a fuller understanding of the role of faith in the healing process. Faith involves more than trusting God to heal us of our illnesses. Faith also involves working with God to assume greater responsibility for our own health maintenance.

THE PEOPLE, PLACES, AND TIMES

Jesus' Ministry. Jesus' ministry brought healing and forgiveness to many. However, His ministry also brought Him constant opposition and death on the Cross.

The scribes and Pharisees were always looking for reasons to discredit Jesus' ministry. When they were not challenging His authority or questioning the source of His authority (Mark 2:6-7), they were criticizing Him because of the company He kept (Mark 2:16b) or trying to catch Him healing on the Sabbath (Mark 3:2). Moreover, the scribes and Pharisees were forever asking questions aimed to damage the reputation of Jesus' disciples (Mark 2:18b). At the heart of their concern was the issue of Jesus' authority to forgive sins.

Jesus Heals the Sick. In the face of increasing hostility and controversy, however, Jesus intentionally continues His ministries of preaching, forgiving sins, and healing the sick. It is in this setting of controversy and tension that the healing of the "one sick of the palsy" (Mark 2:3) takes place. The story teaches that Jesus has the power to heal and forgive sins (Mark 2:9-10).

The healing of the "one sick of the palsy" also sends a subtle message to the scribes and Pharisees. That message is that Jesus is able to do what they, in their religious authority, are unable to do. Jesus can both heal and forgive sins. The story makes it obvious that the scribes' and Pharisees' accusations against Jesus are both false and baseless.

Jesus is more than an effective and popular preacher. He also forgives sins and honors faith. He honors faith by healing us of our illnesses (Mark 2:5), and in some instances by giving us sufficient grace to use our illnesses in the service of God's higher purposes (2 Corinthians 12:7-9).

BACKGROUND

Following His baptism by John in the Jordan River, Jesus spent some time traveling throughout Galilee. His travels brought Him to Capernaum in the northern region of Galilee, which appears to have been a kind of organizing center for His ministry.

Jesus was not long in Capernaum before the townspeople, including the scribes and Pharisees, learned of His presence. A crowd soon gathered. Some have speculated that "the house" in which they gathered (Mark 2:1), where the healing of the one sick of the palsy took place, was the home of Simon and Andrew referred to in Mark 1:29.

Many came, no doubt, wanting to see Jesus perform a miracle. Much to their surprise, however, Jesus was not performing miracles. He was preaching the Word (2:2c). Due to the controversy that was brewing between Jesus and the religious authorities over the issue of the forgiveness of sins, the scribes were particularly interested in trying to trap Jesus in some form of blasphemy. Their motives were not only suspect, but also sinister. Therefore, they strategically positioned themselves in hopes that Jesus might violate some Jewish law or speak with irreverence and disrespect concerning the holiness of God.

While Jesus was preaching, He was presented with an opportunity to demonstrate to the scribes and the Pharisees that He had both the authority to forgive sins (v. 5) and the power to heal (v. 3).

AT-A-GLANCE

1. Jesus Preaches the Word (Mark 2:1-2)
2. Jesus Forgives Sins (vv. 3-7)
3. Jesus Heals (vv. 8-12)

IN DEPTH

1. Jesus Preaches the Word (Mark 2:1-2)

Jesus' ministry involved preaching the Word, forgiving sins, and healing the sick. When we meet Jesus in Mark 2, He is preaching "the word" (v. 2). "The word" is used here to refer to Jesus' message concerning the kingdom.

With great enthusiasm, the townspeople flocked to hear Jesus preach and to witness a possible miracle. They heard the word being preached, and they witnessed a miracle. Mark's description of the crowd that gathered suggests that it filled the house, jammed the doorway, and spilled out into the street. What a tribute to the ministry of Jesus!

We can be grateful today that Jesus' ministry is still alive and well. Through His Church and the faithful service of His followers, the Word is still being preached. By God's grace, people still receive forgiveness of sins. Through God's power, healings still take place.

2. Jesus Forgives Sins (vv. 3-7)

When Jesus entered into Capernaum (v. 1), He did not go with the intentions of performing a miracle. He went to preach the Gospel of the kingdom of God. During the course of His preaching, another ministry opportunity presented itself. Four men carrying "one sick of the palsy" joined the crowd that gathered, presumably at Simon and Andrew's house. Because of the crowd, the men were unable to access Jesus through the doorway of the house. Therefore, to get within touching distance of Jesus, they carried the paralytic ("sick of the palsy") up the outside stairway to the roof of the house. They tore the roof open and lowered the paralytic on his bed down through the opening to where Jesus stood preaching. What a scene!

Was there no concern for the damage done to Simon and Andrew's house? What about the straw-mixed-with-clay-turned-into-dust and other debris that must have fallen on innocent bystanders as the roof was being torn open? What risks were involved in carrying a sick man lying on his bed up to the roof of someone else's house? Suppose they had accidentally fallen through the roof? All these questions aside, authentic faith does not hesitate to risk doing what it has to do to meet with desired results. God honors faith that is expressed in one's conduct.

Indeed, "when Jesus saw their faith," He did an extraordinary thing. Instead of performing a healing, Jesus "said unto the sick of the palsy, 'Son, thy sins be forgiven thee'" (Mark 2:5).

Blinded by their own self-interests and theological shortsightedness, the scribes viewed Jesus' actions as an attempt to claim authority to do what God alone could do. Consequently, they fumed with judgmental arrogance that was visible in their expressions. They reasoned in their hearts, "Why doth this man thus speak blasphemies? Who can forgive sins but God only?" (Mark 2:6b-7).

Based upon Exodus 34:6ff and Isaiah 43:25; 44:22, the scribes held that only God had the authority to forgive sins. In their view, Jesus had done the unpardonable: He had committed blasphemy. Given Jewish law pertaining to blasphemy (see Leviticus 24:15-16), this was a serious charge that was punishable by death.

Obviously, the scribes' position exposed their limited awareness of who Jesus really was—namely, the Son of God who had both the authority to forgive sins and the power to heal.

3. Jesus Heals (vv. 8-12)

Jesus is not unaware of the scribes' reasoning nor of the Scriptures. His verbal response to their body language is quick and direct (Mark 2:8b-10a). Jesus' words convey to the scribes that forgiving sins is no harder than healing. Since Jesus can heal, as the scribes had seen Him do, then He can also forgive sins. Therefore, Jesus turns His attention to the paralytic and commands him, "Arise, and take up thy bed, and go thy way into thine house" (v. 11).

The healing verified Jesus' claim to grant forgiveness. Since the healing was real, the claim to forgive sins is also real. It would appear that Jesus did the healing, which the scribes could see, in order to prove the forgiveness, which they could not see.

According to verse 12, the paralytic immediately arose, took up his bed, and walked out in full view of the crowd. This amazed everyone, and they praised God, saying, "We never saw it on this fashion" (v. 12)—meaning they had never seen anything like this!

Every healing that takes place is cause for rejoicing and praising God. God still heals, *but not always*. Sometimes He works with us to *use our illnesses to serve His higher purposes*. Believers would do well to learn to exercise the kind of faith that recognizes that God is free to heal whom He will. In some instances, He may choose not to heal; but in such cases, believers may still exercise the faith to believe that His grace can sustain us even in the absence of healing. While we may desire healing, God may choose to use our illnesses to serve a purpose that is higher than our healing. Faith can enable us to use our physical illnesses in His service.

SEARCH THE SCRIPTURES

1. "When Jesus saw their faith, he said unto the _____ of the palsy, Son, thy _____ be forgiven _____" (Mark 2:5).

2. "Whether is it easier to say to the sick of the palsy, Thy sins be _____ thee; or to say, _____, and take up thy _____, and walk?" (v. 9)

3. "And immediately he arose, took up the _____, and went forth before them all; insomuch that they were all _____, and glorified God, saying, We never saw it on this _____" (v. 12).

DISCUSS THE MEANING

1. Why did Jesus perform the miracle of forgiveness before performing the miracle of healing (Mark 2:10)?

2. Discuss whether or not there is a difference between a cure and a healing. In what ways does this distinction assist you to better understand the role of faith in the healing process?

3. Given their commitment to uphold Jewish law, were the scribes justified in their accusations against Jesus? Were they doing what they believed to be right, or were they operating from a position of jealousy because they were threatened by Jesus' popularity?

LESSON IN OUR SOCIETY

The now well-known story and biography of Lola Falana, the famed African American actress/singer/dancer, teaches us much about health, healing, and faith. In 1987, Lola Falana was diagnosed with multiple sclerosis. Crippled, partially blinded, and with no medical cure in view, she turned to God and prayed for her healing.

After an extended period of spending time with God and her spiritual mentors, she came to understand the role of faith in the process of healing. She is quoted as saying, "I am not cured, but I am healed."

Lola Falana now tours the country sharing with others about the empowering sufficiency of God's grace that enables us to use our illnesses to serve some higher purpose. According to her own testimony, she has found happiness and peace with the simple things of life. It just may be that this is the ultimate healing—to have inner peace and a growing relationship with God.

May those who have not yet found the physical healing they seek continue in the faith, believing that God does heal physical illnesses. He does not always heal. Sometimes He chooses to use our illnesses to serve His higher purposes for our lives. The satisfaction that comes from exercising the faith to embrace illness in the confidence that our service—however limited due to our illness—pleases God is perhaps the highest form of healing that anyone can experience.

MAKE IT HAPPEN

If you or someone you know is suffering from a physical illness, pray that God might grant wisdom and a deeper understanding of the role of faith in the healing process. Dare to believe that when physical illness prevails, there is more to pray for than a cure. We can pray for God to give us grace to work with Him to use our illness in His service.

FOLLOW THE SPIRIT

What God wants me to do:

_____

_____

REMEMBER YOUR THOUGHTS

Special insights I have learned:

_____

_____

MORE LIGHT ON THE TEXT

Mark 2:1-12

1 And again he entered into Capernaum after some days; and it was noised that he was in the house. 2 And straightway many were gathered together, insomuch that there was no room to receive them, no, not so much as about the door: and he preached the word unto them.

People were drawn to Jesus. His presence, His words, His wisdom, His actions, His attitude, and the grace of God that rested upon Him drew people to the Lord Jesus. As the Son of God, His nature drew people as well. The Greek word *zoe* means the life and nature of God. Jesus Christ was full of *zoe*, the life and nature of God, or the God-kind of life. Therefore, it was this nature that drew people to Him wherever He went. They desired to be close to Him, to be in His presence, to listen to His words, to hear His voice. They wanted to see Him as He touched the lives of the people.

The Lord Jesus preached the Word of God to them. He preached God's wisdom, God's counsel, and God's compassion. Jesus was the Messenger and He was the Message. He was a living example of what He preached and taught. He never spoke or preached a word that He did not live out. He was the living testimony of the Word He preached and taught. He is the Word of God indeed!

3 And they come unto him, bringing one sick of the palsy, which was borne of four. 4 And when they could not come nigh unto him for the press, they uncovered the roof where he was: and when they had broken it up, they let down the bed wherein the sick of the palsy lay.

How refreshing, encouraging, and uplifting it is to us when we have Christian friends who touch our lives with their faith. Friends who love the Lord, love us, and support us in prayer and in encouragement are special gifts to us from God. Friends who will sacrifice themselves on our behalf are precious. When we have genuine Christian friends who support us in these ways, they are more valuable than gold.

We really don't know a lot about these four men who carried the paralyzed man to Christ, but we can recognize faith at work in them. They are men of great faith. The Lord Jesus affirms this in verse 5. Obviously, they believed that the Lord Jesus could and would heal this man, or they would not have made the effort to bring him to the Lord. They were also determined and not easily discouraged. They would not take "No, you can't get to the Master today" for an answer. They were also selfless; they put this man and his needs before concern for themselves and material things. Their actions were not an example of reckless destruction of property. Apparently, they realized that a roof can be repaired. These four men wanted to see to it that this paralyzed man would get to Jesus and receive his healing. They understood that this man's healing was much more important than a roof.

Also, it should be noted that Jesus does not become angry at the four for making a hole in the roof. The Lord Jesus is impressed with their faith, and His actions commend what they did. It is very likely that these men (who were so loving and committed to helping this man get healed) were thoughtful enough to repair the hole they had created. Their actions remind us that people are always much more important than things.

5 When Jesus saw their faith, he said unto the sick of palsy, Son, thy sins be forgiven thee.

The Lord Jesus acknowledges the faith of the four men. He responds to their faith first by speaking words of forgiveness to the paralyzed man: "Son, your sins are forgiven."

6 But there were certain of the scribes sitting there, and reasoning in their hearts, 7 Why doth this man thus speak blasphemies? who can forgive sins but God only?

The scribes who were present immediately begin to criticize Christ's action. They thought that Jesus did not have the authority to forgive sins. They say that forgiveness of sin is a task for God alone. However, they failed to realize Jesus' inherent authority to forgive iniquities. This was and is God the Son, and certainly He can forgive transgressions. Jesus does in fact forgive this man's sins.

8 And immediately when Jesus perceived in his spirit that they so reasoned within themselves, he said unto them, Why reason ye these things in your hearts? 9 Whether is it easier to say to the sick of the palsy, Thy sins be forgiven thee; or to say, Arise, and take up thy bed, and walk?

The Lord Jesus perceived in His spirit what they were thinking. He then questions them. His questions reveal the errors of their thinking and understanding. The Lord Jesus was helping the paralyzed man to receive both God's forgiveness and healing. Thus, the Lord Jesus wanted to minister to the man's spiritual need and then to his physical need.

10 But that you may know that the Son of man hath power on earth to forgive sins, (he saith to the sick of the palsy,) 11 I say unto thee, Arise, and take up thy bed, and go thy way into thine house.

The Lord Jesus points out that He has both the power to forgive sin and the power to heal this man. In receiving Christ's forgiveness, the man has the guilt of sin taken away. In receiving his healing, the man receives from the Lord the gift of wholeness in his body. Forgiveness and wholeness are very precious gifts that our Lord willingly gives to us.

12 And immediately he arose, took up the bed, and went forth before them all; insomuch that they were all amazed, and glorified God, saying, We never saw it on this fashion.

The Lord Jesus, with authority and power, commanded the paralyzed man to arise, take up his bed, and go home. The man obeyed. His obedience was an act of faith. As he responded to Christ's command in faith, he received his healing. In other words, it was through his faith and obedience that he received his healing.

The response of the people who witnessed this miracle was powerful. The people were amazed, astonished, and they glorified God. This and other miracles of the Lord Jesus were signs that pointed people to the Lord and the salvation that He has provided.

DAILY BIBLE READINGS

M: Jesus Heals the Demoniac
Mark 5:1-13

T: He Has Done Everything Well
Mark 7:31-37

W: How Many Loaves Do You Have?
Mark 8:1-5

T: Four Thousand Are Fed
Mark 8:6-10

F: Stretch Out Your Hand
Mark 3:1-6

S: Son, Your Sins Are Forgiven
Mark 2:1-5

S: I Say to You, Stand Up
Mark 2:6-12

Find other relevant information on the miracles of Christ by searching through past issues of *Precepts For Living* using your *Precepts For Living* CD-ROM.

TEACHING TIPS

June 19
Bible Study Guide 3

1. Words You Should Know

A. False Witness (Mark 14:56-57) *pseudomartureo* (Gk.)—To not tell the truth when giving testimony.

B. Buffet (v. 65) *kolaphizo* (Gk.)—Literally, to rap or strike with the fist; a physical form of mistreatment.

C. Consultation (15:1) *sumboulion* (Gk.)—To consult or deliberate.

2. Teacher Preparation

A. Maximize your study and use of this BIBLE STUDY GUIDE.

B. If you can, secure a copy of a commentary on the FOCAL VERSES. These insights will prove extremely helpful.

3. Starting the Lesson

A. Ask the students if they have ever served on a jury. Then, invite those who have done so to share their feelings about the experience.

B. Announce that today's lesson takes us into the courtroom where Jesus is on trial, and the jury appears to have already made its decision before the trial begins.

4. Getting into the Lesson

A. After reading the FOCAL VERSES aloud, ask the students if anything in the passage suggests that Jesus will get a fair trial.

B. Now, discuss with your students the fact that members of the Sanhedrin were trying to protect and preserve their own status through their hostility toward and premature judgment of Jesus.

5. Relating the Lesson to Life

A. Ask the students to share what they might have said if they had been one who witnessed on Jesus' behalf.

B. Knowing the Sanhedrin's prejudgment of Jesus, ask the students if they think their witness on Jesus' behalf would have been effective.

C. Discerning the Sanhedrin's negative predisposition and its increasing hostility toward Jesus, now ask the students if they would have stood up and defended what was right.

D. When the tide of violent opposition is rising against us, what rationale can we embrace in order to be motivated to do what is right? Solicit your students' own personal experiences in which they were threatened or ridiculed for taking a stand.

6. Arousing Action

A. Have the students identify two situations or circumstances in the community or nation where standing for the right thing resulted in abuse.

B. Pray that God will give wisdom and courage to those who stand up for what is right, even in the face of intense hostility and violent opposition.

WORSHIP GUIDE

For the Superintendent or Teacher
Theme: The Trials and Opposition
Theme Song: "Who Will Suffer with the Saviour?"
Scripture: 1 Peter 5:9
Song: "Stand Up, Stand Up for Jesus"
Meditation: Strengthen us, O God, to always stand for what is right, lest we cower behind our fears and allow injustice to have its way. Amen.

THE TRIALS AND OPPOSITION

Bible Background • MARK 14:53-65; 15:1-5
Printed Text • MARK 14:53-65; 15:1-3
Devotional Reading • MARK 14:17-21

LESSON AIM

By the end of the lesson, the students will discuss Jesus' trial and accompanying mistreatment, talk about the cost required to defend what is right, and be given an opportunity to commit their support to some worthy cause.

KEEP IN MIND

"And the chief priests and all the council sought for witness against Jesus to put him to death; and found none" (Mark 14:55).

FOCAL VERSES

Mark 14:53 And they led Jesus away to the high priest: and with him were assembled all the chief priests and the elders and the scribes.

54 And Peter followed him afar off, even into the palace of the high priest: and he sat with the servants, and warmed himself at the fire.

55 And the chief priests and all the council sought for witness against Jesus to put him to death; and found none.

56 For many bare false witness against him, but their witness agreed not together.

57 And there arose certain, and bare false witness against him, saying,

58 We heard him say, I will destroy this temple that is made with hands, and within three days I will build another made without hands.

59 But neither so did their witness agree together.

60 And the high priest stood up in the midst, and asked Jesus, saying, Answerest thou nothing? what is it which these witness against thee?

61 But he held his peace, and answered noth-

LESSON OVERVIEW

LESSON AIM
KEEP IN MIND
FOCAL VERSES
IN FOCUS
THE PEOPLE, PLACES, AND TIMES
BACKGROUND
AT-A-GLANCE
IN DEPTH
SEARCH THE SCRIPTURES
DISCUSS THE MEANING
LESSON IN OUR SOCIETY
MAKE IT HAPPEN
FOLLOW THE SPIRIT
REMEMBER YOUR THOUGHTS
MORE LIGHT ON THE TEXT
DAILY BIBLE READINGS

ing. Again the high priest asked him, and said unto him, Art thou the Christ, the Son of the Blessed?

62 And Jesus said, I am: and ye shall see the Son of man sitting on the right hand of power, and coming in the clouds of heaven.

63 Then the high priest rent his clothes, and saith, What need we any further witnesses?

64 Ye have heard the blasphemy: what think ye? And they all condemned him to be guilty of death.

65 And some began to spit on him, and to cover his face, and to buffet him, and to say unto him, Prophesy: and the servants did strike him with the palms of their hands.

15:1 And bound Jesus, and carried him away, and delivered him to Pilate.

2 And Pilate asked him, Art thou the King of the Jews? And he answering said unto him, Thou sayest it.

3 And the chief priests accused him of many things: but he answered nothing.

IN FOCUS

Many years ago, I played on my high school's basketball team. The school was located in a rural community in Kansas. I was the only African American on the team and was strategically instrumental in helping my school get to the regional play-offs. Unfortunately, we lost the first game in the tournament play-offs by one point. It was a tough but well-played game.

Following the game, my teammates decided to

go to a local restaurant for an after-game meal and a time of relaxed fun and fellowship. Knowing the societal prejudices of that day, I was somewhat reluctant to go, but I did.

The team that beat us that evening had already arrived at the restaurant and were seated a few tables away from us. We did not plan to meet them there; it just happened—probably because this was the most popular restaurant in this small rural community. Not long after we were seated and prepared to place our orders, a man emerged from the kitchen wiping his hands on his white apron. He came straight toward me and whispered in my ear, "We don't serve colored people here. You will have to leave."

I was not surprised. I knew deep within my spirit that this was going to happen. After all, it was 1959. Segregation at lunch counters was alive and well. My level of social consciousness at the time did not give me the courage to begin a lone protest. So, very calmly, but with deep feelings of rejection, I got up and left the restaurant. Later I learned, much to my surprise, that while my own team members—who incidentally did not live in that community—stayed, the teammates of the other team—who lived in that community—did the exact opposite. Upon learning of the reason for my leaving, they all got up and walked out of their own community restaurant. I have long since wondered why my own teammates, who seemingly had less to risk, did not leave also?

What drives some people to stand up for what is right, while others pursue paths of least resistance? Forty-six years have come and gone since that experience in the restaurant of that small rural Kansas community. I would welcome an opportunity to meet with my "old" high-school basketball teammates and the other team players as well to discuss the activities of that night, which are still vivid in my memory.

There are often opportunities for us to take a stand for what is right in our everyday experiences. God's Word tells us to "put on the whole armour of God, that ye may be able to stand against the wiles of the devil" (Ephesians 6:11). In today's passage, Jesus is still calling for us to stand and be a witness for Him and affirm righteousness.

THE PEOPLE, PLACES, AND TIMES

The Religious Hierarchy. By the time we meet Jesus in Mark 14, the hostility from Jerusalem's religious hierarchy has nearly spun out of control. These entrenched religious leaders can no longer tolerate Jesus' subtle, and sometimes blatant, demands for social and religious reform. They had concluded that their authority, their traditions, and their institutions were threatened beyond measure. Mounting tensions between Jesus and the religious authorities could no longer be controlled. From their vantage point, the growing popularity and influence of this radical upstart from the "no account" village of Nazareth had to be crushed once and for all. Jesus must be put to death. Hence, tabling their long-nurtured attempts to entrap Jesus, Jerusalem's religious leaders have Him arrested.

The Arrest. To avoid the possible instigation of a public riot, the arrest took place at night. The temple captains, who apprehended Jesus, took Him quietly and immediately to the high priest, Caiaphas. By early dawn of the next morning, the trial was well under way.

BACKGROUND

Many have tried to give an orderly account of how Jesus' trial unfolded, only to discover countless difficulties in the way He was arrested and adjudicated. The greater part of the difficulties grow out of the fact that while it was the Jewish religious leaders who wanted to execute Jesus, only the Romans had the authority to do so. The religious infractions for which Jesus was being accused under Jewish law did not justify the death penalty under Roman civil law. Consequently, the Jewish authorities were challenged to conduct the trial in such a way as to produce a legal brief that would convince the Romans to execute the death sentence. Jesus' fate had become the subject of a lot of political lobbying, backroom bargaining, and negotiation.

A parallel study of the Gospels will show that Jesus' trial took place in two phases. First, there was a Jewish trial for religious infractions. Second, there was a Roman trial for civil infractions. Each of these two convened three separate times.

The Jewish religious trial convened during (1) the preliminary hearing before Annas (see John 18:12-14, 19-23); (2) the trial before Caiaphas and the Sanhedrin (see Mark 14:53-65); and (3) the continuation and verdict of the trial before Caiaphas and the Sanhedrin (see Mark 15:1).

The Roman civil trial convened during (1) the trial before Pilate (see Mark 15:2-5); (2) the trial before Herod Antipas (see Luke 23:6-12); and (3) the continuation and verdict of the trial before Pilate (see Mark 15:6-15).

In this lesson, we will consider aspects of both the Jewish religious trials (see Mark 14:53-65) and the Roman civil trial (see Mark 15:1b-3).

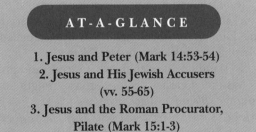

AT-A-GLANCE

1. Jesus and Peter (Mark 14:53-54)
2. Jesus and His Jewish Accusers (vv. 55-65)
3. Jesus and the Roman Procurator, Pilate (Mark 15:1-3)

IN DEPTH

1. Jesus and Peter (Mark 14:53-54)

Peter is to be commended for having followed Jesus "into the palace (i.e., Greek *aule*, **ow-lay**—literally, an exterior courtyard in front of a dwelling or edifice usually open to the air) of the high priest" (v. 54). The text notes that Peter "followed him afar off." At least he followed. While all the other disciples "forsook" Jesus "and fled" (see Mark 14:50), Peter took a stand and trailed Jesus even into the courtyard of Caiaphas' palace. The text suggests that Peter was determined to stay for an indeterminate period of time because "he sat with the servants, and warmed himself at the fire."

Matthew notes that Peter "sat with the servants" to see the end (see Matthew 26:58). Peter wanted to see the final outcome of the trial. While he was not in the room where the inquisition took place, he could see the upstairs room where the Sanhedrin had gathered to decide Jesus' fate.

Given the tension and invoked secrecy that characterized the evening's proceedings, one is tempted to ask, "How did Peter gain access into Caiaphas' courtyard?" According to John's gospel (John 18:15-18), Peter was not the only disciple in Caiaphas' courtyard. Also present was an unnamed disciple who knew Caiaphas, and therefore also knew some of the servants. It was this unnamed disciple who capitalized on his relationship with Caiaphas and the servants to request permission for Peter's admittance.

In the struggle against injustice, it helps to know people who serve in high places, even when they are the perpetrators of injustice. Peter's courage and that of the unnamed disciple stand as models for all who, in the face of potential scorn and ridicule, take a stand for what is right and just. There was little, if anything, that Peter could do to change the direction of things. For the moment, however, Peter did what he could. Although understandably afraid (i.e., he "followed him afar off," Mark 14:54), Peter positioned himself to be ready to do something should the opportunity present itself. One's availability is essential to following Jesus.

While we do not know a lot about Caiaphas' palace, it must have been large enough to comfortably accommodate "all the chief priests and the elders and the scribes" (v. 53b)—a total of 71, including Caiaphas.

The NIV Study Bible. Grand Rapids, Mich.: Zondervan Publishing House, 1995.

2. Jesus and His Jewish Accusers (vv. 55-65)

The Jewish religious leaders had already decided to put Jesus to death, but they had no authority to pull the trigger. Only Roman authorities could execute the death penalty. What the Jewish authorities needed, therefore, was evidence to support their claim that Jesus deserved to be crucified. Therefore, they successfully rounded up the usual suspects: witnesses they could bribe, if necessary, to give testimony concerning Jesus and His claims. The testimonies given, however, were discredited due to lack of agreement. Mark simply says, "And the chief priests and all the council sought for witness against Jesus to put him to death; and found none" (v. 55). Nor was there agreement among those who bore testimony to a definite charge (vv. 58-59).

According to Jewish law (see Numbers 35:30; and Deuteronomy 17:6; 19:15), seeking the death penalty in criminal cases required at least two witnesses whose testimonies agreed. The smallest disagreement or inconsistency was enough to discredit the witnesses' testimonies. While Mark makes reference to the many false witnesses who came forth (vv. 56-58), it is not clear in what sense their testimony was false.

Failure to garner the necessary evidence from witnesses obviously infuriates the members of the Sanhedrin. Their frustration is evidenced by the high priest, who "stood up" (Gk. *anistemi*, **an-IS-tay-mee**—here the word carries the idea of standing up against someone), obviously irritated, and interrogated Jesus, "Are you not going to answer? What is this testimony that these men are bringing against you?" (v. 60b, NIV). This question from Caiaphas was an obvious attempt to provoke Jesus to say something that the council could manipulate into a reason to send Jesus to Pilate. But "In majestic silence, Jesus refused to dignify the self-refuting testimony by any explanation of His own." Mark records that Jesus "held his peace, and answered nothing" (v. 61a). Often the best defense against a false accusation is no defense.

Caiaphas' second attempt to elicit some statement from Jesus is more direct than his first line of questioning: "Are you the Christ, the Son of the Blessed One?" calls for a yes or no response. Jesus answers in the affirmative and adds, "And you will see the Son of Man sitting at the right hand of the Mighty One and coming on the clouds of heaven" (vv. 61-62, NIV). Whatever Jesus may have meant to communicate by His statement, Caiaphas' dramatic response made it clear that he understood it to be blasphemous, and he called for a vote of the council (vv. 63-64a). The vote to convict Jesus carried, and He was thus "condemned...to be guilty of death" (v. 64b).

The council continued to express its rejection and repudiation of Jesus by spitting on Him, hitting Him, and taunting Him in a variety of ways (v. 65). The council soon turned Jesus over to the guards, who continued to beat and to make a mockery of Him. Then they "bound Jesus, and carried him away, and delivered him to Pilate" (Mark 15:1b).

What charges did the Sanhedrin level against Jesus? Mark does not tell, but Luke does. The Sanhedrin charged Jesus on three counts: (1) "perverting the nation," (2) "forbidding to give tribute to Caesar," and (3) that "he himself" claimed to be "Christ a King" (see Luke 23:2).

Hiebert, D. Edmond. *The Gospel of Mark: An Expositional Commentary.* Edited by Greg Kuzmic. Greenville, S.C.: Bob Jones University Press, 1994.

3. Jesus and the Roman Procurator, Pilate (Mark 15:1-3)

Pilate is no doubt already aware of the charges against Jesus, so his initial questioning of Jesus is based upon the third of the Sanhedrin's charges: "Art thou the King of the Jews?" (v. 2).

Jesus' somewhat evasive response prompts "the chief priests" to persist more vigorously in accusing Him of "many things." Still, Jesus remains silent, and His silence amazes Pilate.

To stand up and defend what is right and just, as was noted earlier, requires great strength and courage. *Blessed are those who stand tall and firm in defense of what is right and just. They have a friend and colleague in Jesus.* Jesus Himself, standing before the Sanhedrin and Pilate, demonstrates that it also takes strength and courage to remain silent in the face of undeserved incrimination. *Blessed are those who maintain their composure when facing all kinds of false and vicious accusation. They have a friend and colleague in Jesus.*

May God continue to arm people of good will with the character of heart and the sense of mind needed to fight the good fight, to be involved in the right issues, and to take the right stand.

SEARCH THE SCRIPTURES

1. "And [Peter]...sat with the servants, and _____ himself at the _____ " (Mark 14:54).

2. Who sought to put Jesus to death (v. 55)?
3. What was the first question Pilate asked Jesus (Mark 15:2)?
4. Who accused Jesus of many things (v. 3)?

DISCUSS THE MEANING

1. What happens when Christians do not stand for what is right in a fight against injustice?

2. What does the following phrase mean: "You are either a part of the problem or a part of the solution"?

3. Since God is sovereign, why does He permit some Christians to be martyred in their witness for Him?

LESSON IN OUR SOCIETY

While it may seem otherwise to those who suffer injustice, it is rarely easy to carry out injustice. Those who service injustice always pay a tremendous cost. For example, those who profited from American slavery lived in constant fear of possible food poisoning and slave revolts. Ultimately, racism marginalizes everybody. To quote Dr. Martin Luther King, Jr.: "Injustice anywhere is a threat to justice everywhere." When all is said and done, injustice is also a threat to *humanity* everywhere. The moral laws of the universe declare that in the end, it is far better to take a stand and pay the cost for what is right and just than to take a stand and pay the cost for what is wrong and unjust.

MAKE IT HAPPEN

Have the students identify three social issues or problems facing their community (such as homelessness, domestic violence, theft, etc.), and share ways in which they might take a stand regarding social injustice. Pray that the students will have the courage to take a stand and the strength to maintain their composure when the going gets rough.

FOLLOW THE SPIRIT

What God wants me to do:

_____

_____

REMEMBER YOUR THOUGHTS

Special insights I have learned:

_____

_____

MORE LIGHT ON THE TEXT

Mark 14:53-65; 15:1-3

53 And they led Jesus away to the high priest:

and with him were assembled all the chief priests and the elders and the scribes.

Following His arrest, Jesus was brought before the high priest and his colleagues for interrogation. From John's gospel, we learn that Caiaphas was the high priest at Jesus' trial (John 18:13-14). Caiaphas was the son-in-law of Annas, who presided over the Sanhedrin from A.D. 18 to 36. The Sanhedrin, or council (Gk. **sunedrion**), was made up of 70 members plus the high priest, who served as the president, and functioned as the supreme Jewish tribunal. As the chief governing body of the Jews, the council mediated between the local Jewish populace and Roman occupying authority. It had administrative authority and could order and execute arrests by its own law enforcement officers (cf. Matthew 26:47; Mark 14:43; Acts 4:1ff). Its primary jurisdiction covered civil and religious matters of Jewish law, and criminal matters, to some degree. Capital cases required the confirmation of the Roman procurator (John 18:31), though the procurator's judgment was usually in accordance with the demands of the Sanhedrin. The construction of the words translated as "assembled" (Gk. *sunerchomai*, which means "were brought together") indicates a summoning of an extraordinary session of the Sanhedrin comprising of "the chief priests" (Gk. *archiereus*), "the elders" (Gk. *presbuteros*), and "the scribes" (Gk. *grammateus*).

54 And Peter followed him afar off, even into the palace of the high priest: and he sat with the servants, and warmed himself at the fire.

Peter had boasted that he would stand up for what he believed about Jesus, even if it would cost his life (14:31). But here we see him following "him afar off." Having gained access into the courtyard, Peter opts to melt into the crowd and, from a safe distance, learns what he could of the fate of his teacher and friend. Mark's juxtaposition of Peter's earlier boasting and his present location sets the stage for one of the important lessons of this section—faithful witness in the presence of danger or persecution.

55 And the chief priests and all the council sought for witness against Jesus to put him to

Jesus stood before the high priest and answered nothing.

death; and found none. **56 For many bare false witness against him, but their witness agreed not together. 57 And there arose certain, and bare false witness against him, saying, 58 We heard him say, I will destroy this temple that is made with hands, and within three days I will build another made without hands. 59 But neither so did their witness agree together.**

The theme of the importance of a witness is emphasized by Mark. Here he contrasts true witness with false witness. False witness is characterized by denial and deception. Clearly, the chief priests and the whole council could not build any strong case against Jesus without resorting to extra-judicial sleight of hand. In spite of their strenuously desperate attempts to find any credible witness in order to convict Jesus, none was found. All they could gather was a motley crowd of false witnesses (Gk. *pseudomartureo* meaning "false witness").

The phrase "But neither so did their witness agree together" in the original Greek form is *isai hai marturiar ouk esan* (literally, "their testimonies are not equal"). In other words, their testimonies

did not correspond on the essential points. If the religious leaders were to be remotely true to Deuteronomy 19:15, Jesus could have been set free right then and there for lack of two corroborating witnesses. But the purpose of this trial was not to find the truth, but to convict Jesus by any means. So they had to continue with the charade. Desperate to put something upon Him, the false witnesses tried again with trumped-up charges of blasphemy, but once again they could not corroborate their accusations.

60 And the high priest stood up in the midst, and asked Jesus, saying, Answerest thou nothing? what is it which these witness against thee? 61 But he held his peace, and answered nothing.

The more the witnesses tried to put something on Jesus, the more they failed miserably and the more desperate the situation was becoming. The religious leaders were even more frustrated because amid the clatter and chatter of the witnesses Jesus was saying nothing. As if to make up with bravado what could not be accomplished by evidence, the high priest "stood up in the midst"

(Gk. *anastas eis meson*), as if to intimidate Jesus by his overbearing presence. Jesus would not be moved by this empty show of power, nor would He dignify their baseless charges with an answer. The parallelism in the phrase "held his peace, and answered nothing" (Gk. *esiopa kai ouk apekrinato ouden*) is a way to emphasize the deafening silence with which Jesus responded to this exercise in jurisprudential fraud. The high priest's desperation is at a fever pitch.

61b Again the high priest asked him, and said unto him, Art thou the Christ, the Son of the Blessed? 62 And Jesus said, I am: and ye shall see the Son of man sitting on the right hand of power, and coming in the clouds of heaven.

From Matthew we learn that the high priest prefixed his question with a solemn oath (cf. Matthew 26:63). So far, everything had been false, but this one statement is true. When the high priest said, "Art thou the Christ, the Son of the Blessed?" (Gk. *su ei ho christos ho huios tou eulogetou* literally, "you are the Christ, the Son of the Well Spoken Of"), he spoke an eternal truth. The Bible says that even if the whole world denies Him, He will not deny Himself. At this juncture, there is only one answer to give. And Christ uttered those two words that reverberated throughout the court and reverberate even today: *Ego eimi*, or "I Am." Then He continues by referring to the Second Coming: "and ye shall see the Son of man sitting on the right hand of power, and coming in the clouds of heaven." Christ bears true witness!

63 Then the high priest rent his clothes, and saith, What need we any further witnesses? 64 Ye have heard the blasphemy: what think ye? And they all condemned him to be guilty of death.

Jesus has borne true testimony to Himself. His one testimony stands in contrast to and contradicts the cacophony of all the false voices in that courtyard. The testimony of Jesus about Himself is the truth that sets the world free. The high priest would not receive the truth. In a flamboyant show of ceremonial piety, he tore "his (ceremonial) clothes" (Gk. *chitonas outou*). What the occasion lacked in truth and justice, the high priest made up for with extreme ceremonialism and a pompous display of ecclesiastical grandstanding. Because of Christ's testimony to the truth, the high priest nullified any further need for witnesses. Like a drowning man who must clutch at every straw, he had found something for which he must kill Jesus—blasphemy (Gk. *blasphemia*, meaning "insult to God"). Together with the rest of the chief priests, scribes, the whole council, and the people, "they all" (Gk. *hoi de pantes*) condemned Jesus to death. Promptly, from all sides, every manner of physical and mental abuse was heaped on Jesus, including spitting on Him, hitting Him with open palms, and hurling at Him whatever object was nearby.

65 And some began to spit on him, and to cover his face, and to buffet him, and to say unto him, Prophesy: and the servants did strike him with the palms of their hands.

To "spit" (Gk. *emptuo*) on someone's face is an act of great shaming (cf. Numbers 12:14; Deuteronomy 25:9). The Greek structure of the sentence indicates that it is the high priests and the elders that first began to spit on and strike Jesus. Soon, the crowd joined in. Standing for the truth may cost one dearly, but the alternative is even costlier. Ironically, they requested Jesus to prophesy. It is not surprising that the clan of the Sadducees, who did not believe in the existence of angels and spirits (Acts 23:26), would make a mockery of prophecy.

15:1 And straightway in the morning the chief priests held a consultation with the elders and scribes and the whole council, and bound Jesus, and carried him away, and delivered him to Pilate.

Through the night, Christ was subjected to the most humiliating cruelty known in the land. But the religious leaders still had one more hurdle to cross before they could take Jesus to Golgotha. The judicial authority of the Jewish Sanhedrin did not extend to capital cases. For Jesus' conviction to take effect, they must obtain confirmation of the sentence from the Roman procurator of Judea, Pilate. So the Sanhedrin "held a consultation" to decide how they would present Jesus to

Pilate. Recognized authorities agree that the rare Greek word *sumboulion,* translated as "consultation" in this passage, suggests the idea of a concerted plan of action. Since most of their action the night before was indeed illegal, they needed to ratify it at dawn before they delivered Jesus to the Roman proconsul, Pilate.

2 And Pilate asked him, Art thou the King of the Jews? And he answering said unto him, Thou sayest it.

From Pilate's question, we may be able to deduce the result of the consultation. Pilate was not overly enthused about the constant religious squabbles among the Jews; he was decidedly uninterested in the charges of "malefactor." So, they conspired to impose a treasonable felony charge upon Jesus. They not only lied about Jesus discouraging the payment of taxes to Caesar, but also charged that He was setting up a counter government in which He would be the king. Obviously, this was a charge that Pilate could not ignore. As with the Sanhedrin the night before, this question about His kingship is the one question that Jesus answered. Here again is where His own testimony is important. Jesus is indeed the King, not just of the Jews, but also of the whole world. Yet Jesus, on one hand, and the Jews and Pilate, on the other hand, are speaking of two different kingdoms. From the other Gospel accounts, Jesus made it clear that the worldly kingdom that Pilate and the religious leaders were overly jealous of was not His concern. Christ is King indeed, but not through the instrumentality of human appointment or political maneuvering (John 18:36). He rules in those who have voluntarily chosen to obey Him in humble submission (Luke 17:21; Romans 12:17). But a day is coming when "at the name of Jesus every knee should bow, of things in heav-en, and things in earth, and things under the earth; And that every tongue should confess that Jesus Christ is Lord, to the glory of God the Father" (Philippians 2:10-11).

3 And the chief priests accused him of many things: but he answered nothing.

There is a time to speak and a time to hold one's peace. The chief priests kept heaping accusations on Jesus. The text does not tell us the charges, but they would have to be in terms of something that violated Roman law in order to be considered in Pilate's court. Implicit in the accusation that Jesus threatened to destroy the temple is that He was a violent revolutionary—a terrorist. With His eyes on the big picture of the Father's eternal purpose, Jesus endured the barrage of the chief priests' false accusations with great composure.

DAILY BIBLE READINGS

M: Jesus Predicts Peter's Denial
Mark 14:26-31

T: Jesus Is Betrayed By Judas
Mark 14:43-50

W: False Testimony Is Given About Jesus
Mark 14:53-59

T: Jesus Is Condemned
Mark 14:60-65

F: Peter Denies Jesus
Mark 14:66-72

S: Jesus Goes Before Pilate
Mark 15:1-5

S: Pilate Hands Jesus Over to Die
Mark 15:6-15

Search out all the places the word *Son* is used to verify the deity of Christ by using the concordance and the Greek and Hebrew dictionary on your *Precepts For Living* CD-ROM.

TEACHING TIPS

June 26
Bible Study Guide 4

1. Words You Should Know

A. Sepulchre (Mark 16:2) *mnemeion* (Gk.)—Tomb or cave where bodies were buried. Joseph of Arimathea prepared Jesus' tomb (Mark 16:8; Matthew 27:57-60).

B. Galilee (v. 7) *galilaia* (Gk.)—A racially mixed area in a northern Roman province where Jesus spent most of His ministry.

2. Teacher Preparation

A. To prepare for today's lesson, pray that God will enlighten you with His Word.

B. Study the FOCAL VERSES. Familiarize yourself with the information in the MORE LIGHT ON THE TEXT section.

C. Read the BIBLE BACKGROUND and reflect on the DEVOTIONAL READING.

3. Starting the Lesson

A. Open the class with prayer.

B. Divide the class into groups and debate the evidence or lack of evidence for the Resurrection. You may want to summarize the responses on the chalkboard or newsprint.

C. Read the FOCAL VERSES and the KEEP IN MIND verse together in class. Ask for volunteers to read the IN DEPTH section and explain the verses.

4. Getting into the Lesson

A. Have the students share the new things they learned about Christ's Resurrection. List these things on the chalkboard or on newsprint. Compare the new list with the list of responses from the class discussion in STARTING THE LESSON.

B. Ask the students to discuss situations in their lives when they felt fearful and hopeless like the disciples.

5. Relating the Lesson to Life

A. Discuss the students' responses to the LES-SON IN OUR SOCIETY section.

B. Ask the students to share any insights they have received from today's lesson.

6. Arousing Action

A. Challenge the students to complete the MAKE IT HAPPEN assignment.

B. Ask the students to review today's lesson this week by answering the SEARCH THE SCRIPTURES and DISCUSS THE MEANING questions.

C. Ask if there are any prayer concerns, and then end the session with prayer.

JUNE 26TH

WORSHIP GUIDE

For the Superintendent or Teacher
Theme: The Triumph
Theme Song: "You Are My Dwelling Place"
Scripture: Mark 16:12-15, 18
Song: "A Shield About Me"
Meditation: Lord Jesus, we give honor to You. We thank You for being our hope and giving us resurrection power! Teach us to spread the good news of Your grace and mercy. In Jesus' name we pray. Amen.

THE TRIUMPH

Bible Background • MARK 16
Printed Text • MARK 16:1-8, 12-15
Devotional Reading • MATTHEW 28:16-20

LESSON AIM

By the end of the lesson, the students will know of Christ's resurrection power, and will know that God provides hope in difficult situations. The students will also learn the importance of spreading the Good News of the Gospel.

KEEP IN MIND

"Be not affrighted: Ye seek Jesus of Nazareth, which was crucified: he is risen; he is not here: behold the place where they laid him" (Mark 16:6).

FOCAL VERSES

Mark 16:1 And when the sabbath was past, Mary Magdalene, and Mary the mother of James, and Salome, had bought sweet spices, that they might come and anoint him.

2 And very early in the morning the first day of the week, they came unto the sepulchre at the rising of the sun.

3 And they said among themselves, Who shall roll us away the stone from the door of the sepulchre?

4 And when they looked, they saw that the stone was rolled away: for it was very great.

5 And entering into the sepulchre, they saw a young man sitting on the right side, clothed in a long white garment; and they were affrighted.

6 And he saith unto them, Be not affrighted: Ye seek Jesus of Nazareth, which was crucified: he is risen; he is not here: behold the place where they laid him.

7 But go your way, tell his disciples and Peter

LESSON OVERVIEW

LESSON AIM
KEEP IN MIND
FOCAL VERSES
IN FOCUS
THE PEOPLE, PLACES,
AND TIMES
BACKGROUND
AT-A-GLANCE
IN DEPTH
SEARCH THE SCRIPTURES
DISCUSS THE MEANING
LESSON IN OUR SOCIETY
MAKE IT HAPPEN
FOLLOW THE SPIRIT
REMEMBER YOUR THOUGHTS
MORE LIGHT ON THE TEXT
DAILY BIBLE READINGS

that he goeth before you into Galilee: there shall ye see him, as he said unto you.

8 And they went out quickly, and fled from the sepulchre; for they trembled and were amazed: neither said they any thing to any man; for they were afraid.

16:12 After that he appeared in another form unto two of them, as they walked, and went into the country.

13 And they went and told it unto the residue: neither believed they them.

14 Afterward he appeared unto the eleven as they sat at meat, and upbraided them with their unbelief and hardness of heart, because they believed not them which had seen him after he was risen.

15 And he said unto them, Go ye into all the world, and preach the gospel to every creature.

IN FOCUS

Angie left the funeral feeling deeply depressed. Her husband was gone, and she thought to herself, "What will happen to me now? How will I make ends meet? What about the house, the bills, and the college fund?" Her mind raced over all the financial burdens that were left. Her husband, Jeff, had been a good man and the breadwinner. He had set aside various investment accounts for the children and recently doubled his life insurance policy so the mortgage would be paid off in the event of his death. Angie loved her husband and was thankful for his fine steward-ship. Before he died, Jeff made sure his family's needs were adequately met.

God is our breadwinner, too! He looks after His children in a similar way. During difficult times, God provides both present security and a future hope through our Lord Jesus Christ.

THE PEOPLE, PLACES, AND TIMES

Salome. Her name is a derivative of the Hebrew word *shalom,* which means "peace." Scholars believe she is the sister of Mary, the mother of John and James (Jesus' disciples). She took spices to Jesus' tomb and stood at the Cross during His crucifixion (Mark 15:40; 16:1).

Jesus of Nazareth. This term was used by the apostles to refer to Jesus. Although Jesus was born in Bethlehem, He was raised in Nazareth, a small village in the Roman province of Galilee (the home of His earthly parents, Mary and Joseph). The name "Jesus" was common during His time, and scholars believe the reference to "Jesus of Nazareth" was to differentiate Jesus from others with the same first name; there are also hostile references to the name throughout the Bible (John 1:46; Acts 7:45, 24:5; Matthew 27:16-17).

Comfort, Philip W., and Walter A. Elwell, eds. *Tyndale Bible Dictionary.* Wheaton, Ill.: Tyndale House Publishers, 2001. 938, 1152.

BACKGROUND

Jesus suffered actual physical death on the Cross. A few of His disciples, including women, witnessed His crucifixion. However, most of His followers, fearing Roman retaliation, fled to Jerusalem and locked themselves behind closed doors. Joseph of Arimathea, a prominent member of the Jewish council, went before Pilate and boldly requested Jesus' body for burial preparation. Joseph wrapped Jesus' body and placed it in a tomb. A heavy stone was rolled across the tomb's entrance. Roman soldiers were positioned outside the tomb to guard Jesus' body against theft. Religious leaders believed a group of zealous disciples would steal Christ's body to ensure the appearance of His resurrection. Despite their feeble attempts to thwart the plan of God, Jesus

was raised from the grave. Neither death nor fear can hinder God's hand.

Christ made Himself known in the presence of several witnesses, who gave testimony of His reappearance. The disciples received news of Jesus' return but refused to believe the witnesses. Later, Jesus rebuked them for not believing the testimonies about His resurrection. Nevertheless, He commanded them to go preach the Good News of the Gospel to all people, restoring hope to a lost and dying generation.

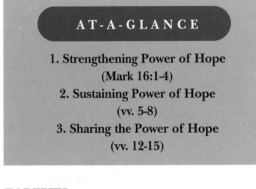

AT-A-GLANCE

1. Strengthening Power of Hope
(Mark 16:1-4)
2. Sustaining Power of Hope
(vv. 5-8)
3. Sharing the Power of Hope
(vv. 12-15)

IN DEPTH

1. Strengthening Power of Hope (Mark 16:1-4)

In Jesus' day, it was a Jewish custom to anoint the body of the dead. The women loved Christ and wanted to do the right thing, so they bought spices after the Sabbath had ended.

When we read this passage of Scripture, we might ask, "Why were women the first to arrive at the tomb? What moved these faithful women to seek the Lord so early in the morning?" The compelling love of Jesus moved these women; they wanted to see their Saviour one more time!

Even in our church culture today, it is women who seek the Lord early in difficult situations. More often than not, it is our mothers and grandmothers whom we seek first for comfort and prayer during times of heartache. It is the "mothers" of the church, the prayer warriors, from whom we seek guidance during times of uncertainty. In every situation, it is wise to seek the Lord early.

The women asked each other, "Who will roll the stone away from the entrance of the tomb?" The stone was huge and too heavy for them to move alone. The women were afraid the stone would prevent them from anointing the body of Jesus.

How many times have we been faced with heavy burdens, or "stones," that require strength beyond our own to move? When we depend on God, He moves obstacles out of our way! Problems are only temporary stumbling blocks. There is no problem too big or too heavy for God to lift or roll away.

God moved the stone. God always sends relief at the right time. Our own strength is not enough. It is important that we depend upon Him. When we are seeking God, He will move any obstruction that blocks or impedes our access to Him.

The stone was not moved so Jesus could exit the tomb. The stone was removed so people could see that He had risen. If we seek God, He will always reveal Himself to us. If we look, we will find that there is enough evidence around us to see the miraculous power of God's workmanship.

Jesus got up from the grave by the power of God! Jesus' resurrection is God's plan to give us victory over death! It is possible the women thought Jesus' body had been stolen from the tomb. Forgetting what Jesus had told them about His resurrection, the women responded to the empty tomb with fear. Even after the privilege of witnessing the phenomenal powers of Christ's miracles before His death, the women approached the tomb with apprehension and disbelief. Often, we are no different; our response to God in many instances is the same as these women's. However, God's sustaining power gives us hope in times of fear and uncertainty. We can rely on His faithfulness to fulfill His promises through our lives.

2. Sustaining Power of Hope (vv. 5-8)

The women were afraid when they saw the angel. Nevertheless, God was anticipating their arrival. God is never caught off guard by our behavior. He is always prepared for our reactions. God understood the women would be alarmed and afraid of finding the tomb empty. God positioned an angel to meet them. He did not leave the women wondering, supposing a thief or a religious leader had taken the body of Jesus. God

wanted the women to know for sure that this was His doing! Isn't that just like God? He makes sure His children can recognize His handiwork! We can always recognize the handiwork of God through the confirmation of His Word.

Jesus was not in the tomb. How often do we find ourselves looking for God in all the wrong places? The angel said, "He has risen! He is not here. See the place where they laid him" (v. 6, NIV). God wanted the women to see the empty tomb for themselves. Why was this important? As witnesses for Christ, it is important that our testimony be rooted in what we know about Jesus. The women were going to be witnesses of the resurrection of Christ. His Resurrection was evidence of His triumphant victory over death. As Christians, we can rest assured that through Christ Jesus, we, too, have victory over death! Jesus took full authority over death and Satan. Those who are in Christ Jesus will be raised from the dead by the resurrecting power of God.

On three occasions before Christ's crucifixion, the apostle Peter denied his relationship with Christ. Peter's blatant denial of Christ led him to feel unworthy, believing he was no longer a disciple. Sometimes when we sin, we allow our guilt and feelings of worthlessness to cause us to separate from the people of God. This passage of Scripture illustrates God's compassion and desire to bring us back into fellowship with Him. God seeks those who have fallen away from the sheepfold; He looks for lost sheep! This is a beautiful illustration of the shepherding care of our Lord Jesus. Jesus knew Peter loved Him and that his heart was sorrowful. The Lord forgave Peter. When we repent, God forgives us and seeks to restore us.

When the angel directed the women to go tell the disciples about Jesus' resurrection, they did not hesitate. Out of obedience and reverential fear of God, they moved swiftly into action. The angel gave instructions for the disciples to meet Jesus in Galilee, which is where Jesus had first called most of His disciples. It was in Galilee that He had told them they would become "fishers of men" (Matthew 4:19).

3. Sharing the Power of Hope (vv. 12-15)

The disciples were hiding in Jerusalem behind

closed doors, fearing for their lives (John 20:29). They were afraid Roman soldiers might kill them. They thought Jesus was dead, and all their hopes were shattered. Fear misdirected their focus and paralyzed their thinking. Their thoughts were now centered on despair, fear, and shattered hope. Fear often blocks our ability to recall God's Word. Whenever we become consumed with fear, immobilized by obstacles, or overwhelmed by our situation, we can easily forget the promises of God. Jesus told the disciples over and over again that He would die and live again. Regardless of what our circumstances look like, we must remember that we can rest on the promises of God.

Jesus rebuked His disciples for their disbelief and not trusting the message of His resurrection. Despite their wavering faith, Jesus commanded them to go preach the Good News of the Gospel to all people, telling the world about Him. Some Christians feel they have nothing to "preach" about because they are not ministers or pastors. However, we do not need a pulpit to tell people about the goodness of Jesus. Our lives should be a walking testimony of our relationship with Christ. When we spend time with Jesus, people will know Him through our conversations, attitudes, and behavior. People need to know that God is the ultimate provider of comfort, joy, and hope!

SEARCH THE SCRIPTURES

1. Why did the women take spices to Jesus' tomb (Mark 16:1)?

2. Who was sitting inside the tomb clothed in white garments (v. 5)?

3. Why did Jesus rebuke the disciples for their unbelief and hardness of heart (v. 14)?

DISCUSS THE MEANING

1. What is the significance of the stone being rolled away from the entrance of the tomb?

2. Why were the women the first to arrive at the tomb of Jesus?

3. Why did the angel instruct the women to tell the disciples and Peter to meet Jesus in Galilee? Why was Peter singled out?

LESSON IN OUR SOCIETY

Death has a peculiar impact on us. It creates enormous anxiety, fear, and discomfort. Death challenges our faith, shakes our hopes, and shatters many of our precious dreams. Much of what we depend on for future security is sometimes connected to the life of someone else. The followers of Jesus placed all their hope and trust in Jesus and laid their lives on the line to follow Him. The disciples left their families, businesses, and social statuses to accompany Him during His earthly ministry. When so much is riding on the survival of one person and that person is no longer around, it can seem like everything is crashing down. Jesus' death created anxiety, fear, and a sense of helplessness in His disciples. However, Jesus rebuked their disbelief and lack of faith. Even death should not have been allowed to impede their trust in God.

How do you respond to traumatic experiences? Do you feel hopeless, insecure, and fearful? Determine to center your hope and faith on Jesus.

MAKE IT HAPPEN

There are many of our friends, people we know from church, coworkers, and family members who are experiencing hopelessness. Pray and ask the Lord to reveal to you at least one individual with whom you can share the Good News of Christ. Make an effort to talk to that person this week.

FOLLOW THE SPIRIT

What God wants me to do:

_____

_____

REMEMBER YOUR THOUGHTS

Special insights I have learned:

_____

_____

MORE LIGHT ON THE TEXT
Mark 16:1-8; 12-15

1 And when the sabbath was past, Mary Magdalene, and Mary the mother of James, and Salome, had bought sweet spices, that they might come and anoint him.

The Sabbath ends at 6:00 p.m. on Saturday.

Thereafter, the people go about their business. Mary and the other women had bought materials in preparation for the anointing of Jesus' body. The Jews did not embalm their dead. Therefore, their bringing "sweet spices" (Gk. *aroma,* from which our English word "aroma" comes) was an act of devotion and love.

2 And very early in the morning the first day of the week, they came unto the sepulchre at the rising of the sun. 3 And they said among themselves, Who shall roll us away the stone from the door of the sepulchre?

Very early Sunday morning, the "first day of the week" (Gk. *mias sabbaton*), but just at "the rising of the sun" (Gk. *anatello helios*), the women came to Jesus' tomb. All along the way, their chief concern was the big stone used to seal the door of the tomb (Mark 15:46). From the construction of the Greek phrase *elegon pros eautas,* it is indicated that they were continuously saying to themselves again and again, "Who will roll away the stone?"

Rolling a circular stone securely into place was a relatively easy task. But rolling it uphill or lifting it out of the doorway was clearly a difficult task.

4 And when they looked, they saw that the stone was rolled away: for it was very great. 5 And entering into the sepulchre, they saw a young man sitting on the right side, clothed in a long white garment; and they were affrighted.

The Greek word *anablepo,* which is translated as "looked," suggests heavy hearts and downcast eyes. But looking up, the women noticed that the stone had already been "rolled away" (Gk. *apokulio*). Unlike Matthew (28:2), Mark makes no attempt to explain how the stone was rolled away. He only emphases its size as "very great" (Gk. *sphodra megas*). Upon entering the tomb, they were confronted with an even more frightening surprise. A "young man" (Gk. *neaniskos*) dressed in a white robe was seated on the right side of where Jesus had been laid. But there was no sign of Jesus! The flood of emotions described by the Greek word *ekthambeo,* translated as "they were affrighted" (alarmed), ranges from astonishment to fear and perplexity. Perhaps it refers to their disappointment in the thought that Jesus' body

might have been stolen or a fleeting thought of doubtful joy that He had actually risen as He had said He would.

6 And he saith unto them, Be not affrighted: Ye seek Jesus of Nazareth, which was crucified: he is risen; he is not here: behold the place where they laid him. 7 But go your way, tell his disciples and Peter that he goeth before you into Galilee: there shall ye see him, as he said unto you.

The angelic being (cf. Matthew 28:2; Luke 24:4) addressed the alarmed women, saying, "He is risen!" This means: "Stop it! Do not go on being astonished." Jesus of Nazareth, who was crucified, is risen! Rather, go tell (Gk. *epo*) Christ's disciples, and especially Peter. There is urgency in the angel's instruction. Rather than stay there gazing into the empty tomb, they were to go get the word out that Jesus is risen indeed! He also recalls for them Jesus' promise of going ahead of them into Galilee after the Resurrection (Mark 14:28; cf. Matthew 26:32).

The women were to carry the news first to the disciples, perhaps to assuage their fears and doubts or, more importantly, because the Gospel is good news to the community of saints. Perhaps, Peter is singled out as the Lord's way of communicating forgiveness for his denial or perhaps to indicate his leadership authority over the community. The Resurrection is the climax of Mark's gospel. Without the Resurrection, Jesus' life and death would have been that of overwhelmingly tragic events. The empty tomb was and is the only explanation that will explain the truth that God raised Jesus of Nazareth from death.

8 And they went out quickly, and fled from the sepulchre; for they trembled and were amazed: neither said they any thing to any man; for they were afraid.

The women had their orders. They "trembled and were amazed" (Gk. *tromos kai ekstasis*) as they fled the tomb. As the angel had instructed, they said nothing to anyone. The angel's words were not enough to calm them. The entire event was too much for them. Apparently, while they had obeyed part of the angelic instruction to go from the tomb, they failed in their mission to communicate the message of Christ's resurrection. However, according to Matthew (28:8) their fear was mingled with joy and they ran to tell the disciples; then the record that they spoke to "no one" would exclude the disciples.

16:12 After that he appeared in another form unto two of them, as they walked, and went into the country. 13 And they went and told it unto the residue: neither believed they them.

Jesus appeared in another form. For the third time on Resurrection Day, Jesus appears to two disciples who were walking along their way into the country. This time He is revealed "in another form" (Gk. *en heteros morphe*), which was different from His pre-Calvary appearance. Luke identifies one of the disciples by name as Cleopas (Luke 24:18). These two went back and reported their Emmaus Road experience to the rest or "unto the residue." But as in the case of Mary Magdalene (vv. 9, 11), they remained unconvinced—"neither believed they them" (Gk. *oude ekeinos pisteuo*).

14 Afterward he appeared unto the eleven as they sat at meat, and upbraided them with their unbelief and hardness of heart, because they believed not them which had seen him after he was risen.

Later, Christ appears to the apostles gathered at their meal. He must deal with the disciples' "unbelief" (Gk. *apistia*) and "hardness of heart" (Gk. *sklerokardia*), which together had prevented them from believing that He had risen from death. The noun form of "upbraided" (Gk. *oneidizo*) means a matter of disgrace or reproach. Clearly the Lord views the disciples' unbelief in His resurrection as a serious matter. All through their time together, He had continued to teach them about His suffering, death, and resurrection (cf. Mark 8:31; 9:31; 10:33-34). How could they miss such an important lesson?

15 And he said unto them, Go ye into all the world, and preach the gospel to every creature.

Go ye!—the Great Commission is found in one form or another in each the four Gospels (Matthew 28:18-20; Mark 16:15-18; Luke 24:44-48; John 20:21, 22). It is that important. The Lord's command to His original followers and to all those who would come to Him through their preaching is to go into all the world and proclaim Christ to all peoples. Moved by the Great Commandment to love God and our neighbors, believers are called to obey the command to go into the world and proclaim the Good News or preach the Gospel to all creation. Let's be about the Lord's business.

DAILY BIBLE READINGS

M: Jesus' Tomb Is Sealed
Matthew 27:62-66

T: He Is Not Here
Matthew 28:1-6b

W: He Has Been Raised
Mark 16:1-8

T: Jesus Appears to the Women
Matthew 28:6c-10

F: Jesus Appears to Other Followers
Mark 16:9-13

S: I Am With You Always
Matthew 28:16-20

S: Go Into All the World
Mark 16:14-20

In the concluding remarks of the Mark 16 Resurrection narrative, believers are told by Christ to: "Go ye into all the world, and preach the gospel to every creature" (Mark 16:15). Use your *Precepts For Living* CD-ROM to find out the full meaning of the word *preach*.

TEACHING TIPS

July 3
Bible Study Guide 5

1. Words You Should Know

A. Blessed (Matthew 5:3-11) *makarios* (Gk.)—Possessing the characteristic of deity; refers to one who is indwelt by God because of Christ and as a result is fully satisfied.

B. Kingdom (v. 3) *basileia* (Gk.)—Royal dominion; the kingdom within one's heart; God's rule within believers.

2. Teacher Preparation

A. Begin by reading Matthew 5—7. Use a modern Bible translation for more understanding or a different way of looking at this passage.

B. Start early in the week going over the Beatitudes. Work through the questions and see how much of the passage you already know. Also, complete the DISCUSS THE MEANING questions so you can think about them all during the week.

C. Materials needed: Bibles, paper, and pencils for each student, chalkboard or newsprint.

3. Starting the Lesson

A. Before class begins, see if anyone in the class can quote the Beatitudes from memory. Divide the SEARCH THE SCRIPTURES and DISCUSS THE MEANING questions among several students. Tell them you will call on them when the class reaches that part of the lesson.

B. Read the IN FOCUS section. Ask some of the students to say whether they are in the fortunate group of Christians who know their blessings and live royally, or if they are often unaware of all that God has done for them. Discuss why some Christians experience more joy and gratitude than others.

C. Pray for the lesson, keeping in mind the LESSON AIM.

4. Getting into the Lesson

A. To help the students understand the history of the Beatitudes and some unfamiliar terms, read BACKGROUND and THE PEOPLE, PLACES, AND TIMES. You may want to place the words defined in WORDS YOU SHOULD KNOW on the chalkboard or on newsprint.

B. Read each section of the lesson according to the AT-A-GLANCE outline. Call on the students selected to answer the questions from the SEARCH THE SCRIPTURES and DISCUSS THE MEANING sections.

5. Relating the Lesson to Life

A. Have a student read LESSON IN OUR SOCIETY aloud.

B. Review the assignment in the MAKE IT HAPPEN section. Have the students make a list and briefly discuss their discoveries.

C. Break up the students into groups of two or three and pray about the situations on each person's paper.

6. Arousing Action

After prayer, have as many students as possible say what changes they plan to make in the way they think, in their attitude, and/or in their behavior as a result of this lesson.

WORSHIP GUIDE

For the Superintendent or Teacher
Theme: The Beatitudes
Theme Song: "Make Me a Blessing"
Scripture: Matthew 5:1-16
Song: "We're Blessed, We're Blessed"
Meditation: Father, thank You for all the precious gifts You give to Your children, who are so undeserving.

THE BEATITUDES

Bible Background • MATTHEW 5:1-16
Printed Text • MATTHEW 5:1-16
Devotional Reading • LUKE 6:17-23

LESSON AIM

By the end of the lesson, the students should have explored the Beatitudes, be motivated to reap the blessings outlined there, and be committed to being an outspoken witness for God.

KEEP IN MIND

"Blessed are they which do hunger and thirst after righteousness: for they shall be filled" (Matthew 5:6).

FOCAL VERSES

Matthew 5:1 And seeing the multitudes, he went up into a mountain: and when he was set, his disciples came unto him:

2 And he opened his mouth, and taught them, saying,

3 Blessed are the poor in spirit: for theirs is the kingdom of heaven.

4 Blessed are they that mourn: for they shall be comforted.

5 Blessed are the meek: for they shall inherit the earth.

6 Blessed are they which do hunger and thirst after righteousness: for they shall be filled.

7 Blessed are the merciful: for they shall obtain mercy.

8 Blessed are the pure in heart: for they shall see God.

9 Blessed are the peacemakers: for they shall be called the children of God.

10 Blessed are they which are persecuted for righteousness' sake: for theirs is the kingdom of heaven.

11 Blessed are ye, when men shall revile you, and persecute you, and shall say all manner of evil against you falsely, for my sake.

12 Rejoice, and be exceeding glad: for great is your reward in heaven: for so persecuted they the prophets which were before you.

13 Ye are the salt of the earth: but if the salt have lost his savour, wherewith shall it be salted? it is thenceforth good for nothing, but to be cast out, and to be trodden under foot of men.

14 Ye are the light of the world. A city that is set on an hill cannot be hid.

15 Neither do men light a candle, and put it under a bushel, but on a candlestick; and it giveth light unto all that are in the house.

16 Let your light so shine before men, that they may see your good works, and glorify your Father which is in heaven.

LESSON OVERVIEW

LESSON AIM
KEEP IN MIND
FOCAL VERSES
IN FOCUS
THE PEOPLE, PLACES, AND TIMES
BACKGROUND
AT-A-GLANCE
IN DEPTH
SEARCH THE SCRIPTURES
DISCUSS THE MEANING
LESSON IN OUR SOCIETY
MAKE IT HAPPEN
FOLLOW THE SPIRIT
REMEMBER YOUR THOUGHTS
MORE LIGHT ON THE TEXT
DAILY BIBLE READINGS

JULY 3RD

IN FOCUS

When Lydia, our firstborn, was a baby, my husband and I agreed to raise her differently. We considered ourselves part of the new generation of African American Christians who wanted to break old traditions and focus primarily on sound biblical principles.

The Christmas Lydia turned 2 years old, we decided to make her Christmas very simple. We wanted to place the main emphasis on the birth of Christ and not merely on an abundance of gifts received on Christmas morning. We thought we were doing a good job of carrying out our wishes because we only bought her two or three nice Christmas gifts.

However, on Christmas morning the Christmas tree was loaded with gifts. We forgot about the gifts Lydia would receive from both of her grandmothers, her aunts, and several people at the church we attended. On Christmas morning, Lydia was surrounded by brightly colored packages. As soon as she opened one we said, "Here Lydia, here's another one." By the time she was all done opening about 15 gifts, she ran gleefully around the Christmas tree from item to item. She didn't know which outfit to try on or which toy to play with first. She was overwhelmed with delight.

Unfortunately, many Christians open the gift of salvation and stop there. The Sermon on the Mount—particularly the first part of the message, the Beatitudes—reminds believers that when we trust Christ for our salvation and enter into the kingdom of God, He provides His children with an abundance of gifts. He wants Christians to be overwhelmed with delight, like a 2-year-old with too many gifts on Christmas morning!

THE PEOPLE, PLACES, AND TIMES

The Mount. Some have speculated that Jesus was near Capernaum at the beginning of His ministry when He delivered the Sermon on the Mount. The writer (Matthew) avoids identifying either a specified time or place. He wanted the attention to be on the sermon and its content, not on the setting.

Mercy. God does not condone sin or ignore it; instead, He pours out mercy and compassion on the person who is constantly falling short. One who is merciful realizes the misery of an unbeliever and shows pity to the sinner, prays for that individual, loves him, and does whatever he or she can to help.

BACKGROUND

Matthew 5—7 is known as the Sermon on the Mount. It is one of five long discourses by Christ found in Matthew's gospel. The Sermon on the Mount is a collection of Jesus' teachings on spiritual maturity. The main theme of the Sermon on the Mount is summarized in one verse: "Be ye

therefore perfect, even as your Father which is in heaven is perfect" (Matthew 5:48). Jesus' sermon explained how His followers could be perfect, meaning mature and complete in Christ and all that God intended for His children to be.

The Sermon on the Mount contrasts a new way of following God with the old way taught by the scribes and Pharisees. The religious leaders emphasized strict observance of the letter of the law. Jesus elaborated on the spirit of the law and displayed the heart of God revealed in the law.

Jesus taught His committed followers the proper character, duties, and attitudes of the Christian disciple, as well as the dangers and rewards of following Christ. He wanted His followers to know what it meant to become a part of the kingdom of God (i.e., yield to God as the king and ruler of one's entire life). This sermon describes life in the kingdom, from entrance into the kingdom here on earth to the final judgment in heaven.

AT-A-GLANCE

1. Kingdom Children: Taught by Jesus (Matthew 5:1-2)
2. Kingdom Children: Blessed by God (vv. 3-6)
3. Kingdom Children: Blessing One Another (vv. 7-10)
4. Kingdom Children: Under Persecution (vv. 10-12)
5. Kingdom Children: Salt and Light in the World (vv. 13-16)

IN DEPTH

1. Kingdom Children: Taught by Jesus (Matthew 5:1-2)

According to Luke, when Jesus preached the Sermon on the Mount, the 12 apostles had already been appointed. The night before, Jesus had gone up into the mountain and prayed. In the morning, just after the Twelve had been chosen, Jesus began this sermon. Other devoted disciples were also part of the crowd on the mountain, along with a multitude of people.

In this sermon, Jesus made God's expectations clear to His apostles and close followers. He also told them what to expect as a result of their allegiance and devotion to God. He preached this sermon to the unbelievers in the crowd as well, encouraging them to join those who were already a part of the kingdom.

Having "opened his mouth" is a common Hebrew expression. It marks the impressiveness and importance of the occasion. The phrase "with Him teaching them" invites the listeners to not merely hear a good sermon but to follow Jesus' teaching as obedient disciples.

2. Kingdom Children: Blessed by God (vv. 3-6)

The beginning of the Sermon on the Mount consists of 10 statements of blessing. These declarations are referred to as the Beatitudes. The word *blessed* introduces someone who is to be congratulated. Many Bible translators use the word *happy* instead of *blessed,* but a temporary mental state like happiness is not what is being described here. "Blessed" is a condition of life and describes one who is fortunate or well-off.

Each of the 10 Beatitudes is spiritual, coming from a generous Heavenly Father. They are gifts that are given when one enters the kingdom of heaven and decides to follow God's instructions instead of the world's dictates. Jesus' sermon addresses those who are "poor in spirit." He is addressing the meek who are humbly trusting God, even though their loyalty may result in oppression and material disadvantage. The emphasis is on dependence on God, not material things. The poor in spirit are individuals who are "empty before God." Daily, they reach up unfilled hands to the Heavenly Father and receive grace.

This "poor in spirit" group has been promised the "kingdom of heaven." This is not an identifiable place on earth or in heaven. If you can, imagine each believer surrounded by the presence of God and His precious gifts. This kind of "place" exists wherever Jesus reigns as King; His power and might are evident.

"They that mourn" are the next group Jesus addresses. The verb *mourn* denotes loud wailing, such as a lament for the dead or grieving over a severe, painful loss. This sorrow is the recognition of the power of sin and of our helplessness to ward it off and escape—a constant, repentant distress cry. This kind of mourning requires a special kind of comfort; therefore, God Himself addresses this cry. God's comfort flows to a believer who is mourning and crying out in distress. This verse is often used to comfort those grieving over a death or a loss, but the verse is really speaking to those who have suffered because of their loyalty to God.

The next group addressed are those who are "meek." Meekness is an inward virtue that displays itself when a person is wronged or abused. A meek person will react not with bitterness, anger, or violence, but instead will respond with mildness, gentleness, and patience.

Jesus is the greatest example of meekness. He refused to throw his weight around, relying totally on God to take vengeance on His enemies. He constantly entrusted Himself to a Heavenly Father who promised that He would get what He was due. For people who have this inner attitude, the divine blessing constantly follows them in this life.

The righteous—those living according to God's standards—are the next group addressed in the Beatitudes. This state should be desired by all believers, like a hungry and thirsty man desires food and water. Hunger and thirst are very commonly used to express strong spiritual desires and needs. The body craves food and water daily. Those in God's kingdom hunger and thirst for forgiveness, and God satisfies that need daily. Men cannot achieve righteousness through their own effort. Once again, the believer has to turn to God and receive the gift of righteousness. The moment faith in Christ is wrought, the believer is declared righteous.

3. Kingdom Children: Blessing One Another (vv. 7-10)

The first three beatitudes focused on Christians' awareness of their own shortcomings and their great need for God. The principles in these beatitudes clearly define the believer's attitude and God's response. The next three beatitudes are more active, particularly in regard to our behavior toward others.

Christians receive God's mercy in abundance. He forgives His undeserving children for a multitude of sins. Mercy is not merely an emotion ("Oh-h-h, I'm so sorry") but a practical action ("Here, let me help").

The phrase "pure in heart" means singleness of heart and refers to a child of God who is honest and has no hidden motives or selfish interests. It denotes one who loves God with all his heart and shows it outwardly in sincere service to others.

Those with a pure heart are promised that they shall see God. Viewing God fully will only be realized in heaven, when we shall see Him just as He is. The greatest joy for the Christian in heaven will be to see God. However, the person who is free from sin, cleansed, and forgiven will begin to see God in His true character and will experience His presence here on earth.

"Peacemakers" are rare in our society. We live in a world of people who pour forth violence, conflict, and anger. The absence of selfish ambition and a concern for the good of others is pleasing to God.

The peacemaker is—first of all—at peace with God. When believers are filled with God's sweet peace, peace with others is a natural result. A peacemaker is a reconciler. This reconciling of men to God is the responsibility of all Christians (2 Corinthians 5:19-20).

4. Kingdom Children: Under Persecution (vv. 10-12)

The Beatitudes emphasize rewards in the kingdom of God. Yet, as God's children display the character of God on earth, not everyone is going to encourage the Christian in his or her positive, godly attitudes. Jesus walked this earth as a perfect man, and yet He endured suffering and persecution; God's children will encounter the same.

The tone of the phrase "they which are persecuted" seems to indicate those who have allowed themselves to be persecuted. They did not flee from persecution but willingly submitted to it when it came to them. And they endured "for righteousness' sake." Their whole lives, their character, and their actions stood as a rebuke to the world, and therefore the world persecuted them. By taking this kind of stand for God in opposition to the world, they displayed the grace and gifts provided in the kingdom of God.

Jesus says that in the face of this kind of persecution, we are to rejoice. Paul and Silas sang hymns of joy while in prison (Acts 16:25). Jesus endured the cross "for the joy that was set before Him" (Hebrews 12:2). "Blessed" are those believers who are persecuted, insulted, and lied about because they dare to take a stand for Christ. Jesus encourages this group to be happy, to be glad. Why? Because those who suffer with Christ will experience the comfort that He experienced. They will also receive a future reward. In heaven, a "crown of reward" is waiting for all who have shared in His sufferings.

Jesus also mentions the prophets, the martyrs of the past who gave up their lives for God. When we suffer persecution for Christ's sake, we can have joy because we are part of this great company of believers.

5. Kingdom Children: Salt and Light in the World (vv. 13-16)

In the Beatitudes, Christ began by explaining how God wants to bless believers. Now, He challenges those who have received God's blessing to be a blessing to the world. "Ye," meaning all of Christ's followers, are to be salt and light in a dark world.

Salt is powerful. One grain can change the taste of a whole lump. Jesus is identifying His small group of followers and saying, "Ye are the salt of the earth"—in other words, "You are a small group, but you will influence the whole world." It was said of the disciples, "These men have turned the world upside down." Salt keeps food from spoiling; however, our world has become a world of decay and rottenness because spiritual salt is lacking. Christ's disciples make the earth a purer and better place to live. But they must be distinctive. Unsalty salt has no use. The rabbis commonly used salt as an image for wisdom (Colossians 4:6). The Greek word for "lost his savour" actually means "became foolish." A foolish disciple has no influence on the world.

Light, like salt, is distinctive. The light—the individual who is displaying good works—exists for the purpose of glorifying God and directing people's attention to Him. Christ is the Light of the world, and believers have Christ inside of them. People are confused, unhappy, bored, and lonely. Therefore, Jesus is challenging His followers to go into dark places where there are troubled lives and give them light.

SEARCH THE SCRIPTURES

1. "Blessed are the ____ in _____: for theirs is the _____ of _____" (Matthew 5:3).

2. "Blessed are they that _____: for they shall be _____" (v. 4).

3. "Blessed are they which do _____ and _____ after _____: for they shall be filled" (v. 6).

4. "Blessed are the peacemakers: for they shall be called the _____ of _____" (v. 9).

5. "Ye are the _____ of the earth" (v. 13).

DISCUSS THE MEANING

1. What does it mean to be "blessed"?

2. Are all Christians experiencing God's blessings? Why or why not?

3. Give modern-day examples of what it means to be light and salt in the world.

LESSON IN OUR SOCIETY

There have been times in America when being a Christian was popular and positive. But Christians have also been rejected and have suffered severe oppression. During the times of popularity, it's easy to witness and take a stand for Christ. But what about when people ridicule you for your faith? In times of opposition and times of peace, remember all that God has and all that God is. All of that is available to His children.

MAKE IT HAPPEN

Reflect on question three of the DISCUSS THE MEANING section. Take the modern-day examples and apply them to your own family, job, neighborhood, or church.

FOLLOW THE SPIRIT

What God wants me to do:

_____

_____

REMEMBER YOUR THOUGHTS

Special insights I have learned:

_____

_____

MORE LIGHT ON THE TEXT
Matthew 5:1-16

Although the passage in Matthew 5—7 has been given a number of titles, such as "Christian charter," "Christian manifesto," or "the design, or pattern, for Christian living," it is generally known as the Sermon on the Mount. This title is derived from the setting of the speech (see 5:1). This passage can correctly be regarded as the inauguration speech of Christ's ministry. It contains some of Jesus' greatest teachings. Indeed, some scholars have regarded it as not only the greatest teaching of Christ, but the greatest teaching of any kind in history. Here, Christ spells out the ethical and moral standards for living in the "kingdom of heaven" that is "at hand" (Matthew 4:17). He enunciates some of the spiritual and practical ways in which one can live both in this present world and in the world to come. These standards and teachings, although directed to Jesus' immediate audience, are relevant for all people of all times.

The first 16 verses (5:1-16), which can be subdivided into three sections, function as the prologue for the Sermon on the Mount. The three divisions are (1) the introduction, which gives the setting of the sermon (vv. 1-2); (2) a series of sayings known as the Beatitudes (vv. 3-12), each of which begins with the word *Blessed,* indicating the favorable, or fortunate, status of a peculiar set of people; and (3) the "ye are" sayings, which describe the calling and role of those who will be members of the new kingdom.

1 And seeing the multitudes, he went up into a mountain: and when he was set, his disciples came unto him: 2 And he opened his mouth, and taught them, saying,

As has been indicated, the narrative in verses 1 and 2 serves as an introduction to the passage. It sets the stage for what will follow in the rest of the sermon. Here we learn that Jesus was teaching from a mountain. The word "and" (Gk. *de,* which can also be translated as "now," "moreover," "but," etc.) that begins this chapter is a conjunction and serves to connect what follows to the previous passage (4:25).

In chapter 4, we read of Christ's ministry of teaching, miracles, and healing throughout the regions of Palestine and Galilee. These events had attracted large crowds to Him. When He saw the multitudes, He "went up into the mountain." Mountains play an important role in Matthew (4:8; 5:1; 8:1; 14:23; 15:29; 17:1; 9, 20; 18:12; 21:21; 24:16; 28:16). Christ's third temptation by the devil was on the mountain (4:8-10), and the mountain will be the setting for His Great Commission at the end of His ministry on earth (28:16-20). Although Matthew does not deem it necessary to name the mountain for this discourse, one can think of two major mountains. **The first would be Mount Sinai, where Moses gave the Law of the Lord to the people of Israel** (Exodus 19-20). The second would be Mount Zion, a site where Isaiah predicted that all nations would be gathered at the end time to hear the Word of God (Isaiah 2:1-4; cf. Micah 4:1-4). If either of these was the mountain, the only spiritual significance it has for the narrative is to show the importance, authenticity, and authority of the message, whereby Christ institutes the reign of God and teaches people about the kingdom. Apart from this, the significance of the mountain here relates to the number of people. The crowd was so great that Jesus needed a higher and broader space where He could address them.

Verse 1 seems to suggest that there were two different types of people in the crowd. The first represented the larger group (mentioned in 4:25), who came from different regions around Jerusalem. The people who made up the second group were Jesus' disciples, among whom were those Jesus had called earlier to follow Him (4:18-22). This smaller group probably sat in a semicircle close to Him, and the rest of the crowd formed a larger semicircle down the slope of the mountain. The word translated as "set" is the Greek word *kathizo* and means "to sit down, settle

down, or sojourn." This means that Jesus sat down as He taught the people, which was customary for teachers in Jewish circles (see 13:2; 23:2; Luke 4:20-21).

"And he opened his mouth, and taught them" is a familiar phrase that is usually used to introduce an important teaching, as it is here and elsewhere in Scripture (see Psalm 78:1-2; Job 33:1-2; Acts 8:35; 10:34; 18:14). The phrase may also demonstrate a conscious and deliberate decision on the part of the Teacher to teach, seizing the opportunity afforded Him by the surging crowd to set forth the fundamental ordinances of the kingdom.

To whom is Jesus speaking? Is He teaching the disciples, the crowd, or both? Whom does "taught them" refer to? At first glance, one might assume that the immediate antecedent is "his disciples" in verse 1. However, at the conclusion of the sermon, one observes that "the people were astonished at his doctrine: for he taught them as one having authority, and not as the scribes" (7:28-29).

3 Blessed are the poor in spirit: for theirs is the kingdom of heaven.

Verse 3 begins the second section consisting of "blessed" sayings, or more correctly, the Beatitudes (vv. 3-12). Each of the verses starts with the word "blessed" (Gk. *makarios,* **mak-ar'-ee-os**), which also means "fortunate" or "happy." The word "beatitude" is derived from the Latin *beatus* (which means "blessed"), the equivalent of *makarios.* Others prefer to title the passage *Macarisms,* from the Greek. This form of saying found here is reminiscent of the Old Testament form of writing found primarily in the poetical books and the Psalter (e.g., Psalm 1:1; 32:1-2; 84:4-5; 144:15; Proverbs 3:13; Daniel 12:12).

Jesus begins His teaching by pronouncing blessings on, or proclaiming God's favor to, the "poor in spirit." As we have already noted, *makarios* may be translated as either "blessed" or "happy." If the former is the case, it means that the "poor in spirit" are blessed because "theirs is the kingdom of heaven." If the latter is the case, then those who are "poor in spirit" (here on earth by implication) will inherit the kingdom of heaven

(God). In the parallel passage in Luke 6:20 (NASB) it reads, "you who are poor," omitting the phrase "in spirit." There, the meaning is clear: It refers to those who are economically bankrupt on earth, deprived of earthly riches, and who will be rewarded in the kingdom of heaven. The Old Testament is full of references to the poor (Deuteronomy 15:11; Psalm 37:14; 72:1-4; Amos 8:4). These passages address those who are poor in material goods and of lowly disposition, which accompanies such deprivation, rather than the "poor in spirit." In these situations, God fights for the cause of the poor and delivers them (cf. 1 Samuel 2:8; Psalm 34:6; 35:10; Isaiah 41:17).

Although the "poor" in the Old Testament were usually the pious (Psalm 69:29-36; Isaiah 61:1), the phrase "poor in spirit" is not found in the Old Testament. The precise meaning of this phrase in Matthew is not clear. There are two distinct options in trying to understand: it refers to those who cultivate the spirit of humility and self-abasement, or it describes those in need, like the poor, whose poverty is an affliction of the spirit. The phrase does not speak of those who are faint-hearted, as some would contend, but speaks of the humble in heart. Thus, it means the humble—those who acknowledge their unworthiness before God and absolute dependence on the Lord. Both the Old Testament and New Testament speak profoundly of the rewards, benefits, and blessings of being humble (Proverbs 16:19; 29:23; Isaiah 57:15; Matthew 18:4; Luke 18:14).

Here the reward is that the kingdom of heaven belongs to them (as we see in Matthew 3:2 and 4:17); they will partake in the reign of the Messiah and enjoy the blessings He brings. Christ is the perfect example of humility and its rewards, as Paul describes in Philippians 2:6-11.

4 Blessed are they that mourn: for they shall be comforted.

While the humble or "poor in spirit" will inherit the "kingdom of heaven" (v. 3), those who mourn will be comforted. What makes them mourn? It is their fallen and sinful condition. Who are "they" referred to here? I believe Jesus includes the godly remnant who weep and lament because of the suffering and humiliation of Israel at the hands of foreign nations, which is the consequence of both personal and (Israel's) corporate sin against the Lord. The psalmist's lament, "Rivers of waters run down mine eyes, because they keep not thy law" (Psalm 119:136), is echoed by Ezekiel (9:4) and describes the desperate condition of Israel's relationship with the Lord. God responds to them through Isaiah (40:1).

The beatitude here in Matthew speaks of the deplorable condition of the world, both then and now. Like Simeon, they were "waiting for the consolation of Israel" when there will be no more pain and sorrow (Luke 2:25). These first two beatitudes are alluded to in Isaiah's messianic blessings (61:1-3), which are fulfilled in Christ (Luke 4:16-19). Christ says that He has come to change mourning into joy and to bestow "the oil of gladness instead of mourning, and a garment of praise instead of a spirit of despair" (Isaiah 61:3, NIV). These blessings, as yet only partially realized, will be fully consummated at the return of the Messiah (Revelation 7:17).

5 Blessed are the meek: for they shall inherit the earth.

The next group to be rewarded are the "meek." The word "meek" (Gk. *praus*) is difficult to define. The nearest synonym is "gentleness," which is better to exemplify than to merely define. Abraham demonstrated a spirit of meekness when he gave Lot first choice of the land, although the promise was made to him (Genesis 13:8-12). *Praus* refers to mildness of disposition, or gentleness of spirit. Meekness toward God is that disposition of spirit in which we accept His dealings with us as good, and therefore submit without dispute or resistance. In the Old Testament, the meek are those who wholly rely on God rather than their own strength to redress injustice. Thus, meekness toward evil people means knowing that God is using the injuries they inflict to purify His elect, and that He will deliver His elect in His time (Isaiah 41:17; Luke 18:1-8).

Gentleness, or meekness, is the opposite of self-assertiveness and self-interest. It stems from trust in God's goodness and control over the situation. A meek person is not occupied with oneself at all. As noted in 1 Peter 3:4, 14-15, meekness can signify absence of pretension, but generally suggests gentleness (Matthew 11:29; James 3:13) and self-control. This is the work of the Holy Spirit, not of the human will (Galatians 5:23). It is a virtue to aspire to, but for the Greeks, it was a vice because of their inability to distinguish it from servitude.

Jesus is the perfect example of meekness, and Matthew throws more light on this word when he uses the same word to describe the way Christ exercises His authority (11:29; 21:5). Meekness has to do with the way we relate to others when we shun the arrogant and vicious ways of the strong.

The meek, rather than the strong, aggressive, harsh, and tyrannical, will inherit the earth, Jesus asserts. The verb "inherit" is often used in Scripture, especially in the Old Testament, in relation to the Promised Land (see Deuteronomy 16:20; Isaiah 57:13; 60:21). The promise here is alluded to by the psalmist in Psalm 37:11 (see also vv. 9, 29), although in the Old Testament texts, "the earth" refers to the land of Canaan to be possessed. The word "earth," or "land," in this beatitude has a broader meaning. As Richard B. Gardner writes, "It is a way of depicting a place to dwell without fear in the new realm of God's kingdom. Such will be the lot of the meek who follow Jesus, who look to God to shape and to guarantee their destiny."

Gardner, Richard. "Matthew." *Believers Church Bible Commentary.* Scottdale, Pa.: Herald Press, 1991. 95.

6 Blessed are they which do hunger and thirst after righteousness: for they shall be filled.

The next group in the Beatitudes whom Matthew congratulates are those who hunger, or long, for righteousness. The language is reminiscent of Old Testament themes. The verbs "hunger" and "thirst" express a strong urge, or desire—a craving for something good like food and water. Here, it expresses a desire to live rightly or to have a good relationship with the Lord. The sons of Korah cried out, "My soul thirsteth for God, for the living God" (Psalm 42:2; cf. 63:1). Eating and drinking is used metaphorically in the Old Testament to express the desire to have a

relationship with God (Isaiah 55:1-3)—a desire that only God satisfies (Psalm 107:9). Therefore, those who "hunger and thirst for righteousness" are the people who yearn for a deeper, right relationship with the Lord (see Matthew 6:33).

Apart from having a personal relationship with God or living uprightly before Him, which this beatitude tends to address, is there any other sense in which the word "righteousness" can be used? The answer lies in the alternative definition of the term as expressed here in the Greek word *dikaiosune* (**dik-ah-yos-oo'-nay**), which means "justification" or "equity" and is from the word *dikaios,* meaning "just." It carries with it the idea of justice—dealing fairly or rightly and equitably with others—with social justice as the undertone. Therefore, this beatitude addresses not only those who hunger and thirst for personal righteousness (i.e., living uprightly before the Lord), but also those who strongly desire that justice be done everywhere and to all mankind.

They yearn for the new kingdom where there is justice, equality, and holiness (2 Peter 3:13); they are not satisfied with the status quo. They desire both personal spiritual growth and change in society. The reward for their yearning is that they will be filled, or satisfied. Note that the verb "filled" (Gk. *chortazo,* **khor-tad'-zo**) is the same word used in Matthew 14:20, after Jesus fed the 5,000 men (cf. Philippians 4:12; Revelation 19:21). They are therefore blessed and will be happy because their desire and curiosity will (most likely) be fulfilled in the actualization of the kingdom.

7 Blessed are the merciful: for they shall obtain mercy.

The simplest way to talk about the beatitude in verse 7 is in terms of reaping and sowing (i.e., you reap what you sow), but here in a positive sense. This beatitude is similar to Psalm 18:25. The word "mercy" contains the idea of both forgiveness and compassion (i.e., showing kindness). Both understandings of mercy (forgiveness and compassion) are common themes in Matthew's gospel (in the Lord's Prayer, 6:12-15; in Jesus' teachings and parables, 9:13; 12:7; 18:33-34). The reward for showing mercy is obtaining (i.e., also receiving)

We should relate to God and others with sincerity of heart and mind.

mercy, not necessarily from other people or from the immediate recipients, but from the Lord. The opposite is equally true: Those who do not show mercy will not be shown mercy (James 2:13). Although showing mercy to others is not always the ground for God's mercy, it can be its "occasional ground," as someone put it (6:14-15). Mercy is part of God's character and is not dependent upon our merciful acts; it is in God's nature and a gift to sinful man.

8 Blessed are the pure in heart: for they shall see God.

"The pure in heart" seems to address genuineness of faith and those who reflect truthfulness and purity of mind without duplicity. This beatitude is a reflection of Psalm 24:3-6, which poses the question of who is able to ascend to the temple and see the Lord. In his answer, the psalmist (most likely David) replies that it is "he that hath clean hands, and a pure heart; who hath not lifted up his soul unto vanity, nor sworn deceitfully" (v. 4). From this psalm, it is apparent that only those who are internally clean (Deuteronomy 10:16; 30:6; etc.) and those who relate to God and others with sincerity of mind—as opposed to merely the externally pious—will see God (James 4:8).

The beatitude speaks of those whose thoughts are pure and free from deceit, as opposed to the hypocrites (Matthew 6:1-18); they will see God. To see God is to experience His presence in an intimate way; to have a close relationship with Him. Moses had this experience with the Lord; hence, God spoke "face-to-face" with him in the wilderness—an experience the psalmist desired and in fact had (Psalm 63:1-2). Abram (Abraham) had such an intimate relationship with the Lord that God "talked with him" (Genesis 17:3) in a heart-to-heart discussion. Isaiah also had this experience, which was terrifying and yet transforming (Isaiah 6:5; cf. Genesis 32:26-30). These were glimpses of the revelation of God's presence, but the complete unveiling of this truth, promise, and blessing to the "pure in heart" is yet future.

9 Blessed are the peacemakers: for they shall be called the children of God.

Among those who are blessed are the "peacemakers," not the "peaceful." Their reward is that they will be called the children of God. The Bible speaks continually of peace in both the Old and New Testaments (e.g., Proverbs 15:1; Isaiah 52:7; Luke 24:36; Romans 10:15; 12:18; 1 Corinthians 7:15; Hebrews 12:14; 1 Peter 3:11). Isaiah prophesied that the Promised Son would be called "Prince of Peace" (Isaiah 9:6-7). In another place he proclaimed: "How beautiful upon the mountains are the feet of him that bringeth good tidings, that publisheth peace; that bringeth good tidings of good, that publisheth salvation; that saith unto Zion, Thy God reigneth!" (52:7).

Jesus is the fulfillment of Isaiah's prophecy and the supreme example of a peacemaker. He brings reconciliation between God and man and between man and man. The Greek word *eirenopoios* (**i-ray-nop-oy-os'**), which is translated as "peacemakers," occurs only here in the New Testament, but related words are found in other parts of the New Testament. For example, James 3:18 says that "the fruit of righteousness is sown in peace of them that make peace." In Ephesians and Colossians, Paul attributes peacemaking to God through the blood of His Son (Ephesians 2:13-16; Colossians 1:19-20).

It is of interest to note that the people Jesus blesses here are neither the peaceful, nor lovers of peace, nor those who only speak of peace, but rather those who work actively to make or bring about peace. With God as their example, they strive to make peace at all costs (sometime sacrificing their own peace or even their lives) and with all persons, whether friends or foes (Matthew 5:45). By imitating the Lord in peacemaking, the peacemakers demonstrate that they are the true children of God. Hence, Jesus says that God will accept them as His own at the consummation of all things.

10 Blessed are they which are persecuted for righteousness' sake: for theirs is the kingdom of heaven.

The next group to receive God's blessings are those who are persecuted for their righteousness, or right deeds, probably referring to the peacemakers and those who fight for justice (v. 6). In a world that is full of hate and prejudice, the peacemakers and those who endeavor to live uprightly in the sight of God are never cherished or welcomed in society. Often, they are persecuted and receive the brunt of society's anger and hatred. Persecution, or oppression, is the mark of discipleship, as Jesus reminded His disciples (John 15:18-25). Encouraging the disciples at Lystra, Iconium, and Antioch to remain true to the faith, Paul and Barnabas remind them, "We must go through many hardships to enter the kingdom of God" (Acts 14:22; see also 2 Timothy 3:12 and 1 Peter 4:13-14). The promise, or blessing, for the "poor in spirit" (Matthew 5:3) is the same here. Indeed, this beatitude tends to tie together all the other beatitudes, for all the virtues therein can be summed up under the theme of righteousness, or right living.

Some interpreters believe that the phrase "for righteousness' sake" refers to the Lord Jesus Christ, and that can also be true (see v. 11). However, it is apparent that Jesus is not referring to Himself here but to those who suffer because they want to walk uprightly.

11 Blessed are ye, when men shall revile you, and persecute you, and shall say all manner of evil against you falsely, for my sake. 12 Rejoice, and be exceeding glad: for great is your reward in heaven: for so persecuted they the prophets which were before you.

Verses 11 and 12 are an expansion of verse 10. They deal with the attitude that believers ought to cultivate when they face persecution and oppression because of their faith in Christ. We notice here that Jesus changes from third person pronouns to second person plural pronouns, which indicates that at this point He is addressing a specific group in the audience. Here, Jesus lists three forms of oppression that the disciples (and all those who believe in Him) would suffer be- cause of their faith and their relationship with the Lord Jesus: revilement, persecution, and slander. The word "revile" (Gk. *oneidizo*, **on-i-did'-zo**), means to defame, rail at, taunt, or reproach. It also means to ridicule somebody because of what that person does, how the person acts or behaves, how the person looks physically, or what the person believes.

The second opposition is "persecution," translated from the Greek word *dioko*. Persecution takes a variety of forms and covers a wide range of hostile actions. It would include harassment, molestation, and maltreatment in various forms. The third form of opposition the disciples will suffer is that people "shall say all manner of evil against [them] falsely" (i.e., slander or false and malicious accusation). In the parallel passage, Luke adds that they would be hated and excluded from the synagogue (Luke 6:22-23).

Jesus urges His disciples to rejoice with exceeding gladness even in the face of their tribulations. He gives two reasons why the disciples should rejoice and be glad. The first is that they will be greatly rewarded for their faith, that their reward will be great in heaven. It should be noted that this reward is not a "rite of passage" into the kingdom; rather, it demonstrates that God is faithful and just to reward those who are faithful and endure to the end. Reward is a common theme in both Jewish circles and in the New Testament (see Matthew 6:1-4; 10:42; 20:1-16). The second reason the disciples can rejoice in tribulation is that they are in the same company with the Old Testament prophets before them who were likewise persecuted (see 2 Chronicles 24:21; Nehemiah 9:26; cf. Matthew 23:29-39; Acts 7:51-52; 1 Thessalonians 2:14-16; Hebrews 11:35-38). Jesus is implying that the disciples, who will share the same fate as the prophets of old, are themselves prophets, persecuted in the same manner as their predecessors. Therefore, this calls for rejoicing, and the apostles understood and applied this later (Acts 5:41; cf. 2 Corinthians 4:17; 1 Peter 1:6-9).

This beatitude does not imply that Christians, or believers, should seek persecution, nor does it permit retreat from it or revenge. Rather, it speaks of steadfast faith in the Lord under any and all circumstances with humility and singleness of heart and continuing reliance on and faithfulness to God, irrespective of what may come our way, good or bad.

13 Ye are the salt of the earth: but if the salt have lost his savour, wherewith shall it be salted? it is thenceforth good for nothing, but to be cast out, and to be trodden under foot of men.

Verses 13 to 16 are still being addressed directly to Christ's followers. This is evident from the second person plural pronoun, which was first used in the previous verse (v. 11). Indeed, the subject "ye" or "you" (Gk. *humeis*, **hoo-mice'**) in both verses 13 and 14 is emphatic and can be translated as "yourselves" (i.e., "you yourselves"). The emphasis demonstrates the importance of the subject and the specificity of the sayings to the disciples.

Here Jesus uses two metaphors—salt and light—to describe the disciples' calling and their responsibilities to the world. Salt and light are two common but very important and useful substances used by mankind in all generations.

There are a number of ways salt was and is used: as a preservative, as a purifying agent (2 Kings 2:20-21), and as a seasoning for food, both for humans (Job 6:6) and for beasts (Isaiah 30:24). In Old Covenant religious practice, salt was used especially for sacrifices (Leviticus 2:13; Ezra 6:9; Ezekiel 43:24). It is not clear in what sense "salt" is being used in this verse. However, we know that salt plays very important roles in our daily lives, and Jesus expects His disciples to fulfill similar roles in the world. If those roles are not fulfilled, the disciples are like salt that has "lost his savour" (i.e., taste or saltiness) and are therefore worthless.

The question "wherewith shall it be salted?" is rhetorical with an obvious answer: nothing! Therefore, Jesus says, since "it is . . . good for nothing," it will be thrown out "to be trodden under foot of men." The Igbos of Nigeria have a similar adage concerning water: "Water is for washing, but if water becomes dirty, what can be used to wash it or purify it?" The answer is again obvious: nothing. The adage continues, "It is then worthless, and only to be thrown or poured away." The phrase "to be cast out, and to be trodden under foot of men" speaks of judgment for those who do not fulfill their calling (cf. Matthew 8:12; 22:13; 25:30), whose lives fail to make a positive Christian impact in the world.

14 Ye are the light of the world. A city that is set on an hill cannot be hid. 15 Neither do men light a candle, and put it under a bushel, but on a candlestick; and it giveth light unto all that are in the house.

The second metaphor used to describe the disciples is "light." They are the "light of the world," Jesus says. He begins by emphasizing the nature and function of light, which is primarily to illuminate large areas to make things visible. Lights are usually visible, and light helps people see where they are going. Jesus qualifies the analogy of light with, "A city that is set on an hill cannot be hid." The idea here is probably taken from the city of Jerusalem, or Zion, which is built on a hill and can be seen from afar, especially at night when the lights from the oil lamps glow. It is also believed that many ancient cities were built with limestone, which made them gleam in the sun and were therefore difficult to conceal.

Continuing with this theme, Jesus says in effect that for candles to be useful, they must be on candlesticks (lampstands) so that they can illuminate large areas, rather than "under a bushel." A bushel was a basin or bowl used for solid measures (e.g., wheat). People would normally light their candles and put them on lampstands so that they might give light to the whole house, not cover them with a bowl. If the flame is covered, it will die and the people will be in the dark. Therefore, the disciples have the same function as light in the world.

Light is a common symbol in the Bible; the Jews saw themselves as the light of the world (Romans 2:19), and the true light is the suffering servant (Isaiah 42:6; 49:6), who ultimately was Christ (Matthew 4:16; John 8:12; 9:5; 12:35; 1 John 1:7).

16 Let your light so shine before men, that they may see your good works, and glorify your Father which is in heaven.

Jesus then spells out the obvious as He drives home His point and the meaning of the metaphor. The disciples as the light of the world must show forth their "light" by letting it shine. They would do this through good works, by living out their lives as set forth in verses 3-10. Although they would face all types of persecutions (vv. 10-12), that should not make them hide their light, which was given for others to see so that they might give glory to their Father in heaven. This is the main objective and purpose of discipleship (1 Peter 2:12; 4:11; cf. 2 Corinthians 4:6) as exemplified by Christ Himself (John 17:4; cf. 13:31; 14:13).

DAILY BIBLE READINGS

M: Jesus Teaches About Discipleship
Luke 6:17-23

T: Instructions on Living the Christian Life
Matthew 5:1-8

W: More Instructions for True Disciples
Matthew 5:9-16

T: Love Your Enemies
Matthew 5:43-48

F: Be Merciful
Luke 6:32-36

S: Do Not Judge
Matthew 7:1-5

S: On Judging Others
Luke 6:37-42

What does it mean to be "blessed"? The study tools in your *Precepts For Living* CD-ROM can help you find out!

TEACHING TIPS

July 10
Bible Study Guide 6

1. Words You Should Know

A. Alms (Matthew 6:1) *eleemosune* (Gk.)—A compassion of benefit toward the poor; giving.

B. Pray (v. 6) *proseuchomai* (Gk.)—To pray to God; make earnest supplication; worship.

C. Forgive (v. 12) *aphiemi* (Gk.)—To send away, or the remission of a punishment due to sinful conduct; the complete removal of the cause of the offense.

2. Teacher Preparation

A. Read the BIBLE BACKGROUND section.

B. Read the DAILY BIBLE READINGS and note how God's people sought Him in numerous situations.

C. Materials needed: 3 x 5" index cards, pencils, small receptacle to hold cards (perhaps a shoe box), chalkboard or newsprint.

3. Starting the Lesson

A. Ask at least three students to open in prayer.

B. Select one student to read the FOCAL VERSES 1-9, and a second student to read the FOCAL VERSES 10-14.

4. Getting into the Lesson

A. Ask the students to read IN FOCUS. Ask if anyone has found themselves in a similar situation. Spend no more than five minutes in discussion.

B. Ask a student to read the BACKGROUND and LESSON IN OUR SOCIETY sections, and discuss what it is that God wants from us.

C. Select three students to read IN DEPTH.

5. Relating the Lesson to Life

A. Review the lesson according to the AT-A-GLANCE outline.

B. After reading section 1, "Our Giving," ask if anyone has ever been in a position where they needed to receive food, clothing, money, etc. How did it make them feel to receive what was needed?

C. After reading section 2, "Our Praying," ask how they feel about repetitious prayers. Spend no more than five minutes in discussion.

D. After reading section 3, "Our Forgiving," ask for a moment of silence so everyone can search their hearts for forgiveness.

6. Arousing Action

A. List on the chalkboard or newsprint what the class considers to be the most important areas of need for prayers today.

B. Have each student write a prayer request on a 3 x 5" card, but do not put their name on the card. Place the cards in the small receptacle.

C. Have the students pair off and pray for one another.

D. Then ask each student to select a 3 x 5" prayer request card from the receptacle (make sure it is not theirs) and each day during the week pray for that request.

E. Remind the students to finish the lesson during their private devotions.

F. Close the class in prayer.

PRACTICES OF PIETY

Bible Background • MATTHEW 6:1-18
Printed Text • MATTHEW 6:1-14
Devotional Reading • LUKE 11:5-13

LESSON AIM

By the end of the lesson, the students will know the right motives in giving, the right model for prayer, the promises and warnings for the right understanding in forgiveness and will commit themselves to modeling the behavior indicated in these texts.

KEEP IN MIND

"Take heed that ye do not your alms before men, to be seen of them: otherwise ye have no reward of your Father which is in heaven" (Matthew 6:1).

FOCAL VERSES

Matthew 6:1 Take heed that ye do not your alms before men, to be seen of them: otherwise ye have no reward of your Father which is in heaven.

2 Therefore when thou doest thine alms, do not sound a trumpet before thee, as the hypocrites do in the synagogues and in the streets, that they may have glory of men. Verily I say unto you, They have their reward.

3 But when thou doest alms, let not thy left hand know what thy right hand doeth:

4 That thine alms may be in secret: and thy Father which seeth in secret himself shall reward thee openly.

5 And when thou prayest, thou shalt not be as the hypocrites are: for they love to pray standing in the synagogues and in the corners of the streets, that they may be seen of men. Verily I say unto you, They have their reward.

6 But thou, when thou prayest, enter into thy closet, and when thou hast shut thy door, pray to

LESSON OVERVIEW

**LESSON AIM
KEEP IN MIND
FOCAL VERSES
IN FOCUS
THE PEOPLE, PLACES,
AND TIMES
BACKGROUND
AT-A-GLANCE
IN DEPTH
SEARCH THE SCRIPTURES
DISCUSS THE MEANING
LESSON IN OUR SOCIETY
MAKE IT HAPPEN
FOLLOW THE SPIRIT
REMEMBER YOUR THOUGHTS
MORE LIGHT ON THE TEXT
DAILY BIBLE READINGS**

thy Father which is in secret; and thy Father which seeth in secret shall reward thee openly.

7 But when ye pray, use not vain repetitions, as the heathen do: for they think that they shall be heard for their much speaking.

8 Be not ye therefore like unto them: for your Father knoweth what things ye have need of, before ye ask him.

9 After this manner therefore pray ye: Our Father which art in heaven, Hallowed be thy name.

10 Thy kingdom come. Thy will be done in earth, as it is in heaven.

11 Give us this day our daily bread.

12 And forgive us our debts, as we forgive our debtors.

13 And lead us not into temptation, but deliver us from evil: For thine is the kingdom, and the power, and the glory, for ever. Amen.

14 For if ye forgive men their trespasses, your heavenly Father will also forgive you:

IN FOCUS

Virginia sat at her desk with her hands folded together, head bowed, and eyes closed. It was her lunch hour, and she had decided to forgo her lunch in favor of prayers. She needed to hear from God. After nine years of employment at the university, it looked as if she was going to be fired.

She had transferred into the position only seven months ago when her former job had been phased out. Up until now, her work record had been impeccable. Now her new supervisor was telling her that her work was unsatisfactory. "Dear Lord," she prayed. "Please give me the strength to endure whatever comes my way and help me to have the right attitude, especially toward my supervisor. I trust in You and not the situation. Show me what to do, Lord."

Have you ever had something happen to you that was not in your control? Where did you turn? Today we want to examine God's teachings on prayer.

THE PEOPLE, PLACES, AND TIMES

Prayer. The communication from the heart of man to the ear of God. Throughout the Old and New Testaments, we find God answering the prayers of those people who needed Him. Abel's blood cried out from the dust of the earth, and God heard him and avenged him (Genesis 4:10-12). The Hebrews, while in Egypt, cried out because of their hard taskmasters, and God sent Moses to deliver them (Exodus 3:1—4:17). David prayed for forgiveness and restoration after being caught in sin, and God heard his prayer (Psalm 51). Elisha prayed for his servant's eyes to be opened to see the army of the Lord, and God made it so (2 Kings 6:17). The disciples asked Jesus to teach them to pray after they had watched Him (Luke 11:2-4). Peter prayed, and Tabitha woke up from the dead (Acts 9:40-41). Both faith (Mark 11:24) and forgiveness (Mark 11:25) are needed in order for prayers to be answered.

BACKGROUND

Jesus taught that the true righteousness of the kingdom must be applied in the everyday activities of life. He cautioned against practicing piety to impress other people. Almsgiving was designed to be a display of mercy, but the Pharisees had distorted the showing of mercy by using it to demonstrate their devotion to religious duties in almsgiving and prayer. Giving without fanfare and quietly praying will receive its rewards.

Just as the Pharisees made a public display in giving, so they did in praying also. They prayed in public places to be seen and heard by men. Jesus says they got their reward in the applause of the people. Instead of condemning prayer of this kind, the Lord purified the practice by directing us into a private place to be alone and pray to our Father. Jesus went on to give us an example of how to pray with certain guidelines.

AT-A-GLANCE

1. Our Giving (Matthew 6:1-4)
2. Our Praying (vv. 5-13)
3. Our Forgiving (v. 14)

IN DEPTH

1. Our Giving (Matthew 6:1-4)

Jesus cautioned against practicing piety to impress other people. The righteousness of the Pharisees was insincere and dishonest. They practice their religion for the accolades of the people. They were hypocrites (play-actors or pretenders) who deliberately used religion to promote their own gain. But true righteousness comes from within. We should not practice our giving for the applause of men, but for the reward of God.

Giving to the poor, praying, and fasting were important traditions to the Pharisees. Jesus, however, warns that our hearts should have the right attitude when we practice our giving. If our motive is to gain the praise of men, we have the wrong attitude. But if our motive is to serve God in love and please Him, then we will give our gifts without calling attention to them. Though all giving doesn't necessarily have to be done anonymously, we should not use our giving to make people think we're more spiritual than we really are.

2. Our Praying (vv. 5-13)

Jesus gave instructions to guide us in our praying. He taught that prayer should be done confidentially. It is not wrong to pray in public, but it is not right to pray in public if you are not in the habit of praying in private. It is not wrong to seek God's help or bless our food. Our Lord prayed privately (Mark 1:35); so did Elisha (2 Kings 4:33) and Daniel (Daniel 6:10). We should pray sincerely (Matthew 6:7-8), not using empty phrases, because God knows what we need before we ask. If we repeat our requests, that doesn't make it a vain repetition; it is when we babble without a sincere heart's desire to seek and do God's will (Matthew 6:9-13).

Jesus gave His followers a model prayer known as the Lord's Prayer. We should use this prayer as a pattern; Jesus said to pray after this manner. The purpose of prayer is to glorify God, and these are the guidelines for prayer: (1) it should involve worship, reverence, and exaltation of our Father; (2) it should concern itself with the work God is engaged in, namely, the establishment of God's kingdom and His will being done on earth; (3) it should be concerned with daily needs; (4) it should contain confession and seek forgiveness; and finally (5) it should seek protection and deliverance from the evil one.

Notice this model prayer begins with the phrase "our Father." We put God's concerns first, then we can bring our own needs. This is the God-appointed way of having our needs met because prayer also prepares us for God's answer.

3. Our Forgiving (v. 14)

We must pray with a forgiving spirit toward others. If you do not forgive repentant offenders, God will not forgive you. Christians must be prepared and willing to forgive the offenses of others; if we don't forgive, our prayers are of no avail. If God would answer the prayers of a person who is unforgiving, then He would be encouraging sin. Forgiveness puts you in right relationship with your brothers and sisters and with God. It enables you to pray effectively; therefore, forgiveness is an important part of prayer.

The basic concept of prayer is forgiveness. Forgive your brother and be forgiven. To be forgiven is to be released from all guilt and condemnation. We all need forgiveness. Forgiving means we should not be bitter or hostile, seek revenge, or hold hard feelings against another person. We should not rejoice when others fall on hard times or experience trouble and trials in their lives. Blessed are the merciful, for they shall obtain mercy (Matthew 5:7).

SEARCH THE SCRIPTURES

1. Is giving to gain recognition from men rewarded by God (Matthew 6:4)?

2. To whom should we pray (v. 6)?

3. How is forgiveness connected to prayer (v. 14)?

DISCUSS THE MEANING

1. When a man does good and shows kindness, does it matter to God what his motive is (Matthew 6:1)?

2. If God knows what we have need of, why pray (v. 8)?

3. What is prayer (v. 9)?

LESSON IN OUR SOCIETY

The Pharisees wanted to be seen praying so that people would see how religious they were. They sought the approval of men. We see the same thing today in our churches and on our televisions. Yet more and more people seek answers through psychic hot lines because they do not want to spend the time developing a relationship with their Creator. If we really want answers to today's complex issues, we must ask God because He sees the complete picture from beginning to end.

MAKE IT HAPPEN

Prayer is needed today more than ever. This week, set aside a specific time each day for prayer. Psalm 63:1 says, "Early will I seek thee." Ask the Father to bring to your mind those people who have hurt you or persecuted you. Then ask Him to help you to forgive those people. If you can contact any of them, do so, and resolve whatever differences you may have. Remember, prayer changes things.

FOLLOW THE SPIRIT

What God wants me to do:

_____

_____

REMEMBER YOUR THOUGHTS

Special insights I have learned:

_____

_____

MORE LIGHT ON THE TEXT
Matthew 6:1-14

In this passage, which is part of the Sermon on the Mount, Jesus talks about two important aspects of the Christian life: almsgiving and prayer. The overall theme is these activities of righteousness should be done with the right motivation. If they are done for the benefit and admiration of others, then they accomplish nothing. In fact, those who do this are called hypocrites. They look pious and righteous, but they are seeking to glorify themselves and not God.

1 Take heed that ye do not your alms before men, to be seen of them: otherwise ye have no reward of your Father which is in heaven.

Verse 1 starts with a warning, "Take heed" (be careful), and then tells us not to bring our alms and seek the attention of others as we bring them. If we seek attention, that will be our reward, and we will have no reward from God.

2 Therefore when thou doest thine alms, do not sound a trumpet before thee, as the hypocrites do in the synagogues and in the streets, that they may have glory of men. Verily I say unto you, They have their reward. 3 But when thou doest alms, let not thy left hand know what thy right hand doeth: 4 That thine alms may be in secret: and thy Father which seeth in secret himself shall reward thee openly.

Jesus issued a more specific warning to those who would actually hire trumpeters to precede them as they marched into the temple to present their offerings. He said these are hypocrites and the immediate rush and attention they receive from the crowds are the extent of their reward. Today we do not hire trumpeters, but sometimes we might find ourselves "blowing our own horns," so to speak, by naming the amounts and frequency of our donations. Also, we might expect to be rewarded and acknowledged by those we give to. If so, our names on the pews or the offering plates will be the extent of our reward. Jesus tells us that to give with an expectation of being noticed and rewarded by people is to give with the wrong attitude.

In verse 3, Jesus tells us we should do our giving in secret, keeping secret what we are doing, even from ourselves to some extent. There is a human tendency to brag, even to ourselves sometimes, to tell ourselves what we can expect from God in response to our generosity. Verse 4 emphasizes the importance of "secrecy," which means we should give because it is the right thing to do, not because we will get something out of it. Even though this verse does assure us that if we do give out of the right motives and without seeking attention, God will see and reward us openly.

5 And when thou prayest, thou shalt not be as the hypocrites are: for they love to pray standing in the synagogues and in the corners of the streets, that they may be seen of men. Verily I say unto you, They have their reward. 6 But thou, when thou prayest, enter into thy closet, and when thou hast shut thy door, pray to thy Father which is in secret; and thy Father which seeth in secret shall reward thee openly.

Verses 5-6 apply this same "secrecy" principle to prayer. Jesus declared that praying to impress others makes people into hypocrites. He described the hypocrites as those who found conspicuous places to stand and pray in the synagogue and even on the street corners. Their objective was to have everyone see them and admire their devotion and dedication. Instead, we should go into a secret closet and, even though no one else may know what we are doing, God will see, know, and reward us. This is not to say we should avoid praying in public, but we should not pray to show the public how pious and spiritual we are. Even in public, our motivation should be to glorify and seek God and God alone.

7 But when ye pray, use not vain repetitions, as the heathen do: for they think that they shall be heard for their much speaking. 8 Be not ye therefore like unto them: for your Father knoweth what things ye have need of, before ye ask him.

In verse 7, Jesus continued His instructions about prayer. Not only are we to avoid praying in order to be seen by others, but we are to avoid the practice that was common to the Gentiles of using lots of words to try to impress or manipulate God. The Gentiles had so many gods and so many names for them that they would try to list them all to make sure they included the right one. Also, they would try to flatter the gods in order to convince them to answer the prayer. Jesus said specifically not to be like them. He assures us that God, our Father, the omniscient One, knows already what we need even before we ask. And God cannot be manipulated. God stands ready to answer our prayers and bless us because of the love He has for us.

9 After this manner therefore pray ye: Our Father which art in heaven, Hallowed be thy name.

In verses 9-14, He tells us how we should pray. Jesus gives us the model of prayer we commonly call the Lord's Prayer. It is also recorded in Luke 11:1-4. According to Luke's gospel, Jesus gives this prayer in response to a request from one of the disciples (Luke 11:1). Matthew does not include this request, but he includes a longer and more developed version of the prayer. It was not intended to replace the corporate prayer in the synagogue, but to give His disciples a model for their own private prayer time. Books have been written analyzing this prayer. It is so rich in meaning and subject to various interpretations. Although it is short, it is a powerful model for the way that we should pray in our own prayer closets.

Jesus started by affirming that God is the Father, the one in the heavens. This was typical of many formal Jewish prayers. We know that Jesus referred to God as "Abba," which is an affectionate, familiar term, similar to our current use of the term "dad" or "daddy." It shows the kind of relationship He had with God, the Father. We too should seek to have that same kind of closeness and intimacy in our relationship with God.

Fatherhood is a very sensitive and delicate issue in the African American community. So many forces have conspired, from the lingering effects of slavery to the current evils of racism and other forms of oppression, against African American men. The result is that many homes and families are headed by women. There are some negative feelings associated with the term "father" for this reason and others. So many theologians now are questioning whether we really should address God as Father, since it does evoke such powerfully negative feelings in so many.

But we cannot take away the fact that this is how Jesus addressed God—as Father (Daddy). This picture of what the father/son, father/daughter relationship can be like can guide us as we work to repair the damage and heal the pain in the African American community. The seams of our families can be mended and made strong by using God, the perfect, all-loving, all-caring Father, as a model.

After this opening address, the Lord's Prayer contains seven petitions. There are three "you" or God petitions—things we are praying God will do for His glory. These are followed by four "we" peti-tions—things we want God to do for His children.

The first "you" petition, "Hallowed be thy name," would more accurately be stated, "Let thy name be hallowed." This means that God's name should be sanctified, revered, and considered holy. For Jewish people, the name of God was considered so holy it could not be spoken or even written in its entirety. The name of God was treated with reverence because, for them, it was synonymous with God. For us, the prayer is a request that in all the earth the name of God would speak of God's holiness and kingdom.

10 Thy kingdom come. Thy will be done in earth, as it is in heaven.

This refers to the end times, when there will be fulfillment of all prophecies and expectations. At that time, God's kingdom will prevail, and God will rule and reign on earth as He does in heaven. This is what we look forward to as Christians, and we seek to make it a reality in our daily lives as we wait for the kingdom to come in totality.

The second half of this verse continues with the desire for the coming of the kingdom, that is, God's ultimate will for the earth and humanity. As we pray these words, we have to consider what we are doing day-to-day to bring the kingdom and God's will to fruition on earth.

At this point, the "we" petitions begin as we request things from God.

11 Give us this day our daily bread.

Some scholars have debated over whether this means literal bread in terms of our daily physical needs, or whether "daily bread" should be taken in the spiritual sense, or even in the understanding of what will be consumed at the heavenly banquet. The majority opinion seems to be that when we pray for our daily bread, we are praying to have our physical needs met, as they arise, on a daily basis. It doesn't necessarily mean we will be able to build bigger barns to store it all, but we will have enough for the day.

12 And forgive us our debts, as we forgive our debtors.

Whether we use the word "debts," "trespasses," or "sins," it is pretty clear that we want to be forgiven for the wrong things we do. The flip side of the coin is that we, too, must be willing to forgive the wrongs done to us.

13 And lead us not into temptation, but deliver us from evil: For thine is the kingdom, and the power, and the glory, for ever. Amen.

This is a difficult passage to understand, because it implies God actively "leads" us into temptation. The epistle of James cautions us never to say that God is tempting us (James 1:13-14). Most scholars agree that this means God doesn't allow us to be tempted or tested beyond our ability to persevere. There is a very popular saying people quote, especially in times of trial: "God won't put more on you than you can bear."

Then the prayer continues with a request to be delivered from evil. The more accurate translation of the Greek word *poneros* (**pon-ay-ros**) used here is "evil one." When times of testing do come, as they will, then we pray to be delivered from the evil one—Satan. He comes only to steal, kill, and destroy (John 10:10). These two petitions go together.

Some people feel Christians should not undergo trials and temptations. But Jesus said we would have tribulation in the world (John 16:33). We should be of good cheer in the midst of them, however, because we know that He has overcome the world. So when we are tempted, when we suffer, when we are tossed and driven by the storms of life, we pray for the strength to bear it, to come through it, and to be delivered from the evil one.

14 For if ye forgive men their trespasses, your heavenly Father will also forgive you:

Finally, Jesus goes back to the subject of forgiveness in verse 14. This verse is not part of the prayer, but is included again to emphasize the importance of forgiveness and the fact that it must go two ways in the life of the Christian.

We sing and pray the Lord's Prayer so often that it can become rote and lose its meaning for us. But when we look at it with fresh eyes, it can come alive again and give us, as Jesus intended, clear instructions on how to pray effectively.

How serious are we in wanting God's kingdom to come and His will to be done? Do we live as kingdom people, aware of who and whose we are? How easy or difficult is it for us to forgive others when they do something wrong to us? How satisfied are we with having just our daily needs met, as opposed to all our wants and desires met? These are all questions which arise when we take time to really reflect and meditate on the Lord's Prayer.

DAILY BIBLE READINGS

M: The Importance of Prayer
James 5:13-18
T: Have Faith and Pray
Mark 11:20-25
W: God Answers Prayer
Matthew 7:7-11
T: Perseverance in Prayer
Luke 11:5-13
F: Concerning Almsgiving and Prayer
Matthew 6:1-8
S: The Lord's Prayer
Matthew 6:9-15
S: Concerning Fasting and Treasures
Matthew 6:16-21

Do you have a personal testimony of how God has answered a prayer? Why not share it with the *Precepts* Discussion Group located on your *Precepts For Living* CD-ROM?

TEACHING TIPS

July 17
Bible Study Guide 7

1. Words You Should Know

A. Mysteries (Matthew 13:11) *musterion* (Gk.)—A hidden thing or a secret that is not obvious to many people.

B. Waxed gross (v. 15) *pachuno* (Gk.)—To make thick or to fatten. Metaphorically, it means to make stupid.

C. Converted (v. 15) *epistrepho* (Gk.)—To cause to return or bring back.

2. Teacher Preparation

A. Read the LESSON AIM.

B. Read the DEVOTIONAL READING (Mark 4:10-20) to see how his spiritual walk went from a shallow to a deep-rooted faith.

C. Familiarize yourself with general gardening terminology to better help the students understand the roles that the soil (or heart), pots (situations or circumstances), and weather conditions (trials and tribulations) play in a plant's growth.

D. Bring along two sets of headphones and/or earplugs. Be prepared to discuss how these devices can hinder or foster hearing.

3. Starting the Lesson

A. Open the session with prayer. Thank God for the ability to see and hear eternal truths not perceived by eyes and ears but with and by the Holy Spirit.

B. Ask volunteers to wear the headphones and/or earplugs for at least five minutes.

C. Generate a discussion on pet peeves surrounding hearing and listening, and how technology helps or hinders communication. After five minutes, ask the volunteers to discuss how much of the discussion they heard and understood while wearing the headphones and/or earplugs.

4. Getting into the Lesson

A. Have volunteers read the FOCAL VERSES.

B. Read in unison the LESSON AIM and the KEEP IN MIND verse.

C. It is important for the students to understand that the Word of God is always good seed, but the earth (one's heart) determines how and if it grows. Ask the students to discuss their past or present gardening or farming experience and identify some factors that contribute to their success or failure. Ask the students: How is having a "green thumb" similar to having a hearing heart? How can a person cultivate a heart receptive to the Gospel?

5. Relating the Lesson to Life

A. Have the students read and discuss the IN FOCUS story.

B. Discuss how it relates to today's LESSON AIM.

C. Discuss how technology today helps us better hear the Word of God, and why we should use such resources.

6. Arousing Action

A. Have the students identify the shallow, hard, or thorny areas that hinder the productivity of the Word of God in their lives.

B. Challenge them to tap into the power of the Holy Spirit to help them overcome these areas.

C. Close the session with prayer.

WORSHIP GUIDE

For the Superintendent or Teacher
Theme: The Purpose of the Parables
Theme Song: "Wonderful Words of Life"
Scripture: Matthew 13:9-17
Song: "How Firm a Foundation"
Meditation: Lord, thank You for Your Holy Word. May it always be a lamp unto our feet and a light unto our path. Amen.

THE PURPOSE OF THE PARABLES

Bible Background • MATTHEW 13:1-23
Printed Text • MATTHEW 13:9-17
Devotional Reading • MARK 4:10-20

LESSON AIM

By the end of the lesson, the students will understand that a person's initial receptivity and response to the Word of God directly impacts spiritual growth and development and their ability to endure and overcome trials and temptations.

KEEP IN MIND

"Who hath ears to hear, let him hear" (Matthew 13:9).

FOCAL VERSES

Matthew 13:9 Who hath ears to hear, let him hear.

10 And the disciples came, and said unto him, Why speakest thou unto them in parables?

11 He answered and said unto them, Because it is given unto you to know the mysteries of the kingdom of heaven, but to them it is not given.

12 For whosoever hath, to him shall be given, and he shall have more abundance: but whosoever hath not, from him shall be taken away even that he hath.

13 Therefore speak I to them in parables: because they seeing see not; and hearing they hear not, neither do they understand.

14 And in them is fulfilled the prophecy of Esaias, which saith, By hearing ye shall hear, and shall not understand; and seeing ye shall see, and shall not perceive:

15 For this people's heart is waxed gross, and their ears are dull of hearing, and their eyes they have closed; lest at any time they should see with their eyes, and hear with their ears, and should

---

LESSON OVERVIEW

LESSON AIM
KEEP IN MIND
FOCAL VERSES
IN FOCUS
THE PEOPLE, PLACES, AND TIMES
BACKGROUND
AT-A-GLANCE
IN DEPTH
SEARCH THE SCRIPTURES
DISCUSS THE MEANING
LESSON IN OUR SOCIETY
MAKE IT HAPPEN
FOLLOW THE SPIRIT
REMEMBER YOUR THOUGHTS
MORE LIGHT ON THE TEXT
DAILY BIBLE READINGS

---

understand with their heart, and should be converted, and I should heal them.

16 But blessed are your eyes, for they see: and your ears, for they hear.

17 For verily I say unto you, That many prophets and righteous men have desired to see those things which ye see, and have not seen them; and to hear those things which ye hear, and have not heard them.

IN FOCUS

Jackie lost her hearing following a childhood illness. In the ensuing years, she used hearing aids, determined never to allow her disability to short-circuit her achievements. One day a colleague told her about cochlear ear implants, which could greatly improve her ability to hear and speak clearly.

After much thought, Jackie decided not to have the surgery concluding the device was too new and the risk was too high.

One day as Jackie sat in the kitchen reading the daily newspaper, her son fell into the family pool. Unaware of his distress, Jackie sat quietly and continued to read her paper. Her son's screams for help went unheard. Fortunately, her husband was nearby and heard the child's screams and rescued him from the pool. It was then that she decided to consider her options to improve her hearing. Her goal was to hear better and understand her children, especially when they were out of her sight. Today, with the cochlear implant in her right ear and a hearing aid in the left, she is increasingly able to hear more sound.

Jackie's experience proves that there are varying degrees of hearing. Today, we will discover how Jesus used the parable of the sower to effectively illustrate that point.

THE PEOPLE, PLACES, AND TIMES

Multitudes. Many people flocked to hear Jesus' teaching and to witness and experience His miracles. However, they were not interested in developing long-term relationships or being discipled. To these people, Jesus continually spoke in parables.

Parables. Even back in biblical times, people loved storytelling. In fact, it was one of the major modes of entertainment of that time. Like general stories, parables are entertaining enough to attract crowds. But when told by Jesus, their main purpose was to deliver biblical truth in easy-to-swallow nuggets.

BACKGROUND

Usually referenced by his surname, John Mark was an associate of the apostle Paul and Barnabas. He traveled with them on an early missionary trip, but later turned back (Acts 12:25; 13:13). His seeming desertion led the apostle Paul to deny him the opportunity to partner with him in ministry again. Barnabas disagreed with Paul. When all was said and done, Paul chose to travel with Silas, and Barnabas traveled with Mark. However, the broken fellowship was apparently healed, as evidenced by the apostle Paul's remarks, including his comment to Timothy that Mark "was profitable for ministry" (Colossians 4:10; Philemon 1:24; 2 Timothy 4:11). Mark's ministry journey is illustrative of how, with God's help, we can move from unproductive to productive lives that prove beneficial to ourselves and others.

Farming and fishing were two key industries during Mark's ministry. In his time, farmers scattered seed by hand, which resulted in some landing in undesirable places (the wayside and stony ground). Jesus knew that on one level, the multitudes would understand the sowing and reaping analogy of the parable of the sower. They would

also be familiar with concerns about ground condition, predators, and the like, and their effect upon the harvest. He also knew that despite their religiosity, many among the multitudes were spiritually cold and unresponsive (Matthew 13:14).

> ### AT-A-GLANCE
>
> **1. Sharing Secrets with Friends**
> **(Mark 13:9-12)**
> **2. Looking Beyond Outward Appearances**
> **(vv. 13-15)**
> **3. New Testament Blessings Through**
> **Christ (v. 17)**

IN DEPTH

1. Sharing Secrets with Friends (Mark 13:9-12)

The disciples, having shared many personal and private times with Jesus, knew that He was a master storyteller. Yet because of their personal affiliation, they also knew He could—and often did—speak clearly when He wanted to impart important spiritual truths. Thus, they were confused when Jesus had the opportunity to speak to multitudes (likely tens of thousands), He opted for an obscure language. Jesus explained that He did so because there was an important difference between the multitudes and the disciples. The former were merely curious followers; the latter were close associates and friends. Because of their intimate relationships, they were privy to information—secrets—not shared with the multitudes.

That Jesus made the distinction is important for two reasons. First, it underscores the reality that knowing about Christ and His works is vastly different from knowing Him and sharing in His life (Philippians 3:10). Second, it emphasizes the importance of developing a more intimate relationship with Jesus Christ.

2. Looking Beyond Outward Appearances (vv. 13-15)

Jesus used the analogies of eyes and ears. But it was apparent that He was not speaking about the physical organs or their physical functioning. Actually, He was talking about the people's spiritual condition, as evidenced by hearts that had "waxed gross," or had become callous to spiritual things. This is astonishing when you consider that devout Jews and even teachers of the law were among the multitudes that occasionally followed Him. By their outward piety and job function, it could have been assumed that they were spiritually in tune with God. However, that was not so. Jesus' depiction of the multitudes was a necessary reminder that God's righteousness is an inward matter of the heart. The parable of the sower makes the point that ground that looks good may actually be too shallow, hard, or unresponsive to produce the desired harvest.

3. New Testament Blessings Through Christ (v. 17)

Not only did Jesus want His disciples to know that they were not to judge by outward appearance, He also wanted them to know that they were experiencing a blessing by associating with Him.

Likewise, today we experience blessings through our relationship with Jesus Christ. For "as it is written, Eye hath not seen, nor ear heard, neither have entered into the heart of man, the things which God hath prepared for them that love him. But God hath revealed them unto us by his Spirit: for the Spirit searcheth all things, yea, the deep things of God" (1 Corinthians 2:9-10).

SEARCH THE SCRIPTURES

1. What devoured the seeds on the wayside (Mark 13:4)?

2. Why did the sun scorch the seed that fell on stony places (v. 6)?

3. What did the thorns do to the seed (v. 7)?

4. What happened to the seeds that fell on good ground (v. 8)?

DISCUSS THE MEANING

1. Why did Jesus tell stories like the parable of the sower (Mark 13:13-14)?

2. How does Jesus define "eyes that see and ears that hear" (v. 16)?

LESSON IN OUR SOCIETY

"Did you hear me?" How many times a day do you find yourself asking that question? All kinds of distractions can hinder communication and foster ill will. Take cell phones for example. They were designed to make communication faster and easier, but oftentimes they are major distractions to drivers and pedestrians. They can hinder the owner's ability to perceive—or hear—other things when not used prudently. What other means of communication (i.e., listening to the radio, watching television) may have caused your ears to become dull to His voice?

MAKE IT HAPPEN

Are you listening fully to God, or are your spiritual ears clogged? Have trials, temptations, or cares caused you to tune out the Holy Spirit? Are you ready and willing to be plugged back in by first hearing His call to repentance?

FOLLOW THE SPIRIT

What God wants me to do:

_____

_____

REMEMBER YOUR THOUGHTS

Special insights I have learned:

_____

_____

MORE LIGHT ON THE TEXT
Matthew 13:9-17

The word "parable" comes from the Greek word *parabole* (**par-ab-ol-ay'**). It literally means to place beside for purposes of comparison or illustration. A parable is usually a fictitious story or narrative drawn from nature or human experience that is told to convey some truth, or to illustrate and represent some real-life situation. The use of parables is a common southwest Asian teaching method used to introduce the unfamiliar through the familiar. Parables were often used by Jesus to help explain or convey moral and spiritual truths, which apart from the parable may have been more difficult to understand.

Spiros Zodhiates has observed that Jesus used parables in two ways: (1) "to reveal truth to His disciples...and (2) to veil truth from those whom He knew would not believe even if they understood the meaning of the parable." The disciples' question in Matthew 13:10 suggests that they understood Jesus to be using the parable of the sower to veil a truth that the common people already found difficult to understand. It would appear that the disciples felt that in this instance (vv. 1-9), the meaning of the parable was unclear. Therefore, the disciples questioned why Jesus would speak so clearly to them (i.e., the disciples) and so unclearly to the general public (i.e., those uncommitted to Jesus). Why would Jesus further veil and obscure the truth in a parable? "Why speakest thou unto them in parables?" (v. 10b). Matthew 13:11-17 is Jesus' response to the disciples' question.

Zodhiates, Spiros, ed. *The Complete Word Study Dictionary: New Testament.* Chattanooga, Tenn.: AMG Publishers, 1993. 1097.

9 Who hath ears to hear, let him hear.

Thinking through what one has heard is an important aspect of learning that is often neglected by the learner. This neglect is sometimes motivated not by a failure to understand what is taught, but by unreadiness to act upon what is taught. This is particularly true when what is taught makes demands upon those being taught. For example, people tend to forget, or find difficult to understand, information that calls for a change in their behavior or in their perception of important issues. In the final analysis, learning is more than a matter of understanding; it is also a matter of wanting to understand. Jesus discerns that His hearers, like the people in the prophet Isaiah's days, do not want to understand. They neither think through what they have heard, nor do they want to think through what they have heard. They refuse to believe, to receive divine instruction, and to make a commitment to Jesus. In turn, their refusal to make a commitment to Jesus impeded their capacity to understand His teachings.

Those who do not want to hear what is said rarely understand what is said—even when what is said is simplified and illustrated in a parable. Failure to accept Jesus also hampers one's ability to understand Jesus' parables. Jesus' parables are best understood within the context of a committed relationship with Jesus.

Knowing this, Jesus goes a second mile and pleads with His hearers to give serious consideration to what He has said. Jesus desires that they appropriate what He has said into their own behavior and way of seeing things. Jesus wants His hearers to listen for more than academic reasons. He wants them to think through what they have heard to the extent that it finds expression in their thoughts, behavior, and relationship with Him. If the people are to understand Jesus' parables, they must make a commitment to Him.

Jesus' concern is both implicit and summarized in the idiom, "He that has ears to hear, let him hear."

10 And the disciples came, and said unto him, Why speakest thou unto them in parables?

Unlike the disciples in Mark's gospel, who asked about the parable (Mark 4:10), and unlike the disciples in Luke's gospel, who asked about the meaning of the parable (Luke 8:9), the disciples in Matthew's gospel asked, "Why speakest thou unto them in parables?" It would appear that in Matthew's gospel, the disciples already know the meaning of the parable of the sower. They wanted to know why Jesus chose to further veil in a parable the truth His hearers already found difficult to understand. Therefore, they come to Jesus, presumably in private, wanting to know why Jesus keeps speaking to the uncommitted in parables.

11 He answered and said unto them, Because it is given unto you to know the mysteries of the kingdom of heaven, but to them it is not given.

Jesus' response makes it immediately clear that the disciples are able to understand what those uncommitted to Jesus cannot understand. Knowledge of "the mysteries of the kingdom of heaven" has been given to the disciples. Such knowledge has not been given to those uncommitted to Jesus. The disciples have something that those uncommitted to Jesus do not have. The disciples have the gift of understanding, while those uncommitted to Jesus are void of this gift.

Matthew's emphatic and perfect tense use of the Greek phrase translated as "has been given unto you" denotes that the gift of understanding is not a passing experience. The gift of understanding remains with those who continue in their commitment to Jesus.

The gift of understanding, however, does not necessarily imply immediate understanding of Jesus' parables. Rather, it means that through continued devotion to Jesus, understanding will come. Understanding will come as a gift from God. Matthew's use of the word "mysteries" (from the Greek word *musterion*, **moos-TAY-ree-on**—literally, "to shut the mouth," as to keep a secret) further underscores the fact that the gift of understanding is from God. A mystery is something that only God can work out—that is why it is a mystery.

God works out "the mysteries of the kingdom of heaven." The mysteries God works out, He makes understandable and gives such understanding as a gift for which the disciples should be grateful.

12 For whosoever hath, to him shall be given, and he shall have more abundance: but whosoever hath not, from him shall be taken away even that he hath.

Contrary to popular opinion, this verse is not about possessing material things. It is not about the rich and the poor. Verse 12 is about possessing spiritual truths. Truth properly used by those who possess it grows. Truth that goes unused, or is abused, tends to vanish from the view of those by whom it is misused.

Here Jesus identifies two kinds of persons: (1) those who have received His message and therefore know "the mysteries of the kingdom of heaven," and (2) those who have refused to receive His message and are therefore not fully aware of "the mysteries of the kingdom of heaven." Both will have their reward. Those who have received His message will receive more truth and grow by it. For those who have refused to receive Jesus' message, what limited truth they may have will soon dissipate.

Those who have received His message—namely, the disciples—are warned against taking the gift of understanding for granted. They should consider themselves privileged and behave in ways that express their gratitude. They can do this

by recognizing that while much understanding has been given to them, much more will be given as a result of properly using what they have.

The exact opposite is to be expected by those who have refused to receive Jesus and His message. These people are unable to fully understand the parables of Jesus. Moreover, even the limited understanding afforded them—through Jewish law, for example—"shall be taken away."

This statement from Jesus sounds both a note of warning and a note of encouragement. It is an encouragement to those who make use of the gift of understanding that God has given them. They will receive even greater understanding. It is a warning to those who refuse to accept the whole of Jesus' message because any limited knowledge they may have of Jesus' message will fade from their understanding for lack of use. "And that," says Jesus, "is why I speak to the uncommitted in parables."

13 Therefore speak I to them in parables: because they seeing see not; and hearing they hear not, neither do they understand.

According to Matthew, Jesus speaks to the uncommitted in parables because the uncommitted do not listen or do not want to understand after listening. They are spiritually insensitive. Although seeing, they do not really see; and although hearing, they do not really hear. They do not understand. They are willfully narrow-minded.

Those who willfully set themselves against God cannot understand the message of the parables that come from God through Jesus Christ. While they may be in the habit of seeing and hearing parables and may even appreciate what they see and hear, they have no appreciation for or comprehension of the parables' deeper meanings and message.

The willful narrow-mindedness of the uncommitted is further illustrated by Matthew's reference to Isaiah 6:9-10 in verses 14-15, which follow.

14 And in them is fulfilled the prophecy of Esaias, which saith, By hearing ye shall hear, and shall not understand; and seeing ye shall see, and shall not perceive: 15 For this people's heart is

waxed gross, and their ears are dull of hearing, and their eyes they have closed; lest at any time they should see with their eyes, and hear with their ears, and should understand with their heart, and should be converted, and I should heal them.

Here Matthew records Jesus' appeal to the prophecy of Esaias (Isaiah 6:9-10) in order to further illustrate the narrow-mindedness of the uncommitted. According to Isaiah, "this people's heart is waxed gross, and their ears are dull of hearing, and their eyes they have closed." In essence, they are unwilling to repent and are therefore unable to see, hear, and understand.

Matthew wants his readers to know that the condition of the uncommitted is the result of their own doing (i.e., "their eyes, they have closed"). This is not what God wants for them. Indeed, they were to repent and believe they would see, hear, understand, and be healed.

God always responds to those who turn away from worldliness and self-centeredness, and turn to Him and His ways. Sin is a destructive condition that only God can rectify. When people turn to God in repentance, He heals them of their sinful condition.

Matthew's use of the word "heal" (Gk. *iaomai*, **ee-ah-om-ahee**) normally refers to physical healing, but here is used metaphorically to refer to the healing of moral diseases, such as the healing of a sin-sick soul.

16 But blessed are your eyes, for they see: and your ears, for they hear. 17 For verily I say unto you, That many prophets and righteous men have desired to see those things which ye see, and have not seen them; and to hear those things which ye hear, and have not heard them.

The text now turns to focus not upon the uncommitted, "but" (Gk. adversative) upon the disciples. The disciples are singled out as those who have received and continue to receive God's

blessings: "Blessed are your eyes, for they see: and your ears, for they hear." In other words, God has blessed the disciples in that they are spiritually perceptive and aware. They see, hear, and are making progress in their understanding of "the mysteries of the kingdom of heaven." Indeed, they are seeing, hearing, and in the process of understanding what the prophets before them prophesied. Therefore, the disciples should be grateful to be able to participate in the things "that many prophets and righteous men have desired to see" and hear.

The prophets foretold the things that the disciples were now receiving. What the disciples were experiencing in the ministry of Jesus, the prophets only envisioned. The disciples were, indeed, blessed—as are all those who commit to following Jesus and who read and study His parables.

DAILY BIBLE READINGS

M: Truth in a Parable
Psalm 78:1-7
T: Keep Looking and Listening
Isaiah 6:1-10
W: The Parable of the Sower
Mark 4:1-9
T: The Purpose and Explanation of Parables
Mark 4:10-20
F: Let Anyone with Ears Listen
Matthew 13:1-9
S: Blessed Are Your Eyes and Ears
Matthew 13:10-17
S: The Parable of the Sower Explained
Matthew 13:18-23

What did Jesus and Isaiah really mean when they used the words *understand* and *understanding* (Matthew 13:14-15; Isaiah 6:9)? Find out by using the reference tools in your *Precepts For Living* CD-ROM.

TEACHING TIPS

July 24
Bible Study Guide 8

1. Words You Should Know

A. Reckon (Matthew 18:24) *sunairo* (Gk.)—To bring together; to settle an account.

B. Wroth (v. 34) *orgizo* (Gk.)—To be very angry.

2. Teacher Preparation

A. Begin preparing for this lesson by reading the DAILY BIBLE READINGS throughout the week as a part of your daily devotions. Also, take time to review the DEVOTIONAL READING and read Matthew 1—18.

B. Study the FOCAL VERSES and the lesson commentary in this BIBLE STUDY GUIDE. Then adapt the lesson to best fit your class.

C. Materials needed: Bibles, pencils, pens, and paper.

3. Starting the Lesson

A. Before the students arrive, write the lesson title, The Unforgiving Servant; the AT-A-GLANCE outline; and the word *forgiveness* on the chalkboard.

B. Open the class with prayer, concentrating on the LESSON AIM.

C. Ask the students what comes to their minds when they think of the word *forgiveness.* Allow several students to share their thoughts on forgiveness.

D. Have a student read the IN FOCUS section, and discuss it briefly.

4. Getting into the Lesson

A. BACKGROUND and THE PEOPLE, PLACES, AND TIMES will help the students gain a better understanding of the context for today's lesson. Have two students read these sections, and allow the class to discuss them briefly.

B. Next, divide the students into three groups; assign each group a section of the IN-DEPTH commentary according to the AT-A-GLANCE outline. Have each group read and discuss their section. Then have them prepare and present a dramatized version of their commentary to the class.

Encourage them to be creative, share the main points, and have fun doing it.

C. After the dramatized presentation, do the SEARCH THE SCRIPTURES and DISCUSS THE MEANING questions to promote further understanding of the lesson.

5. Relating the Lesson to Life

A. Have a student read the LESSON IN OUR SOCIETY section. It will help the students see how the lesson applies to our modern-day society.

B. Ask the students to share any insights they may have received from today's lesson.

6. Arousing Action

A. Have the students read the MAKE IT HAPPEN section silently.

B. Give the students time to write the name of the person whom God has impressed on their hearts.

C. Challenge the students to incorporate the MAKE IT HAPPEN suggestion in their own lives.

D. Close the class by praying in unison the prayer the Lord taught His disciples (Matthew 6:9-13).

JULY 24TH

WORSHIP GUIDE

For the Superintendent or Teacher
Theme: The Unforgiving Servant
Theme Song: "Rock of Ages, Cleft for Me"
Scripture: Matthew 18:21-35
Song: "And Can It Be That I Should Gain?"
Meditation: Dear Father, thank You for Your unlimited and unconditional forgiveness. Help me to extend this same type of forgiveness to others. Amen.

THE UNFORGIVING SERVANT

Bible Background • MATTHEW 18:21-35
Printed Text • MATTHEW 18:21-35
Devotional Reading • 2 CORINTHIANS 2:5-11

LESSON AIM

By the end of the lesson, the students will be able to explain Jesus' principle on forgiving one another. The students will also be able to sympathize with those who need forgiveness and determine to share God's love and forgiveness with at least one other person during the coming week.

KEEP IN MIND

"Then the Lord of that servant was moved with compassion, and loosed him, and forgave him the debt" (Matthew 18:27).

FOCAL VERSES

Matthew 18:21 Then came Peter to him, and said, Lord, how oft shall my brother sin against me, and I forgive him? till seven times?

22 Jesus saith unto him, I say not unto thee, Until seven times: but, Until seventy times seven.

23 Therefore is the kingdom of heaven likened unto a certain king, which would take account of his servants.

24 And when he had begun to reckon, one was brought unto him, which owed him ten thousand talents.

25 But forasmuch as he had not to pay, his lord commanded him to be sold, and his wife, and children, and all that he had, and payment to be made.

26 The servant therefore fell down, and worshipped him, saying, Lord, have patience with me, and I will pay thee all.

27 Then the lord of that servant was moved with

LESSON OVERVIEW

LESSON AIM
KEEP IN MIND
FOCAL VERSES
IN FOCUS
THE PEOPLE, PLACES,
AND TIMES
BACKGROUND
AT-A-GLANCE
IN DEPTH
SEARCH THE SCRIPTURES
DISCUSS THE MEANING
LESSON IN OUR SOCIETY
MAKE IT HAPPEN
FOLLOW THE SPIRIT
REMEMBER YOUR THOUGHTS
MORE LIGHT ON THE TEXT
DAILY BIBLE READINGS

compassion, and loosed him, and forgave him the debt.

28 But the same servant went out, and found one of his fellowservants, which owed him an hundred pence: and he laid hands on him, and took him by the throat, saying, Pay me that thou owest.

29 And his fellowservant fell down at his feet, and besought him, saying, Have patience with me, and I will pay thee all.

30 And he would not: but went and cast him into prison, till he should pay the debt.

31 So when his fellowservants saw what was done, they were very sorry, and came and told unto their lord all that was done.

32 Then his lord, after that he had called him, said unto him, O thou wicked servant, I forgave thee all that debt, because thou desiredst me:

33 Shouldest not thou also have had compassion on thy fellowservant, even as I had pity on thee?

34 And his lord was wroth, and delivered him to the tormentors, till he should pay all that was due unto him.

35 So likewise shall my heavenly Father do also unto you, if ye from your hearts forgive not every one his brother their trespasses.

IN FOCUS

Jeremy's mind raced like a VCR on rewind as he sat on a 747 destined for Japan. Twenty-five years ago, Jeremy had flown this same route from the

United States to Japan in order to serve in the United States Navy. Time does heal and brings drastic changes in one's life. During Jeremy's first journey to Japan, he had been young, immature, self-centered, and far from God.

Now, 25 years later, Jeremy had not only grown older, but had grown to experience God's unlimited and unconditional love and forgiveness. It took a drastic tragedy for Jeremy to come to this truth. One night, Jeremy returned home drunk from an evening with his coworkers, and filled with rage, he killed his girlfriend. Although it was an accident, Jeremy spent some time in a military prison. His girlfriend's parents were Christian, God-fearing people. As a result of her parents' love and forgiveness toward him, he didn't have to spend his life in a foreign prison. Their love and forgiveness also led Jeremy to seek the God that they knew.

Jeremy sought and found that Christ's death and Resurrection made it possible for him to experience God's love and forgiveness for all his past sins, even murder. Jeremy now shares his testimony wherever he goes, especially in prisons throughout the world. Flying to Japan 25 years later is giving Jeremy a chance to share God's love and forgiveness in the same prison where he had served time. Jeremy had experienced God's love and forgiveness and wanted others to know the same. God's love and forgiveness are the focus of our study this week.

THE PEOPLE, PLACES, AND TIMES

Forgiveness. The concept of forgiveness during Jesus' time was connected with atonement and God's grace. When the word *forgive* was used, it implied that atonement was made. The atonement was possible because of a holy sacrifice. This sacrifice was possible only because Christ shed His holy blood as the means of making atonement with God (Leviticus 17:11). God's forgiveness, therefore, is only possible because of His grace. Forgiveness is rooted in the nature of God as gracious.

Jesus' birth, life, death, and Resurrection brought a new dimension to forgiveness. Our forgiveness rests on God's grace through the atoning work of Christ. The atoning work of Christ makes it possible for all men to practice unlimited forgiveness.

BACKGROUND

In the middle of His fourth discourse to the disciples and the multitudes, Jesus began talking about man's relationship with one another (Matthew 18:15). He presented the procedure on how Christians should work out disputes among themselves. If a problem can't be resolved between two Christians, they should have one or two other Christians listen to the problem. If the problem is still not resolved, one must then bring it to the church. If the Christian in the wrong still refuses to follow the church's resolutions, then he should be treated as one who doesn't know God. Jesus concludes this teaching on relationships between Christians by reminding them that if two or three come together and pray in His Name, it will be done (Matthew 18:20).

It was this teaching on resolving disputes with other Christians that led Peter to ask the question in Matthew 18:21 about the number of times one should forgive another.

AT-A-GLANCE

1. Unlimited Forgiveness
(Matthew 18:21-22)
2. A Forgiving King (vv. 23-27)
3. An Unforgiving Servant (vv. 28-35)

IN DEPTH

1. Unlimited Forgiveness (Matthew 18:21-22)

"Forgiveness" is often defined as treating the one who is forgiven as though the offense was not committed. It also involves declaring that one does not harbor malice or unkindness toward the other person. Jesus often taught about forgiveness for one another. Apparently, Peter listened carefully to Jesus' teaching concerning the forgiveness of a brother (vv. 15-20). He desired further explanation on the number of times one should forgive another person. He asked Jesus, "Lord, how oft shall my brother sin against me, and I forgive him? till seven times?" (v. 21).

Identifying the number of times one should forgive another person is probably derived from a Jewish custom that teaches one should forgive another three times, but not the fourth. Peter asked if the number should be increased to seven times. He thought that he was being generous when he suggested "till seven times." But Jesus' response clarified that the issue is not the number of times. The issue is that one should give unlimited forgiveness to others. He said, "I say not unto thee, Until seven times: but, Until seventy times seven." Although seventy times seven equals 490 times, Jesus did not intend for Peter to take his answer in any exact mathematical sense. He clearly meant unlimited forgiveness. We are not to limit our forgiveness to any fixed number of times. We must continually extend forgiveness to one another.

2. A Forgiving King (vv. 23-27)

Jesus often used parables, which are stories related to everyday living, to illustrate a truth that He wanted to teach. Here, He uses the parable about the relationship between a king and his servant. Jesus began by stating, "Therefore"; that is, since there is unlimited forgiveness in the kingdom of heaven, let us look at an example of unlimited forgiveness on earth.

A king desired to settle his accounts with his servants, but he discovered that one of the servants could not settle a large debt. The servant's debt was 10 thousand talents (v. 24). A talent was a sum of money, or weight of silver or gold, amounting to three thousand shekels. If the servant owed 10 thousand silver talents, he owed over 15 million dollars. His debt was immensely large.

The king ordered that the servant, his family, and his possessions be sold into slavery in order to repay the debt. He was following an ancient custom among the Hebrews that settled debts (see Leviticus 25:39; 2 Kings 4:1).

But the servant fell upon his knees before him and pleaded, "Lord, have patience with me, and I will pay thee all" (v. 26). The king was moved with compassion, took pity upon him, and canceled the indebtedness (v. 27). He knew that the ser-

vant could never fully repay his debt. Therefore, looking at the distressed situation that the family was in, he forgave the whole debt. The king demonstrated unlimited forgiveness. The king's response parallels God's response to man's request for forgiveness. God, in His mercy, forgives our sins because we can never repay the debt we owe to Him. And God continually demonstrates unlimited forgiveness to us when we confess.

3. An Unforgiving Servant (vv. 28-35)

When a wrong is done to a man, his memory is often too short. This was the manner in which the king's servant, who was shown great mercy and forgiveness, dealt with another servant who owed him money. The king's servant soon discovered that one of his fellow servants owed him a hundred denarii (v. 28). A "denarii" was a Roman coin totaling 15 to 20 dollars. This was a small amount compared to what the first servant had been forgiven by the king. Instead of his showing mercy to his fellow servant, he took him by the throat and said, "Pay me that thou owest" (v. 28). This fellow servant also fell to his knees and begged him to be patient with him until he could repay his debt (v. 29).

One would think that the first servant would have sympathized with his fellow servant from his own experience, but he did not. Instead, he threw the fellow servant into prison until the debt was paid. Those who observed his behavior were shocked. They knew the mercy and the forgiveness which had been demonstrated to him by the king. Therefore, the fellow servants went to the king and told him everything that had happened (v. 31).

The king immediately sent for the first servant. Upon the servant's arrival, the king said, "O thou wicked servant, I forgave thee all that debt, because thou desiredst me: Shouldest not thou also have had compassion on thy fellowservant, even as I had pity on thee?" (vv. 32-33). The king called him "wicked" and reminded him of the mercy and forgiveness that he had received concerning his own debt. The king was angry and showed no more mercy to him this time. Instead, he had the unforgiving servant delivered to the "tormentors, till he should pay all that was due unto him" (v. 34).

Jesus summarized the parable's principle on forgiveness by closing with the statement, "So likewise shall my heavenly Father do also unto you, if ye from your hearts forgive not every one his brother their trespasses" (v. 35). In other words, if we desire to experience God's forgiveness, we must be willing to forgive others, forever. God has unconditionally forgiven our multitude of sins. How much more should we be able to forgive the wrong done to us by someone else? We are instructed to forgive from our hearts, which implies that we cannot harbor a grudge against another person and say that we have forgiven him. We are commanded to forgive each other with unlimited forgiveness, just as God has forgiven us.

SEARCH THE SCRIPTURES

1. Peter asked if he should forgive his brothers up to *SEVEN* times (Matthew 18:21).

2. The king wanted to *SETTLE* his accounts with his servants (vv. 23-24).

3. The king took *pity* on his servant who could not pay him back (v. 27).

4. But the first servant *fell* to take pity on his fellow servant who owed him (v. 30).

5. God will not show forgiveness to us if we do not show *forgiveness* to others (v. 35).

DISCUSS THE MEANING

1. What did Jesus mean when He said that we should forgive "seventy times seven" (Matthew 18:22)?

2. Why were the other servants disgusted with the first servant's behavior (v. 31)?

3. What is meant by the statement, "So likewise shall my heavenly Father do also unto you" (v. 35)?

LESSON IN OUR SOCIETY

The debates on capital punishment find Christians and non-Christians on both sides of the issue. After our lesson today on unlimited forgiveness, one wonders if Christians should be against capital punishment. We, as Christians, should be able to demonstrate unlimited forgiveness to those who have done us wrong, whether they repent or not.

Yes, even when a person refuses to repent, as one who has experienced God's unconditional forgiveness, we must demonstrate unconditional forgiveness.

MAKE IT HAPPEN

The world doesn't understand how Christians can practice unlimited and unconditional forgiveness. But God has given us His Holy Spirit, who gives us power to practice unlimited and unconditional forgiveness. Pray, asking God to teach you how to practice it as a way of life. Then think of one person at your job, school, or in your neighborhood who does not know about God's love and forgiveness. Ask God to give you an opportunity to share it with that specific person this week.

FOLLOW THE SPIRIT

What He wants me to do:

_____

_____

REMEMBER YOUR THOUGHTS

Special insights I have learned:

_____

_____

MORE LIGHT ON THE TEXT
Matthew 18:21-35

Jesus has just finished teaching the disciples how to deal with disputes in the church, where one brother has offended another. First, the one offended is to directly approach the one who has caused the offense for settlement. If that does not work, the one offended is to bring in two witnesses. If that fails, the church is to be involved. If the offender refuses to change, then he should be disciplined (vv. 15-17). In verses 18-20, Jesus speaks of the power the church has because of His permanent presence in it.

21 Then came Peter to him, and said, Lord, how oft shall my brother sin against me, and I forgive him? till seven times? 22 Jesus saith unto him, I say not unto thee, Until seven times: but, Until seventy times seven.

Matthew introduces the next sequence of

events with the conjunction "then" (Gk. *tote*) and links the preceding event with the ones that follow. *Tote* is used to introduce that which follows in time, and therefore can be rendered "at that time" or "after that" and so on. Perhaps, prompted by the teaching of forgiveness, Peter approaches Jesus and asks a follow-up question about forgiveness using a practical example. The issue is not referring to the decision of the church, but personal forgiveness (compare Matthew 6:14-15; Mark 11:25; Luke 17:3-4). "How oft shall my brother sin against me, and I forgive him?" Peter asks, and interjects, "Till seven times?" In the rabbinical community, the agreement was that a brother might be forgiven for a repeated sin three times; after that, there is no forgiveness.

Why did Peter come up with seven? Is he trying to be magnanimous by suggesting "seven times"? Alternatively, is he following a common thread of the use of seven in the Bible? It is generally suggested that the number seven indicates completeness, using the Genesis creation account as the basis (Genesis 2:1-3; compare Leviticus 4:6; 26:21; Numbers 19:4; Joshua 6:4; Proverbs 24:16). The Greek word translated as "my brother" is *adelphos* and refers to a blood-related sibling or anyone of the same religious society, as in verse 15.

Jesus' reply, "I say not unto thee," suggests that this situation had been discussed earlier and perhaps Peter had not understood it clearly. Jesus then says, not "seven times," but "until seventy times seven." In Luke 17:3-4, Jesus says, "If thy brother trespass. . . .against thee seven times in a day, and seven times in a day turn again to thee, saying, 'I repent; thou shalt forgive him'."

What does Jesus mean by "seventy times seven?" Reading it with a Greek or English understanding, "seventy times seven" equals 490, but with the Roman numerals LXX, which renders Hebrew, it means 70 plus 7 or 77. Jesus alludes to Genesis 4:24, transforming Lamech's revenge into a principle for forgiveness. However, in this context, Jesus is not setting 490 or 77 times as the upper limit for forgiveness, but teaches that frequency or quantity should not qualify regarding forgiveness. The parable that follows vividly illustrates the extent, rather than the frequency, of forgiveness. It further shows that we are forgiven far more than we can ever forgive.

23 Therefore is the kingdom of heaven likened unto a certain king, which would take account of his servants.

Jesus illustrates His point with a parable. "Therefore," since Jesus requires His disciples to forgive those who offend them, the kingdom of heaven can be compared to a king who removes the record of his debtors.

God is represented in the parable by an earthly king. Those in the kingdom are the servants (Gk. *doulos*), literally "slaves," serving a great king. The servants may include high-ranking officials in a huge colonial empire, since the sum of the amount owed is huge (v. 24). The king decides to "take account" (Gk. *sunairo*, **soon-ah'-ee-ro**), which means "to compare accounts" (see also 25:19).

24 And when he had begun to reckon, one was brought unto him, which owed him ten thousand talents. 25 But forasmuch as he had not to pay, his lord commanded him to be sold, and his wife, and children, and all that he had, and payment to be made. 26 The servant therefore fell down, and worshipped him, saying, Lord, have patience with me, and I will pay thee all.

One of the officials who owes ten thousand talents is brought to the attention of the king. One "talent" (Gk. *talanton*) is about 75 pounds. In today's currency, a talent of gold would be worth about $29,085.00; therefore 10,000 talents would be worth $290,085,000.00. A talent of silver is estimated at $1,920.00, and 10,000 talents would be worth $19,920,000. Given the fluctuating price of precious metals, coupled with inflation, these figures would run into tens of millions of dollars. However, the amount is used to compare the extent of the forgiveness and mercy shown to the servant-debtor and the amount owed to him by his fellow servant to whom he shows no mercy.

The servant appears before the king and is not able to pay the king what he owes. The king orders that he, his family (his wife and children), and all their possessions be sold to recover the debt. The practice of being sold into slavery for a debt is consistent with the practice in Old

Testament times (Leviticus 25:39; 2 Kings 4:1). It is the most severe and humiliating punishment for anyone to endure. The aim of selling the entire family is not to recover the full amount owed, but to punish. If the top price for a slave is one talent or less, as some suggest, then the total price of the family would not be enough to cover the debt. This is a punishment, and such slaves, therefore, must be freed in the year of jubilee (Leviticus 25:10, 28).

The servant, desperate and hopeless, falls down on his knees and pleads for time. "Be patient with me, I will pay back everything," he says. The phrase "fell down, and worshiped him" comes from the Greek word *proskuneo*, which also means to go on one's knees, to kneel before someone, or to prostrate oneself in homage (Matthew 20:20). The servant's falling down and worshiping serves a dual purpose: Paying homage is a sign of a desperate plea to his lord (master). As we noted last week, this honor is reserved for kings and people of higher positions in society.

27 Then the lord of that servant was moved with compassion, and loosed him, and forgave him the debt.

Seeing his desperation, helplessness, and inability to pay such a huge amount, his lord is moved with compassion and forgives him of the whole amount he owed. To be "moved with compassion" (Gk. *splagchnizomai*, **splangkh-nid'-zom-ahee**) means "to have sympathy" or "to pity." The king is moved with pity, and he forgives him the "debt" (Gk. *daneion*, **dan'-i-on**), which is better translated as "loan." The lord treats the debt as a bad loan and writes it off. The servant doesn't have to pay it back. He is totally freed from any obligation.

The phrase "loosed him" (Gk. *apoluo*) means "to untie"; it suggests that he was arrested and bound before being brought before the king and was completely released (set free) when the king forgave him. In this case, the debt was treated at first as embezzlement, but now the king cancels it like a bad loan and forgives the servant.

28 But the same servant went out, and found one of his fellowservants, which owed him an hundred pence: and he laid his hands on him, and

took him by the throat, saying, Pay me that thou owest. 29 And his fellowservant fell down at his feet, and besought him, saying, Have patience with me, and I will pay thee all. 30 And he would not: but went and cast him into prison, till he should pay the debt.

Verses 28-31 give a completely opposite picture of verses 24-27. The servant who received mercy from his master for the huge amount of "money" owed shows no mercy to his fellow servant who owed a few talents. The Lord links the preceding story with the conjunction, "but," which immediately strikes a note of contrast with and introduces the next phase of the parable.

Having been forgiven his debt, the servant probably rushes out of the king's court with celebration of joy. He finds another servant, lower in rank than he, in the outer courtyard, who owes him 100 "pence" (i.e., 100 denarii, NIV). One penny is the equivalent of $0.17, and one hundred pence is $17.00. The amount might be high, based on their standard, but it was very insignificant when compared with the amount forgiven him.

Immediately, he mercilessly grabs the servant by the throat, choking him and demanding that the debt be paid immediately. His fellow servant pleads with him to be patient with him and says that he will eventually pay him everything he owes. The similarity of the plea (v. 29) to his own plea to the king (v. 26) does not move this unforgiving man. Rather than showing mercy, he has him thrown into a debtor's prison and orders that he be remanded there until he pays the amount in full.

31 So when his fellowservants saw what was done, they were very sorry, and came and told unto their lord all that was done.

The other servants, who witnessed what had happened, are distressed at such cruelty, and go out to report to the master. The phrase "they were very sorry" is the Greek phrase *elupethesan sphodra*, which means "greatly grieved." They are not merely sorry, but are severely touched in the heart to the point of grieving. They are not merely sympathetic; they empathize with the fellow servant, and show it by reporting it to their master.

The word rendered as "told" (Gk. *diasapheo*) is a strong verb, which means "to explain" or "to narrate." It is used only twice in the New Testament—here and in Matthew 13:36. They explain in detail what the unforgiving servant has done.

32 Then his lord, after that he had called him, and said unto him, O thou wicked servant, I forgave thee all that debt, because thou desiredst me: 33 Shouldest not thou also have had compassion on thy fellowservant, even as I had pity on thee? 34 And his lord was wroth, and delivered him to the tormentors, till he should pay all that was due unto him.

On hearing this report, the master calls in the unforgiving servant and reprimands him, denouncing him for what he has done and calling him a "wicked servant." He asks him why he cannot forgive his fellow servant as he has been forgiven. Of course, he has no answer, and the master expects no answer. There is no amount of explanation that would exonerate him for his wicked action.

The master is so upset that instead of selling him (v. 25), he turns him over to the "tormentors" (Gk. *basanistes*), which means "torturers." The word refers to jailers who have charge of the prisoners and who torture them when asked to do so. The servant was to be tortured in prison until he paid back all that he owed, which was impossible.

35 So likewise shall my heavenly Father do also unto you, if ye from your hearts forgive not every one his brother their trespasses.

Jesus concludes the parable by comparing the reaction of the master to the unmerciful servant with what God will do to those who do not forgive others their trespasses. This parable demonstrates the necessity of forgiveness and how we should treat one another. Jesus advocates that we forgive from our "hearts" those who have wronged us. The phrase "from your heart" here means genuine and sincere forgiveness. Concluding His teaching on prayer, Jesus tells His disciples that they ought to forgive others, as they have been forgiven, lest our Father will not forgive your sins (Matthew 6:12, 14-15).

This parable, as we have already said, does not deal with the frequency but with the extent of forgiveness we have received from our Heavenly Father through the death of His Son. We are forgiven far more than we can ever forgive. Therefore, as Christians, we have been forgiven much, and we should forgive much.

DAILY BIBLE READINGS

M: We Sin, But God Forgives
Daniel 9:3-10
T: God Does Forgive Our Sins
Psalm 32:1-5
W: God Is a Forgiving God
Psalm 86:1-7
T: You Must Forgive
Luke 17:1-5
F: Forgive the Offender
2 Corinthians 2:5-11
S: About Forgiveness
Matthew 18:21-27
S: The Unforgiving Servant
Matthew 18:28-35

Use your *Precepts For Living* CD-ROM to quickly find all the places that "forgive" and "forgiveness" occur in the Bible.

TEACHING TIPS

July 31
Bible Study Guide 9

1. Words You Should Know

A. Separate (Matthew 25:2) *aphorizo* (Gk.)—A formal parting. Also, to remove from a mixture or combination; to isolate.

B. Righteous (v. 37) *dikaios* (Gk.)—Morally upright; just.

2. Teacher Preparation

A. Study the DEVOTIONAL READING and the FOCAL VERSES three times, utilizing different translations so that you can respond to the students' questions.

B. Meditate on Matthew 25 and bring three different translations to class.

C. Be prepared to share with your students an experience in which you ministered to the less fortunate.

D. Materials needed: Bibles, pens, and paper.

3. Starting the Lesson

A. Open the class with prayer and ask God for clarity and understanding.

B. Have three students read the FOCAL VERSES in different translations.

C. Ask the students to share their ideas on ministering to the less fortunate and to tell how often, if at all, they get involved with helping these people.

4. Getting into the Lesson

A. Have the students read the IN FOCUS and BACKGROUND sections. Discuss how the information relates to the lives of your students.

B. Read the IN DEPTH section. Have the students discuss whether the information changes their focus regarding ministry to the less fortunate.

5. Relating the Lesson to Life

A. Have the students read the LESSON IN OUR SOCIETY section.

B. Ask the students to complete the SEARCH THE SCRIPTURES and DISCUSS THE MEANING questions. Discuss how they would change their goals to include helping the needy.

6. Arousing Action

A. Give the students paper divided into three columns labeled PAST, PRESENT, and FUTURE. Under each heading, have the students list activities that include sharing with the less fortunate.

B. After the students complete the activity, have them share what they wrote and how they could do some things differently in the future (i.e., implement a change from their past and present activities).

C. Close with prayer.

FINAL ACCOUNTING

Bible Background • MATTHEW 25:31-46
Printed Text • MATTHEW 25:31-46
Devotional Reading • LUKE 6:27-31

LESSON AIM

By the end of the lesson, the students will learn that how they treat others is a direct reflection on how they treat Christ; they will learn the difference between serving self and serving God; and they will decide to put into practice Christ's teachings presented in this text.

KEEP IN MIND

"And the King shall answer and say unto them, Verily I say unto you, Inasmuch as ye have done it unto one of the least of these my brethren, ye have done it unto me" (Matthew 25:40).

LESSON OVERVIEW

LESSON AIM
KEEP IN MIND
FOCAL VERSES
IN FOCUS
THE PEOPLE, PLACES, AND TIMES
BACKGROUND
AT-A-GLANCE
IN DEPTH
SEARCH THE SCRIPTURES
DISCUSS THE MEANING
LESSON IN OUR SOCIETY
MAKE IT HAPPEN
FOLLOW THE SPIRIT
REMEMBER YOUR THOUGHTS
MORE LIGHT ON THE TEXT
DAILY BIBLE READINGS

FOCAL VERSES

Matthew 25:31 When the Son of man shall come in his glory, and all the holy angels with him, then shall he sit upon the throne of his glory:

32 And before him shall be gathered all nations: and he shall separate them one from another, as a shepherd divideth his sheep from the goats:

33 And he shall set the sheep on his right hand, but the goats on the left.

34 Then shall the King say unto them on his right hand, Come, ye blessed of my Father, inherit the kingdom prepared for you from the foundation of the world:

35 For I was an hungred, and ye gave me meat: I was thirsty, and ye gave me drink: I was a stranger, and ye took me in:

36 Naked, and ye clothed me: I was sick, and ye visited me: I was in prison, and ye came unto me.

37 Then shall the righteous answer him, saying, Lord, when saw we thee an hungred, and fed thee? or thirsty, and gave thee drink?

38 When saw we thee a stranger, and took thee in? or naked, and clothed thee?

39 Or when saw we thee sick, or in prison, and came unto thee?

40 And the King shall answer and say unto them, Verily I say unto you, Inasmuch as ye have done it unto one of the least of these my brethren, ye have done it unto me.

41 Then shall he say also unto them on the left hand, Depart from me, ye cursed, into everlasting fire, prepared for the devil and his angels:

42 For I was an hungred, and ye gave me no meat: I was thirsty, and ye gave me no drink:

43 I was a stranger, and ye took me not in: naked, and ye clothed me not: sick, and in prison, and ye visited me not.

44 Then shall they also answer him, saying, Lord, when saw we thee an hungred, or athirst, or a stranger, or naked, or sick, or in prison, and did not minister unto thee?

45 Then shall he answer them, saying, Verily I say unto you, Inasmuch as ye did it not to one of the least of these, ye did it not to me.

46 And these shall go away into everlasting punishment: but the righteous into life eternal.

IN FOCUS

Anita and Dena were sisters who lived within a block of each other. Their parents were deceased, and they made their homes in their grandmother's and mother's homes, which had been built by their father. The homes had served their purpose. They were places where strangers and guests alike were welcomed. There was always a home-cooked meal for anyone who crossed the threshold. The sisters were keeping the family tradition, but the collapse of their houses and the neighborhood was forcing them to move. The houses were deteriorating faster than they could be repaired. Drug dealers had moved into the neighborhood, all the older neighbors had died, and the environment was just not the same.

Trying to let go of the past and look to the future, the sisters started searching for new homes for their families. Not wanting to separate, they looked for homes in the same community. A member of Anita's church called her one day and said she had located a new home for her and her sister in a new community. After much prayer and deliberation about whether to stay or leave their family homes, the sisters were led to move to the new community. They were the last to leave their beloved neighborhood.

The new community had love, peace, and families who cared about each other. Just as they had for those they left behind, the sisters once again opened their doors to those in need. The gunshots that rang out at night, the drug dealers who invaded their neighborhoods, and the gangbangers who caused their children and families to fear for their very lives were no longer there. God had separated them from the evil and brought them back into a place of peace.

THE PEOPLE, PLACES, AND TIMES

Parable of the Sheep and the Goats. God's judgment on the nations (Matthew 25:32) was a standard part of Jewish expectations for the future. God would ultimately separate the "sheep" from the "goats," but the distinction between the two groups can be seen in various contrasts. For instance, the sheep and goats graze together; however, shepherds in Palestine separated them at night because sheep preferred the outdoors, while goats needed to be kept in a warm place. Sheep were of higher value, while goats were regarded as a lower-value stock. In

some instances, sheep represent good and goats represent trouble—thus, the comparison in Matthew 25:33. With these examples in mind, we can understand why Jesus used sheep and goats in His parable about separation and judgment.

Righteous Deeds. Jesus gave a list of standard righteous deeds found in covenant ethics and which included visiting the incarcerated (vv. 35-36). Terms of the Old Covenant also included visiting the sick, helping the poor, and welcoming strangers into one's home. Caring for the less fortunate was so important that it was considered like treating Christ in the same manner.

BACKGROUND

The judgment of the sheep and goats occurs to determine who may enter the kingdom of God. The basis of the judgment is the relationship of men to Christ as demonstrated by their treatment of those who are in need (Matthew 25:34-36). Those who are saved (sheep) enter the kingdom prepared for them (v. 34), while the lost (goats) go away into "everlasting punishment" (hell, v. 46). In the end, the kingdom consists only of the saved.

AT-A-GLANCE

1. The Great Appearing
(Matthew 25:31)
2. The Great Division
(vv. 32-40)
3. The Great Condemnation
(vv. 41-46)

IN DEPTH

1. The Great Appearing (Matthew 25:31)

Jesus uses His Second Coming as the basis for this teaching. The great appearing of Jesus serves as an entrance into active Christian compassion. Unlike other places where Jesus uses mainly parables, in this passage Jesus combines the idea that He will literally come back.

Several things come to the forefront in this

passage. First, the text states, "When the Son of man shall come." Although we do not know when, the time has been set. Next, the Second Coming will be "in his glory." Jesus came the first time clothed in a veil of flesh, wrapped in swaddling clothes, and sleeping in a manger. But this time His glorious reflection will be splendidly displayed to the ends of the earth. Finally, He will come with "all the holy angels with him." When Jesus came the first time, the angels sang and glory filled the heavens. However, in this great appearing, all the holy angels will be with Him. Can you imagine tens of millions of angels with Him? What a glorious sight! The fact that they are with Him also tells us that they will be at His command, and He will not hesitate to use the power at His disposal.

This time Jesus is not coming to serve, but to receive the service due to Him. The text tells us that "then shall he sit upon the throne of his glory." The throne clearly indicates His lordship and royalty. Though He is coming in glory, He is at rest in His display of power. Only Christ can appear with such power, yet remain seated.

At Jesus' first coming, very few came to worship Him (shepherds, wise men). This time, all the nations shall be gathered before the presence of the One who sits on the throne.

2. The Great Division (vv. 32-40)

When Jesus appears, there will be a great division. We read that He will separate the people one from another as the shepherd divides the sheep from the goats. Jesus uses the symbolic language of a parable to refer to the separation of evil men from good men, or people of faith from unbelievers, as separating His "sheep" from the "goats."

All nations, whether powerful or powerless, will stand before His throne to be judged. This judgment will not be based on earthly possessions or racial superiority, but on whether they belong to Him. The basis of the division is participation in the nature of Christ. One cannot help but think back to the fact that as the Lamb of God, Jesus is implying that the sheep share in His nature. By not saying "his goats," but rather "the goats," Jesus sets them apart already.

What makes the sheep His sheep? It is implied here that they are participants in His nature—they have His character. Furthermore, it means that they belong to Him. Hence, the use of the possessive pronoun—they are His, they belong to Jesus. The "goats" are not His. By their very nature they remain outside His nature. Recall Jesus' rebuke of the Jews: "You are of your father the devil." Therefore, the division is based on whose spiritual DNA one has. The goats do not share in the transforming spiritual genes provided by the Lamb of God.

Not only were they separated by participation according to their nature, they were also separated based on their manifest character. These two groups are separated based on what they did or did not do. Many people claim to be born of God, but do not act accordingly. Those who have been infused with the new nature from the Son of man will show they belong to Him by their active compassion. The Shepherd does not ask them what they did because He already knows what they did based on their connection to Him. Rather, the judge states exactly what separates them from the sheep.

He says several things. First, He invites the sheep to Himself with, "Come, ye blessed of my Father." The invitation affirms them as members of His family. Second, He invites them to "inherit the kingdom prepared for you from the foundation of the world." The fact that He calls it an inheritance shows that He sees them as joint heirs and not strangers. This connection by itself separates them from the pain of judgment (see Romans 8:1). This inheritance, which has been prepared from the foundation of the world, reminds us of why God created humanity in the beginning and of His generous offer to Adam to become the ruler of all that God made. The group that He metaphorically calls "sheep" are now to inherit what God prepared from the foundation of the world.

3. The Great Condemnation (vv. 41-46)

Jesus will say to those on the left, who are parabolically referred to as goats, "Depart from me," while in direct contrast His word to the sheep is, "Come." This command to depart has the ring of finality to it and can be traced back to the fact that this group had also rejected Him. Those who refuse to participate in His nature and who will not become related to Him will hear, "Depart from me."

Second, unlike their counterparts who have been blessed, He says, "Ye cursed." To be cursed by God is dangerous. God has nothing good to say about them because they chose a nature that contradicts God's nature and thereby rejected the new nature, which was freely given to them in Christ Jesus.

Third, they were to go "into everlasting fire" (v. 41). The duration of their departure is not merely for a millennium, but "everlasting." Thus, they have chosen for themselves eternal separation from God.

Oh, that we understood the danger of being separated from God. Note that in this text, the Shepherd separates them from their fellow human beings and then separates them from Himself. What a separation! But here is the clincher: This is not just a departure into nothingness, but a departure into fire, pain, and everlasting suffering. This place was prepared for the devil and his angels. These people, who have willingly participated in the nature of the devil, are eternally separated from their divine inheritance and destiny.

There are exactly five types of need which the King uses as the basis of the judgment. Those who are pronounced as blessed are defined by their actions of compassion and outreach. They gave openly to strangers, covered the naked, and went to visit others they reached beyond themselves, showing the character of Jesus.

No doubt the goats would have cared for those around them if there was a clear manifestation that this was indeed Christ clothed as a beggar. Both the believers and nonbelievers would have fed the hungry, given water to the thirsty, taken the stranger in, clothed the naked, and visited the sick and the imprisoned if they knew it was Jesus. But the basic difference is, those who had His nature were naturally drawn to care for others, even without knowing it was actually Jesus they were serving.

We must treat everyone in need as we would

treat the Lord. Jesus comes to us in such ways that we do not readily recognize Him. We are called to care for the least of these, for Jesus is very clear that He represents them and that our treatment of them reflects our treatment of Him. Our giving and our caring must grow out of the fact that we are His. Are you reflecting the nature of Jesus? What distinguishes those who have the nature of Jesus from the world is our propensity toward showing care for others.

SEARCH THE SCRIPTURES

1. "And _____ shall set the _____ on his _____ hand, but the _____ on the _____" (Matthew 25:33).

2. "_____, and ye _____ me: I was _____, and ye _____ me: I was in _____, and ye _____ unto me" (v. 36).

3. "Then shall the _____ answer him, saying, Lord, when saw we thee an _____, and _____ thee? or _____, and gave thee _____?" (v. 37).

4. "Then shall he say also unto them on the _____ hand, _____ from me, ye _____, into _____ _____, prepared for the _____ _____ _____ _____" (v. 41).

5. "I was a _____, and ye took me not in: _____, and ye _____ me not: _____, and in _____, and ye _____ me not" (v. 43).

DISCUSS THE MEANING

1. Have you ever been approached by someone in the street asking for food? Why did you decide to give or not give them food or money?

2. For Thanksgiving or Christmas, have you ever volunteered to serve food or spend time with people who do not have a home or family? Have you ever volunteered at any other time?

3. Have you ever visited anyone in prison or in the hospital? Did you go because you felt obligated to or because you really cared about them?

4. Have you ever cared for anyone you really didn't know because they were in need? Do you always have to know the circumstances of the person and the legitimacy of the problem before you help them?

5. What is the distinction between the sheep and the goats? Which group do you belong to?

We show love for Christ by doing for others.

LESSON IN OUR SOCIETY

There are people in our communities that need our help. We don't see them because we view them as part of the landscape. We wish they would go away, but Jesus taught us that "inasmuch as ye have done it unto one of the least of these, my brethren, ye have done it unto me" (Matthew 25:40). The way we treat those in need is how we treat our Lord and Saviour. If we have no regard for our fellow man, we have no regard for our Father in heaven.

Christ did not say, "Let me check your references, your resume, and your ability to pay Me back." He said, "Come unto me, all ye that labour and are heavy laden, and I will give you rest" (Matthew 11:28). We make and set conditions, but God forgives our sins and meets our needs. If we really believed in God, we would not set conditions before we released our ability to care. God loves and takes care of us unconditionally, and He blesses us continually. As recipients of grace, we can show our love for Christ by what we do for others.

MAKE IT HAPPEN

All of us have the opportunity to donate clothes, feed the hungry, go to a shelter and provide assistance, get involved in a prison ministry, or visit the hospitalized. We often leave these duties to the deacons and missionaries of the church; however, we are all disciples of Christ and share in the same responsibility.

If you are not already part of a ministry that helps meet these needs, join one. If your church does not have this type of outreach, start one. It's up to you. Are you a sheep—or a goat?

FOLLOW THE SPIRIT

What God wants me to do:

_____

_____

REMEMBER YOUR THOUGHTS

Special insights I have learned:

_____

_____

MORE LIGHT ON THE TEXT

Matthew 25:31-46

31 When the Son of man shall come in his glory, and all the holy angels with him, then shall he sit upon the throne of his glory: 32 And before him shall be gathered all nations: and he shall separate them one from another, as a shepherd divideth his sheep from the goats: 33 And he shall set the sheep on his right hand, but the goats on the left.

This passage of Scripture is not so much a parable as it is prophecy. It does, however, have some traits of a parable because it details the shepherd, sheep, and goats. The point here is to describe the events of Jesus' Second Coming.

When Christ returns, He will come back in His full glory, the same glory that clothed Him before He descended from heaven. His angels will accompany Him and will help gather all the people together at the same time. The Jews and Gentiles will not assemble in two different groups.

Once more, Jesus teaches in a context with which the Jews were familiar. Sheep and goats grazed together during the daytime but were separated at night. In this passage, the sheep go one way and the goats go another. The right side symbolizes blessing, honor, and favor; the left side symbolizes worthlessness and condemnation.

34 Then shall the King say unto them on his right hand, Come, ye blessed of my Father, inherit the kingdom prepared for you from the foundation of the world:

Here, Jesus refers to Himself as "King" for the first and only time in Scripture. He called Himself by other titles and in so doing used the first person, e.g., "I am the good shepherd" (John 10:11). In this verse, He uses the third person.

Once they have been separated out totally, Jesus will address the sheep, inviting them into God's kingdom. Matthew uses the Greek word *kleronomeo* (**klay-ron-om-eh'-o**) meaning "to possess" and signaling to the sheep to take possession of the kingdom. Jesus calls them blessed, not because of what they received (grace), but for what they did with what they received. He further says that this place has been prepared specifically for them since the beginning of the world.

35 For I was an hungred, and ye gave me meat: I was thirsty, and ye gave me drink: I was a stranger, and ye took me in: 36 Naked, and ye clothed me: I was sick, and ye visited me: I was in prison, and ye came unto me.

Jesus lists some of the acts of compassion the sheep performed. The need for compassion still exists today, and many people feed the hungry, satisfy the thirsty, house the homeless, clothe the destitute, and visit the sick and imprisoned. But the service is not as crucial as the motivation behind it.

Some people get involved because of tax benefits, a guilty conscience, or obligations within a group or organization. God will not honor their deeds because their motives were not pure.

37 Then shall the righteous answer him, saying, Lord, when saw we thee an hungred, and fed thee? or thirsty, and gave thee drink? 38 When saw we thee a stranger, and took thee in? or naked, and clothed thee? 39 Or when saw we thee sick, or in prison, and came unto thee?

Few people have seen Jesus with unmistakable certainty. Though possible, it's a bit unlikely that anyone living today has had a face-to-face encounter with the Saviour. Conversely, we may have seen Christ in others or recognized an opportunity to serve Him by ministering to others.

This was the question of the justified ones. According to what they knew about Christ, He was never hungry, thirsty, a stranger, naked, sick, or imprisoned. Thus, confusion filled their minds. Evidently, they sacrificed themselves to attend to someone else, and their unselfishness pleased God.

40 And the King shall answer and say unto them, Verily I say unto you, Inasmuch as ye have done it unto one of the least of these my brethren, ye have done it unto me.

Jesus calms the sheep by referring them to their merciful deeds born of God's love for them. The brothers of Christ were not only His siblings; they included all people who inhabited the land and shared a bond with Christ through His sufferings and afflictions.

Jesus stresses the "least" of His brothers, highlighting the humility exercised by the righteous in serving those thought unworthy of service. He then identifies with those people, making their pain, sorrow, and suffering His own.

41 Then shall he say also unto them on the left hand, Depart from me, ye cursed, into everlasting fire, prepared for the devil and his angels: 42 For I was an hungred, and ye gave me no meat: I was thirsty, and ye gave me no drink: 43 I was a stranger, and ye took me not in: naked, and ye

clothed me not: sick, and in prison, and ye visited me not.

The Lord uses the same standards for both groups and parallels them to each other. Whereas Jesus invites those on the right to come, He commands those on the left to depart. Just as God made the kingdom of heaven ready for the righteous, He made the everlasting fire ready for the unrighteous.

Originally, the everlasting fire was designated for Satan and his followers. But since the entrance of sin into the world and the introduction of death by sin, man was destined to join Satan in this inferno. God did not prepare this place for mankind because He is "not willing that any should perish" (2 Peter 3:9). But since God is just, man's disobedience demanded that he be punished unless he made proper atonement. Christ made that atonement, so man must live through the One who paid his debt. Otherwise, he must suffer God's judgment.

44 Then shall they also answer him, saying, Lord, when saw we thee an hungred, or athirst, or a stranger, or naked, or sick, or in prison, and did not minister unto thee? 45 Then shall he answer them, saying, Verily I say unto you, Inasmuch as ye did it not to one of the least of these, ye did it not to me. 46 And these shall go away into everlasting punishment: but the righteous into life eternal.

The goats' reply echoes the sheep's, but there may be a difference in the tone. While the sheep may have been pleasantly surprised by Jesus' report, the goats were desperately shocked by His convicting words. They pleaded hopelessly after hearing their sentence, but the King had rendered His ruling.

This contrast brings another issue to the surface. Neither the sheep nor the goats appear puzzled by their destination, but they seem bewildered by the reason for going there. None of them expected to live or die based on how they treated Jesus because no one may have believed they ever had the opportunity.

A similar circumstance exists today. Many people are not aware of the good they do through the Holy Spirit, and many don't recognize the chance to love as Christ loved and to serve Him by serving others.

Furthermore, some people believe they are sheep, when God sees them as goats. Jesus reiterates that the service done unto others was also done unto Him. If anyone masks a deed of goodwill behind an expectation of selfish gain, it carries no spiritual value.

DAILY BIBLE READINGS

M: God Wants Us to Do Good
Psalm 14
T: Do Not Withhold Good
Proverbs 3:27-33
W: The Golden Rule
Luke 6:27-31
T: Do Good, Be Generous, Share
1 Timothy 6:13-19
F: Help Your Brother or Sister
1 John 3:11-17
S: You Did It to Me
Matthew 25:31-40
S: You Did It Not to Me
Matthew 25:41-46

Do you want to be strengthened spiritually? Then you must regularly read God's Word! Why not set yourself up on a systematic plan to read through the Bible by using the Bible Reading Planner included as a feature of the *Precepts For Living* CD-ROM?

TEACHING TIPS

August 7
Bible Study Guide 10

1. Words You Should Know

A. Esaias (Luke 4:17) *hesaias* (Gk.)—Isaiah, the prophet.

B. Minister (v. 20) *huperetes* (Gk.)—An assistant to the ruler of the local synagogue.

C. Brow of the Hill (v. 29) *ophrus oros* (Gk.)—Mountain.

2. Teacher Preparation

A. Read today's lesson text and also read the prophecy as it appears in Isaiah 61. Think about how that promise has been fulfilled and is being fulfilled through those who follow Jesus Christ.

B. Glance through each of the Gospels and make a list of the miracles Jesus performed and the ways that He brought forth good news.

3. Starting the Lesson

Read today's IN FOCUS story about Eloise and her experience with Sister Grimes. Discuss how people sometimes want to believe the worst about others. Talk about the ways we can guard against getting discouraged when others refuse to support our changes for the better.

4. Getting into the Lesson

A. Point out that Jesus' experience in Nazareth was not unique. Many people have experienced receiving "no honor" from hometown folk. Emphasize the fact that Jesus knew the Scriptures, which supported His position.

B. Point out the importance of keeping our eyes and hearts fixed on the Lord and focused on whether or not He is pleased with our behavior.

5. Relating the Lesson to Life

A. Review THE PEOPLE, PLACES, AND TIMES section. Discuss the role of the synagogue in the Jewish community, from both a religious and social perspective. Also, discuss how Jesus often met with confrontation in the synagogues.

B. Give the students an opportunity to answer the questions in SEARCH THE SCRIPTURES.

C. Today's DISCUSS THE MEANING section calls for class members to put themselves in Nazareth on that day. Ask members if they feel they would have asked Jesus for a sign also. Talk about why people are often enraged when the truth is spoken to them.

D. The LESSON IN OUR SOCIETY section focuses on spiritual growth—the ways we are hindered and may hinder others. Discuss God's ability to create great results from meager beginnings.

6. Arousing Action

A. Ask the students to think of someone who is trying to turn his or her life around and needs encouragement. What could happen if no one comes forward to offer support and encouragement to that person?

B. Give the students an opportunity to complete the FOLLOW THE SPIRIT and REMEMBER YOUR THOUGHTS sections.

AUG 7TH

LUKE'S MISSION STATEMENT

Bible Background • LUKE 4:14-30
Printed Text • LUKE 4:16-24, 28-30
Devotional Reading • MATTHEW 13:54-58

LESSON AIM

By the end of the lesson, the students will gain insight into the nature and scope of Jesus' call and revisit the early days of Jesus' fulfilling ministry. Also, they will determine to identify and/or affirm God's will for their lives and set about realizing it just as Jesus did.

KEEP IN MIND

"The Spirit of the Lord is upon me, because he hath anointed me to preach the gospel to the poor; he hath sent me to heal the brokenhearted, to preach deliverance to the captives, and recovering of sight to the blind, to set at liberty them that are bruised" (Luke 4:18).

FOCAL VERSES

Luke 4:16 And he came to Nazareth, where he had been brought up: and, as his custom was, he went into the synagogue on the sabbath day, and stood up for to read.

17 And there was delivered unto him the book of the prophet Esaias. And when he had opened the book, he found the place where it was written,

18 The Spirit of the Lord is upon me, because he hath anointed me to preach the gospel to the poor; he hath sent me to heal the brokenhearted, to preach deliverance to the captives, and recovering of sight to the blind, to set at liberty them that are bruised,

19 To preach the acceptable year of the Lord.

20 And he closed the book, and he gave it again to the minister, and sat down. And the eyes of all

LESSON OVERVIEW

LESSON AIM
KEEP IN MIND
FOCAL VERSES
IN FOCUS
THE PEOPLE, PLACES,
AND TIMES
BACKGROUND
AT-A-GLANCE
IN DEPTH
SEARCH THE SCRIPTURES
DISCUSS THE MEANING
LESSON IN OUR SOCIETY
MAKE IT HAPPEN
FOLLOW THE SPIRIT
REMEMBER YOUR THOUGHTS
MORE LIGHT ON THE TEXT
DAILY BIBLE READINGS

them that were in the synagogue were fastened on him.

21 And he began to say unto them, This day is this scripture fulfilled in your ears.

22 And all bare him witness, and wondered at the gracious words which proceeded out of his mouth. And they said, Is not this Joseph's son?

23 And he said unto them, Ye will surely say unto me this proverb, Physician, heal thyself: whatsoever we have heard done in Capernaum, do also here in thy country.

24 And he said, Verily I say unto you, No prophet is accepted in his own country.

4:28 And all they in the synagogue, when they heard these things, were filled with wrath,

29 And rose up, and thrust him out of the city, and led him unto the brow of the hill whereon their city was built, that they might cast him down headlong.

30 But he passing through the midst of them went his way.

IN FOCUS

Eloise was so heartbroken that she didn't know if she would ever walk through the doors of that church again. The ministry she had started—to help teenage girls in the church stay focused and in school—was doing really well; that is, until Sister Grimes came and insulted her. To make matters worse, she did it in front of the girls!

Just when it seemed that things were going so

well, out of nowhere, Sister Grimes walked up to her and said, "I don't know what kind of role model you're supposed to be. Humph! I remember when you left town to have that baby and you were just 16 yourself!"

It made Eloise sad that, even after 30 years, people were still wanting to believe such a vicious lie about her. She was so shocked by Sister Grimes' words that she didn't even bother to correct her.

The words hurt, even after three decades had passed. To this day, only a few people knew that she went away because she had been diagnosed with leukemia. The doctors found a way for her to receive treatment at a special children's hospital that her parents could never have afforded. For whatever reason, her parents didn't want anyone outside the family to know about her illness. They didn't even tell the school why she moved to another city. Thinking back on it, Eloise still believes that telling everyone about the leukemia couldn't have been worse than enduring the lies about her being pregnant.

THE PEOPLE, PLACES, AND TIMES

Synagogue. The local meeting place and assembly hall for Jews during the days of the New Testament writings. This type of synagogue had its origin in the time after Solomon's temple was destroyed and many of the Hebrews were sent into exile. It became necessary to develop local centers of worship and instruction. Even after their return from exile and the Jerusalem temple was rebuilt, these local centers of worship continued.

Most communities of size had at least one synagogue, and some had several. Jewish sources hold that a synagogue was to be built wherever there were 10 or more Jewish men. The primary meeting was held on the Sabbath. The usual worship service consisted of the recitation of the *Shema* (Deuteronomy 6:4-9), prayers, Scripture readings from the Law and the Prophets, a sermon, and a benediction.

Local elders were given the responsibility for oversight of the synagogue. Often they appointed a ruler and a layman who cared for the building and selected those who participated in the worship service. The ruler was assisted by an attendant.

Jesus in the Synagogues. On many occasions, Jesus encountered opposition and conflict in the synagogues. The incident at Nazareth is just one example. Early in His ministry, He encountered opposition in the synagogue at Capernaum because He healed a man there (Mark 1:21-28; Luke 4:31-37). The ruler of one synagogue was angered because Jesus healed a woman on the Sabbath (Luke 13:10-16). Jesus' statement that He was the fulfillment of the Isaiah prophecy angered those who heard Him in the synagogue at Nazareth. His preaching and teaching often evoked negative reactions (Matthew 13:54-58; Mark 6:1-6).

Jesus issued a stern warning against those who paraded their self-righteousness in the synagogue, calling them hypocrites. As opposition grew, He warned His disciples of a time in the future when they, too, would be persecuted in the synagogues (Matthew 10:17; 23:34; Mark 13:9; Luke 12:11; 21:12).

BACKGROUND

At the age of about 30, Jesus began His public ministry. He had already submitted Himself to baptism to demonstrate His faithfulness and obedience, even though He was without sin.

Following His baptism, the Holy Ghost led Him into the wilderness, where He endured 40 days and nights of fasting and isolation. This was a period of physical weakness but spiritual strength. Three times Satan tried to tempt Jesus, making Him offers that might appeal to His humanness. By the power of the Holy Ghost, Jesus endured this period and refused the devil's temptations.

The power of the Holy Ghost, which had given Jesus the victory over Satan in the wilderness, led Him to Galilee. There, He was able to teach in the synagogues and He was well received, gaining popularity among the people there. Jesus must have been encouraged by His reception. He was glorified by all those around Him.

The accolades Jesus received in Galilee did not represent the true glory of Jesus, which was to come. Still, Jesus' ministry began and ended with Him being glorified.

IN DEPTH

1. Prophecy Fulfilled in Jesus (Luke 4:16-21)

From His glorious reception at Galilee, Jesus' premiere stop on His preaching circuit was His hometown, Nazareth. Perhaps because they felt no close identity with Him, He sought first to bring the Good News to His own people. The phrase "where he had been brought up" gives the impression that Jesus had not been in Nazareth for a while prior to this visit (Luke 4:16).

Jesus had been raised by devout Jewish parents who reared Him to participate in the tenets of His faith. Therefore, as His custom was, He went to the synagogue on the Sabbath day. It was normal and usual for Him to participate in worship.

During the synagogue service, the first scriptural reading was from the Torah. These readings followed a schedule of 155 specific lessons, which were designed to allow completion of the entire Pentateuch in three years. In both Palestine and Babylon, the verses were read from the Hebrew text. This was followed by an Aramaic translation, the familiar language of the Middle East. The reading from the Torah was followed by a reading from the Prophets. Scholars are uncertain as to how the reading from the Prophets was chosen. Perhaps the particular reading was left to the discretion of the man reading. Anyone could be invited to read the Scripture lesson for the synagogue services. The reading was followed by a sermon if a competent teacher was present.

It is possible that Jesus Himself chose the particular passage to be read after He was given "the book of the prophet Esaias" (Isaiah), as indicated by the phrase, "he found the place where it was written" (v. 17). The reading from Isaiah points back to Jesus' baptism, when He was anointed for His ministry. The nature of His ministry is given in this prophecy by Isaiah. His purpose was to bring Good News to the poor, the brokenhearted, the captives, the blind, and the oppressed (bruised). The Gospel is Good News to those whose hope lies in Almighty God to act on their behalf. Jesus identified Himself with the social, religious, and economic outcasts of His day. The acceptable year of the Lord had been launched in the person and ministry of Jesus.

When He finished reading, Jesus handed the book over to the minister, one who served as an assistant to the head of the synagogue (a role somewhat similar to that of a deacon in the early church). After His reading, the congregation was still. All eyes were fastened on Him. Jesus broke through the silence with a simple, yet powerful declaration, "This day is this scripture fulfilled in your ears" (v. 21). There He was, standing before them. Jesus of Nazareth was the Messiah of God's promise.

2. Hometown Boy Rejected (vv. 22-24)

Initially, those who heard His words responded favorably to Him. They wondered at the gracious words He had just spoken. Still, they were confused about His identity. They could not move beyond the fact that He was Joseph's son. How could a carpenter's son declare Himself to be the Son of God?

Apparently He knew their thoughts, that they were saying to Him, "Physician, heal thyself" (v. 23). Some Bible scholars interpret His statement as reflecting future deeds rather than something that had already taken place. Nevertheless, the message is clear. Jesus was being challenged to do for those in His hometown what He had done for those in neighboring towns. He will have to substantiate His words with action. Since He claimed Himself to be the Messiah, He should be able to perform miracles that one might expect from the Son of God.

No prophet is accepted in his own country. Luke categorizes Jesus' rejection as being the same as the rejection experienced by the Old Testament prophets. Jesus refused to give in to the people's demands for a sign. He cited two incidents from the Old Testament to justify His refusal.

3. Move to Kill Jesus (vv. 28-30)

When the people heard Jesus' words, they were filled with wrath. Very early in Jesus' ministry, people began to display a desire to mold Him into the kind of Messiah they thought He should be instead of accepting Him as God's perfect gift. Even today, many people attempt to mold Jesus according to their own expectations. The people of Nazareth were so enraged that they sought to kill Jesus. Perhaps they were so angry because Jesus had told them the truth and it hit home. Nothing angers like the truth! They managed to take Him out of the city where they led Him to the "brow of the hill" (v. 29). Although the city itself is built on a slope, the supposed site of the brow is a precipice that ranges from 80 to 300 feet high, located southeast of Nazareth. They attempted to throw Jesus off this hill.

Of course, their attempt was not successful. It was not time for Jesus' ministry to end. Luke credits their failure to divine intervention as Jesus was able to pass through the midst of them and go His way.

SEARCH THE SCRIPTURES

1. What did Jesus do once He arrived at Nazareth (Luke 4:16)?

2. From what book of prophecy did Jesus read (v. 17)?

3. What responsibilities had Jesus been given because the Spirit of the Lord was upon Him (vv. 18-19)?

4. What did Jesus do when He had finished reading? How did the people react to what Jesus had read (v. 20)?

5. What words did Jesus speak to break the silence (v. 21)?

6. What was the people's initial reaction to Jesus' statement (v. 22)?

7. What question did they ask about His background (v. 22)?

8. How did Jesus respond to their question (vv. 23-24)?

9. How did the people respond to Jesus' explanation (v. 28)?

10. How did Jesus escape (v. 30)?

DISCUSS THE MEANING

1. Why was it so difficult for the people to believe that Jesus was indeed the Messiah who had been prophesied in the Old Testament? Do you think the people were totally unjustified in requesting a sign? Would they have believed Jesus even if they had been given a sign?

2. Why were the people so enraged by the example Jesus gave them concerning Elisha and Elijah? Why were they so angry that they wanted to kill Jesus?

LESSON IN OUR SOCIETY

It is often difficult for us to allow someone to grow as God intends. As soon as a person makes a step toward correcting negative behavior with positive behavior, he or she is often ridiculed by others. Instead of support, the one seeking the strength to make a life change often receives criticism for daring to be different. Perhaps that is because many people's vision of God is too small. Sometimes people find it difficult to believe that, through the power of the Holy Spirit, ordinary people can, and do, grow into extraordinary people.

The people at Nazareth would not allow Jesus to move beyond their image of Him as a carpenter's son. They missed out on a great blessing because of their limited sight. We, too, can miss out on great things if we attempt to limit people according to our own narrow visions.

MAKE IT HAPPEN

Is there something you wish to change in your life but are afraid to because you fear the criticism or ridicule of others? It may be something as inconsequential as changing your hair color. Or it might be as serious as eliminating a bad habit or fulfilling a call that God extended to you long ago. Write down the barriers that inhibit your ability to make a change for the better in your life. Ask yourself, "What is the worst thing that could happen if I go ahead and _____?" Then, ask God for the strength and guidance to help you take that leap.

FOLLOW THE SPIRIT

What God wants me to do:

_____

_____

REMEMBER YOUR THOUGHTS

Special insights I have learned:

_____

_____

MORE LIGHT ON THE TEXT
Luke 4:16-24, 28-30

Jesus has been baptized (Luke 3:21) and is led into the wilderness by the Spirit where the devil tempts Him for 40 days (4:1-13). Having overcome all the temptations of the devil and being filled with the power of the Holy Spirit, Jesus returns to the region of Galilee, where He officially begins His ministry (cf. Matthew 4:12; Mark 1:14). He is now about 30 years old (Luke 3:23). According to the Jewish law, this is the age priests begin their duties (Numbers 4:23; 1 Chronicles 23:3).

From the context, Jesus has been teaching in other cities in this region (e.g., Capernaum; see Luke 4:23), especially in their synagogues, before He goes to His own hometown of Nazareth. His fame has spread all over the place because of the miracles and the authority with which he taught them (Luke 4:14-15; Mark 1:21-28; 3:32ff).

16 And he came to Nazareth, where he had been brought up: and, as his custom was, he went into the synagogue on the sabbath day, and stood up for to read.

Continuing His itinerary in the Galilee region, Jesus comes to Nazareth, His hometown. Nazareth was a town in the southern part of Galilee where Jesus spent His boyhood years (Matthew 2:23). Nazareth was a small, but beautifully secluded, town nestled in the southernmost hills of the Lebanon mountain range. It was situated in the territory belonging to Zebulun. The origin of the city is unknown, and Nazareth itself was probably insignificant. It is never mentioned in the Old Testament.

It is said that Nazareth lay close to the important trade routes of Palestine and overlooked the Plain of Esdraelon, through which caravans passed as they traveled from Gilead to the south and west. North of the city was the main road from Ptolemais to the Decapolis, along which the Roman legions frequently traveled. This fact probably accounts for the origin of the name "Nazareth" in the Aramaic, meaning "watchtower."

However, geographically Nazareth itself was situated in a valley about 366 meters (1,200 feet) above sea level overlooking the Esdraelon Valley.

To the north and east were steep hills, while on the west the hills rose to an impressive 488 meters (1,600 feet). The city, therefore, was somewhat isolated from nearby traffic. This apparent isolation as a frontier town on the southern border of Zebulun contributed to the fact that Nazareth was regarded as a less important part of the national and religious life of Israel. Coupled with its seclusion, Nazareth had a bad reputation both morally and religiously. It is also believed that Nazareth had a certain crude dialect in the Galilean region. All this seems to make Nazareth notorious, and probably prompted Nathanael, when he first learned of Jesus of Nazareth, to ask, "Can there any good thing come out of Nazareth?" (John 1:46). The city became known in the New Testament because of Christ.

At Nazareth, Jesus went into the synagogue on the Sabbath day, a habit He had formed from childhood (Luke 2:41-50). He grew up in the city and in the synagogue; He was therefore a familiar face. He also was familiar with the worship rituals. It was customary during a synagogue service on the Sabbath for seven people to read from the Scriptures: a priest, a Levite, and five ordinary Jews. Therefore, it was not strange that Christ is handed the Scripture to read. Of course, He must have done that many times before.

17 And there was delivered unto him the book of the prophet Esaias. And when he had opened the book, he found the place where it was written,

As we have already noted, the reading of Scripture formed an integral part of the temple or synagogue worship. Indeed, Scripture reading remains the most important part of worship in the Jewish religion even today. Before and during Jesus' time, the Jewish people read the Scripture systematically. They read from the Law and from the Prophets.

Jesus is then handed the book of the prophet Esaias (Isaiah). In the Hebrew scrolls, the prophetic books were in single volumes (except the 12 minor prophets). Jesus unrolls the scroll to the prophetic passage, which summarizes His earthly mission. Whether Jesus looked for a passage He wished to read, or He just opened the book and His eye fell upon that particular passage, or it was the passage assigned for that Sabbath day, we do not know. Most likely, Jesus was reading from the assigned lesson from the prophet for the day. Jesus would probably comply with and adapt to the set routine of the synagogue rather than disrupt it.

18 The Spirit of the Lord is upon me, because he hath anointed me to preach the gospel to the poor; he hath sent me to heal the brokenhearted, to preach deliverance to the captives, and recovering of sight to the blind, to set at liberty them that are bruised. 19 To preach the acceptable year of the Lord.

He reads from Isaiah 61:1-2 and includes a single phrase from 58:6. He probably read in Hebrew and translated into Aramaic, the common spoken language at the time. He reads, "The Spirit of the Lord is upon me," which means that He is filled with the power of the Holy Spirit. As we see in verse 21, Jesus identifies Himself as the subject of Isaiah's prophecy. Here, He says that He has the Holy Spirit for a specific ministry. We should note that He has the Holy Spirit because He has been "anointed." This seems to indicate that the filling or the possession of the Holy Spirit is consequent to the anointing. The word "anointed" here is translated as the Greek word *chrio* (**khree'-o**), which means to consecrate, ordain, or set apart a person for a particular service.

In the Old Testament, persons or things were anointed, as symbolized by the pouring of oil to signify holiness and separation unto God—for example, the tabernacle and its furniture (Exodus 30:22ff), priests (Exodus 28:41), kings (Judges 9:8; 2 Samuel 2:4; 1 Kings 1:34), and prophets (1 Kings 19:16). The anointing also symbolized authority, appointment, and equipping for a special function or service to God. It was usually associated with the outpouring of the Spirit of God (1 Samuel 10:1, 9; 16:13; Isaiah 61:1). The anointing was always regarded as an act of God, and it was sometimes used to mean the bestowal of divine favor (Psalm 23:5; 92:10). The same idea is also carried over into the New Testament (Acts 10:38; 1 John 2:20, 27) and generally refers to the anointing of the Holy Spirit. As we see in this passage and other places in the New

Testament, anointing is also frequently related to healing. The disciples of Jesus anointed the sick (Mark 16:18), and James instructed the elders to anoint the sick with oil for healing purposes (James 5:14).

Here the writer declares that Jesus has been consecrated, as evidenced by the power of the Holy Spirit for a twofold ministry—to preach and to heal. He is called "to preach the gospel" (Gk. *euaggelizo*, **yoo-ang-ghel-id'-zo**), that is, to announce good news, or glad tidings, to the "poor" (Gk. *ptochos*). This probably includes the physically and spiritually poor. He is called to preach "deliverance to the captives"—those who were bound and imprisoned in sin, sickness, and death (Acts 10:38; Ephesians 4:8-10; Hebrews 2:14-15). He is also sent to "preach" (proclaim to all) "the acceptable year of the Lord." The year of the Lord is typified by the year of Jubilee when liberty was proclaimed to all people on the Day of Atonement as instituted by God (Leviticus 25:8-13, 28). The atonement of Christ is fully embraced when the poor, the sick, the sinful, and the helpless are restored to prosperity, health, holiness, power, and dominion over Satan and receive membership and communion in the family of God.

The second function of the anointing is for healing. Here is meant both spiritual and physical healing. Jesus is sent "to heal the brokenhearted." This includes those who are broken in mind and soul or psychologically sick (Acts 10:38). He will bring comfort and hope to the destitute in heart. This is the work of the Holy Spirit, whom Christ promised His disciples before He ascended, and which is demonstrated repeatedly in the Gospels. The anointing is also for the "recovering of sight to the blind"—body, spirit, and soul—for those in darkness (Matthew 4:16; Luke 1:79; 2:32; John 1:4-9; 9:32-33; Acts 26:18). Jesus is also sent to liberate those "that are bruised" (Gk. *thrauo*, meaning shattered or completely crushed in life). This speaks of the oppressed and broken (Isaiah 58:6-14; cf. Mark 5:1-20; Luke 13:16). Although this passage refers to the immediate situation of Israel's captivity, the reality is to be fulfilled in the future by Christ's ministry.

20 And he closed the book, and he gave it again to the minister, and sat down. And the eyes of all them that were in the synagogue were fastened on him. 21 And he began to say unto them, This day is this scripture fulfilled in your ears.

Luke now resumes his narrative. After reading the lesson for the day, Jesus "closed the book," which might be better rendered as "rolled" (or "folded together") the parchment, then handed it back to the minister, sat down, and was about to start a sermon. It was customary in the Jewish religious tradition that after the reading from the Scripture, the reader would sit down to preach a sermon on the passage (Luke 2:46; 5:3; Matthew 5:1; 13:1-2; 15:29; 24:3). As He sat down to preach, all the people in the synagogue focused their attention on Him. Jesus explained to them the Scripture. We do not have the full content of Jesus' teaching, but only a summary of the main theme of Christ's words: "This day is this scripture fulfilled in your ears."

Jesus declares to them that the words which He has read to them have finally been fulfilled in their presence; in essence He says that He, Jesus, is the One anointed by God, endued with the Holy Spirit, spoken of in the Old Testament to proclaim the Good News of salvation and deliverance and to heal all manner of diseases. He was sent to proclaim the "acceptable year of the Lord" (v. 19)—the Messianic age and the year of Jubilee, an age ushered in by His presence, a period in which God has planned to grant salvation to all types of people.

22 And all bare him witness, and wondered at the gracious words which proceeded out of his mouth. And they said, Is not this Joseph's son?

At first, the people's reaction was that of wonder and excitement, as the following words "witness," "wondered," and "gracious" suggest. All have a positive connotation. To "witness" (Gk. *martureo*, **mar-too-reh'-o**) simply means to give an honorable report of what one has seen or heard. It also has the idea of affirming a truth or bearing testimony. "Wondered" (Gk. *thaumazo*, **thou-mad'-zo**) means to admire, marvel, or to have admiration. Jesus spoke with such grace and authority that the people marveled at His words. His words

and His claim were so startling and amazing to them that they began to question within themselves, "Is not this Joseph's son?"

Although they had known Him, they had never heard such words from Him in the 30 years He had lived among them. Moreover, they reflected on Jesus' background and family—He was only the son of Joseph, an ordinary person. How could He make such a claim? This was the turning point. They changed from an attitude of awe and wonder to doubt, skepticism, and prejudice. They must have thought, "How can Jesus, whose father, Joseph, is poor, be the One anointed to preach to the poor?" Jesus endured such prejudice repeatedly as recorded in the Scriptures (cf. Mark 6:3; John 1:46; 7:52).

23 And he said unto them, Ye will surely say unto me this proverb, Physician, heal thyself: whatsoever we have heard done in Capernaum, do also here in thy country. 24 And he said, Verily I say unto you, No prophet is accepted in his own country.

Jesus observes their skeptical attitude and says to them, "Ye will surely say unto me this proverb, Physician, heal thyself." The origin of the proverb is not given; however, it seems to be a common saying, understood by everyone. It sounds also like a prophetic saying fulfilled at His crucifixion (Luke 23:39). The people also wanted Jesus to perform the same miracles He had done at Capernaum, one of the cities of Galilee. This probably would prove to them the genuineness of His claim as God's anointed. The gospels of Matthew and Mark have records of Christ's successful ministry in Capernaum (Matthew 4:13; Mark 1:21-28). Earlier, in Luke 4:14-15, Luke himself records Christ's extensive and successful ministry in Galilee, including His work at Capernaum. The saying reminds us of Satan's demands of Jesus for miraculous feats before His public ministry. Here Jesus expresses either the reply He expects the people to make in response to His message, or what He knows they are individually thinking. As in the wilderness encounter with the devil, Jesus refused their demands.

Jesus continues by telling them an important fact, which is probably another common saying among the people—namely, that a prophet is never accepted in his own country. Jesus introduces this fact with the common formula, "Verily I say unto you" (Gk. *amen lego humin*), often used to introduce a solemn assertion. This is used six times in the gospel of Luke but more frequently in Matthew and Mark. The saying simply means that people who have achieved some fame or honor in life are never acknowledged at home. No one is popular in his own hometown. This also anticipates the rejection Jesus would face in His earthly ministry (especially among the Jews), like the prophets who were also rejected by their own people.

28 And all they in the synagogue, when they heard these things, were filled with wrath, 29 And rose up, and thrust him out of the city, and led him unto the brow of the hill whereon their city was built, that they might cast him down headlong. 30 But he passing through the midst of them went his way,

Jesus' answer infuriated all the people in the synagogue. The word "wrath" (Gk. *thumos*, **thoo-mos'**) is described as fierce indignation or a forceful, vindictive anger. Such fierce anger is usually associated with, or often results in, hatred and bitterness. Here "all" the people, without exception, are angered at His words. They take Him out of the synagogue and out of the city to a hilltop to throw Him from the cliff. They "thrust him out of the city" means that they drag Him from the synagogue to the outskirts of the city. They take Him to the mountain peak around Nazareth and are about to "cast (throw) him down headlong," but He walks through them and goes His own way. We are not told how He actually did this. In any case, He departs from them unharmed without any further incident. He spiritually disarms them by the power of the Spirit. He goes up to Capernaum and continues His teaching.

It is significant that they looked for a miracle and He demonstrated the same, though not on their own terms, but on His own. He walked away because it was not yet time for Him to lay down His life. Hence, He foiled their wicked plan through His divine power. Jesus says that He lays down His own life voluntarily; no one takes it from Him (John 10:17ff; 15:13).

DAILY BIBLE READINGS

M: The Year of the Lord's Favor
Leviticus 25:8-12

T: Elijah Revives the Widow's Son
1 Kings 17:17-24

W: Jesus Is Rejected in Nazareth
Matthew 13:54-58

T: Jesus Teaches in His Hometown
Mark 6:1-6

F: Jesus Reads Isaiah's Words
Luke 4:14-19

S: Today This Scripture Has Been Fulfilled
Luke 4:20-24

S: All in the Synagogue Were Enraged
Luke 4:25-30

Why not use the Gk. and Hebrew dictionary in your *Precepts For Living* CD-ROM to gain a better understanding of the word *hear*? Do a cross-reference check on Matthew 13:9 to find everywhere "hear" occurs in the Bible!

TEACHING TIPS

August 14
Bible Study Guide 11

1. Words You Should Know

A. Ruler of the synagogue (Luke 8:41) *archisunagogus* (Gk.)—The senior official in a synagogue of New Testament times. His functions were to take care of the physical arrangements for the worship services, to manage the maintenance of the building, and to determine who would be called to read from the Torah.

B. Virtue (v. 46) *dunamis* (Gk.)—Refers to miraculous power or a mighty work.

C. Faith (v. 48) *pistis* (Gk.)—In the New Testament tradition, it means trust and belief in God and His Son, Jesus the Christ.

2. Teacher Preparation

A. Read Luke 7—9 for background information. As you study, remember Luke's emphasis on Jesus' concern for the society's outcasts.

B. Remind yourself that the subjects of the Scripture are two women. Then, reflect on the implications for women today.

3. Starting the Lesson

A. Open the session with prayer. Then ask the students if they have ever been treated like an outcast and, if so, invite them to share how it made them feel.

B. Remind the students of the obvious differences between the two recipients of Jesus' healing: Jairus's daughter was in a position of honor, while the woman with the issue of blood was in a position of disgrace. Yet, Jesus heals them both. Ask the students to consider what conclusions we can draw about Jesus' concern for all people.

4. Getting into the Lesson

A. Read the LESSON AIM as a group.

B. Have each student silently read the FOCAL VERSES.

C. After the Scripture reading, remind the students that in Jesus' day, women were to be seen and not heard; yet, Jesus took time for them. Be sure to center the discussion around the events before and after their encounters with Jesus.

5. Relating the Lesson to Life

A. Challenge the students with the idea that real desire expresses itself in action. Explain that tenacity pays off.

B. Jairus is a model of a concerned, loving father who allowed his daughter to meet Jesus. Statistics show us that when a father is present and is an active participant in his family's life, children fare much better in society than they do in families without a father. Ask the students to consider how our sons and dsughters might fare if there were more fathers like Jairus.

6. Arousing Action

A. Ask each student to pick out one positive attribute of the main characters in today's passage and implement it in their own lives.

B. Challenge your students to make an extra effort to practice what they heard Jesus preach, teach, and do.

WORSHIP GUIDE

For the Superintendent or Teacher
Theme: Jairus's Daughter Restored and a Woman Healed
Theme Song: "Pass Me Not, O Gentle Saviour"
Scripture: Mark 10:46-52
Song: "Have a Little Talk with Jesus"
Meditation: God, help us to know that no matter who we are, Your healing power is available to all of us because You are an equal-opportunity God. Help us to have a faith that makes us whole. Amen.

JAIRUS'S DAUGHTER RESTORED AND A WOMEN HEALED

Bible Background • LUKE 8:40-56
Printed Text • LUKE 8:40-56
Devotional Reading • MATTHEW 9:18-26

LESSON AIM

By the end of the lesson, the students should know that Jesus is not a respecter of persons, but that He is willing to save all who believe, and everyone who trusts in Jesus can go to Him for healing.

KEEP IN MIND

"And he said unto her, Daughter, be of good comfort: thy faith hath made thee whole; go in peace" (Luke 8:48).

FOCAL VERSES

Luke 8:40 And it came to pass, that, when Jesus was returned, the people gladly received him: for they were all waiting for him.

41 And behold, there came a man named Jairus, and he was a ruler of the synagogue: and he fell down at Jesus' feet, and besought him that he would come into his house:

42 For he had one only daughter, about twelve years of age, and she lay a dying. But as he went the people thronged him.

43 And a woman having an issue of blood twelve years, which had spent all her living upon physicians, neither could be healed of any,

44 Came behind him, and touched the border of his garment: and immediately her issue of blood stanched.

45 And Jesus said, Who touched me? When all denied, Peter and they that were with him said, Master, the multitude throng thee and press thee and sayest thou, Who touched me?

LESSON OVERVIEW

LESSON AIM
KEEP IN MIND
FOCAL VERSES
IN FOCUS
THE PEOPLE, PLACES, AND TIMES
BACKGROUND
AT-A-GLANCE
IN DEPTH
SEARCH THE SCRIPTURES
DISCUSS THE MEANING
LESSON IN OUR SOCIETY
MAKE IT HAPPEN
FOLLOW THE SPIRIT
REMEMBER YOUR THOUGHTS
MORE LIGHT ON THE TEXT
DAILY BIBLE READINGS

46 And Jesus said, Somebody hath touched me: for I perceive that virtue is gone out of me.

47 And when the woman saw that she was not hid, she came trembling, and falling down before him, she declared unto him before all the people for what cause she had touched him, and how she was healed immediately.

48 And he said unto her, Daughter, be of good comfort: thy faith hath made thee whole; go in peace.

49 While he yet spake, there cometh one from the ruler of the synagogue's house, saying to him, Thy daughter is dead; trouble not the Master.

50 But when Jesus heard it, he answered him, saying, Fear not: believe only, and she shall be made whole.

51 And when he came into the house, he suffered no man to go in, save Peter, and James, and John, and the father and the mother of the maiden.

52 And all wept, and bewailed her: but he said, Weep not; she is not dead, but sleepeth.

53 And they laughed him to scorn, knowing that she was dead.

54 And he put them all out, and took her by the hand, and called, saying, Maid, arise.

55 And her spirit came again, and she arose straightway: and he commanded to give her meat.

AUG 14TH

56 And her parents were astonished: but he charged them that they should tell no man what was done.

IN FOCUS

Michael was a young pastor recently appointed to a new church. His new church was a middle-class congregation of 400 people located in the suburbs. Most of his parishioners were doing well for themselves and, therefore, had moved out of the inner city to escape its many challenges. Just as Michael was beginning his ministry there, a poor family, the Smiths, moved into the area after being displaced in the inner city due to gentrification. The Smiths began attending Pastor Michael's church, and they expressed to him that Mr. Smith had mental challenges that led to frequent periods of unemployment, alcohol abuse, and other unproductive behavior.

Mr. and Mrs. Smith went to Pastor Michael for counseling regarding their situation. They needed help from the church, and Pastor Michael was prepared to give them as much help as they needed. However, much to his dismay, many people in the church did not seem to care about the Smith family's struggles. Some members had been attending church all of their lives—first in the inner city and now in a middle-class suburb—but they failed to lift a helping hand for a family that was of a lower economic status and in need of healing. The people in the congregation had the collective strength to make a difference in the lives of the Smith family; yet they would not because they lacked that one essential Christian characteristic—compassion.

When Pastor Michael realized this self-centered focus was shared by many of the people he was serving, he immediately preached and taught on Jesus' ministry of compassion. He taught that God is love, and that those who love God ought also to love their neighbor. He worked persistently to transform his "cold" congregation into a "sensitive, loving" flock.

Within six weeks, members of the congregation began to ask their pastor what they could do to help the Smith family overcome their adversity. As time progressed, the church members also began to reach out with helping hands to other

needy families. As a result, the church established a new ministry called "A Ministry of Compassion."

In today's lesson, Jesus heals two people who held very different positions in society and confirms that He is no respecter of persons.

THE PEOPLE, PLACES, AND TIMES

Issue of Blood. This phrase always refers to vaginal bleeding. A woman with normal menstruation was considered unclean for seven days, along with anything that came into contact with her. A woman who bled longer than seven days was unclean as long as she was bleeding, plus seven additional days. All of the Gospels, except for John, give an account of Jesus' miraculous healing of the woman who had hemorrhaged for 12 years. By touching Jesus' garment, the woman was actually violating the Old Testament laws concerning menstruation and making Jesus' garment unclean. However, her courageous act of faith in Jesus healed her.

Comfort, Philip, and Walter Elwell, eds. *Tyndale Bible Dictionary.* Wheaton, Ill.: Tyndale House Publishers, 2001. 595.

Jairus. The leader of the Capernaum synagogue who sought Jesus among the crowds and petitioned Him to come and heal his critically ill daughter. Jairus was the administrative head and president of the board of elders responsible for the management of the synagogue and the conduct of the services. He mainly was responsible for allocating duties and seeing that they were carried out well and in order. As the ruler of the synagogue, he was one of the most important and respected men in the community.

BACKGROUND

Jesus' ministry was both demanding and physically draining. He was truly compassionate for all, and His compassion was a defining characteristic of His ministry. Jesus cared about everyone: the rich and the poor, men and women, Jews and Gentiles. He practiced an inclusive love for all humanity.

In today's Scripture, Jesus broke the Jewish traditions that would have shunned and unfavorably treated the poor, bleeding woman while treating favorably Jairus's daughter. Note several things in this account. First, the hemorrhaging woman and Jairus's daughter are opposites in economic and social standing. However, it was the woman with the least honor and status whom Jesus healed first. The one with the higher status and honor, He healed last. Jesus made no economic or social distinction as to who can experience the "new life" He gives. Jairus and the bleeding woman were both aggressive and assertive in requesting Jesus' help. However, the hemorrhaging woman who was healed is not mentioned by name; she had no status and no one to defend her. Yet, Jesus restored her and she was given more than her recovered health. On the other hand, Jairus's daughter, a girl of privilege, honor, and status, was restored as well. Jesus' actions further illustrated the inclusive and egalitarian nature of His compassionate ministry.

AT-A-GLANCE

1. Jesus Responds to a Distressed Father
(Luke 8:40-42)
2. Jesus Restores a Diseased Woman
(vv. 43-48)
3. Jesus Resurrects a Dead Girl
(vv. 49-56)

IN DEPTH

1. Jesus Responds to a Distressed Father (Luke 8:40-42)

Jesus had just returned from the region of Gerasa when He was intercepted by Jairus, a ruler of the Capernaum synagogue. Jairus pleaded with Jesus to come to his house to heal his dying daughter. Jesus responded to his request by following him to his house. Jairus was an honored man in his community who was well-respected and had considerable influence. He was probably used to people coming to him for help. Instead, he now found himself in need of great help. His daughter was deathly ill. Having no one else to turn to, Jairus cast aside his privileged and honored status and pleaded with Jesus for assistance on his daughter's behalf. Jairus had to put aside his pride

and humble himself before the Saviour. More importantly, he put aside his religious arrogance in order to open his mind to the possibility of divine power at work in a controversial person like Jesus. He knew that his resources were exhausted, and now he had only one last option—Jesus.

Jesus responded to Jairus's plea because He understood his hopelessness and despair. Jesus responded because Jairus reached out to Him. Similarly, if we reach out to Jesus, He will surely respond to our every need.

2. Jesus Restores a Diseased Woman (vv. 43-48)

While Jesus was on His way to Jairus's house, a destitute, diseased, and nameless woman came up behind Him and touched His garment. Because of her illness, she was not supposed to be near other people, let alone a rabbi like Jesus. However, her need was too great and the opportunity was too awesome for her to let it pass. Worse yet, she had spent all of her money on physicians and she was still no better.

In order for her to be restored to wholeness, she had to break traditional and cultural prejudices, do something revolutionary, and go for her healing. Just by touching the border of His garment, the nameless woman was cured of her affliction. By her actions, she broke the honor code of her day that relegated even healthy women to second-class citizenship and totally ostracized women who had any kind of sickness. When she acted in faith, Jesus felt "power" flow from Himself, and He stopped and asked the question, "Who touched me?" The woman ran to Him and confessed that she was the one who had touched Him. Jesus then gave her something that all of us need. He said, "Daughter, be of good comfort: thy faith hath made thee whole; go in peace."

Jesus not only cured her, He also made her a whole person—restoring her both physically and socially. While suffering 12 years physically, she had also suffered emotionally because her health caused her to be ostracized from her community. Now, since Jesus made her "whole," she was restored back into the Israelite community, and even more importantly, she entered into the kingdom of God. Her faith, complete trust, and belief in Jesus was the catalyst for her restoration.

The word *wholeness* implies we are complete—lacking nothing. To be "whole" means to be complete as God made you. Everyone needs to emulate this woman, whose faith in Jesus was so great that she believed there was power in everything and anything connected with Jesus, including His robe. When you have faith in Jesus Christ, then you have access to power that can transform you into a whole person. At some point in our lives we can feel like victims: unloved, unwanted, dishonored, guilt-laden, and broken. However, there is restoration available! Strive this day to embrace your heritage and to have a faith in Jesus that will make you truly complete in every way.

3. Jesus Resurrects a Dead Girl (vv. 49-56)

As Jesus affirmed and restored the hemorrhaging woman, someone came from Jairus's house and told him that his daughter was dead and not to bother Jesus anymore. But when Jesus heard the death announcement, He disregarded it and told Jairus not to fear but to believe, and his daughter would be made whole also. When they approached the house, Jesus went in with Peter, James, John, and the dead girl's father and mother. Jesus reminded the weeping group that had gathered in the dead girl's room that she was not dead but only sleeping. When they scornfully laughed, Jesus put all of them out of the room. He then took the dead girl by the hand and told her to rise. Her spirit came back into her and she sat up alive. To her parents' astonishment, Jesus brought her back to life through His resurrection power.

In the preceding healing story, the woman touched Jesus and was restored. This time, however, Jesus touched the girl and she was resurrected! These two acts of healing suggest that Jesus does not show favoritism and that He can restore and resurrect anyone, no matter what their social status. Everyone is good enough to be made "whole." Compassionate ministry understands that people of every socioeconomic level are human. Compassionate ministry rejects what society says about certain individuals and accepts what Jesus says about the intrinsic worth of each individual. In Matthew 25:40, Jesus affirms His solidarity with the disadvantaged: "Verily I say unto you,

Inasmuch as ye have done it unto one of the least of these my brethren, ye have done it unto me."

The church cannot afford to neglect Jesus' message and mission to the poor and disadvantaged. If we as Christians allow Jesus to touch us, take us by the hand, and tell us to rise up, then we also will experience a resurrection of purpose as well as power and allow God to use us as instruments in His liberation of lost souls.

SEARCH THE SCRIPTURES

1. What did Jairus ask Jesus to do for him (Luke 8:41-42)? *Come to his house & heal his daughter*

2. Who intercepted Jesus as He followed Jairus to his house (vv. 43-44)? *Woman with the issue of blood*

3. What was the woman's condition, and how long had she suffered (v. 43)? *Hemorrhaged 12 years*

4. How did Jesus know someone had touched Him (v. 46)? *Virtue is gone out of him*

5. What made the woman whole (v. 48)? *thy Faith*

6. When Jesus learned that Jairus's daughter had died, what was His response (v. 50)? *Fear not, believe only*

7. How did Jesus resurrect Jairus's daughter (v. 55)? *Commened her to arise*

DISCUSS THE MEANING

1. In Luke 8:48, Jesus told the woman, "Daughter, be of good comfort: thy faith hath made thee whole; go in peace." What does the word *whole* mean to you? Can you attend church every Sunday, claim to be saved, and still not be whole? Explain.

2. In our text today, Jesus heals two people who held very different positions in society. Jairus's daughter held a high status, while the bleeding woman held a very low status. Yet Jesus called the bleeding woman "daughter." What do these two healing accounts tell us about how Jesus views people? *No favoritism*

3. What methods does your church utilize to evangelize and minister to the poor, the abused, the drug addicts, the mentally and physically challenged, the gangbangers, and the street people?

LESSON IN OUR SOCIETY

Women have always played a vital role in the ministry of Jesus and in the development of the church. This account of double healing lets us know that even while Jewish society, at this time, did not fully value women as it should, Jesus did. Therefore, if Jesus did, then the Church should as well. By example, Jesus gives us a mandate to restore and resurrect people from all walks of life.

MAKE IT HAPPEN

Anything or anyone connected to Jesus has power! Scripture says, "If ye abide in me, and my words abide in you, ye shall ask what ye will, and it shall be done unto you" (John 15:7). This week, make it your responsibility not to judge people by their outward appearance or social status, but rather on their intrinsic worth as a human being.

FOLLOW THE SPIRIT

What God wants me to do:

_____

_____

REMEMBER YOUR THOUGHTS

Special insights I have learned:

_____

_____

pick up here

MORE LIGHT ON THE TEXT
Luke 8:40-56

40 And it came to pass, that, when Jesus was returned, the people gladly received him: for they were all waiting for him.

"When Jesus was returned" refers to His coming back to the place He had left to go to the east side of the sea (see Luke 8:22; cp. Matthew 8:18). The place is most likely Capernaum, which served as His headquarters since His rejection from Nazareth (Luke 4:31; Matthew 9:1; Mark 5:21). The word "people" (Gk. *ochlos*, **okh-los**) means a crowd or a multitude of people were pressing each other. The multitude received Him gladly, for they were eagerly "waiting for" (Gk. *prosdokao*, **pros-dok-ah-o**) or expecting Him. The crowd was expecting a lot from Jesus since they had seen or heard about His deeds.

41 And, behold, there came a man named Jairus, and he was a ruler of the synagogue: and he fell down at Jesus' feet, and besought him that he would come into his house:

Jairus was "a ruler of the synagogue" and a prominent man in the city. Without constraint, he "fell down at Jesus' feet." His attitude indicated his great distress and his genuine desire to have Jesus come to his house.

42 For he had one only daughter, about twelve years of age, and she lay a dying. But as he went the people thronged him.

Jairus' 12-year-old only daughter "lay a dying" (Gk. *apothnesko*, **ap-oth-nace-ko**). The use of the imperfect tense indicates that Jairus's daughter was not dead at this point, but had what appeared to be a terminal illness. There was no hope for her to be healed. As Jesus went, the multitude "thronged" Him (see 8:14), or pressed round Him. The verb "thronged" (Gk. *sumpnigo*, **soom-pnee-go**) has the idea of pressing together. It means literally that the crowd was suffocating Jesus.

43 And a woman having an issue of blood twelve years, which had spent all her living upon physicians, neither could be healed of any,

In this crowded situation, there was also a woman who was in a desperate condition. She had been suffering for 12 years and had spent all of her money seeking a cure. Instead of getting better, her health continued to deteriorate. Her sickness was incurable and must have caused her a lot of distress. It had both physical and social consequences. She was ceremonially unclean and thus was not permitted to take any part in the temple worship or touch anybody (see Leviticus 15:18-27). Her uncleanness was considered to be contagious. She was not at the right place according to the law.

44 Came behind him, and touched the border of his garment: and immediately her issue of blood stanched.

The woman believed so strongly that the power of God was working through Jesus (see v. 48) that she thought that if she could only touch Him, she would be healed. She came from behind and touched the border of His garment, certainly hoping that nobody would notice her. It was probably the nature of her sickness that caused her to make this clandestine approach. Still, she was instantly healed of her sickness. Used here, the verb "stanched" (Gk. *histemi*, **his-tay-mee**) intransitively means "to stand still" or "to cease," thus, her illness ceased to be.

45 And Jesus said, Who touched me? When all denied, Peter and they that were with him said, Master, the multitude throng thee and press thee, and sayest thou, Who touched me?

Jesus perceived that someone had touched Him, and He insisted on knowing who it was. The disciples could not understand Jesus' question. When the people around Him denied touching Him, Peter exclaimed that with the pressure of the people they were all touching Him. So, it seemed silly to ask who had touched Him.

46 And Jesus said, Somebody hath touched me: for I perceive that virtue is gone out of me.

Jesus insisted that someone had touched Him. He knew that someone had touched Him in a more than casual or superficial way. He was conscious that "virtue is gone out" of Him (cf. Luke 5:17; 6:19). The word "virtue" (Gk. *dunamis*, **doo-nam-is**) means "power" or "force." The phrase seems to indicate that Jesus did not heal without some cost to Himself.

Jesus certainly knew who touched Him (cf. v. 47; John 2:24-25; 6:61). He wanted to bring the woman out into the open for her own good. In order for her to get back to a normal life, it was necessary that her healing be widely known.

Note: Don't hold back on telling about your healing

47 And when the woman saw that she was not hid, she came trembling, and falling down before him, she declared unto him before all the people for what cause she had touched him, and how she was healed immediately.

The woman came forward when she "saw that she was not hid." She knelt before Him in terror and confessed in front of all the people why she had touched Him. The word "trembling" (Gk. *tremo*, **trem-o**) means "to tremble with fear" or "to be afraid." In fear, she admitted her action and probably wondered what was going to happen. Would her healing be taken away? What would the people think?

48 And he said unto her, Daughter, be of good comfort: thy faith hath made thee whole; go in peace.

First, Jesus comforted her: "Daughter, be of good comfort." There was no need to fear. He then related her healing directly to her faith (cf. 7:50; 17:19). She had a genuine faith and not a mere superstition.

The word "peace" (Gk. *eirene*, **i-ray-nay**) denotes a plenitude of life and salvation. It is the messianic gift par excellence (cf. 1:79; 2:14, 29; 7:50; 10:5-6; 11:21; 12:51; 14:32; 19:38, 42; 24:36; Isaiah 9:5-6; Micah 5:4-5).

49 While he yet spake, there cometh one from the ruler of the synagogue's house, saying to him, Thy daughter is dead; trouble not the Master.

Someone from Jairus's house came at that point to report the death of the young child. There was no further need to "trouble. . . the Master." The word "trouble" (Gk. *skullo*, **skool-lo**) means "to weary" or "to trouble." The substance of the message was, "It is too late. The situation has gone beyond Jesus' ability to do anything about it. Jesus' power cannot extend beyond death."

50 But when Jesus heard it, he answered him, saying, Fear not: believe only, and she shall be made whole.

Jesus heard it and exhorted Jairus to fear not and believe (Gk. *pisteuo*, **pist-yoo-o**) meaning literally to "stop fearing," "believe," or "have faith." The tense of the verb (aorist imperative) indicates that Jesus was demanding an act of faith from Jairus (cf. Mark 5:36). He needed to make a quick decision. Jairus believed that Jesus had the power to heal his daughter. He was challenged not to lose that belief, but to persist in faith. By doing so, Jairus witnessed the almighty power of Jesus resurrect his daughter.

51 And when he came into the house, he suffered no man to go in, save Peter, and James, and John, and the father and the mother of the maiden.

When they arrived at the home of Jairus, Jesus permitted no one to come in except the child's parents and three of His disciples: Peter, James, and John. These three disciples were associated in a particular way with Jesus' ministry. They were with Him on the Mount of Transfiguration (Luke 9:28-36) and in the Garden of Gethsemane (Matthew 26:37; Mark 14:33).

52 And all wept, and bewailed her: but he said, Weep not; she is not dead, but sleepeth.

The phrase "all wept, and bewailed" certainly included the household, the neighbors, and professional mourners, as was the custom of the time in Israel (see Luke 7:12; Matthew 9:23; 2 Chronicles 35:25). They were engaged in noisy grief. Jesus quieted them with the words, "She is not dead, but sleepeth." "Sleepeth" (Gk. *katheudo*, **kath-yoo-do**) is used primarily of natural sleep. Here Jesus is using the term figuratively to talk about the child's death (cf. John 11:11-14; Acts 7:60; 13:36; 1 Corinthians 15:18-20; 1 Thessalonians 4:13-15). In that sense, to use the word "sleep" in this case indicates that her death was only temporary.

53 And they laughed him to scorn, knowing that she was dead.

The mourners scoffed at Jesus. They knew that the child was dead. The word "knowing" (Gk. *eido*, **i-do**) denotes a fullness of knowledge. The mourners knew from observation, so there was no doubt that the child was dead.

54 And he put them all out, and took her by the hand, and called, saying, Maid, arise.

The mourners, wailing, went in with Jesus; but He put them all out. Jesus took the child by the hand and ordered her to arise (Gk. *egeiro*, **eg-i-ro**, literally, to "arise from sleep, sitting, lying or sickness"; cf. Matthew 2:14; 9:5, 7, 19; James 5:15).

55 And her spirit came again, and she arose straightway: and he commanded to give her meat.

The essence which gives life and animation to her body returned (cf. 1 Kings 17:21-22). The word "spirit" (Gk. *pneuma*, **pnyoo-mah**) means "wind" or "breath." Here it has the meaning of "soul."

Jesus raised Jairus's daughter instantaneously; then He ordered the parents to give her food.

56 And her parents were astonished: but he charged them that they should tell no man what was done.

The child's parents were amazed at the miracle. Jesus requested that the parents not report what He had done to anyone. It was difficult to keep quiet after such a miracle. Besides, there were many witnesses (see vv. 52-53). Why this secrecy? Maybe the report would increase the hostility of the leaders against Jesus and cause them to seek to kill Him before His time came. Or possibly the crowd would increase so much that it would limit Jesus' effective service and provoke a revolution. Another possibility was to remember that many things would not be understood until after Jesus' own Resurrection (1 Corinthians 13:9-10).

DAILY BIBLE READINGS

M: A Centurion's Servant Is Healed
Luke 7:1-10

T: A Girl Restored, A Woman Healed
Matthew 9:18-26

W: Two Blind Men Healed by Faith
Matthew 9:27-31

T: A Hemorrhaging Woman Is Healed
Mark 5:24b-34

F: A Girl Is Restored to Life
Mark 5:35-43

S: A Sick Woman Is Healed
Luke 8:40-48

S: Jairus's Daughter Is Alive
Luke 8:49-56

Has God healed you or someone else in your family? Here is another opportunity for you to encourage others by sharing a positive testimony using the *Precepts* Discussion Group feature on your *Precepts For Living* CD-ROM.

TEACHING TIPS

August 21
Bible Study Guide 12

1. Words You Should Know

A. Neighbour (Luke 10:27, 29, 36) *plesion* (Gk.)—A friend or any other person when two people are concerned.

B. Priest (v. 31) *hiereus* (Gk.)—One responsible for worship and sacrifices at the temple.

C. Levite (v. 32) *Levites* (Gk.)—A lay associate of the priest. Levites assisted priests in temple duties such as providing music for the worship service and security in the temple buildings.

D. Samaritan (v. 33) *Samareites* (Gk.)—A person who lived in the city or region of Samaria.

2. Teacher Preparation

A. Read the DEVOTIONAL READING (Matthew 22:34-40) and study the FOCAL VERSES as you prepare for the lesson.

B. Explore the BIBLE STUDY GUIDE for this lesson. Note salient points in the IN FOCUS and IN DEPTH sections.

C. Materials needed: Bibles, pens, and paper.

3. Starting the Lesson

A. Begin the lesson with prayer.

B. Read the KEEP IN MIND verse and the LESSON AIM aloud. Next, ask a student volunteer to read the FOCAL VERSES.

4. Getting into the Lesson

A. To set the stage for the lesson, ask the students whether they would give to a beggar on the street or stop to help someone who appeared stranded on the road. Why or why not? Then ask whether they believe that beggars should be in shelters or get public assistance rather than beg.

B. Have the students read the IN FOCUS and BACKGROUND sections of the lesson.

C. Now, read and discuss the IN DEPTH section. After a brief discussion, ask the students: "Who is your neighbor?"

5. Relating the Lesson to Life

A. Lead the students back into the discussion of whether they would give to beggars or help others in distress. Then, have them explain what circumstances would or would not prompt them to help.

B. Ask the students their definition of "a good neighbor" and how they can demonstrate those attributes.

C. Now, have the students complete the SEARCH THE SCRIPTURES and DISCUSS THE MEANING sections.

D. Conclude by reading the LESSON IN OUR SOCIETY section. Discuss.

6. Arousing Action

A. Review the MAKE IT HAPPEN section and challenge the students to put the suggestions into practice.

B. Discuss any special insights the students received from the lesson today and how these insights might affect them in the future.

C. Encourage the students to read the suggested DAILY BIBLE READINGS for daily devotions. Close with prayer.

WORSHIP GUIDE

For the Superintendent or Teacher
Theme: The Good Samaritan
Theme Song: "Just a Closer Walk with Thee"
Scripture: Deuteronomy 15:7-11; Luke 10:25-37
Song: "I Want to Be a Follower of Christ"
Meditation: Thank You, Lord, for inspiring us to want to help our fellow man, not for rewards, but because we are children of God. Thank You also for allowing our lives to be a light for others to follow.
Amen.

THE GOOD SAMARITAN

Bible Background • LUKE 10:25-37
Printed Text • LUKE 10:25-37
Devotional Reading • MATTHEW 22:34-40

LESSON AIM

By the end of the lesson, the students will learn how to give of themselves unselfishly and commit to being a good neighbor.

KEEP IN MIND

"And he answering said, Thou shalt love the Lord thy God with all thy heart, with all thy soul, and with all thy strength, and with all thy mind; and thy neighbour as thyself" (Luke 10:27).

FOCAL VERSES

Luke 10:25 And, behold, a certain lawyer stood up, and tempted him, saying, Master, what shall I do to inherit eternal life?

26 He said unto him, What is written in the law? how readest thou?

27 And he answering said, Thou shalt love the Lord thy God with all thy heart, and with all thy soul, and with all thy strength, and with all thy mind; and thy neighbour as thyself.

28 And he said unto him, Thou hast answered right: this do, and thou shalt live.

29 But he, willing to justify himself, said unto Jesus, And who is my neighbour?

30 And Jesus answering said, A certain man went down from Jerusalem to Jericho, and fell among thieves, which stripped him of his raiment, and wounded him, and departed, leaving him half dead.

31 And by chance there came down a certain priest that way: and when he saw him, he passed by on the other side.

32 And likewise a Levite, when he was at the

LESSON OVERVIEW

LESSON AIM
KEEP IN MIND
FOCAL VERSES
IN FOCUS
THE PEOPLE, PLACES, AND TIMES
BACKGROUND
AT-A-GLANCE
IN DEPTH
SEARCH THE SCRIPTURES
DISCUSS THE MEANING
LESSON IN OUR SOCIETY
MAKE IT HAPPEN
FOLLOW THE SPIRIT
REMEMBER YOUR THOUGHTS
MORE LIGHT ON THE TEXT
DAILY BIBLE READINGS

place, came and looked on him, and passed by on the other side.

33 But a certain Samaritan, as he journeyed, came where he was: and when he saw him, he had compassion on him,

34 And went to him, and bound up his wounds, pouring in oil and wine, and set him on his own beast, and brought him to an inn, and took care of him.

35 And on the morrow when he departed, he took out two pence, and gave them to the host, and said unto him, Take care of him; and whatsoever thou spendest more, when I come again, I will repay thee.

36 Which now of these three, thinkest thou, was neighbour unto him that fell among the thieves?

37 And he said, He that shewed mercy on him. Then said Jesus unto him, Go, and do thou likewise.

IN FOCUS

Jesse always traveled from one part of town to the other without worrying whether her car would make it. One day on her lunch hour, she took what she thought would be a quick trip to pay a bill. On her way back to the office, she proceeded onto the exit ramp and had to stop because of a backup of cars on the ramp. As the light turned green, her car stalled and would not move. After several attempts to restart the car to no avail, she put her hazard lights on to prevent anyone from driving up directly

AUG 21ST

behind her dead car. She kept looking in her rearview mirror to see that approaching cars were slowing down in time to see her dilemma and then go around. She prayed that no one would hit her from behind while they tried to quickly get on the exit ramp.

She looked again in her mirror as a police car approached. Jesse finally felt relieved, but the officer ignored her, went around her in the left lane, and kept going. "Perhaps he is going to turn around," she surmised. She waited, but he never came back. Later, a large, dark car with wide mirrors approached. She recognized it as an unmarked police car. Again, the driver looked over, went around her, and scurried on. Jesse felt defeated because she now felt that if a policeman wouldn't stop, then no one else would either.

After what seemed like an eternity, a man in an old, large Cadillac-like car stopped behind her and honked his horn. She whispered to herself in a panic, "Doesn't he see my flashers? I can't move this car!"

The man pulled from behind her, over to the right, and got out of his car. He was large in stature and wore dark sunglasses and a baseball cap. In his right hand, he had a cell phone and was talking to someone. Though he was neatly dressed, he still frightened Jesse.

As he approached her vehicle he asked, "What's the matter—car won't start? Lift your hood," he instructed. With some trepidation she acquiesced, but after he fiddled with some wires under the hood the car still did not start. "Let me push you out of the way. Put your car in neutral and steer to the right toward the curb," he further instructed. Next, the man handed her his cell phone to call someone for help. She took the phone and called her office to let them know that she was stranded on an exit ramp, but no one was there who could come to her aid.

The gentleman asked her where she worked and offered to take her back to the office. Jesse prayed and considered her other options; she could stay there and wait until someone at work could come to her rescue, whenever that might be, or allow this good Samaritan to give her a ride back to the office. As the Holy Spirit led her, she prayerfully got into the man's car, where there was gospel music playing. They introduced themselves to each other, and he gave her his business card. As it turned out, the man was the pastor of the church on the next block over from her office.

As they arrived at her place of employment, Jesse thanked him for helping her. The man told her to be sure to have her car towed before nightfall so that it would not be vandalized. As he drove off, she looked after him and said to herself, "God sends angels in all kinds of packages."

In today's lesson we see how Jesus uses the parable of the good Samaritan to illustrate how to show compassion and love for our fellow man.

THE PEOPLE, PLACES, AND TIMES

The Road to Jericho. Travel from Jerusalem to Jericho was by way of a steeply descending road that wound through rocky places that easily hid robbers. Jericho was lower in elevation than Jerusalem, and they were about 17 miles from each other. One had to contend not only with the steepness of the road, but also with ravines, caves, and sharp turns that hindered the traveler. The road was especially dangerous because robbers were common and often attacked a person traveling alone, thus earning the road the name, "path of blood." Many people during that time did not have extra clothes; therefore, clothing was a valuable item to steal.

Laws of Purity. Priests believed that a person was not to touch a corpse because it was impure. Even Pharisees believed that if the shadow of a corpse fell on a person, the person became impure. Priests and Levites were expected to observe high standards of ritual purity for their sacred ministry. When the priest saw the traveler, he did not know whether the man was dead or alive. Therefore, because of the laws governing purity, he did not want to risk defilement by touching him. Such laws were not as strict for Levites, but the Levite also wanted to avoid defilement since any approach to the wounded man would have seriously compromised his position.

BACKGROUND

Samaria was the name given to the northern kingdom and its capital city in ancient Palestine.

The city of Samaria was located north of present-day Jerusalem and east of the Mediterranean Sea. The city was first built on a hill overlooking a main road to Jerusalem, the capital of King David. It was chosen by Omri, king of Israel, to be the capital of the northern kingdom.

After the Assyrians conquered the northern kingdom, they carried off many of its inhabitants, replacing some of them with people from other conquered lands. The people of the region, which became known as Samaria, practiced a form of Judaism and preserved the so-called Samaritan Pentateuch. They claimed it represented an older text of the first five books of the Bible than did the Jewish Torah.

In New Testament times, the Samaritans were considered heretics and were hostile toward the Jews. They were the descendants of colonists whom the Assyrian kings relocated to Palestine after the fall of the northern kingdom in 722 B.C. They were despised by the Jews because of their mixed Jewish-Gentile blood (mixed race) and their different worship, which was centered on Mount Gerizim. Mount Gerizim was the site of the temple the Samaritans had built when they were not allowed to participate in the building of the new temple in Jerusalem.

Modern-day Samaritans practice a religion similar to that of the biblical Jews. Although they are few in number, they still make their home around the ancient temple site of Mount Gerizim, near modern Nabulus, in the area now known as the West Bank.

AT-A-GLANCE

1. Jesus Is a Neighbor (Luke 10:25-32)
2. Neighbors With Compassion (vv. 33-35)
3. Neighbors Without Compassion (vv. 36-37)

IN DEPTH

Stare here 8-17-05

1. Jesus Is a Neighbor (Luke 10:25-32)

In His parables, Jesus negated the barriers that the Jews, Levites, Samaritans, and Pharisees had created between various classes of people. He was told that He couldn't heal on the Sabbath (John 9:13-16). He was told that certain classes of people didn't mix and that He shouldn't speak to a woman, as He had done in Samaria (John 4:9). Again and again, Jesus demonstrated that some Pharisaic traditions were created to keep people apart instead of allowing them to fellowship with each other.

The parable of the good Samaritan showed that everyone is our neighbor. It does not matter whether one is rich, middle-class, or poor; everyone is called to receive Jesus as Lord and Saviour. God does not abide by man-made laws, designed to create divisions and facilitate strife among people of various classes.

The rulers of Jesus' time were often busy promoting their own agendas, and they tried to condemn Jesus because His teaching promoted sharing, caring, and loving one another regardless of one's class or social status.

Jesus is the greatest neighbor, and by His example He shows us how to start breaking down the barriers of separation we have established with our own social groups. Jesus was a neighbor to the poor just as He was to the rich. Jesus isolates no one and relates to everyone, regardless of their background.

2. Neighbors With Compassion (vv. 33-35)

Even though Jewish teachers used the word *neighbor* to mean "fellow Israelite," they were selective in their relationships with non-Jewish people, who also lived in the land. The parable of the good Samaritan is particularly meaningful because it demonstrates how one man ignored his beliefs and background to help someone of another race.

The Samaritan not only traveled down to Jericho, but also showed practical compassion for another person. Helping someone in need was more important to the Samaritan than his religious beliefs or past encounters with this other man's race.

How many times have you been in a situation in which someone of another race stopped to help you, while members of your own race passed you by? You may have been hesitant, but they gave you the help you needed and did what they could to make sure you were all right. As Christians, we too have to lay aside our differences and learn to willingly help our fellow man. Christ is our example. He illustrated agape love and the principle of helping in the parable of the good Samaritan. How many times has God reached down to help you?

3. Neighbors Without Compassion (vv. 36-37)

The hatred between the Samaritans and Jews dates back to Old Testament times. The division between the two groups was so deep that the Jews publicly cursed the Samaritans and prayed that God would not grant them eternal life. In 128 B.C., the Jews attacked and destroyed the Samaritans' temple, trying to force them back into line. Sometime between 9 and 6 B.C., during the Passover, the Samaritans defiled the Jewish temple by spreading men's bones over it. Does this not sound like a modern-day feud?

Race and location keep neighbors from meeting each other, even in some churches. The Samaritans were a mixed race and were thought to be defiled because of this. They were not the kind of people you would want to associate with. Today, it is not uncommon in many upper-class neighborhoods to look down upon or ostracize people of a certain race or social class. We often look upon anyone who is not a part of our group as an outsider.

This is interesting because, although we worship God, we often forget that Jesus consorted with all those people we would consider outcasts. We dislike people because of how they look on the outside. Jesus, however, looks past the outside covering and loves us still. Because He is omniscient (knows everything), He discerns that those people we ignore may have much to offer the kingdom of God. Jesus does not decide whether He is going to associate Himself with us based on the neighborhoods we live in. Instead, His desire for us is that we live righteously, showing love to everyone we encounter.

The priest represented the highest religious leadership among the Jews, and the Levite was an associate of the priest. The Samaritan, however, was seen as a foreigner and someone who would not be moved to show any type of compassion for the Jews. Not only did he stop, he bandaged the man's wounds, put him on his own animal, and took him to a safe haven for care. The Jews held the Samaritans in contempt. It was unthinkable that a Samaritan would demonstrate the most mercy. The priest and the Levite let their relationship with the Samaritans override any demonstration of compassion because he was not their kind.

"Who is my neighbor?" The lawyer already knew the answer: Anyone he could help. He knew what to do; the real question was, would he lay aside his personal feelings to help someone in need? Because of his social stature, the lawyer thought he had a right to eternal life and had proven it by his own righteousness. Jesus knew that the telling of this parable forced the lawyer to follow the moral example of a Samaritan in Jesus' story. The lawyer was also forced to answer the question, "Who is my neighbor?" As he considered the answer, he thought of all those people he had wrongly categorized, and he came to realize that even the lowest class of people deserve compassion.

Will you do what the Lord requires of you, or will you ignore Him like the Levite and Pharisee and continue pursuing your own agenda?

SEARCH THE SCRIPTURES

1. What did Jesus do to illustrate how to be a good neighbor (Luke 10:30)?

2. How did Jesus respond when the lawyer asked Him how he could have eternal life (v. 27)?

3. When the Samaritan saw the injured man, what made him stop to help (v. 33)?

4. What did Jesus encourage the lawyer to practice (v. 37)?

5. Who is my neighbor (v. 37)?

DISCUSS THE MEANING

1. What is the relationship between the priest, the Levite, and the Samaritan?

2. What is the significance of the priest and Levite passing the injured man on the road?

3. What is the importance of the Samaritan stopping?

4. We are given an idea why the priest and Levite did not stop in THE PEOPLE, PLACES,

AND TIMES section. What reason would the policeman and undercover policeman portrayed in the IN FOCUS section have for not stopping?

LESSON IN OUR SOCIETY

Sometimes we will not stop to help someone because we think they will harm us. We are afraid that stopping may do more injury than good. We suspect others of being involved in illicit behavior such as drug dealing or running a scam to steal money or property. We look at race, location, and the appearance of the person before determining whether help should be given. We look at all of these things, but God examines our hearts first. God stops and listens to our cries of distress no matter what condition we are in and comes to our rescue.

The next time you pass someone who is injured or is stopped on the side of the road, put yourself in their place. Wouldn't you want someone to stop and help you?

MAKE IT HAPPEN

Society has taught us to be watchful and mistrustful of any stranger. We consider our neighbors to be only the people who live on our street, and outside of that we don't volunteer to help.

These are still dangerous times. If you are traveling and see an injured person or someone needing help with a vehicle, pray for discernment, asking God for guidance, and if the Holy Spirit dictates, stop and offer assistance. If you don't feel comfortable enough to stop, call the police to get the person some help. You might also set up a meeting with a representative from the police department to come speak with your church ministry or watch group about how to give and receive roadside assistance.

FOLLOW THE SPIRIT

What God wants me to do:

_____

_____

REMEMBER YOUR THOUGHTS

Special insights I have learned:

_____

_____

MORE LIGHT ON THE TEXT
Luke 10:25-37

25 And, behold, a certain lawyer stood up, and tempted him, saying, Master, what shall I do to inherit eternal life? 26 He said unto him, What is written in the law? how readest thou?

Once again, a teacher of the Law attempts to match his finite or limited knowledge of the Word of God with the infinite or unfathomable knowledge of the Son of God. Luke tells us that a certain lawyer tempted Him. The Greek word for "tempted" is *ekpeirazo* (**ek-pi-rad'-zo**) and means "to test or try." Jesus faced these sorts of tests from religious leaders several times in Scripture. The purpose was to acquire some reason to convict Jesus of blasphemy and ultimately to execute Him.

By calling Him "Master" (Gk. *didaskalos*, **did-as'-kal-os**, meaning "teacher"), the lawyer acknowledges Jesus' authority and familiarity with the Word. The use of this word is not an acknowledgment that Jesus is the only begotten of the Father. He concedes only what many believe about Christ today: that He was simply a great teacher.

The lawyer inquires about his ability to attain everlasting life: What work did he need to perform in order to live forever? We must keep in mind that the religious leaders during Jesus' earthly ministry were steeped in tradition and man-made amendments to the Law. The Pharisees, scribes, and elders ranked God's commandments and rules. Emphasizing some, they minimized others. In comparing this passage to Matthew's account of the incident (Matthew 22), we see that significance is attached to the greatest commandment.

Why was the lawyer testing Jesus? He wanted to see if the Lord agreed with the assessment made by the teachers of the Law regarding which of God's commandments was the greatest—the one that would lead to eternal life.

However, Jesus puts the ball back in his court. He asks the man for his personal interpretation and opinion: "How readest thou?" Because of the lawyer's expertise in the law and his likely (though unstated) association with the religious leaders, he responds with confidence and assurance.

The Good Samaritan showed that God's love embraces all people.

27 And he answering said, Thou shalt love the Lord thy God with all thy heart, and with all thy soul, and with all thy strength, and with all thy mind; and thy neighbour as thyself. 28 And he said unto him, Thou hast answered right: this do, and thou shalt live.

The lawyer quotes the words of Moses from Deuteronomy 6:5 and Leviticus 19:18, respectively. Jesus says that all of the Old Testament prophecy and Law hang on these two demands (Matthew 22:40).

The Master further affirms the lawyer's response by commending his answer and exhorting him to do as he stated. Jesus tells him that he shall live if he does so, but the lawyer needed to understand that the only way he could love God with his complete being and his neighbor as himself was through faith in Christ. No acts or deeds born of human will and intellect would suffice. Up to this point, the lawyer did not understand this concept because of his deep roots in the traditional interpretations of the Law.

The essence of Jesus' statement is that by keeping the Law perfectly at all times, one may live forever. However, because no one besides the

Saviour could keep the Law perfectly at all times, no one would live forever.

Observe again the underlying intent of the lawyer's question, "What works can I do to earn everlasting life?" Jesus gave the answer: Maintain God's Law (the same one that you know and teach) without ever failing. Although his reply received Christ's stamp of approval, the lawyer becomes dissatisfied with what has transpired. He knows that man cannot keep the Law and is destined to die. He isn't expecting Jesus to turn the tables on him, so he feels compelled to pick at Him more.

29 But he, willing to justify himself, said unto Jesus, And who is my neighbour?

The phrase "willing to justify himself" indicates that the lawyer was resolved and determined to show that he was righteous. The Greek word translated as "justify" is *dikaioo* (**dik-ah-yo'-o**), which means to show, exhibit, declare, or pronounce one to be righteous, whether he is or wishes himself to be considered.

He wants Jesus to confirm his limited definition of "neighbor." The teachers of the Law, the

Pharisees, the chief priests, and other religious leaders were an aristocratic group, members of an elite fraternity. They felt they were better than the common folk of the land. Thus, not everyone was their neighbor. Their status allowed them to pick and choose their neighbors according to class and race.

30 And Jesus answering said, A certain man went down from Jerusalem to Jericho, and fell among thieves, which stripped him of his raiment, and wounded him, and departed, leaving him half dead.

Jerusalem and Jericho were centers of religious activity: Jerusalem was the base of Judaism (and later the Christian church) and Jericho served as the home of hundreds of priests. No more than 18 miles separated these towns. The main road connecting them was notorious for its high crime rate, as the rugged landscape provided good hideouts for robbers awaiting commuters traveling the steep path. In this story, some thieves attacked a traveler on his way to Jericho, tore his clothes from him, beat him, and left him on the road to die.

31 And by chance there came down a certain priest that way: and when he saw him, he passed by on the other side. 32 And likewise a Levite, when he was at the place, came and looked on him, and passed by on the other side.

The priest was headed toward Jericho, which was likely his home. We should also understand that since he was leaving Jerusalem, the site of the temple, the priest had concluded his ministerial duties for the day. He noticed the man lying on the road, but he offered no help. He placed a limit on his services and deemed anything done outside the walls of the temple to be beyond his capability and/or obligation.

It's also possible that three other excuses ran through the priest's mind: First, he feared for his own life; second, he didn't have the time, energy, or resources to help the man the way he needed to; and third, he figured that someone else would take care of the man. How many times do we, as Christians, use these excuses to avoid helping someone in need?

When the Levite came along the same path headed in the same direction, he went to the victim and looked him over. Then he decided to pass over to the other side. Instead of assessing the damage and taking action, he took inventory and remained inactive.

One prevailing argument for the behavior of the priest and the Levite contends that they did not want to defile themselves by interacting with a stranger, who was doubtlessly bruised and bloody. Jewish customs—not God's Word—forbid the Jews from such contact, and the priest and Levite displayed their preference for man's rules over godly love and mercy.

33 But a certain Samaritan, as he journeyed, came where he was: and when he saw him, he had compassion on him, 34 And went to him, and bound up his wounds, pouring in oil and wine, and set him on his own beast, and brought him to an inn, and took care of him. 35 And on the morrow when he departed, he took out two pence, and gave them to the host, and said unto him, Take care of him; and whatsoever thou spendest more, when I come again, I will repay thee.

The significance of the Samaritan in this parable cannot be overstated. Jews despised these people because they were products of crossbreeding between the Assyrian conquerors of Israel and their Jewish captives. Because of the Samaritans' ancestry, Jews believed that their faith was diluted, thereby making them unclean and detestable. Not only did "the Jews have no dealings with [them]" (John 4:9), but they also believed the Samaritans to be demon-possessed (John 8:48).

The Samaritan had compassion on the man. He didn't merely sympathize or empathize with him but felt compelled to perform an act of mercy to deliver him from his dire situation. The thieves had left him half dead, so the Samaritan attempted to save the man's life.

This show of compassion mirrors that of Jesus in three instances: healing a multitude of sick people (Matthew 14:14), feeding the 4,000 (Matthew 15:32), and healing two blind men (Matthew 20:34). In each of these scenes, a feeling of pity prompted a work of mercy.

The Samaritan attended to the man's injuries,

substituting personal possessions for medical equipment. (We must keep in mind that Luke was a physician, so he was careful to include details of the trauma.) Notice the sacrifices the Samaritan made. He bandaged the victim's wounds, likely with strips of his own clothing. To the man's bruises he applied oil and wine, which served as household remedies. He set him on his own beast, which probably meant that the Samaritan walked to the inn. He rearranged his schedule to spend the night with the man. Lastly, he gave the innkeeper a down payment for any expenses with a pledge to return and pay the balance. "Two pence" (Gk. *duo denarion,* **doo-o day-nar'-ee-on**) equaled two days' wages for a laborer of that era.

This was an extraordinary show of godly love. The Samaritan took the initiative to put his own needs aside and serve someone else. Furthermore, he followed through on what he started, giving of his time, possessions, money, heart, and honor for another human being. Preservation of a man's life became his most important priority, not the rules and norms established by man.

36 Which now of these three, thinkest thou, was neighbour unto him that fell among the thieves? 37 And he said, He that shewed mercy on him. Then said Jesus unto him, Go, and do thou likewise.

Jesus again puts the lawyer on the spot. He asks the lawyer for his opinion on who acted neighborly, based on the lawyer's knowledge of the Law and his response in verse 27. Jesus seemed to do His best teaching when He allowed His audience to realize the truth for themselves instead of disclosing it Himself.

The lawyer, as Luke's narrative indicates, does not use the word "Samaritan." Although he understands the message behind Jesus' parable, the same arrogance that spurred him to justify himself in verse 29 would not allow him to confess verbally that the Samaritan acted more righteously than the priest or the Levite.

His obstinacy showed how humans will refuse to give credit where credit is due, even when there is no debate. In the lawyer's eyes, Samaritans could do nothing noble or admirable, a misconception that led to this being labeled the parable of the good Samaritan. The play on words shows how God can use what's thought of as the "worst" of society to do what's best for His kingdom.

Jesus then reinforces His answer in verse 28. He advises the lawyer to do as the one who showed mercy on the beaten man had done, trying to get him to realize that keeping the letter of the Law is not enough to inherit eternal life. Love, mercy, and grace must exceed the limits of the Law, and those seeking everlasting life must exhibit these traits through faith in Jesus Christ.

DAILY BIBLE READINGS

M: The Great Commandment
Deuteronomy 6:1-9
T: Love Your Neighbor
Leviticus 19:11-18
W: The Greatest Commandment
Matthew 22:34-40
T: The First Commandment
Mark 12:28-34
F: Love Your Neighbor as Yourself
Luke 10:25-29
S: The Parable of the Good Samaritan
Luke 10:30-37
S: Love Fulfills the Law
Romans 13:8-14

Use the reference tools on your *Precepts For Living* CD-ROM to find out more about the city of Samaria.

TEACHING TIPS

August 28
Bible Study Guide 13

1. Words You Should Know

A. Parable (Luke 14:7) *parabole* (Gk.)—A method of speech in which moral or spiritual truth is illustrated by an analogy derived from common experience in life; a fictitious story usually conveying a moral or spiritual truth.

B. Kingdom of God (v. 15) *basileia theos* (Gk.)—The redemptive reign of God dynamically active to establish His rule among men.

C. Servant (v. 21) *doulos* (Gk.)—Someone who serves a higher authority, either voluntarily or involuntarily.

2. Teacher Preparation

A. Read Luke 13—15 for background information on the text.

B. Also read the DEVOTIONAL READING (1 Peter 5:3-10) and study the FOCAL VERSES carefully.

C. Review today's BIBLE STUDY GUIDE and answer the SEARCH THE SCRIPTURES and DISCUSS THE MEANING questions.

3. Starting the Lesson

A. Begin with prayer, keeping the LESSON AIM in mind.

B. Have each student read a verse until all of the FOCAL VERSES are read.

C. Ask your students to reflect on the passage and apply it to their daily life.

D. Give the students a few minutes to read the IN FOCUS story and the BACKGROUND section so they will be aware of how this lesson impacts their own lives.

E. Have your students answer the questions in the SEARCH THE SCRIPTURES and DISCUSS THE MEANING sections.

4. Getting into the Lesson

A. Explain to the students that a parable is a simple narrative used to convey a profound truth.

B. Have the students read THE PEOPLE, PLACES, AND TIMES section.

5. Relating the Lesson to Life

A. Ask the students to share any African American parables that helped them while growing up.

B. Have the students define the term *humility* and ask them if they practice it.

C. Ask the students how they can learn *when* or *when not* to practice humility.

6. Arousing Action

A. Encourage your students to perform some task this week, without seeking recognition or honor. Invite them to focus on doing God's will in anonymity, knowing that God "which seeth in secret himself shall reward thee openly" (Matthew 6:4).

B. Remind them that being a Christian is not about seeking honor, but rather striving to do God's will.

C. Urge the students to invite people to the church as Jesus was inviting people into the kingdom of God.

HUMILITY AND HOSPITALITY

Bible Background • LUKE 14:7-24
Printed Text • LUKE 14:7-11, 15-24
Devotional Reading • 1 PETER 5:3-10

LESSON AIM

By the end of the lesson, the students should be able to see the benefits of humility and the importance of inviting everyone to take part in the Church of Jesus Christ and, ultimately, the kingdom of God. They should also learn that if God welcomes everyone who accepts His invitation, then so should we.

KEEP IN MIND

"And the lord said unto the servant, Go out into the highways and hedges, and compel them to come in, that my house may be filled" (Luke 14:23).

FOCAL VERSES

Luke 14:7 And he put forth a parable to those which were bidden, when he marked how they chose out the chief rooms; saying unto them,

8 When thou art bidden of any man to a wedding, sit not down in the highest room; lest a more honourable man than thou be bidden of him;

9 And he that bade thee and him come and say to thee, Give this man place: and thou begin with shame to take the lowest room.

10 But when thou art bidden, go and sit down in the lowest room; that when he that bade thee cometh, he may say unto thee, Friend, go up higher: then shalt thou have worship in the presence of them that sit at meat with thee.

11 For whosoever exalteth himself shall be abased; and he that humbleth himself shall be exalted.

LESSON OVERVIEW

LESSON AIM
KEEP IN MIND
FOCAL VERSES
IN FOCUS
THE PEOPLE, PLACES, AND TIMES
BACKGROUND
AT-A-GLANCE
IN DEPTH
SEARCH THE SCRIPTURES
DISCUSS THE MEANING
LESSON IN OUR SOCIETY
MAKE IT HAPPEN
FOLLOW THE SPIRIT
REMEMBER YOUR THOUGHTS
MORE LIGHT ON THE TEXT
DAILY BIBLE READINGS

14:15 And when one of them that sat at meat with him heard these things, he said unto him, Blessed is he that shall eat bread in the kingdom of God.

16 Then said he unto him, A certain man made a great supper, and bade many:

17 And sent his servant at supper time to say to them that were bidden, Come; for all things are now ready.

18 And they all with one consent began to make excuse. The first said unto him, I have bought a piece of ground, and I must needs go and see it: I pray thee have me excused.

19 And another said, I have bought five yoke of oxen, and I go to prove them: I pray thee have me excused.

20 And another said, I have married a wife, and therefore I cannot come.

21 So that servant came, and shewed his lord these things. Then the master of the house being angry said to his servant, Go out quickly into the streets and lanes of the city, and bring in hither the poor, and the maimed, and the halt, and the blind.

22 And the servant said, Lord, it is done as thou hast commanded, and yet there is room.

23 And the lord said unto the servant, Go out into the highways and hedges, and compel them to come in, that my house may be filled.

24 For I say unto you, That none of those men which were bidden shall taste of my supper.

474

IN FOCUS

A legend was told that many years ago, there lived a man so spiritual that angels came from heaven to see how one could be so godly. This kind and gentle soul simply went about his life radiating love. Two phrases summed up his outlook: He gave and he forgave. Yet, these words never fell from his lips; they were expressed in his ready smile, his kindness, love, and goodwill.

Because of his countenance, the angels asked the Creator, "Oh, Lord, grant him the gift of miracles!" God replied, "I consent. Ask for him whatever you wish."

"What do you desire?" cried the angels to this humble servant.

"What can I wish for?" asked the holy man. "That God give me His grace? He's already done that."

The angels insisted, "You must ask for a miracle, or one will be forced upon you."

"Very well," said the man. "My wish is that I do a great deal of good without ever knowing it."

The angels were even more perplexed. They took counsel together and developed the following plan: Each time the man's shadow fell behind him or at his side, it would have the power to cure disease, soothe pain, and comfort sorrow.

And so it came to pass, as this gentle man walked life's paths, his shadow caused withered plants to bloom, produced clear water in muddy streams, and gave joy to unhappy people. The people, respecting his humility, followed him closely, never speaking about his miracles. Little by little, they even came to forget his name and called him only "the holy man."

The point of this parable is that by radiating love and kindness, each of us has the power to do good without realizing it. The secret of being a saint is being a saint in secret.

In today's lesson, we learn that exercising humility is a requirement of being a disciple. Jesus said, "He that humbleth himself shall be exalted" (Luke 14:11). When we do God's will in a spirit of humility, we glorify God, bless our community, and put ourselves in a position where God will exalt us.

THE PEOPLE, PLACES, AND TIMES

The Pharisees. A religious sect active in Palestine during the New Testament period. The Pharisees are consistently depicted in the Gospels as Jesus' antagonists. It is commonly held that the Pharisees represented mainstream Judaism early in the first century and that they were characterized by a variety of morally objectionable features. Many Bible dictionaries and similar works of reference depict the Pharisees as greedy, hypocritical, lacking a sense of justice, overly concerned with fulfilling the literal details of the law, and insensitive to the spiritual significance of the Old Testament. However, modern scholars have uncovered some new information about the Pharisees. Namely, they were not all of questionable character, and they only represented a small movement in a highly diversified society. They may have been Jesus' main antagonists as described in the Gospels, but there were other religious sects in the Jewish aristocracy that may have antagonized Jesus' movement as well. According to the Jewish historian, Josephus, the Pharisees were "extremely influential among the townsfolk; and all prayers and sacred rites of divine worship [were] performed according to their exposition."

Comfort, Philip W., and Walter A. Elwell, eds. *Tyndale Bible Dictionary.* Wheaton, Ill.: Tyndale House Publishers, 2001. 1026-1027.

BACKGROUND

Jesus had many confrontations with his main antagonists, the Pharisees. In today's text, He is eating at the house of one of the chief Pharisees and He teaches them about humility and hospitality. Although they invited Jesus to their homes, the Pharisees treated Jesus with contempt. They often verbally engaged Him while in the synagogue to entrap Him.

The Pharisees were adversaries of Jesus because He threatened their status in and grip on the Jewish social order. In both Northern and Southern Israel, the Pharisees were a powerful religious-political organization. Jesus threatened their influence because He was the common peoples' champion. Jesus exposed the Pharisees' flawed and oppressive theology and their selfish ambition for power.

In today's text, Jesus chastises them for not being humble or useful in bringing the kingdom of God into reality. He also reminds them through a parable that if the current religious leaders do not accept God's invitation to be a part of the kingdom of God, then those whom many considered unclean and sinners will be the invited guests at the messianic banquet.

AT-A-GLANCE

1. Expectations of Christians
(Luke 14:7-11)
2. Excuses by Christians (vv. 15-20)
3. Executing God's Plan (vv. 21-24)

IN DEPTH

1. Expectations of Christians (Luke 14:7-11)

Jesus noticed how the invited guests at the Pharisee's house chose the best seats in the house for themselves. He disdained their ambition, their desire to be seen, and their desire to be first. He then instructs the religious leaders on the value of humility. To be humble is to be confident in one's abilities, while at the same time not thinking too highly of oneself. True humility can be attained when we match our lives with Jesus' life (cf. Philippians 2:5-11). When we do that, and see how far we are from His high standards, we cannot help but abandon any exaggerated arrogance on our part. If humility was good enough for Jesus, surely it is good enough for us. Jesus expects all His disciples, including today's religious leaders, to emulate His humility.

Jesus clearly states that a person who exalts himself will be brought down, but he who humbles himself will be exalted (Luke 14:11). We know of many in the church who have exalted themselves only to be brought down due to some ethical infraction. We also know of many who have humbled themselves and worked on behalf of the good of the community. And as a result, they and their churches have been exalted. The benefits of practicing humility and the implications continue for us today. Let us minis-

ter to our brothers and sisters for the sake of the Gospel and not for publicity, notoriety, or fame.

2. Excuses by Christians (vv. 15-20)

While Jesus is still talking with the Pharisees, someone brings up how blessed it will be to eat bread in the kingdom of God. (Most likely, this Pharisee is referring to the 'messianic banquet,' which will occur when the Messiah establishes God's kingdom on earth.) Jesus then tells a parable about how the people who are invited to a banquet first appear to be willing to attend it, but when they are told that the banquet hall is ready, they make excuses about why they cannot attend. They say that they are busy with possessions, people, finances, or family obligations; those who refused the invitation all want excused absences. The servant explains the situation to his lord. Upon hearing that his invitations have been rejected, the lord commands his servant to go into the streets, highways, and hedges to invite all who would come, regardless of their socioeconomic status. This parable is an indictment against the Pharisees, professional religionists who rejected Jesus' invitation to join His kingdom movement. Based on the parable, the "righteous" were invited first, but when they refused to attend because of excuses, those considered to be unrighteous were invited in their place.

The warning in this parable is that we must never become so busy or preoccupied that we refuse to accept God's invitation. Today, God invites us to make disciples, preach His Word, pastor His churches, start prison ministries, and start men's ministries, women's ministries, and youth ministries. If we continue to refuse God's invitation, He may simply choose someone else to do His work. It is time to examine our lives and our churches to eliminate all individual and collective excuses for not serving God wholeheartedly.

As African Americans, we know God has blessed us despite the suffering we have had to endure in America. We know that if our lives are going to change for the better, then we must initiate the change. So let us serve God wholeheartedly, spread the power of love, and preach the Good News of the Gospel. Let us accept God's invitation and do God's will with a greater commitment than we have ever had before.

3. Executing God's Plan (vv. 21-24)

In the parable, after the initial invitees rejected the lord's invitation, the servant was told to go where he had not gone before and compel outsiders to attend the great banquet. It was a revolutionary and radical step for the lord to resort to such a tactic. The point is, the lord's house was going to be filled with people no matter what.

We can learn from the way the servant in the parable fulfilled his lord's wishes. The servant's activity is really a metaphor for evangelism. He models the behavior that all of God's children need to have: the ability to follow orders to invite anyone and everyone to come into the Lord's kingdom.

The servant's mission in the story is essentially the Church's mission today. We are not to be selective when we invite people to Christ, but we are to be inclusive. The poor, the crippled, the blind, and the lame all have value in God's kingdom. The parable shows us the inclusive nature of God. He does not show favoritism. He welcomes everyone who receives Him as Lord of their lives. He does not exclude anyone from His call, yet people still reject Him.

Jesus gave the Great Commission in Matthew 28:19: "Go ye therefore, and teach all nations, baptizing them in the name of the Father, and of the Son, and of the Holy Ghost." As Christians, it is our mission to go into the streets, lanes, highways, and hedges to compel our brothers and sisters to come into the kingdom of God. It is our mission to go into the projects, the ghettos, and the urban jungles to compel our brothers and sisters to receive Christ as Lord and Saviour. In this parable, Jesus paints a picture of executing the plan of God, which is to welcome the oppressed and dispossessed—even if it means doing so at the expense of the self-righteous.

SEARCH THE SCRIPTURES

1. Where did Jesus say one should sit when invited to a banquet in order not to be embarrassed later (Luke 14:8-9)?

2. What happens when you exalt yourself? What happens when you humble yourself (v. 11)?

3. Why did the invited guests refuse to respond to the invitation of the rich man (vv. 18-21)?

4. When the invited guests refused the invitation, what did the rich man tell his servant to do (v. 21)?

5. Were the guests who refused the rich man's invitation given a second chance or an opportunity to change their minds (v. 24)?

DISCUSS THE MEANING

1. Why did Jesus have a problem with the Pharisees' selfish ambition?

2. Why did Jesus try to teach them about humility?

3. In what ways can you practice humility? Is humility always a good thing (see Proverbs 11:2; 15:33; 22:4; 1 Peter 5:5)?

4. Excuses prevented the invited guests from taking advantage of a great opportunity. How dangerous are excuses? How are excuses preventing the church from taking advantage of great opportunities?

LESSON IN OUR SOCIETY

Humility is one characteristic all God's people should practice. To be humble does not mean that one puts oneself down, but rather that one seeks to help others in any way possible without fanfare and notoriety. The kingdom of God is not made up of big "I's" and little "you's." It is made up of people of equal standing in God's eyes. As we follow the example of Jesus Christ, we can remain humble in all that we do. Today's lesson teaches us that humility is the quickest way to execute God's salvation plan for those who accept His invitation.

MAKE IT HAPPEN

Decide today that you will live a life of humility. Understand the hospitality of God by recognizing how He welcomes all who accept His will for their lives. Today, decide to walk in humility and welcome all who will come into the church, remembering that God has accepted you in spite of your imperfections. If God has accepted and forgiven you, then you ought to forgive and accept others.

No matter what you do for a living, when you keep in perspective how much Jesus has done, and is still doing for you, you can't help but remain humble. Purpose in your heart to show someone else the same mercy God has shown you.

FOLLOW THE SPIRIT
What God wants me to do:

_____

_____

REMEMBER YOUR THOUGHTS
Special insights I have learned:

_____

_____

MORE LIGHT ON THE TEXT
Luke 14:7-11, 15-24
7 And he put forth a parable to those which were bidden, when he marked how they chose out the chief rooms; saying unto them,

The ancient Jews considered it a virtuous deed to invite prominent teachers to share in the Sabbath meal, and well-known teachers often participated in dialogues at these banquets. Jesus had been invited to share in the Sabbath meal at the house of a prominent Pharisee (Matthew 14:1) when he "marked" how the guests "chose out the chief rooms." The word "marked" is translated from the Greek *epecho* and means to fix the mind upon, give heed to, or pay attention to. In other words, the Lord noticed how the guests vied for the "chief rooms" (Gk. *protoklisia*). *Protos* means "first" or "chief" and *klisia* means a place of reclining at a table (on couches), as the wealthy people did in New Testament times. So this compound refers to places of honor at the table.

The *triclinia,* or Grecian table used in those times, consisted of three sections that were placed together to form a flat-bottomed letter U. The space enclosed by the table was left vacant so that the servants might enter it to serve the guests, who reclined on couches around the outer margin of the table. The central seat of each of these three sections was deemed a place of honor. Jesus noticed the antics of the guests as they competed for the prominent seats and may have found them amusing.

8 When thou art bidden of any man to a wedding, sit not down in the highest room; lest a more honourable man than thou be bidden of him; 9 And he that bade thee and him come and say to thee, Give this man place; and thou begin with shame to take the lowest room.

Although the Lord's teaching is described as a parable, it is really more in the nature of practical advice. In fact, the teaching is an elaboration on the advice given by King Solomon in Proverbs 26:6-7. Jesus mentions another kind of feast than the one in progress, so that His teaching would not be taken personally by the host or the guests.

The wedding Jesus speaks of here is from the Greek word *gamos,* meaning "wedding feast." The Lord often uses the wedding feast motif to characterize the relationship between God and His people (Matthew 22:2ff; 25:1-10). The metaphor looks back to the teaching of Old Testament prophets, especially Isaiah 54:4ff and Hosea 2:19.

The words here used by our Lord teach how to avoid shame and to gain honor. They also form a parable that is intended to teach the great spiritual truth that true humility leads to exaltation. "Sit not down in the highest room" (Gk. *me kataklithes eis ten protoklisian*) is more correctly translated as "do not recline in a place of honor." Jesus considers the possibility that a person "more honorable" (Gk. *entimos*), or held in higher esteem, arrives late to the feast. In this case, someone would have to move, and the person moved from the choice seat would find every place full except the "lowest room" (Gk. *eschatos topos*), literally meaning "the last place." The person's new seat would be a cause of "shame" (Gk. *aischune*) meaning public humiliation and embarrassment.

10 But when thou art bidden, go and sit down in the lowest room; that when he that bade thee cometh, he may say unto thee, Friend, go up higher: then shalt thou have worship in the presence of them that sit at meat with thee.

Jesus advises the guests to "sit down in the lowest room" instead of rushing to the places of honor. If the wedding host recognizes you as a person worthy of honor, he will invite you to a higher place. The invitation to a higher seat will bring the invitee "worship" (Gk. *doxa*) meaning "glory." In this case, the word refers to favorable human thought or opinion.

11 For whosoever exalteth himself shall be abased; and he that humbleth himself shall be exalted.

This is one of our Lord's favorite sayings (Luke 18:14; Matthew 23:12). People see humiliation as the just punishment for arrogance, but God takes pleasure in elevating truly humble people to positions of respect and honor. The spiritual lesson is that one must not seek self-promotion, but be content in lowly places, from where he or she can be invited to higher places.

14:15 And when one of them that sat at meat with him heard these things, he said unto him, Blessed is he that shall eat bread in the kingdom of God.

The parable of the "great banquet" originally applied to Israel and the nation's rejection of God's call to them, but now applies to the Church of Christ. The subject of the parable is actually the day of resurrection and heavenly glory. Those who had been expected to attend God's banquet had turned the Host down, so now He would invite the outcasts.

The parable is precipitated by one of the guests at the banquet Jesus had attended. Jesus had explained how extending hospitality to the less fortunate would result in heavenly reward at the resurrection of the righteous. Hearing this the guest exclaimed, "Blessed is he that shall eat bread in the kingdom of God." "Blessed" is from the Greek word *makarios* and refers to a state where God is present and involved in a person's life, and the hand of God directs all of that person's affairs for a divine purpose.

The expression "kingdom of God" (Gk. *basileia theos*) refers back to the prophecies of Daniel (2:44; 7:13-14) and represents the everlasting kingdom that God would set up and give to Christ. The language implies that God Himself will set a feast for those who fed the poor, and this implication agreed with the Jewish notion that the kingdom of God would be ushered in with a great festival.

16 Then said he unto him, A certain man made a great supper, and bade many: 17 And sent his servant at supper time to say to them that were bidden, Come; for all things are now ready.

Responding to the man's excited exclamation, Jesus launches into another parable. This one points to the day of resurrection in the future glory. According to Jewish custom in biblical times, when guests were invited to a feast they were told the day of the feast but not the exact time. Just before the feast was to begin, the host sent his servant to each of the guests to inform them that the festivities were about to begin. The point is that each of the guests in this parable had already agreed to attend the banquet.

18 And they all with one consent began to make excuse. The first said unto him, I have bought a piece of ground, and I must needs go and see it: I pray thee have me excused.

Instead of attending the feast as agreed, all of the guests insulted the host as each one of them "began to make excuse." "Make excuse" is from the Greek word *paraiteomai* meaning to decline, to beg to be excused, or to refuse a request. The phrase "with one consent" (Gk. *apo mia*) means to be in agreement with at the same time.

All the excuses are weak. The first man said he had to go see a field he had just purchased. No doubt he had seen the field before he bought it.

19 And another said, I have bought five yoke of oxen, and I go to prove them: I pray thee have me excused.

The second man's excuse was that he had just bought five new oxen that he needed to prove. To "prove" (Gk. *dokimazo*) meant to test a thing or try it out. Turning down the invitation so that he could try out his new possession demonstrates a preoccupation with a new toy rather than urgent business.

20 And another said, I have married a wife, and therefore I cannot come.

The third man's excuse was the weakest of all. Jewish weddings were such elaborate affairs that the man had to know well in advance that he was getting married and should not have accepted the first invitation. Having a new wife would have pre-vented the man from going to war (Deuteronomy 24:5), but certainly not from attending a banquet.

These three excuses show that after first accept-ing the invitation, the guests had made their engagements, either for business or pleasure, with-out the least regard for the host of the banquet. The parable is intended to teach that men forego their rights to heaven for trifles. The three excuses warn us not to be hindered by the love of posses-sions, the affairs of business, or social tics.

21 So that servant came, and shewed his lord these things. Then the master of the house being angry said to his servant, Go out quickly into the streets and lanes of the city, and bring in hither the poor, and the maimed, and the halt, and the blind.

"Master of the house" (Gk. *oikodespotes*) refers to both the head of the family and the master of the house, or landowner. In this case the host became angry because the insults were a personal insult. He ordered his servant to go out to the streets and lanes to invite guests. "Streets" (Gk. *plateia*) were broader than the usual neighborhood road and were traveled by a wider variety of people. "Lanes" (Gk. *rhume*) were small side paths that the unfor-tunates and outcasts were likely to frequent. The people invited from the streets and lanes were like-ly to be the same people Jesus invited (v. 13).

22 And the servant said, Lord, it is done as thou hast commanded, and yet there is room. 23 And the lord said unto the servant, Go out into the high-ways and hedges, and compel them to come in, that my house may be filled.

The servant is now sent to those who live with-out the city and are found upon the highways and in the hedges of the vineyards and gardens. The second- and third-class citizens are depicted as needing to be compelled; this is because they count themselves unworthy of the invitation. These latter classes of people are probably a direct reference to the Gentiles. But they were to be com-pelled to come by moral, not by physical means. Physical constraint would have been contrary to all custom, as well as impossible for one servant to enforce. The fact that the house is not full after the initial foray demonstrates the roominess of heaven and the vastness of divine hospitality.

24 For I say unto you, That none of those men which were bidden shall taste of my supper.

Those who were originally invited to the feast were excluded by their own actions. They had refused to come, so now they would not receive the slightest taste. Here the word "taste" (Gk. *geuomai*) is used metaphorically of receiving a sensation or impression of anything, or experiencing anything. The "supper" is used in the figurative sense of Christ's heavenly kingdom (see Revelation 3:20). No one who rejects the invitation to this heavenly feast will ever experience even the slightest hint of heaven.

DAILY BIBLE READINGS

M: Bear with One Another in Love
Ephesians 4:1-6
T: Imitate Christ's Humility
Philippians 2:1-8
W: Clothe Yourself with Humility
1 Peter 5:3-10
T: Parable of the Wedding Banquet
Matthew 22:1-10
F: Jesus Heals the Man with Dropsy
Luke 14:1-6
S: Humility and Hospitality
Luke 14:7-14
S: Parable of the Great Dinner
Luke 14:15-24

With your *Precepts For Living* CD-ROM you can do a cross-refer-ence check on Luke 14:11. You'll find other places in the Bible that use the word *humble*. Use the Gk. and Hebrew dictionary to see what the Greek form of the word means.

NOTES

NOTES

NOTES

NOTES

NOTES

NOTES

NOTES

NOTES